Anger, Aggression, and Interventions for Interpersonal Violence

Anger, Aggression, and Interventions for Interpersonal Violence

Edited by
Timothy A. Cavell
Kenya T. Malcolm
University of Arkansas

 Routledge
Taylor & Francis Group
New York   London

KH

Cover design by Tomai Maridou

CIP information for this volume may be obtained by contacting the Library of Congress

Anger, aggression, and interventions for interpersonal violence

     p. cm.

ISBN 978-0-8058-5554-8 — 0-8058-5554-8 (cloth)
ISBN 978-0-8058-6152-5 — 0-8058-6152-1 (pbk.)
ISBN 978-1-4106-1505-3 (e book)

Books published by Lawrence Erlbaum Associates are printed on acid-free paper, and their bindings are chosen for strength and durability.

Printed in the United States of America
10 9 8 7 6 5 4 3 2

7/29/08

To the memory of Marie Wilson Howells,
a benefactor and champion of psychological inquiry.

Table of Contents

List of Contributors

Sandra T. Azar *The Pennsylvania State University*
Karen L. Bierman *The Pennsylvania State University*
Jeannette Bischkopf *Freie Universität, Berlin*
Charles M. Borduin *University of Missouri—Columbia*
Monica Brooker *Wichita State University*
Brad J. Bushman *University of Michigan*
Carol Cannella *St. John's University*
Marc Carriere *University of Windsor, Ontario, Canada*
Timothy A. Cavell *University of Arkansas*
Kahni Clements *Indiana University*
Ray DiGiuseppe *St. John's University*
Leslie S. Greenberg *York University, Toronto, Ontario*
Alexandra Groff *Western Psychiatric Institute and Clinic, Pittsburgh, PA*
Amy Holtzworth-Monroe *Indiana University*
Cindy Harmon-Jones *College Station, Texas*
Eddie Harmon-Jones *University of Wisconsin—Madison*
Julie A. Hubbard *University of Delaware*
Howard Kassinove *Hofstra University*
Jill Kelter *St. John's University*
David J. Kolko *University of Pittsburgh School of Medicine*
Jeffrey M. Lohr *University of Arkansas*
Kerry N. Makin-Byrd *The Pennsylvania State University*
Kenya T. Malcolm *University of Arkansas*
Oommen K. Mammen *Western Psychiatric Institute and Clinic, Pittsburgh, PA*
Meghan D. McAuliffe *University of Delaware*
Michael T. Morrow *University of Delaware*
Raymond W. Novaco *University of California, Irvine*
Bunmi O. Olatunji *University of Arkansas*
Paul A. Pilkonis *Western Psychiatric Institute and Clinic, Pittsburgh, PA*
Sandra C. Paivio *University of Windsor, Ontario, Canada*
Ronnie M. Rubin *University of Delaware*
Lynn Schrepferman *Wichita State University*
James Snyder *Wichita State University*
Mike Stoolmiller *Oregon Social Learning Center, Marquette, MI*
David A. Wolfe *CAMH Centre for Prevention Science, London, Ontario, Canada*

Preface

Euripides (c. 480–406 BC), often described as the father of the psychological drama, was a prolific but not very popular playwright in ancient Greece. While his contemporaries wrote larger-than-life stories about great battles and heroic warriors, Euripides' told tales of ordinary folks struggling with the same issues that befall most persons. He was generally dismissed by his contemporaries, especially Aristophanes, who continually ridiculed Euripides and his work. Euripides' insensitivity to popular ideals led eventually to his being exiled from Greece. He died while living in Macedonia, the victim of a violent death. Reportedly, the king of Macedonia found reason to unleash upon Euripides a ferocious pack of hunting dogs that tore him limb from limb.

Modern critics see Euripides as an iconoclast, a truth seeker who saw beyond and through widely held notions about valor and honor. For him, the most compelling battles were waged between two lovers or between one's heart and mind. Among the issues he addressed was the role of anger in human interaction. His writings reveal a tendency to view anger as corrosive: "Those whom God wishes to destroy, he first makes angry." He also recognized the convoluted functions that anger can have within interpersonal relationships: "What anger worse or slower to abate than lovers love when it turns to hate."

We are not tragedians, but we are truth seekers. And we are interested in how anger can distort interpersonal relationships, transforming what was once heartfelt desire into hurtful rage. We offer here a book that is distinct in its mission. We asked our contributors to consider whether the treatment of interpersonal violence should reflect its common occurrence across a range of social contexts and developmental periods. More specifically, we challenged our panel of experts to confront the complex relation between anger and aggression. In asking our contributors to re-visit this age-old question, we, like Euripides, risk producing a work that could be viewed as pedestrian or pessimistic. Only time will tell how our volume will be received, but we are pleased to offer it and eager to participate in whatever debates and exchanges it might engender. And we are fairly optimistic about avoiding political exile or canine-led disaster.

When first we proposed this book, we conducted a search for texts published since 1990 using the following combinations of keywords and conjunctions: "anger" OR "aggression" AND "intervention" OR "violence." We found listings for 45 books, more than half of which were either self-help books or practitioner guidebooks that lacked the underpinnings of sound, empirical research. The remaining volumes were meant for researchers or for both researchers and practitioners. Most of these texts focused on a particular population (e.g., youth, women) or on a specific interpersonal or relationship context (e.g., workplace). We counted only eight books devoted to anger or to aggression that also covered a range of client populations or relationship domains. Seven of these eight focused on anger only or on aggression only, although a number of themes (e.g., bio-genetics, cognitive theory, social interactionist theory, life-span development) were used to bind chapters together. We found only one text that considered broadly the twin concerns of anger *and* aggression: *Anger, Aggression, and Violence: An Interdisciplinary Approach.* The book was authored by Paul Robbins and McFarland & Company published it in 2000. A quick inspection of this book revealed, however, that its focus was not the *relation* between anger and aggression, much less the implications of that relation for treating interpersonal violence. It would seem, therefore, that our book is unique in what it offers the reader. Our book should appeal to most but not all practitioners. Those clinicians who are seeking a detailed treatment protocol will need to look elsewhere. However, practitioners who know of and use such protocols will benefit greatly from the wisdom, the experience, and the science that permeate these pages. Our book will also appeal to most but not all researchers who identify interpersonal violence, anger, or aggression as topics of interest. Scholars looking for a comprehensive review addressing a single type of interpersonal violence or a very specific approach to treating interpersonal violence will not be satisfied. Our book holds greater value for those who see grappling with thorny issues, such as the relation between anger and aggression, as a chance to broaden their thinking and enhance their future investigations.

ACKNOWLEDGMENTS

Many individuals contributed to the development and ultimate production of this book, and we want to acknowledge their help and support. We note first those individuals and families who struggle with the problem of interpersonal violence and who are brave enough to seek assistance from unfamiliar professionals such as ourselves.

We next wish to acknowledge the hard work and dedication of our contributing authors. They were able to blend scholarly expertise and professional demeanor in ways that make the job of editor easier and more rewarding.

We thank our colleagues in the Department of Psychology at the University of Arkansas, in particular Doug Behrend, Dave Schroeder, Eric Knowles, and Joel Freund. We offer a special thank you to the estate of Marie Wilson Howells. The Howells endowment was established to promote research and scholarship in psychology at the University of Arkansas, and support from this endowment was instrumental in bringing this book to fruition.

We certainly wish to acknowledge those friends and family members who heard far too long about "the anger and aggression book." Kenya Malcolm thanks daughters Dorienne and Natalie for their loving ways and for exposing their mother to the full array of human emotions. She also thanks their father, Robert, for working from home so that she can have time to enjoy projects like this. Tim Cavell appreciates the patience shown by his three children—Hannah, Hope, and Graham—as well as their daily reminders of his fatherly joys and tasks. And he is most appreciative of the love, support, and care provided by his wife, Lauri.

Finally, we are grateful to the fine folks at Lawrence Erlbaum Associates who saw promise in our proposal and who persevered to make this book a quality volume. We note in particular the support and guidance of Susan Milmoe, Steve Rutter, Nicole Buchman, and Sondra Guideman.

—*Timothy A. Cavell*
—*Kenya T. Malcolm*

Introduction: The Anger–Aggression Relation

Timothy A. Cavell
Kenya T. Malcolm

This book is about interpersonal violence—what clinical scientists know about it and what mental health practitioners can do about it. For those who are not scientists or practitioners, the question of what's to be done about interpersonal violence brings a mix of reactions. Some decry the fact that interpersonal violence continues to plague so-called "civilized" societies and that more is not being done to end this tragedy; others merely shrug and opine that interpersonal violence has always been part of the human enterprise. The purpose of this book is not to reconcile these divergent views of human nature (see instead Buss & Shackelford, 1997) but to advance the way practitioners and researchers conceptualize interventions for violent clients. Though narrower, it is still an ambitious goal.

Interpersonal violence has different names depending on the interpersonal context or relationship involved. Common labels are *child abuse, intimate-partner violence, youth violence, elder abuse, sibling aggression, school bullying,* and *workplace violence.* Perpetrators and victims of interpersonal violence can include husbands, wives, romantic partners, parents, children, siblings, coworkers, and classmates. The World Health Organization has defined *interpersonal violence* as "violence between family members and intimates, and violence between acquaintances and strangers that is not intended to further the aims of any formally defined group or cause" (Waters et al., 2004, p. 2). In this volume, we focus primarily on violence among family members and intimates.

Acts of interpersonal violence are both tragic and costly. In the United States, the direct costs of interpersonal violence (for medical care, legal services, incarceration, etc.) have been estimated at nearly $2 billion a year or about 0.02% of the country's annual gross domestic product (GDP; Waters et al., 2004). When indirect costs (for lost earnings, lost productivity, psychological costs, etc.) are added, the estimates rise sharply and reach 3.3% to 6.5% of the annual GDP. However, there are also data indicating that interventions can lower the incidence of interpersonal violence and do so in ways that easily offset the cost of intervention (Waters et al., 2004). Some interventions are policy-level actions (e.g., federal laws, public health campaigns), some are community-wide prevention programs, and others are psychotherapeutic strategies.

This book is concerned with the third type of intervention. Public health initiatives are designed to reduce the overall incidence and prevalence of various maladies, but workaday clinicians and the clients they serve evaluate treatment success one case at a time. Published outcome studies document that clinically meaningful gains are achievable in cases of interpersonal violence but that there is also substantial room for improvement. We hope that our text can improve on what is known about therapeutic interventions for families and couples affected by interpersonal violence. Our plan for doing so was twofold: (a) Assemble a panel of experts, and (b) foster among them a spirit of creative problem solving.

Harris (2004) has suggested that creative problem solving is achieved by one of five methods. Listed below are these five methods along with Harris's example of each:

- Evolution—incremental improvement (e.g., the latest versions of computers, autos).
- Revolution—reject current strategies (e.g., abandon pesticides as a termite deterrent and shift to strategies that are nontoxic).
- Changing direction—redefine the problem (deterring skateboarders via fences vs. deterring skateboarding via altered walkways and inclines).
- Synthesis—combine two or more disparate ideas (e.g., dinner + theater).
- Reapplication—unfixate from preconceived notions (e.g., paint to prevent loosening of screws).

We emphasized the last two methods. We wanted a text that considered—under one title—different forms of interpersonal violence and their corresponding treatments. We also wanted our contributors to reexamine their basic assumptions about the relation between anger and aggression and the implications of that relation for intervention work. Interventions that target interpersonal violence tend to be fairly specific to the relationship or to the developmental context in which it occurs. Thus, abusive parents, violent spouses, and aggressive children are likely to receive different treatments, even if they worked with the same practitioner. This makes sense given that developmental, contextual, and relationship factors contribute to the onset, frequency, and severity of interpersonal violence. But it is also possible that interpersonal violence has core features that transcend the specific context in which it is found. One such feature is the link between anger and aggression.

THE COMPLEX RELATION BETWEEN ANGER AND AGGRESSION

Researchers invoke an array of constructs to explain the origins and patterned use of violence, and these differences are reflected in the varying approaches to treating interpersonal violence. Commonly studied are psychological factors, including interpersonal and emotional skill deficits, poor coping strategies, past traumas, insecure attachment tendencies, psychiatric disorders, family stressors, and substance abuse problems. Other potential mechanisms are thought to reside in the environment—in contexts that model, shape, and reinforce (or fail to restrict) aggressive behavior. Also assumed to be operating are broader contextual variables such as poverty, prejudice, social norms in support of violence, violence-filled media, and inadequate legal protections for victims. Some of these putative causal factors are far removed temporally from the violent actions that lead to treatment (e.g., past child abuse), some are considered relatively stable (e.g., personality traits), and some are beyond the control of most therapists (e.g., poverty). As a result, currently available treatments usually target factors that promote or precipitate dysregulated anger or contextual determinants of aggressive behavior. We believe there is value in attempting to reconcile these two approaches.

When someone acts aggressively, there is often a presumption of underlying anger; conversely, when someone is extremely angry, there is a tendency to anticipate impending aggression. These are reasonable presumptions given that anger and aggression are often linked temporally and functionally. Ample research documents that strong feelings of anger commonly precede aggressive actions and that aggressive behavior can serve to maintain or intensify feelings of anger. However, the relation between anger and aggression is neither simple nor complete; anger does not always lead to aggression, nor does aggression require the presence of anger (Averill, 1982). Each can occur independently of the other and the determinants of anger are not identical to the factors that give rise to aggression. The relation between anger and aggression can also vary greatly across individuals. For example, children who are prone to using aggression are less likely to differentiate between anger and other negative feelings or to see a clear distinction between feeling angry and acting aggressively (Lemerise & Dodge, 1993). One might also presume that the relation between anger and aggression can shift over time for a given individual. This notion lies at the heart of interventions that try to modify how clients respond when angry.

One might also presume that the study of anger and the study of aggression are necessarily linked, but this is hardly the case. Scholars in both camps identify with the goal of understanding, predicting, and reducing interpersonal violence, but there is little effort to integrate the two bodies of knowledge. Far more common is to increment what is known specifically about anger (i.e., an internal, affective experience) or about aggression (i.e., an overt behavior shaped by external contingencies). This tendency toward balkanization is magnified when intervention researchers design treatments that fit a specific interpersonal or developmental context. For some interpersonal contexts, treatment is designed to reduce aggressive behavior, with little or no attention given to anger *per se*. Thus parents of conduct problem children are usually trained to restrict their child's aggression but not to enhance their child's ability to regulate anger. In other interpersonal contexts, the clear emphasis is on anger as the focus of treatment. For example, psychological interventions for violent husbands generally place greater emphasis on anger management issues than on ways to impose reliable sanctions for aggressive behavior (Salazar & Cook, 2002). But is there room for integration? Is there value in having parents blend strict discipline with strategies that help children cope with angry feelings? And how can practitioners augment anger-focused interventions with strategies that effectively limit perpetrators' use of violence? Earlier we acknowledged that context-specific treatments are a reasonable response to research indicating that interpersonal violence manifests itself in varying forms and for various reasons. But we also believe there is promise in considering commonalities across different forms of interpersonal violence. In this text, that common lens is the relation between anger and aggression.

All interventions designed to treat interpersonal violence make assumptions about anger and its relation to the display and treatment of aggression. Sometimes these assumptions are made explicitly; at other times, the assumptions are tacit and must be inferred from what is or is not addressed therapeutically. For example, interventions that downplay the role of anger make an implicit assumption that anger is secondary and perhaps epiphenomenal to the actual perpetration of aggression and violence. Other models place heavy emphasis on anger and assume that successful treatment is unlikely unless angry feelings are front and center. Some intervention researchers recognize the apparent schism in the treatment of anger and aggression and have fashioned multicomponent intervention programs (e.g., Kazdin, Siegel, & Bass, 1992). But the stacking of treatments for anger and aggression is not the same as developing treatment models that carefully consider the complex relation between anger and aggression and that make explicit how this relation affects treatment goals and strategies.

ORGANIZATIONAL OVERVIEW

We divided our text into four sections. Part I addresses general models for treating clients with anger-related problems. Discussed here are cognitive-behavioral interventions that dominate the treatment arena, plus newer approaches that give practitioners promising alternatives for working with angry and aggressive clients. Part II considers the function of anger as a basic human emotion and the features that distinguish it from other emotions, both positive and negative. Also addressed in this part is the value of having clients experience and express angry feelings as part of therapy. Part III considers the anger–aggression relation among children and adolescents. Contributors discuss the role of anger and other emotions in the development and treatment of aggression and the impact of targeted interventions on anger-related problems. The final part focuses on violent families, including those with abusive parents and battering spouses. Clinical work with violence-prone families is a daunting enterprise and the complex relation between anger and aggression is but one of the challenges practitioners face.

Readers will also find within each part a commentary specific to the chapters in that part. Our commentators were asked to offer their thoughts and reactions to each chapter, identifying perhaps common themes or additional insights and findings not mentioned by the authors. Readers will find the commentaries to be a useful tool for consolidating and integrating the wealth of information contained in each part.

Anger, Aggression, and General Models of Intervention

Our book opens with Novaco's thoughtful discussion of anger dysregulation and the intricacies of treating clients who present with anger-related problems. Novaco coined the term *anger management* over 30 years ago (Novaco, 1975), and his experience and broad perspective are evident in his account of the key issues, core themes, and important developments in the field. Readers unfamiliar with psychological interventions for clients who are angry and violent will find this chapter an excellent starting point. Novaco is sensitive to the problems faced by angry clients and their therapists, and he carefully integrates the conceptual with the practical. Perhaps most helpful is his emphasis on separating the goal of preventing anger dyscontrol from the task of interrupting anger escalation.

For Novaco, anger control is a "proactive posture, not merely an intercession on the spot" (p. 20). A first step toward that posture is to help clients separate their anger from their threat system, which can happen only if therapy represents a safe place for reflection and exploration.

In chapter 2, DiGiuseppe, Cannella, and Kelter cover exposure-based interventions for angry clients. DiGiuseppe has been at the forefront of scholars debating the question of whether anger disorders should have their own diagnostic category, akin to categories for mood and anxiety disorders (DiGiuseppe & Tafrate, in press). The focus of this chapter is on the use of exposure strategies (e.g., verbal insults or "barbs") when treating angry clients. DiGiuseppe et al. discuss promising findings in support of exposure but question whether the findings can be explained by the principles of classical conditioning. They argue that instrumental learning is a better framework for understanding these outcomes. Practitioners will find useful the clinical case descriptions as well as the authors' recommendations for using exposure specifically with angry clients. For example, DiGiuseppe et al. advise against efforts to maximize habituation by having clients focus on angry feelings, as is done with anxious clients.

Rounding out Part I is Kassinove's provocative commentary on these first two chapters. Widely known for his work on the treatment of anger problems (e.g., Kassinove & Tafrate, 2002), Kassinove—like Novaco and DiGiuseppe—laments that so little research on anger and anger problems has informed the working clinician: "Research done on 21-year-old college students who score high on a single anger questionnaire does not seem applicable to 50-year-old adults with more complex lives and comorbid issues who are seen in private practices or inpatient settings" (p. 79). Standing in the way of real progress, says Kassinove, is confusion about how to define anger and how to separate it from the construct of aggression. He also finds fault with definitions of anger that invoke internal structures and processes that are difficult to measure (e.g., thoughts, beliefs, intentions). Kassinove proposes, as an alternative to treatments drawn from a cognitive-behavioral perspective, an approach he labels *verbal-behavior therapy* (VBT). In VBT, anger would be narrowly defined as the display of angry statements that are functionally linked to violent motor behavior. The task of the VBT therapist would be to help clients replace these statements with more adaptive verbalizations (e.g., assertiveness skills) that are functionally separate from violent outcomes.

Natural and Therapeutic Functions of Anger Experience and Anger Expression

In chapter 4, readers are presented an up-to-date look at research on anger as a primary human emotion. Harmon-Jones and Harmon-Jones note that anger is not a "thing" but a collective of basic processes (e.g., feelings, facial expressions, appraisals, action plans, physiology). Their discussion of these processes reveals the complex origins and functions of anger experiences. Like Kassinove, Harmon-Jones and Harmon-Jones question whether cognitive appraisals are a necessary component to definitions of anger. They also review studies indicating that anger—unlike fear and sadness—is associated with approach motivation and with more positive subjective feelings such as self-assurance, determination, and strength.

In chapter 5, Olatunji, Lohr, and Bushman discuss the concept of venting—the deliberate release of angry feelings with the goal of preventing more uncontrolled and violent displays of anger. Venting is based on the psychodynamic notion of catharsis, the relieving of anger-induced pressure in one's psyche. Bushman has conducted a number of studies examining the impact of venting on subsequent anger and aggression (e.g., Bushman, 2002), and Olatunji and Lohr have encouraged practitioners to be wary of pseudoscientific intervention strategies when treating angry clients (Lilienfeld, Lynn, & Lohr, 2003; Olatunji, & Lohr, 2005). In this chapter, they examine evidence that venting leads to less anger and to a lower likelihood of aggression. They report, despite popular beliefs to the contrary, that there is little scientific support for this hypothesis and caution practitioners about the risks of using venting exercises. They promote instead treatment approaches (e.g., cognitive-behavioral) that have a more solid scientific foundation.

The value of having clients experience angry feelings in session is further considered in the chapter by Paivio and Carriere. These authors introduce readers to emotion-focused therapy (EFT; Greenberg & Paivio, 1997) and outline its underlying assumptions. Their discussion focuses on the application of EFT to clients whose anger is tied to the trauma of childhood abuse. From an EFT perspective, clients' anger problems are not limited to issues of under- or overcontrol; also critical to assess and treat are clients whose problems involve limited awareness and inappropriate expression of anger. Paivio and Carriere pay special attention to the many variants of anger experience and expression, arguing that some are adaptive whereas others are clearly maladaptive. In contrast to the research on venting, the EFT model offers practitioners a more nuanced (and less negative) frame for understanding the role of anger experience and anger expression in therapy.

Providing commentary on these three chapters are Greenberg and Bischkopf. Greenberg has written extensively on experiential forms of therapy, and in this chapter he and his coauthor directly address the debate over whether having clients access and express angry feelings is therapeutic. Greenberg and Bischkopf frame the debate in this way: "Is it better in psychotherapy to support expression or containment?" (p. 169).

These commentators recognize the dangers of encouraging cathartic release, but like Harmon-Jones and Harmon-Jones, they also view anger as having adaptive value. For Greenberg and Bischkopf, anger is too complex a phenomenon to be captured by the simple indices of frequency, intensity, and duration. Also needed is an appreciation for the meaning of anger, and many clients will need assistance before they can use anger experiences in service of sense making and adaptive problem solving. Thus a key issue in this debate is the distinction between anger expression in everyday life and anger expression in therapy. Because clients are often confused by their anger, carefully processing those feelings *in session* can help them to develop more adaptive responses to anger episodes outside of therapy.

The Anger–Aggression Relation in Violent Children and Adolescents

The next set of chapters focuses on the role of anger in the development of aggressive behavior and the treatment of aggressive, antisocial children and adolescents. In chapter 8, Snyder, Schrepferman, Brooker, and Stoolmiller use data from an ongoing longitudinal study to examine the role of anger displays in children's conflicts with parents and with peers. In previous work, Snyder and colleagues found evidence that children use coercion with parents to the extent it "works" better than other influence tactics (e.g., Snyder & Patterson, 1995). Typically the payoffs for child coercion involve parents backing down from a request or giving in to a child's demand. In this chapter, the authors expand on this theme, using their findings to describe a preliminary working model of how children's anger displays interact with and amplify social contingencies in the development of aggressive behavior. Particularly intriguing are findings indicating that angry displays and coercive exchanges occur at a much greater rate with peers than with parents. It appears that for vulnerable children, the peer context adds substantially to their "basic training" in aggressive behavior.

The next chapter is by Karen Bierman, known for developing and evaluating interventions for angry, aggressive children who are also rejected by their peers. Her recent work has involved the FAST Track delinquency prevention project, a large multisite trial targeting aggressive children from Grade 1 untill Grade 10 (Conduct Problems Prevention Research Group, 2004). Bierman examines the role of emotion processes in the development of aggressive, antisocial behavior and the extent to which current intervention models address issues of emotion dysregulation. She notes potential limitations in these models, in particular the lack of emphasis on children's cognitive and emotional responses during moments of heightened arousal.

Suggestions for addressing these limitations echo those made by other contributors who work primarily with angry adults: (a) attend to issues of emotional safety when working therapeutically with angry, aggressive children (see Novaco), (b) help children appreciate the meaning of their anger when generating alternative response options (see Paivio & Carriere), and (c) provide opportunities for graduated exposure to and processing of interpersonal situations that represent increasingly difficult emotional demands (see DiGiuseppe et al.).

The third chapter in this part centers on multisytemic therapy (MST). Any discussion involving the treatment of violent teens would be incomplete without consideration of this impressive intervention model. For nearly two decades, proponents of MST have rigorously tested their model and shown it to be a robust intervention for severely delinquent youth (Henggeler & Borduin, 1990). The chapter is written by Charles Borduin, one of the original co-developers of MST. Borduin asks what role does anger play in the work of MST therapists and what impact does MST have on the anger-related problems of delinquent youth? He first offers a primer on the principles of MST and a brief description of its service delivery format, which is highly innovative. The typical MST therapist works intensively for 3 to 4 months with a small caseload of families, is available around the clock for consultation, and usually conducts therapy sessions in the home, at school, or in the neighborhood. Borduin describes how anger is conceptualized within the MST model and reports on studies that evaluated the impact of MST on youths' angry outbursts.

Commentary on these chapters is provided by Hubbard, McAuliffe, Rubin, and Morrow. Hubbard has conducted a number of enterprising studies on the relation between child anger and aggression, often using multiple indices of child anger (e.g., Hubbard et al., 2002, 2004). Hubbard and her coauthors are pleased that intervention researchers are giving greater attention to children's anger, and they welcome conceptual models that move the study of childhood aggression away from a strictly social-information-processing (SIP) framework. Briefly discussed is the affective social competence model (Halberstadt, Denham, & Dunsmore, 2001), which Hubbard and colleagues see as a useful conceptualization of children's socioemotional functioning. Readers will find especially helpful their recommendations for enhancing future intervention work with aggressive children.

The Anger–Aggression Relation in Violent Families

Mammen and colleagues begin the last set of chapters with an innovative approach to conceptualizing and treating one type of family violence—child physical abuse (CPA). They suggest that parents who perpetrate

CPA can benefit from treatments that specifically target *anger attacks*. Anger attacks are defined as episodes of rapid onset, intense anger that are ego-dystonic and that covary with harsh and abusive parenting (Mammen et al., 1999). Somewhat akin to Kassinove's recommendation to treat anger displays that are functionally linked to overt aggression, Mammen and colleagues see value in directly treating anger attacks that can escalate into episodes of physical abuse. Distinctly different from Kassinove, however, is the fact that these investigators have a strong interest in the use of serotonergic antidepressants as effective interventions for recurring anger attacks.

In the next chapter, Holtzworth-Munroe and Clements consider the relation between anger and intimate-partner violence. They recognize the potential value in understanding this relation but are also aware that feminist theorists view reports of anger as post hoc justifications for male batterers' abuse of power against women. Expanding on a similar, earlier review of this literature (Eckhardt, Barbour, & Stuart, 1997), Holtzworth-Munroe and Clements give a thorough accounting of the state of the science. Their chapter offers valuable information to practitioners and researchers unfamiliar with issues that can confound the study and treatment of intimate-partner violence. These include various measurement issues and options, the difference between anger and hostility, the relation between marital violence and marital distress, and the clinical significance of subtypes of male batterers (e.g., Holtzworth-Munroe, Meehan, Herron, Rehman, & Stuart, 2003).

The challenge of conducting therapy with violence-prone families is the focus of chapter 14. Azar and Makin-Byrd draw on previous research to suggest that a strong working alliance and the capacity to resolve therapeutic ruptures are critical to successful interventions. Azar and Makin-Byrd extend this notion to families affected by violence (e.g., child abuse, partner battering, aggressive children) by proposing that therapeutic ruptures are often the product of biased perceptions on the part of therapists. The authors outline potential "cultural" differences between therapists and members of violence-prone families and discuss how these differences can lead to clashes in assumptive beliefs and fundamental values that are hard to detect. The authors hypothesize that subtle value clashes can partly explain high dropout rates and underwhelming outcome findings common to studies of family violence. Readers are given a number of useful recommendations for recognizing and working through value clashes that can disrupt therapy process.

Commenting on these three chapters is David Wolfe, widely known for his scholarly work on the tragedy of family and relationship violence (e.g., Wolfe, 1999). Wolfe applauds the clinical wisdom offered by these contributors and extends further their discussion of the anger–aggression relation. He presents an excellent summation of research linking mood, affect, and memory as it relates to anger and family violence. For Wolfe, it is important to understand that emotional regulatory deficits and cognitive distortions cocontribute to recurring patterns of interpersonal violence. Both are by-products of living in homes marked by violence:

> Modeling of aggressive problem-solving tactics via marital violence and corporal punishment, rehearsal and reinforcement (or lack of effective punishment) of aggressive behavior with siblings and peers, the absence of opportunities to learn appropriate problem-resolution approaches, and the establishment of a cognitive viewpoint that adheres to strict family roles and low self-efficacy all contribute to impaired self-regulation and disinhibition of aggressive behavior. (see pp. 396)

Recent work by Wolfe and his colleagues documents the developmental connections between early experiences of child maltreatment and later violence with an intimate partner. He describes data that reveal clear associations between childhood abuse and a propensity in adolescence for violent romantic relationships (Wolfe, Wekerle, Scott, Straatman, & Grasley, 2004). Maltreated youth struggle to form and sustain relationships that are not tainted by mistrust, hostility, and the presumption that there will always be victims and victimizers.

EMERGING THEMES, REMAINING QUESTIONS

In many ways, the chapters in this text represent a preliminary data set designed to answer the following question, "Are current models and methods for treating interpersonal violence operating from a common view of anger and aggression?" When we began this project, we were unsure of the answer to that question. Complicating matters was the fact that treatments for violent clients vary greatly across interpersonal and developmental contexts. We also learned from our search of the literature that clearly stated assumptions about the relation between anger and aggression are hard to find. Still, the question seemed worth asking, regardless of the answer. If there was a consensus view about anger and aggression, then our text would help to illuminate that common ground. But if clarity and consensus were lacking, then our text could offer new avenues for those looking to advance research and practice related to the problem of interpersonal violence.

The "data" are now in and the clear answer—for now—is, "There is no consensus view about anger and aggression." Although we had our suspicions, we were surprised at how little is actually known about the emotion we call anger and its relation to aggression, and how much disagreement there is about the role of anger in the treatment of interpersonal violence. We were surprised to find that those who study and treat one form of interpersonal violence often have little knowledge of or input into treatments for other forms of interpersonal violence. We were surprised at how seldom investigators consider possible links between the treatment of anger-related problems and the treatment of other disorders, particularly anxiety and mood disorders. And we were surprised to learn that in some treatment models little if any attention is given to clients' actual experience of anger, whereas in other treatment models the contextual factors that occasion clients' use of aggression is given short shrift. But we also find exciting the possibilities that arise form these informational gaps and disconnects. It is our hope that future investigators will actively pursue these possibilities, providing future practitioners with more effective ways to counter the dilemma of interpersonal violence.

To aid in that effort, we list four key themes or questions to emerge from our collection of chapters. Readers who focus on select chapters only (due to an interest in one particular form of interpersonal violence) might miss these overarching issues. They would also miss the rich diversity of viewpoints on these issues generated by our panel of scholars. Therefore, we thought it wise to give an early snapshot of emerging themes and remaining questions.

How to Define Anger?

Several contributors noted that anger is a core emotion and that it manifests itself in multiple domains (e.g., cognitive, verbal, behavioral, physiological). Beyond that point, however, there was little agreement about how to define or measure anger. Some contributors seemed unfazed by the fuzzy nature of the construct; others argued that a clear, agreed-upon definition of anger is the single most important challenge to advancing the treatment of interpersonal violence. So how should we define anger? Is anger viewed most productively as an affective state, as an enduring mood, as a stable personality trait, or as some combination of these? Is it better to ignore the subjective aspects of anger and focus solely on its overt, measurable features (e.g., facial expressions, angry vocalizations), as suggested by Kassinove? Or is it important to include in one's definition the phenomenology and underlying meaning of anger, as suggested by Paivio and Carriere? These questions are not merely academic exercises; they go to the very heart of how we conceptualize and treat clients' anger episodes and violence proneness.

How to Understand the Relation Between Anger and Aggression?

The chapters in this text provide an invaluable guide for those interested in the complex relation between anger and aggression. But considerably more research is needed before we can appreciate the parameters and dynamics of that relation. We were struck by how little attention has been devoted to this question in recent years, especially given how much greater attention has been devoted solely to the topic of anger or to the topic of aggression. Indeed, one gets the impression that previous researchers had grown weary of trying to explain the relation between anger and aggression and so they turned their attention to just one or the other. Fortunately, our contributors agreed to wrestle once again with the thorny issue of how anger and aggression are related and what that relation means for treating interpersonal violence. What we learned from their work is that a clear, consensus understanding of this relation does not exist at the present time. What did emerge, however, was strong agreement that plumbing deeper the nature of this relation should yield valuable insights for both researchers and practitioners.

Is There Value in the Distinction Between Proactive and Reactive Aggression?

When our contributors directly addressed the anger–aggression relation, they often did so in the context of this familiar dichotomy. Many observed that anger and aggression are likely to covary, particularly when aggressive behavior is marked by heightened emotional arousal and a desire to lash out at those who are seen as harmful or threatening. It is worth noting, however, that most contributors tended to dismiss the validity and utility of the proactive–reactive aggression dichotomy. Some noted the lack of clinical specificity afforded by this distinction; others cited Bushman and Anderson's (2001) cogent critique of the research supporting this dichotomy. But there were notable exceptions to this dismissive position, and these came from scholars whose work has focused almost exclusively on aggressive children. Both Bierman and Hubbard (along with her coauthors) continue to see value in distinguishing proactive from reactive forms of aggression. Perhaps a shared interest in studying developing patterns of aggression makes the proactive-reactive distinction particularly useful to these scholars. In making their case for further study in this area, Hubbard et al. note (a) that highly correlated variables can still be distinct if they relate differently to other variables, (b) that longitudinal studies of reactive and proactive aggression are needed to understand fully the nature of these two constructs, and (c) that psycho-physiological profiles associated with reactive and proactive aggression have not received adequate attention from researchers.

Target Anger or Aggression?

As noted earlier, treatments for interpersonal violence tend to lean in one of two directions: Target clients' tendency to become dysregulated when angry or target their tendency to engage in overtly aggressive acts. The first approach places a premium on understanding anger-related difficulties from the perspective of emotional understanding and emotion regulation. The second approach is based more on operant and social learning theories of aggression and the contextual factors that maintain patterns of antisocial or prosocial behavior. Both approaches have solid research traditions, yet rarely are these traditions considered in tandem. Treatments that emphasize the goal of restricting aggression typically target aggressive children or violent youth for whom parents and other adult stakeholders (e.g., teachers) continue to play a critical helping role. But how do interventionists working with adult clients understand and approach the goal of containing aggression outside of session? To whom do victims look for protection from and containment of aggressive acts? Are interventionists who pay close attention to clients' anger experiences overlooking powerful external forces? Or is it the case that practitioners who focus heavily on the consequences of aggression fail to appreciate the challenge of altering clients' primary strategies for dealing with angry arousal? How would interventions that truly integrate the treatment of anger and aggression differ from existing approaches?

CONCLUSION

We are interested in advancing treatments for interpersonal violence, especially in cases where violence occurs among family members or between romantic partners. Angry feelings are hard to avoid in close relationships and anger is more common when those relationships are marked by chronic dissatisfaction. Aggression is one strategy that individuals can use to escape or avoid the discomfort of emotion-laden conflict. With repeated use and rewards, aggression can develop into a primary response to relationship-based anger. It would seem, therefore, that treatments for interpersonal violence would have to address the overlearned and functional relation between angry feelings and aggressive acts. Our contributors offer a state-of-the-science rendering of what is known about this complex relation and what practitioners can do to help those clients caught in its pernicious trap. Readers will learn that understanding the functions of anger and the payoffs for aggression is a critical step to effective intervention.

Readers will also learn that clients' anger-related problems are often part of a larger clinical picture that includes comorbid symptoms and multiple and chronic life stressors. They will learn that solving serious anger and aggression problems is more than counting to 10 or venting pent-up feelings: It might involve helping clients understand the role of emotions generally and anger specifically, and it might mean clients' use of prescribed SSRIs (Selective Serotonin Reuptake Inhibitors). Readers will also learn that anger and aggression "works" for some clients and to ignore the reinforcing (and nonpunitive) consequences of interpersonal violence could be a serious clinical mistake. Readers will also learn that effective therapy will likely require that clients invest in skills that are a feasible replacement for established patterns of anger and violence, what Novaco calls a proactive posture. And readers will learn that clients will likely resist change efforts, for reasons that are sometimes hard to detect and understand, but that successful outcomes may well depend on therapists' ability to work through such conflicts and miscommunications.

In proposing this text, we made certain assumptions. We assumed that current views of the relation between anger and aggression are outdated and underspecified and that interventions for interpersonal violence would benefit from greater understanding of the anger–aggression relation. We also assumed that interventions for interpersonal violence would benefit from efforts to integrate treatments for aggression and treatments for anger. Finally, we assumed that interventions for interpersonal violence would be advanced when the relation between anger and aggression is considered across different forms of interpersonal violence and their corresponding treatments. It is our hope that greater understanding of the anger–aggression relation can help to identify critical change mechanisms and core intervention principles that can enhance practitioners' efforts to counter the tragedy of interpersonal violence.

REFERENCES

Averill, J. R. (1982). *Anger and aggression: An essay on emotion.* New York: Springer-Verlag.

Bushman, B. J. (2002). Does venting anger feed or extinguish the flame? Catharsis, rumination, distraction, anger, and aggressive responding. *Personality and Social Psychology Bulletin, 28,* 724–731.

Bushman, B. J., & Anderson, C. A. (2001). Is it time to pull the plug on hostile versus instrumental aggression dichotomy? *Psychological Review, 108(1),* 273–279.

Buss, D. M., & Shackelford, T. K. (1997). Human aggression in evolutionary perspective. *Clinical Psychology Review, 17*, 605–619.

Conduct Problems Prevention Research Group. (2004). The effects of the fast track program on serious problem outcomes at the end of elementary school. *Journal of Clinical Child and Adolescent Psychology, 33*, 650–661.

DiGiuseppe, R., & Tafrate, R. C. (in press). *Understanding anger and anger disorders.* New York: Oxford University Press.

Eckhardt, C. I., Barbour, K. A., & Stuart, G. L. (1997). Anger and hostility in maritally violent men: Conceptual distinctions, measurement issues, and literature review. *Clinical Psychology Review, 17*(4), 333–358.

Greenberg, L. S., & Paivio, S. C. (1997). *Working with emotions in psychotherapy.* New York: Guilford.

Harris, R. A. (2004). *Creative problem solving: A step-by-step approach.* Los Angeles: Pyrczak.

Halberstadt, A. G., Denham, S. A., & Dunsmore, J. C. (2001). Affective social competence. *Social Development, 10*, 79–119.

Henggeler, S. W., & Borduin, C. M. (1990). *Family therapy and beyond: A multisystemic approach to treating the behavior problems of children and adolescents.* Pacific Grove, CA: Brooks/Cole.

Holtzworth-Munroe, A., Meehan, J. C., Herron, K., Rehman, U., & Stuart, G. L. (2003). Do subtypes of maritally violent men continue to differ over time? *Journal of Consulting and Clinical Psychology, 71*(4), 728–740.

Hubbard, J. A., Parker, E. H., Ramsden, S. R., Flanagan, K. D., Relyea, N., Dearing, K. F., et al. (2004). The relations between observational, physiological, and self-report measures of children's anger. *Social Development, 13*, 14–39.

Hubbard, J. A., Smithmyer, C. M., Ramsden, S. R., Parker, E. H., Flanagan, K. D., Dearing, K. F., et al. (2002). Observational, physiological, and self-report measures of children's anger: Relations to reactive versus proactive aggression. *Child Development, 73*, 1101–1118.

Kassinove, H., & Tafrate, R. C. (2002). *Anger management: The complete practitioner's guidebook for the treatment of anger.* Atascadero, CA: Impact.

Kazdin, A. E., Siegel, T. C., & Bass, D. (1992). Cognitive problem-solving skills training and parent management training in the treatment of antisocial behavior in children. *Journal of Consulting and Clinical Psychology, 60*, 733–747.

Lemerise, E. A., & Dodge, K. A. (1993). The development of anger and hostile interactions. In M. Lewis & J. M. Haviland (Eds.), *Handbook of emotions* (pp. 537–546). New York: Guilford.

Lilienfeld, S. O., Lynn, S. J., & Lohr, J. M. (2003). *Science and pseudoscience in clinical psychology.* New York: Guilford.

Mammen, O. K., Shear, M. K., Pilkonis, P. A., Kolko, D. J., Thase, M. E., & Greeno, C. G. (1999). Anger attacks: Correlates and significance of an underrecognized symptom. *Journal of Clinical Psychiatry, 60*(9), 633–642.

Novaco, R. W. (1975). *Anger control: The development and evaluation of an experimental treatment.* Lexington, MA: Heath.

Olatunji, B. O., & Lohr, J. M. (2005). Nonspecific factors and the efficacy of psychosocial treatments for anger. *The Scientific Review of Mental Health Practice, 3*, 3–18.

Salazar, L. F., & Cook, S. L. (2002). Violence against women: Is psychology part of the problem or the solution? A content analysis of psychological research from 1990 through 1999. *Journal of Community & Applied Social Psychology, 12*, 410–421.

Snyder, J. J., & Patterson, G. R. (1995). Individual differences in social aggression: A test of a reinforcement model of socialization in the natural environment. *Behavior Therapy, 26*, 371–391.

Waters, H., Hyder, A. Rajkotia, Y., Basu, S. Rehwinkel, J. A., & Butchart, A. (2004). *The economic dimensions of interpersonal violence*. Geneva, Switzerland: World Health Organization, Department of Injuries and Violence Prevention.

Wolfe, D. A. (1999). *Child abuse: Implications for child development and psychopathology (2nd ed.)*. Thousand Oaks, CA: Sage.

Wolfe, D. A., Wekerle, C., Scott, K., Straatman, A., & Grasley, C. (2004). Predicting abuse in adolescent dating relationships over one year: The role of child maltreatment and trauma. *Journal of Abnormal Psychology, 113*, 406–415.

I

ANGER, AGGRESSION, AND GENERAL MODELS OF INTERVENTION

1

Anger Dysregulation

Raymond W. Novaco

Our scientific spirit and concern for humanity implore us to attenuate violence, and that ambition easily reaches for anger control. Because aggressive behavior is so often activated by anger, the societal call for anger control fits with quotidian conflict resolution agenda and the broadly based quest for interpersonal harmony. Far more than seeking to enhance civility, social gatekeepers prudently look for ways of reducing violence risk, particularly in view of the familiar shortcomings of institutional corrections systems. As well, interest in anger control has extended beyond wanting remedies for violent behavior. There is now widespread recognition that this turbulent emotion, when experienced recurrently, has health impairment consequences.

Anger control has been a vexing issue that has been addressed in disparate ways by great thinkers across historical periods and by social scientists, clinicians, and community caretakers alike. While acknowledging anger's troublesome facets and by-products, we remain mindful of its personal and social value. Humans are hard-wired for anger because of its survival functions. There can be no sensible thoughts to negate it, much as the Stoics and the Victorians tried. Nevertheless, the aggression-producing, harm-doing capacity of anger is unmistakable, and so is its potential to adversely affect prudent thought, core relationships, work performance, and physical well-being. The problem conditions, however, are not derivative of anger per se, but instead result from anger dysregulation.

SOCIETAL AGENDA AND ANGER CONTROL DIALECTICS

Anger adds fine color to the human personality, and it enables perseverance in the face of hardship. Its interest value captivates our attention, and its threat significance commands it. Anger episodes, social scripted as

3

they are, make for amusement in portrayal, as we know that the shrapnel of everyday existence can jostle the most sanguine disposition. People become attached to their anger routines, which can be oddly satisfying. The psychosocial symbolism of anger casts it as energizing, empowering, signaling, justifying, rectifying, and relieving. Hence, interventions aimed at anger reduction might be disparagingly viewed as totalitarian ploys to stifle individuality and the human spirit. The term anger management might, in an Orwellian sense, connote invasive control over the will to determine one's own destiny. Social gatekeepers—parents, school principals, employers, police, and magistrates—of course, are not charmed by the mastery-toned elements of anger, but rather are sensitized to and unsettled by the contrary social metaphors of anger as eruptive, unbridled, savage, venous, burning, and consuming.

Because anger is too easily transformed into destructive aggression, it beckons for self-regulation. However, many of those who have anger regulatory difficulties that impair their social functioning are otherwise beset with adversities that attenuate control capacity. High-anger people often lead lives with multiple sources of anger aggression instigation. Although they are architects as well as recipients of their misfortunes, their anger troubles can be reflective of trauma, hardship, chaotic social relationships, and perhaps mental disorder. For those high in avenues of friction, impoverished in support structures, and short in countervailing resources for inhibitory controls, anger easily becomes a default response. It carries the aura of repelling threat and provides fortification of self-worth.

Important to note, in the context of the present volume, it is the embeddedness of anger in an admixture of adversities that sharply distinguishes this emotion in clinical populations from the anger reactions observed in the subject pools of university laboratories. Achieving change in clinically problematic conditions is a bit more complicated than offering distraction, supplying a cool drink, hitting a bop bag, or providing mitigating information about a perceived slight from an experimental confederate. Garden-variety anger reactions, whether laboratory grown or real life based, are qualitatively different from those rooted in longstanding distress. With seriously angry people, simply engaging them in the process of treatment is fraught with many obstacles. As Howells and Day (2003) have cogently articulated, the complexity of clinical cases, clients' inferences about their problems, clients' personal goals, mandatory treatment issues, institutional settings, cultural differences, and gender differences all bear on client responsivity to provided programs. Readiness for anger treatment often must be fostered therapeutically.

In contemporary society, seemingly omnipresent injunctions for "anger management" have taken many forms from the judicial proscriptive to the satirical. Becoming prosaic risks trivialization of anger problems and of the change process, and it has inculcated mistaken views of interventions as mechanized procedures — that is, "putting him through an anger management course." To be sure, anger control has been a societal agenda at least since classical philosophers grappled with the regulation of inner life and the enhancement of virtue. Anger was perhaps the prototype of the view of emotions as "passions" that seized the personality, disturbed judgment, altered bodily conditions, and imperiled behavior. Plato and Aristotle, in seeking the perfection of character and temperament, viewed moderation in anger as desirable. The Stoics, in contrast, precluded the viability of anger, as readily seen in the writings of Seneca and Epictetus. Roman and Greek philosopher/historians such as Cicero and Plutarch, also sought eradication of anger in the quest for tranquility of mind.[1] Predating the Greek and Roman Stoics were Buddhist teachings about the path to enlightenment, seeking to train the mind to gain inner strength. The military strategies attributed to Sun Tzu (4th century, 1983) saw anger as a fault on which military commanders could capitalize. The long-standing injunctions for anger control in the domains of work and family in American history are superbly presented by Stearns and Stearns (1986). Present-day cognitive-behavioral intervention advocates should not lose sight of this ancestry.

Whether we have made any advances in proscriptions for anger control in the past two millennia might be an unsettling question, and addressing it is a daunting task beyond the present scope. Yet, a brief example is useful here. The classical eradicationist view is perhaps best exemplified in the writings of Lucius Seneca (44/1817), who in first-century Rome was an adviser to Caligula and a tutor of Nero.[2] Seneca wrote systematically about anger control, and much of his important treatise on morals identified key elements stipulated by contemporary cognitive and social/personality psychology concerning emotions. The conception of anger as a product of threat perceptions, as having confirmatory bias characteristics (i.e., the perception of events is biased toward fit with existing anger schemas), as being primed by aversive precursors, and as having social-distancing effects (i.e., expressing anger keeps people

---

[1]It is exceedingly difficult to summarize the writings of philosophers on anger, even for a single historical period. Fortunately, for the classicists, there is a masterful book by Harris (2001) and a very fine edited volume by Braund and Most (2003).

[2]Seneca's friction with Nero, culminating in the odious emperor forcing him to commit suicide, is summarized in an account given by Roger L'Strange in the introduction to the Harper & Brothers edition of the Morals (Seneca, 44/1817). Nero's deadly brutality, including toward his mother and wives, ended in his own suicide by stabbing himself in the throat (cf. Hibbert, 1985, who also provides an excerpt of Seneca's condemnation of the savagery of gladiatorial contests).

away), which are part of the present author's view of anger, can be found in Seneca (44/1817). Like other Stoic philosophers, who negated the value of emotions, his view of anger was almost exclusively negative. Seneca recognized the powerful role of cognition as a determinant of anger, advocated cognitive shift and reframing to minimize anger, and saw the merit of a calm response to outrageous insult. However, he discounted the functional value of anger and failed to recognize the importance of the intensity dimension, which thereby led him to miss the principle of regulation. Seneca often confused anger with aggression (despite having differentiated them), did not inform us about the etiology of anger dysregulation, and did not understand how anger can be entrenched in personality and pose resistance to change efforts.[3]

People having serious anger problems often do not embrace treatment, largely due to the value that they ascribe to anger in dealing with life's adversities. Because anger can be comingled with many other clinical problems (e.g., personality disorder, psychoses, substance abuse, dementia), getting leverage for therapeutic change can be an elusive goal, particularly when referrals for anger treatment entail some element of coercion. Efforts to achieve clinical change are challenged by the adaptive functions of anger as a normal emotion, such that it is not easily relinquished. Anger can be ingrained in personal identity. Moreover, when derivative of a traumatic life history, it serves protective needs, but its social-distancing function is an obstacle to therapeutic change efforts.

Because anger activation may be a precursor of aggressive behavior, it often presents safety concerns for mental health professionals, wary to engage it as a treatment focus. Assaultiveness is indisputably a significant problem for those providing care to psychiatric patients, which is discussed more fully later. However, though many high-anger patients may present with a hard exterior, they can be psychologically fragile—especially those having histories of recurrent abuse or trauma and those for whom abandonment and rejection have been significant life themes. Anger and aggression as character armor can mask felt vulnerability, as can be generated by the foreboding punitive actions of powerful social systems.

The instrumental value of anger and aggression can make for their intractability; hence therapeutic change agents should bear in mind functionality themes. Detaching someone from anger/aggression routines smartly proceeds from recognition of the functions served by them, both

---

[3]Another Stoic philosopher, Epictitus, was commonly quoted in early cognitive therapy writings, such as by Albert Ellis and Donald Meichenbaum. In his book on anger, Ellis (1977) oddly missed Seneca, and his approach to anger is to see it as largely derivative of irrational beliefs and its remediation as predicated on modifying those beliefs.

manifest and latent. Functional analysis of anger was a springboard for early cognitive-behavioral anger treatment (Novaco, 1975, 1976), and keeping sight of functionality is an implicit premise in the "Aggression Replacement Training" work of Arnold Goldstein and his colleagues (Goldstein & Glick, 1987; Goldstein & Keller, 1987; Goldstein, Nensen, Daleflod, & Kalt, 2004). When we seek to diminish anger or encourage its moderation, strive to promote prosocial behavior as an alternative to reactive aggression, and generally aim to displace values conducive to violence, we should be cognizant of the broad array of influences that sustain violent behavior and anger activation.

As the notion of functionality is intrinsic to the systems-oriented approach to anger that is advocated here, it is useful to first present some thoughts on functions of violence and of anger. The theme of symbolic control of anger and aggression emerges when functions are examined.

FUNCTIONS OF VIOLENCE

One of the most incisive observations in social science was that of Robert Merton (1957), who stated that persistence was evidence of function. Indeed, Merton (1938) saw the social order as an impulse management device, a way of regulating biologically based tensions. Violence, of course, has certainly been persistent.[4] Its functions can be construed in terms of two broad categories: *core survival value functions* and *extended social system value functions* (see Table 1.1). The elaboration of these categories and their partitioning is not done here, as the point is to highlight contextual influences and symbolic structures that sustain violent behavior.

Violence is harm-doing behavior. In the service of survival maintenance (viz. defense of self, loved ones, and resources needed to sustain well-being) there is exoneration for necessitated harm-doing. Humans, though, are unique in the animal kingdom in using aggression not only for defense of self, family, and sustenance, but also in defense of symbols. Humans territorialize ideas as well as real estate. Thus, warfare has often been about the defense of symbols and their promulgation. Democracy

---

[4]The wooly-headed canard that, as humans, we are more violent now than we have ever been is easily dispelled by elementary attention to history. The Assyrians, Romans, Turks, European monarchies, Mongolians, and Zulus, to take a few dynastic examples, perpetrated ample brutality. Consider that Genghis Khan virtually depopulated northern China in the 13th Century when he slaughtered tens of millions of Chinese or that there were approximately 2 million causalities in the battles of the Somme and of Verdun in 1916 in World War I. The history of Renaissance Florence is filled with artistic achievement, but it is also replete with killing.

TABLE 1.1
Functions of Violence

Core Survival Functions (manifest functions)	
Survival maintenance	• defense of self and loved ones • for humans, defense of symbols and their promulgation
Acquisition and defense of resources	• given finite resources or differential demand for resources, violence has utility • given that human nature is flawed, violence will be used by some, to get what is needed or desired, despite proscribed norms and punishments

Extended Social System Value Functions (latent functions)	
Societal unification and sustaining of social bonds	• violence as external threat encourages activities that promote efficient defense and well being of the community • reinforces social bonds encouraging procreation
Social system ordering and regulation	• induces hierarchical ordering of social system, legitimizing control mechanisms for minimizing conflict • regulatory structures (laws, police, courts) are reinforced by violence and thereby given greater legitimacy for extension to nonviolent rule breaking
Sustains conceptions of "good" and "just"	• demarcates "evil" people and "bad" behavior • violence is intrinsic to the norm of retaliatory and redressing of grievances
Ventilation/discharge	• gives expression to anger and distress, having cathartic value
Freedom representational	• represents demonstration of freedom, liberty, autonomy, and power
Entertainment	• in direct and vicarious forms, it produces arousal and enhancement of sensation • violence is a commodity having economic value

and national pride have served to justify and motivate war at least since the funeral oration of Pericles, as recounted by Thucydides, in fifth-century BC (Thucydides, 1960). However, in the vein of core survival needs, violence also functions to acquire resources—material, status, and so on. It is used to get what is needed or desired. Given finite resources or differential demand for bountiful resources, violence has utility for their acquisition.

These survival maintenance functions are transparent. What are less obvious, but nevertheless identifiable, are the extended social system value functions served by violence. These are not elaborated here, but the simple idea to register is that there are social-context considerations to be given to the occurrence of violence, and factors bearing on its enactment may be not so conspicuous. For example, violence, in the form of external threat, serves purposes of societal unification and reinforcement of social bonds. It encourages activities that promote efficient defense and community coalition, as well as procreation and the production of capital resources. This is the use to which the tags of the "Great Satans" and "Evil Empires" have been put. Governmental leaders have always known the value of having external enemies, which not only mobilize the populace against the designated external foe but also serve to distract attention away from internal problems.

System-ordering effects result from violence. In animal species, both intraspecific and interspecific aggression has long been understood by ethologists to have species-preserving functions (Cloudsley-Thompson, 1965; Eibl-Eibesfeldt, 1967; Lorenz, 1966). Aggression induces a hierarchical structuring of the social group. In humans, it also legitimizes external controls for the minimization of conflict and optimizing of production. Social scientists have been aware of that certainly since Hobbes's (1651/1958) social contract theory, for which the authority of the sovereign was predicated on violence control. Violence fosters establishment of regulatory mechanisms (laws, agencies, punishments) that instill internal control of impulses. Structures established to curtail violence (laws, police, courts) are in turn reinforced by violence, and are thereby granted greater legitimacy in extension to nonviolent rule breaking or civil disputes. Scherer, Abeles, and Fischer (1975) discussed the system-enhancing functions of conflict and also asserted that conflict resolution helps a system to adapt to its environment.

Associated with the system regulatory function of punitive correction is that violence is intrinsic to the norm of retaliation and the redressing of grievances. Embedded in this norm of *lex talionis* is the theme of "justification." Retaliatory harm-doing behavior (whether that be in the form of a "just war," interpersonal defense, or judicial punishment) is deemed justified by unprovoked or unwarranted aggression. Violence in this context also sustains conceptions of "good" and "just" by demarcating "evil" people and "bad" behavior meriting punitive treatment. Malicious people, who do unjustified violence, are thought to justly deserve retaliatory responses that may be violent in response.

The justification theme is strongly driven by symbolic structures. What is judged to be the transgression, affront, or wickedness is shaped by schema or macro knowledge structures. The threat schema of a social group can heighten attention to transgressions or signals of malicious intent. Violations or encroachments might be exacerbated or excused by status variables that mark the action as especially onerous or, alternatively, as forgivable. Justification is a core theme in the activation of anger and aggression, being rooted in ancient religious texts, such as the Bible and the Koran, as well as classical mythologies about deities and historical accounts of the behavior of ancient rulers.[5] Anger, as well, is very much infused with themes of justification, and even righteousness—exemplified by God's anger in the Dies Ire (Days of Rage) segment of the Latin Mass of the Dead. Retaliatory aggression recruits anger as an energizer.

There are other latent functions of violence related to symbolic structures. One is that violence also has a freedom representational function—which can perhaps be viewed as an opponent process (Solomon, 1980) to societal efforts to constrain aggressive behavior. Violence constitutes a deviation from prevailing regulatory codes and thereby represents demonstration of freedom, autonomy, liberty, and power separate from sovereignty. The point of departure for revolutions is a violent act, which itself takes on powerful symbolic signification and longevity, reflected in societal celebrations.

Still another latent function is that violence has entertainment value. In both direct and vicarious forms, it produces arousal and the enhancement of sensation. At least since gladiatorial contests in the Roman Coliseum, violence has been a commodity having economic value. For audiences, of course, the product is served as a vicarious experience. Drama, film, music, and other art forms give portrayals of violence that provided amusement and aesthetic appreciation. As Konecni (1991) has argued, actors' anger and enacted violence have demonstrable effects on spectators, including audience empathy and identification with the characters.

---

[5]Biblical examples of the justification theme can be found in its various books, such as the Psalms and Zephaniah, as well as in Ezekiel, where one finds the passage (25:17) recited by Samuel Jackson's character in the movie *Pulp Fiction*, "and I will execute great vengeance upon thee with furious rebukes." Stone narrative examples are seen in the palace wall reliefs of seventh-century BC Assyrian kings Sennacherib and Ashurpanipal (now in the British Museum in London), which depict massive savagery by these kings who considered themselves gods.

As a concluding note to this discussion of violence functions, something should be said about the "hostile versus instrumental aggression" canard. This distinction is often made to differentiate aggressive behavior that is enacted for the purpose of doing harm/damage to the attacked person/target from aggression that is motivated by noninjurious goals, such as economic gain or status enhancement. This is a bogus distinction, as aggression is inherently instrumental (including being an expression of anger), so the idea of noninstrumental aggression makes little sense. Other relabelings of this distinction, such as "annoyance motivated" versus "incentive motivated" or "reactive" versus "proactive" have been offered. These bifurcated classifications of aggression that hinge on ambiguously differentiated goal distinctions can be bypassed by simply thinking of aggression as occurring with or without anger (Novaco, 1998).

A most thorough discussion of this issue was proffered by Bushman and Anderson (2001), who concluded that it was time to "pull the plug" on the dichotomy.

ANGER FUNCTIONS

Akin to aggressive behavior, anger has functional value for survival. In the face of adversity, it can mobilize physical and psychological resources, energize behaviors for corrective action, and facilitate perseverance. Anger serves as a guardian to self-esteem, operates as a means of communicating negative sentiment, potentiates the ability to redress grievances, and boosts determination to overcome obstacles to our happiness and aspirations. The acceptability of its expression and the form that its expression takes vary socioculturally (e.g., Averill, 1982; Kassinove, Sukhodolsky, Tsytsarev, & Solovyova, 1997; Malgady, Rogler, & Cortes, 1996). Attending to how anger functions provides knowledge about this emotional state or syndrome and also can inform clinical intervention strategies that aim to diminish anger responding.

In the major aggression theories of Berkowitz (1962), Feshbach (1964, 1971), and Bandura (1973, 1983) respectively, anger arousal is assigned response-energizing, response-motivating, and response-activating functions. Anger is viewed in each of those theories as an emotional response that facilitates aggression, rather than as a necessary condition—which remains the standard position among aggression scholars. However, in his subsequent theorizing, Berkowitz's (1990, 1993) view is that anger occurs parallel to aggression and that both are produced by "negative affect" induced by unpleasant external events.

In the field of emotion, anger was prominently addressed by Darwin (1872/1998), both throughout that volume and in a chapter detailing its vicissitudes (i.e., defiance, indignation, rage, and hatred). Many theories of emotion have enlarged upon the Darwinian view of emotions as reactions to basic survival problems created by the environment and on Cannon's (1915) idea that internal changes prepare the body for fight or flight behavior. These core ideas are exemplified in Plutchik (1980), as well as in Lazarus (1968). From Cannon to Lang (1995), emotion has commonly been viewed as an action disposition. As well, emotional expression in understood to have communicative value, which Darwin (1872/1998) recognized and which has received extensive research attention from Ekman (2003), Izard (1977), and others.

The psychodynamic view of aggression, discussed more fully later regarding anger regulation, though not disposed toward a functional perspective, tends to see anger—or more exactly "hostility"—as a motivational force for human destructiveness. One finds that view in core psychoanalytic writings on aggression from Freud (1930/1961) to Saul (1956). Bowlby's (1973) discussion of anger is sparse—it occupies a very small proportion of the text, despite its inclusion in the book's subtitle. However, Bowlby saw anger as functional when it served to fortify attachment bonds and dysfunctional when it weakened them.

The social constructivist approach of Averill (1982, 1990) is very important. He views anger as a socially constituted syndrome—a transitory social role governed by social rules. His constructivist viewpoint emphasizes the idea that the meaning and function of emotions are primarily determined by the social systems in which they occur and of which they are an integral part. Emotions are interpreted as passions, rather than actions—that is, as something that happens to one, rather than something that one does. He articulated this analysis with relevant biological and psychological systems, and his scholarly book covered historical, philosophical, legal, and scientific literature.

The identification of anger functions by Novaco (1976) was undertaken with an eye toward treatment provision. The central idea was that the inherent instrumentality of anger and aggression would be an impediment to therapeutic change efforts. Thus, clinical assessment should incorporate ideographic functional analysis of anger patterns. Encapsulating and recasting that earlier formulation, anger can be seen to have the following functions: It *energizes* behavior as a high arousal state, increasing the amplitude of responding; it *focuses* attention on situational elements having threat significance; it *expresses* or communicates negative sentiment, to convey displeasure and to prompt conflict resolution; it *defends* the self by social distancing and fear suppression, and it also defends self-worth by externalizing attributions of blame for misfortune; it *potentiates* a sense of personal control or empowerment, among social groups as well as individuals; it *instigates* aggressive behavior due to its survival relevance, symbolic linkages, and learned connections; it *signals* information about personal state and situational significance, which is relevant to self-monitoring; and it *dramatizes* a social-role enactment, in the sense of anger expression being dramaturgy played out in accord with social scripts.

By understanding how anger functions for an individual identified as having a problem meriting treatment, the attempt at intervention can more smartly proceed by addressing the needs being served by the troublesome anger responding routines. Functional analysis has long underpinned the experimental analysis of behavior approach to human aggression, as applied, for example, by Marcus, Vollmer, Swanson, Roane, and Ringdal (2001) to persons with developmental disabilities. It has also been applied to deliberate self-harm (Gratz, 2003). As well, Daffern and Howells (2002) have argued for a functional-assessment approach to inpatient aggression to guide selection of management strategies and psychological intervention.

To provide some elaboration here of one not so obvious treatment-related aspect of an anger functions orientation, consider the "signaling" function mentioned previously. The assertion is that anger serves as a discriminative cue of an unwanted state of affairs. Anger is a sign of agitated distress or tension, acute or chronic, arising from aversive circumstances.

Anger activation varies in Central to anger regulation is self-monitoring. One must detect a signal of departure from homeostasis in order to correct the deviation. Anger activation varies in frequency, intensity, duration, and mode of expression, which can be considered anger problem parameters (cf. Novaco & Jarvis, 2002)—that is, response dimensions on which we can gauge whether someone can be understood to have an anger problem. The intensity dimension functions as a qualitative discrimination, because we partly judge that we are *angry*, as opposed to being "upset," "bothered," or "annoyed" by virtue of the affect intensity. Unlike frequency, which is quite variable culturally, degree of intensity is much more clearly indicative of dysfunction, because physiological arousal is an intrinsic element. It is well established scientifically that high arousal disrupts performance, especially mental processes involved in complex tasks. In addition to having cognitive interference effects, high-intensity anger leads to impulsive behavior, as it overrides inhibitory controls. People often judge their anger intensity from their behavior in an anger episode, although this is more the case for men than for women (Frost & Averill, 1982); however, there are many internal cues, both somatic and cognitive, that demarcate anger intensity. With regard to engaging clients in anger treatment, the intensity of anger is a gateway parameter as high-intensity anger is easily designated as unwanted. Moderating anger intensity is a therapeutic goal that quite readily receives endorsement.

A CONTEXTUAL PERSPECTIVE ON
ANGER CONTROL PROBLEMS

Personal narratives about anger experiences provide the observational base from which we understand anger as a subjective emotion. Indeed, anger incident accounts that unfold the phenomenology of provocation episodes can mesmerize an audience, being a routine ploy of comedians. The attributional bias inherent in self-centered portrayals is transparent, but there is another bias common in anger incident accounts that is not so readily detected. When people report anger experiences, they most typically tell about things that have "happened to them," describing elements physically and temporary proximate to the anger arousal—that is, they ascribe the provocation to aspects of the immediate situation in which anger was activated. Provocation sources are ordinarily identified as the aversive behavior of others, such as insults, unfair treatments, or deliberate thwartings. Anger is then prototypically experienced as a justified response to some "wrong" that has been done, portrayed in the telling as being something about which anger is quite fitting. Thus, subjective accounts of anger experiences can be seen to have a "proximity bias" (Novaco, 1993).

The seductive quality of anger narratives is misleading about sources of anger arousal and about variables influencing its course. This does not just pertain to ordinary discourse. A number of studies on activators of anger have been based on daily diary data and classifications of open-ended incident descriptions, whereby respondents confine their account of the anger instigation to proximate situations. Assigning the causes of anger to discrete occurrences has occurred in the community and student studies by Averill (1982), the autobiographical narrative studies by Baumeister, Stillwell, and Wotman (1990), and the student questionnaire studies of Ben-Zur and Breznitz (1991) and M. B. Harris (1993), as well as the informative Kassinove et al. (1997) cross-cultural study. These investigations have applied a discrete-event, main-effects conception to anger activation, rather than a search for higher order interactions. Yet, self-report questionnaires can be constructed to examine the variance in anger reactions associated with situations, modes of response, and individual differences, as did Endler and Hunt (1968), who found that nearly 30% of total variance was associated with interactions.

Viewing anger from a contextual perspective and incorporating system theory concepts captures the dynamics of anger in a way that is helpful to treatment and prevents clinicians from getting stuck in the head—that is, restrict their purview to intrapsychic factors. Intervention for persons troubled by anger can usefully proceed by examining the environmental, interpersonal, and dispositional subsystems that shape anger reactions.

Moreover, whereas anger dyscontrol can result from long-term exposure to adverse life circumstances, acute trauma, psychosis, or biochemical imbalance, recurrent anger can be seen to be a product of *agentic* behavior. People often select high-conflict settings or continue to inhabit high-stress environments that set the stage for their anger experiences. Habitually hostile and aggressive people can create systemic conditions that fuel continued anger responding that is resistant to change. Alternatively, many clients are beset with exposure to toxic psychosocial environments, from which they seem to have little freedom of movement. Recognition of the confluence of multilevel risk factors affecting violence, is well exemplified by the multisystemic treatment of juvenile offenders and their families conducted by Borduin and others (cf. reviews by Borduin, 1999; Curtis, Ronan, & Borduin, 2004), which has links to the social ecological model of Bronfenbrenner (1979, 1986), who emphasized interconnected systems and reciprocal influences.

Therapeutic focus on intrapsychic variables is transparently inadequate when the person remains immersed in anger-engendering contexts. In contrast, systems concepts, highlighted later, call attention to anger dynamics and system interplay. Here, the presentation is brief, but a fuller presentation can be found in Robins and Novaco (1999), where the systems perspective is also applied to two clinical cases.

As a point of departure, it is useful to view anger as grounded in long-term *adaptations* to internal and external environmental demands, involving a range of environmental fields from the biological to the sociocultural. Thus, individual, group, and aggregate-level factors affect anger as the person, group, or organization responds to demands pertinent to survival. Because anger has important adaptive functions in affecting behavior, as previously discussed, it thereby affects the social and physical environmental systems in which the person has membership. Threat, conflict, frustration, or surprise disturbs *homeostasis*, prompting attempts to adapt to the challenge and to reestablish *equilibrium*. However, in the context of a perceived threat, anger can operate as a "default" response to which the person resorts in the absence of more sophisticated or optimal coping strategies. Anger is a cue that something needs to change, but it is also engaged as a means of changing the aversive conditions. Successful adaptation, of course, is predicated on knowing what to change and when to change it.

Anger experiences are *embedded* or nested within overlapping systems, such as the work setting, the work organization, the regional economy, and the sociocultural value structure. By recognizing anger embeddedness, attention is given to elements of social-cultural and physical environmental envelopes that impart anger-inducing potential to the behavior settings nested within them. Though we more commonly recognize acute (proximal) potentiators of anger, such as inconsiderate behavior by others or noxious interruptions, we are less immediately cognizant of ambient conditions, because they lack perceptual salience. Yet, for example, perturbations in the regional economy, such as aggregate job loss, are associated in time series with rates of violent behavior in the community (Catalano, Novaco, & McConnell, 1997, 2002). Background adversities, such as aggregate economic strain, personal work pressures, family conflicts, or routine traffic congestion, operate as distal sources of tension, which can *transfer* across these life domains. Interdomain transfer effects are exemplified by negative mood at home in the evening being very significantly influenced by travel impedance on the commute home from work, controlling for many personal demographic, residence, and job variables (Novaco, Kliewer, & Broquet, 1991). Indeed, one of the most important phenomena involving anger and aggression is *excitation transfer* (Zillmann, 1971, 1979; Zillmann & Bryant, 1974). This pertains to the carryover of undissipated arousal, originating from some prior source, to a new situation having a new source of arousal; the carryover then heightens the probability of aggression toward that new and more proximate source. As undissipated arousal accumulates, the transfer results in anger responses of exaggerated intensity to the proximate activator.

In viewing anger contextually, emphasis is given to *interdependencies* between systems and system components. The causes, experiences, and sequelae of anger are reciprocally influenced. For example, in a coercive family system, as reflected in much research by Patterson and his colleagues (Patterson, 1984, 1986), parental anger arises during disciplinary confrontations as an effort to control a child's antagonistic behavior. The parent's anger display not only can prompt further antagonistic behavior from the child but also models anger as a response to noncompliance or being thwarted, thus reinforcing the coercive character of the milieu. As Patterson (1986) concluded after complex model testing, "parental nattering and explosive reactions during discipline confrontations were bidirectionally related to the target child's coercive exchanges with family members" (p. 441).

The interrelatedness of system components provides for *positive and negative feedback* among the interdependent structures. When a system moves away from equilibrium, negative feedback serves to *counteract the deviation*. The counteraction or inhibition of the deviation hinges on signal detection, as occurs with a thermostat, which is analogous to the function of cognitive systems in self-monitoring anger reactions to achieve anger control. Human biological systems are replete with negative-feedback loops, but the thermostat and cooling system is a very apt example, because "heat" is the most central metaphor of anger (Lakoff & Kovecses, 1987). The cathartic expression of anger also has an equilibrium-restorative function, provided that contextual conditions for the catharsis are met. As this is a frequently misunderstood phenomenon, it merits concerted attention in addressing anger regulation.

Among the most important concepts pertaining to anger/aggression dynamics and anger treatment is *escalation*. Anger reactions can escalate through positive feedback that *amplifies deviation* from equilibrium, whereby succeeding events intensify the conditions that gave rise to those events. Anger displays in a situation of conflict tend to evoke anger and aggression in response, which then justify the original anger and increase the probability of heightened antagonism. Such anger/aggression *escalation* effects are well-known in conflict scenarios, whether interpersonal or international. Anger arousal tends to give rise to thoughts that justify the anger, which in turn, through associative cognitive networks, increase the likelihood that future events are appraised in ways that facilitate anger. Not to get stuck in the head, one can see deviation amplification occur in a larger positive-feedback loop of behavioral, geographical, and mate selection choices that create environments and adaptive pressures that may reinforce anger activation and the mode of response. People with problems controlling anger are likely to lose friends that they insult, yet will maintain interpersonal associations with others who tolerate or even support their anger. Over time, their schemas will shift increasingly toward appraisals consistent with anger, and a repertoire of conditioned anger responses will evolve. Occupational, recreational, friendship, and family choices and activities may then depend on anger-tolerant contexts.

Another very key concept in dealing with anger dyscontrol is *automaticity*—when a component of a system no longer requires input from another component in order to be activated. Thoughts, emotions, and behaviors can occur without the need for, and indeed may be outside the control of, conscious attention. Many interactions over a long period of time (practice) are typically necessary to achieve automaticity, as occurs in the acquisition of skills. Similarly, anger and aggression can become automatized as coping responses. A related concept is that of aggressive scripts, best articulated by Huesmann (1998). Aggressive scripts, which program antagonistic behavior and exacerbate anger difficulties, are socially and contextually learned. As social-interaction patterns solidify and categorizations of provocation are schematized, anger can be evoked with considerable automaticity in reaction to minimal threat cues. Alternatively, one can learn to automatize nonanger responses, which is a core objective of anger treatment.

For many treatment-seeking clients, anger has come to be an "automatic" response that is troublesome, akin to the classical notion of emotion as a "passion" that takes control of the personality (cf. Averill, 1982). Anger reactions may thus be experienced subjectively as being uncontrollable and inevitable. As inputs that give rise to anger recur, such as intrusive hostile thoughts, they can be activated by increasingly more subtle environmental cues and reflect a lack of regulatory ability to inhibit the anger. The involvement of anger in posttraumatic stress disorder is a dysregulatory aspect of automaticity in response to survival threat (Chemtob, Novaco, Hamada, Gross, & Smith, 1997; Novaco & Chemtob, 2002).

A principal psychosocial metaphor associated with anger is that is "eruptive," exemplified by Mt. Vesuvius imagery (Novaco, 1975). The explosiveness aspect, though, perhaps overrides the transformational aspect that occurs in conjunction with a *threshold* effect. A threshold in a system is a point at which some part of the system changes in a qualitative way. When this occurs, a new property is said to have emerged. An easy and highly relevant example is that of water boiling at 100 degrees Celsius, transforming a fluid into an emergent hot gas that will pressurize a container. There is no better metaphor for anger than hot fluid in a container. When "heat" (social friction) reaches a critical point, an explosion of anger emerges as a new property.

Threshold effects are relevant to anger regulatory self-monitoring, as well as to detection of violence risk by organizational systems. The conversion of restrained anger to chaotically expressed aggression has colloquially been described as the "last straw." Strongly and frequently inhibited aggression can convert to explosive behavior, as has been demonstrated to occur with violent offenders later assessed as having "overcontrolled hostility" (R. Blackburn, 1968; Megargee, 1966). The violent episode is precipitated by a stressful event, such as a job loss, a supervisory confrontation, or a relationship breakup that ruptures the "overcontrol" containment. This feature is pertinent to how Malay amok episodes have been traditionally understood (cf. Carr & Tan, 1976; Spores, 1988), and to the contemporary Western civilization syndrome glibly termed as "going postal."[6] Davey, Day, and Howells (2005) review the issue of anger overcontrol pertinent to serious violent offenders, discussing it in terms of emotion regulation theory and treatment readiness issues. As well, among hospitalized psychiatric patients, the occurrence of assaultive

---

[6]Perhaps the first multiple-murder episode by a postal worker occurred on August 20, 1986, at 7:00 a.m. in Edmond, Oklahoma, when Patrick Sherrill came to work with several pistols in a cloth sack. First he shot 2 supervisors and a man fleeing out the back door; he then killed 11 more and wounded 6 others before shooting himself in the head. He had been reprimanded the day before by his immediate supervisor and had also told a union steward that his employers were giving him a hard time. However, there had been previous workplace violence episodes, including the assassination of San Francisco mayor George Moscone and city councilman Harvey Milk by Dan White in 1978.

behavior has been thought to have "spontaneous" and "unpredictable" qualities (cf. Novaco, 1994; Volavka, 2002), erupting without an apparent trigger. However, someone who dwells in a setting that is inherently frustrative—and is also devoid of affirmations of self-worth and offers ample time for rumination—may be provoked to assault by events appearing to be relatively minor, as when a hospital patient is denied a request, temporarily loses a privilege, or has an expected visitor fail to show (Novaco, 1997).

The *emergent property* at threshold may also be something constructively beneficial. In dealing with many types of clinical problems, motivation for change is seen to emerge when the person "hits bottom." People with severe anger problems are often resistant to change, which can be seen as exhibiting system *inertia*. Treatment of anger proceeds successfully when two thresholds are met: (a) when the client recognizes that costs of anger outweigh the benefits of anger/aggression habits, and (b) when the client commits to engage with the therapist. However, treatment engagement may be followed by disengagement, necessitating reengagement efforts. Howells and Day (2003) have turned the "treatment resistance" notion on its head, asserting instead that the treatment engagement problem be understood as a matter of "readiness."

The intrapersonal, dispositional systems addressed by anger treatment are the cognitive, physiological, and behavioral domains, with attention given to their links to the environmental contexts in which the person functions. Cognitive dispositions for anger include knowledge structures, which are organized schematically, and appraisal processes. Anger schemas are cognitive structures about environment–behavior relationships entailing rules governing responses to threatening situations. The anger–threat relationship is discussed more fully in the next section. Things can have provocation value by virtue of their symbolic significance, such as social-group identifiers or fighting words. Physiological dispositions for anger include activation in the cardiovascular, endocrine, cortical, and limbic systems, and by tension in the skeletal musculature. Neurobiological mechanisms include the amygdala, the prefrontal cortex, and serotonin. Behavioral dispositions include instrumentally conditioned and observationally learned repertoires of anger-expressive behavior, including aggression but also avoidance behavior. Implicit in the cognitive labeling of anger is an inclination to act antagonistically toward the source of the provocation. However, an avoidant style of responding, found in personality and psychosomatic disorders, can foment anger by leaving the provocation unchanged or exacerbated.

These dispositional subsystems are highly interactive or interdependent. Hostile interpretations influence physiological arousal levels, high arousal activates aggression and overrides inhibition, and antagonistic behavior escalates aversive events and shapes anger schemas and behavioral routines that become encoded as scripted habits. The intrapersonal dispositional system interfaces with the environmental, such as when anger and aggression drive away pacific people, leaving one with angry/aggressive companions or with those for whom antagonism is congruent. That distilled companion set is unlikely to be prosocial achievement oriented or be disposed to offer constructive support in times of need; instead they would be those who not only incite anger but from whom one continues to learn anger-responding and anger-engendering ways of thinking about life challenges and one's social relationships.

Anger is diminished as one automatizes a thinking style that is incongruent with anger, develops increasingly more adaptive alternative responses to environmental demands, chooses low-conflict environments, maintains supportive social relationships, and invests in the future. There is dynamic interaction between these interdependent components—a change in each component of the system facilitates changes in other components. In the course of treatment, new properties can emerge (e.g., perspective taking, self-calming), become automatized and give rise to yet other emergent properties (e.g., humility, higher frustration tolerance, formation of positive relationships) that are antidotes to anger responses. The inability to control anger reflects absence in appreciation, affiliation, and acceptance. Anger control is a proactive posture, not merely an intercession on the spot of arousal. The core principles and concepts of this contextual perspective are given in Table 1.2.

ANGER AND THREAT

Anger is intrinsically associated with threat sensing. Implicit in the notion of threat is potential harm to the subject—an elementary point, but one that is perhaps lost when "angry faces" are used as experimental stimuli in physiological research on threat. Anger is aroused when threat is detected, malevolence is inferred, and approach or attack motivation is engaged. It is amplified by justification schema.

Threat detection occurs through elaborate neurocognitive systems that are progressively being identified. The neural architecture specialized for the processing of emotion and emotion–cognition interactions includes the limbic system, and particularly the amgydala (e.g., LeDoux, 1984, 1989, 1993). The activation of the amygdala is centrally involved in detecting events as threats (Aggleton & Mishkin, 1986; McGaugh, 2003). Neurobiological mechanisms associated with amygdala involvement in aversive emotion have been addressed by McGaugh and his colleagues (e.g., Cahill & McGaugh, 1990; Cahill, Roozendaal, & McGaugh, 1997;

TABLE 1.2
Contextual Perspective on Anger Regulation

Core Principles
• Anger is a dynamic phenomenon shaped by contextual conditions; this orientation stands in contrast to viewing anger as a reaction to proximal events, thoughts, and contingencies. • Anger engagement is centrally linked to survival functions; its value is dependent on its regulation in serving both acute and long-term needs. • Anger is grounded in long-term adaptations to internal and external environmental demands, in a range of environmental fields from the biological to the sociocultural.

Regulatory Systems Concepts	
embeddedness:	Anger systems are embedded or nested in overlapping systems.
interdependence:	The causes, experiences, and sequelae of anger are reciprocally influenced.
threshold effects:	Anger activation can occur in a continuous, gradual manner or emerge as a "sudden leap."
nonlinearity:	Changes that occur in anger level or anger expression are not necessarily incremental.
automaticity:	With repeated practice or trauma, anger may become automatized as a coping response.
escalation:	Anger engagement can increase the probability of its precursors. Angry behaviors tend to produce further aversive experiences.
negative feedback:	For anger regulation, proficiency hinges on self-monitoring skills and the person's provocation coping repertoire. It also hinges on values attached to the departure from homeostasis.
inertia:	The functionality of anger as a survival response fosters resistance to change.
equifinality:	The causes of anger and aggression are multifactorial; conversely, therapeutic changes can be produced through multiple routes.
optimization:	To achieve anger regulation as a treatment outcome, the therapeutic course should target the enhancement of coping skills to fit the person's existing resources, life space, activities, and goals.

McGaugh, 1995). Lang (1995) has proposed that emotion is controlled by appetitive and aversive motive systems in the brain, with the amygdala serving as a key site for the aversive motivational system. Anger is seen by Lang as a product of subcortical structures related to harm avoidance and as primed by this motivational system—that is, associative linkages to anger have greater access, and anger is more likely, when the aversive motivational system is engaged by stimuli signifying present danger or reminders of trauma.

In contrast to Lang's work pointing to aversive or avoidance motivation, the impressive work of Harmon-Jones on frontal brain activity (Harmon-Jones, 2004; Harmon-Jones & Allen, 1999; Harmon-Jones & Sigelman, 2001) has linked anger with left-prefrontal cortical activity, which has typically been associated with positive affect and approach motivation. However, the anger conditions he has studied are not traumatic ones. Earlier, it had been conjectured by Davidson that the anterior regions of the two cerebral hemispheres were specialized for approach (left hemisphere) and withdrawal (right hemisphere) and that cortical asymmetry was associated with approach-versus avoidance-related affects (Davidson, 1993, 1998). Recently, Hewig, Hagemann, Seifert, Naumann, and Bartussek (2004) in complex testing of affective valence (positive-negative), motivational direction (approach-withdrawal), and behavioral activation (activation-inhibition) hypotheses regarding frontal cortical asymmetry primarily found support for the motivational direction hypothesis. Subjects with greater left-frontal cortical activity had higher STAXI anger-out scores, and those with greater right-frontal activity had higher anger control scores. However, it should be noted that there was no anger induction in their study—participants were not made angry; they were administered an anger disposition scale. Thus, although it is known is that the limbic system, cortical structures, and neurotransmitters such a norepinephine, serotonin, and dopamine are involved in anger activation (e.g., Anderson & Silver, 1998; Davidson, Putnam, & Larson, 2000), the neural structures and circuitry in anger dysregulation remains to be disentangled.

Anger is directed by attention. To get angry about something one must pay attention to it. Anger is associated with selective attention to cues having high provocation value. A principal function of cognitive systems is to guide behavior, and attention itself is guided by integrated cognitive structures, known as schemas, which are mental representations that incorporate rules about environment–behavior relationships. Summary theoretical presentations on cognitive processing pertinent to anger and aggression can be found in Huesmann (1998) and Novaco and Welsh (1989), as well as Beck (1999). Evidence of attentional bias associated with anger was obtained on Stroop task performance interference by Eckhardt and Cohen (1997) and by van Honk et al. (2001), being particular noteworthy in the former study, which induced anger by insult and measured it as a trait characteristic.

What receives attention is a product of the cognitive network that assigns meaning to events and the complex stimuli that configure them. Expectations guide attentional search for cues relevant to particular needs or goals. Once a repertoire of anger schemas has been developed, events (e.g., being asked a question by someone) and their characteristics (e.g., the *way* the question was asked, *when* it was asked, or *who* asked it) are encoded or interpreted as having meaning in accord with the preexisting schema.

Since the Stoic philosophers, especially Seneca (44/1817), anger has been understood to be strongly determined by personal interpretations of events. When threat signals are detected, higher level cognitive reasoning elaborates this information, in what are termed appraisal processes (Lazarus, 1994; Ortony, Clore, & Collins, 1988). The concept of appraisal is that of interpretation, judgment, or meaning embedded in the perception of something—not as a cognitive event occurring after that something has happened. Appraisal of provocation is *in* the seeing or hearing (cf. Novaco, 1986). Appraisal, though, is an ongoing process, so various reappraisals of experience will occur and will correspondingly affect whether or not the probability of aggression is lessened, maintained, or intensified. Rumination about provoking circumstances will extend or revivify anger reactions. As well, the occurrence of certain thoughts can prime semantically related ideas that are part of an anger schema. Imagined violence among hospitalized psychiatric patients was found by Grisso, Davis, Vesselinov, Appelbaum, and Monahan (2000) to be strongly related to anger and to postdischarge community violence.

Because of their survival function, the threat-sensing aspect of anger schemas carries urgent priority and can preempt other information processing. Associated with anger reactions and high-anger dispositions is an interpretive bias to infer malevolence that feeds the reciprocal connection between anger and aggression. This conjecture (Novaco, 1978, 1979) was tested and supported in comparison group studies by Nasby, Hayden, and DePaulo (1980) with emotionally disturbed boys and by Copello and Tata (1990) with violent offenders in a high-security hospital. This is consistent with findings by Dodge and his colleagues on hostile attributional bias among aggressive boys (e.g., Dodge & Coie, 1987; Dodge & Somberg, 1987). Moreover, someone who has been targeted by physical attack will likely show selective attention to anger-related threat cues, as can be seen in the elaborate neurophysiological evidence of Pollak and Tolley-Schell (2003) regarding the attentional processing of physically abused children to angry faces. They conjectured that poorly modulated attentional control during anger displays contributes to the social-cognitive biases found in abused children (see also, Pollak & Kistler, 2002).

Perceived malevolence is one of the most common forms of anger-inducing appraisal. When another person's behavior is interpreted as intending to be harmful to self, anger and aggression schemas are activated. Perceiving malevolence pulls for anger by involving the important theme of justification, which includes the externalization of blame. Weiner's approach to emotion through attributional analysis has emphasized that anger is experienced when a personally relevant negative outcome is attributed to factors controllable by others (e.g., Weiner, 2001; Weiner, Graham, & Chandler, 1982). When harm or injustice has been done, social norms of retaliation and retribution are engaged. Pertinent here is Averill's (1982) view of anger as a socially constituted syndrome or a transitory social role governed by social rules. Thus, provocation meaning and function would be determined by the social systems in which it occurs and of which it is an integral part.

Justification is a core theme in the activation of anger and aggression. Anger is also a blaming reaction, directed against deserving targets. Anger expression and physical aggression are subjectively experienced as applying a legitimate punitive response for transgression or as ways of correcting injustice. Justification is often accompanied by entitlement, which entrenches the anger. Sometimes, of course, justifications are embe-llished so as to exonerate blame for destructive outcomes of expressed anger.

Linking anger to threat perception carries several implications for understanding anger dysregulation (Novaco & Chemtob, 2002; Novaco & Welsh, 1989). Persons with high-anger dispositions are highly vigilant in threat sensing and quick in response. Threat sensing is confirmation-biased—anything that could be perceived as harmful or malevolent is rapidly designated as such, and the anger responses are highly automatized. The rapid engagement of anger preempts alternative appraisals of the triggering event and considerations of alternative action plans. The strong arousal overrides inhibitory controls of aggressive behavior, and the threat-anger-aggression responses forge a positive-feedback loop—the more threat is perceived, the more anger and aggression; and, conversely, the more anger and aggression, the greater the readiness to perceive threat and the likelihood of new inputs that will constitute threat. Anger and aggression generate unfriendly responses from others.

To facilitate anger regulation, treatment procedures should strive to disconnect anger from the threat system. This aspect of therapeutic intervention, which applies to both individual and group-based treatment, is elaborated in a later section.

ANGER REGULATION

Emotion regulation has become a major topic in the fields of developmental psychology, personality and social psychology, and cognitive neuroscience. In its most elementary sense, emotion regulation is a process whereby engagement or activation of one system component modulates the state of another system component. The neuroscience research provides strong exemplars, as reflected in the works discussed previously and that of others, such as Damasio (1995). In developmental psychology, emotion regulation theory and research is displayed in the work of Cole and Zahn-Waxler (1992), Dodge (1989), Eisenberg and her colleagues (e.g., Eisenberg, & Fabes, 1992; Eisenberg, Spinard, & Smith, 2004), and Campos, Frankel, and Camras (2004). Links to attachment theory can be seen in Mikulincer (1998) and Mikulincer, Shaver, and Pereg (2003). In personality and social psychology, some exemplifications are the control process theory of Carver and Scheier (1990) and Muraven and Baumeister's (2000) view of self-control as a consumable resource. The impressive work of Gross (e.g., Gross, 1998, 2002; Gross & John, 2003) has spanned the fields of cognition and emotion, social psychology, clinical psychology, and neuroscience. Philippot and Feldman (2004) provide broad coverage of this developing topic.

For the most part, theory and research on emotion regulation has not attended to the dynamic complexities of anger. Though it has examined generic regulation processes or strategies, such as suppression, reappraisal, distraction, comfort seeking, and withdrawal, the focus has not been on psychotherapeutic relevance. Here, in contrast, a clinical orientation is adopted in discussing anger regulation. In doing so, attention is given to some core psychoanalytic works, where the study of anger and aggression has important roots, reflected in ongoing research and clinical issues, such as repressed/suppressed anger and catharsis.

ANGER CONTROL IN PSYCHOANALYTICAL THEORY

The landmark work in human aggression research is the *Frustration and Aggression* monograph by Dollard, Doob, Miller, Mowrer, and Sears (1939), the heuristic source of which is psychoanalytic theory. The history of that lineage in aggression research and other historical background pertinent to anger and clinical intervention is given in Taylor and Novaco (2005). The present text adds to that account, addressing repressed anger and catharsis.

Anger was a sparse topic in psychoanalytic writings, and Freud never provided a coherent view of anger. He gave greatest emphasis to it in writing about Michelangelo's statue of Moses (Freud, 1914/1985).[7] Menninger (1938), one of Freud's major exponents, presented many clinical and journalistic stories of persons who "boil over with rage" and later asserted that the human child "usually begins his life in anger" (Menninger, 1942); but he did not give explicit attention to anger and rarely used the word in his books. The famous treatise on aggression by Hartmann, Kris, and Loewenstein (1949) virtually omits the word *anger*, which appears in one incidental comment describing a child's hypothetical behavior. Anna Freud's (1949) article on aggression in that same volume had emotional development in its title, but the word *anger* does not appear anywhere in the text. Horney (1939) broke from the Freudian emphasis on libidinal frustration in the etiology of the neuroses, as she conjectured that hostile impulses toward parents may be aroused in the child in many ways, including lack of respect, injustice, unreasonable demands, unreliability, coercion, and manipulation. It was one of her disciples, Rubin (1969), who gave anger top billing, and he advocated an outlook on anger that recognized its normality. However, he was preoccupied with the blocking, freezing, twisting, subverting, or otherwise "perverting" of anger, hence he leaned rather far in the ventilationist direction.

There are many examples of the inattention to anger by psychoanalytic scholars in the decades after Freud (see Taylor & Novaco, 2005), but Redl and Wineman (1951, 1952) did grant anger some priority. In their theoretical framework, developed in conjunction with the treatment of children having conduct disorders, they posited an impulse system and control system hydraulic model. Problematic manifestations of anger were understood in terms of breakdowns in the control system. Despite the cogency of their work, anger remained an undiscovered topic in psychoanalytic writings. For example, Crocker's (1955) lengthy case study of a highly aggressive 13-year-old boy, with "severe temper tantrums," which was published in the flagship journal, *The Psychoanalytic Study of the Child*, was approached in formulation and in treatment in terms of ego mastery of libidinal development—indeed, to an astounding degree.

Two concepts bequeathed by the psychoanalytic perspective have had continued play in cognitive-behavioral research and clinical intervention. The first is that of *repressed anger*, which bears on how the relationship between anger and depression is understood. The second is that of *catharsis*,

---

[7]Freud's original publication of this essay on Moses was done anonymously in 1914 in the journal *Imago*. The Michelangelo statue of Moses, which mesmerized Freud on visits to Rome, is in the church of San Pietro in Vincoli (St. Peter in Chains). Gay (1988) provides Freud's account of having stood daily in front of the statue during one 3-week visit. Freud concluded that it was Michelangelo's intent to portray Moses as having subdued his inner tempest. He renewed that interpretation in a postscript in 1927 (Freud, 1914/1985, pp. 237–238).

which bears on the relationship between anger and aggression, as well on therapeutic techniques for dealing with anger.

Repressed Anger

The classic psychoanalytic position on aggression is that "outward aggression is an expression of the death instinct in the service of Eros," and that "any restrictions of aggression directed outwards increases self-destruction" (Freud, 1930/1961, p. 66). It is this postulate that underlies the psychodynamic view that depression is anger turned inward. The idea of retroflected anger or "hostility turned inward" appeared in *Mourning and Melancholia* (Freud, 1917/1963) and was carried forward by Menninger (1938) and by Storr (1968) in conceptualizing the psychopathology of depression. It is also central to Madow's (1972) understanding of the role of anger in numerous somatic disorders, as well as depression and suicide. At the societal level, Grier and Cobbs (1968) portrayed the rage of African-American individuals in precisely these terms. Freud's view was that the self-reproaches of the melancholiac are really against a loved object but are redirected to the patient's own ego. This notion was based on his observations about mourning and grief, whereby the bereaved person's unconscious anger toward the deceased could not be allowed into consciousness, hence the inverted hostility. The concept was later extended by Freud and his followers to apply to libidinal object relations and loss in general. Even Bowlby (1973) gives credence to this term. Bandura (1973) cogently disputed psychodynamic accounts of aggression, but vestiges of this view of depression as "repressed anger" remain. It is not a concept that has empirical support, nor is it a useful one, except perhaps to persuade a depressed or avoidant person to become energized in coping with aversive events.

At the outset, "repression" should not be confused with "suppression"; however, failure to distinguish repressed anger from suppressed anger pervades the literature. Many investigators conveniently slip from Freudian theory, which stipulates repression, to self-report measures of "introjected hostility" or "anger in." Freud (1917/1963), in accounting for melancholia, describes the hostility as unconscious. The psychoanalytic concept of "repression" signifies denial, rejection, and keeping something out of consciousness (cf. Freud, 1915/1963). Thus, if someone is repressing anger, then they are not aware of it. To the contrary, people who are depressed commonly report anger and do so straightaway. That does not signify repression. Anger suppression or inhibition of anger expression is, in contrast, a viable concept that is not elaborated here. Instead, some basic points are made concerning anger and depression in conjunction with the notions of anger "direction" and "inwardly directed hostility."

Anger is often a strong accompaniment to depression (e.g., Fava & Rosenbaum, 1999; Koh, Kim, & Park, 2002; Posternak & Zimmerman, 2002), as is the case for hostility with depression (e.g., Scocco, Meneghel, Caon, Dello Buono, & De Leo, 2001; Yesavage, 1983). In conjunction with trauma, anger is a common result (cf. Beckham, Moore, & Reynolds, 2000; Novaco & Chemtob, 1998), and anger's integral association with post-traumatic stress disorder is discussed later. Returning to the context of bereavement, in Lindemann's (1944) classic study of bereaved persons, he found irritability and anger to be normal reactions, yet he described what he termed "morbid grief reactions" in which the grief process was distorted by intensified hostility, including furious hostility toward specific persons. Longitudinal research on bereavement by Clayton and Darvish (1979) regarding the course of depressive symptoms found that, for those who remain depressed after 13 months, feelings of anger about the death intensified; but the anger was frequently directed at the deceased, the hospital, and the physician—it was seldom self-directed.

Early research regarding hostility directedness, conducted with psychiatric patients, found *both* inwardly *and* outwardly directed hostility to be associated with depression (I. M. Blackburn, 1974; Lyketsos, Blackburn, & Tsiantis, 1978; Schless, Mendles, Kipperman, & Cochrane, 1974; Weissman, Klerman, & Paykel, 1971). Recent research by Koh et al. (2002), with multiple anger measures, compared depressive disorder patients with anxiety disorder and somatoform disorder patients and with healthy controls. Degree of depression was highly correlated with the anger measures for the patient groups and for the healthy controls. The group-differentiating anger dimension, however, was *anger-out*, and there were no group differences for anger-in. Depressive disorder patients had significantly higher anger-out scores on that Spielberger anger expression measure (Spielberger et al., 1983) and significantly higher anger/hostility on two other measures. The data of Riley, Treiber, and Woods (1989) show depressed patients to be higher in anger than normal controls on multiple measures, regardless of directedness. Inwardly directed hostility occurs simultaneously with depressed mood (Newman & Hirt, 1983) and, though it does decline in response to treatment for depression, the outwardly directed hostility remains (I. Blackburn, 1974; Lyketsos et al., 1978). Suppressed anger, of course, has many deleterious effects, particularly as it has been robustly associated with elevated blood pressure and sustained hypertension in laboratory, field, and clinical studies (cf. Robins & Novaco, 2000). In headache patients, anger suppression has been linked to depression (Materazzo, Cathcart, & Pritchard, 2000).

Depressive episodes often involve psychomotor agitation, brooding, and irritability. Beyond these demarcating symptoms, Fava, Anderson, and Rosenbaum (1990) reported on a series of cases with major depressive disorder for whom sudden "spells" of anger occurred, which were said to resemble panic attacks. Subsequently, in a study with 127 medication-free outpatients with major unipolar depression, Fava et al. (1993) found that 44% of them reported having "anger attacks," and those who did scored significantly higher on psychometric scales of hostility. In review articles, Fava has asserted that approximately one third of depressed outpatients experience anger attacks (Fava, 1998; Fava & Rosenbaum, 1999). Mammen et al. (1999) found a rate of 60% at a specialty clinic for pregnant or postpartum women, and anger attacks were significantly associated with diagnoses of unipolar depression. Leaving aside the issue of whether "anger attacks" constitute a phenomenon any different from simply having a strong anger reaction, the point here is that anger is associated with depression, and those who are depressed readily report anger experiences.

The association between depression and anger extends to aggressive behavior and violence. High anger and hostility in domestically violent men is accompanied by depression (Maiuro, Cahn, Vitaliano, Wagner, & Zegree, 1988). More centrally, aggression is manifested in the self-harming and suicidal behavior of depressed persons, and certainly in the behavior of those with bipolar disorders. Scocco et al. (2001), with a large sample of elderly persons in the community, found that the presence of suicidal feelings was significantly differentiated by the Brief Symptom Inventory (BSI) "hostility" scale (which is really an *anger* measure), and, controlling for depression, anxiety, health status, marital status, and use of hypnotics, there was nearly a threefold increase in risk in suicidal feelings associated with that "hostility" measure. Studies by Hillbrand and his colleagues with forensic patients have demonstrated that self-destructiveness and interpersonal violence coexist, as a substantial number of violent patients alternate between self-harm and attacks on others (Hillbrand, 1995; Hillbrand, Krystal, Sharpe, & Foster 1994). Yesavage (1983) found that suicidal and other self-destructive acts by hospitalized depressives did not correlate with degree of depression but were significantly related to hostility, both self-reported and observer rated.

Finally, regarding whether depressed persons are violent, the important MacArthur study of violence risk (Monahan et al., 2001), which involved over 1,100 discharged psychiatric patients in three U.S. metropolitan areas, provides persuasive data. This comprehensive study found that postdischarge violence in the community at 20 weeks and at 1 year varied significantly as a function of diagnostic category, and the violence rate was highest for persons with a diagnosis of depression. The 1-year prevalence rate of violence was 28.5% for patients with depression, 22.0% for those with bipolar disorder, and 14.8% for those with schizophrenia. However, in variable-centered analyses of violence risk factors, depression was not significant, whereas anger was significant.

In summary, anger coexists with depression. Persons who are clinically depressed report anger expressiveness as well as anger suppression, they report anger directed at others as well as anger directed at self, and they act violently toward others as well as engage in self-harm. The psychoanalytic conjecture that the etiology of depression is the result of *repressed* anger is without empirical foundation. In contrast, anger suppression—the conscious inhibition of anger expression—remains a valuable concept, particularly as it does not always indicate dysfunction.

Catharsis

Catharsis is a controversial and poorly understood topic that emerged from psychoanalytic writings and the frustration–aggression hypothesis. Because of its importance in understanding the relationship between anger and aggression and because part of the controversy involves prescriptions for handling anger, it merits our attention. The topic of catharsis is multiplex, being associated with aspects of theater, psychotherapy, contact sports, media violence, and assorted folklore about dealing with aggressive urges—including assorted bash-toys, bop-bags, and commercialized voodoo gadgets. In clinical practice, it is unfortunately associated with huckster pseudotherapies that are transparently not grounded in thorough understanding of the person. However, it is not without value in psychotherapy. Displaced aggression can have merit, as when an out-of-sight inanimate object is a substitute target for a person (e.g., a misbehaving child), especially when the displaced aggression is a clinically formulated strategy and when the substitute behavior is a short-term alternative until greater anger control is instituted. In a cognitive-behavioral therapy (CBT) anger treatment program, catharsis has a minimal role, at best; but it is worth unraveling the issues, especially because clients may believe in the value of catharsis as tension release (see chap. 5, this volume).

The concept of catharsis is typically traced historically to Aristotle (e.g. Berkowitz, 1970; Bushman, Baumeister, & Stack, 1999; Konecni, 1991), who thought that in watching tragedies, members of the audience would be purged of distressed emotions, such as pity, fear, and anger, by vicariously experiencing the tragic performance. Aristotle's *Poetics* is usually cited as the source, but there is more on the subject in his *Politics*. The idea of tension reduction through outward expression was fundamental to psychoanalytic therapy and later to other psychodynamic approaches, including Gestalt therapy, emphasizing the expression of blocked, "dammed-up," or unfinished emotions. Catharsis was Freud's "talking cure" (initially suggested to him by Breuer as a procedure to be used in conjunction with hypnosis). Cathartic therapy was aimed at bringing an original distressing experience into consciousness to enable the person to discharge or "abreact" the blocked, troublesome affect causing the client's symptoms. Support for the catharsis concept also came from animal ethologists (positing aggressive instinct), such as Lorenz (1966), who viewed aggressive behavior as having energy-discharge or tension-reduction functions. In generalizing his animal behavior theories to human, Lorenz prescribed cathartic activity, including sports, as an aggression control strategy.

This hydraulic model—equilibrium is restored by relieving pressure thorough discharge, which thereby prevents hazardous eruption—adopted for anger and aggression, can promote an overvaluing of "ventilation" as an approach to anger control. This is exemplified in the outlook advocated by Rubin (1969). To be sure, there is considerable folklore about catharsis. Many people believe that it is better to vent than to swallow, simmer, and fume. Various cinematic and stage scenes, product advertisements, song lyrics, and famous-person advice statements solidify that view. Berkowitz (1970, 1993) and others, such as Tavris (1982), and more recently Bushman and his colleagues (Bushman, 2002; Bushman et al., 1999; Bushman, Baumieister, & Phillips, 2001; chap. 5, this volume), have argued against the value of venting, given the evidence contrary to its efficacy. However, they have made a bit too much of the ventilationist theme in being critical of clinical approaches that make use of cathartic techniques for anger management (e,g., Bach & Wyden, 1968).

Before addressing matters of clinical relevance, some commonly missed elements of the scientific controversy merit attention. Research on catharsis was stimulated by the *Frustration and Aggression* monograph (Dollard et al., 1939), where it was stated that "The occurrence of any act of aggression is assumed to reduce the instigation to aggression" (p. 50). Catharsis is the expression/release of internal tension, and the "cathartic effect" is the reduction of this tension, reflected in a decreased probability of subsequent aggression and lowered arousal level. In critiques of catharsis, Berkowitz (1970, 1993) and others (e.g., Quanty, 1976; Tavris, 1982) gave too much space to studies involving observed or imagined aggression, as opposed to direct action. In this regard, Konecni (1984) urged that the differences between the Aristotelian catharsis paradigm and that of Plato be recognized. The Aristotelian version involves the *observation* of violence, whereas the version of Plato (in *The Republic*) instead concerns the *performance* of aggressive actions, done when one is *angry* and delivered *against the anger instigator*. Konecni, who had conducted laboratory research on catharsis (Konecni, 1975a; Konecni & Ebbesen, 1976), identified methodological problems in many experiments on catharsis and came to the conclusion that many investigators, using poorly formulated research designs, "expected the manipulation of Aristotelian independent variables to produce decreases in Platonic dependent measures" (Konecni, 1984, p. 31).

It would be tangential here to attempt a full discussion of catharsis research issues, and it is far better in any case to refer to Konecni's (1975a, 1984) handling of that task. Important to note, though, one will also find in his writings a bidirectional causality model of anger and aggression (see also Konecni, 1975b), whereby level of anger is a determinant of aggressive behavior, and the expression of aggression can decrease level of anger, thus decreasing subsequent aggression—the "cathartic effect." It is also clear from Konecni's theory and empirical findings that (a) both anger and aggression can be decreased by nonaggressive activities; (b) the cathartic effect pertains to the *immediate* consequences of aggression by angered persons; and (c) over time, "aggression breeds aggression." The latter is expected by virtue of the anger-reducing reinforcement contingencies for aggressive behavior, enduring cognitive concomitants of anger that lead to reinstigation of aggression, and the development of aggressive response patterns in anticipation of anger cues. Konecni (1991) provides an exposition and extension of his model to the theater staging and direction of dramatic performances. More generally, his bidirectional causality postulate is pertinent to the "interrelatedness" of anger and aggression—a theme here in advocating a systems contextual perspective for understanding anger.

Before proceeding to the more recent research by Bushman and his colleagues (Bushman, 2002; Bushman et al., 1999, 2001), which bears on catharsis beliefs relevant to both clients and therapists, it should be noted that catharsis investigators have oddly ignored that Dollard et al. (1939) did say: (a) that the cathartic reduction in subsequent aggression is more or less temporary, and (b) that the repetition of a mode of release may produce learning of it (see their footnote, p. 50). Critics of the catharsis hypothesis have also not grappled with the points raised by Holt (1970) regarding the constructive versus destructive expressions of anger, and his criticism of energy-discharge or tension-reduction models. Holt had asserted that the "clearing of the air" in constructive anger expression is primarily about getting cognitive clarification or restructuring to remove the instigation to aggression and to restore mutual empathy. When anger is constructively expressed, people not only express feelings, they also communicate their definition of the situation and indicate desired changes.

People do believe that venting anger will make them feel better, and those who are attached to this belief are more likely to do so (Bushman et al., 2001). Media messages touting the value of catharsis induce the inclination to vent anger (Bushman et al., 1999). When the participants in the later study and also in Bushman (2002) were made angry and then (some) were given the opportunity to hit a punching bag, most of them enjoyed it. Those that did hit the punching bag exhibited more subsequent aggression against the person who made them angry at the start, which is contrary to beliefs about the cathartic value of venting. However, it is not a full test of the catharsis hypothesis, because, in hitting a punching bag, the cathartic activity is not directed against the anger instigator. Also missed is postcatharsis arousal assessment, as multiple studies by Hokanson and his colleagues (e.g., Hokanson, 1961a, 1961b; Hokanson & Burgess, 1962a, 1962b; Hokanson & Shetler, 1961) have found that following aggression *directly* against an anger instigator, there *is* a lowering of physiological arousal—a cathartic effect.

What gets lost in laboratory catharsis research is the ecological-validity issue—the psychotherapeutic context. The "ventilationist" argument is a straw man, banking on so-called cathartic anger expression associated with fringe therapies, for which California is infamous. Pillow punching, battaca bashing, primal screaming, and so forth, are gadget-play tactics that do not constitute much of a therapeutic game plan. When a therapist, guided by a grounded clinical formulation, encourages the expression of "blocked" feelings, the therapeutic interest may be more in the inhibitory forces than in the anger expression itself. The person's restraints on anger expression are perhaps indicative of conflicting thoughts and feelings that are preventing a full examination of the troubles that have brought the person to therapy. By having the person feel safe in expressing anger, whether that be in a structured role play or through a procedure that looks like a game (to get around the censor), the therapist may be seeking to convey that the oppositional forces are not so terrifying and that anger expression, in the context of a supportive relationship, can be safe. What is important is not getting the anger "out," per se, but putting on the table the multilayered issues (e.g., matters pertaining to guilt and shame) associated with the blocking of the anger expression and the intensity, duration, and complications of the feelings involved. Getting the anger out can be a ploy for revealing the entangled distress and worrisome thoughts that are choking the person and impairing ability to move forward in life.

To be sure, therapists have used "catharsis" in ways that are unhelpful. Benjamin (1990) provides a fine set of examples of such uses that detract from viable therapeutic goals and recapitulate an ineffective interpersonal relationship style. She emphasizes that when attention is given to the interpersonal consequences of anger expression (e.g., facilitating a patient's differentiation from a destructive parent, learning about one's interactive patterns, and promoting a constructive reframing of the self) and to the interpersonal meaning of the anger, then there is therapeutic value.

In contrast to what happens in laboratory settings, in a proper therapeutic context, the expression of anger is monitored and discussed.

Whether in the therapy room or in vivo, whatever the person does as a cathartic activity would ideally be prescribed and extensively discussed—what was experienced during the activity and what sense the person made of it. Assurances of safety would of course be a paramount consideration. The source of the anger instigation would be discussed, as would the sensations and thoughts associated with the cathartic activity. The person would be encouraged to examine the meaning of the experience, including his or her interpretations of the aversive event and its larger significance. Important to note, the person would be helped to discover alternative strategies for dealing with the problem. In a proper therapy, unlike what happens in the lab or in a weekend encounter group, the person comes back, anger experiences are discussed, and long-term goals are addressed.

Cognitive-Behavioral Treatment Emphases for Anger Regulation

The CBT of anger has been developed primarily for anger dysregulation related to aggressive behavior. However, the just discussed comorbidity of anger with depression and the overcontrol of anger are easily accommodated. As well, the provision of clinically formulated cathartic opportunities might even be considered to help the client to regulate explosive outbursts. Indeed, the first presentation of the stress inoculation approach to anger (Novaco, 1977) involved a case of a seriously angry but depressed man, whose anger at work was suppressed, whereas at home he erupted with impulsive verbal and physical aggression. The effect of the latter on his children (whose behavior was rather unruly) induced him to seek therapy. In the early stages of anger treatment, displaced cathartic activity was sometimes used (hitting a tire in the backyard, rather than hitting his sons). The major emphases, however, were on cognitive restructuring, somatic-arousal reduction, and behavioral coping skills for provoking situations. As cognitive and arousal regulation procedures took hold, he was taught behavioral skills to manage the disruptive behavior of his children (e.g., how to defuse fights between his sons), and "cathartic" aggression was soon displaced as a primeval coping strategy and as pointless, because anger frequency and intensity diminished and self-effectance was bolstered.

Anger has been found to predict physical aggression by psychiatric-hospital patients, prior to admission (Craig, 1982; McNeil, Eisner, & Binder, 2003; Novaco, 1994), in the hospital (Novaco, 1994; Novaco & Taylor, 2004; Wang & Diamond, 1999) and, important to note, in the community after discharge (Monahan et al., 2001). Within hospital, anger and aggression incur a great cost. High levels of direct-care staff injuries have been reported in studies done in secure hospitals (e.g., Bensley et al., 1997;

Carmel & Hunter, 1989; National Audit Office, 2003). Because anger can activate aggressive behavior, anger control is indispensable for aggression control. In addition to detriments associated with aggression, anger arousal is also problematic because it can interfere with information processing and, thereby, impair judgment and problem solving. Recurrent anger detracts from adaptive functioning in the contexts of work, family, and social relationships. An angry person is not optimally alert, thoughtful, empathic, prudent, or appreciative. Anger is also problematic as an internal stressor, causing wear and tear on the body when recurrently activated, as reflected in its well-established link to cardiovascular disease (Siegman & Smith, 1994; Strike & Steptoe, 2004).

Anger regulation concerns the person's capacity to modulate the experience and expression of anger in accord with environmental demands, performance priorities, and survival needs. Regulation of anger *experience* has priority for control, as it concerns activation or reactivity, which can have automaticity features. The regulation of anger *expression* pertains to manifestations, which have socially governed display rules, and consequences, over which there is some degree of voluntary control.

A misleading aspect of the notion of "anger management" is that it implies that treatment is centrally about what to do when one gets angry. Instead, a very significant objective of anger treatment is about how not to get angry in the first place—hence the priority given to regulatory controls for anger experience or activation. The parameters or state markers for anger activation that receive attention in CBT anger treatment are: *reactivity* (frequency of onset and how easily anger is triggered), *latency* (how rapidly activated), *intensity* (how strongly engaged), and *duration* (persistence of arousal). Treatment aims to minimize anger reactivity, intensity, and duration and to moderate anger expression to reduce the costs of anger dyscontrol.

Regulation implies executive capacity, for which a key component is signal detection. Hence, a fundamental skill in CBT anger treatment is self-monitoring—detecting the cognitive, arousal, and behavioral signs of anger, as well as recognizing situational elements that can prime anger and aggressive responding. Self-monitoring is centrally important for obviating or interrupting self-confirming vicious cycles of anger–aggression escalation by inducing the person to detect disconfirming evidence (e.g., lack of hostile intent), to consider mitigating circumstances, or to reframe the episode. When anger activation is "hot," such self-regulation is very difficult. Hence, anger treatment procedures give extensive attention to the acquisition of self-monitoring skills. Kassinove and Tafrate (2002) provide many devices for self-monitoring training. Protocol-based procedural detail is provided in Taylor and Novaco (2005) for implementation with persons having intellectual disabilities.

Regulation, in the context of anger control, also implies a motivated effort to modulate internal states and impulses. This involves skills and strategies, but there is the prior requirement of *goals* and *values* congruent with anger control. Impulse control is derived from values associated with control, intrinsically involving a temporal perspective or time horizon (Wilson & Herrnstein, 1985). The rewards for anger control are in the future. This necessitates prioritization of goals, with which most clients need assistance. It also involves wisdom—what is good/bad for self and others—which requires safety and trust in the therapeutic relationship to foster.

To facilitate anger regulation, anger treatment procedures strive to disconnect anger from the threat system. This is done first through the provision of safety, patience, and psychological space for reflection, exploration, and choice. The client's view of anger is normalized, to obviate worries about being a "bad" or unworthy person. The therapist will acknowledge the legitimacy of the client's feelings, affirming his or her self-worth. Building trust in the therapeutic relationship is pivotal. As self-regulation hinges on knowledge, therapy promotes education about anger and discovery of the client's personal anger patterns or "anger signature." Much is done to augment self-monitoring and to encourage the moderation of anger intensity. As tension or strain may surface in the course of treatment, the therapist models and reinforces nonanger alternative responding so as to build replacements for the automatized angry reactions that had been the client's default coping style.

Anger Assessment

Because anger is often embedded with other distressed emotions, accessing it is not straightforward, which presents clinical assessment challenges. There are multiple sources of reactivity bias in anger assessment. People who have long-standing anger difficulties are characteristically suspicious and distrustful, and anger testers may be viewed as representative of a threatening system deserving guarded responses. Important to note, the psychosocial symbolism associated with anger (particularly its boiling/eruptive and savage/nonrational aspects) can deter respondents from disclosing anger and the actions to which anger might dispose them. Moreover, anger can be a protected part of the person, centrally involving matters of self-worth, and is thus not readily revealed or surrendered. As a patient once commented in reflecting about life in an institution, "All you've got is your anger." Disclosing anger may be perceived to carry the psychological cost of losing power and, what may be for that person, the last remaining symbol of personal freedom and self-worth.

In general, anger assessment should be undertaken with multiple measures, seeking convergence or triangulation across different instruments and modes of assessment, as well as different time points because of fluctuating contextual conditions. Three main self-report measures of anger appearing in current clinical investigations are the Spielberger State–Trait Anger Expression Inventory (STAXI; Spielberger, 1996), the Buss–Perry Aggression Questionnaire (AQ; Buss & Perry, 1992; Buss & Warren, 2000), and the Novaco Anger Scale and Provocation Inventory (NAS-PI; Novaco, 1994, 2003). A thorough review of instruments for the assessment of anger and hostility can be found in Eckhardt, Norlander, and Deffenbacher (2004). The focus of anger assessment should be on the construct, not the instrument. Efforts should be made to minimize factors likely to induce reactivity and impair validity, such as juxtaposition with stressful events, potential disapproval, loss of privileges, or increased detention. Anger scores for a particular person are most meaningful in relation to comparable population—college students having lives of minimal adversity quite readily report anger, whereas forensic patients who ruminate about grievances throughout the day and assault people are not so forthcoming in anger reports. Repeated-measures testing is also advisable, as a person's previous scores provide a reference frame. Finally, high-anger self-report scores are generally less ambiguous than low scores.

When anger assessment is done in conjunction with treatment, the therapist should have collated anger assessment data to construct a formulation of the client's anger regulatory problem and the treatment targets. That information should be derived from multiple sources and modes of assessment: (a) clinical interview with the client, significant others, and clinical team or case workers; (b) self-report psychometric scales, such as the STAXI, AQ, and NAS-PI, and also anger diary recordings, for which there are various formats; (c) behavioral observation ratings, which can be provided by trained observers, such as ward or residential staff (cf. Suris et al, 2004); (d) coding of case files and incident reports (e.g., Novaco & Taylor, 2004); and (e) structured provocation testing, which can done via imaginal provocation procedures (cf. Novaco, 1975; Taylor, Novaco, Guinan, & Street, 2004).

ANGER TREATMENT

The provision of therapy for clients troubled by anger must address a turbulent emotion associated with subjective distress and perhaps physical health impairment, but the impetus for treatment is commonly that the person has been flagged for the detrimental effects that his or her anger is having on personal relationships or the manifold consequences of aggressive behavior. Because anger is often entrenched in personal identity and may be derivative of a traumatic life history, it can be hard to dislodge.

However, though some high-anger patients present with a hard exterior, they can be psychologically fragile, especially those having histories of recurrent abuse or trauma, or when abandonment and rejection have been significant life themes. Because anger often appears in an admixture of distressed emotions and long-standing personal hardships, as one commonly sees with hospitalized patients or incarcerated offenders, getting leverage for change can be elusive.

Anger management is a workplace metaphor. Conceivably, anger might be managed like a troublesome problem on the shop floor or, alternatively, as a crucial resource or asset. Prescriptions for job conduct from Dale Carnegie on winning friends and influencing people and later from T-group sensitivity trainers, left little room for anger. Rampages by disgruntled employees in the workplace violence script adopted so frequently in the United States have solidified this metaphor, as has the overarching litigation-inspired need to manage risks. Murderous rage venting on high school campuses reinforced this further. Yet, undeniably, we are hard-wired for anger, because it has survival value. Anger is a fundamental resource not to be squandered by unnecessary activation and expenditure. In the face of adversity, it can mobilize psychological resources, energize behaviors for corrective action, and facilitate perseverance. However, its unmistakable link to aggressive behavior and its detrimental effect on physical health and social relationships render the need for its regulation a legitimate societal concern.

The term *anger management* has become common parlance, but it is a rubric for widely varying interventions offer by practitioners in diverse settings on several continents. The term was coined in Novaco (1975)—cf. *Oxford English Dictionary*—when CBT for anger was first developed. That initial therapy evolved to adopt a stress inoculation approach (Novaco, 1977), as influenced by Meichenbaum's work on anxiety (cf. Meichenbaum, 1985). Subsequent anger intervention studies followed the stress inoculation format (which has graded exposure in a provocation hierarchy as a core procedure), and others added to it (e.g., Feindler & Ecton, 1986). Although Deffenbacher and his colleagues have taken a more generic CBT approach (e.g., Deffenbacher, Dahlen, Lynch, Morris, & Gowensmith, 2000; Deffenbacher, Lynch, Oetting, & Kemper, 1996; Deffenbacher, Story, Stark, Hogg, & Brandon, 1987), as have Kassinove and Tafrate (2002). The stress inoculation approach remains the present author's preferred method of individual treatment, and its efficacy has been demonstrated in controlled studies with high-anger patients having serious disorders: Vietnam veterans with severe combat-related post-traumatic stress disorder (Chemtob et al., 1997) and hospitalized forensic patients with intellectual disabilities (Thorne, 2005; Taylor, Novaco, Gillmer, & Thorne, 2002).

Clinical interventions for anger, however, can be seen to occur at several levels, which vary in their degree of complexity. Novaco, Ramm, and Black (2000) thus distinguished levels of therapeutic intervention for anger, differentiating (a) general clinical care for anger, (b) anger management, and (c) anger treatment. Anger treatment is distinguished from the other levels of intervention by its theoretical grounding, systematization, complexity, and depth of therapeutic approach. It is best provided on an individual basis and may require a preparatory phase to facilitate treatment engagement. Although Kassinove and Tafrate (2002) titled their book *Anger Management,* their level of intervention is anger treatment.

General clinical care for anger identifies it as a clinical need and addresses it through counseling, psychotherapeutic, and psychopharmacological provisions, including client education, support groups, and eclectic treatments, without a formal intervention structure. In contrast, *anger management* typically refers to a structured CBT intervention, originally applied as an individual therapy (Novaco, 1975), but is now often provided in a group mode. That provision is largely psycho-educational in format, as occurs in court-referred or school-based programs, prison settings, and general-public workshops. Such programs typically follow a topical sequence, covering situational activators ("triggers"), how thoughts and beliefs influence anger, self-observation, relaxation techniques, problem solving, conflict resolution strategies, and other CBT coping skills, such as calming self-statements, communication of emotions, and appropriate assertiveness. There is wide variation in "anger management" programs, which are marketed commodities.

In contrast, anger treatment entails greater depth of engagement. Increased depth is associated with thoroughness of assessment, attention to core needs of the clients, greater individual tailoring to client needs, greater specialization in techniques, and the need for clinical coordination and supervision. Anger treatment targets enduring change in cognitive, arousal, and behavioral systems, achieved through changing valuations of anger and augmenting self-monitoring capacity. Because it addresses anger as grounded and embedded in aversive and often traumatic life experiences, it entails the evocation of distressed emotions—that is, fear, sadness, and shame, as well as anger. Therapeutic work centrally involves the learning of new modes of responding to cues previously evocative of anger in the context of relating to the therapist, and it periodically elicits negative sentiment on the part of the therapist to the frustrating, resistive, and unappreciative behavior of the client.

The specialized form of CBT anger treatment called the stress inoculation approach involves the following key components: (a) client education about anger, stress, and aggression; (b) self-monitoring of anger frequency, intensity, and situational triggers; (c) construction of a personal anger provocation hierarchy, created from the self-monitoring data and used for the practice and testing of coping skills; (d) arousal reduction techniques of progressive muscle relaxation, breathing-focused relaxation, and guided imagery training; (e) cognitive restructuring of anger schemas by altering attentional focus, modifying appraisals, and using self-instruction; (f) training behavioral coping skills in communication, diplomacy, respectful assertiveness, and strategic withdrawal, as modeled and rehearsed with the therapist; and (g) practicing the cognitive, arousal regulatory, and behavioral coping skills while visualizing and role-playing progressively more intense anger-arousing scenes from the personal hierarchies. The inoculation procedure is a therapist-guided, graded exposure to provocation stimuli to facilitate anger control. This occurs "in vitro" through imaginal and role-play provocations in the clinic, and "in vivo" through planned testing of coping skills in anger-inducing situations, as established by the hierarchy collaboratively constructed by the client and therapist.

Provocation hierarchy scenarios are designed to capture the client's sensitivities to provoking elements, such as the antagonist's tone of voice or nuances of facial expression. Each scenario ends with provocative aspects of the situation (i.e., not giving the client's reaction), so that it serves as a stimulus scene. The therapist directs this graduated exposure to provocation, knowing the moderating variables that will exacerbate or buffer the magnitude of the anger reaction, in case the scene needs to be intensified or attenuated in potency. Prior to the presentation of hierarchy items, whether in imaginal or role-play mode, anger control coping is rehearsed, and arousal reduction is induced through deep breathing and muscle relaxation. Success with a hierarchy item occurs when the client indicates little or no anger to the scene and can envision or enact effective coping in dealing with the provocation. Treatment conclusion is demarcated by the completion of the hierarchy and agreed resolution with the client.

An effort is made to anticipate circumstances in the client's life that could remain anger provoking and the obstacles to anger control that might arise. People having anger difficulties are often without adequate supportive relationships to provide reinforcement for anger control. Follow-up sessions are typically arranged for relapse prevention, to ascertain what coping skills have proven to be most efficacious, and to boost treatment in areas in need of further work. Because of the reputations acquired by high-anger people, the reactions of others to them can be slow to change. This can lead to relapse and require further therapeutic attention at follow-up.

It should be noted that CBT anger treatment is an adjunctive therapy for a targeted clinical problem and thus is not meant to address other or more general psychotherapeutic needs. Given the functionality of anger and aggression, therapeutic work must replace a client's old problematic routines with new coping skills that enhance well-being. Many people referred for serious anger problems will also be experiencing a primary comorbid Axis I or II disorder (e.g., substance misuse, schizophrenia, personality disorder), which may directly affect the nature and course of the anger problem. Disentanglement of the comorbidity contribution within the cognitive, arousal, and behavioral domains becomes a key aspect of anger assessment and a significant component of the overall formulation. Treatment content will be required to take these factors into account, through either parallel interventions or synthesis of intervention focus and content.

People who are violent are often referred for anger treatment (e.g., incarcerated offenders and spousal abusers or enraged drivers in the community). It is all too easy to refer violent offenders for "anger management," thus it is crucial to identify whether the violent behavior is a product of anger dyscontrol. Across categories of clients, the key issues of appropriateness for CBT anger treatment are: (a) the extent to which the person has an anger regulatory problem, implying that acquisition or augmentation of anger control capacity would reduce psychological distress, aggression, or other offending behavior, or a physical health problem, such as high blood pressure; (b) whether the person recognizes, or can be induced to see, the costs of his or her anger/aggression routines and is thus motivated to engage in treatment; and (c) the person can sit and attend for approximately 45 minutes. The latter criterion applies especially to hospitalized psychiatric patients. Those who are acutely psychotic or whose delusions significantly interfere with daily functioning are not suitable candidates. Persons with substance abuse disorders also require prior treatment to engage in anger therapy. Individual psychotherapy is inadequate when the person has serious comorbid disorders and/or remains immersed in anger-engendering contexts, and coordinated efforts of a multidisciplinary treatment team are required.

An enlightened presentation of the many issues involved in readiness for anger therapy can be found in Howells and Day (2003), who discuss matters of therapeutic alliance, responsivity, and prospective modification of therapeutic approach. In addition to what they denote, it can also be said that prospective participants in anger treatment often lack a number of prerequisites for optimal involvement in a self-regulatory, coping skills intervention program. Clients may have had some training in arousal control and thus may not have difficulty in identifying emotions or differentiating degrees of anger intensity. But they may be unaccustomed to making self-observations about their thoughts, feelings, and behavior in rudimentary self-monitoring. Many may not recognize the degree to which thoughts, emotions, and behavior are interconnected. For others, however, such educational aspects of the preparatory phase are of less importance than the engagement issues.

In the treatment of hospitalized forensic patients by the present author and his colleagues (Renwick, Black, Ramm, & Novaco, 1997; Taylor et al., 2002; Taylor et al., 2005), a preparatory phase has thus been constructed to "prime" the patient motivationally and to establish basic skills of emotion identification, self-monitoring, communication about anger experiences, and arousal reduction. It serves to build trust in the therapist and the treatment program, providing an atmosphere conducive to personal disclosure and to the collaboration required by this therapeutic approach. The latter includes building a common language about the model of anger that guides the treatment (Novaco, 1994). Though designed to be relatively nonprobing and nonchallenging, for some institutionalized patients it can elicit distress, as it raises vulnerability issues for them. Consequently, intersession follow-up meetings with patients may be needed to support them in coping with the impact of the sessions. Because the preparatory phase can be pitched to the client as a "trial period," its conclusion then leads to a more explicit and informed choice by the client about starting treatment proper. In effect, there is a bit of sleight-of-hand at play here in presenting the "preparatory phase" to the client as something to "try out," in the sense of it not being the "real treatment," when indeed it is. Procedural detail on anger treatment preparatory phase is given in Taylor and Novaco (2005).

The designated recipients of real-life anger interventions have been highly diverse in problem condition—for example, domestic-violence perpetrators, traffic offenders, children with conduct problems, quarrelsome neighbors, explosive felons, and persons with various psychiatric disorders being offered anger management as supplementary care. In contrast, a great many recipients of anger treatment in controlled studies have been college student volunteers, which unfortunately results in disproportionate attention to such studies with quasi-clinical clients in meta-analyses. As six meta-analyses have now been published (Beck & Fernandez, 1998; Del Vecchio & O'Leary, 2004; DiGuiseppe & Tafrate, 2003; Edmondson & Conger, 1996; Sukhodolsky, Kassinove, & Gorman, 2004; Tafrate, 1995), there may be more meta-analyses of anger treatment than the number of high-quality clinical trials justify. Overall, these meta-analytic studies have found medium to strong effect sizes, indicating that approximately 75% of those receiving anger treatment improved compared to controls. Meta-analytic reviews fail to include case study reports and multiple baseline studies with clinical populations, for whom CBT and stress inoculation for anger has produced significant clinical gains.

The cognitive-behavioral treatment of anger has been shown to have applicability to a wide range of client populations. Anger dysregulation is associated with many clinical disorders, and in addition to it being indicative of subjective distress, self-report of anger is predictive of violent behavior. Hospitalized patients with long-standing aggression histories, mental disorder, and even intellectual disabilities can be engaged in CBT anger treatment and have been shown to benefit. Though therapeutic mechanisms underlying treatment gains are not clear, nor their sustainability or generalizability, we are fortified in seeking further advances in providing remedies for this important clinical problem of anger dyscontrol.

REFERENCES

Aggleton, J. P., & Mishkin, M. (1986). The amygdala: Sensory gateway to the emotions. In R. Plutchik & H. Kellerman (Eds.), *Emotion: Theory, research and experience* (*Vol. 3*, pp. 281–299). Orlando, FL: Academic Press.

Anderson, K., & Silver, J. H. (1998). Modulation of anger and aggression. *Seminars in Clinical Neropsychiatry, 3*, 232–241.

Averill, J. R. (1982). *Anger and aggression: An essay on emotion.* New York: Springer-Verlag.

Averill, J. R. (1990). Emotion in relation to systems of behavior. In N. L. Stein, B. Leventhal, & T. Trabasso (Eds.), *Psychological and biological approaches to emotion* (pp. 385–404). Hillsdale, NJ: Lawrence Erlbaum Associates.

Bach, G. R., & Wyden, P. (1968). *The intimate enemy: How to fight fair in love and marriage.* New York: Avon.

Bandura, A. (1973). Aggression: A social learning analysis. Englewood Cliffs, NJ: Prentice-Hall.

Bandura, A. (1983). Psychological mechanisms in aggression. In R. Geen & E. Donnerstein (Eds.), *Aggression: Theoretical and empirical reviews* (pp. 1–40). New York: Academic Press.

Baumeister, R. F., Stillwell, A., & Wotman, S. R. (1990). Victim and perpetrator accounts of interpersonal conflict: Autobiographical narratives about anger. *Journal of Personality and Social Psychology, 59*, 994–1005.

Beck, A. T. (1999). *Prisoner's of hate: The cognitive basis of anger, hostility, and violence.* New York: HarperCollins Perennial.

Beck, R, & Fernandez, E. (1998). Cognitive-behavioral therapy in the treatment of anger. A meta-analysis. *Cognitive Therapy and Research, 22*, 63–74.

Beckham, J. C., Moore, S. D., & Reynolds, V. (2000). Interpersonal hostility and violence in Vietnam combat veterans with chronic posttraumatic stress disorder: A review of theoretical models and empirical evidence. *Aggression and Violent Behavior, 5*, 451–466.

Benjamin, L. S. (1990). Interpersonal analysis of the cathartic model. In R. Plutchik & H. Kellerman (Eds.), *Emotion: Theory, research, and experience: Vol. 5. Emotion, psychopathology, and psychotherapy* (pp. 209–229). San Diego, CA: Academic Press.

Bensley, L., Nelson, N., Kauffman, J., Silverstein, B., Kalot, J., & Sheilds, J. W. (1997). Injuries due to assults on psychiatric hospital employees in Washington State. *American Journal of Industrial Medicine, 31*, 91–99.

Ben-Zur, H., & Breznitz, S. (1991). What makes people angry: Dimensions of anger-evoking events. *Journal of Research in Personality, 25*, 1–22.

Berkowitz, L. (1962). *Aggression: A social psychological analysis.* New York: McGraw-Hill.

Berkowitz, L. (1970). Experimental investigations of hostility catharsis. *Journal of Consulting and Clinical Psychology, 35*, 1–7.

Berkowitz, L. (1990). On the formation and regulation of anger and aggression. *American Psychologist, 45*, 494–503.

Berkowitz, L. (1993). *Aggression: Its causes, consequences, and control.* New York: McGraw-Hill.

Blackburn, R. (1968). Personality in relation to extreme aggression in psychiatric offenders. *British Journal of Psychiatry, 114*, 821–828.

Blackburn, I. M. (1974). The pattern of hostility in affective illness. *British Journal of Psychiatry, 125*, 141–145.

Borduin, C. M. (1999). Multisystemic treatment of criminality and violence in adolescents. *Journal of the American Academy of Child and Adolescent Psychiatry, 38*, 242–249.

Bowlby, J. (1973). *Attachment and loss: Vol II. Separation: Anxiety and anger.* New York: Basic Books.

Braund, S., & Most, G. W. (2003). *Ancient anger: Perspectives from Homer to Galen.* Yale Classical Studies, Vol. XXXII Cambridge, England: Cambridge University Press.

Bronfenbrenner, U. (1979). *The ecology of human development: Experiments by nature and design.* Cambridge, MA: Harvard University Press.

Bronfenbrenner, U. (1986). Ecology of the family as a context for human development: Research perspectives. *Developmental Psychology, 22*, 723–742.

Bushman, B. (2002). Does venting anger feed or extinguish the flame? Catharsis, rumination, distraction, anger, and aggressive responding. *Personality and Social Psychology Bulletin, 28*, 724–731.

Bushman, B. J., & Anderson, C. A. (2001). Is it time to pull the plug on the hostile versus instrumental aggression dichotomy? *Psychological Review, 108*, 273–279.

Bushman, B. J., Baumeister, R. F., & Phillips, C. M. (2001). Do people aggress to improve their mood? Catharsis beliefs, affect regulation opportunity, and aggressive responding. *Journal of Personality and Social Psychology, 81*, 17–32.

Bushman, B. J., Baumeister, R. F., & Stack, A. D. (1999). Catharsis, aggression, and persuasive influence: Self-fulfilling or self-defeating prophecies? *Journal of Personality and Social Psychology, 76*, 367–376.

Buss, A. H., & Perry, M. (1992). The Aggression Questionnaire. *Journal of Personality and Social Psychology, 63*, 452–459.

Buss, A. H., & Warren, W. L. (2000). *The Aggression Questionnaire (AQ): Manual.* Los Angeles: Western Psychological Services.

Cahill, L., & McGaugh, J. (1990). *Amygdaloid complex lesions differently affect retention of tasks using appetitive and aversive reinforcement.* Behavioral Neuroscience, 104, 523–534.

Cahill, L., Roozendahl, B., & McGaugh, L. (1997). The neurobiology of memory for aversive emotional events. In M. E. Bouton & M. S. Fanselow (Eds.), *Learning, motivation, and cognition: The functional behaviorism of Robert* C. Bolles (pp. 369–384). Washington, DC: American Psychological Association.

Campos, J. J., Frankel, C. B., & Camras, L. (2004). On the nature of emotion regulation. *Child Development, 75*, 377–394.

Cannon, W. B. (1915). *Bodily changes in pain, hunger, fear, and rage.* New York: Appleton.

Carmel, H., & Hunter, M. (1989). Staff injuries from patient violence. *Hospital and Community Psychiatry, 40*, 41–46.

Carr, J. E., & Tan, E. K. (1976). In search of the true amok: Amok as viewed within the Malay culture. *American Journal of Psychiatry, 133*, 1295–1299.

Carver, C. S., & Scheier, M. F. (1990). Origins and functions of positive and negative affect: A control-process view. *Psychological Review, 97*, 19–35.

Catalano, R., Novaco, R., & McConnell, W. (1997). A model of the net effect of job loss on violence. *Journal of Personality and Social Psychology, 72*, 1440–1447.

Catalano, R., Novaco, R. W., & McConnell, W. (2002). Layoffs and violence revisited. *Aggressive Behavior, 28*, 233–247.

Chemtob, C. M., Novaco, R. W., Hamada, R. S., Gross, D. M., & Smith, G. (1997). Anger regulation deficits in combat-related post-traumatic stress disorder. *Journal of Traumatic Stress, 10*, 17–36.

Clayton, P. J., & Darvish, H. S. (1979). Course of depressive symptoms following the stress of bereavement. In J. E. Barrett, R. M. Rose, & G. Klerman (Eds.), *Stress and mental disorder.* (pp. 121–136). New York: Raven.

Cloudsley-Thompson, J. L. (1965). *Animal conflict and adaptation.* Chester Springs, PA: Dufour Editions.

Cole, P. M., & Zahn-Waxler, C. (1992). *Emotion dysregulation in disruptive behavior disorders.* In D. Cicchetti & S. L. Toth (Eds.), *Developmental perspectives on depression.* (pp. 173–209). Rochester, NY: University of Rochester Press.

Copello, A. G., & Tata, P. R. (1990). Violent behaviour and interpretative bias: An experimental study of the resolution of ambiguity in violent offenders. *British Journal of Clinical Psychology, 29*, 417–428.

Craig, T. J. (1982). An epidemiological study of problems associated with violence among psychiatric patients. *American Journal of Psychiatry, 139*, 1262–1266.

Crocker, D. (1955). The study of a problem of aggression. *The Psychoanalytic Study of the Child, X*, 330–335.

Curtis, N. M., Ronan, K. R., & Borduin, C. M. (2004). Multisystemic treatment: A meta-analysis of outcome studies. *Journal of Family Psychology, 18*, 411–419.

Daffern, M., & Howells, K. (2002). Psychiatric inpatient aggression: A review of structural and functional assessment approaches. *Aggression and Violent Behavior, 7*, 477–497.

Damasio, A. R. (1995). Toward a neurobiology of emotion and feeling: Operational concepts and hypotheses. *The Neuroscientist, 1*, 19–25.

Darwin, C. (1998). *The expression of emotions in animals and man (3rd ed.).* London: HarperCollins. (Original work published 1998).

Davey, L., Day, A., & Howells, K. (2005). Anger, over-control and serious violent offending. *Aggression and Violent Behavior, 10*, 624–635.

Davidson, R. J. (1993). The neuropsychology of emotion and affective style. In M. Lewis & J. M. Haviland (Eds.), *Handbook of emotions* (pp. 143–154). New York: Guilford.

Davidson, R. J. (1998). Affective style and affective disorders: Perspectives from affective neuroscience. *Cognition and Emotion, 12*, 307–330.

Davidson, R. J., Putnam, K. M., & Larson, C. L. (2000). Dysfunction in the neural circuitry of emotion regulation—a possible prelude to violence. *Science, 289*, 591–594.

Deffenbacher, J. L., Dahlen, E. R., Lynch, R. S., Morris, C. D., & Gowensmith, W. N. (2000). An application of Beck's cognitive therapy to general anger reduction. *Cognitive Therapy and Research, 24*, 689–697.

Deffenbacher, J. L., Lynch, R. S., Oetting, E. R., & Kemper, C. C. (1996). Anger reduction in early adolescents. *Journal of Counseling Psychology, 43*, 149–157.

Deffenbacher, J. L., Story, D. A., Stark, R. S., Hogg, J. A., & Brandon, A. D. (1987). Cognitive-relaxation and social skills interventions in the treatment of general anger. *Journal of Counseling Psychology, 34*, 171–176.

Del Vecchio, T., & O'Leary, K. D. (2004). Effectiveness of anger treatments for specific anger problems: A meta-analytic review. *Clinical Psychology Review, 24*, 15–34.

DiGuiseppe, R., & Tafrate, R. C. (2003). Anger treatments for adults: A meta-analytic review. *Clinical Psychology: Science and Practice, 10*, 70–84.

Dodge, K. A. (1989). Coordinating responses to aversive stimuli: Introduction to a special section on the development of emotion regulation. *Developmental Psychology, 25*, 339–342.

Dodge, K. A., & Coie, J. D. (1987). Social information processing factors in reactive and proactive aggression in children's peer groups. *Journal of Personality and Social Psychology, 53*, 1146–1158.

Dodge, K. A., & Somberg, D. R. (1987). Hostile attributional biases among aggressive boys are exacerbated under conditions of threat to the self. *Child Development, 58*, 213–224.

Dollard, J., Doob, L. W., Miller, N. E., Mowrer, O. H., & Sears, R. R. (1939). *Frustration and aggression.* New Haven, CT: Yale University Press.

Eckhardt, C. I., & Cohen, D. J. (1997). Attention to anger-relevant and irrelevant stimuli following naturalistic insult. *Personality and Individual Differences, 23*, 619–629.

Eckhardt, C., Norlander, B., & Deffenbacher, J. (2004). The assessment of anger and hostility: A critical review. *Aggression and Violent Behavior, 9*, 17–43.

Edmonson, C. B., & Conger, J. C. (1996). A review of treatment efficacy for individuals with anger problems: Conceptual, assessment, and methodological issues. *Clinical Psychology Review, 16*, 251–275.

Eibl-Eibesfeldt, I. (1967). Ontogenetic and maturational studies of aggressive behavior. In C. E. Clemente & D. B. Lindsley (Eds.), *Aggression and defense: Neural mechanisms and social patterns.* Berkeley: University of California Press.

Eisenberg, N., & Fabes, R. A. (1992). Emotion, regulation, and the development of social competence. In M. S. Clark (Ed.), *Review of personality and social psychology: Vol. 14. Emotion and social behavior* (pp. 119–150). Newbury Park, CA: Sage.

Eisenberg, N., Spinard, T. L., & Smith, C. L. (2004). Emotion-related regulation: Its conceptualization, relations to social functioning, and socialization. In P. Philippot & R. S. Feldman (Eds.), *The regulation of emotion* (pp. 277–306). Lawrence Mahwah, NJ: Lawrence Erlbaum Associates.

Ekman, P. (2003). *Emotions revealed: Recognizing faces and feelings to improve communication and emotional life.* New York: Times Books.

Ellis, A. (1977). *How to live with and without anger.* New York: Readers' Digest Press.

Endler, N. S., & Hunt, J. M. (1968). S–R inventories of hostility and comparisons of the proportions of variance from persons, responses, and situations for hostility and anxiousness. *Journal of Personality and Social Psychology, 9,* 309–315.

Fava, M. (1998). Depression with anger attacks. *Journal of Clinical Psychiatry, 59 (Suppl. 18),* 18–22.

Fava, M., Anderson, K., & Rosenbaum, J. F. (1990). "Anger attacks": Possible variants of panic and major depressive disorders. *American Journal of Psychiatry, 147,* 867–870.

Fava, M., & Rosenbaum, J. F. (1999). Anger attacks in patients with depression. *Journal of Clinical Psychiatry, 60 (Suppl. 15),* 12–24.

Fava, M., Rosenbaum, J. F., Pava, J. A., McCarthy, M. K., Steingard, R. J., & Bouffides, E., (1993). Anger attacks in unipolar depression. Part 1: Clinical correlates and response to fluoxetine treatment. *American Journal of Psychiatry, 150,* 1158–1163.

Feindler, E. L., & Ecton, R. B. (1986). *Adolescent anger control: Cognitive-behavioral techniques.* New York: Pergamon.

Fehbach, S. (1964). The function of aggression and the regulation of aggressive drive. *Psychological Review, 71,* 257–272.

Feshbach, S. (1971). Dynamics and morality of violence and aggression. *America Psychologist, 26,* 281–292.

Freud, A. (1949). Aggression in relation to emotional development; normal and pathological. *The Psychoanalytic Study of the Child, III/IV,* 37–42.

Freud, S. (1961). *Civilization and its discontents.* New York: W. W. Norton. (Original work published 1930).

Freud, S. (1963). Instincts and their vicissitudes. In S. Freud, *General psychological theory* (P. Rieff, Ed.). New York: Collier Books. (Original work published 1915)

Freud, S. (1963). Mourning and melancholia. In S. Freud, *General psychological theory* (P. Rieff, Ed.). New York: Collier Books. (Original work published 1917)

Freud, S. (1963). Repression. In S. Freud, *General psychological theory* (P. Rerff, Ed.). New York: Collier Books. (Original work published 1915)

Freud, S. (1985). The Moses of Michelangelo. In A. Dickson (Ed.), The Pelican Freud Library J. Strachey, Trans.) (Vol. 13, pp. 211–238). Harmondsworth, England: Penguin. (Original work published 1914)

Frost, W. D., & Averill, J. R. (1982). Differences between men and women in the everyday experience of anger. In J. R. Averill (Ed.), *Anger and aggression: An essay on emotion* (pp. 281–316). New York: Springer-Verlag.

Gay, P. (1988). Freud: A life for our time. New York: Norton.

Goldstein, A. P., & Glick, B. (1987). *Aggression replacement training: A comprehensive intervention for adolescent youth.* New York: Plenum.

Goldstein, A. P., & Keller, H. R. (1987). *Aggressive behavior: Assessment and intervention.* Oxford, England: Pergamon.

Goldstein, A. P., Nensen, R., Daleflod, B., & Kalt, M. (2004). *New perspectives on aggression replacement training.* Chichester, England: Wiley.

Gratz, K. L. (2003). Risk factors for and functions of deliberate self-harm: An empirical and conceptual review. *Clinical Psychology: Science and Practice, 10,* 192–205.

Grier, W. H., & Cobbs, P. M. (1968). *Black rage*. New York: Basic Books.

Grisso, T., Davis, J., Vesselinov, R., Appelbaum, P. S., & Monahan, J. (2000). Violent thoughts and violent behavior following hospitalization for mental disorder. *Journal of Consulting and Clinical Psychology, 68*, 388–398.

Gross, J. J. (1998). The emerging field of emotion regulation: An integrative review. *Review of General Psychology, 2*, 271–299.

Gross, J. J. (2002). Emotion regulation: Affective, cognitive, and social consequences. *Psychophysiology, 39*, 281–291.

Gross, J. J., & John, O. P. (2003). Individual differences in two emotion regulation processes: Implications for affect, relationships, and well-being. *Personality and Social Psychology, 85*, 348–362.

Harmon-Jones, E. (2004). Contributions from research on anger and cognitive dissonance to understanding the motivational functions of asymmetrical frontal brain activity. *Biology Psychology, 67*, 51–76.

Harmon-Jones, E., & Allen, J. J. B. (1998) Anger and frontal brain activity: EEG asymmetry consistent with approach motivation despite negative affective valance. *Journal of Personality and Social Psychology, 74*, 1310–1316.

Harmon-Jones, E., & Sigelman, J. (2001). State anger and prefrontal brain activity: Evidence that insult-related relative left-prefrontal activation is associated eith experienced anger and aggression. *Journal of Personality and Social Psychology, 80*, 797–803.

Harris, M. B. (1993). How provoking! What makes men and women angry? *Aggressive Behavior, 19*, 199–211.

Harris, W. V. (2001). *Restraining rage: The ideology of anger control in classical antiquity.* Cambridge, MA: Harvard University Press.

Hartmann, H., Kris, E., & Loewenstein, R. M. (1949). Notes on the theory of aggression. *The Psychoanalytic Study of the Child, III/IV*, 9–36.

Hewig, J., Hagemann, D., Seifert, J., Naumann, E., & Bartussek, D. (2004). On the selective relation of frontal cortical asymmetry and anger-out versus anger-control. *Journal of Personality and Social Psychology, 87*, 926–939.

Hibbert, C. (1985). *Rome: The biography of a city*. Middlesex, England: Penguin.

Hillbrand, M. (1995). Aggression against self and aggression against others in violent psychiatric patients. *Journal of Consulting and Clinical Psychology, 63*, 668–671.

Hillbrand, M., Krystal, J., H., Sharpe, K. S., & Foster, H. G. (1994). Clinical predictors of self-mutilation in hospitalized forensic patients. *Journal of Nervous and Mental Disease, 182*, 9–13.

Hinton, D., Hsia, C., Um, K., & Otto, M. W. (2003). Anger-associated panic attacks in Cambodian refugees with PTSD; a multiple baseline examination of clinical data. *Behaviour Research and Therapy, 41*, 647–654.

Hobbes, T. (1951/1958). *Leviathan. Parts I and II.* Englewood Cliffs, NJ: Prentice-Hall.

Hokanson, J. E. (1961a). Vascular and psychogalvanic effects of experimentally aroused anger. *Journal of Personality, 29*, 30–39.

Hokanson, J. E. (1961b). The effects of frustration and anxiety on overt aggression. *Journal of Abnormal and Social Psychology, 62*, 346–351.

Hokanson, J. E., & Burgess, M. (1962a). The effects of three types of aggression on vascular processes. *Journal of Abnormal and Social Psychology, 64*, 446–449.

Hokanson, J. E., & Burgess, M. (1962b). The effects of status, type of frustration, and aggression on vascular processes. *Journal of Abnormal and Social Psychology, 65*, 232–237.

Hokanson, J. E., & Shetler, S. (1961). The effects of overt aggression on physiological arousal level. *Journal of Abnormal and Social Psychology, 63*, 446–448.

Holt, R.R. (1970). On the interpersonal and intrapersonal consequences of expressing or not expressing anger. *Journal of Consulting and Clinical Psychology, 35*, 8–12.

Horney, K. (1939). *New ways in psychoanalysis.* New York: Norton.

Howells, K., & Day, A. (2003). Readiness for anger management: Clinical and theoretical issues. *Clinical Psychology Review, 23*, 319–337.

Huesmann, L. R. (1998). The role of social information processing and cognitive schema in the acquisition and maintenance of habitual aggressive behavior. In R. G. Geen & E. Donnerstein (Eds.), *Human aggression: Theories, research, and implications for social policy.* (pp. 73–109). San Diego, CA: Academic Press.

Izard, C. E. (1977). *Human emotions.* New York: Plenum.

Kassinove, H., Sukhodolsky, D. G., Tsytsarev, S. V., & Solovyova, S. (1997). Self-reported anger episodes in Russia and America. *Journal of Social Behavior and Personality, 12*, 301–324.

Kassinove, H., & Tafrate, R. C. (2002). *Anger management: The complete treatment guidebook for practitioners.* Atascadero, CA: Impact.

Koh, K. B., Kim, C. H., & Park, J. K. (2002). Predominance of anger in depressive disorders compared with anxiety disorders and somatoform disorders. *Journal of Clinical Psychiatry, 63*, 486–492.

Konecni, V. J. (1975a). Annoyance, type, and duration of postannoyance activity, and aggression: "The cathartic effect." *Journal of Experimental Psychology: General, 104*, 76–102.

Konecni, V. J. (1975b). The mediation of aggressive behavior: Arousal level versus anger and cognitive labeling. *Journal of Personality and Social Psychology, 32*, 706–712.

Konecni, V. J. (1984). Methodological issues in human aggression research. In R. M. Kaplan, V. J. Konecni, & R. W. Novaco (Eds.), *Aggression in children and youth* (pp. 1–43). The Hague, Netherlands: Nijhoff.

Konecni, V. J. (1991). Psychological aspects of the expression of anger and violence on the stage. *Comparative Drama, 25*, 215–241.

Konecni, V. J., & Ebbesen, E. B. (1976). Disinhibition vs. the cathartic effect: Artifact and substance. *Journal of Personality and Social Psychology, 34*, 352–365.

Lakoff, G., & Kovecses, Z. (1987). The cognitive model of anger inherent in American English. In D. Holland & N. Quinn (Eds.), *Cultural models in language and thought* (pp. 195–221). Cambridge, England: Cambridge University Press.

Lang, P. J. (1995). The emotion probe: Studies of motivation and attention. *American Psychologist, 50*, 372–385.

Lazarus, R. S. (1968). Emotions and adaptation: Conceptual and empirical relations. In W. J. Arnold (Eds.), *Nebraska Symposium on Motivation (Vol. 16, pp. 175–270).* Lincoln: University of Nebraska Press.

Lazarus, R. (1994) Appraisal: The long and short of it. In P. Ekman & R. J. Davidson (Eds.), *The nature of emotion* (pp. 208–215).

LeDoux, J. E. (1984). Cognition and emotion: Processing functions and brain systems. In M. S. Gazzaniga (Ed.), *Handbook of cognitive neuroscience* (pp. 357–368). New York: Plenum.

LeDoux, J. E. (1989). Cognitive-emotional interactions in the brain. *Cognition and Emotion, 3,* 267–289.

LeDoux, J. E. (1993). Emotional networks in the brain. In M. Lewis & J. M. Haviland (Eds.), *Handbook of emotions* (pp. 109–118). New York: Guilford.

Lindemann, E. (1944). Symptomayology and management of acute grief. *American Journal of Psychiatry, 101,* 141–148.

Lorenz, K. (1966). *On aggression.* New York: Harcourt, Brace, & World.

Lyketsos, G. C., Blackburn, I. M., & Tsiantis, J. (1978). The movement of hostility during recovery from depression. *Psychological Medicine, 8,* 145–149.

Madow, L. (1972). *Anger.* New York: Scribner's.

Maiuro, R. D., Cahn, T. S., Vitaliano, P. P., Wagner, B. C., & Zegree, J. B. (1988). Anger, hostility, and depression in domestically violent versus generally assaultive men and nonviolent control subjects. *Journal of Consulting and Clinical Psychology, 56,* 17–23.

Malgady, R. G., Rogler, L. H., & Cortes, D. E. (1996). Cultural expression of psychiatric symptoms: Idioms of anger among Puerto Ricans. *Psychological Assessment, 8,* 265–268.

Mammen, O. K., Shear, M. K., Pilkonis, P. A., Kolko, D. J., Thase, M. E., & Greeno, C. G.(1999). Anger attacks: Correlates and significance of an unrecognized symptom. *Journal of Clinical Psychiatry, 60,* 633–642.

Marcus, B. A., Vollmer, T. R., Swanson, V., Roane, H. R., & Ringdahl, J. E. (2001), An experimental analysis of aggression. *Behavior Modification, 25,* 189–213.

Materazzo, F., Cathcart, S., & Pritchard, D. (2000). Anger, depression, and coping interactions in headache activity and adjustment: A controlled study. *Journal of Psychosomatic Research, 49,* 69–75.

McGaugh, J. L. (1995). Emotional activation, neuromodulatory systems, and memory. In D. L. Schachter (Ed.), *Memory distortion: How minds, brains, and societies reconstruct the past* (pp. 255–273). Cambridge, MA: Harvard University Press.

McGaugh, J. L. (2003). *Memory and emotion.* New York: Columbia University Press.

McNeil, D. E., Eisner, J. P., & Binder, R. L. (2003). The relationship between aggressive attributional style and violence by psychiatric patients. *Journal of Consulting and Clinical Psychology, 71,* 399–403.

Megargee, E. I. (1966). Undercontrolled and overcontrolled personality types in extreme antisocial aggression. *Psychological Monographs, 80,* (Whole No. 611).

Meichenbaum, D. (1985). *Stress inoculation training.* Oxford, England: Pergamon.

Menninger, K. (1938). *Man against himself.* New York: Harcourt.

Menninger, K. (1942). *Love against hate.* New York: Harcourt.

Merton, R. K. (1938). Social structure and anomie. *American Sociological Review, 3,* 672–682.

Merton, R. K. (1957). *Social theory and social structure.* New York: The Free Press.

Mikulincer, M. (1998). Adult attachment style and individual differences in functional versus dysfunctional experiences of anger. *Journal of Personality and Social Psychology, 74,* 513–524.

Mikulincer, M., Shaver, P. R., & Pereg, D. (2003). Attachment theory and affect regulation: The dynamics, development, and cognitive consequences of attachment-related strategies. *Motivation and Emotion, 27,* 77–102.

Monahan, J., Steadman, H. J., Silver, E., Appelbaum, P. S., Robbins, P. C., Mulvey, et al. (2001). *Rethinking risk assessment:The MacArthur study of mental disorder and violence.* Oxford, England: Oxford University Press.

Muraven, M., & Baumeister, R. F. (2000). Self-regulation and depletion of limited resources: Does self-control resemble a muscle? *Psychological Bulletin, 126,* 247–259.

Nasby, W., Hayden, B., DePaulo, B. M. (1980). Attributional bias among aggressive boys to interpret unambiguous social stimuli as displays of hostility. *Journal of Abnormal Psychology, 89,* 459–468.

National Audit Office. (2003). *A safer place to work: Protecting NHS hospital and ambulance staff from violence and aggression.* (Report No. HC 527, by the Comptroller and Auditor General). London: Author.

Newman, R. S., & Hirt, M. (1983). The psychoanalytic theory of depression: Symptoms as a function of aggressive wishes and level of articulation. *Journal of Abnormal Psychology, 92,* 42–48.

Novaco, R. W. (1975). *Anger control: The development and evaluation of an experimental treatment.* Lexington, MA: Heath.

Novaco, R. W. (1976). The functions and regulation of the arousal of anger. *American Journal of Psychiatry, 133,* 1124–1128.

Novaco, R. W. (1977). Stress inoculation: A cognitive therapy for anger and its application to a case of depression. *Journal of Consulting and Clinical Psychology, 45,* 600–608.

Novaco, R. W. (1978) Anger and coping with stress. In J. Foreyt & Rathjen (Eds.), *Cognitive behavior therapy: Research and applications* (pp. 135–173). New York: Plenum Press.

Novaco, R. W. (1979). The cognitive regulation of anger and stress. In, P. Kendall & S. Hollon (Eds.), *Cognitive behavioral interventions: Theory, research, and procedures* (pp. 241–285). New York: Academic Press.

Novaco, R. W. (1986). Anger as a social and clinical problem. In R. Blanchard & C. Blanchard (Eds.), *Advances in the study of agression.* Vol. 2 (pp. 1–67). New York: Academic Press.

Novaco, R. W. (1993). Clinicians ought to view anger contextually, *Behavior Change, 10,* 208-218).

Novaco, R. W. (1994). Anger as a risk factor for violence among the mentally disordered. In J. Monahan & H. Steadman (Eds.), *Violence and mental disorder: Developments in risk assessment.* (pp. 21–59) Chicago: University of Chicago Press.

Novaco, R. W. (1997). Remediating anger and aggression with violent offenders. *Legal and Criminological Psychology, 2,* 77–88.

Novaco, R. W. (1998). Aggression. In H. S. Friedman (Ed.), *Encyclopedia of mental health* (pp. 13–26). San Diego, CA: Academic Press.

Novaco, R. W. (2003). *The Novaco Anger Scale and Provocation Inventory (NAS-PI).* Los Angeles: Western Psychological Services.

Novaco, R. W., & Chemtob, C. M. (1998). Anger and trauma: Conceptualization, assessment, and treatment. In V. M. Follette, J. I. Ruzek, & F. Abueg (Eds.), *Cognitive-behavioral therapies for trauma* (pp. 162–190). New York: Guilford.

Novaco, R. W., & Chemtob, C. M. (2002). Anger and combat-related posttraumatic stress disorder. *Journal of Traumatic Stress, 15,* 123–132.

Novaco, R. W., & Jarvis, K. L. (2002). Brief cognitive behavioral intervention for anger. In F. Bond & W. Dryden (Eds.), Handbook of brief cognitive behavioral therapy (pp. 77–100). London: Wiley.

Novaco, R. W., Kliewer, W., & Broquet, A. (1991). Home environment consequences of commute travel impedance. *American Journal of Community Psychology, 19,* 881–909.

Novaco, R. W., Ramm, M., & Black, L. (2000). Anger treatment with offenders. In C. Hollin (Ed.), *Handbook of offender assessment and treatment* (pp. 281–296). London: Wiley.

Novaco, R. W., & Welsh, W. N. (1989). Anger disturbances: Cognitive mediation and clinical prescriptions. In K. Howells & C. R. Hollin (Eds.), *Clinical approaches to violence* (pp. 39–60). London: Wiley.

Novaco, R. W. & Taylor, J. L. (2004). Assessment of anger and aggression in offenders with developmental disabilities. *Psychological Assessment, 16,* 42–50.

Ortony, A., Clore, G. L., & Collins, A. (1988). *The cognitive structure of emotions.* Cambridge, England: Cambridge University Press.

Patterson, G. R. (1984). Siblings: Fellow travelers in coercive family processes. In R. J. Blanchard & D. C. Blanchard (Eds.), *Advances in the study of aggression.* (Vol. 1, (pp. 173–215). New York: Academic Press.

Patterson, G. R. (1986). Performance models for antisocial boys. *American Psychologist, 41,* 432–444.

Philippot, P., & Feldman, R. S. (2004). *The regulation of emotion.* Mahwah, NJ: Lawrence Erlbaum Associates.

Plutchik, R. (1980). *Emotion: A psychoevolutionary synthesis.* New York: Harper & Row.

Pollak, S. D., & Kistler, D. J. (2002). Early experience is associated with the development of categorical representations for facial expressions of emotion. *Proceedings of the National Academy of Sciences, 99,* 9072–9076.

Pollak, S. D., & Tolley-Schell, S. A. (2003). Selective attention to facial emotion in physically abused children. *Journal of Abnormal Psychology, 112,* 323–338.

Posternak, M. A., & Zimmerman, M. (2002). Anger and aggression in psychiatric outpatients. *Journal of Clinical Psychiatry, 63,* 665–672.

Quanty, M. B. (1976). Aggression catharsis: Experimental investigations and implications. In R. G. Geen & E. C. O'Neal (Eds.), *Perspectives on aggression* (pp. 99–132). New York: Academic Press.

Redl, F., & Wineman, D. (1951). *Children who hate.* New York: The Free Press.

Redl, F., & Wineman, D. (1952). *Controls from within.* New York: The Free Press.

Renwick, S., Black, L., Ramm, M., & Novaco, R. W. (1997). Anger treatment with forensic hospital patients. *Legal and Criminological Psychology, 2,* 103–116.

Riley, W. T., Treiber, F. A., & Woods, M. G. (1989). Anger and hostility in depression. *The Journal of Nervous and Mental Disease, 177,* 668–674.

Robins, S., & Novaco, R. W. (1999). Systems conceptualization and treatment of anger. *Journal of Clinical Psychology, 55,* 325–337.

Robins, S., & Novaco, R. W. (2000). Anger control as a health promotion mechanism. In D. I. Mostofsky & D. H. Barlow (Eds.), *The management of anxiety in medical disorders* (pp. 361–377). Boston: Allyn & Bacon.

Rubin, T. I. (1969). *The angry book.* London: Macmillan.

Saul, L. J. (1956). *The hostile mind.* New York: Random House.

Scherer, K. L., Abeles, R. P., & Fisher, C. S. (1975). *Human aggression and conflict: Interdisciplinary perspectives.* Englewood Cliffs, NJ: Prentice-Hall.

Schless, A. P., Mendles, J., Kipperman, A., & Cochrane, C. (1974). Depression and hostility. *Journal of Nervous and Mental Disease, 159,* 91–100.

Scocco, P., Meneghel, G., Caon, F., Dello Buono, M., De Leo, D. (2001). Death ideation and its correlates: Survey of an over-65–year-old population. *Journal of Nervous and Mental Disease, 189,* 210–218.

Seneca, L. (1817). *Seneca's morals.* New York: Harper & Brothers. (Original work published 44).

Siegman, A. W., & Smith, T. W. (1994). *Anger, hostility, and the heart.* Hillsdale, NJ: Lawrence Erlbaum Associates.

Solomon, R. (1980). The opponent-process theory of acquired motivation. *American Psychologist, 35,* 691–712.

Spielberger, C. D. (1996). *State–Trait Anger Expression Inventory Professional Manual.* Lutz, FL: Psychological Assessment Resources.

Spielberger, C. D., Jacobs, G., Russell, S. & Crane, R. (1983). Assessment of anger: The State–Trait Anger Scale. In J. D. Butcher & C. D. Spielberger (Eds.), *Advances in personality assessment* (Vol. 2. pp. 157–187). Hillsdale, NJ: Lawrence Erlbaum Associates.

Spores, J. C. (1988). *Running amok: An historical inquiry* (Monograph No. 82, Southeast Asia Series). Athens: Ohio University Center for International Studies.

Stearns, C. Z., & Stearns, P. (1986). *Anger: The struggle for emotional control in America's history.* Chicago: University of Chicago Press.

Storr, A. (1968). *Human aggression.* New York: Bantam.

Strike, P. C., & Steptoe, A. (2004). Psychosocial factors in the development of coronary artery disease. *Progress in Cardiovascular Disease, 46,* 337–347.

Sukhodolsky, D. G., Kassinove, H., & Gorman, B. S. (2004). Cognitive-behavior therapy for anger in children and adolescents: A meta-analysis. *Aggression and Violent Behavior, 9,* 247–269.

Sun Tzu. (1983). *The art of war* (Foreword by J. Clavell). New York: Delta.

Suris, A., Lind, L., Emmett, G., Borman, P. D., Kashner, M., & Barratt, E. S. (2004). Measures of aggressive behavior: Overview of clinical and research instruments. *Aggression and Violent Behavior, 9,* 165–227.

Tafrate, R. C. (1995). Evaluation of treatment strategies for adult anger disorders. In H. Kassinove (Ed.), *Anger disorders: Definition, diagnosis, and treatment* (pp. 109–129). Washington, DC: Taylor & Francis.

Tavris, C. (1982). *Anger: The misunderstood emotion.* New York: Simon & Schuster.

Taylor, J. L., & Novaco, R. W. (2005). *Anger treatment for people with developmental disabilities: A theory, evidence, and manual based approach.* London: Wiley.

Taylor, J. L., Novaco, R. W., Gillmer, B. T., Robertson, A., & Thorne, I. (2005). A controlled trial of individual cognitive-behavioural anger treatment for people with intellectual disabilities and histories of aggression. *British Journal of Clinical Psychology, 44* (p. 3), 367–384.

Taylor, J. L., Novaco, R. W., Gillmer, B., & Thorne, I. (2002). Cognitive-behavioural treatment of anger intensity in offenders with intellectual disabilities. *Journal of Applied Research in Intellectual Disabilities, 15,* 151–165.

Taylor, J. L., Novaco, R. W., Guinan, C., & Street, N. (2004). Development of an imaginal provocation test to evaluate treatment for anger problems in people with intellectual disabilities. *Clinical Psychology and Psychotherapy, 11,* 233–246.

Thucydides. (1960). *The history of the Peloponnesian War.* New York: Oxford University Press.

van Honk, J., Tuiten, A., van den Hout, M., Putnam, P., de Haan, E., & Stam, H. (2001). Selective attention to unmasked and masked threatening words: relationships to trait anger and anxiety. *Personality and Individual Differences, 30,* 711–720.

Volavka, J. (2002). *The neurobiology of violence.* Washington, DC: American Psychiatric.

Wang, E. W., & Diamond, P. M. (1999). Empirically identifying factors related to violence risk in corrections. *Behavioral Sciences and the Law, 17,* 377–389.

Weiner, B. (2001). Responsibility for social trangressions: An attributional analysis. In B. F. Malle, L. J. Moses, & D. A. Baldwin (Eds.), *Intentions and intentionality: Foundations of social cognition.* (pp. 331–344). Cambridge, MA: MIT Press.

Weiner, B., Graham, S., & Chandler, C. (1982). Pity, anger, and guilt: An attributional analysis. *Personality and Social Psychology Bulletin, 8,* 226–232.

Weissman, M. M., Klerman, G. L., & Paykel, E. S. (1971). Clinical evaluation of hostility in depression. *American Journal of Psychiatry, 128,* 261–266.

Wilson, J. Q., & Herrnstein, R. J. (1985). *Crime and human nature.* New York: Simon & Schuster.

Yesavage, J. E. (1983). Direct and indirect hostility and self-destructive behavior by hospitalized depressives. *Acta Psychiatrica Scandinavica, 68,* 345–350.

Zillmann, D. (1971). Excitation transfer in communication-mediated aggressive behavior. *Journal of Experimental Social Psychology, 7,* 419–434.

Zillmann, D. (1979). *Hostility and aggression.* Hillsdale, NJ: Lawrence Erlbaum Associates.

Zillmann, D., & Bryant, J. (1974). Effect of residual excitation on the emotional response to provocation and delayed aggressive behavior. *Journal of Personality and Social Psychology, 30,* 782–791.

Effective Anger Treatments Require a Functional Analysis of the Anger Response

Ray DiGiuseppe, Carol Cannella, and Jill Kelter

Psychiatric outpatients present with anger problems as frequently as they do with anxiety and depression (Posternak & Zimmerman, 2002). In fact, more than a quarter of outpatients reported a significant anger symptom (DiGiuseppe, McDermut, Fuller, & Zimmerman, 2005). Clinicians report seeing the same number of clients with anger problems as they do clients with anxiety disorders (Lachmund, DiGiuseppe, & Fuller, 2005). Despite the frequency with which clients present with anger problems and clinicians report seeing angry clients, research on effective treatments for anger problems lags behind research on the treatments for other emotional problems. Several meta-analytic reviews on anger treatments (R. Beck & Fernandez, 1998; Del Vecchio & O'Leary, 2004; DiGiuseppe & Tafrate, 2003; Edmondson & Conger, 1996; Sukhodolsky, Kassinove, & Gorman, 2004; Tafrate, 1995) have drawn upon relatively few studies, none of which have included patients seeking treatment for anger problems. The majority of interventions used to treat disturbed anger included relaxation, cognitive restructuring, assertiveness training and, of course, exposure-based interventions. Research supports the efficacy of these cognitive-behavior therapies (CBTs) for anger problems and the degree of change produced by treatment was usually of a large magnitude. However, the effect sizes reported for anger treatment studies have been smaller than those typically reported for anxiety and depression interventions. If we were to examine the effectiveness of anger treatment in domestic-violence perpetrators, the degree of change produced by our interventions drops considerably. As Norcross and Kobayashi (1999) lamented, we cannot treat anger as successfully as we do other emotional problems. We still need new, creative, and more effective interventions.

Perhaps this state of affairs has arisen because most anger-specific CBT interventions were derived from effective interventions for anxiety and depression. Anger treatments have not been developed from an understanding of disturbed anger.

Consider, for example, anger treatments that incorporate exposure-based interventions where clients are presented with anger-arousing stimuli. Exposure-based interventions were first devised to treat anxiety disorders and may be considered the treatment of choice for many anxiety disorders (Foa & Kozak, 1986). Many anger treatment studies use exposure-based interventions and implement them in the same manner in which they are implemented in the treatment of anxiety. The crossover of these treatments from anxiety to anger was based on the assumptions that anger and anxiety are learned in the same manner and that exposure interventions should, therefore, work similarly with anxiety and anger problems.

Similarly, cognitive interventions for anger have been developed based on the work of A. T. Beck (1999), Ellis (1977), and D'Zurilla and Nezu (1999). As a result, the cognitive constructs targeted in these interventions closely resemble the cognitions targeted in interventions for anxiety and depression. Theory and research in the cognitive mediation of anger has focused on the same negative distortions, irrational beliefs, and social problem-solving skill deficits proposed to mediate other emotions. This is understandable because angry clients often have comorbid emotional problems. However, perhaps angry clients experience the cognitions that mediate other emotional excesses because they experience those other emotional excesses as well as dysfunctional anger. Few unique cognitive interventions appear to be aimed at cognitive processes or content based on cognitive models of anger. The one cognitive concept that appears unique to generating anger instead of other emotions is the hostile attribution concept identified by Crick and Dodge (1994).

It is quite clear that psychology has adopted treatments for anger based on little knowledge of the mechanisms that mediate anger. This chapter explores how people learn to become angry and suggests that interventions should be built upon this knowledge and not upon the models of other emotions.

CONDITIONING OF ANGER

Classical Conditioning of Anger and Aggression

Classical conditioning is one mechanism through which emotional expression is acquired. Specifically, research has firmly established that humans and other animals learn to connect fear and anxiety through the mechanisms of classical conditioning (Ledoux, 1996, 2002). Pairing a conditioned stimulus (CS) with an unconditioned stimulus (UCS) that automatically arouses pain, discomfort, or disgust results in fear being aroused the next time that CS is presented. Pavlov believed that organisms could increase their ability to adapt and survive if they could learn to associate CS with UCS that innately trigger an unconditioned response (UCR). Pavlov proposed 13 innate UCRs that could be used in this way, including the religious instinct, the sexual reflex, fear, disgust, guarding reflexes, and the urge to aggress (see Windholz, 1987). Because of Pavlov's theoretical assertion that aggression could be classically conditioned, influential psychologists for generations have attributed the learning of angry or aggressive responses to classical conditioning (Berkowitz, 1983; Ulrich & Wolfe, 1969). Despite these assertions, a negligible amount of research has explored Pavlov's original conjecture concerning anger and aggression. In 1945 after a series of studies, Seward concluded that "there was no evidence that aggressiveness occurred as a classically conditioned response" (p. 38). A few authors reported to have classically conditioned aggression in fish, specifically Blue Gourmis (Hollis, Cadieux, & Colbert, 1995) and fighting Beta fish (Bronstein, 1988). In both studies, the CS was paired with stimuli that elicited aggression toward other males competing for mating territory.

We have also failed to uncover a stimulus that could serve as a UCS to consistently arouse anger or aggression as the UCR. Pain is a possible choice for such a UCS but not all pain leads to anger or aggression. The failure to identify a clear UCS that will always lead to the UCR of anger and aggression suggests that classical conditioning may not account for the mechanism by which people learn to become angry.

Some studies have paired a CS with a UCS that elicited an innate aggressive attack in rats (Creer, Hitzing, & Schaeffer, 1966; Farris, Gideon, & Ulrich, 1970; Lyon & Ozolins, 1970; Vernon & Ulrich, 1966; Ulrich, Hutchinson, & Azrin, 1965). During these aggressive attacks, the rats showed facial features that Darwin (1872/1965) associated with anger. However, these studies involved the pairing of the CSs directly with painful shock to the animal. These studies administered shock, as the UCS, to animals and concluded that pain-elicited aggression was a natural reflex. The pain was the UCS and aggression the UCR. The conclusion that pain-elicited aggression was an unlearned response (Hutchinson, Ulrich, & Azrin, 1965) made this connection the most likely beginning for a Pavlovian conditioning model of learned aggression and anger. To complete the classical conditioning model, researchers then paired the shock and pain (UCS) with a tone or some other CS.

Only one study attempted to classically condition aggression in primates. Using squirrel monkeys, Dunham and Carr (1976) found that in this species, conditioning to shock depended on the degree to which the pain-elicited aggressive response (e.g., biting) predicted or resulted in a long shock-free period. That is, if the aggression elected by the shock resulted in a longer period of no shock, the aggression response was more easily learned. When they administered the trials randomly in time, no conditioned response (CR) was learned. This animal research appeared between 1965 and 1976 and then seems to have stopped.

Though some of these researchers suggested (e.g., Vernon & Ulrich, 1966) that this form of learning could account for the human learning of aggression, noticeably absent are studies that attempted to classically condition aggression or anger in humans. In fact, we uncovered just one study that investigated pain-elicited aggression in humans. Heacock, Thurber, and Vale (1975) administered shock to seven pairs of people who had the opportunity to retaliate. Subjects were instructed to initiate shock to each other. However, one person in the pair could retaliate only when a cue light was turned on. One person in each of four pairs discontinued the experiment because of either crying or failure to participate. When subjects did not respond to the opportunity to retaliate, they were told "You are not following directions." This study failed to follow a procedure that resembled classical conditioning. The authors concluded that their results may have been due to the subjects' wishes to obey authority. Although this study did display that retaliation occurred, we do not believe that it can be taken as support for the classical conditioning of anger or aggression in humans. It is unlikely that in today's world of concern for ethics in research and mandatory Institutional Review Boards, research on the condition of pain-elicited aggression in humans will reemerge.

Some studies reported studying angry faces as CSs compared with faces expressing other emotions in fear conditioning. Faces displaying different emotions were paired with fear-eliciting stimuli. These studies indicated that when the CS was an angry face, the CR had greater resistance to extinction than when learning was associated with human faces expressing other emotions (Dimberg, 1986; Dimberg & Oehman, 1983; Oehman & Dimberg, 1978; Zafiropoulou & Pappa, 2002). These results suggest that humans have a strong preparedness to learn to fear angry faces rather than faces expressing other emotions. However, these studies fail to tell us whether CSs can be associated with anger or aggression as a CR.

Pain-elicited aggression is unlikely to account for much of the learning of human anger. Only a portion of the cases of anger we have encountered includes a history of victimization by aggression. Many angry clients have no such history. Thus, some other mechanism is necessary to account for their anger. Also, when a history of victimization by aggression is present, the situations or people that trigger anger appear to have no relationship to those who perpetrated the aggression against the client. Classical conditioning by pain-elicited aggression might be the mechanism that accounts for the anger in people with post traumatic stress disorder (PTSD) who have experienced abuse or combat. However, many people who are angry about the abuse they have experienced during childhood did not respond to their abuse with aggression because they were too young and weak to attack an abusing adult. Fear was most likely their immediate UCR. Therefore, people who experience anger as a symptom of PTSD when the trauma occurred in childhood would have learned to associate fear with the stimuli associated with the abuse. It is more likely that their anger would result from cognitive appraisal processes that occurred after the abuse.

The entire literature on the classical conditioning of anger and aggression is minuscule compared with the literature on classical conditioning of the fear response. It is interesting that no citations for research in pain-elicited aggression have appeared in almost 30 years. Perhaps interest in this area ceased because it failed to explain the learning of anger and aggression. It is important that no other UCSs have been associated with anger or aggression given the ubiquity of these reactions in all species and the importance of human anger and aggression as social problems. As the work of LeDeux (1996, 2002) has shown, science knows a great deal about fear conditioning in humans and other species as demonstrated by hundreds of published studies. The specific neural pathways of fear conditioning and the neurotransmitters that operate these pathways are well established. Science has a deep understanding of the urge to flee and how that urge is transferred to other stimuli in adaptive and maladaptive ways.

Why, then, has knowledge of classically conditioning the urge to fight and the emotion that often accompanies it progressed so little? Based on the lack of evidence, it is tempting to conclude that the classical conditioning of anger and aggression cannot occur. Perhaps many more researchers have tried to establish the classical conditioning of anger or aggression and our review encountered the "file drawer problem." This refers to the fact that scientific journals rarely publish negative findings and negative research reports remain in their investigators' file drawers. Perhaps classical conditioning is not a good model to explain how humans learn to become angry. Does this matter?

We believe that there is more at stake here than the Ivory Tower ideas of the long-deceased Russian theorist, Ivan Pavlov. The principles of Pavlovian conditioning and the knowledge that has accumulated in the last hundred years have led to helpful interventions for the treatment of anxiety disorders. Based on this knowledge, a number of treatments have been developed that either pair CSs with relaxation or other incompatible responses or use exposure-based interventions. Exposure to feared stimuli is a unifying principle of psychotherapy and has been used across theoretically disparate orientations such as behavioral, psychodynamic, and Gestalt therapies. Exposure treatments (i.e., therapies that involve the presentation of a specific, arousal-inducing stimulus as part of the treatment) represent the treatment of choice based on empirical evidence.

In exposure-based treatments for anxiety, the treatment is more effective if clients receive instructions to feel their emotions fully. The more clients attend to their feelings and report feeling anxious while experiencing the exposure imagery, the better the treatment outcome. Research also indicates that clients should experience exposure to the stimuli for a long time until they experience a reduction in their anxiety (see Foa & Kozak, 1986). If clients distract themselves from the imagery or leave the *in vivo* stimuli prematurely, they successfully escape or avoid the feared stimulus, thereby experiencing negative reinforcement through the removal of an unpleasant stimulus. This results in a strengthening of the relationship between the CS and the CR. Clients are instructed to face the feared stimuli in imagery or reality until they feel their anxiety has diminished.

Since the inception of behavior therapy and Wolpe's (1958) demonstration of the effectiveness of systematic desensitization and other exposure treatments, a debate has raged regarding the mechanism underlying effective exposure intervention for anxiety. Originally, Wolpe proposed that reciprocal inhibition accounted for the effectiveness of exposure-based interventions. Counterconditioning, habituation, extinction, and cognitive techniques such as increasing self-efficacy and cognitive restructuring (see Tryon, 2003, for a review) have also been proposed to explain the results. Tryon concluded that research on these proposed mechanisms of learning have failed to support any of the proposed mechanisms for the effectiveness of exposure interventions. Several new explanations for the success of exposure treatments have relied on neural network theories (Tryon, 2003) and emotional processing models (Foa & Kozak, 1986) as such explanations may best account for the behavior change in treating anxiety disorders.

These new emotional processing models (Foa & Kozak, 1986) assume that once people experience trauma or a connection between neutral stimuli and a harmful event, all knowledge about the stimuli and responses become part of a memory-fear structure. The emotional processing model proposes that memories associated with or triggered by fear consist of a cognitive network of information. The neural network created by the trauma or fear experience links together the eliciting stimuli present when the trauma occurred, thoughts about these stimuli, meaningful associations about the stimuli and thoughts, and the behavioral and physiological responses to the trauma. The firing or arousal of any one of these elements triggers all of the others.

Changes in the fear structure occur in three stages. First, the fear needs to be aroused through exposure to the arousing stimuli. If the fear structure is not activated, it is presumed that change will not occur. The second step is fear habituation. Continued arousal for a period of up to 60 or even 90 minutes within an exposure treatment session produces habituation of the physiological responses associated with anxiety. Finally, the association of the stimuli with the lowered arousal, which occurs with habituation, provides information concerning the frequency of danger or the valence of a threat. If the stimulus has been present through exposure and habituation has occurred, the reduced arousal conveys knowledge that danger is infrequent or that the threat is of a low valence. Finally, this new learning should result in a lowering of affect across sessions. In the next exposure session, lower arousal is expected. Research has demonstrated that emotional processing appears to account for the changes associated with exposure treatments of anxiety disorders. Barlow (1991) proposed that this information-processing model could be applied to other negative emotions such as sadness and anger. Given the number of similarities between anger and anxiety, this model might explain the treatment of anger responses.

Several interventions designed to treat anger have included exposure elements and have significantly reduced anger. Many clinicians have devised these treatments on the assumption that anger and anxiety are similar emotions and, therefore, interventions used to treat anxiety should work for anger. However, research in anger treatments has only recently focused on exposure-based interventions, and very little research has attempted to devise an exposure-based intervention on a particular theory of learning or emotional processing. Gostouspour (2001) used data from the treatment outcome studies and effect sizes reported in our meta-analytic review of anger treatments (DiGiuseppe & Tafrate, 2003). She predicted, as shown in the anxiety treatment literature and based on classical conditioning and emotional processing principles, that the more clients received instructions to feel their anger, the more they would have focused on the emotion of anger and the more effective the treatments would be. Gostouspour coded each study for whether or not the method section reported that the therapists instructed the clients to feel their anger. This dichotomous variable was then used to predict the effect sizes of the treatment. Having clients focus on the feeling of anger resulted in a –.52 correlation. The more clients focused on their anger, the worse the treatment outcome. This finding suggests that although exposure remains a crucial part of anger treatments, instructing clients to maximize their degree of anger may lessen the treatment effectiveness. Different procedures may maximize exposure effectiveness and different mechanisms may underlie its effects. This study has several flaws, however. It was done as a retrospective review and many of the studies reviewed may have used instructions to focus on the emotion of anger and failed to report it. For studies that did report such instructions, it is unclear how successful the instructions were. Assessing clients' experience of their emotional state directly during the exposure treatment, as had been done with anxiety treatments, would represent a better test of this treatment principle.

A slightly different conclusion is reached when examining the effect sizes of similar interventions with and without an exposure component. Interventions that focus on the development of relaxation skills and those that use relaxation skills plus imaginal exposure seem to show different levels of effectiveness. For example, in anger management training (AMT; Hazaleus & Deffenbacher, 1986; Suinn, 1990), relaxation skills are practiced in response to anger scenes developed by the client. Clients are asked to feel their anger in response to the scenes, thus providing a context for the use of relaxation skills. Several meta-analytic reviews compared AMT to progressive muscle relaxation and noted increased effectiveness in protocols that included an exposure component. The inclusion of instructions to associate relaxation with images of anger-provoking scenes is directly analogous to the anxiety treatments. However, we do not know if the clients' experience of anger is related to greater treatment efficacy as is observed with anxiety treatments.

In an attempt to explore the feasibility of using imaginal exposure for anger reduction, Grodnitzky and Tafrate (2000) provided a better test of the mechanism of action proposed by Foa and Kozak (1986). Using a small group of adult outpatients, Grodnitzky, and Tafrate measured state anger within and across sessions while participants rehearsed imaginal scenes of anger-provoking stimuli. Over the course of the study, the majority of patients met a criterion for clinically significant improvement on important indices of anger. They believed that visual analysis of the process measures, which included patient reports of daily exposure practice sessions, matched the pattern of habituation within and across sessions suggested by the emotional processing model. However, due to the small sample size, they reported no analyses that indicated that habituation was related to more successful outcomes.

Another attempt to assess whether emotional processing accounted for the effects of imaginal exposure interventions was done by Walley (2002). Her treatment and research were designed to correspond to work done with exposure interventions for anxiety. The treatment included the development of a hierarchy of anger-provoking situations. Participants were instructed to imagine the scenes and to report the level of their anger every 5 minutes throughout the exposure imagery. They held the image for at least 30 minutes or until they had a substantial drop in their angry feelings. The participants received instructions to focus on the feelings, but not to respond with aggression. Walley's research participants rated their level of state anger. The hypothesis that habituation within and between sessions, as measured by clients' ratings of state anger, would correlate with outcomes on measures of anger and aggressive behavior was not supported. Again, exposure was a successful intervention for anger (clients showed improvements), but the mechanisms of emotional processing did not seem to account for the effect. So far, these early attempts using imaginal exposure in treating anger have failed to find evidence that the emotional processing theory, which explains the use of similar treatments in anxiety disorders, is the mechanism for these anger treatment effects.

Tafrate and Kassinove (1998) developed an exposure treatment for anger that involved presenting angry men with verbal insults or barbs. They created a pool of insults or negative statements that elicited their angry outbursts. In the individual treatment sessions, the therapist read a list of these barbs to the subjects in an angry tone over the course of 15 sessions. In each session, 10 barbs were directed at the client and then repeated. While experiencing the barbs, the men were instructed to rehearse rational, irrational, or irrelevant self-statements. The authors devised their experiment to test whether cognitive change or classical conditioning extinction accounted for treatment effects. If anger were under cognitive control, the group who recited rational statements would benefit more from the exposure than those who recited irrational or irrelevant statements. If the three groups faired equally well, exposure alone would have accounted for the treatment effects and the emotional processing of a conditioning response would have accounted for any treatment gains. All three groups benefitted from the barb technique, suggesting that exposure alone can reduce anger. However, the men who rehearsed the rational statements improved significantly more on some dependent measures. The barb technique may not have been a good test of extinction or of Foa and Kozak's emotional processing. In each case, the participants rehearsed some type of statements. This would have distracted the participants from focusing on the anger-arousing stimuli and the experience of anger rather than focusing on the emotion. Also, new barb stimuli were continually directed at the participants. Thus, extinction or emotional processing would have had to occur to a class of stimuli as opposed to one stimulus scene as happens in exposure treatment of anxiety. Learning to have a different emotional reaction to a class of stimuli rather than one specific stimulus may be an advantage because generalization is programmed into the treatment from the beginning. Although exposure to a class of stimuli may encourage generalization to situations out of therapy much better than exposure to one stimulus at a time, this procedure deviates from the traditional use of exposure interventions, which usually expose the client to one emotionally arousing stimulus at a time for a prolonged period. Because the individual sessions lasted only a half hour, Tafrate and Kassinove's (1998) intervention did not last long enough to test the emotional processing model, and they did not measure anger arousal within and between sessions to assess if high arousal followed by habituation predicted change.

A study by McVey (2000) from the same laboratory tested the barb technique in one 3-hour massed learning trial under three conditions. One group received the barb exposure with response prevention. Participants were instructed to "focus on the feeling," and to "experience the anger." Another group received barb exposure while rehearsing rational self-statements. A third group received barb exposure while rehearsing irrelevant self-statements. The prolonged exposure trial and the instructions to focus on the feeling in this design provided a much better test of the emotional processing hypothesis. The inclusion of a group who rehearsed rational statements provided a test of the cognitive processing model. The rehearsal of rational and irrelevant self statements would have diminished arousal. The rational statements were incompatible with anger arousal and the irrelevant statements would have distracted participants from focusing on the barbs or their feelings. Participants in all groups showed statistically and clinically significant reductions on the measures of anger from pretreatment to follow-up. Also, none of the three treatments differed at follow-up. The fact that the group instructed to focus on their anger feelings failed to improve significantly more than the other groups receiving exposure suggests that the emotional processing model fails to account for the benefit of exposure treatments of anger.

In a third study from this group using the same barb technique, Terracciano (2000) compared research participants who received the barbs while rehearsing rational self-statements to participants who received the barbs alone. He found that barb exposure produced a significant pre to posttest reduction in anger, but no differences in outcome occurred between groups. Thus, the barb technique worked regardless of the presence of cognitive rehearsal.

No studies have appeared using the barb technique while measuring anger arousal within and between sessions to observe habituation. Thus, they have not provided a direct test of emotional processing as the mechanism of change. However, because exposure to barbs works with all types of cognitive rehearsal that distracts the client from feeling the emotional arousal, it seems that the existing research on the intervention fails to support the hypothesis that emotional processing accounts for the change in anger.

The studies just reviewed showed that exposure can be an effective intervention for anger. However, no consistent pattern of results emerged concerning what mechanism accounts for this success. Although Grodnitzky and Tafrate (2000) present some support for habituation as the mechanism of change, their study included only six subjects and no direct link between anger arousal habituation and anger outcome measures was made. Walley's (2002) study most directly tested the emotional processing hypothesis and failed to find support that emotional processing accounted for the change. Several reasons may account for this failure. In the studies by Kassinove and colleagues, the anger-provoking barbs may not be equivalent to the stimulus used in exposure to anxiety. The barbs are usually delivered every couple of minutes. Each new barb may start a new trial of exposure, which is then ended when a new barb is presented. Thus, clients were not exposed to one stimulus for a long time, but to many examples of a class of stimuli. Possibly, emotional processing may occur with anger if clients were exposed to one long image or presentation of one barb. Perhaps the presentation of barbs has not been long enough for habituation to occur. Although early attempts to utilize exposure techniques have resulted in helping clients reduce anger, most of the research reported previously failed to present anger provoking stimuli for a sufficiently long period as recommended by Foa and Kozak (1986). Longer exposure periods may produce habituation. However, there is also the possibility that focusing on the emotion of anger may produce cognitive ruminations that blame the perpetrator pictured in the stimulus and these self-statements may reinforce angry attitudes and counteract any decrease in anger produced by habituation.

Perhaps people do not learn to associate anger with eliciting stimuli in the same way they learn to become anxious. Several researchers who have used exposure to reduce anger have reported they are reluctant to have clients focus for long periods on anger-provoking stimuli while instructed to focus on their experience of anger. Such instructions may increase anger (Brondolo, DiGiuseppe, & Tafrate, 1997; Deffenbacher, & McKay, 2000). Anger is an emotion related to approach behaviors, whereas anxiety is most associated with avoidance (see chap. 4, this volume). Perhaps avoidance is best learned through classical conditioning processes. Anger is more associated with the brain's seeking system (Pankseep, 1998), the area of the brain that searches out positive reinforcers and directs approach behaviors. This is consistent with the theoretical and empirical research that identifies anger as related to high self-efficacy or self-esteem (Baumeister & Boden, 1998; DiGiuseppe & Froh, 2002; Frijda, 1986). Many clinical models of anger have suggested that anger is aroused by low self-esteem but these models have not been supported (Baumeister & Boden, 1998). Perhaps anger is learned by instrumental or operant learning paradigms that emphasize learning based on consequences. When people become angry, they experience thoughts of justification and self-righteousness. These thoughts could provide reinforcement for the anger arousal. Also, when angry, people may rehearse vengeful images that can be experienced as rewarding. Although exposure interventions do appear to work, more research is needed to learn what characteristics of the intervention will maximize its effectiveness. We do not recommend that practitioners use prolonged exposure with instruction to focus on the angry feelings until more research appears to support its usefulness. However, exposure models have been effective, and constructing exposure interventions on operant models of learning may lead to more successful interventions.

In this section, we have reviewed the literature on classical conditioning and anger. Although classical conditioning has been enormously helpful in understanding the learning of fear and disgust and in developing treatments for anxiety disorders, it has shed little light on how people learn to become angry. Perhaps operant learning or cognitive models of emotional arousal will lead to a better understanding of anger.

Instrumental Conditioning of Anger

Hundreds of research articles have documented the role of reinforcement and modeling in the learning of aggressive behaviors. However, a review of this literature is beyond the scope of this book (see Connor, 2002, for a comprehensive review). Despite this voluminous literature, we know little about how these same variables affect the arousal of angry emotions. Two factors seem to account for this. The first is the separation of anger from aggression as topics of investigation and targets of treatment, and the second is the questionable distinction between instrumental and affective/reactive aggression. In the literature concerning learning and anxiety, psychologists conceptualize avoidance or escape behaviors as motivated by fear. The emotion motivates avoidance and the behavior follows to relieve the negative experience of fear. Psychologists do not propose that escape and avoidance behaviors are separate topics of investigation independent of the emotion of fear, or that fear is an independent topic to be studied without consideration of the behaviors that it motivates. Fear and the escape and avoidance behaviors that fear motivates are studied as a system. Perhaps anger and aggression should be studied the same way. Anger and aggression may have been more easily separated as topics of investigation because, as noted previously, people become angry more often than they behave aggressively. Research has shown that perhaps 1 in 10 anger episodes lead to an aggressive response; thus, most episodes of anger do not lead to aggression (see DiGiuseppe & Tafrate, 2006). This low rate of aggression in response to anger may have occurred because of the way researchers have defined aggression. The term *aggression* is usually limited in such research to verbally harsh or insulting comments or dramatic, physical contact with objects or people. However, anger may lead to many behaviors such as pouting, angry facial expressions, intimidating gestures, and indirect or passive aggressive behaviors that are usually not measured. The facial- or body-language expression of anger may serve to coerce people into compliance and thus be reinforced. Indirect or passive-aggressive responses may accomplish revenge without getting noticed. Thus, they result in reinforcement. The focus on extreme, outward, or dramatic forms of aggression has led to a poor understanding of the relationship between anger and behavior and how both are learned. A continuum of aggression responses may result from anger to satisfy the motives of coercion and revenge that anger itself arouses.

The distinction between instrumental and reactive aggression has further promoted this separation of anger and aggression. The social-learning models of aggression popular in psychology today best explains instrumental aggression. If the person has attained goals with aggressive behavior, he or she is more likely to do so in the future, and if a person sees that others can attain the goal through aggression, that person is likely to use aggressive means to acquire the goal as well. This has been considered instrumental aggression and no emotional arousal is needed. Factored into this model of aggression is the probability of punishment or retaliation from the victim or his or her group, or criminal detection and prosecution by society. Such theories are used to explain how the person learns to behave aggressively and assumes the aggression is motivated by acquisition of concrete reinforcers. It also assumes that no emotional arousal is necessary for the aggression to occur. If the aggression is aimed at achieving some object, the explanation of instrumental aggression works. But reactive aggression can also achieve desired outcomes.

The principles of reinforcement and modeling explain how people learn to attain food. They do things that they observe others doing to get food or for which they have been reinforced for getting food. Such a model explains how people learn food acquisition, but fails to explain when people display these behaviors to get food. For that we need the construct of hunger and the brain mechanism that arouses the human motivation of hunger, which starts the process of seeking food and makes the attainment of food reinforcing.

Operant learning models have long made the distinction between skill acquisition and performance. How people learn a behavior is different from when they display that behavior. Operant models of aggression appear to have failed to make this distinction. An operant model works less well in explaining when the person uses aggression for other, intangible types of rewards such as power, status, revenge, or compliance. In these situations, affect is usually involved. Does the reinforcement of aggression also reinforce the experience of anger?

Several stages are necessary for the learning of aggression to occur. Consider the case of Harold, who was referred to our anger treatment center for infecting his company's computer network with a virus. Harold, a 51-year-old White man, worked for a large insurance company as a computer programmer. Despite being the most senior member in his department, management passed Harold over for promotion several times. Harold became considerably angry when his company hired someone from outside to head his department. Managers had told Harold that they did not consider him to be management material. Although he would continue to receive regular raises and bonuses, they would not promote him. Harold felt that the company did not appreciate his years of loyalty and hard work. He felt angry and strongly wanted revenge on the company. Although Harold was an excellent programmer and knew a great deal about the workings of the company's system, he had little experience with computer viruses. Harold had learned about viruses and virus detection from talking to colleagues who worked in that area. Once Harold became angry, he decided to seek revenge, and used his knowledge of computer viruses to disable the company's system.

Learning occurred at several points along the way to Harold's successfully implanting a virus into his company's computer system. First, Harold learned to use computers for many years in his job as a computer programmer and had learned about viruses by talking to others. Second, Harold had learned that a failed computer caused financial loss to a company and great embarrassment to the vice president of information technology. Third, Harold learned to feel excessively angry about failure to attain certain levels of success. He had to learn to think of himself as unappreciated and treated unjustly if others did not follow rules that he thought of as fair. Fourth, Harold had learned that anger was associated with a desire to "even the score" and bring harm to the target of his anger. Fifth, although Harold had learned Items 3 and 4 just mentioned, he still needed a target at which to be angry; performance of these learned responses required a specific motive to activate that learning. Harold needed to be angry enough with someone to want to harm that person. Sixth, once anger and revenge were aroused, Harold further instructed himself on the finer details of computer viruses to accomplish his goals. The motivation of revenge provided the reinforcement that turned his acquired knowledge into performance.

We propose that people learn anger primarily through operant rather than classical conditioning. Anger has many positively reinforcing characteristics. Since the time of Aristotle (1943) and Seneca (Basore, 1958), people have referred to anger as a moral emotion that is associated with self-righteous attitudes. When angry, people perceive themselves as morally correct. This alone has some self-reinforcing components. Anger also provides a sense of power and control over the perceived indiscretions of others. Angry outbursts may result in compliance by others. In addition, anger promotes a desire for revenge. People enjoy revenge and will spend time, money, and effort to achieve it; when attained they savor it. These are characteristics of positive reinforcement.

Despite the distinction between affective/reactive and instrumental aggression, the arousal of anger and the resulting display of angry facial and bodily gestures, the verbal intonations, the angry content, and the angry behaviors often have the effect of coercion. As mentioned earlier, the human species seems prepared to learn to fear angry facial expressions. Thus, getting angry arouses fear in others, often resulting in their submission to the person who displays anger. This results in the attainment of what one wants in the short run. Anger arousal can also be negatively reinforced. This same pattern of anger and coercion can result in negative reinforcement to the annoying things others do, and anger results in the cessation of an aversive stimulus. Displays of anger often succeed in silencing others or compelling them to cease behaviors we find unpleasant, distracting, or annoying. Examples of this can be found in many families where an anger outburst stops a spouse or child from continuing a behavior that annoys the angry person.

The distinction between affective and instrumental aggression may have prevented the development of research on anger as an instrumental or operantly learned system. According to this distinction, reinforcement occurs in the instrumental nonaffective aggression. Recently, Bushman and Anderson (2001) have questioned the utility and validity of this distinction. Our own research on the assessment of anger has focused on the motives associated with anger using our Anger Disorders Scale (DiGiuseppe & Tafrate, 2004). People usually experience one of four motives when angry: correcting the situation, attaining revenge, escaping the discomfort of the arousal, and coercing others into submission. The first rarely occurs in clinical cases so we dropped it from our scale. Factor analysis for the subscales of our measure resulted in three higher order factors, each associated with one of the remaining three motives. Verbal aggression and many anger arousal qualities loaded with coercion to form one factor. A cluster analysis of our data produced one cluster that we labeled the *dysphoric mate cluster*, which had high loadings of verbal aggression and coercion, and was typical of people who seek couples therapy. Thus, the anger experiences and verbal aggression are associated with using anger to coerce others, an instrumental aggressive act.

Other forms of aggression such as physical, relational, passive, and indirect aggression were associated with the motive of revenge, based on results of our factor analysis (DiGiuseppe & Tafrate, 2004) and cluster analysis (DiGiuseppe & Tafrate, 2006). Revenge is the one reinforcing aspect of anger that has been avoided by most modern perspectives on this emotion. Modern psychology has failed to identify the association of revenge and anger and the strong compelling reinforcement attained by revenge. This is surprising given that a rich literature exists on the topic of revenge in Western civilization since the time of Sophocles's *Ajax*. To learn about revenge, watch the Opera *Rigoletto*, read the classic *The Iliad*, go see the musical *Sweeney Todd—The Demon Barber of Fleet Street*, or visit nearly any academic department of your local university. As a field, psychology has neglected the study of this motive. Recent research has uncovered activity in the reinforcement areas of the brain in research participants who imagined getting revenge (Knutson, 2004). Again, such findings indicate that the arousal of anger is both affective and instrumental. We concur with Bushman and Anderson (2001) that the distinction between affective and instrumental aggression has outlived its usefulness. One could even go further and propose that all anger is learned primarily by instrumental conditioning.

Becoming angry can also encourage others to avoid certain topics or issues. Such negative reinforcement may explain the lack of introspection and insight usually attributed to angry clients. Psychoanalytic theory (Freud, 1920) and Gestalt therapy (Perls, 1969) have proposed that people lack awareness and keep things out of consciousness. Barlow (1991) and Ellis (2003) proposed that avoiding negative emotions is a major cause of psychopathology. Recently, Hayes (Hayes & Gifford, 1997) has proposed to link this process (which he calls experiential avoidance) to many forms of behavioral disorders. Anger may be one way that people successfully avoid facing unpleasant situations and keep psychological pain out of consciousness. Becoming angry and expressing it through facial or bodily gestures or vocal tones may intimidate others and discourage them from talking about uncomfortable topics. Thus, successfully displayed anger leads to intimidation, which then leads others to avoid topics, thereby allowing those topics to remain out of consciousness.

The case of Janis exemplifies how anger can be negatively reinforced and can keep topics out of awareness. She came to our anger group because she feared that she would hurt her 2-year-old son. She frequently got angry when the child did not sleep or made demands on her. Janis had several other stressors in her life that depleted her coping resources. She had been physically abused as a child, moved often, and married a man whom she did not love because she sought financial security. Janis had little insight into her reasons for marrying, for her frequent moves to new cities, or for any of her life choices. She failed to understand why she was so angry with her son, whom she reported to love very much. Whenever a group member questioned her on aspects of her life, Janis snarled back at them or looked away in anger and pouted. Group members quickly stopped asking her about herself and no demands were placed on her to confront uncomfortable topics. Eventually, Janis reported that she responded with sarcasm and insults when her husband approached her about the distance in their relationship and about her relationship with her abusing parents. Janis was aware that she did not want to talk about these issues and resented other people's attempts to meddle in her life. We eventually helped Janis recognize that her anger intimidated others, leading them to avoid all criticism of her or the mentioning of unpleasant topics. This had allowed Janis to avoid facing important issues in her life.

If the classical conditioning of anger and aggression relies on the link between a UCS and a UCR as the base of future learning, the operant conditioning of anger relies on a reinforcer for anger. How does this early learning occur? Berkowitz (2003) has proposed a revised frustration–aggression hypothesis. His theory maintains that frustration leads to a negative affect and to escape from or attack of an unpleasant stimulus. If young children respond to this initial motivation to attack and their affectively aroused behavior is successful in either attaining the reward that has eluded them or ending unpleasant stimuli, both their affect and their behavior are reinforced. Successful arousal may lead to the development of a habit of anger arousal and angry action instead of fear or escape. Developmentally, anger is one of the first emotions to be successfully coded in infants. Also, aggressive behaviors tend to peak in the preschool years, at about 2½ years of age. Thus, anger and aggression are established early in life. Once these responses are established, adjustment occurs through learning to inhibit these responses or appropriately control them in socially acceptable ways. Conceptualizing anger as controlled by operant rather than classical conditioning has several implications for treatments. First is the focus on problem solving in therapy. Our experience is that angry people often focus on the short-term positive consequences of their anger to the exclusion of focusing on the long-term negative consequences of their arousal. Teaching the consequences of anger makes one aware of the contingencies that are operating. Helping clients to become aware of all of the long- and short-term consequences of their anger often produces dramatic change in their emotional and behavioral responses (DiGiuseppe & Tafrate, 2003). If angry clients focus on attaining revenge or compliance with their short-term goals, anger will prevail. Focusing on the quality of life instead of inflicting pain on one's enemy, or focusing on the long-term quality of intimate relationships instead of one's immediate desires, allows for other reactions besides anger. Teaching alternative-solution thinking allows for new responses to attain more desirable outcomes.

Using an operant model to understand anger also changes the way we implement exposure interventions for anger. Exposure interventions should instruct the client to learn to associate a new competing and incompatible response with the triggers of one's anger. An operant model would pair the previous anger trigger with a new response (e.g. relaxation), some form of cognitive acceptance, or a means to remain calm in the face of challenging triggers. Repeated pairings of the stimuli with the new response will make for more effective learning. Such repeated pairings may account for the success of the barb technique mentioned previously. In this treatment, a new example of a class of stimuli (e.g., new insults) are paired with calm nonresponding—a response incompatible with the angry aggressive response. Relaxation, assertiveness, and social skills are all new behaviors that we recommend teaching angry clients. Once taught, these responses also require rehearsal. Instructions designed to maximize habituation, such as focusing on the anger, have the potential to be counterproductive because they ask the client to rehearse the anger response after the presentation of the stimuli. Also, the adoption of an operant model focuses on the cognitions that self-reinforce anger, such as the justification thoughts identified by Novaco (2003) and moral correctness. Thoughts and images about attaining revenge are reinforcing and could be replaced with thoughts and images of other reinforcers such as successful resolution of conflict or relaxation images.

CONCLUSIONS

We have not presented an inclusive explanation of how anger develops and which interventions may help treat disturbed anger. What we have tried to focus on is that treatments for anger need to be based on an understanding of the learning and cognitive processes that arouse and maintain anger. This is preferable to basing interventions on successful treatments of other emotional disorders. Classical conditioning and emotional processing models from the anxiety treatment literature do not appear to successfully explain anger treatments and have led to marginally effective interventions. The operant learning paradigm better explains the learning of anger responses. Anger is represented in the areas of the brain associated with approach behaviors and is associated with thoughts of self-efficacy and high self-esteem. Anger appears to be reinforced by the actions that it motivates, such as coercion, revenge, and the removal of unpleasant stimuli, by thoughts related to moral justification, and by images of revenge and coercion. Based on this model, effective anger interventions would focus on social problem-solving training that helps people become aware of the long-term negative consequences of their anger and identifies new responses. Behavioral rehearsal interventions that teach these new responses via modeling, coaching, and feedback would also be helpful. To encourage reduction in anger arousal, clients could learn relaxation responses and use discrimination training to learn to perform these responses when confronted with previous anger-provoking stimuli. Thus, exposure-based interventions teach the client to confront an anger-provoking stimulus and quickly perform a new reaction before anger arousal is achieved. Additional research on the effectiveness of interventions based on these principles is needed to establish the value of these suggestions.

REFERENCES

Aristotle. (1943). Nicomachean ethics. In L. R. Loomis (Ed.), *On man in the universe: Metaphysics, parts of animals, ethics, politics, poetics* (pp. 85–245). New York: Black.

Barlow, D. H. (1991). Disorders of emotion. *Psychological Inquiry, 2(1)*, 58–71.

Basore, J. W. (1958). *Seneca: Moral essays, (Vol. 1)*. Cambridge, MA: Harvard University Press.

Baumeister, R. F., & Boden, J. M. (1998). Aggression and the self: High self-esteem, low self-control, and ego threat. In R. G. Geen & E. Donnerstein (Eds.), *Human aggression: Theories, research, and implications for social policy.* (pp. 111–138). New York: Academic Press.

Beck, A. T. (1999). *Prisoners of hate: The cognitive basis of anger, hostility, and violence.* New York: HarperCollins.

Beck, R., & Fernandez, E. (1998). Cognitive-behavioral self-regulation of the frequency, duration, and intensity of anger. *Journal of Psychopathology and Behavior Assessment, 20(3)*, 217–229.

Berkowitz, L. (1983). Aversively stimulated aggression: Some parallels and differences in research with animals and humans. *American Psychologist, 38(11)*, 1135–1144.

Berkowitz, L. (2003). Affect, aggression and antisocial behavior. In R. J. Davidson, K. R. Scherer, H. H. Goldsmith (Eds.), *Handbook of affective sciences (pp. 804–823).* New York: Oxford University Press.

Brondolo, E., DiGiuseppe, R., & Tafrate, R. C. (1997). Exposure-based treatment for anger problems: Focus on the feeling. *Cognitive & Behavioral Practice, 4(1)*, 75–98.

Bronstein, P. M. (1988). Socially mediated learning in male Betta splendens: III. Rapid acquisition. *Aggressive Behavior, 14(6)*, 415–424.

Bushman, B. J., & Anderson, C. A. (2001). Is it time to pull the plug on hostile versus instrumental aggression dichotomy? *Psychological Review, 108(1)*, 273–279.

Connor, D. E. (2002). *Aggression and antisocial behavior in children and adolescents: Research and treatment.* New York: Guilford.

Creer, T. L., Hitzing, E. W., Schaeffer, R. W. (1966). Classical conditioning of reflexive fighting. *Psychonomic Science, 4(3)*, 89–90.

Crick, N. R., & Dodge, K., A. (1994). A review and reformulation of social information-processing mechanisms in children's social adjustment. *Psychological Bulletin, 115(1)*, 74–101.

Darwin, C. (1965). *The expression of the emotions in man and animals.* Chicago: University of Chicago Press. (Original work published 1872)

Deffenbacher, J. L., & McKay, M. (2000). *Overcoming situational and general anger: Client manual.* Oakland, New Harbinger Publications. Department of Psychology.

Del Vecchio, T. , & O'Leary, K. D. (2004). Effectiveness of anger treatments for specific anger problems: A meta-analytic review. *Clinical Psychology Review, 24*(1), 15–34.

DiGiuseppe, R. A., & Froh, J. J. (2002). What cognitions predict state anger? *Journal of Rational-Emotive and Cognitive-Behavior Therapy, 20,* 133–150.

DiGiuseppe, R. A., Fuller, J. R., Mc Dermut, W., & Zimmerman, M. (2005 November). *Comorbity of DSM-IV TR Axis I Disorders in patients with Anger Symptoms.* Paper presented at the 38th Annual Convention fo the Association for Behavioral and Cognitive Therapies. Washington: DC.

DiGiuseppe, R., & Tafrate, R. (2003). Anger treatment for adults: A meta-analytic review. *Clinical Psychology: Science and Practice, 10,* 70–84.

DiGiuseppe, R., & Tafrate, R. C. (2004). *Anger Disorders Scale: Manual.* Toronto, Ontario, Canada: Multi Health Systems, Inc.

DiGiuseppe, R., & Tafrate, R. C. (2006). *Understanding anger disorders.* New York: Oxford University Press.

Dimberg, U. (1986). Facial expressions as excitatory and inhibitory stimuli for conditioned autonomic responses. *Biological-Psychology, 22(1),* 37–57.

Dimberg, U., & Oehman, A. (1983). The effects of directional facial cues on electrodermal conditioning to facial stimuli. *Psychophysiology, 20(2),* 160–167.

Dunham, P. J., & Carr, A. (1976). Pain-elicited aggression in the squirrel monkey: An implicit avoidance contingency. *Animal Learning and Behavior, 4(1–A),* 89–95.

D'Zurilla, T. J., & Nezu, A. (1999). *Problem solving therapy: A social competence approach to clinical intervention.* New York: Springer.

Edmondson, C., & Conger, J. (1996). A review of treatment efficacy for individuals with anger problems: Conceptual, assessment, and methodological issues. *Clinical Psychology Review, 16(3),* 251–275.

Ellis, A. (1977). *How to live with and without anger.* New York: Readers' Digest Press.

Ellis, A. (2003). *Overcoming resistance, (2nd ed.).* New York: Springer.

Farris, H. E., Gideon, B. E., & Ulrich, R. E. (1970). Classical conditioning of aggression: A developmental study. *Psychological Record, 20(1),* 63–67.

Foa, E. B., & Kozak, M. J. (1986). Emotional processing of fear: Exposure to correct information. *Psychological Bulletin, 99,* 20–35.

Freud, S. (1920). *A general introduction to psychoanalysis* (G. S. Hall, Trans.). New York: Boni and Liveright.

Frijda, N. H. (1986). *The emotions.* Cambridge, England: Cambridge University Press.

Goshtasbpour, F. (2001). A meta-analytic review of the components of adult anger management treatments. St. John's University. (New York), *Dissertation Abstracts International: Section B: The Sciences and Engineering, 62(1-B),* 548.

Grodnitzsky, G., & Tafrate, R. (2000). Imaginal exposure for anger reduction in adult outpatients: A pilot study. *Journal of Behavior Therapy and Experimental Psychiatry, 31(3–4),* 259–279.

Hayes, S. C., & Gifford, E. V. (1997). The trouble with language: Experiential avoidance, rules, and the nature of verbal events. *Psychological Science, 8(3),* 170–173.

Hazaleus, S. L., & Deffenbacher, J. L. (1986). Relaxation and cognitive treatments of anger. *Journal of Consulting and Clinical Psychology, 54,* 222–226.

Heacock, D., Thurber, S., & Vale, D. (1975). Shock elicited aggression by human subjects. *Journal of Social Psychology, 95(1),* 55–59.

Hollis, K. L. , Cadieux, E. L., & Colbert, M. M. (1995). The biological function of Pavlovian conditioning: A mechanism for mating success in the blue gourami (*Trichogaster trichopterus*). *Journal of Comparative Psychology, 103(2),* 115–121.

Hutchinson, R. R., Ulrich, R. E., & Azrin, N. H. (1965). Efects of age and related factors on the pain-elicited aggression reaction. *Journal of Comparative and Physiological Psychology, 59(3),* 365–369.

Knutson, B. (2004). Sweet revenge? *Science, 305(8),* 1246–1247.

Lachmund, E., & DiGiuseppe, R., & Fuller, J. R. (2005). Clinicians' diagnosis of a case with anger problems. *Journal of Psychiatric Research, 39*(4), 439–447.

LeDoux, J. E. (1996). *The emotional brain: The mysterious underpinnings of emotional life.* New York: Simon & Schuster.

LeDoux, J. E. (2002). *The synaptic self.* New York: Simon & Schuster.

Lyon, D. O., & Ozolins, D. (1970). Pavlovian conditioning of shock-elicited aggression: A discrimination procedure. *Journal of the Experimental Analysis of Behavior, 13(3),* 325–331.

McVey, M. E. (2000). Exposure and response prevention versus rational self-statements in the treatment of angry men. *Dissertation Abstracts International Section A: Humanities and Social Sciences, 61(6-A),* 2197.

Norcross, J., & Kobayashi, (1999). Treating anger in psychotherapy: Introduction and case. *Journal of Clinical Psychology, 55(3),* 275–282.

Novaco, R. W. (2003). *Novaco Anger Scale and provocation inventory.* Los Angles, Western Psychological Services.

Oehman, A., Dimberg, U. (1978). Facial expressions as conditioned stimuli for electrodermal responses: A case of "preparedness"? *Journal of personality and Social Psychology, 36*(11), 1251–1258.

Panksepp, J. (1998). *Affective neuroscience: The foundation of human and animal emotions.* New York: Oxford University Press.

Perls, F. S. (1969). *Gestalt therapy verbatim.* New York: Bantam.

Posternak, M. A., & Zimmerman, M. (2002). Anger and aggression in psychiatric outpatients. *Journal of Clinical Psychiatry, 63,* 665–672.

Seward, J. P. (1945). Aggressive behavior in the rat: I. General characteristics; age and sex differences. *Journal of Comparative Psychology, 38,* 175–197.

Suinn, R. (1990). *Anxiety management training: A behavior therapy.* New York: Plenum.

Sukhodolsky, D. G., Kassinove, H., & Gorman, B. S. (2004). Cognitive-behavioral therapy for anger in children and adolescents: A meta-analysis. *Aggression and Violent Behavior, 9,* 247–269.

Tafrate, R. (1995). Evaluation of treatment strategies for adult anger disorders. In H. Kassinove (Eds.), *Anger disorders: Definitions, diagnosis and treatment.* (pp. 109–130). Washington, DC: Taylor & Francis.

Tafrate, R. C., & Kassinove, H. (1998). Anger control in men: Barb exposure with rational, irrational, and irrelevant self-statements. *Journal of cognitive Psychotherapy, 12*(3), 187–211.

Terracciano, S. (2000). Effects of barb exposure and rational statement rehearsal on anger and articulated thoughts in angry married men: Extinction or cognitive restructuring? *Dissertation Abstracts International: B. The Physical Sciences and Engineering, 61(6–B)*, 3294.

Tryon, W. (2003, November). *Possible mechanism for why desensitizations and exposure therapy work.* Poster presented at the annual convention of the Association for the Advancement of Behavior Therapy, Boston.

Ulrich, R., Hutchinson, R. R., & Azrin, N. H. (1965). Pain-elicited aggression. *Psychological Record, 15(1)*, 111–126.

Ulrich, R., & Wolfe, M. (1969). Research and theory on aggression and violence. *Science Teacher, 36(5)*, 24–28.

Vernon, W., & Ulrich, R. (1966). Classical conditioning of pain-elicited aggression. *Science, 152(3722)*, 668–669.

Walley, J. C. (2002). Imaginal exposure and response prevention for anger and aggressive behavior. *Dissertation Abstracts International: Section B. The Sciences and Engineering, 63(4-B)*, 2080.

Windholz, G. (1987). Pavlov's conceptualization of unconditional reflexes, or instincts, within the framework of the theory of higher nervous activity. *Pavlovian Journal of Biological Science, 22(4)*, 123–131.

Wolpe, J. (1958). *Psychotherapy by reciprocal inhibition.* Stanford, CA: Stanford University Press.

Zafiropoulou, M., & Pappa, E. (2002). The role of preparedness and social environment in developing social phobia. *The Journal of the Hellenic Psychological Society, 9(3)*, 365–377.

Finding a Useful Model for the Treatment of Anger and Aggression

Howard Kassinove

As noted by DiGiuseppe and colleagues (chap. 2, this volume), there is little doubt that anger is a frequent phenomenon in clinical practice. Indeed, after 30-plus years of private practice and employment in two mental health centers, I now realize that anger was a significant part of the clinical picture in at least one third of the adult cases I treated. Regrettably, although some formal diagnoses have been proposed to highlight anger as a phenomenon of importance (Eckhardt & Deffenbacher, 1995), the lack of official categories in the *DSM* does not encourage the line clinician to think of anger as a primary problem. We have also devoted much less scientific attention to anger than to the similar emotions of anxiety and depression (Kassinove & Sukhodolsky, 1995). This situation has limited our understanding of anger and its relationship to aggression and interpersonal violence. In the two preceding chapters, Novaco cogently presented his ideas about the nature and treatment of anger dysregulation and DiGiuseppe and colleagues focused on a functional analytic perspective to the problem. Their contributions have helped us to understand the nature of anger and its consequences, and to develop programs of intervention. Nevertheless, a number of important questions remain. Because of space limitations, this commentary selectively addresses only some of these.

To begin, I certainly agree with much of what Novaco presents in his comprehensive perspective. He has been examining anger for more than 30 years and his contributions to the analysis, etiology, and treatment of the problem are legendary. He notes that anger and aggression are partially hard-wired responses that have had survival functions for members of our species. Anger is related to sensing environmental threats, selectively attending to stimuli that are high in provocation value, inferring malevolent intent (as guided by cognitive schemas), and an increase in the motivation to attack. Cognitive processes that lead us to believe that our thoughts about the trigger are justified serve to amplify anger, as do a number of neurobiological structures and processes. In addition, at the behavioral level there are many well-known positive and reinforcing outcomes of anger and aggression, such as immediate social compliance by others, achieving some short-term goals, a satisfying sense of power and control, protection of personal resources, and so on. At the same time, some of the longer-term outcomes are quite negative, such as increases in coronary events and unsatisfying interpersonal relationships. Nevertheless, if we look at the whole picture there are actually many reasons (i.e., causes) for us to become angry and behave aggressively. The problem, in the modern social world, is the dysregulation of anger. When it is too strong or too weak, and when it is activated inappropriately, it leads to trouble. Dysregulated anger, Novaco (chap. 1, this volume) writes, can be "too easily transformed into destructive aggression" (p. 4) and can "adversely affect prudent thought, core relationships, work performance, and physical well-being" (p. 3).

The goal, both for Novaco and for DiGiuseppe and colleagues, is to understand the etiology, manifestations, and maintaining forces of anger and aggressive behavior so that effective intervention programs can be developed. Because anger is so widespread, these programs have to be applicable to a wide range of angry and aggressive adults whether they are students, clients in industrial settings, outpatients, inpatients, incarcerated criminal justice offenders, and so on. Unfortunately, as Novaco notes, many studies in the field have been done using university students and he questions whether knowledge gained from these subjects applies to anger in other, more disturbed clinical populations. He also questions whether some of the simple techniques examined in published studies, such as offering mildly angry and generally well-functioning young adults (i.e., students) a distraction or by providing information to explain away an interpersonal slight from a confederate, apply to anger and aggression in seriously disturbed people who have long problem histories and who suffer from many current stressors. DiGiuseppe and colleagues (chap. 2, this volume) also recognize this problem when they list six meta-analytic reviews from which it is concluded that current treatments for anger are effective. Regarding the subjects used in the studies reviewed, they write, "none of which have included patients seeking treatment for anger problems" (p. 5). Of course, this is an important issue and in recognition of the problem some researchers have used clinical analogues. In university samples, for example, Deffenbacher and colleagues select students who are high on trait anger and who specify that they want treatment for their anger (e.g., Deffenbacher, Huff, Lynch, Oetting, & Salvatore, 2000; Deffenbacher, Oetting, Huff, & Thwaites, 1995). Their work has contributed substantially to our base of knowledge. Nevertheless, practitioners have long believed that it is not helpful to read the scientific literature partly because of this very issue of ecological validity. For the line mental health worker, research done on 21-year-old college students who score high on a single anger questionnaire does not seem applicable to 50-year-old adults with more complex lives and comorbid issues who are seen in private practices or inpatient settings.

The comorbidity issue is also quite significant, as anger has been shown to be associated with a variety of other problems. In his samples, for example, Deffenbacher has shown that anger is related to alcohol intake, impulsiveness, minor automobile accidents, and a variety of risky behaviors (e.g., Deffenbacher, Filetti, Richards, Lynch, & Oetting, 2003). Our own work also demonstrates this point. We (Kassinove & Tafrate) used the Tafrate, Kassinove, and Dundin (2002) data set to examine the presence of other disorders in angry community adults from ages 25 to 52. Based on scores on the Millon Clinical Multiaxial Inventory (Millon, Davis, & Millon, 1997), when compared to lower-trait-anger adults, greater psychopathology was found in adults higher on trait anger. Elevations were noted on drug dependence, alcohol dependence, and anxiety, which appeared in approximately one third of the high-anger subjects. Indications of posttraumatic stress disorders (PTSD), depression, and delusional disorders were also more frequent in the higher-anger group. Angry adults, we concluded, are likely to present with a wide range of *DSM* Axis I (i.e., psychological) problems. Our unpublished data also showed a greater likelihood that higher-anger community adults had been arrested (65% vs. 25%), were incarcerated (35% vs. 12%), were dissatisfied with their employment (45% vs. 17%), and had more verbal and physical conflicts in their relationships (18% vs. 0% and 10% vs. 0%, respectively). Indeed, the occurrence of comorbid substance use has been described by a number of anger researchers and is the focus of Reilly and Shopshire's (2002) treatment program.

INDIVIDUAL EPISODES OF ANGER AND THE PROXIMITY BIAS

In treatment, it is the individual episode of anger that is repeatedly discussed with patients the goal of developing increased understanding and better coping responses. Thus, it is important to catalog personal perceptions of such episodes and there is a long history of doing so (e.g., Anastasi, Cohen, & Spatz, 1948; Gates, 1926). In fact, much of what we have learned about anger comes from questionnaire or interview studies that have asked adults to report about personal events that were followed by anger.

In these studies, the subjects typically report about recent, unexpected, and unwanted behaviors by others that they perceived as aversive, such as being directly or indirectly insulted, neglected, and so on. For Novaco (chap. 1, this volume), such studies have a "proximity bias" because subjects are unlikely to see causation in the long-term, naturally selected, adaptive functions of anger or to attribute their anger to larger issues such as continued exposure to stressful and aversive life events, acute trauma, psychosis, some form of chemical disorder, and so on. Rather, respondents consistently see others in the immediate environment as the cause of their anger. Because of this bias, these studies provide only limited understanding of anger and aggression.

I suspect that most researchers would agree with Novaco's position that anger experiences and displays are actually embedded in a large network of overlapping and interdependent systems (including value structures, economic forces, work and family pressures, traffic congestion, history of the species, biological reactivity and physical limitations, etc.), all of which set the stage for more or less anger (Kassinove & Eckhardt, 1995). These systems provide positive and negative feedback, which further affect the frequency, intensity, and duration of anger. In contrast to this broad view, DiGiuseppe and colleagues (chap. 2, this volume) place great emphasis on "understanding the learning and cognitive processes that arouse and maintain anger" (p. 72). Although they devote much of their space to showing that an operant analysis yields a better understanding of anger than does a respondent analysis or an emotional processing analysis, they certainly would not discount many of the other anger-initiating or dysregulating forces highlighted by Novaco. The question for practitioners is to determine which of the larger factors existing outside of conscious awareness and not reported in interview studies can be usefully included in treatment programs, and which cannot.

FREQUENCY, INTENSITY, AND
DURATION OF ANGER

Anger varies in frequency, intensity, duration, and mode of expression. As Novaco notes (chap. 1, this volume), each of these can be considered anger problem parameters that might allow us to determine whether someone has an anger problem. For example, from the perspective of a spouse or a colleague it might be clear that anger is causing problems for a mate or a coworker. Unfortunately, as noted earlier, others are typically seen as the cause of personal anger. Thus, practitioners often hear reports such as, "I don't have an anger problem. It's her fault. If she would just do what I ask, then I wouldn't be angry. Why don't you fix her?" For this reason, Novaco notes that the intensity dimension may be the most important signal for treatment acceptance. We typically judge that we are angry or furious, as opposed to simply being annoyed, by virtue of personally experienced intensity and intensity is associated with physiological arousal that disrupts performance, especially mental processes involved in complex tasks, leads to impulsive behavior, and so forth. If high anger intensity leads to being aware of being personally overwhelmed, then acceptance of treatment may be increased. This hypothesis seems reasonable but remains to be empirically examined. In the interim, we also focus on intensity in our program (Kassinove & Tafrate, 2002). We have found that an anger thermometer helps patients develop an anger vocabulary and this allows them to discriminate lower from higher intensity levels, variations of which they have often been unaware.

At the same time, the frequency and duration of anger, along with the mode of responding (e.g., aggressive), are significant. The longer-term activation of bodily responses (e.g., excessive hormone secretions) may be exactly what is responsible for the increased coronary and hypertensive related outcomes associated with anger (e.g., Williams et al., 2000). Unfortunately, clinical experience has shown that patients rarely respond to lessons about long-term anger effects any more than adolescents respond to lectures that cigarette smoking may lead to cancer 25 years in the future. Thus, anger and aggression intensity in the here and now may be the practitioner's best ally in treatment acceptance.

Anger is seen in Novaco's model, at least partially, as a product of provocations, perceptions of threat, and confirmatory bias characteristics. His description is similar to both our own anger episode model (Kassinove & Tafrate, 2002) and that which is described by DiGiuseppe and colleagues. These models have led almost all anger researchers to promote learning- theory-based techniques to disengage the stimulus provocation from the anger or aggression response, as well as cognitive techniques developed by Ellis (1994), Beck (1976), and others, to deal with the threat perceptions and confirmatory cognitive biases.

Once anger is aroused, Novaco and most others posit that it is a potential instigator for aggression. This construction of events, of course, assumes that anger and aggression are different phenomena, an arguable point that is discussed in some depth later. Nevertheless, given this potential, Novaco has tackled the question of what it is that increases the anger provoking value of stimuli. The interdependent factors he writes about include social-significance variables (e.g., fighting words), physiological dispositions (e.g., activation of the cardiovascular and endocrine systems), neurobiological mechanisms (e.g., the amygdala, prefrontal cortex, and serotonin), and behavioral dispositions that are produced by instrumentally and observational learning.

THE AUTOMATICITY OF ANGER

Novaco notes that much of the anger and aggression seen clinically is a function of *automaticity*. Self-reports of angry thoughts and observed aggressive behaviors often seem to emerge without conscious control as automatic coping responses. Again, the importance of this notion is built into our treatment program as we promote telling patients that much anger occurs on "automatic pilot." A barb technique is used to disengage automatic angry responding to perceived aversive stimuli, labeled as triggers. The barb procedure involves the controlled delivery of aversive verbalizations to patients and, by one of a number of means, to delay their automatic anger response. Whether the delay is provided by taking deep breaths, by calmly responding with rational-emotive-based rational verbalizations (Ellis, 1994), or by counting to 10, building in a delay breaks the automatic anger response and allows for a thoughtful reply to the verbal barb. DiGiuseppe and colleagues, in chapter 2 of this volume, question whether the barb technique can appropriately be called an exposure procedure and make the case that it cannot. Their point, that patients are not exposed to the same stimulus without interruption for an extended period of time, is well taken. Nevertheless, use of this technique to deal with anger automaticity is based on the initial paper by Kaufman and Wagner (1972), the stress inoculation work of Novaco (1975, 1977), and the empirical support provided by Tafrate and Kassinove (1998) and others. How we will eventually categorize the procedure remains for future analysis. Clinically, we have used this technique effectively with university students, community adults, and outpatients. Whether it is equally useful with inpatients, severely disturbed older adults with long problem histories and many current stressors remains to be examined. In those samples, it may be less effective and practitioner safety issues may be more critical. Thus, it is important to learn about the efficacy of various anger reduction procedures in different environments.

NEXT STEPS

Novaco has produced a line of research and a comprehensive model that takes into consideration a wide array of forces that lead to the activation of anger and aggression. His work has been the stimulus for advances in treatment and is to be applauded. Nevertheless, it is time for further questions to be addressed. For example, are all of the dimensions that he lists of relevance to practitioners? It is one thing to provide a descriptive, scientific analysis of the etiology of anger and aggression that includes the long-term stress produced by substandard living conditions or congested traffic, or behaviors naturally selected to preserve a species and regulated by biophysical structures and processes. It is quite another thing to determine how to modify dysregulated anger within the current life of a single individual. Certainly, clinicians will have great difficulty modifying hard-wired responses of patients, especially those with serious comorbidity. Indeed, such regulation may be near impossible when anger management programs are but 10 or 15 sessions in length. As professional educators, consider how we might respond if asked how many sessions it would take for a native English speaker to learn to speak fluent Portuguese? What would be learned in the time span of one college semester, beyond the basics? With so many reinforcements to speak English it is hard to learn Portuguese, even when such learning is highly desired. For the past 15 years, I have been trying to learn to speak Russian. Although I have made progress, it is very difficult given that I live and work in an English-speaking environment, cannot practice with regularity, have more than 60 years of reinforcement for learning English, watch television in English, and so on. In the same manner, how much anger reduction or regulation can be learned in 10 to 40 sessions when practitioners are up against opposing forces such as long-term reinforced histories of angry and aggressive responding, hard-wired predispositions to react with aggression, significant current stressors, constant modeling of anger and aggression on television, and so forth? Perhaps it is time to be honest about the length of treatment that is needed to produce *important* changes in anger reactions in clinical populations.

In further analyses, we must now also ask if anger and aggression are truly a function of *both* external variables (e.g., insults) and internal variables (e.g., schemas, choice, and agency). And, now that a list of eliciting and maintaining variables has been identified, can we determine the percentage of variation in anger or aggression that is accounted for by each of the variables in specific populations? We may find, for example, that neurobiological variables account for more of the variance in psychotic or low-IQ adults whereas cognitive and learning variables may be more important in high-functioning adults seen in private practices. Scholars seem to disagree about the power of various interventions, as when Novaco questions techniques such as distraction or providing information to explain away the minor negative behavior of a perceived offender. Such disagreement may emerge because of the different populations served by anger researchers and practitioners. Obviously, angry adults who work as corporate executives have different learning abilities and coping resources than do psychotic inpatients. Both groups, I believe, deserve our attention.

THE CONFUSING PROBLEM OF
"ANGER" AND "AGGRESSION"

As part of his interesting and thoughtful historical review, Novaco (chap. 1, this volume) writes that "Seneca often confused anger with aggression" (p. 6). In chapter 2 of this volume, DiGiuseppe and colleagues also highlight the importance of the "separation of anger from aggression as topics of investigation and targets for treatment" (p. 66). Unfortunately, we are still confusing the two, and adequate definitions are not provided by either Novaco or DiGiuseppe in this volume (see Kassinove & Tafrate, 2006, for a discussion of the problem). Until such definitions are agreed upon, we will be unable to determine whether anger is a precursor to aggression or whether the two are best conceived of as a single concept.

Novaco also writes that Konecni sees the relationship of anger to aggression as bidirectional. Anger may determine aggressive behavior and the expression of aggression may *reduce* anger and, thus, subsequent aggression. This leads Novaco to argue for some degree of merit in the hypothesis of catharsis or ventilation. His proposal is thoughtful and intriguing, and rests on the idea that the experimental work that has negated the value of ventilation has not been ecologically sound. I agree.

For a variety of obvious reasons, we have to clearly differentiate between the concepts of anger and aggression. Is it not basic that the science and practice of psychology, and psychotherapy, can progress only with clear definitions and precise measurement of the important variables? The functional analysis of anger proposed by DiGiuseppe and colleagues, and the beliefs of Novaco (e.g., "aggressive behavior is so often activated by anger," chap. 1, this volume, p. 3) are likely to bear fruit for the field only if anger is defined clearly and is differentiated from aggression, violence, and related terms.

In the science of psychology, we have accepted many hypothetical constructs that have no counterparts in the real world. We have also known for a long time (e.g., Nunnally, 1967) that constructs are simply heuristics or guides for exploring *observables*. Just as anxiety does not "exist," neither does anger. Perhaps, it would be better to view anger as an *emotion* (i.e., a construct) that is composed of a constellation of observable motor behaviors (e.g., avoidance and/or approach responses; muscle or motor expressions such as a furrowed brow, glaring, pursing of the lips, throwing objects, pushing or hitting others, etc.), observable and measurable changes in the biophysiology of the body (e.g., increase heart rate, hormone production, etc.), and cognitive processes (observable by only a single individual who reports on internal experiences). Perhaps, however, it would be better to view anger as a *feeling*, which has traditionally referred only to subjective experiences (Izard, 1977). In this case, anger would refer to conscious awareness of bodily arousal (but not the arousal itself), conscious awareness of thoughts and images about the anger trigger (e.g., "I thought he was my best friend. He should have included me. I can just imagine that he's having a good time at the party while I am sitting here alone."), and thoughts of revenge or retaliation (e.g., "I am never going to invite her to my house again and I will tell others about how selfish she is."). The former perspective would fit the model of anger as an emotion whereas the latter would be simply a verbal-cognitive perspective that has become so popular in recent years.

Aggression traditionally refers to gross motor behavior, with the *intent* to harm. Thus, motor behavior that inadvertently hurts others (e.g., pain caused by a dentist) is not aggression, but the intentional corporal punishment of a misbehaving child is aggression. If a child is pushed out of the way of an unseen car, in order to save the child's life, the push is not considered to be an act of aggression even if the child is bruised in the process. The intent was to help. However, if a child is slapped in the face by a parent who discovers that the child broke a vase, the intent is to harm the child and aggression is an acceptable label. Intent, a cognitive construct, has long been part of the definition of aggression, thus setting the stage for cognitive analyses of the problem and cognitive modes of intervention.

If anger is thoughtfully differentiated from aggression and violence (the latter two are also not differentiated in the literature), this would help us to understand their relationships. However, if anger is defined as an emotion that includes observable gross motor behavior (as is done in many scholarly reports) we run into obvious troubles. Anger researchers will surely find an inflated relationship, and conclude that anger causes or instigates aggression because of the overlapping elements of motor behavior in both the predictor and the criterion. On the other hand, if anger is defined as a private feeling that we learn about by self-report of internal cognitive processes, then we are faced with measurement issues. Introspection, although still popular to the layperson, has not yielded much scientific fruit.

To show the definition problem in some detail, consider the following hypothetical scenario. A wife discovers that her husband has been stealing money from their joint bank account. Her response might be categorized along three variables. First, in a series of graded steps, her personal reaction might vary from a limited view captured by, "Your *behavior* was wrong" to a broader, more generalized and vengeful view captured by "I always knew that *you are a total jerk*, just like your father was, and I am going to get even with you." Second, she might just think this to herself, or she might say it aloud to her husband or others, or she might forcefully scream it at him. Finally, she might or might not engage in associated motor behaviors such as pushing him, throwing a pencil at him, throwing a plate against the wall, throwing a plate at him, or hitting him with a pot (note the increasing intensity of her behavior). She might also behave indirectly by spitting in his soup before she serves it to him. In the matrix of many possibilities produced by the three variables, would we all agree on which represent anger and which represent aggression? Some might say that anger consists only or primarily of the (unmeasurable) private thoughts. But this anger could only be approached by introspection and verbal reports, which may or may not reflect the thoughts. We can never know what others are thinking and it is unlikely that a woman living with an abusive husband would verbalize honestly to him.

Others might say that anger consists of the measurable *verbal* reports and that, as a feeling, it does not include the gross motor behaviors. They would then define aggression as observable motor behavior. If we adopt these definitions, we would be able to examine the nature of anger (the frequency of specific verbalizations) and its relationship to aggression and violence (i.e., measurable gross motor behaviors). In this analysis, I have ignored the biophysical processes, some of which can be experimentally (drug) induced and verbally reported on (e.g., a racing heart rate) and some of which cannot (e.g., dichotomous and catastrophizing thoughts; see Salzinger, 1995). I have also ignored the issue of so-called "verbal aggression," in which the only motor behavior is verbal behavior. By this kind of analysis, verbal aggression is an oxymoron because there is no gross motor behavior.

A fundamental question is whether the whole set of behaviors that we refer to as anger and aggression can be adequately explained without referring to hypothesized cognitive processes at all. For cognition to be an important part of the anger definition and the anger-causes-aggression equation, we must show that by including cognition we add more to our understanding than by excluding it. This is suggested by the law of parsimony. The functional analysis provided by DiGiuseppe and colleagues (chap. 2, this volume) suggests that "treatments for anger need to be based on an understanding of the learning *and cognitive processes* that arouse and maintain anger" (italics added). Although it is popular today to speak of such mental processes, Skinnerians would have difficulty ascribing causation to cognitive processes such as irrational ideas, schemas, and so on. In fact, an operant analysis can explain both anger and aggressive behavior in the absence of a concept of intent. Such an analysis has already been provided by Salzinger (1995).

Anger and aggression may well be the same phenomenon, differing simply in strength (Salzinger, 1995). Without definitional agreement, we will continue to wander with uncertainty as we try to understand and treat interpersonal violence. The science and practice of psychology, and psychotherapy, can progress only with clear definitions and precise measurement of the variables in question. Again, a functional analysis of anger is likely to bear important fruit for the field only if anger is defined clearly and is differentiated from aggression and violence.

FUNCTIONAL ANALYSIS AND CAUSATION

DiGiuseppe and colleagues (chap. 2, this volume) focus on the importance of a functional analysis to aid in understanding anger. I agree with their position and believe that it is time to move in that direction. However, they include unmeasurable cognitive variables, as does Novaco when he includes "agency." Thus, it is wise to review some points about causation.

A functional view tends to focus on efficient causation. For those unfamiliar with this term, Aristotle listed four types of causes: material, efficient, formal, and final (Rychlak, 1997). A *material* cause refers to substances that set limits on behavior, such as the fact that we are made of flesh. Thus, no matter how much we exercise we will never be as strong as steel and will never be able to withstand an aggressive force (as produced by a bullet and handgun) as well as will steel. We will suffer because we are made of flesh. *Efficient* causes refer to changes and include how and why things move or remain stationary. The analysis is temporal in nature. When a hammer strikes a nail (the preceding event), the nail moves into the wood (the consequence). The strength of the stimulus (i.e., force of the blow) causes the nail to move. We don't speak of any kind of process that exists in between the strike of the hammer and the movement of the nail. We don't say that the nail was motivated to move, or agentically decided to move, or wanted to move, or needed to move. We simply describe the functional relationship of the two events. The third type, *formal causes*, refers to patterns, essences, shapes, and styles. Thus, nails move into wood more easily because they are long and thin, and have a point. Lastly, *final causes* refer to intentions, reasons, wishes, desires, hopes, and so forth. That is, we hit the nail because we intend to build a bookcase. We use a nail because we believe that the bookcase will be stronger than if we use glue alone. Final causes add mental processes to the model. Of note, however, is the fact that each of these intentions is linked to the learning history of the person and can be explained by operant psychology without the use of final causes. Much of this proposed final part of the causal chain is outside of the reach of science. Perhaps the final cause, for example, as to why we build a bookcase, is that god wanted a bookcase in the room. Because such propositions are not measurable, scientists stick to the examination of the other types of causes and leave final causation for philosophers to ponder. Unfortunately, the rise of cognitive-behaviorism has revived the acceptance of unmeasurable cognitive variables.

With regard to the central issue in this text, aggressive behavior, our goal is to examine the role played by these four causes. Do we aggress because we have fists, because we have first been hit by another person, because the length of our arm allows us to reach and punch another person, because we have been successful when we aggressed in the past and reaped desired rewards, or because we are impelled by moral justification and want or desire to aggress? As noted earlier, traditional S–R (stimulus–response) behavioral psychologists have focused on material and efficient causation. Cognitive psychologists have added the mental dimension of final causation.

The quest by DiGiuseppe and colleagues (chap. 2, this volume) to examine the functional relationship of the anger response is certainly a step in the right direction. Nunnally (1967) noted long ago that the results of science are inevitably reported as functional relationships among measured variables. However, to include final causes and cognitive processes is problematic because of measurement problems.

THE NONCOGNITIVE, BEHAVIORAL PATH

What accounts for the etiology and maintenance of anger and interpersonal aggression? DiGiuseppe and colleagues (chap. 2, this volume) support a functional analysis of the problem. Good! However, based on paper-and-pencil tests and interview data, they devote much space to the mental concept of *motives,* the promotion of *thoughts* of revenge and so on. Likewise, Novaco (chap. 1, this volume) supports a free-will concept of "agency" and most researchers define aggression as *intentionally* harmful motor behaviors. Admittedly, in our own professional work we also use mental concepts such as irrational ideas (Kassinove & Tafrate, 2002). In daily clinical work, after all, we have no choice but to speak to patients in the vernacular.

As scientists, however, we must ask what the radical behaviorists would say? Is there a more parsimonious alternate to the mental explanations perspective to account for anger, aggression, and interpersonal violence? Radical behaviorists do not totally discount mental life. Rather, they recognize that it is private, cannot be reliably and publicly assessed, and is best left out of a scientific analysis. Thus, they explain anger, aggression, and interpersonal violence by reference to environmental variables. Skinner (1990) noted that psychologists have spent a significant amount of time looking inside the person for a free, initiating mind to explain behavior. That effort has been to little avail and, in many ways, psychology is differentiated from philosophy with regard to how we handle the notion of a free mind that supposedly begins the behavior chain of anger, aggression, and violence.

In his search for causal elements, three types of variation and selection were accepted by Skinner (1990). To be helpful to practitioners who work with angry patients, these would have to explain the etiology of anger and interpersonal violence and would hopefully lead to effective treatments. The first, natural selection, accounts for the evolution of our species and species-wide behavior. In animals, the fight reaction in response to threats often led to reinforcements that strengthened a set of fighting behaviors. Strong, immediate aggressive behavior that led to harm against challengers and predators allowed for self-protection, protection of the young, access to food, shelter, and desired mates, and so on. Of course, if the flight reaction would have been a better alternative, the animal may have died during a fight. In this manner, animals with survival behaviors were selected. Natural selection, however, prepared us only for a physical and social environment that resembled the past environment. In modern society, we are rarely faced with enemies who are out to kill us. Food and shelter are quite readily available, as are a selection of mates. We are typically faced with less threatening aversive triggers such as insults, being left out of a group, passed over for a promotion, and the like. In modern, lawful societies, the strong responses of screaming and motor aggression that were useful in the uncivilized world are no longer necessary. To behave very strongly against a boss, teacher, or spouse (e.g., to scream or hit) will likely lead to trouble.

Operant conditioning, the second type of variation and selection, accounts for acquired behaviors of the individual person. As the person develops, within the limits of hard-wired natural selection, a repertoire of behaviors develop that we often call "personality." When a school bully demands that other children relinquish their lunch money to him, and they do so, bullying behavior is strengthened. When a boss yells at employees, and the employees do what is asked (at least when the boss is present), yelling is strengthened. When a husband pouts, moves slowly, and talks only when spoken to, his wife may ask what is wrong. If it takes multiple probes on her part to get him to talk, his pouting is strengthened further. By comparison to natural selection, operant conditioning works quickly, allowing for the development of anger intervention strategies for the individual.

A major problem, as Skinner (1990) noted, is that selection must wait for variation. That is, before prosocial or antisocial behavior can be selected it must first appear. How do anger and aggression first appear? Where do they come from and why are they maintained in spite of the many documented negative outcomes? According to behavior theory, the initiation of (angry and aggressive) behavior in a single person became easy when our vocal musculature came under operant control. Children, adolescents, and adults could be told what to do. Most of us are taught (told and reinforced) to treat others with kindness, to be fair, and so forth. In some cases, however, gang members and others with a history of bullying and violence are taught (told) about how to gain short-term reinforcements quickly. They are taught by their aggressive peers to argue, yell, threaten, push, shove, slap, and so on, and these behaviors often lead to immediate gratification. Thus, they are strengthened. Not all aggression, of course, is reinforced. But, enough of it is to make it highly resistant to extinction. As noted by DiGiuseppe and colleagues (chap. 2, this volume), and others (Kassinove & Tafrate, 2002), the short-term outcomes of anger and aggression are often positive and reinforcing (e.g., compliance with the demands of bullies) whereas the longer-term outcomes are the ones that are negative (e.g., loss of friendships, incarceration, etc.). For most of us, the reinforcing strength of the short-term positive outcomes is far more powerful than the negative long-term effects. Thus, anger and aggression become part of the repertoire of behavior.

A third kind of variation and selection involves cultures. Cultures reinforce and prepare members of the group for a world in which the culture developed. However, when members of the culture move to a different environment, they often fail when they try to use the same skills that were previously successful (see Diamond, 1994, 1999). In the world of bullies, gangs, and other groups where aggression has been rewarded, we cannot expect that such thugs will move to a middle-class, prosocial world and adapt easily. They will likely stick to the behaviors that worked in the past. Indeed, gang members in prison will not be reinforced if they assertively say, "I feel annoyed when I think of what you said to me." Rather, they are likely to be beaten up. Threats to others are more likely to establish their dominance, increase their access to desired goods, and protect them. Those are the strongly reinforced behaviors they hold when they enter our intervention programs.

Operant psychology posits that private events follow the same laws of learning as do public events. That is, our thoughts, motives, images, desires, and so on, are a function of events in the environment. Although they may be part of a chain of events, in experimental terms they are dependent variables. If anger is a private event, a fundamental question for both scientists and practitioners is whether such private (cognitive) events can have a controlling and initiating influence on externally observed behavior such as interpersonal aggression? As noted earlier, radical behaviorists do not negate the "reality" of consciousness, irrational ideas, images, fantasies, hostile thoughts, ruminations, and so forth. Rather, their goal is to discover whether they can realistically be assessed and modified in psychotherapy, and whether such modification (typically judged by self-report data; "I don't hate her anymore and I've given up my desire to hurt her") will lead to a lowered probability of motor aggression and violence.

In both of the previous chapters, it was noted that, traditionally, aggression that follows anger has been labeled as emotional aggression whereas aggression that occurs in the relative absence of anger is labeled as instrumental aggression. For example, aggression that occurs as a part of gang violence (behavior fostered by peer pressure and modeling that is often not the result of festering anger) is considered to be instrumental. The aggressor may not be angry and may have no hostile attitude toward the victim. Rather, the aggression occurs as a result of the social environment and peer reinforcement. In contrast, many observations of aggressive behavior are *verbally reported to be preceded* by anger, by thoughts of malevolent actions by others directed at the self, and by fantasies of revenge. Bushman and Anderson (2001) have argued that this distinction has outlived its usefulness, as there is great overlap of the two models. Novaco (chap. 1, this volume) and DiGiuseppe and colleagues agree (chap. 2, this volume), as do I. As pointed out in the operant analysis of anger and aggression by Salzinger (1995), the stimuli that elicit anger and aggression are much the same and they are both maintained by reinforcing consequences. Without a distinction between instrumental and hostile aggression, we may simply examine the other, noncognitive causal forces that lead to aggression. This is the operant approach promoted by DiGiuseppe and colleagues (chap. 2, this volume), and I agree that this model is likely to lead to useful intervention strategies. Of course, in a full analysis of aggressive behavior, it does seem important to examine, and add to the equation, the role of cultural and biogenetic forces that may lead to interpersonal aggression.

A PROPOSAL

There is an alternate perspective to the view that cognitive-behavior therapy (CBT) is the best model for anger/aggression/violence interventions. I propose that it would be wise to begin to think of the field not as CBT but as VBT—*Verbal-behavior therapy*. Because verbal behavior is observable by others and measurable, we can easily examine the relationship of various verbalizations that might be defined as "anger" (e.g., "I feel really pissed off." or "I feel really pissed off and want to get even with him."), or lower-level motor behaviors that have previously been defined as manifestations of anger (e.g., pointing at another person, glaring, etc.), to stronger observable behaviors that are cataloged as "aggression" (pushing, shoving, slapping, punching, stabbing, shooting, etc.). This proposal for anger researchers would be consonant with the approach taken by Miller and Rollnick (2002), who have been examining *commitment language*. They have identified four patient verbalization themes that seem to be predictive of behavioral change. Labeled as *change talk statements*, they include verbalization of problem recognition, expression of concern, intention to change, and optimism. In the beginning phase of treatment, the goal is to increase these classes of verbalizations. Evidence for the connection between commitment language and behavioral outcomes has been reviewed by Amrhein, Miller, Yahne, Palmer, and Fulcher (2003).

The goal in this proposal is to learn about the functional relationships between measurable verbal variables and observable and measurable anger/aggression variables. A *function* is a mathematical description of what is called a *relationship* by the layperson. A mathematical function, of course, is far more precise as the relationship may be direct, inverted, curvilinear, and so on. For example, there is a functional relationship between air temperature and the amount of clothing that is worn. As temperature rises, we tend to wear less and the relationship can be described mathematically. For psychologists, this notion of functional relationships plays an essential role in predicting and controlling human behaviors, such as aggression. However, as noted previously, the predictor and the criterion must be independent of each other for the true function to be understood.

Kassinove and Tafrate (2006) have suggested that the following definitions may help us to answer questions about the relationship of anger to interpersonal aggression:

> Anger can be considered as the private event. It refers to an experienced negative feeling state that varies in intensity (labeled from annoyance, through anger and, then, to fury) and duration (fleeting states to enduring grudges). It may be experienced infrequently or frequently, and is associated with other private events such as negative images and thoughts about the trigger, cognitive misinterpretations, and desires to warn, intimidate, control, attack, or gain retribution. This anger may exist simply as anger-in (Spielberger, 1999). Because it is private and unmeasurable (except by self-report), we can only speculate as to whether the anger/private event (awareness, thoughts, images and motives) is functionally associated with physiological and motor reactions.

This definition does not negate the reality of experience. We may simply never know if a functional relationship exists between private mental life and external variables labeled as aggression or violence. Of course, there are many verbalizations (e.g., "I am really seething") and lower-level motor behaviors (e.g., pursing of the lips) that we do label as signs of anger. These are both observable and measurable and can be put into a prediction equation.

Aggression can be considered to refer to various classes of gross motor behavior, catalogued by some system of intensity, surrounding circumstances, etc. It refers to public behaviors that can be observed, measured, counted, etc. Violence, although alternate definitions exist, usually refers to group behavior, as in the violent behavior of gangs.

These definitions of anger and aggression allow for the differentiation of milder behaviors labeled as anger from stronger behaviors labeled as aggression. If adopted, these definitions would allow us to examine further the relationship of these two variables in a manner similar to the study of commitment language referred to earlier. Although the problems of introspection and self-report would remain, we could easily examine the link between verbal behaviors (e.g., "I want to get even") to gross motor behaviors (e.g., as pushing, shoving, murder, etc.). Thus, we could examine the functional relationship, without resorting to private mental states. There is no need in a proposal for VBT to negate the reality of private events. After all, everyone reports that they exist. Rather, the goal is to focus on measurable elements of human behavior in order to catalog functional relationships that are important for clinical change.

In a modern world, intervention techniques such as verbal assertiveness (e.g., "I feel rather annoyed when I think of what you did. I'd like to talk with you about it.") make more sense than strong motor responses (i.e., aggression) against perceived anger triggers. Assertiveness training, so popular when the field of behavior therapy began, fits the model of examining the relationship of verbalizations to later motor behaviors. What is the relationship of various verbalizations to those stronger motor behaviors we call aggression? Which specific verbal responses are likely to increase aggression (perhaps, "You're a jerk.") and which may decrease the probability of aggression (perhaps "I feel uncomfortable. I'd like to talk to you.")? In what environments might such verbalizations be effective? The analysis of anger, aggression, and interpersonal violence in a VBT model may yield important outcomes missed by the current, popular CBT model.

CONCLUSIONS

The chapters by Novaco and DiGiuseppe and colleagues (chaps. 1 and 2, this volume, respectively) make important contributions to our understanding of anger, aggression, and interpersonal violence. Novaco notes that these are hard-wired responses that are embedded in a variety of psychosocial systems. They have had survival value for the species, and often lead to positive outcomes. He notes that the problem consists of the dysregulation of anger and believes that anger may be a precursor to aggression. His presentation about the history of the study of anger is both enlightening and thought provoking. Novaco highlights a number of problems, including that so many studies have been done on college students with relatively mild levels of anger, and that anger has often been judged by responses on paper-and-pencil tests administered at one point in time. This leads him to question whether the results are applicable to older patients, with comorbid problems, who live in stressful environments. DiGiuseppe and colleagues review prior analyses of anger and conclude that a functional analysis of anger, aggression, and interpersonal violence from the viewpoint of operant psychology will likely lead to better treatments than if we try simply to use knowledge gained from the study of other emotions such anxiety and depression. Their view is that learning and cognitive analyses will lead to an enhanced understanding of the issues.

In this commentary, I have stressed my agreement with much of what is presented by Novaco and DiGiuseppe and colleagues. Their positive contributions cannot be overstated. At the same time, the importance of clear and nonoverlapping definitions of anger and aggression has also been stressed. Without such definitions, problems remain. First, we will continue to focus on unmeasurable private cognitive events, based on questionable self-report data. Second, we will continue to find a stronger than is true relationship between anger and aggression because both are often defined by gross motor behaviors such as pushing or shoving. That is, pushing and shoving are currently considered to be signs of both anger and aggression. A proposal that we turn our focus from CBT to VBT was made. By focusing on the relationship of measurable verbal behaviors (e.g., "I think of hurting you.") to measurable gross motor behaviors (e.g., punching), we are likely to make more progress in the discovery of the functional relationships suggested by DiGiuseppe and colleagues. Interpersonal anger-aggression-violence is likely a function of natural selection, operant conditioning, and the development of cultures. Certainly, it is difficult to overcome the forces of natural selection. However, placing angry-aggressive-violent patients in environments that do not reinforce such behaviors, building in delays before responding to the common and relatively mild aversive behaviors that we face in modern society (e.g., being ignored by others), and teaching better verbal and motor responses, may yield significant outcomes to enhance interpersonal functioning.

ACKNOWLEDGMENT

I express my appreciation for the thoughtful advice provided by Kurt Salzinger and Raymond Chip Tafrate on various elements of this commentary.

REFERENCES

Anastasi, A., Cohen, N., & Spatz, D. (1948). A study of fear and anger in college students through the controlled diary method. *Journal of Genetic Psychology, 73,* 243–249.

Amrhein, P. C., Miller, W. R., Yahne, C. E., Palmer, M., & Fulcher, L. (2003). Client commitment language during motivational interviewing predicts drug use outcomes. *Journal of Consulting and Clinical Psychology, 71,* 862–878.

Beck, A. T. (1976). *Cognitive therapy and the emotional disorders.* New York: International Universities Press.

Bushman, B. J., & Anderson, C. A. (2001). Is it time to pull the plug on the hostile versus instrumental aggression dichotomy? *Psychological Review, 108,* 273–279.

Deffenbacher, J. L., Filetti, L. B., Richards, T. L., Lynch, R. S., & Oetting, E. R. (2003). Characteristics of two groups of angry drivers. *Journal of Counseling Psychology, 50,* 123–132.

Deffenbacher, J. L., Huff, M. E., Lynch, R. S., Oetting, E. R., & Salvatore, N. F. (2000). Characteristics and treatment of high-anger drivers. *Journal of Counseling Psychology, 47,* 5–17.

Deffenbacher, J. L., Oetting, E. R., Huff, M. E., & Thwaites, G. A. (1995). Fifteen-month follow-up of social skills and cognitive-relaxation approaches to general anger reduction. *Journal of Counseling Psychology, 42,* 400–405.

Diamond, J. (1999). *Guns, germs and steel: The fate of human societies.* New York: Norton.

Diamond, J. (2004). *Collapse: How societies choose to fail or succeed.* New York: Viking.

Ellis, A. E. (1994). *Reason and emotion in psychotherapy: Revised and updated.* New York: Carol.

Eckhardt, C. I. & Deffenbacher, J. L. (1995). Diagnosis of anger disorders. In H. Kassinove (Ed.), *Anger disorders: Definition, diagnosis, and treatment* (pp. 27–47). Philadelphia: Taylor & Francis.

Gates, G. S. (1926). An observational study of anger. *Journal of Experimental Psychology, 9,* 325–331.

Izard, C. E. (1977). *Human emotions.* New York: Plenum.

Kassinove, H., & Eckhardt, C. I. (1995). An anger model and a look to the future. In H. Kassinove (Ed.), *Anger disorders: Assessment, diagnosis, and treatment* (pp. 197–204) Washington, DC: Taylor & Francis International.

Kassinove, H., & Sukhodolsky, D. G. (1995). Anger disorders: Basic science and practice issues. In H. Kassinove (Ed.), *Anger disorders: Assessment, diagnosis, and treatment* (pp. 1–26). Washington, DC: Taylor & Francis International.

Kassinove, H., & Tafrate, R.C. (2002). *Anger management: The complete practitioners guidebook for the treatment of anger.* Atascadero, CA: Impact.

Kassinove, K., & Tafrate, R. (2006). Anger related disorders: Basic issues, models, and diagnostic considerations. In E. Feindler (Ed.), *Comparative treatments of anger disorders* (pp. 1–27). NewYork: Springer.

Kaufman, L., & Wagner, B. R. (1972). Barb: A systematic treatment technology for temper control disorders. *Behavior Therapy, 3,* 84–90.

Miller, W. R., & Rollnick, S. (2002). *Motivational interviewing: Preparing people for change* (2nd ed.). New York: Guilford.

Millon, T., Davis, R., & Millon, C. (1997). *Millon Clinical Multiaxial Inventory–III Manual* (3rd ed.). Minneapolis, MN: National Computer Systems.

Novaco, R. W. (1975). *Anger control: The development and evaluation of an experimental treatment.* Lexington, MA: Heath.

Novaco, R. W. (1977). Stress inoculation: A cognitive therapy for anger and its application to a case of depression. *Journal of Consulting and Clinical Psychology, 45*, 600–608.

Nunnally, J. C. (1967). *Psychometric theory.* New York: McGraw-Hill.

Reilly, P., & Shopshire, M. S. (2002). *Anger management for substance abuse and mental health clients.* Rockville, MD: U.S. Department of Health and Human Services.

Rychlak, J. F. (1997). *In defense of human consciousness.* Washington, DC: APA Press.

Salzinger, K. (1995). A behavior-analytic view of anger and aggression. In H. Kassinove (Ed.), *Anger disorders: Definition, diagnosis, and treatment* (pp. 69–79). Philadelphia: Taylor & Francis.

Skinner, B. F. (1990). Can psychology be a science of mind? *American Psychologist, 45*, 1206–1210.

Tafrate, R., & Kassinove, H. (1998). Anger control in men: Barb exposure with rational, irrational, and irrelevant self-statements. *The Journal of Cognitive Psychotherapy, 12*, 187–211.

Tafrate, R.C., & Kassinove, H. (2006). Cognitive behavioral treatment for the case of Anthony. In E. Feindler (Ed). *Comparative treatments of anger disorders* (pp. 115–137). New York: Springer.

Tafrate, R.C., Kassinove, H., & Dundin, R. (2002). Anger episodes of angry community residents. *Journal of Clinical Psychology, 58*, 1573–1590.

Williams, J. E., Paton, C. C., Siegler, I. C., Eigenbrod, M. L., Nieto, F. J., & Tyroler, H. A. (2000). Anger proneness predicts coronary heart disease risk. Prospective analysis from the Atherosclerosis Risk in Communities (ARIC) Study. *Circulation, 101*(17), 2034–2039.

II

NATURAL AND THERAPEUTIC
FUNCTIONS OF ANGER
AND ITS EXPRESSION

Anger: Causes and Components

Eddie Harmon-Jones and Cindy Harmon-Jones

Emotions can be considered processes that involve involuntary action readiness (Frijda, 1986). Basic emotions, such as anger, provide organisms with relatively complex and biologically prepared behavioral potentials that assist in coping with major challenges to their welfare (Panksepp, 1998). However, these inherited behavioral potentials only suggest ways of behaving as organisms evolved to have larger, more complex brains. Thus, although humans may possess the same emotional instincts as other animals, we may not be as controlled by the dictates of emotions and thus we have more choices (Panksepp, 1994). Consequently, our emotions can be regulated and thus may not directly affect behavior.

An emotion is not a "thing" but is best considered a process that is made up of basic processes such as feelings of pleasure or displeasure, facial-expression components, particular appraisals, and particular action plans and activation states (Frijda, 1993). Anger is a relatively unpleasant feeling, and it is described using words like *annoyed, angry,* and *enraged,* which in our view, express differences in intensity (cf. Lewis, 1993, however, who suggested that rage and anger are qualitatively different). When left uncontrolled or uninhibited, its facial expression involves the muscles of the brow moving inward and downward, thus "creating a frown and a foreboding appearance around the eyes, which seem to be fixed in a hard stare toward the object of anger. The nostrils dilate and the wings of the nose flare out. The lips are opened and drawn back in a rectangle-like shape, revealing clinched teeth. Often the face flushes red" (Izard, 1977, p. 330). Because humans are taught to control anger and its expression, the expressions of anger vary considerably from one person to another, but "on the face of an angry person there is almost always one or more of the innate components of the natural expression which signals his or her internal state" (Izard, 1977, p. 330).

In this chapter, we review recent research and theoretical advances in the study of basic processes involved in anger. Anger has been suggested to serve a variety of adaptive functions. It organizes and regulates several psychological processes, such as self-defense and mastery. It also regulates social and interpersonal behaviors, and organizes behaviors to assist with goal-directed action. However, because anger may give rise to mal-adaptive cognitions and behaviors, individuals and societies often attempt to regulate anger as a way of preventing intra- and interpersonal negative consequences, such as aggression.

We focus our review on the causes of anger, its subjective feeling and motivational components, and some of its neural components. In doing so, we consider all of the component processes typically involved in anger — its feelings, appraisals (under causes), action plans and activation states (under motivation), and physiology. However, we do not review the literature on angry facial expressions, as it is beyond the scope of this chapter (for a recent review, see Russell & Fernández-Dols, 1997).

SUBJECTIVE FEELINGS AND ANGER

The conception of anger advanced in this chapter is much broader than some others, which suggest that there are different kinds of anger. For example, Ellsworth and Scherer (2003, p. 575) wrote, "Rather than a single emotion of anger, there can be many varieties of 'almost anger' and many nuances of the anger experience."

We do not reject such a possibility, but instead suggest a broader view that proposes that there is an important commonality overriding the "nuances" of anger experience. Spielberger et al. (Speilberger, Jacobs, Russell, & Crane, 1983; Spielberger, Reheiser, & Sydeman, 1995) reflected this notion in regarding *anger* as encompassing low-intensity feelings such as irritation or annoyance as well as high-intensity feelings such as fury and rage. A factor analysis of the items in his State Anger scale (such as "I am furious" and "I feel irritated") obtained only a single factor, suggesting that the feelings tapped by these items reflected a unitary affective state varying in intensity. Spielberger's (Spielberger et al., 1983, 1995) distinction between "anger-in" and "anger-out," it should be noted, refers to differences in the *predisposition (i.e., trait) to openly express* the motoric concomitants of anger rather than qualitative differences in the nature of the angry feelings (Spielberger et al., 1995). Our conception of anger experience is in accord with the prototype view of emotion concepts advanced by Shaver, Schwartz, Kirson, and O'Connor (1987). Shaver et al. found that the anger prototype indicates that a variety of feelings labeled *irritation, annoyance, exasperation, disgust,* and *hate* are often included within the general notion of anger. In summary, there is some justification to not regarding the various "nuances" of anger experience as distinctly different emotional or affective states.

It is often held that emotions, unlike moods, are about something in particular; they have a more definite cause and/or a more specific target. However, this clarity and/or focus is a matter of degree, as Frijda (1986, pp. 59–60) recognized, and people can vary in the extent to which they believe they know what produced the mood they are experiencing. As Frijda put it, the distinction between mood and emotion is "unsharp" (p. 60). If people can vary in the extent to which they have a clear conception of the cause of their affective arousal, where do we place the cutting point on this continuum, putting mood on one side and emotion on the other?

Valence

Anger is often regarded as a negative emotion by laypersons as well as psychological scientists. However, what is meant by negative is not always clearly defined in the literature. Emotions can be regarded as positive or negative (a) *because of the conditions that evoked the emotion;* (b) *because of the emotion's adaptive consequences;* or (c) *because of the emotion's subjective feel.*

Thus, the emotion of anger can be viewed as negative when considering the conditions that evoked the emotion, because anger is evoked by aversive events. Anger could be viewed as either positive or negative when considering its adaptive consequences, depending on the outcome of the situation in which anger occurred. However, one would also need to define for whom the consequences are adaptive—the individual expressing the anger or the individual or group receiving it, and whether the consequences are adaptive in the short term or long term. Finally, anger could be viewed as either positive or negative when considering the subjective feel or evaluation of the emotion, depending on whether an individual likes or dislikes the subjective experience of anger.

In considering the valence of an emotion, the definition of emotion must also be considered. Although there is no completely accepted definition of emotion, some scientists focus on the stimulus conditions when defining an emotion (e.g., negative situation blamed on another causes anger), whereas other scientists focus on the responses evoked when defining an emotion (e.g., anger involves certain physiological changes, behavioral expressions, and subjective feelings). The stimulus-based definitions indicate that the individual's evaluation of the stimulus causing the emotion determines the valence of the emotion (Lazarus, 1991). Thus, most appraisal theorists regard whether the emotion-evoking situation is appraised as positive or negative as the most important and frequent way of distinguishing positive from negative emotions. By this definition, then, anger is a negative emotion.

Response-based definitions of emotion indicate that the individual's subjective evaluation of the feeling determines the valence of the emotion. When anger is examined as a subjective experience, however, it is not necessarily negative; it can be subjectively accepted or rejected. Anger can be evaluated positively by the person experiencing the emotion, as when an individual says, "I like how it feels when I am furious." Although many persons find the experience of anger unpleasant, some individuals may find it relatively more pleasant.

In general, both state and trait studies examining the valence of anger indicate that most individuals regard anger as a negative experience. However, there are some individuals who routinely find the experience of anger more positive or less negative than other individuals find anger (Harmon-Jones, 2004). Moreover, these individual differences in attitudes toward anger relate positively to Buss and Perry (1992) trait anger and trait hostility (as measured by the Positive and Negative Affect Schedule–Expanded [PANAS–X], of Watson & Clark, 1991), although the correlations are not so high as to suggest redundancy. These individual differences in attitude toward anger also relate negatively to trait fear (as measured by PANAS–X). Attitude toward anger does not relate to self-reported affect intensity or social desirability. Thus, although the valence of anger is predominantly negative, some individuals find it less negative than others, and these attitudes toward anger may have important consequences.

Relationship to Other Emotional Experiences

In a given situation, anger may be the primary or even sole emotional experience. However, often times, anger occurs amid other negative emotions, as many conceptual perspectives recognize (e.g., Berkowitz, 1989). For example, in a recent experiment, anger was manipulated using an interpersonal insult and self-reported affect was measured following the insult (Harmon-Jones, Vaughn-Scott, Mohr, Sigelman, & Harmon-Jones, 2004). In addition to reporting feeling more anger, insult condition participants reported feeling more active, alert, determined, proud, and strong than the no-insult control condition participants. These latter items are from the PANAS measure of activated positive affect (Watson, Clark, & Tellegen, 1988). On the surface, these results suggest that the insult manipulation caused more activated positive affect. Such an interpretation would be consistent with the idea that the activated positive affect scale is measuring approach motivation (Watson, 2000). However, another interpretation is that the words did not reflect feelings of positivity in this situation in which anger was present.

These results for activated positive affect have since been replicated using a different anger manipulation. In addition, trait behavioral activation system (BAS; Gray, 1987) sensitivity was positively related to both reported anger and reported activated positive affect, providing convergent evidence. Moreover, anger and activated positive affect were positively correlated (Harmon-Jones, Harmon-Jones et al., 2005).

MOTIVATIONAL COMPONENTS OF ANGER

A number of theorists have suggested that anger is an emotion that evokes behavioral tendencies of approach (e.g., Darwin, 1872/1965; Ekman & Friesen, 1975; Plutchik, 1980; Young, 1943). Of course, emotions are complex phenomena and discrete emotions may elicit both approach and withdrawal tendencies. However, we believe that the dominant behavioral tendency associated with anger is approach.

Behavioral and Subjective Evidence

Indeed, research has indicated that anger is often associated with attack (e.g., Berkowitz, 1993). Moreover, Depue and Iacono (1989) have suggested that irritable aggression is part of the behavioral facilitation system, a biobehavioral system similar to the BAS (Gray, 1987), which has been found to be associated with relative left prefrontal cortical activity (Harmon-Jones & Allen, 1997; Sutton & Davidson, 1997), a cortical region thought to be involved in approach motivation. Whether anger results in a general tendency to approach as compared to a specific tendency to aggress is currently a topic of debate with some suggesting the former (Lewis, 1993) and some the latter (Berkowitz, 1999).

In support of the idea of anger evoking approach motivation, Lewis, Alessandri, and Sullivan (1990; Lewis, Sullivan, Ramsey, & Alessandri, 1992), in studies on contingency learning, found that infants who displayed anger during extinction demonstrated the highest levels of joy, interest, and a required arm pull operant when the learning portion of the task was reinstated. Thus, subsequent to frustrating events, anger may maintain and increase task engagement and approach motivation.

In other research with adult humans, Baron (1977) demonstrated that angry individuals are reinforced positively by signs of their tormentor's pain. The participants who had been deliberately provoked by another individual had an opportunity to assault him in return. Indications that their first attacks were hurting their target led to increased aggression for previously provoked participants, but to reduced aggression for unprovoked participants. The initial signs of their victim's suffering showed the angry persons they were approaching their aggressive goal and thus evoked even stronger assaults from them. Other research is consistent with these findings (e.g., Berkowitz, Cochran, & Embree, 1981).

Additional support for the idea that anger is associated with approach motivation comes from research testing the conceptual model that integrated reactance theory with learned helplessness theory (Wortman & Brehm, 1975). According to this model, how individuals respond to uncontrollable outcomes depends on their expectation of being able to control the outcome and the importance of the outcome. When an individual expects to be able to control outcomes that are important, and those outcomes are found to be uncontrollable, psychological reactance should be aroused. Thus, for individuals who initially expect control, the first few bouts of uncontrollable outcomes should arouse reactance, a motivational state aimed at restoring control. After several exposures to uncontrollable outcomes, these individuals should become convinced that they cannot control the outcomes and should show decreased motivation (i.e., learned helplessness). In other words, reactance will precede helplessness for individuals who initially expect control. In one study testing this model, individuals who exhibited angry feelings in response to one unsolvable problem had better performance and were presumably more approach motivated on a subsequent cognitive task than did participants who exhibited less anger (Mikulincer, 1988).

Other research has revealed that state anger relates to high levels of self-assurance, physical strength, and bravery (Izard, 1991), inclinations associated with approach motivation. Additionally, Lerner and Keltner (2001) found that anger (both trait and state) is associated with optimistic expectations, whereas fear is associated with pessimistic expectations. Moreover, happiness was associated with optimism, making anger and happiness appear more similar to each other in their relationship with optimism than fear and anger. Although Lerner and Keltner interpreted their findings as being due to the appraisals associated with anger, it seems equally plausible that it was the approach motivational character of anger that caused the relationship of anger and optimism. That is, anger creates optimism because anger engages the approach motivational system and produces greater optimistic expectations.

Other evidence supporting the idea that anger is associated with an approach orientation comes from research on bipolar disorder. The emotions of euphoria and anger often occur during manic episodes of bipolar disorder (Cassidy, Forest, Murry, & Carroll, 1998; Depue & Iacono, 1989; Tyrer & Shopsin, 1982). Both euphoria and anger may be approach-oriented processes, and a dysregulated or hyperactive approach system may underlie mania (Depue & Iacono, 1989; Fowles, 1993). Research suggests that hypomania/mania involves increased left frontal brain activity and approach motivational tendencies. In this research, it has been found that individuals who have suffered damage to the right frontal cortex are more likely to evidence mania (see review by Robinson & Downhill, 1995). Thus, this research is consistent with the view that mania may be associated with increased left frontal activity and increased approach tendencies, because the approach motivation functions of the left frontal cortex are released and not restrained by the withdrawal system in the right frontal cortex. Furthermore, lithium carbonate, a treatment for bipolar disorder, reduces aggression (Malone, Delaney, Luebbert, Cater, & Campbell, 2000), suggesting that anger and aggression correlate with the other symptoms of bipolar disorder. In addition, trait anger has been found to relate to high levels of assertiveness and competitiveness (Buss & Perry, 1992).

Recently, two additional individual-differences studies were conducted to test the hypothesis that trait anger is related to trait approach motivation, or more specifically, to trait BAS sensitivity (Harmon-Jones, 2003). In both studies, trait BAS sensitivity, as assessed by Carver and White's (1994) scale, was positively related to trait anger, as assessed by the Buss and Perry (1992) aggression questionnaire. One of the two studies found that trait anger also related to trait behavioral inhibition system (BIS) sensitivity. In both studies, general negative affect was statistically controlled. This was done because anger's association with general negative affect (Berkowitz, 1999, 2000; Watson, 2000) may cause the association of BIS and anger. That is, the affect of anger has two subcomponents: a nonspecific component that reflects the contribution of general negative affect (Berkowitz, 1999; Watson, 2000) and a more specific component that reflects the unique qualities of anger (Watson, 2000). In other words, at the simple correlation level, anger may be associated with BIS, but when controlling for negative affect, anger will not be associated with BIS but will only be associated with BAS. Results supported this prediction in both studies. Additional results in Study 2 revealed that BAS was positively correlated with physical aggression, and simultaneously regressing aggression onto BAS, BIS, and general negative affect revealed that physical aggression was positively related to BAS, negatively related to BIS, and positively related to negative affect. Carver (2004) has also found that trait BAS predicts state anger in response to situational anger manipulations. These results support the hypothesis that anger is related to approach motivation.

CAUSES OF ANGER

Researchers have often considered anger to be the result of physical or psychological restraint or of interference with goal-directed activity (Darwin,

1872/1965; Izard, 1977; Lewis, 1993). This action-oriented approach to understanding the cause of anger is consistent with postulations advanced by other major theoretical perspectives.

Reinforcement Approaches

For example, neo-behaviorists suggested that the actual or signaled arrival or termination of pleasant or unpleasant events (positive or negative reinforcers) was the primary cause of emotions (Mowrer, 1960). Gray (1987) extended these ideas by including stimulus omissions and interactions with individuals' resources, such as ability to deal with events (see also Rolls, 1999). According to these models, angry emotions (like frustration, anger, and rage) occur as a result of the omission of a positive reinforcer or the termination of a positive reinforcer. Along these lines, Lewis (1993) proposed that the thwarting of a goal-directed action is an unlearned cause of anger. In one experiment, after 2- to 8-month-old infants were conditioned to move one of their arms in order to see a picture of another baby's smiling face, the infants were exposed to an extinction phase in which the arm movement no longer revealed the happy picture. This "frustrating" event caused the majority of the infants to exhibit angerlike facial expressions (Lewis et al., 1990).

Similarly, in considering the causes of anger, Berkowitz (1989) extended the original frustration-aggression model (Dollard, Doob, Miller, Mowrer, & Sears, 1939) with a cognitive neo-associative model of anger and aggression. According to this model, any unpleasant situation, including pain, discomfort, frustration, or social stress, provokes negative affect. This negative affect is associated with fight-*and*-flight motivation. The individual's prior experiences have formed associations that provide cues relating to the present situation. If these cues lead him or her to desire primarily to escape, then the flight system is activated and the person experiences mostly fear. If the cues lead him or her to desire to attack, then the fight system is activated and he or she experiences mostly anger.

Cognitive Appraisal Approaches

The other main theoretical approach aimed at understanding the causes of anger is the cognitive approach. Much of the recent theorizing on causes of anger has come out of this literature. These theorists propose that emotions are caused by an individual's appraisal of a situation. According to appraisal theorists, persons constantly evaluate (appraise) the situations in which they find themselves. A central assumption of appraisal theories is that it is not the situation itself that causes emotion, but rather the ways in which the individual appraises the situation (e.g., Roseman, Spindel, & Jose, 1990).

All appraisal theorists agree that anger is evoked in negatively appraised situations. These situations are often described as situations where the individual's goals are blocked. To clarify what is meant by "goals," some theorists state that the instigating circumstance must be evaluated as personally significant in some way, so that it has goal relevance, if there is to be an angry reaction (Lazarus, 1991; Scherer, 2001). Goals are defined very broadly by some researchers, including not only consciously sought goals, but also basic needs. Thus, pain or discomfort could be considered as blocking the individual's goal to be comfortable. Roseman (1991) defined an anger-evoking situation as one appraised as delivering the absence of a reward or the presence of punishment, whereas Lazarus and Scherer defined an anger-evoking situation as one appraised as containing an obstruction to goal attainment.

Negatively appraised situations are associated with all of the emotions considered to be negative, including fear, sadness, and anger. Theorists have sought the necessary conditions required in order to cause anger, rather than a different negative emotion, to be evoked. One condition that has been proposed as necessary for anger to occur is an appraisal of "other-blame," that is, an assessment by the individual that someone or something has wrongly caused the negative situation to occur (Lazarus, 1991; Ortony, Clore, & Collins, 1988). Some appraisal theorists have proposed that anger occurs only when the individual appraises the evoking event as wrong, unfair, or improper (Frijda, Kuipers, & ter Schure, 1989; Roseman, 1991; Shaver et al., 1987). Lazarus proposed that, in order for anger to occur, the individual must perceive a threat against self-esteem.

Another characteristic that appraisal theorists have proposed as necessary for anger is an appraisal of *high coping potential* in the negative situation. By this, they mean that individuals become angry when they believe that they have a high likelihood of being able to rectify the negative situation and to prevent the undesired consequences (Lazarus, 1991; Scherer, 2001; Stein & Levine, 1989). In negative situations where the individual appraises low coping potential, by contrast, these theorists propose that sadness, fear, or anxiety is experienced instead of anger.

Problems With the Appraisal Accounts

Appraisal theorizing has attracted much interest in recent years and has dominated recent thinking about the causes of emotions in general. On one hand, the idea that anger results from an appraisal that the situation is (a) negative, (b) threatens self-esteem, (c) is caused by others, and (d) is one that we expect to be able to rectify has intuitive appeal. That is, many of us can easily recall instances where we experienced anger and it seemed that the anger resulted from such appraisals. However, our intuitions may be wrong.

Indeed, the appraisal literature has been criticized for failing to provide evidence as to whether appraisals cause emotion or whether emotion motivates the individual to make appraisals. Frijda (1993; Frijda & Zeelenberg, 2001) and Parkinson and Manstead (1992) have noted that, because of the verbal-report methods employed in most investigations in this area, it is unclear whether the identified appraisal characteristics preceded or followed the arousal of the emotional experience. "Nothing in the data resists the interpretation that the relevant appraisals were consequences rather than precedents of the emotional reactions" (Parkinson & Manstead, 1992, p. 129).

Other scientists have questioned the necessity of specific appraisals for anger (Berkowitz & Harmon-Jones, 2004a, 2004b). For example, Berkowitz and Harmon-Jones have argued that once the fight system and anger are activated, the person begins to make appraisals and to do other cognitive processing of the situation, in order to determine who or what to attack, and how or whether to follow through behaviorally with these impulses. This conception differs from the appraisal models in that it proposes that an appraisal of the provoking situation is not necessary in order to produce emotion. They do believe that appraisals are involved in the experience of anger, but see these as coming later in the process, and occurring with anger, or being provoked by anger, rather than being the cause of anger. They propose that Berkowitz's cognitive neo-associative model better accounts for all of the data, including atypical anger occurrences that do not fit well into models that assume the necessity of self-relevance, goals, and blameworthy behavior by another person. They also take issue with appraisal theorists definitions of "goals," "cognitions," and "appraisals" that are sometimes so overly broad that they are untestable (e.g., the "goal" of not experiencing discomfort).

Regarding the necessity of the appraisal of other-blame for anger, it has been suggested that, although other-blame does often occur along with anger, it is the emotion of anger that motivates the individual to seek someone or something to blame for the negative situation. Fridja (1993) reports a number of instances where angry persons blamed, and even aggressed against, inanimate objects in a way that many would characterize as irrational, lending support to the idea that blaming is motivated by anger rather than the other way around.

Lazarus's (1991) claim that self-esteem threats are necessary for anger elicitation has also been questioned. Whereas self-esteem threats may be common in anger-evoking situations, studies have shown that persons sometimes report experiencing anger in response to frustration of transient goals that would not be expected to have high personal relevance. Moreover, it is not likely that the 2-month-old infants in Lewis and colleagues' experiments (1990) were concerned about self-esteem (though Lazarus would contend that such evidence should not be considered).

Finally, the claim that high coping potential is necessary for the experience of anger has recently been challenged by an experiment in which coping potential was manipulated and found to affect cortical activation (see later) but not the subjective experience of anger (Harmon-Jones, Sigelman, Bohlig, & Harmon-Jones, 2003).

NEURAL COMPONENTS OF ANGER

Much recent research has examined the relation between anger and asymmetrical frontal cortical activity because past research had suggested that left frontal cortical activity was associated with approach motivation, whereas right frontal cortical activity was associated with withdrawal motivation. In one of the first studies along these lines, Harmon-Jones and Allen (1998) found that trait anger related to increased left frontal activity and decreased right frontal activity. More recently, Harmon-Jones (2004) addressed an alternative explanation for these results. The alternative explanation suggested that persons with high levels of trait anger might experience anger as a positive emotion, and this positive feeling or attitude toward anger could be responsible for anger being associated with relative left frontal activity. After developing a valid and reliable assessment of attitude toward anger, a study was conducted to assess whether resting baseline asymmetrical activity related to trait anger and attitude toward anger. Results indicated that anger related to relative left frontal activity and not attitude toward anger. Moreover, further analyses revealed that the relationship between trait anger and left frontal activity was not due to anger being associated with a positive attitude toward anger.

To address the limitations of the aforementioned correlational studies, experiments have been conducted in which anger is manipulated and its effects on regional brain activity are examined. In Harmon-Jones and Sigelman (2001), participants were randomly assigned to a condition in which another person insulted them or to a condition in which another person treated them in a neutral manner. Immediately following the treatment, EEG (electroencephalogram) data were collected. As predicted, individuals who were insulted evidenced greater relative left frontal activity than individuals who were not insulted. Additional analyses revealed that within the insult condition, reported anger and aggression were positively correlated with relative left frontal activity. Neither of these correlations was significant in the no-insult condition. These results suggest that relative left frontal activation was associated with more anger and aggression in the condition in which anger was evoked. This research thus provides the first demonstration of a relationship between state anger and relative left frontal activation.

Recent experimental evidence has replicated these results and also revealed that state anger evokes both increased left and decreased right frontal activity. Moreover, a manipulation of sympathy for the person who would later insult the participant revealed that sympathy reduced the effects of insult on left and right frontal activity (Harmon-Jones et al., 2004). This research suggests that experiencing sympathy for another individual may reduce aggression toward that individual (e.g., see review by Miller & Eisenberg, 1988) by reducing the relative left frontal activity associated with anger.

In the two experiments just described, the designs were tailored in such a way as to evoke anger that was approach oriented. Although most instances of anger involve approach inclinations, as discussed earlier, not all instances of anger are associated with approach motivation. To manipulate approach motivation independently of anger, Harmon-Jones et al. (2003) performed an experiment in which the ability to cope with the anger-producing event was manipulated. Based on past research that has revealed that coping potential affects motivational intensity (Brehm & Self, 1996), it was predicted that the expectation of being able to take action to resolve the anger-producing event would increase approach motivational intensity relative to expecting to be unable to take action.

In the experiment, two conditions were run and they differed with regard to whether it was possible for participants to act to change the event that caused the anger, to manipulate coping potential or the expectation of acting to change the situation. Both conditions evoked significant increases in anger (over baseline) and they were not significantly different from each other. More important and consistent with predictions, results indicated that participants who expected to engage in the approach-related action evidenced greater left frontal activity than participants who expected to be unable to engage in approach-related action. Moreover, within the action-possible condition, participants who evidenced greater left frontal activity in response to the angering event also evidenced greater self-reported anger, providing support for the idea that anger is often an approach-related emotional response. In the condition where action was not possible, greater left frontal activity did not relate to greater anger. In our view, this is because, although anger usually leads to approach motivation, when action is not possible, approach motivation remains low, even if angry feelings are high. Finally, within the action-possible condition, participants who evidenced greater left frontal activity in response to the event were more likely to engage in behaviors that would reduce the possibility of the angering event from occurring in the future (i.e., they were more likely to sign the petition and to take petitions with them for others to sign to prevent a possible tuition increase at their university). This finding suggests that greater approach motivation, as reflected in greater left frontal cortical activity, was associated with more action to correct the negative situation.

This research suggests that the left frontal region is most accurately described as a region sensitive to approach motivational intensity. It was only when anger was associated with an opportunity to behave in a manner to resolve the anger-producing event that participants evidenced the increased relative left frontal activation. The effect of increased left frontal cortical activation being evoked during instances of anger where approach-related action is possible has been replicated (Harmon-Jones, Lueck, Fearn, & Harmon-Jones, 2006). The results of these two experiments should not be taken to indicate that such explicit manipulations of action possibility are always necessary. Manipulations of action possibility may only potentiate the effects of emotion manipulations on asymmetrical frontal cortical activity. Indeed, in a recent study, participants were exposed to anger-inducing pictures (and other pictures) and given no explicit manipulations of action expectancy. Across all participants, a null effect of relative left frontal asymmetry occurred. However, individual differences in trait anger related to relative left frontal activity to the anger-inducing pictures, such that individuals high in trait anger showed greater left frontal activity to anger-producing pictures (controlling for activity to neutral pictures; Harmon-Jones, in press).

Other research is consistent with the hypothesis that anger is associated with left frontal activity. For example, d'Alfonso, van Honk, Hermans, Postma, and de Haan (2000) recently used slow repetitive transcranial magnetic stimulation (rTMS) to inhibit the left or right prefrontal cortex. Slow rTMS reduces cortical excitability, so that rTMS applied to the right prefrontal cortex decreases its activation and causes the left prefrontal cortex to become more active, whereas rTMS applied to the left prefrontal cortex causes activation of the right prefrontal cortex. They found that rTMS applied to the right prefrontal cortex caused selective attention toward angry faces whereas rTMS applied to the left prefrontal cortex caused selective attention away from angry faces. Thus, an increase in left prefrontal activity led participants to attentionally approach angry faces, as in an aggressive confrontation. In contrast, an increase in right prefrontal activity led participants to attentionally avoid angry faces, as in a fear-based avoidance. The interpretation of these results is supported by research demonstrating that attention toward angry faces is associated with high levels of self-reported anger and that attention away from angry faces is associated with high levels of cortisol (van Honk, Tuiten, de Haan, van den Hout, & Stam, 2001; van Honk et al., 1998, 1999).

Research on Anger Using Other Brain-Imaging Methods

The reviewed research has revealed that the left frontal cortical region is involved in approach motivated anger. Few studies using brain-imaging technologies other than EEG have been conducted.[1] In one, positron emission tomography (PET[2]; oxygen-15-labeled carbon dioxide) was measured while men were exposed to personally created angry or neutral mental imagery scripts. Results revealed that as compared to neutral imagery, anger imagery caused an increase in the left orbital frontal cortex, the right anterior cingulate cortex, the bilateral anterior temporal poles, left precentral gyrus, bilateral medial frontal cortex, and bilateral cerebellum. Thus, the increase in activity in the left orbital frontal cortex is consistent with the anger research results obtained using EEG. However, Dougherty et al. (1999) interpreted the increase in left orbital frontal cortical activity as corresponding "to inhibition of aggressive behavior in the face of anger" (p. 471). Whereas this interpretation is consistent with some speculations of the role of the left orbital frontal cortex in response inhibition (Mega, Cummings, Salloway, & Malloy, 1997), it is inconsistent with the EEG results showing that increased left frontal activity is associated with increased aggression and approach behavior (e.g., Harmon-Jones & Sigelman, 2001; Harmon-Jones et al., 2003). The interpretation that the left frontal cortical region is involved in the inhibition of anger and aggression is also inconsistent with lesion data suggesting that mania results from damage to the right frontal region (e.g., Robinson & Downhill, 1995) and results obtained when the left relative to right frontal cortex is activated and angry attentional processes are measured (e.g., d'Alfonso et al., 2000). However, EEG is likely assessing dorsolateral frontal cortical activity and not orbital frontal activity, and left orbital frontal activity may be involved in the inhibition of anger, whereas left dorsalateral frontal activity may be involved in approach motivations like anger.

Of course, it may be difficult to compare anger induced by imagery to anger induced by insulting feedback or goal blocking, as in the EEG experiments. In the imagery experiments, there was no report of a significant association between reported anger and regional brain activity. In the EEG experiments, self-reported anger has been found to correlate significantly with relative left frontal activity. Such correlations assist in determining whether the brain activation is related to emotional experience or some other nonemotional variable.

---

[1]Whereas there have been several studies examining neural responses to photographs of angry faces, there have been only a very few studies examining neural activity associated with the experience or expression of anger. Because the former type of studies are likely assessing neural processes associated with the perception of emotional stimuli and not necessarily the experience or expression of emotion, these studies are not reviewed.

[2]Positron emission tomography (PET) is a powerful imaging technique that accurately scans the cellular function of the human body by detecting radiation from the emissions of positrons. Positrons are tiny particles that are present in a radioactive substance that is administered to the patient or participant.

CONCLUSION

Empirical and theoretical developments on the causes of anger were reviewed. Although cognitive appraisal models of anger have received much attention, reinforcement and neo-associative models have been supported as well. Indeed, as Berkowitz's neo-associative model would suggest, appraisals may not be necessary to cause anger and they may only intensify it. In addition, recent research and theory regarding the subjective feelings and motivational components of anger were reviewed. Much of it suggests that anger is a negative feeling state that is also associated with subjective feelings such as bravery, self-assurance, determination, and strength, terms that some emotion models would call positive. These recent results suggest that more research is needed to understand how the situational context affects the valence of subjective feeling states and how these states relate to behavioral and physiological measures of anger and aggression. Finally, much recent research and theory has suggested that anger is associated with approach motivation, and that anger associated with strong approach inclinations is associated with greater left frontal and lesser right frontal cortical activation. Future research is necessary to understand the states and traits that might cause anger to instead be associated with other motivational tendencies and patterns of brain activity. Given these recent advances in research and theory, a more complete understanding of anger is emerging. Such may assist in its regulation and control.

ACKNOWLEDGMENTS

Portions of the research described within this chapter were supported by a grant from the National Science Foundation (BCS 0350435) and by a grant from the National Institute of Mental Health (R03 MH60747-01).

REFERENCES

Baron, R. A. (1977). Effects of victim's pain cues, victim's race, and level of prior instigation upon physical aggression. *Journal of Applied Social Psychology, 9,* 103–114.

Berkowitz, L. (1989). Frustration–aggression hypothesis: Examination and reformulation. *Psychological Bulletin, 106,* 59–73.

Berkowitz, L. (1993). *Aggression: Its causes, consequences, and control.* New York: McGraw-Hill.

Berkowitz, L. (1999). Anger. In T. Dalgleish & M. Power (Eds.), *Handbook of cognition and emotion* (pp. 411–428). Chichester, England: Wiley.

Berkowitz, L. (2000). *Causes and consequences of feelings.* Cambridge, England: Cambridge University Press.

Berkowitz, L., Cochran, S., & Embree, M. (1981). Physical pain and the goal of aversively stimulated aggression. *Journal of Personality and Social Psychology, 40,* 687–700.

Berkowitz, L., & Harmon-Jones, E. (2004a). More thoughts about anger determinants. *Emotion, 4,* 151–155.

Berkowitz, L., & Harmon-Jones, E. (2004b). Toward an understanding of the determinants of anger. *Emotion, 4,* 107–130.

Brehm, J. W., & Self, E. (1989). The intensity of motivation. In M. R. Rosenzweig & L. W. Porter, *Annual review of psychology* (Vol. 40, pp. 109–131). Palo Alto, CA: Annual Reviews.

Buss, A. H., & Perry, M. (1992). The aggression questionnaire. *Journal of Personality and Social Psychology, 63,* 452–459.

Carver, C. S. (2004). Negative affects deriving from the behavioral approach system. *Emotion, 4,* 3–22.

Carver, C. S., & White, T. L. (1994). Behavioral inhibition, behavioral activation, and affective responses to impending reward and punishment: The BIS/BAS scales. *Journal of Personality and Social Psychology, 67,* 319–333.

Cassidy, F., Forest, K., Murry, E., & Carroll, B. J. (1998). A factor analysis of the signs and symptoms of mania. *Archives of General Psychiatry, 55,* 27–32.

d'Alfonso, A. A. L., van Honk, J., Hermans, E., Postma, A., & de Haan, E. H. F. (2000). Laterality effects in selective attention to threat after repetitive transcranial magnetic stimulation at the prefrontal cortex in female subjects. *Neuroscience Letters, 280,* 195–198.

Darwin, C. (1965). *The expression of the emotions in man and animals.* Chicago: University of Chicago Press. (Original work published 1872)

Depue, R. A. & Iacono, W. G. (1989). Neurobehavioral aspects of affective disorders. *Annual Review of Psychology, 40,* 457–492.

Dollard, J., Doob, L., Miller, N., Mowrer, O., & Sears, R. (1939). *Frustration and aggression.* New Haven, CT: Yale University Press.

Dougherty, D. D., Shin, L. M., Alpert, N. M., Pitman, R. K., Orr, S. P., Lasko, M., Macklin, M. L., et al. (1999). Anger in healthy men: A PET study using script-driven imagery. *Biological Psychiatry, 46,* 466–472.

Ekman, P., & Friesen, W. V. (1975). *Unmasking the face: A guide to recognizing emotions from facial clues.* Englewood Cliffs, NJ: Prentice-Hall.

Ellsworth, P. C., & Scherer, K. R. (2003). Appraisal processes in emotion. In R. J. Davidson, H. Goldsmith, & K. R. Scherer (Eds.), *Handbook of the affective sciences* (pp. 572–595). New York: Oxford University Press.

Fowles, D. C. (1993). Behavioral variables in psychopathology: A psychobiological perspective. In P. B. Sutker & H. E. Adams (Eds.), *Comprehensive handbook of psychopathology* (2nd ed., pp. 57–82). New York: Plenum.

Frijda, N. H. (1986). *The emotions.* Cambridge, England: Cambridge University Press.

Frijda, N. H. (1993). The place of appraisal in emotion. *Cognition and Emotion, 7,* 357–387.

Frijda, N. H., Kuipers, P., & ter Schure, E. (1989). Relations among emotion, appraisal, and emotional action readiness. *Journal of Personality and Social Psychology, 57,* 212–228.

Frijda, N. H., & Zeelenberg, M. (2001). Appraisal: What is the dependent? In K. R. Scherer, A. Schorr, & T. Johnstone (Eds.), *Appraisal processes in emotion* (pp. 141–155). Oxford, England: Oxford University Press.

Gray, J. A. (1987). *The psychology of fear and stress*. London: Cambridge University Press.

Harmon-Jones, E. (2003). Anger and the behavioural approach system. *Personality and Individual Differences, 35*, 995–1005.

Harmon-Jones, E. (2004). On the relationship of anterior brain activity and anger: Examining the role of attitude toward anger. *Cognition and Emotion, 18*, 337–361.

Harmon-Jones, E. (in press). Trait anger predicts relative left frontal cortical activation to anger-inducing stimuli. *International Journal of Psychophysiology*.

Harmon-Jones, E., Harmon-Jones, C., Abramson, L., Nelson, B. W., Rupsis, M. M., Burck, A. L., Fearn, M., et al. (2005). *Behavioral approach sensitivity, hypomania, anger, and a construct once called positive affect*. Manuscript in preparation.

Harmon-Jones, E., & Allen, J. J. B. (1997). Behavioral activation sensitivity and resting frontal EEG asymmetry: Covariation of putative indicators related to risk for mood disorders. *Journal of Abnormal Psychology, 106*, 159–163.

Harmon-Jones, E., & Allen, J. J. B. (1998). Anger and prefrontal brain activity: EEG asymmetry consistent with approach motivation despite negative affective valence. *Journal of Personality and Social Psychology, 74*, 1310–1316.

Harmon-Jones, E., Lueck, L., Fearn, M., & Harmon-Jones, C., (2006). The effect of personal relevance and approach-related action expectation on relative left frontal cortical activity. *Psychological Science, 17*, 434–440.

Harmon-Jones, E., & Sigelman, J. (2001). State anger and prefrontal brain activity: Evidence that insult-related relative left prefrontal activation is associated with experienced anger and aggression. *Journal of Personality and Social Psychology, 80*, 797–803.

Harmon-Jones, E., Sigelman, J. D., Bohlig, A., & Harmon-Jones, C. (2003). Anger, coping, and frontal cortical activity: The effect of coping potential on anger-induced left frontal activity. *Cognition and Emotion, 17*, 1–24.

Harmon-Jones, E., Vaughn-Scott, K., Mohr, S., Sigelman, J., & Harmon-Jones, C. (2004). The effect of manipulated sympathy and anger on left and right frontal cortical activity. *Emotion, 4*, 95–101.

Izard, C. E. (1977). *Human emotions*. New York: Plenum.

Izard, C. E. (1991). *The psychology of emotions*. New York: Plenum.

Lazarus, R. S. (1991). *Emotion and adaptation*. New York: Oxford University Press.

Lerner, J. S., & Keltner, D. (2001). Fear, anger, and risk. *Journal of Personality and Social Psychology, 81*, 146–159.

Lewis, M. (1993). The development of anger and rage. In R. A. Glick & S. P. Roose (Eds.), *Rage, power, and aggression* (pp. 148–168). New Haven, CT: Yale University Press.

Lewis, M., Alessandri, S. M., & Sullivan, M. W. (1990). Violation of expectancy, loss of control, and anger expressions in young infants. *Developmental Psychology, 26*, 745–751.

Lewis, M., Sullivan, M. W., Ramsey, D. S., & Alessandri, S. M. (1992). Individual differences in anger and sad expressions during extinction: Antecedents and consequences. *Infant Behavior and Development, 15*, 443–452.

Malone, R. P., Delaney, M. A., Luebbert, J. F., Cater, J., & Campbell, M. (2000). A double-blind placebo-controlled study of lithium in hospitalized aggressive children and adolescents with conduct disorder. *Archives of General Psychiatry, 57*, 649–654.

Mega, M. S., Cummings, J. L., Salloway, S., & Malloy, P. (1997). The limbic system: An anatomic, phylogenetic, and clinical perspective. *Journal of Neuropsychiatry and Clinical Neuroscience, 9*, 315–330.

Mikulincer, M. (1988). Reactance and helplessness following exposure to unsolvable problems: The effects of attributional style. *Journal of Personality and Social Psychology, 54*, 679–686.

Miller, P. A., & Eisenberg, N. (1988). The relation of empathy to aggressive and externalizing/antisocial behavior. *Psychological Bulletin, 103*, 324–344.

Mowrer, O. H. (1960). *Learning theory and behavior.* New York: Wiley.

Ortony, A., Clore, G. L., & Collins, A. (1988). *The cognitive structure of emotions.* New York: Cambridge University. Press.

Panksepp, J. (1994). The basics of basic emotions. In P. Ekman & R. J. Davidson (Eds.), *The nature of emotion: Fundamental questions* (pp. 20–24). New York: Oxford University Press.

Panksepp, J. (1998). *Affective neuroscience: The foundations of human and animal emotions.* New York: Oxford University Press.

Parkinson, B., & Manstead, A. S. R. (1992). Appraisal as a cause of emotion. In M. S. Clark (Ed.), *Review of personality and social psychology* (Vol. 13, pp. 122–149). Newbury Park, CA: Sage.

Plutchik, R. (1980). *Emotion: A psychoevolutionary synthesis.* New York: Harper & Row.

Robinson, R. G., & Downhill, J. E. (1995). Lateralization of psychopathology in response to focal brain injury. In R. J. Davidson & K. Hugdahl (Eds.), *Brain asymmetry* (pp. 693–711). Cambridge, MA: MIT Press.

Rolls, E. T. (1999). *The brain and emotion.* Oxford, England: Oxford University Press.

Roseman, I. J. (1991). Appraisal determinants of discrete emotions. *Cognition and Emotion, 5*, 161–200.

Roseman, I. J., Spindel, M. S., & Jose, P. E. (1990). Appraisals of emotion-eliciting events: Testing a theory of discrete emotions. *Journal of Personality and Social Psychology, 59*, 899–915.

Russell, J. A., & Fernández-Dols, J. M. (1997). *The psychology of facial expression.* Paris: Cambridge University Press.

Scherer, K. R. (2001). Appraisal considered as a process of multilevel sequential checking. In K. R. Scherer, A. Schorr, & T. Johnstone (Eds.) *Appraisal processes in emotion* (pp. 92–120). Oxford, England: Oxford University Press.

Shaver, P., Schwartz, J., Kirson, D., & O'Connor, C. (1987). Emotion knowledge: Further exploration of a prototype approach. *Journal of Personality and Social Psychology, 52*, 1061–1086.

Spielberger, C. D., Jacobs, G. A., Russell, S. F., & Crane, R. S. (1983). Assessment of anger: The State-Trait Anger scale. In J. N. Butcher & C. D. Spielberger (Eds.), *Advances in personality assessment* (Vol. 2, pp. 159–187). Hillsdale, NJ: Lawrence Erlbaum Associates.

Spielberger, C. D., Reheiser, E. C., & Sydeman, S. J. (1995). Measuring the experience, expression, and control of anger. In H. Kassinove (Ed.), *Anger disorders: Definition, diagnosis, and treatment* (pp. 49–67). Washington, DC: Taylor & Francis.

Stein, N. L., & Levine, L. J. (1989). The causal organization of emotional knowledge: A developmental study. *Cognition and Emotion, 3,* 343–378.

Sutton, S. K., & Davidson, R. J. (1997). Prefrontal brain asymmetry: A biological substrate of the behavioral approach and inhibition systems. *Psychological Science, 8,* 204–210.

Tyrer, S., & Shopsin, B. (1982). Symptoms and assessment of mania. In E. S. Paykel (Ed.), *Handbook of affective disorders* (pp. 12–23). New York: Guilford.

van Honk, J., Tuiten, A., de Haan, E., van den Hout, M., & Stam, H. (2001). Attentional biases for angry faces: Relationships to trait anger and anxiety. *Cognition and Emotion, 15,* 279–297.

van Honk, J., Tuiten, A., van den Hout, M., Koppeschaar, H., Thijssen, J., de Haan, E., et al. (1998). Baseline salivary cortisol levels and preconscious selective attention for threat: A pilot study. *Psychoneuroendocrinology, 23,* 741–747.

van Honk, J., Tuiten, A., Verbaten, R., van den Hout, M., Koppeschaar, H., Thijssen, J., et al. (1999). Correlations among salivary testosterone, mood, and selective attention to threat in humans. *Hormones and Behavior, 36,* 17–24.

Watson, D. (2000). *Mood and temperament.* New York: Guilford.

Watson, D., & Clark, L. A. (1991). *The PANAS–X: Preliminary manual for the Positive and Negative Affect Schedule–Expanded Form.* Unpublished manuscript.

Watson, D., Clark, L. A., & Tellegen, A. (1988). Development and validation of brief measures of positive and negative affect: The PANAS scales. *Journal of Personality and Social Psychology, 54,* 1063–1070.

Wortman, C. B., & Brehm, J. W. (1975). Responses to uncontrollable outcomes: An integration of reactance theory and the learned helplessness model. In L. Berkowitz (Ed.), *Advances in experimental social psychology* (Vol. 8, pp. 278–336). New York: Academic Press.

Young, P. T. (1943). *Emotion in man and animal: Its nature and relation to attitude and motive.* New York: Wiley.

The Pseudopsychology of Venting in the Treatment of Anger: Implications and Alternatives for Mental Health Practice

Bunmi O. Olatunji, Jeffrey M. Lohr, and Brad J. Bushman

Anger varies in terms of frequency, intensity, and duration. Some people feel angry most of the time, whereas others report rarely feeling angry. Anger can vary from mild irritation to intense fury and rage, and as transient or as relatively enduring. Anger is generally defined as a negative emotion that is associated with specific subjective, physiological, interpretive, and behavioral characteristics in response to frustration or injury (Kassinove & Tafrate, 2002). The experience of anger can be elicited by both external and internal events. Anger may be a response to the actions of a specific individual (e.g., being fired by a supervisor) or an environmental stressor (e.g., a traffic jam). Anger may also manifest as a result of chronic worrying or rumination as well as memories of trauma. Although typically considered a negative emotion, anger is a completely normal and functional emotion. From an evolutionary perspective, anger is an adaptive response to threats in that it promotes a sense of empowerment that facilitates self-defense. However, when anger is expressed in a maladaptive fashion, it can be very destructive and lead to a variety of interpersonal problems.

Anger Experience and Its Consequences

When people get angry, their heart rate, blood pressure, and energy hormones (i.e., adrenaline) increase (Kassinove & Tafrate, 2002). One way that this physiological arousal is expressed is via aggression. Aggression may include verbal attacks, threats, physical punishment, or restriction. It is not yet clear if anger causes aggression given that people can behave aggressively without feeling angry. However, when present, anger seems to facilitate aggression. Suppressed anger may also facilitate hostility, an attitude that involves disliking others and evaluating them negatively. Studies suggest that the triad of anger, aggression, and hostility are often related to physical (e.g., Lohr & Hamberger, 1990) and psychological (e.g., Tafrate, Kassinove, & Dundin, 2002) symptoms, including coronary heart disease (Williams et al., 2000). Anger has also been proposed to co-occur with Type A behavior as well as aggressive and risky behavior while driving (Deffenbacher, Huff, Lynch, Oetting, & Natalie, 2000). Others have argued that anger is a potential mediator of domestic violence and substance abuse disorders (e.g., Barbour, Eckhardt, Davison, & Kassinove, 1998).

Although anger is often associated with significant dysfunction, "anger disorders" are not currently recognized by the *Diagnostic and Statistical Manual of Mental Disorders* (4th ed.; DSM–IV; American Psychiatric Association, 1994). However, Eckardt and Deffenbacher (1995) have proposed that three anger disorders be included in the *DSM:* (a) adjustment disorder with angry mood, (b) situational anger disorder, and (c) general anger disorder. Although their anger-based diagnostic model attempts to bridge one of the many gaps in the anger literature, the clinical reality is that anger is typically associated with other diagnosable psychiatric conditions such as intermittent explosive disorder, posttraumatic stress disorder, borderline personality disorder, antisocial personality disorder, paranoid personality disorder, and conduct disorder (Kassinove & Tafrate, 2002). The mediating role of anger in exacerbating psychiatric conditions and the negative consequences of anger have prompted theoretical interest in the mechanisms that facilitate its reduction in treatment and in the larger social context.

DIRECTED EXPRESSION OF ANGER

Catharsis as Mechanism

A common presumption is that the mechanism of catharsis, acting aggressively or even viewing aggression, is an effective means of reducing anger and aggressive feelings. The word *catharsis* comes from the Greek word *katharsis,* which literally translated means a cleansing or purging. The first recorded mention of catharsis occurred in Aristotle's *Poetics.* Aristotle taught that viewing tragic plays gave people emotional release (katharsis) from negative feelings such as pity and fear. In Greek drama, the tragic hero did not just grow old and retire—he often suffered a violent demise. By watching the characters in the play experience tragic events, the viewer's own negative feelings were presumably purged and cleansed. This emotional cleansing was believed to benefit both the individual and society. Catharsis also played an important role in ancient religious and magical healing rituals. By venting their emotions, people presumably called forth and expelled the demons and evil spirits that possessed their bodies.

The ancient notion of catharsis was revived by Sigmund Freud (1930/1961), who believed that repressed negative emotions could build up inside an individual and cause psychological symptoms, such as hysteria (nervous outbursts). Breuer and Freud (1893–1895/1955) proposed that the treatment of hysteria required the discharge of the emotional state previously associated with trauma. Breuer and Freud believed that expressing hostility was much better than bottling it up inside. Freud's therapeutic ideas on emotional catharsis form the basis of the hydraulic model of anger. The hydraulic model suggests that frustrations lead to anger and that anger, in turn, builds up inside an individual, like hydraulic pressure inside a closed environment, until it is released or vented in some way. The modern theories of catharsis are based on this hydraulic model. Thus, catharsis is seen as a way of relieving the pressure that anger creates inside the psyche. The core idea is that it is better to let the anger out in increments, as opposed to repressing it where it will build up to the point at which a more dangerous explosion results.

"Venting" as Social Expression

The concept of catharsis has infiltrated our everyday language. Angry people are said to be like pressure cookers, and their anger is like the steam vapor inside the cooker (Lakoff & Kovecses, 1983). As anger increases, the pressure of the steam rises. Anger is said to "well up inside" and angry individuals are described as reaching the "boiling point." Other related expressions include keeping anger "bottled up" so that one does not "explode," "blow up," "erupt," or "go through the roof." To prevent such outcomes, people are encouraged to "vent their anger," "blow off steam," "let it out," and "get it off their chest." The metaphor of a pressure cooker is a concrete way to describe the function of anger and catharsis. But anger is not a fluid that starts off inside the body and can constructively be moved outside the body. The pressure cooker metaphor and the hydraulic model are based on a false analogy.

Evidence for the Effects of Venting in the Social Context

Some experts claim that venting pent-up anger is one solution to the problem of violence in our society. For example, psychoanalyst Abraham Zaleznik has offered the following advice for curbing workplace violence:

"Part of what enables companies to operate efficiently is a spirit of cooperation, which is undermined by unresolved feelings of anger and frustration. For both the individual and the company's good, then, we must change the corporate code. We must build in breathing room and create opportunities for people to blow off some steam" (Raudsepp, 1993, p. 116). Dr. Ernst Weberschrnitt, a psychiatrist whose practice includes members of the corporate elite, has advised senior executives to confront each other and vent their pent-up hostilities (Bart, 1999). Some companies now have anger web pages and "rap sessions" that allow employees to vent anger and blow off steam.

Physiological Arousal Reduction

It is not surprising that many people say that venting provides emotional release. After venting, people report feeling relieved of tension and arousal and there is a kernel of truth in these statements. In their survey of all the published research on catharsis, Geen and Quanty (1977) concluded that venting one's anger directly against the person who provoked you does often produce a reduction in blood pressure. More recent research has produced findings that are consistent with these conclusions. However, there are two important qualifiers to this general finding. First, venting does not work in situations that produce anxiety. For example, venting is likely to increase blood pressure in situations in which the target holds a higher social status (e.g., a boss). If the target can retaliate by aggressing against you, venting does not reduce arousal. Second, venting anger against a substitute target also does not reduce arousal. If you displace aggression against an innocent person or against an inanimate "safe" object, venting does not reduce arousal.

Subsequent Reduction of Anger and Aggression

Does venting anger reduce anger and subsequent aggression? This is perhaps the most important question. If venting really does get anger "out of your system," then venting should result in a reduction of both anger and aggression. Almost as soon as psychology researchers began conducting scientific tests of catharsis theory, this theory ran into trouble. One of the first experiments on the topic was published by Hornberger (1959). Participants in the study received an insulting remark from a confederate who pretended to be another participant but who was actually working for the researchers and following predetermined instructions. Some participants were set to work pounding nails for 10 minutes—an activity that resembles many of the "venting" techniques believed to be cathartic and recommended even today. For comparison purposes, participants in a control group received the same insult but did not get a chance to vent their anger by pounding nails. All participants then had a chance to criticize the person who had insulted them (though indirectly, to another person). This was the crucial measure of verbal aggression. If hammering nails had led to a beneficial catharsis, then those participants should have been less critical and hostile toward the confederate compared to participants who were not allowed to vent their anger. Unfortunately for catharsis theory, the results showed precisely the opposite effect. Those who hammered nails were more hostile toward the confederate than were those who did not pound nails.

Similar results were obtained when researchers had participants vent directly toward the person who induced their anger. Goldman, Keck, and O'Leary (1969) secretly instructed a "teacher" on how to frustrate his "student." Students had to make a number of complex objects (e.g., dustpan, sailboat) by folding pieces of paper. The teacher gave instructions much too fast for students to follow, purposely made several "slips" while demonstrating how to make the objects, and did not give students enough time to make the objects. These behaviors understandably provoked anger toward the teacher. Midway through the lecture, some of the students (randomly determined) were given a chance to vent their anger by giving the teacher negative ratings on an evaluation form. Later, researchers measured how much residual hostility students felt toward the teacher on a final evaluation form that would "go on his record." Again, the results directly contradicted catharsis theory. Students who had vented their anger continued to be quite hostile toward the teacher; they also felt more hostile than students who had been frustrated but had not been permitted to vent.

The long-term effects of venting were studied by Patterson (1974). He reasoned that if playing football is a good way to vent one's hostility, then football players should show long-term reductions in hostility. Patterson gave a questionnaire measure of hostility to a group of high school football players 1 week before the start of football season and 1 week after the season ended. The same measures were obtained from a control group of physical education students. Physical education students showed no change in hostility from the first to the second measure. However, football players showed change from before to after the season but opposite to what advocates of venting would predict. That is, football players showed a significant increase in hostility rather than a decrease.

If catharsis theory were valid, then greater levels of aggression should occur early in one's participation in an aggressive sporting event because anger should recede with additional time to vent. Results from several studies, however, indicate that aggression increases during such sporting events (Harrell, 1981; Russell, 1981). Similarly, repeated meetings between rival teams are accompanied by more rather than less aggression (Russell, 1983). These findings contradict catharsis theory but are consistent with the idea that expressing anger and aggression promotes further aggression.

Early studies also looked at venting among people who had lost their jobs (Ebbesen, Duncan, & Konecni, 1975). By the flip of a coin, roughly half of a group of technicians discharged from their jobs were given the opportunity to express verbally their hostility toward their former employers. Individuals who had vented were later more aggressive in their descriptions of their former employers compared to those who had not vented. This finding is relevant today, because, as mentioned earlier, some employers offer workers an opportunity to express their disgruntlement and complaints in various ways, such as on venting web pages or in "rap sessions."

These early studies posed a major problem for those who believed in the value of venting. Almost no study yielded results to support catharsis theory. In study after the study, the conclusion was the same: Expressing anger does not reduce aggressive tendencies and likely makes it worse. As a result, Bandura (1973) called for a moratorium on the study of catharsis theory and the use of venting in therapy. Four years later, Geen and Quanty (1977) published their influential review "The Catharsis of Aggression: An Evaluation of a Hypothesis" in the prestigious *Advances in Experimental Social Psychology*. After reviewing the relevant data, these scientists concluded that venting anger does not reduce aggression. If anything, they concluded, it makes people more aggressive afterward. Thus, the scientific community has largely rejected and abandoned catharsis theory and is looking to understand why the opposite effect occurs (i.e., venting anger increases aggression). Unfortunately, however, many voices among the mass media and pop psychology continue to suggest there is value in catharsis theory so the message reaching the general public is that catharsis is an effective, healthy way of handling angry impulses.

A Well-Learned Habit That Is Hard to Break

Bad habits are hard to break. Most people have heard the old joke, "How do you get to Carnegie Hall?" The answer is: "Practice, practice, practice." So for the question, "How do you become an angry, aggressive person?", the answer is the same: "Practice, practice, practice." Venting anger makes you an angrier, aggressive person. Expressing anger teaches people to behave more aggressively. People learn to respond to unpleasant situations by hitting, kicking, screaming, and cursing. Because venting is an aggressive activity, it sustains anger by stimulating physiological arousal, aggressive thoughts, angry feelings, and aggressive impulses. There are a number of psychological processes that maintain anger as a habitual response.

Short-Term Arousal Reduction: It Feels Less Bad and Might Even Feel Good

One reason why catharsis theory persists might be the belief or observation that venting makes people feel better. Research has shown that people often vent because they expect it will improve their mood (Bushman, Baumeister, & Phillips, 2001). Does this prove that venting anger is a healthy behavior? Good feelings often reinforce unhealthy behaviors. People also feel good after eating chocolate and after taking illegal street drugs, even though these behaviors are unhealthy. When a pleasant emotional response follows a behavior, it reinforces that behavior and makes it more likely to occur in the future. This principle is known as the law of effect (Thorndike, 1927). The good feeling that follows illegal drug use reinforces subsequent drug use. Perhaps because venting temporarily decreases arousal, people often report that it makes them feel better inside. However, this emotional improvement is short-lived and it does not translate into less aggression— it translates into more aggression (Bushman, 2002; Bushman, Baumeister, & Stack, 1999). At best, venting may make you feel better for a short time, but that comes from enjoying the angry actions rather than from any meaningful reduction in angry feelings or aggressive tendencies. At worst, venting fosters the illusion that it is healthy to express one's anger. The good feeling that follows venting anger reinforces subsequent venting and violence. People mistake their enjoyment of these aggressive acts for some beneficial or therapeutic outcome. But because these acts feel good, people are willing to try them.

Post Hoc, Ergo Propter Hoc: The Subtle Role of Dissipation

When people become angry, they become fully charged like an electronic capacitor. Although the initial level of anger can be quite intense, the level of anger eventually dissipates until it is gone. The fact that anger does eventually dissipate with time, regardless of what people do, might also foster the illusion that venting works. People become angry, they vent, and the anger in due time goes away. People therefore assume that venting works. What people fail to realize is that the anger would have dissipated had they not vented. Moreover, it would have dissipated more quickly had they not vented and tried to control their anger instead. Anger can be controlled by reducing the arousal state, such as by taking deep breaths or by relaxing (e.g., Novaco, 1975). Even taking a time-out or counting to 10 will help, because it allows anger to dissipate (e.g., Nye, 1993). Anger can also be controlled by mental tactics, such as by reframing the problem, or by distracting oneself and turning attention to other, more pleasant topics (e.g., Wilde, 2001). In short, any act (e.g., making love, performing a good deed) can help if it is incompatible with anger and makes it impossible to sustain the angry state (e.g., Baron, 1976).

People Believe in Venting

Popular beliefs about venting as a way of handling anger persist even though psychological research has shown it to be ineffective. Perhaps such beliefs are maintained because of a self-fulfilling prophecy: The expected behavior comes to pass simply because people believe that it will. We may then ask: If people believe in the value of venting, might their beliefs actually cause venting to have beneficial value? In other words, even though research scientists have shown catharsis theory to be false, might individuals' belief in it make it come true? A second and more serious scenario is also possible. Belief in catharsis could cause people to choose to vent anger but with the effect of increasing, rather than decreasing, their angry feelings, aggressive inclinations, and aggressive behavior. Endorsement of catharsis by pop psychology and popular media would thus have the potential to increase aggression.

Two studies were conducted to test the influence of popular-media messages supporting catharsis (Bushman et al., 1999). In the first study, participants read fake newspaper articles reporting that the catharsis hypothesis had been proven true (or, in the other condition, had been proven false). Participants were then asked to write an essay on abortion and were told that their essays would be graded. Randomly, half of the participants received negative evaluations and a handwritten comment stating, "This is one of the worst essays I have read!" The other half received good evaluations. Afterwards, participants' desire to vent their anger on a punching bag was measured. It was found that media messages advocating catharsis persuaded people to believe in catharsis and to act on this belief (by choosing to hit a punching bag to reduce their anger). In other words, media endorsements of catharsis lead people to "prophesy" that venting is good and to act on this prophecy.

But does the prophecy come to pass? Is it a self-fulfilling or a self-defeating prophecy? The second study answered these important questions. After reading one of the bogus catharsis articles, participants wrote an essay on abortion, had their essay negatively evaluated, and indicated how much they wanted to hit a punching bag. Some participants then hit the punching bag; others sat quietly for a few minutes. Next, aggressive behavior was assessed by having participants play a game in which the "winner" got to blast the "loser" with loud, unpleasant, stressful noise. Level of aggression was based on the volume and duration of the noise delivered in each round. Some participants were led to believe that their competitor was the same person who had negatively evaluated (and insulted) their essay. Others were led to believe that it was a completely different person. If the self-fulfilling prophecy hypothesis is correct, then participants who read the procatharsis article would be less aggressive after they had blown off steam by hitting the punching bag. This would suggest that popular beliefs in catharsis might be sustained by self-fulfilling prophecies and fueled by media advocacy of catharsis. However, results showed that participants were more aggressive after hitting the punching bag, even those who had been led to believe that venting was productive. In other words, belief in venting created a self-defeating prophecy. Participants hit the punching bag in the expectation that it would make them less hostile, but they ended up more hostile and aggressive. Even more disturbing is that hitting the punching bag made participants more aggressive toward an innocent person, someone who had not criticized or insulted them.

Many people do claim that they feel better after venting. Unfortunately, these good feelings can lead to more rather than less aggression. A catharsis effect was not found even when participants were led to believe in it and to act on that belief. If the catharsis theory were true at all, under any circumstances, it should be obtained when people believe that it is true. These research findings indicate exactly the opposite: Media endorsement of catharsis generated self-defeating prophecies. Venting might seem to be the most natural response to frustrations and other unpleasant events, and catharsis theory is a plausible justification of it. However, the evidence indicates that catharsis theory is false and that it is worse than useless because it produces harmful effects. In short, it is potentially dangerous if actively promoted by the mental health profession.

MODIFICATION OF ANGER: PSEUDOPSYCHOLOGICAL BELIEFS REGARDING VENTING

Catharsis and Self-Help

The number of self-help, pop-psychology books that advocate catharsis is another sign of how widespread this concept is. One example is the book *Facing the Fire: Experiencing and Expressing Anger Appropriately*, by John Lee (1993). Lee gives readers the following advice for "safely" venting pent-up anger and frustrations:

> Punch a pillow or a punching bag. And while you do it, yell and curse and moan and holler. . . . Punch with all the frenzy you can. If you are angry at

a particular person, imagine his or her face on the pillow or punching bag, and vent your rage physically and verbally. You will be doing violence to a pillow or punching bag so that you can stop doing violence to yourself by holding in poisonous anger. You are not hitting a person. You are hitting the ghost of that person—a ghost from the past, a ghost alive in you that must be exorcized in a concrete, physical way. (p. 96)

Lee also recommends that angry people twist a towel, hit a couch with a plastic baseball bat, throw rocks, and break glass to get rid of their pent-up anger and frustrations.

With self-proclaimed experts such as Lee advocating the benefits of venting anger, it is hardly surprising that many people come to believe that venting is healthy and productive. The ways of dealing with anger suggested in self-help sources may be harmless in and of themselves. Beating on a pillow, breaking an extra dish, or smashing a frozen milk carton is harmless as far as they go. They may even feel good. The crucial question, however, is what effect these actions have on anger and on how the angry person subsequently treats others. If this advice led to a reduction in subsequent aggression, it would be a valuable contribution to society. On the other hand, if following this advice has no beneficial effect or it makes people more aggressive, then the advice could be harmful and even dangerous.

Catharsis and Psychotherapy

Psychology has contributed some expert opinions in support of the belief that venting anger can be beneficial. The best-known version of this view is probably Freud's catharsis theory, described earlier. The catharsis theory was an important foundation of psychoanalytic therapy and was asserted as crucial in his earliest works. In Freud's view, emotional responses remained potent until they could be felt and expressed, and so refusing to express anger caused the destructive feelings to remain inside the person, where they could cause psychological damage. In his early writings, Freud proposed that all human behaviors stem from the life or self-preservation instinct, called *eros*. He denied the presence of an instinct to explain the darker side of human nature. He wrote: "I cannot bring myself to assume the existence of a special aggressive instinct alongside the familiar instincts of self-preservation and of sex, on an equal footing with them" (Freud, 1909/1961, p. 18). Following the atrocities of World War I, however, Freud changed his mind and proposed the existence of a death or self-destruction instinct, called *thanatos*. He viewed aggression as the redirection or displacement of the self-destructive death instinct away from the self toward others. He wrote that people are "creatures among whose instinctual endowments is to be reckoned a powerful share of aggressiveness"

(Freud, 1930/1961, p. 65). In a famous exchange of letters between Sigmund Freud and Albert Einstein, Freud wrote that if the death instinct "forces are turned to destruction in the external world, the living creature will be relieved and the effect must be beneficial" (Freud, 1990, p. 18).

More modern psychotherapies also advocate venting anger. The goal of focused expressive therapy (Daldrup, Engle, Holiman, & Beutler, 1994), for example, is to resolve "unfinished business" in a patient's relationship with another person by expressing "blocked feelings." Venting is also central to a psychological intervention called primal scream therapy (Casriel, 1972), in which patients yell, scream, and curse to vent their anger. They also use padded mats placed on the floor to thrash about and pound and kick while they are screaming, much like an infant would in a crib. In an excerpt from a group therapy session described in Casriel's book, a therapist tells one patient who is mad at her daughter to push out the anger by screaming as loud as you can. Each therapy session ends with a group scream to remove any residual, pent-up anger.

The Empirical Status of Venting in Anger Treatment

Claims that venting anger is healthy and constructive have been made by newspaper columnists, poets, writers, pop psychologists, and even some well-intentioned (but misguided) therapists. However, a review of the empirical literature indicates that venting is ineffective and in some cases harmful. Warren and Kurlychek (1981) reviewed studies in which participants engaged in verbal, written, or physical acts of aggression and concluded that the rehearsal of verbal and physical aggression toward an antagonist typically leads to increases not decreases in hostile attitudes and behaviors. In a review of studies that examined anger expression, Lewis and Bucher (1992) concluded that catharsis leads to an increase in anger expression. The authors further noted that catharsis-based interventions need to be abandoned as therapeutic tools in mental health practice.

EFFICACY OF ALTERNATIVE TREATMENTS FOR ANGER

Because treatments predicated on venting do not appear to be an effective strategy for reducing anger, practitioners should consider treatments based on proven psychological theories and objective scientific evidence for their efficacy. For example, the existing literature seems to suggest that cognitive-behavioral treatments (CBTs) are more promising for treating anger problems (Beck & Fernandez, 1998). CBT techniques are derived from scientifically supported theoretical models (e.g., Deacon & Abramowitz, 2004) that emphasize the importance of learning history and associated thought processes (Chambless & Ollendick, 2001; Deacon & Abramowitz, 2004). Evidence-based treatments for treating anger include but are not limited to relaxation, progressive muscle relaxation, systematic desensitization, meditation, biofeedback, self-instructional training, cognitive restructuring, social-skills training, problem solving, assertiveness training, exposure, flooding, education, and stress inoculation (DiGiuseppe & Tafrate, 2003).

Some researchers have proposed that anger and anxiety share many clinical features and that interventions effective in treating anxiety disorders can also be used to treat anger problems (Brondolo, DiGiuseppe, & Tafrate, 1997). This line of research predominantly followed from Novaco's (1975) adaptation of Meichenbaum's stress inoculation training (SIT), initially developed for treating anxiety disorders, to the treatment of anger (Masters, Burish, Hollon, & Rimm, 1987). SIT is a form of CBT that consists of three phases (Meichenbaum, 1996). In the initial conceptualization phase, clients are educated about stress. Clients are encouraged to view stressful situations as problems-to-be-solved and are taught how to breakdown global stressors into specific coping goals. The second phase of SIT focuses on skills acquisition and rehearsal. Coping skills (i.e., self-instructional training, problem solving) are taught and rehearsed in the context of potential stressors. The final phase of application and follow-through provides opportunities for the clients to apply learned coping skills to stressors via imagery and behavioral rehearsal, modeling, or role playing. SIT was derived from the theory that anxiety and stress occurs when the demands on a system exceed its resources or when there are no adaptive responses available to meet the demands. The adaptation of SIT for anger was predicated on the assumption that dysfunctional anger responses occur in a similar fashion.

Since the inception of anger treatment, numerous studies providing support for the efficacy of CBT techniques for anger have been published in peer-reviewed journals. In an attempt to integrate these studies, multiple meta-analytic studies have been conducted to assess the efficacy of CBT interventions. Meta-analytic reviews allow researchers to synthesize quantitatively the results from multiple studies in an effort to characterize the general effectiveness of various interventions. Thus, effect sizes can be estimated across different populations, methodologies, and research teams. Table 5.1 provides a review of six meta- analyses.

Is CBT Effective for Anger Reduction?

The findings of various meta-analytic reviews indicate that CBT is generally effective for the treatment of anger. However, meta-analytic reviews have also begun to address the all important question of, "what anger treatment by whom is most effective for which individual with that specific anger problem, and under which set of circumstances?" (see Paul, 1967). Overall, meta-analytic findings seem to suggest that behavioral-based interventions are generally the most effective for treating anger. That is, anger treatments that teach actual behaviors appear to yield better outcomes than those that are based on modifying internal processes (Sukhodolsky, Kassinove & Gorman, 2004). However, the relative effectiveness of behavioral interventions may depend on the modality of assessment (self-report v. observed and questionnaire v. physiological assessment). It also appears that the efficacy of CBT for anger may be symptom dependent. For example, analysis of effect sizes within treatment groups shows that cognitive interventions are highly effective for driving-related anger problems, whereas behavioral treatment is more effective for treating state anger (Spielberger, 1996). Meta-analytic findings also suggest that CBT for anger-related problems may be more effective for adults than for adolescents and children (Sukhodolsky et al., 2004).

Incremental Efficacy and the Role of Nonspecific Factors in Anger Treatment

Although meta-analytic studies are generally in support of the effectiveness of CBT for anger, such studies contain limitations that restrict inferences regarding efficacy. Important to note, meta-analytic studies evaluating the efficacy of CBT for anger typically do not quantify the degree of internal validity of the experimental controls within the studies reviewed (e.g., Olatunji & Lohr, 2005). Furthermore, significant heterogeneity of variance and significant differences among effect sizes for different dependent measures also mitigate clear inferences regarding efficacy. Because of these limitations, it is possible that observed variance among treatments is attributable to the degree that nonspecific factors are experimentally controlled. Indeed, it has been shown that the type of experimental control is significantly related to the magnitude of the overall effectiveness of CBT for anger, with studies using no-treatment control comparisons showing greater effectiveness (Sukhodolsky et al., 2004).

Nonspecific factors have been receiving increased attention in the analysis of treatment efficacy (Borkovec & Castonguay, 1998; Chambless & Hollon, 1998). According to Critelli and Neuman (1984), nonspecific factors include (a) factors without specific activity, (b) unspecified but active factors, and (c) common factors. Factors without specific activity are those for which there is no specific mechanism of action that has an effect on treatment. Unspecified factors are those treatment factors that have not been specified as the active ingredients of a particular treatment. Common factors are those that are not specific to particular treatments,

TABLE 5.1

A Review of Meta-Analytic Findings of Alternative Treatments for Anger

Citation	Studies Examined	Interventions Examined	M Effect Size	Caveats
Tafrate (1995)	Published empirical papers	Cognitive Relaxation Skills training Multicomponent treatment	.93 1.16 .82 1.00	Results varied depending on specific type of therapy (e.g., social skills vs. assertiveness training).
Edmonson & Congor (1996)	Included wider range of outcome variables	Relaxation Social skills Cognitive-relaxation Cognitive	.82 .80 .76 .64	Results varied depnding on method of assessment (e.g., physiologic symptoms, behavior, subjective experience of anger).
Beck & Fernadez (1998)	Included studies using children as well as unpublished doctoral dissertations	CBT- most included cognitive therapy and relaxation	.70	Results varied with population and suggest that CBT is more effective with adults than children.
DiGiuseppe & Tafrate (2003)	50 studies with control groups and 7 studies with within-group data	Anger management Problem Solving Group process Combined treatment Relaxation Humor Meditation Psychoeducation	1.33 .82 .76 .76 .74 .33 .23 .22	Results varied depending on measurement of outcome. Magnitude of change was not significant for self-esteem or relationships.
Del Vecchio & O'Leary (2004)	Noninstitutionalized adults with anger; published articles	Relaxation Cognitive CBT Miscellaneous	.90 .82 .68 .61	CBT and CT were effective for trait anger and relaxation was more effective for state anger.
Sukhodolsky, Kassinova, & Gorman (2004)	Studies using children and adolescents; published and unpublished articles	Skills training Problem solving Affective education Multimodal intervention	.79 .67 .36 .74	Skills training and relaxation were most effective for aggressive behavior. Problem solving was more effective for subjective feelings of anger.

but are common to most types of treatments. Nonspecific factors include (but are not limited to) suggestion, persuasion, treatment credibility, therapist attention, expectancy, effort justification, and therapist allegiance (Lohr, Olatunji, Parker, & DeMaio, 2005). An incrementally efficacious anger treatment would be one that produces effects greater than those produced by nonspecific factors (Olatunji & Lohr, 2005).

In addition to consideration of the quality of the controls for nonspecific factors, anger treatment outcome research can also be improved by incorporating component-controlled evaluations to identify the specific mechanisms of change. Although the characteristic features of CBT for anger-related problems vary substantially across studies, they may be defined as cognitive restructuring, relaxation training, problem solving, and social-skills training. Following the analysis provided by Borkovec and Castonguay (1998), an ideal evaluation of the efficacy of treatment "X" for anger would include: (a) X versus wait list control; (b) X versus attention control; (c) X versus nonspecific factors; (d) X component-controlled research; and (e) X versus next-best treatment. To determine the specific, active features of CBT for anger, dismantling designs (i.e., studies that take apart the multiple components of a given treatment) may also be necessary. For instance, the cognitive component of CBT for anger is said to involve the reconstruction of maladaptive thoughts that may inadvertently reinforce anger. The behavioral component involves arousal reduction, problem-solving skills, and social skills training. Needed are studies in which the experimental design allows for a clear analysis of the separate and combined effects of the cognitive and behavioral components of anger treatments.

Constructing the appropriate combination of components relative to nonspecific control conditions could allow for multiple component comparisons. Recent research suggests that feedback, modeling, and homework may be key components of effective CBT treatment for anger (Sukhodolsky et al., 2004). That is, the effectiveness of CBT for anger increases as the amount of feedback, modeling, and homework (and feedback to homework) increases. Additional research comparing feedback, modeling, and homework as independent and combined treatments for anger will be needed. Such comparisons allow for strong experimental tests of the effects of alternative anger treatment components, key components, and the combined treatment components (Lohr, DeMaio, & McGlynn, 2003). Such methodological considerations will ultimately promote evidence-based anger treatment by identifying incrementally (over and above nonspecific factors) and specifically (over and above other treatments) efficacious anger treatments. By using anger interventions in which the evidence for efficacy is based on strong experimental tests, practitioners can hopefully improve patients' ability to effectively regulate maladaptive anger reactions by promoting efficient coping strategies, and at worse do no harm.

THE BEST INTENTIONS ON THE ROAD TO HELL

The evidence that cognitive-behavioral interventions are efficacious for anger reduction is encouraging, even if we are still uncertain as to the process by which it has beneficial effects. However, it is also essential to consider not only benefits of treatments but also costs. The first rule of the helping profession is *Primum Non Nocere:* First Do No Harm. To date, there is no documented harm caused by CBT for anger-related problems. The same cannot be said for some treatments predicated on the venting of anger. In fact, research evidence indicates that treatments that are based on venting anger can cause more harm than good.

The Case of Kip Kinkle

Among the many examples of the negative consequences of applying techniques based on venting rather than evidenced-based interventions is the case of an Oregon high school student treated by a psychologist for anger problems (Frontline, 2000). Kip Kinkle, a 16-year-old student, had trouble dealing with his anger. He wrote about this in his journal: "I know everyone thinks this way sometimes, but I am so full of rage that I feel I could snap at any moment. I think about it everyday. Blowing the school up or just taking the easy way out, and walk into a pep assembly with guns. In either case, people that are breathing will stop breathing."

Kip's mother took him to see a psychologist because she was worried about him. In his treatment notes, the psychologist wrote: "Kip reported he often feels angry but doesn't know why he feels this emotion. Kip reported he makes explosives from gasoline and other household items and detonates them at a nearby quarry to vent feelings of anger. If he has a 'bad day' at school, he feels better after detonating an explosive." The psychologists put Kip on an anger treatment plan that consisted of, 'blowing off steam," but in a less dangerous manner. The psychologist wrote: "He is not practicing specific techniques for managing anger. Suggested he consider riding his bike, running, shooting baskets or tearing old magazines (old phone books or newspapers) when angry." Tragically, venting anger was not an effective strategy for Kip. On May 20, 1998, he killed both parents in their home. The next day, he entered his school cafeteria and sprayed students with 50 rounds from a semiautomatic rifle, killing 2 students and wounding 25 others. One cannot blame the psychologist for Kip Kinkle's behavior, but the advice to tear up old magazines, phone books, or newspapers when angry has no empirical support and could have made him even angrier.

Attachment Therapy

Mercer, Sarner, and Rosa (2003) provide compelling analysis of the dangers of a specific fringe therapy based on catharsis theory in mental health practice. In their detailed case study, they offer critical analysis of attachment therapy (AT), of mental health clinicians who employ it, and of the dynamics of its promotion in clinical practice. AT generally consists of recognition and modification of maladaptive thoughts, psychodrama (reacting early life events), helping the child to find ways to give voice and support to the wounded inner child, and "nurturing" where parents hold the child in their laps and offer reassurance. AT emphasizes healing emotional wounds through holding techniques. "Therapeutic" holding is often used as a means of allowing the child access to intense emotions. AT is largely predicated on catharsis theory in that the child experiences rage while being physically restrained, which allegedly leads to a decrease in the need to act out (Mercer et al., 2003). The case is that of 10-year-old Candace Newmaker, adopted daughter of Jeanne Newmaker, who died at the hands of three unlicensed mental health practitioners in Evergreen, Colorado, in April of 2000. The death resulted from a lack of oxygen (suffocation) that occurred in the process of applying AT for reactive attachment disorder (RAD) at the behest of the girl's mother. The therapists made a videotape of the procedure, which was subsequently entered into evidence after which the mental health workers and the mother were all convicted of felonies or plea-bargained for lesser charges. The facts of the case clearly show that the perpetrators were minimally trained or unlicensed practitioners. However, it is naive to think that the tragedy occurred solely because of incompetent personnel. Neither licensure nor formal training is a guarantee against applying ineffective or harmful treatments (c.f. Herbert et al., 2000).

The construct of *attachment* is a substantive one originally introduced by John Bowlby (1982) in the analysis of the development of early interpersonal relationships. However, the rationale for AT is built on a semantic confusion of the attachment construct. The development of psychopathology is complex and multifaceted; understanding these phenomena requires cautious analysis and comprehensive assessment by competent diagnosticians. In the usual application of AT, however, ill-defined and overinclusive "symptoms" of attachment disorder lead to its overdiagnosis and mistreatment. Robert W. Zaslow, who first proposed the attachment disorder concept, implemented "rage reduction therapy" in the treatment of autism (Zaslow & Breger, 1969).

Zaslow recommended using severely restrictive procedures to elicit the catharsis of anger and rage, which, in turn, would facilitate attachment with parents and other adults. These practices include, but are not limited to, sustained rigid postures, sustained holding by the therapist, and birth reenactments (rebirthing) involving swaddling and bodily compression. The only conclusion to be drawn about the efficacy of AT is one of extreme caution: There is no evidence to justify the application of AT, but there is documentation that the physically restrictive procedures of AT can cause physical injury and death. The case of Candace Newmaker and AT is an object lesson for the mental health profession. Because there is no equivalent of the Food and Drug Administration to guard the public from ineffective or harmful psychosocial interventions, it is up to the mental health profession to do so. Perhaps the use of AT and other venting procedures should be regarded by the mental health profession as malfeasance or malpractice and as grounds for sanctions.

CONCLUSIONS

Based on the research reviewed in this chapter, it appears that catharsis theory has done more harm than good. It justifies and perpetuates the myth that venting anger is good practice when in fact venting it tends to promote anger and increase the likelihood of aggression and violence. Cathartic striking of an inanimate object is often described as safe and harmless. But the phrase "safe expression" of anger is an oxymoron. Although it is safer than expressing anger directly toward the person who provoked you (especially if that person is large in stature), it is not safe to express anger, even against inanimate objects. In the heat of anger, the distinction between a pillow and a person can become fuzzy. When people are highly aroused, they do not plan their actions. Instead, they fall back on what they have learned to do in similar situations. If a person has learned to react to frustrating events by venting (e.g., by hitting something), it makes little difference whether the target is animate or inanimate.

Many individuals believe that it is healthy and constructive to vent anger and messages supporting catharsis are commonly found in the media. The immediate (but short-lived) good feeling that follows venting also can reinforce the idea that it is beneficial. Even though venting feels good, however, it has negative effects on the individual doing it.

Despite limited evidence regarding efficacy, the promotion and dissemination of venting techniques for anger reduction is still prevalent in the mental health field. Acknowledging the disparity between the popularity of venting techniques and the lack of research evidence supporting its efficacy is only the first step. Evidence-based treatments should be considered the standard of care for anger-related problems. Currently, the neglect of important methodological issues in anger treatment outcome research has contributed to an incomplete understanding of the efficacy of treatments for anger (DiGiuseppe & Tafrate, 2003), and nonspecific factors could account for a substantial amount of change in anger treatment (e.g., Olatunji & Lohr, 2005; Tafrate, 1995). Future anger outcome research should also incorporate component-controlled conditions that allow for the separation of the putative effects of anger interventions and the subsequent identification of specific mechanisms of change.

The empirical literature suggests that CBT interventions are effective in the reduction of dysfunctional anger. CBT interventions may be more appropriate for anger reduction because they emphasize specific procedures, structure the content of those procedures, and design those procedures based on theories of change. With increasing demands of practitioner accountability, the application of CBT to anger problems should be actively encouraged. This may require that managed care companies limit their coverage of psychological services for anger dysfunction to treatments with empirical support. According to Dawes (1994), "the rapid growth and professionalization of the field of psychology has led it to abandon a commitment it made at the inception of its growth. That commitment was to establish a profession that would be based on research findings, employing insofar as possible, well-validated techniques and principles" (p. vii). Indeed, a large body of research on established principles is available to promote evidence-based anger treatment. However, some mental health practitioners continue to endorse and incorporate venting techniques that lack scientific support. The incorporation of such techniques directly challenges the integrity of mental health practice and places the public at risk. By appealing to evidenced-based treatments for anger, practitioners will be more likely to maximize the likelihood of first doing no harm, and then providing clinically meaningful benefits.

REFERENCES

American Psychiatric Association. (1994). *Diagnostic and statistical manual of mental disorders (4th edition)*. Washington DC: Author.

Bandura, A. (1973). *Aggression: A social learning theory analysis*. Englewood Cliffs, NJ: Prentice-Hall.

Barbour, C., Eckhardt, C., Davison, J., & Kassinove, H. (1998). The experience and expression of anger in maritally violent and maritally discordant-nonviolent men. *Behavior Therapy, 29*, 173–191.

Baron , R. A. (1976). The reduction of human aggression: A field study of the influence of incompatible responses. *Journal of Applied Social Psychology, 6*, 260–274.

Bart, P. (1999, May 3). Venting their rage. (The public feuding and legal actions by Michael Eisner and Jeffrey Katzenberg of Walt Disney Co., while criticized by many, may be psychologically beneficial for both executives). *Variety, Volume 374*, i11 p. 4 (1).

Beck, R., & Fernandez, E. (1998). Cognitive-behavioral therapy in the treatment of anger: A meta-analysis. *Cognitive Therapy and Research, 22*, 63–74.

Borkovec, T. G., & Castonguay, L. G. (1998). What is the scientific meaning of "empirically supported therapy?" *Journal of Consulting and Clinical Psychology, 66*, 136–142.

Bowlby, J. (1982). *Attachment*. New York: Basic Books.

Breuer, J., & Freud, S. (1955). *Magic, science, and religion*. Garden City, NY: Doubleday. (Original work published 1893–1895)

Brondolo, E., DiGiuseppe, R., & Tafrate, R. (1997). Exposure-based treatment for anger problems: Focus on the feeling. *Cognitive and Behavioral Practice, 4*, 75–98.

Bushman, B. J. (2002). Does venting anger feed or extinguish the flame? Catharsis, rumination, distraction, anger, and aggressive responding. *Personality and Social Psychology Bulletin, 28*, 724–731.

Bushman, B. J., Baumeister, R. F., & Phillips, C. M. (2001). Do people aggress to improve their mood? Catharsis, relief, affect regulation opportunity, and aggressive responding. *Journal of Personality and Social Psychology, 81*, 17–32.

Bushman, B. J., Baumeister, R. F., & Stack, A. D. (1999). Catharsis, aggression, and persuasive influence: Self-fulfilling or self-defeating prophecies. *Journal of Personality and Social Psychology, 76*, 367–376.

Casriel, D. (1972). *A scream away from happiness*. New York: Gross & Dunlap.

Chambless, D. L., & Hollon, S. D. (1998). Defining empirically supported therapies. *Journal of Consulting and Clinical Psychology, 66*, 7–18.

Chambless, D. L., & Ollendick, T. H. (2001). Empirically supported psychological interventions: Controversies and evidence. *Annual Review of Psychology, 52*, 685–716.

Critelli, J. W., & Neumann, K. F. (1984). The placebo: Conceptual analysis of a construct transition. *American Psychologist, 39*, 32–39.

Daldrup, R. J., Engle, D., Holiman, M., & Beutler, L. E. (1994). The intensification and resolution of blocked affect in an experiential psychotherapy. *British Journal of Clinical Psychology, 33*, 129–141.

Dawes, R. M. (1994). *House of cards: Psychology and psychotherapy built on myth*. New York: The Free Press.

Deacon, B. J., & Abramowitz, J. S. (2004). Cognitive and behavioral treatments for anxiety disorders: A review of meta-analytic findings. *Journal of Clinical Psychology, 60*, 429–441.

Deffenbacher, J. L., Huff, M. E., Lynch, R. S., Oetting, E. R., & Natalie, F. (2000). Characteristics and treatment of high-anger drivers. *Journal of Counseling Psychology, 47*, 5–17.

Del Vecchio, T., & O'Leary, D. (2004). Effectiveness of anger treatments for specific anger problems: A meta-analytic review. *Clinical Psychology Review, 24*, 15–34.

DiGiuseppe, R., & Tafrate, R. C. (2003). Anger treatment for adults: A meta-analytic review. *Clinical Psychology: Science & Practice, 10*, 70–84.

Ebbesen, E. B., Duncan, B., & Konecni, V. J. (1975). Effects of content of verbal aggression on future verbal aggression: A field experiment. *Journal of Experimental Social Psychology, 11,* 192–204.

Eckhardt, C. I., & Deffenbacher, J. L. (1995). Diagnosis of anger disorders. In H. Kassinove (Ed.), *Anger disorders: Definition, diagnosis, and treatment* (pp. 27–48). Washington, DC: Taylor & Francis.

Edmonson, C. B., & Conger, J. C. (1996). A review of treatment efficacy for individuals with anger problems: Conceptual, assessment, and methodological issues. *Clinical Psychology Review, 16,* 251–275.

Freud S. (1909/1961). *Analysis of a Phobia in a five-year-old boy* (standard ed.). London: Norton.

Freud, S. (1930/1961). *Civilization and its discontents* (Standard ed.). London: Norton. (Original work published 1930)

Freud, S. (1970). Why war? In E. I. Megargee & J. E. Hokanson (Eds.), *The dynamics of aggression: Individual, group, and international analyses* (pp. 10–21). New York: Harper & Row.

Frontline (2000). *The killer at Thurston High.* Boston: WGBH.

Geen, R. G., & Quanty, M. B. (1977). The catharsis of aggression: An evaluation of a hypothesis. In L. Berkowitz (Ed.), *Advances in experimental social psychology* (Vol. 10, pp. 1–37). New York: Academic Press.

Goldman, M., Keck, J.W., & O'Leary, C. J. (1969). Hostility reduction and performance. *Psychological Reports, 25,* 503–512.

Harrell, W. A. (1981). Verbal aggressiveness in spectators at professional hockey games: The effects of tolerance of violence and amount of exposure to hockey. *Human Relations, 34,* 643–655.

Herbert, J. D., Lilienfeld, S. O., Lohr, J. M., Montgomery, R. W., O'Donohue, W. T., Rosen, G. M., et al. (2000). Science and pseudoscience in the development and promotion of eye movement desensitization and reprocessing: Implications for clinical psychology. *Clinical Psychology Review, 20,* 945–971.

Hornberger, R. H. (1959). The differential reduction of aggressive responses as a function of interpolated activities. *American Psychologist, 14,* 354.

Kassinove, H., & Tafrate, R. C. (2002). *Anger management: The complete treatment guidebook for practitioners.* California: Impact.

Lakoff, G., & Kovecses, Z. (1983). *The cognitive model of anger inherent in American English* (Report No. 10). Berkeley, CA: Berkeley Cognitive Science Program.

Lee, J. (1993). *Facing the fire: Experiencing and expressing anger appropriately.* New York: Bantam.

Lewis, W. A., & Bucher, A. M. (1992). Anger, catharsis, the reformulated frustration–aggression hypothesis, and health consequences. *Psychotherapy: Theory, Research, Practice, Training, 29,* 385–392.

Lohr, J. M., DeMaio, C., & McGlynn, F. D. (2003). Specific and nonspecific treatment factors in the experimental analysis of behavioral treatment efficacy. *Behavior Modification, 27,* 322–367.

Lohr, J. M., & Hamberger, K. L. (1990). Cognitive-behavioral modification of coronary-prone behaviors: Proposal for a treatment model and review of the evidence. *Journal of Rational-Emotive and Cognitive-Behavior Therapy, 8,* 103–126.

Lohr, J. M., Olatunji, B. O., Parker, L., & DeMaio, C. (2005). Experimental analysis of specific treatment factors: Efficacy and practice implications. *Journal of Clinical Psychology, 61,* 819–834.

Masters, J. C., Burish, T. G., Hollon, S. D., & Rimm, D. C (1987). *Behavior therapy: Techniques and empirical findings* (3rd Ed.). New York: Harcourt Brace Jovanovich College.

Meichenbaum, D. (1996). Stress inoculation training for coping with stressors. *The Clinical Psychologist, 49,* 4–7.

Mercer, J., Sarner, L., & Rosa, L. (2003). *Attachment therapy on trial: The torture and death of Candace Newmaker.* Westport, CT: Praeger.

Novaco, R. (1975). *Anger control: The development and evaluation of an experimental treatment.* Lexington, MA: Lexington Books.

Nye, B. (1993). *Understanding and managing your anger and aggression.* Washington: BCA.

Olatunji, B. O., & Lohr, J. M. (2005). Nonspecific factors and the efficacy of psychosocial treatments for anger. *The Scientific Review of Mental Health Practice, 3,* 3–18.

Patterson, A. H. (1974, September). *Hostility catharsis: A naturalistic experiment.* Paper presented at the annual convention of the American Psychological Association, New Orleans.

Paul, G. (1967). Outcome research in psychotheraphy. *Journal of Consulting Psychology, 31,* 109–118.

Raudsepp, E. (1993, July). Is a bad temper hurting your career? Stress can cause suppressed anger. Here's how to rechannel it constructively. *Hydrocarbon Processing, 72,* 116.

Russell, G. W. (1981). Aggression in sports. In P. F. Brain & D. Benton (Eds.)., *Multidisciplinary approaches to aggression research.* (pp. 431–446). Amsterdam: Elsevier/North-Holland Biomedical Press.

Russell, G. W. (1983). Crowd size and density in relation to athletic aggression and performance. *Social Behavior and Personality, 11,* 1.

Spielberger, C. D. (1996). *State-Trait Anger Expression Inventory, research edition: Professional manual.* Odessa, FL: Psychological Assessment Resources.

Sukhodolsky, D. G., Kassinove, H., & Gorman, B. S. (2004). Cognitive-behavioral therapy for anger in children and adolescents: A meta-analysis. *Aggression and Violent Behavior, 9,* 247–269.

Tafrate, R. C. (1995). Evaluation of treatment strategies for adult anger disorders. In H. Kassinove (Ed.), *Anger disorders: Definition, diagnosis, and treatment* (pp. 109–130). Washington, DC: Taylor & Francis.

Tafrate, R. C., Kassinove, H., & Dundin, L. (2002). Anger episodes in high- and low-trait-anger community adults. *Journal of Clinical Psychology, 58,* 1573–1590.

Thorndike, E. L. (1927). The law of effect. *American Journal of Psychology, 39,* 212–222.

Warren, R., & Kurlychek, R. T. (1981). Treatment of maladaptive anger and aggression: Catharsis vs behavior therapy. *Corrective and Social Psychiatry & Journal of Behavior Technology, Methods, and Therapy, 27,* 135–139.

Wilde, J. (2001). Interventions for children with anger problems. *Journal of Rational-Emotive and Cognitive Behavior Therapy, 19,* 191–197.

Williams, J. E., Paton, C. C., Siegler, I. C., Eigenbrodt, M. L., Nieto, F. J., & Tryoler, H. A. (2000). Anger proneness predicts coronary heart disease risk. *Circulation, 101,* 2034–2039.

Zaslow, R. W., & Breger, L. (1969). A theory and treatment of autism. In L. Breger (Ed.), *Cognitive clinical psychology* (pp. 246–291). Englewood Cliffs, NJ: Prentice-Hall.

Contributions of Emotion-Focused Therapy to the Understanding and Treatment of Anger and Aggression

Sandra C. Paivio and Marc Carriere

This chapter presents the unique contributions of emotion-focused therapy (EFT) and research (e.g., Carriere, 2003; Greenberg & Paivio, 1997; Paivio, 1999) to the understanding and treatment of anger and aggression. This approach is grounded in current experiential therapy theory (e.g., Greenberg, Rice, & Elliott, 1993) which, in turn, draws on developments in cognitive science (e.g., Brewin, 2001) and recent emotion theory and research (e.g., Damasio, 1999; Izard, 1990; LeDoux, 1995). We first outline the fundamental assumptions and principles underlying the approach, followed by contributions of the approach to assessment and intervention with anger problems. Clinical principles are discussed as they apply specifically to the treatment of child abuse trauma because addressing anger and anger problems is central to clinical work with this client group. We conclude by presenting recent research on anger expression in this type of therapy.

Most recent theory and research on anger problems are from the cognitive-behavioral perspective and focus exclusively on the management of dysregulated anger. EFT provides a distinct perspective by emphasizing anger as a healthy resource and anger problems that include its overcontrol and avoidance. Thus EFT has the potential to expand our understanding of anger problems and their treatment.

Fundamental Assumptions Underlying EFT

First, the concept of "experiencing" is fundamental to all experiential therapies, including EFT, and is defined as client attention to, symbolization, and exploration of their moment-by-moment subjective experience (feelings and associated meanings). Client experiencing is the primary source of new information in EFT. This is in contrast to cognitive-behavioral or psycho-dynamic approaches in which psycho-education, skills training, challenges to maladaptive cognitions, or interpretations offered by the therapist are the main sources of new information. Reliance on internal experience as a source of wisdom is considered particularly important in self-development and interpersonal functioning. Anger, in particular, is a powerful emotion that has a profound impact on self-organization and interpersonal relations (Greenberg & Paivio, 1997). Clients in EFT are directed to attend to and express angry feelings as they emerge in the session and to explore the meaning of their anger. This could include memories, images, thoughts or beliefs about self and others, values, standards, goals, desires, bodily experience, action tendencies, as well as fears about or injunctions against anger expression.

The second assumption underlying EFT is that effective intervention requires a highly differentiated perspective of particular emotional experiences and processes. In the case of anger, expressed rage at the source of trauma is not the same as rage that is suppressed, and these are not the same as rage masking fear of abandonment, anger at self in the form or self-criticism, or anger at criticism from others. These anger experiences have different affective, cognitive, motivational, and behavioral components, and each requires a different approach to intervention.

Third, such a differentiated perspective is inherently integrative. Although awareness of internal experience and processes likely is necessary in order to change each of the aforementioned problems, it might not be sufficient. Appropriate intervention, therefore, needs to draw on the strengths of divergent treatment models. For example, interventions that promote the exploration and understanding of particular anger experience are characteristic of experiential therapies such as EFT. Recognition of the internal cues that escalate anger into rage could be a part of that process and a necessary first step in defusing the anger. However, this awareness likely needs to be followed by the practice of anger management skills, such as relaxation, breathing, time-out, or assertive expression, that are more characteristic of cognitive-behavioral (CBT) approaches.

Assumptions About Emotion

Assumptions about emotion that underlie EFT largely derive from current emotion theory and research (e.g., Damasio, 1999; Fridja, 1986; Izard,

1990; LeDoux, 1995). Above all, emotions are viewed as comprising an adaptive orienting system and as playing a key role in the individual's experience of reality, sense of self, and orientation toward others (Greenberg & Paivio, 1997). Anger as a basic affect then is a healthy resource that provides energy and a sense of empowerment; readies individuals to defend themselves against threat or harm, or to correct perceived wrong-doing; and signals others to back off.

Second, emotions are associated with a multimodal network of information or meaning system that comprises an emotion structure (Foa & Kozak, 1996) or scheme (Greenberg & Paivio, 1997). Specific emotions are associated with specific areas of brain activation and specific information (LeDoux, 1996) in the form of action tendencies (motivation), bodily experiences, thoughts, images, memories, and learned rules for expression. Anger involves changes in breathing and vascular, vocal, muscular, and facial responses that ready a person to thrust forward and attack the intruder. Emotions like anger organize for action but do not directly produce behavior; rather, emotion interacts with cognition and experience to produce behavior (Greenberg & Paivio, 1997). As a result of one's prior experiences, for example, anger can be related to the belief that its expression is futile or dangerous.

Third, activation of emotion in therapy is necessary in order to access, explore, and change the associated information and construct new meaning. This is similar to the concept of "emotional processing" that is central to exposure therapies (Foa & Kozak, 1996) whereby the activation of fear is required for desensitization to occur through exposure to new information. Research supports emotional processing as a mechanism of change in trauma therapies (e.g., Jaycox, Foa & Morral, 1998; Paivio, Hall, Holowaty, Jellis, & Tran, 2001). A similar change process is inherent in the concept of a corrective emotional experience that is central to psychodynamic approaches (Bernier & Dozier, 2002). Accordingly, the client "relearns" or reprocesses problematic emotions in the context of a supportive therapeutic relationship. This allows the emotion to be changed or corrected through a new interpersonal experience with the therapist. Problematic anger experience and processes, therefore, must be activated in the therapy session in order for change to occur. For example, clients frequently inhibit their legitimate anger toward abusive or neglectful others for fear of losing control, being like the offender, or unfairly blaming the other. An EFT therapist validates client concerns and, at the same time, promotes acknowledgement and expression of these legitimate angry feelings. Change consists of clients feeling entitled to anger experience, learning that it can be expressed without harm, accessing and exploring the meaning of their anger, and, when necessary, challenging and modifying the associated maladaptive meaning.

Assumptions About Emotion Regulation

According to Gross (1999), healthy emotion regulation requires the capacity to (a) experience the full range of emotions, (b) modulate the intensity of emotional experience, and (c) express emotions appropriately. These capacities provide access to the information associated with specific emotions and increase the likelihood that associated needs (e.g., for contact and comfort, protection, or respectful treatment) will be met. Anger regulation problems, therefore, include both anger that is absent and anger that is chronic and pervasive. For example, clients who are not able to experience their anger can collapse into powerlessness and be unable to stand up for themselves. Alternatively, clients who are chronically angry and not in touch with more vulnerable emotions, such as sadness or fear, can push others away and fail to receive needed support.

Anger regulation problems also include both overwhelming rage and anger that is lacking in conviction or energy. Both are problems with modulation and, in both instances, the adaptive information associated with anger is not available to guide action and it is not communicated. The construct of experiencing is relevant here. Again, this refers to the process of attending to, exploring, and symbolizing the meaning of internal experience. This process cannot occur without some degree of emotional arousal; however, arousal must subside for the highest quality exploration and meaning construction to occur (Klein, Mathieu-Coughlan, & Kiesler, 1986). For example, the person in a fit of rage is too overtaken by emotion to allow the adaptive information contained therein to be symbolized and processed. The client expressing anger that is more modulated is better able to symbolize and reflect upon its meaning. Conversely, without sufficient arousal, exploration is superficial, externally focused, intellectual, or abstract.

Finally, anger regulation problems also concern problems with verbal or behavioral expression such that anger is expressed aggressively, passively, or inaccurately. Anger that is inappropriately expressed does not have the desired effect on the environment, and individuals' needs for respectful treatment or distance are not met. Clients whose displays of anger include violence and acting out need to be taught more appropriate and productive ways of expressing their feelings. The process can involve helping them to relax and take a "step back" from their anger before acting out as soon as it is felt. Clients whose anger is too passive or suppressed need to explore their fears about anger experience and, again, learn to express it appropriately.

ASSESSMENT OF ANGER PROBLEMS

An EFT approach to assessment of emotional experiences, in general, and anger experience, in particular, involves an integration of global and process diagnoses. Process diagnosis of anger involves identifying different types of anger experience or states and the associated cognitive-affective processing difficulties as they occur in the therapy session. A taxonomy of different types of emotion states and emotional processing difficulties has been developed (Greenberg & Paivio, 1997; Greenberg & Safran, 1989) and is described in the following section. First, we discuss the sources of information that comprise accurate assessment of emotional experience.

Sources of Information for Assessment of Anger Experience

Accurate assessment of client emotional experience and processes requires several sources of information. From an EFT perspective, accurate emotion assessment is a bottom-up rather than top-down, theory-driven process. Thus the primary source of information is empathic attunement to the client's moment-by-moment experience in the session. Problems with underregulated, chronic, defensive, or avoided anger can be observed and discussed as they occur in the session. The second source of information is knowledge of human emotions. For example, anger in response to violation or abuse is a normal and healthy self-protective response, whereas anger at one's self for being the victim of abuse is problematic. Accurate assessment of emotional processes also requires information about the particular client's behavioral and learning history. The anger expressed in session by a client with a history of angry outbursts and aggressive behavior is understood differently from the anger of an individual who chronically suppresses anger experience, or uses anger to cover more vulnerable feelings or to control others. In EFT, this information typically is accumulated over the course of therapy sessions. However, information also can derive from more formal assessment procedures. Numerous measures have been developed to assess the affective, cognitive, and behavioral dimensions of anger experience and different types of anger responses (e.g., assertive, aggressive, anger-in) typically exhibited in daily functioning (e.g., Novaco, 1994; Spielberger, Syderman, Owen, & Marsh, 1999). The final source of information for accurate emotion assessment is knowledge of particular personality styles and disorders. For example, individuals with narcissistic tendencies tend to respond to personal slights with intense anger that is thought to cover a more vulnerable or insecure sense of self (Benjamin, 1996); the intense anger of individuals with borderline tendencies, on the other hand, frequently is a response to fear of abandonment (Linehan, 1993).

Types of Anger, Anger-Processing Difficulties, and Intervention Principles

The following taxonomy of different types of anger and cognitive-affective processing difficulties is intended as a useful heuristic that guides appropriate intervention (Greenberg & Paivio, 1997). Different types of anger can co-occur in the same individual and the same session. Clinical judgement about which process to focus on, again, is determined by empathic attunement to the client's moment-by-moment experience, as well as knowledge of the particular client, personality styles, and disorders. We present the types of anger problems that most frequently occur in EFT, bearing in mind that this approach focuses primarily on heightening experiential awareness rather than behavioral control. In instances where anger dysregulation is the primary problem, appropriate intervention requires the integration of evidence-based cognitive-behavioral anger management strategies (e.g., Deffenbacher, 1999; DiGuiseppe, 1999). This section focuses on general principles of intervention. Specific strategies are discussed in the section on anger problems in therapy for child abuse trauma.

The first type of anger is an immediate and direct response to perceived environmental threat that is not reducible to cognitive-affective components. This type of anger is a basic affect that can be either adaptive or maladaptive. Anger at interpersonal violation and maltreatment is considered a *primary adaptive* response because it functions to mobilize self-protective resources and action. Processing difficulties concerning this type of primary anger involve difficulties modulating its intensity that result in either dysregulation or overcontrol. In either case, the information associated with the anger experience is unavailable to guide adaptive behavior. Examples include overwhelming rage and perhaps aggressive behavior at the source of victimization, on the one hand, and various forms of experiential avoidance such as numbness, injunctions against and chronic suppression of anger experience and expression, on the other hand. Many child abuse survivors, for example, chronically avoid their own anger for fear of losing control or behaving like the perpetrator. Negative consequences include a pervasive sense of victimization and powerlessness, self-blame, recurrent bouts of depression, difficulties with assertiveness, and difficulties establishing appropriate interpersonal boundaries. Appropriate intervention for underregulated or overcontrolled primary adaptive anger involves reducing or increasing arousal, respectively, in order to access anger and the associated adaptive information, and promoting appropriate assertive expression at maltreatment.

Difficulties with primary adaptive anger also can be in the realm of appropriate expression whereby individuals are able to experience anger at appropriate levels of intensity but lack assertive expression skills. Intervention in these cases obviously involves modeling or directly teaching anger expression skills. EFT generally relies on modeling or emotion coaching through the use of empathic responding. However, this is another instance where effective intervention could involve the integration of CBT assertiveness training strategies.

Primary maladaptive anger, on the other hand, is an immediate but overgeneralized response to perceived environmental threat. This type of anger frequently is associated with posttraumatic stress reactions. A rape victim, for example, can react with rage at being touched by men. This type of maladaptive anger may or may not be associated with aggressive behavior. Intervention in these instances again could involve integration of CBT and EFT procedures that include counter/conditioning the maladaptive response and, at the same time, validating angry feelings and focusing the expression of healthy and legitimate anger toward the specific source of trauma or harm.

The third category is *secondary* or *defensive* anger. The processing difficulty here is that anger is a secondary reaction to maladaptive cognitions or masks more core emotion, such as sadness, fear, or shame. Examples are anger in reaction to erroneous attributions of malicious intent or perseverating on thoughts that perpetuate anger or help escalate anger into rage; or defensive anger and aggression in response to fear of abandonment observed in some clients with borderline personality (Linehan, 1993) or in some male batterers (Holtzworth-Munroe, 2000). Another type of maladaptive secondary anger is hostility toward self as a result of self-critical thoughts and self-statements. These forms of anger generally are long-lasting rather than immediate and fleeting responses to violation. In these instances, anger experience is not to be accessed as a healthy resource but rather needs to be changed. Secondary anger can be explored to promote awareness of and modify maladaptive thought processes or change maladaptive meaning. Self-critical clients need to become aware of the self-critical process, that is, both the content and harshness of negative self-statements and the experiential impact of these statements. This experiential awareness can help motivate a shift to a more self-affirming stance. Defensive anger that masks more vulnerable feelings should be bypassed in order to access the more core emotional experience and the information associated with it. For example, the client who routinely expresses anger at signs of interpersonal slight needs to gain access to underlying feelings of hurt, rejection, or sadness that give rise to the defensive anger.

The fourth type is *instrumental* anger that is used, consciously or unconsciously, to manipulate or control others. In some instances, aggressive behavior, with or without angry affect, serves the same function as in the case of some types of spousal abuse (Holtzworth-Munroe, 2000). Again, this type of anger and/or behavior is maladaptive and needs to be changed. Appropriate intervention involves confronting and interpreting the instrumental function of the anger and teaching more adaptive ways to get needs met. Both secondary and instrumental anger can be problematic at the level of intensity and intervention needs to include teaching anger management strategies. All of the aforementioned types of anger can be problematic at the level of chronicity or frequency such that anger is the dominant emotion experienced or expressed. In these cases, the individuals frequently have limited awareness of and access to other feelings and intervention consists of implicit emotion coaching and/or explicit emotion awareness training. The former consists of empathic responses that direct client attention to and help them to accurately label their feelings. The latter consists of awareness strategies such as those included in dialectical behavior therapy (Linehan, 1993). The following section discusses how these principles are applied in therapy with survivors of child abuse trauma. Types of anger, anger difficulties, and intervention principles are summarized in Table 6.1.

ANGER IN EMOTION-FOCUSED THERAPY FOR RESOLVING CHILD ABUSE TRAUMA

Anger and anger-related problems are central to experiences of childhood maltreatment and to the resultant adult disturbances. Anger and other problems frequently observed in this client group are attributable to the following three primary and interrelated sources of disturbance: exposure to trauma, negative experiences with attachment figures, and reliance on experiential avoidance as a coping strategy. Each of these sources must be addressed in therapy.

Childhood experiences that involve repeated exposure to violence and trauma are thought to be encoded in memory (particularly the right-brain experiential system) and these memories are activated in response to current stimuli that resemble the trauma (van der Kolk, 1996). These experiences have been linked with posttraumatic stress disorder (PTSD), other anxiety disorders, and cognitive disruptions. Cognitive disruptions include enduring perceptions of self as vulnerable or flawed, others as

TABLE 6.1
Types of Anger, Anger Difficulties, and Intervention Principles

Type of Anger	Difficulties	Intervention Principles
Adaptive		
Primary	Underregulation overcontrol	Reduce or increase arousal
	Inappropriate expression	Model/teach expression skills
Maladaptive		
Primary	Overgeneralized response	Countercondition; validate, focus
		adaptive anger
Secondary	Reaction to maladaptive	Explore and modify cognitions
	cognitions (e.g., anger toward self or others)	
Defensive	Masks more core emotion	Bypass and access core emotion
Instrumental	Used to control others	Confront, access needs, teach more
		adaptive ways to get needs met
All Maladaptive		
	Underregulation	Reduce arousal
	Chronicity/frequency	Increase access to other emotions

151

dangerous and untrustworthy, and the world as basically hostile and unsafe (Janoff-Bulman, 1992). Chronic PTSD symptoms include both "rage at the source" or perpetrator of abuse and experiential avoidance as a strategy for coping with overwhelming affect. There is considerable evidence to suggest that, although avoidance is effective in the short term, in the long run, it perpetuates trauma symptoms (Foa & Jaycox, 1999). Avoidance interferes with emotional processing of trauma feelings and memories; that is, information is unavailable for exploration and modification through exposure to new information. Rage about the abuse and toward the perpetrator is suppressed only to resurface as an overgeneralized response to interpersonal stimuli that resemble the original events. Alternatively, chronically suppressed anger can result in feelings of powerlessness and victimization, hypertension, and secondary anxiety or depression.

Second, experiences of violation, maltreatment, and betrayal at the hands of caregivers generate intense negative feelings, including sadness, fear, and shame, as well as anger. Again, the latter include primary adaptive anger at violation and defensive anger covering more vulnerable experience. These negative experiences with attachment figures also can be internalized as negative representations of self and others. These serve as enduring prototypes that negatively influence perceptions of self and others and interpersonal behavior. Several studies have documented a link between childhood abuse and low self-esteem and enduring difficulties with interpersonal intimacy and trust (e.g., Elam & Kleist, 1999; Mullen, Martin, Anderson, Romans, & Herbison, 1996). These difficulties can manifest in a variety of anger-related problems including hostility toward self in the form of self-criticism and self-blame, chronically overgeneralized anger, defensive anger to cover more vulnerable experiences of fear or shame, suppressed anger for fear of punishment or loss of control, and outbursts of rage. These anger problems, in turn, can interfere with interpersonal intimacy.

The third source of disturbance related to childhood maltreatment is absence of support or "emotional coaching" (Gottman, 1997) to help cope with the intense negative feelings that are generated by abuse and neglect. This results in affect regulation difficulties including both underregulation and overcontrol of emotional experience. Problems with underregulated shame, anxiety, depression, and anger are well documented (e.g., Gilbert, Pehl, & Allan, 1994) and individuals frequently cope with overwhelming affect through avoidance. Again, chronic reliance on experiential avoidance as a coping strategy is thought to perpetuate trauma symptoms (Foa, 2000), resulting in immune system breakdown and poor health outcomes (Pennebaker, Kiecolt-Glaser, & Glaser, 1988), as well as cardiovascular disease (Mills & Dimsdale, 1993). Chronic experiential avoidance also is thought to contribute to the development of alexithymia, which is characterized by impaired awareness of and ability to label emotional experience (Taylor, Bagby, & Parker, 1997). Alexithymia, in turn, has been linked with histories of childhood abuse, social-skills deficits, difficulties with intimacy, and aggressive and self-harm behaviors (Turner & Paivio, 2002; van der Kolk & Fisler, 1994). Paivio and McCullough (2004) studied a sample of female undergraduate students and found that alexithymia mediated the relationship between a history of childhood abuse and engagement in self-harm behaviors, such as self-cutting or -burning. These behaviors also have been linked specifically to difficulties with anger experience and expression (e.g., Osuch, Noll, & Putnam, 1999; Suyemoto & MacDonald, 1995). The following sections specify how emotion-focused trauma therapy (EFTT) with abuse survivors addresses the aforementioned sources of disturbance.

Mechanisms of Change in EFTT

The primary mechanisms of change in EFTT are exposure and "emotional processing" of trauma memories, and provision of a safe and empathic therapeutic relationship. Similar change principles are common across most therapies for child abuse trauma (e.g., Briere, 1996; Courtois, 1991; Herman, 1992; Myers et al., 2002). In EFTT, the therapeutic relationship is both directly and indirectly curative in that it helps to counteract early attachment injuries and empathic failures, and provides a safe context for accessing and exploring painful trauma material. Emotional processing of trauma memories typically requires the activation of core emotion structures so that the associated maladaptive information is available for exploration and modification through exposure to new information (Foa, 2000). Change processes include both desensitization and construction of new meaning. Clients learn that they can tolerate previously avoided painful material and develop a new view of self, others, and traumatic events. Trauma therapies such as EFTT involve accessing, exploring, and modifying maladaptive emotions and meanings associated with fear, shame, and anger. Maladaptive anger includes overgeneralized and defensive anger and anger at self in the form of self-criticism or self-blame.

Although modifying maladaptive emotion is a mechanism of change in many trauma therapies, an important feature that distinguishes EFTT from other approaches is the emphasis on accessing previously inhibited primary adaptive emotions, such anger at violation and sadness at loss. Information associated with these emotions is the primary source of new information (rather than therapist-offered psycho-education, challenges to maladaptive cognitions, or interpretations) that is used to modify maladaptive emotion structures and construct new meaning. Healthy anger concerning violation and abuse, in particular, is incompatible with and can counteract fear, shame, and self-blame, and can contribute to assertiveness, self-empowerment, and appropriately holding abusive/ neglectful others, rather than self, accountable for harm.

Interventions in EFTT

EFTT interventions related to problematic anger focus first on differentiating different types of anger experience. Interventions then are intended to bypass, reduce, or explore defensive anger, or to access healthy adaptive anger. EFTT intervention principles can be combined with CBT techniques (e.g., confrontation, skills training) in order to address problems with instrumental anger or anger dysregulation.

First, empathic responding to client moment-by-moment experience is the primary intervention used in EFTT and the basis for all procedures. Empathic responding contributes to emotion regulation and reprocessing memories of child abuse in two main ways (Paivio & Laurent, 2001). First, empathic responses can help modulate the intensity of emotional experience. The soothing presence of a therapist whose responses validate and communicate understanding of intense anger at violation, for example, can relieve isolation and distress and thus help to reduce arousal. On the other hand, evocative empathic responses that use personal, specific, concrete, and connotative language (e.g., "How dare he treat you like a piece of garbage!") can help to increase arousal and fully access inhibited anger and associated meanings. Again optimal arousal is necessary for meaning exploration.

The second major role of empathic responding is to increase client awareness of emotional experience. Empathic responses can direct client attention to inhibited adaptive anger or indicators of other feelings underlying defensive anger (e.g., "So her criticism really hurts your feelings, like you can never please her."). Empathic responses also can help clients to accurately label and symbolize the meaning of emotional experience. For example, clients frequently enter therapy feeling powerless and victimized and their anger takes the form of undifferentiated hurt, blame, and complaint about maltreatment. A therapist response such as, "You must feel so resentful every time he shuts you out like that," helps to differentiate anger from other feelings and open up the client's anger experience for expression and exploration. Such a therapist response also gives the client permission to feel angry and models the appropriately modulated expression of anger. On the other hand, empathic responses can direct client attention to the thoughts that generate maladaptive secondary anger. For example, a therapist response such as "So what makes you so angry is believing that she is deliberately disregarding your wishes" makes the meaning of anger experience available for exploration and change. Increasing client awareness of the cognitive-affective processes (as well as external stimuli) that generate anger is a first step in learning to manage maladaptive anger and to use anger as a healthy resource.

Gestalt-derived two-chair dialogues (Greenberg et al., Elliott, 1993) and experiential focusing (Gendlin, 1996) techniques also are used to explore and modify various cognitive-affective processing difficulties that frequently are observed in therapy with child abuse survivors. These include self-interruption of anger experience by collapsing into power-lessness, avoiding or inhibiting anger expression for fear of losing control, acting like or unfairly blaming the perpetrator, anger directed at the self in the form of harsh self-criticism, and lack of clarity about emotional experience that contributes to distress. Other experts (e.g., Deffenbacher, 1999) have suggested that Gestalt-type dialogues can be used in CBT to explore how maladaptive anger occurs or escalates. In EFTT, the afore-mentioned self-related processes interfere with the full experience and expression of healthy anger and sadness about the abuse and, therefore, with resolving child abuse issues. In two-chair dialogues for self-criticism, for example, clients are encouraged to specify and feel the impact of harsh criticisms directed at the self. This increases experiential awareness and helps to elicit healthy self-protective resources to challenge or counteract maladaptive self-criticism or self-blame. Similarly, these interventions are used to increase client awareness of how they block or stifle their own experience and the associated feelings of tension and oppression. This can help to elicit healthy resources such as anger at violation or sadness at loss.

Finally, EFTT incorporates exposure-based procedures in order to access and explore trauma feelings and memories, and resolve issues with abusive/neglectful others. This emphasis on the interpersonal process of resolving issues with past attachment figures distinguishes EFTT from other therapies for child abuse trauma that focus on modifying self-concept and current symptoms and interpersonal problems (e.g., Briere, 1996; Myers et al., 2002; Wolfsdorf & Zlotnik, 2001). Typically, the client is encouraged to imaginally confront perpetrators of past abuse and neglect in an empty chair and express current thoughts and feelings about the abuse directly to these imagined others. This quickly accesses core mate-rial, including fear and avoidance, making it available for exploration. However, imaginal confrontation can be stressful and many clients are unwilling or unable to engage in it. When this is the case, memories of the trauma and feelings toward the perpetrator are explored exclusively in interaction with the therapist. The primary intervention here is advanced evocative empathy. Regardless of the intervention, a crucial step in resolving these issues is full experience and expression of previously inhibited anger at maltreatment (and sadness at loss) and associated meanings. Anger experience activates a sense of entitlement to unmet needs for dignity, respect, or protection, for example, and appropriately holding abusive or neglectful others accountable for harm. Once clients' thoughts and feelings are fully expressed and validated by the therapist, they are better able to let go of resentments and unmet needs. From a stronger and more self-affiliative stance they are better able to access empathic resources and, thereby, develop a more differentiated perspective and increased understanding or forgiveness of abusive or neglectful others. The other no longer is seen as an all-powerful ogre but in a more realistic light and the client may develop a real appreciation for their struggles and limitations.

Criteria for Healthy Anger Expression

EFTT defines healthy anger expression according to specific criteria that are consistent with the definition of primary adaptive emotion (Greenberg & Paivio, 1997) presented earlier. First, anger must be directed outward toward the perpetrator of harm, rather than inward toward the self, and concerns specific harms, transgressions, or violations. The anger is an immediate and direct response to harm rather than stemming from a series of thoughts or other feelings. Second, anger must be differentiated from other emotions, such as sadness, guilt, or fear, so that the information specific to anger is available for integration and construction of new meaning. Anger expression mixed with tears or fear, for example, does not allow the individual full access to the cognitive, motivational, or somatic information associated with anger experience. Third, anger is expressed assertively with ownership of experience, rather than aggressively or passively. For example, clients use "I" statements rather than referring to themselves in the third person or attacking or hurling insults at others. Fourth, the intensity of anger expression must be appropriate to the situation. Although this can range from annoyance to rage, high arousal is thought to interfere with meaning exploration, which is one of the criteria for healthy anger expression (Gendlin, 1991). Thus intense anger experience must be modulated and subside in order to be explored for its meaning. Markers of appropriate intensity include verbal and nonverbal indicators of arousal, including appropriate body posture, vocal quality, and facial expressions congruent with anger. Fifth, healthy anger expression is not merely venting or cathartic but must include some elaboration and exploration of meaning and role in the individual's life. It is not simply a verbal tirade but is worked with in an attempt to understand it. Criteria for healthy anger expression are summarized in Table 6.2.

TABLE 6.2
Criteria for Healthy Anger Expression

---

1. (a) Immediate and direct response to harm, rather than response to thoughts or other feelings
   (b) Directed outward toward perpetrator, rather than inward toward the self, for *specific harms*
2. Differentiated from other emotions (e.g., sadness, guilt, fear)
3. Expressed assertively with ownership of experience, rather than aggressively or passively
4. Intensity of expression is appropriate to the situation
5. Includes elaboration and exploration of meaning, rather than simple venting

---

The aforementioned criteria are compatible with those that would be applied in CBT assertiveness training (Kubany, et al., 2004). However, there are several features that distinguish the processes in EFTT from those in CBT. Most notably, the process does not involve explicit teaching or skills training; rather, the therapist guides the process of exploring (and expressing) anger experience or blocks to anger experience as they emerge in the session. Again, this typically is accomplished largely through the use of empathic responding and Gestalt-derived interventions. The therapist acts as an emotion coach helping the client to attend to, to accurately label, and to symbolize the meaning of their presently felt anger experience. The process is not role play or rehearsal for real-life communication but rather focuses on accessing internal information that is used in the construction of new meaning. Dialogues with imagined significant others are not intended as behavioral practice for real-life confrontation but rather to help elicit core emotional experience and "work through" feelings and meanings concerning important others. Once the client is clearer about their own experience, they are in a better position to behave in ways that are consistent with that experience.

RESEARCH ON THE BENEFITS OF ANGER EXPRESSION IN THERAPY

Several studies support the benefits of anger expression in EFTT and similar approaches. First, indirect support comes from results of outcome and process-outcome studies that support the treatment model, in general, with its emphasis on anger expression. Results of one outcome study (Paivio & Greenberg, 1995) supported this approach with a general clinical sample ($N = 32$) who were dealing with unresolved interpersonal issues (usually attachment injuries) from the past. Results of two other studies (Jarry & Paivio, 2004; Paivio & Nieuwenhuis, 2001) supported the approach with men and women who were dealing with child abuse trauma ($N = 37$ and $N = 32$, respectively). It should be noted that individuals reporting currently severe problems with anger dysregulation and aggressive or self-harm behavior are not considered suitable for this type therapy and were excluded from the above samples. The most frequently reported target complaints of clients in all studies included unresolved anger toward abusive, neglectful, or controlling significant others, current distrust or nonassertiveness in interpersonal relationships, and hostility toward self. All studies reported statistically and clinically significant improvements on multiple dimensions of change, including reduced depression, posttraumatic stress symptoms, anxiety, and interpersonal problems, as well as increased self-esteem and resolution of issues with significant others who were the focus of therapy. Average pre–post effect sizes for individual studies ranged from 1.79 to 1.84 standard deviations (SD) and treatment gains were maintained at 6-month follow-up. These effects far exceed the criterion of .8 SD specified by the APA Task Force on the Promotion and Dissemination of Psychological Procedures (American Psychological Association [APA], 1995). Similar results were reported for a similar process-experiential (PE) therapy for depression (Pos, Greenberg, Goldman, & Korman, 2003; Watson, et al., 2003) in which expression of inhibited anger in loss-related depressions was a key therapy process. Furthermore, results of analyses testing the null hypothesis in the Watson et al. study indicated that PE and CBT were equally effective in treating depression.

Furthermore, process-outcome studies support emotional expression as a mechanism of change in this type of therapy. For example, Greenberg and Malcolm (2002) reported that intense emotional expression was one of the factors that discriminated good-outcome from poor-outcome cases in short-term experiential therapy for resolving "unfinished business" with significant others from the past. This therapy model specifically encourages the expression of adaptive anger at violation and sadness at loss and formed the basis of EFTT. In EFTT, Paivio et al. (2001) found that emotional engagement with child abuse material during the imaginal confrontation intervention contributed to client change, beyond contributions made by the therapeutic relationship. Emotional engagement was measured using observer ratings of videotaped episodes of therapy sessions ($N = 37$) and frequently included intense expression of anger at abuse. Preliminary results from a more recent study of EFTT (Paivio, 2004) similarly indicated that client ($n = 23$) postsession reports of emotional engagement during imaginal confrontation, averaged across therapy sessions, predicted treatment outcome.

Direct support for the benefits of anger expression comes from two studies that specifically examined the role of anger in EFTT. Both studies used archival data from the same sample (Paivio & Nieuwenhuis, 2001) of moderately distressed men and women who were dealing with childhood emotional, physical, or sexual abuse. Again, individuals reporting severe problems with anger dysregulation and aggressive behavior were excluded from the sample.

In one study (Holowaty, 2004), mid-and posttest questionnaires asked clients to identify helpful aspects of therapy and to estimate the location of helpful episodes. These client-identified helpful episodes (HE) then were located in therapy videotapes and compared to a group of control episodes (CE) that were matched for stage of therapy ($n = 29$, each). Observer ratings of HE and CE were compared in terms of content and emotional processes. The Emotional Arousal Scale (Machado, Beutler, & Greenberg, 1999) was used to identify the predominant emotion expressed and the level of arousal (rated on a 5-point scale) in each episode. Results indicated that anger was the most predominant emotion expressed in both HE and CE (followed by sadness, fear, and shame). In 50% of all episodes, anger was the predominant emotion expressed. Furthermore, results indicated that the level of emotional arousal was significantly higher in HE compared to CE. Thus intense expression of emotion, particularly anger, was a distinguishing feature of events that clients found helpful in EFTT.

Another study more directly examined the contributions of anger expression to resolution of child abuse trauma in EFTT (Carriere, 2003). Client dialogue during videotaped therapy episodes that contained the imaginal confrontation procedure was analyzed using the Quality of Anger Expression Scale (QAES). The sample for analysis consisted of three episodes each for 33 clients who completed EFTT (total $N = 99$ episodes). The QAES is a psychometrically sound, observer-rated measure that was developed for this study. It consists of five mutually exclusive categories that correspond to the criteria for healthy anger expression presented earlier (externally directed, differentiated from other emotions, assertively expressed, expressed with appropriate intensity, includes some exploration of meaning). Results indicated nontrivial (i.e., $r > .30$; Cohen, 1988) correlations between healthy anger expression and resolution of abuse issues and interpersonal dimensions of change, particularly at follow-up. These results are preliminary but promising and provide support for the assertion that healthy anger expression can have a beneficial effect on psychotherapeutic outcome in EFTT. This study also is the first to quantify specific dimensions of anger believed to be healthy and important for survivors of childhood abuse.

SUMMARY AND CONCLUSIONS

This chapter outlined the fundamental assumptions and principles underlying EFT. These derive from current experiential therapy theory and
research (e.g., Greenberg & Paivio, 1997; Paivio & Greenberg, 1995) which,
in turn, draws on current emotion theory and research (e.g., Damasio, 1999;
Izard, 1990; LeDoux, 1995) and incorporates principles of emotional processing similar to those in exposure therapy (Foa & Kozak, 1986). EFT also
assumes that emotion regulation problems, in general, and anger problems,
in particular, are multifaceted and include not only difficulties with modulation (both underregulation and overcontrol), but problems with limited
awareness and inappropriate expression. An EFT approach to intervention
with anger problems addresses each of these facets.

The chapter then outlined the EFT approach to assessment of emotion
problems, particularly problems with anger. We outlined five sources of
information that contribute to accurate assessment of emotion states. EFT
assessment is a bottom-up process that particularly emphasizes empathic
attunement to clients' currently felt subjective experience as the primary
source of information. Also presented was a taxonomy of different anger
states and associated difficulties in cognitive-affective processing. This taxonomy guides appropriate intervention. Processing difficulties include
chronic or overgeneralized anger, defensive anger that masks more vulnerable experience, secondary anger generated by maladaptive cognitions
(including anger directed at the self), and instrumental anger intended to
manipulate or control others. All of these forms of anger are maladaptive
and intervention involves modifying, bypassing, or changing anger experience. However, anger problems also include primary adaptive anger that is
avoided or overcontrolled. Here EFT intervention involves accessing anger
experience so that the associated adaptive information can be integrated
into self-organization and used to construct new meaning.

The chapter then focused on clinical principles as they apply to survivors of child abuse trauma. We argued that a variety of anger-related
problems are central to experiences of childhood abuse and to the lasting
effects of these experiences. EFTT, therefore, addresses these different
anger problems as a central part of therapy with this client group. We also
specified the intervention strategies used in EFTT to address these problems. EFTT particularly relies on advanced empathic responding and
includes more structured Gestalt-derived dialogues and experiential
focusing techniques. These are used to explore and change maladaptive
anger experience and to access and explore previously inhibited adaptive
experience, including anger. We specified the role of healthy anger experience and expression in resolving child abuse issues and operationally
defined healthy anger expression according to five criteria. Accordingly,

healthy anger is externally directed, differentiated from other emotions, assertively expressed, expressed with appropriate intensity, and includes some exploration of meaning. Finally, we presented indirect and direct evidence supporting the benefits of adaptive anger expression in EFTT.

In sum, most recent theory and research on anger problems are from the cognitive-behavioral perspective and focus exclusively on the management of dysregulated anger. EFT provides a distinct perspective by emphasizing (a) anger as a healthy resource and (b) problems that include not only anger dysregulation, but avoidance of adaptive anger experience. Thus EFT has the potential to expand our understanding of anger problems and their treatment. The importance of such an expanded perspective is particularly evident in therapy with survivors of child abuse trauma where complex anger problems play a central role in disturbance.

REFERENCES

Benjamin, L. S. (1996). *Interpersonal diagnosis and treatment of personality disorders* (2nd ed). New York: Guilford.

Bernier, A., & Dozier, M. (2002). The client–counselor match and the corrective emotional experience: Evidence from interpersonal and attachment research. *Psychotherapy: Theory, Research, Practice, Training, 39,* 32–43.

Brewin, C. R. (2001). A cognitive neuroscience account of posttraumatic stress disorder and its treatment. *Behavior Research & Therapy, 39,* 373–393.

Briere, J. (1996). *Therapy for adults molested as children (2nd ed., expanded and revised).* New York: Springer.

Carriere, M. F. (2003). *Anger expression as a predictor of outcome in emotion focused therapy for adult survivors of childhood abuse. Unpublished master's thesis,* University of Windsor, Windsor, Ontario, Canada.

Cohen, J. (1988). *Statistical power analysis for the behavioral sciences* (2nd ed.). Hillsdale, NJ: Lawrence Erlbaum Associates.

Courtois, C. (1991). Theory, sequencing, and strategy in treating adult survivors. In J. Briere (Ed.), *Treating victims of childhood sexual abuse* (pp. 47–60). San Francisco: Jossey-Bass.

Damasio, A. R. (1999). *The feeling of what happens: Body and emotion in the making of consciousness.* New York: Harcourt.

Deffenbacher, J. L. (1999). Cognitive-behavioral conceptualization and treatment of anger. *JCLP/In Session: Psychotherapy in Practice, 55,* 295–309.

DiGuiseppe, R. (1999). End piece: Reflections on the treatment of anger. *JCLP/In Session: Psychotherapy in Practice, 55,* 373–379.

Elam, G. A., & Kleist, D. M. (1999). Research on the long-term effects of child abuse. *The Family Journal: Counseling and Therapy for Couples and Families, 7,* 154–160.

Franklin, C. L., Posternak, M. A., & Zimmerman, M. (2002). The impact of subjective and expressed anger on the functioning of psychiatric outpatients with post-traumatic stress disorder. *Journal of Interpersonal Violence, 12,* 1263–1273.

Foa, E. G. (2000). Psychosocial treatment of posttraumatic stress disorder. *Journal of Clinical Psychiatry, 61,* (Suppl. 5), 43–51.

Foa, E. G., & Jaycox, (1999). Cognitive-behavioral therapy and treatment of post-traumatic stress disorder. In D. Spiegel, (Ed.), *Efficacy and cost-effectiveness of psychotherapy. (Clinical Practice, 45)* (pp. 23–61). Washington, DC: American Psychiatric Association.

Foa, E. G., & Kozak, M. J. (1996). Emotional processing of fear: Exposure to corrective information. *Psychological Bulletin, 99,* 20–35.

Fridja, N. H. (1986). *The emotions.* Cambridge, UK: Cambridge University Press.

Gendlin, E. T. (1991). On emotion in therapy. In J. D. Safran & L.S. Greenberg (Eds.), *Emotion, psychotherapy, & change* (pp. 255–279). New York: Guilford.

Gendlin, E. T. (1996). *A focusing approach to psychotherapy.* New York: Guilford.

Gilbert, P. J., Pehl, J., & Allan, S. (1994). The phenomenology of shame and guilt: An empirical investigation. *British Journal of Medical Psychology, 67,* 23–36.

Gottman, J. M. (1997). *The heart of parenting: Raising an emotionally intelligent child.* New York: Simon & Schuster.

Greenberg, L. S., & Malcolm, W. (2002). Resolving unfinished business: Relating process to outcome. *Journal of Consulting and Clinical Psychology, 70,* 406–416.

Greenberg, L. S., & Paivio, S. C. (1997). *Working with emotions in psychotherapy.* New York: Guilford.

Greenberg, L. S., Rice, L. N., & Elliott, R. (1993). *Facilitating emotional change.* New York: Basic Books.

Greenberg, L. S., & Safran, J. D. (1989). Emotion in psychotheraphy. *American Psychologist, 44,* 19–29.

Gross, J. (1999). Emotion regulation: Past, present, and future. *Cognition and Emotion, 13,* 551–573.

Herman, J. L. (1992). *Trauma and recovery.* New York: Basic Books.

Holowaty, K. A. M. (2004, June). *Characteristics of client-identified helpful aspects of emotion focused trauma therapy for reprocessing memories of childhood abuse.* Paper presented at the 35th Annual Meeting of the Society for Psychotherapy Research, Rome.

Holtzworth-Munroe, A. (2000). A typology of men who are violent toward their female partners: Making sense of the heterogeneity in husband violence. *Current Directions in Psychological Science, 9,* 140–143.

Izard, C. E. (1990). Personality, emotion expression, and rapport. *Psychological inquiry, 1,* 315–317.

Janoff, Bulman, R. (1992) Shattered assumptions: Towards a new psychology of Trauma. New York: Free press.

Jarry, J., & Paivio, S. C. (June, 2004). *Comparative outcome of two versions of emotion focused trauma therapy for reprocessing memories of childhood abuse: A dismantling study.* Paper presented at the 35th Annual Meeting of the Society for Psychotherapy Research, Rome.

Jaycox, L. H., Foa, E. B., & Morral, A. R. (1998). Influences of emotional engagement and habituation on exposure theraphy for PTSD. *Journal of Consulting and Clinical Psychology, 66,* 185–192.

Jaycox, L. H., Zoellner, L., & Foa, E. B. (2002). Cognitive-behavior therapy for PTSD in rape survivors. *Journal of Clinical Psychology, 58,* 891–906.

Klein, M. H., Mathieu-Coughlan, P., & Kiesler, D. J. (1986). The experiencing scales. In L. S. Greenberg & W. M. Pinsof (Eds.), *The psychotherapeutic process: A research handbook (Guilford clinical psychology and psychotherapy series)* (pp. 21–71). New York: Guilford.

Kubany, E. S., Hill, E. E., Owens, J. A., Iannce-Spencer, C., McCaig, M. A., & Tucmayne, K. J. (2004). Cognitive trauma therapy for battered women with PTSD (CTT-BW). *Journal of Consulting and Clinical Psychology, 72,* 3–18.

LeDoux, J. E. (1995). Emotion: Clues from the brain. *Annual Review of Psychology, 46,* 209–235.

Linehan, M. M. (1993). *Cognitive-behavioral treatment of borderline personality disorder.* New York: Guilford.

Machado, P. P., Beutler, L. E., & Greenberg, L. S. (1999). Emotion recognition in psychotherapy: Impact of therapist level of experience and emotional awareness. *Journal of Clinical Psychology, 55,* 39–57.

Mills, P. J., & Dimsdale, J. E. (1993). Anger suppression: Its relationship to beta-adrenergic receptor sensitivity and stress-induced changes in blood pressure. *Psychological Medicine, 23,* 673–678.

Myers, J. E. B., Berliner, L., Briere, J., Hendrix, C. T., Jenny, C., & Reid, T. A. (2002). *The APSAC handbook on childhood maltreatment.* London: Sage.

Novaco, R. W. (1994). Anger as a risk factor for violence among the mentally disturbed. In J. Monahan & H. J. Steadman, (Eds.), *Violence and mental disorder: Developments in risk assessment* (The John D. and Catherine T. McArthur Foundation series on mental health and development) (pp. 21–59). Chicago: University of Chicago Press.

Osuch, E. A., Noll, J. G., & Putnam, F. W. (1999). The motivations fro self-injury in psychiatric inpatients Psychiatry: Interpersonal and Biological Process, 64, 334–346.

Paivio, S. C. (1999). Experiential conceptualization and treatment of anger. *Journal of Clinical Psychology 55,* 311–324.

Paivio, S. C. (2004, June). *Comparative processes of two versions of emotion focused trauma therapy for reprocessing memories of childhood abuse.* Paper presented at the 35th Annual Meeting of the Society for Psychotherapy Research, Rome.

Paivio, S. C., & Greenberg, L. S. (1995). Resolving "unfinished business": Efficacy of experiential psychotherapy using empty-chair dialogue. *Journal of Consulting and Clinical Psychology, 63,* 419–425.

Paivio, S. C., Hall, I. E., Holowaty, K. A. M., Jellis, J. B., & Tran, N. (2001). Imaginal confrontation for resolving childhood abuse issues. *Psychotherapy Research, 11,* 433–453.

Paivio, S. C., & Laurent, C. (2001). Empathy and emotion regulation: Reprocessing memories of childhood abuse. *Journal of Clinical Psychology, 57,* 213–226.

Paivio, S. C., & Nieuwenhuis, J. A. (2001). Efficacy of emotion focused therapy for adult survivors of childhood abuse: A preliminary study. *Journal of Traumatic Stress, 14,* 115–134.

Pennebaker, J. W., Kiecolt-Glaser, J. K., & Glaser, R. (1988). Disclosure of trauma and immune function: Health implications for psychotherapy. *Journal of Consulting and Clinical Psychology, 56,* 239–245.

Pos, A. E., Greenberg, L. S., Goldman, R.N., & Korman, L. M. (2003). Emotional processing during experiential treatment of depression. *Journal of Consulting and Clinical Psychology, 71*, 1007–1016.

Resnick, P. A., & Schnicke, M. K. (1993). *Cognitive processing therapy for rape victims: A treatment manual*. Newbury Park, CA: Sage.

Spielberger, C. D., Syderman, S. J., Owen, A. E., & Marsh, B. J. (1999). Measuring anxiety and anger with the state-trait anxiety inventory (STAI) and state-trait anger expression inventory (STAXI). In M. E. Maruish (Ed.), *The use of psychological testing for treatment planning and outcome assessment* (2nd ed., pp. 993–1021). Mahwah, NJ: Lawrence Erlbaum Associates.

Suyemoto, K., & McDonald, M. (1995). Self-cutting in female adolescents. *Psychotherapy, 32*, 162–171.

Taylor, G., Bagby, M., & Parker, J. (1997). *Disorders of affect regulation: Alexthymia in medical and psychiatric illness*. Cambridge, Uk: Cambridge University Press.

Turner, A.M. & Paivio, S. C. (2001). *Relations among childhood trauma, alexithmia, social anxiety and social support*. Poster presented at the American Psychological Association, Chicago, IL.

van der Kolk, B. (1996). The body keeps the score: Approaches to the psychobiology of posttraumatic stress disorder. In B. A. van der Kolk, A. C. McFarlane, & L. Weisaeth (Eds.) *Traumatic stress: The effects of overwhelming experience on mind, body, and society*. New York: Guilford.

van der Kolk, B. A., & Fisler, R. E. (1994). Childhood abuse and neglect and loss of self-regulation. *Bulletin of the Meninger Clinic, 58*, 145–168.

Watson, J. C., Gordon, L. B., Stermac, L., Kalogerakus, F., & Stackley, P. (2003). Comparing the efficacy of process-experiential with cognitive-behavioral therapy in the treatment of depression. *Journal of Consulting and Clinical Psychology, 71*, 773–781.

Wolfsdorf, B. A., & Zlotnik, C. (2001). Affect management in group therapy for men and women with posttraumatic stress disorder and histories of childhood sexual abuse. *Journal of Clinical Psychology, 57*, 169–181.

Anger in Psychotherapy: To Express or Not to Express? That Is the Question

Leslie S. Greenberg and Jeannette Bischkopf

In the chapters addressed by this commentary, one focuses on basic processes involved in anger whereas the other two discuss anger in psychotherapy. Harmon-Jones and Harmon-Jones (Chap. 4, this volume) show that anger is best considered a multicomponent process and they review research on its components—appraisals, feelings, action plans, activation states, and physiology. Summarizing the research on subjective feelings of anger, these authors favor the notion of describing the various "nuances" of anger experience rather than categorizing distinctly different emotional or affective states. They suggest linking the valence of an emotion more closely to its definition. For example, what is meant by negative is not always clearly defined in the literature. Although most individuals regard anger as a negative experience, people differ in their attitudes toward anger. Thus, when researching anger as a negative emotion, other subjective experiences related to anger may not be recognized and our understanding of the anger experience is therefore incomplete. For example, they report a recent study (Harmon-Jones, Lueck, Fearn, & Harmon-Jones, 2005) in which anger and activated positive affect were positively correlated. Harmon-Jones and Harmon-Jones also see anger as an approach emotion and essentially take a functional view of emotion and anger—that anger serves a biological and often adaptive function. Their review is a rich source of information on basic processes of anger as seen from a neuro-affective science perspective. It led us to further questions and a discussion of how our therapeutic decisions, interventions, or even treatment approaches can be best informed by an understanding of these basic neuro-affective processes.

By contrast to the neuro-affective perspective offered by the Harmon-Joneses, the chapters by Paivio and Carriere (chap. 6, this volume) and by

Olatunji, Lohr, and Bushman (chap. 5, this volume) review research evidence on the experience and resolution of anger in psychotherapy. Olatunji et al. provide an overview of cognitive-behavioral anger treatments and their effectiveness, whereas Paivio and Carriere demonstrate how anger can be conceptualized and worked with within an emotion-focused approach. Olatunji et al. argue that venting in the treatment of anger maybe harmful, whereas Paivio and Carriere offer a more detailed view of when and for whom anger expression in psychotherapy may be effective. Paivio and Carriere, for example, discuss the contributions of anger expression to resolution of child abuse trauma and the role of expression of inhibited anger in loss-related depressions. Both chapters papers provide an impressive amount of data regarding the effectiveness of anger treatments. Olatunji et al. show that anger management approaches are effective, especially for undercontrolled anger and for specific problems including driving anger and workplace anger. Paivio and Carriere demonstrate the role of anger in emotion-focused trauma therapy. In order to understand when and for whom anger control (in contrast to anger expression) is the most effective way of treatment, we need to take a broader perspective in which anger, in line with the Harmon-Jones perspective, is viewed as a complex phenomenon.

In this commentary, we suggest such an approach and expand on several points that flow from issues raised in the preceding chapters. Our discussion is focused on the role of emotion regulation and on allowing for complexity in the conceptualization and treatment of anger.

The question of whether inhibition is beneficial or detrimental can be seen to be one of the major differences between more intrapsychic therapies (humanistic and psychodynamic) focused more on the transformation of underlying determinants of distressing emotional experience and more cognitive-behavioral therapies (CBTs) focused more on coping with distress. The intrapsychic models are based on the central assumption that inhibitions are unhealthy for an individual. CBT, on the other hand, often makes use of distraction and other inhibitory techniques to divert a client's attention away from a feeling or desire to be extinguished, and toward a therapeutically contracted behavior. In general, however, therapists of most persuasions discourage inhibition of awareness of emotions, desires, and goals. Psychodynamic and humanistic-experiential therapists, however, also generally discourage behavioral inhibition of emotional expression and actions in the therapy session related to affective goals, and often encourage creative integration of emotion-based action dispositions into a person's life.

From this perspective the expression of emotions is viewed as beneficial to mental and physical health. Although research on catharsis is not unequivocal, it appears that expressing emotion reduces physiological and psychological arousal when the action is performed in a context that includes a cognitive working-through component (Greenberg & Safran, 1987). For example, encouraging the expression of both sadness and anger in relation to unresolved grief that includes a component of explaining or helping the client make sense of the process and purpose of a grief reaction, in addition to simply supporting emotional expression, is generally beneficial. The benefits of emotion experience and expression rather than inhibition are evidenced in the work of Pennebaker and his colleagues, who showed that expressive writing of undisclosed trauma experiences result in better physical health relative to writing about a neutral topic such as one's weekly schedule.

CBT therapists, on the other hand, encourage inhibition of undesired behaviors. On this side of the issue, there is evidence that cognitive, emotional, and behavioral inhibition plays a central role in mental and social health. A substantial portion of referrals for psychotherapy are for problems with impulse control, addictions, acting-out behaviors, self-harm behavior, pain management, and other areas where clients' inability to inhibit their behavior or cognitive experience is a major factor in their dysfunction. Here the focus is on emotional behavior in the world. From this perspective, too intense emotional displays are seen to be disruptive or unhealthy (Consedine, Magai, & Bonanno, 2002), too much disclosure is seen as possibly resulting in increased negative emotion (Afifi & Guerrero, 2000; Bushman, 2002; Larsen & Prizmic, 2004) or negative social consequences (Bonanno & Kaltman, 1999; Roloff & Ifert, 2000). The chronic experience of negative affect such as anger or sadness is also seen to cause health problems (Bonanno & Kaltman, 1999; Friedman & Booth-Kewley, 1987; Kennedy-Moore & Watson, 1999; Mayne, 1999). From this perspective, if expression intensifies a person's arousal, inhibition is seen to be preferable and results in better health.

REGULATING EMOTIONS

Therapists and psychologists have long pondered the value of expression versus the active suppression of a feeling. Whether, or under what conditions, expression or inhibition is problematic or beneficial is not clear. In clinical work, inhibition has often been considered a negative tendency, resulting in psychological problems due to nonexpression of the inhibited emotion, thought, or behavior (Pennebaker, 1997). Suppression of memories of a traumatic event in childhood has been associated with problems such as depression and addiction (Brown, Scheflin, & Hammond, 1998; Williams, 1995). Cognitive researchers on the other hand have documented how necessary inhibition is to human functioning, facilitating abilities such as selective attention, decisional action, and the like. Similarly, clients frequently seek out or are referred to therapists for things they wish to inhibit, including behaviors (drinking, acting-out behaviors, etc.), thoughts (worries, ruminations, obsessive thinking), and uncomfortable emotional states (e.g., anger, anxiety, and depression).

So the question raised by these chapters is one of "Which is a more positive (or negative force) in human lives: expression or inhibition of anger?" There is empirical evidence to support both positions (Arbuthnott, Arbuthnott, & Thompson, 2006). Suppression of the experience and expression of emotion in general and anger more specifically is associated with poorer mental and physical health (Smyth, 1998), and problems with inhibition are associated with schizophrenia, attention deficit hyperactivity disorder, and obsessive-compulsive disorder (Bannon, Gonsalvez, Croft, & Boyce, 2002; Barkley, 1997).

Freud (1915/1957) first theorized that unacknowledged goals and emotions, kept out of our awareness through repression and dissociation, led to psychological symptoms and that catharsis was its cure. He however later abandoned this theory in favor of a signal anxiety theory. Rogers (1942) early on noted that release and expression of emotion led to improvement and later refined that formulation into the importance of deepening experience in promoting therapeutic change. Perls, Hefferline, and Goodman (1951) regarded avoidance of painful emotions as central to dysfunction. In intrapsychic approaches to therapy, inhibition or interruption of emotion and especially of anger often has been seen as a negative force, one that leads to dysfunction. As a consequence, psychodynamic and humanistic therapists have developed methods to bring such disavowed goals and emotions into awareness, with the aim of integrating them into the person's awareness, action, and life. Recently, emotion-focused theorists have asserted that it is the informational and self-regulatory value in expressing emotion more than the cathartic value that is helpful in psychotherapy (Greenberg 2002; Greenberg, Rice, & Elliott, 1993). According to this view, anger, rather than being seen as "a-thing-to-be-managed" (Roffman, 2004) or "a-thing-to-be-get-rid-of" is seen as serving a reorienting function and as providing meaning. In the chapters by Harmon-Jones and Harmon-Jones and by Paivio and Carriere (chaps. 4 and 6, this volume, respectively) anger is seen as having this function.

Cognitive researchers, on the other hand, have observed several beneficial inhibitory processes in the context of cognitive tasks. For example, inhibition has been found to operate to prevent distracting sources of information from impairing performance on a current goal, essentially enabling selective attention and action. In this view, inhibition is a valuable process, one that enables selective attention and efficient action toward a particular goal, and deficiencies in inhibition are associated with serious psychological disorders. Olatunji et al, in their chapter on the pseudopsychology of venting (chap. 5, this volume), support this view and review a number of social-psychological experiments showing the detrimental effects of venting.

These two contradictory views essentially focus on expression or suppression of the same material, namely emotions and thoughts. So the question is what is best in psychotherapy? Is it helpful in psychotherapy to bring inhibited material to awareness and encourage its expression, or is it better in therapy to support inhibition, to help clients to pursue their consciously chosen goals more effectively? Is it better in psychotherapy to support expression or containment? Clearly the chapters we reviewed come down on different sides of this argument, with Paivio and Carriere arguing that expression in therapy is useful and Olatunji and colleagues arguing that venting is counterproductive.

In reviewing these chapters on anger, it is important to keep a few key issues in mind to help address the dilemma of expression versus inhibition and/or containment. First, in discussing the value of expression, it is important to discern whether it is anger expression, in the world and everyday life or anger expression in therapy related to unresolved concerns. Focusing on the destructiveness of venting, Olatunji et al. question if there can be safe anger expression in any context and caution that the distinction between hitting a pillow and a person can become fuzzy in the heat of anger. There are a few problems with this notion, however; a major one is that no distinction is being made between anger expression in therapy versus anger expression in real life. In fact, most of what they refer to is focused on the expression of anger in life rather than as part of a process of change in therapy. Taking a simple learning perspective, it also is implied that whatever people experience and learn in psychotherapy (anger expression) is directly transferred into extrasession behavior (i.e., anger in their lives). In this view, anger expression in therapy is seen as leading to aggression or being equivalent to violent behavior and is associated with loss of control. In addition, anger expression and safety seem to Olatunji et al. to be incompatible. This implies that all anger has to be controlled because its expression is unsafe.

We see this as another of the central misunderstandings and problems surrounding the concept of anger. This type of uniform view of anger expression as involving explosive or destructive behavior that needs to be inhibited, and the dichotomization of anger expression into good or bad, narrows our understanding of anger. Positive uses of anger and its role in assertiveness (Kahn & Greenberg, 1980) have hardly been studied and are often neglected when assessing anger. With regard to violence, there is evidence for inhibited as well as expressed anger being an antecedent for violent behavior (Davey, Dey, & Howells, 2005). Tangney, Wagner, Barlow,

Marschall, and Gramzow (1996) differentiated between constructive and destructive responses to anger. The tendency to suppress anger often is a destructive response that may lead to the continuation of interpersonal conflict (due to either vengeful rumination or interpersonal withdrawal). Depression can be also be associated with "anger attacks"; intense anger arousal that has been likened to panic attacks (Fava, Anderson, & Rosenbaum, 1990; see also Mammen, Pilkonis, Kolko, & Groff, chap. 12, this volume). Brody, Haag, Kirk, and Solomon (1999) found that recovered depressed people, compared to never depressed people, had higher levels of anger suppression and fear of anger expression. These were related to fear of damaging a relationship one was dependent on and previous experiences of having intense anger (anger attacks). Clearly inhibited or too little anger can be as much of a problem as expressed or too much anger.

VARIETIES OF ANGER EXPERIENCE AND EXPRESSION

An important distinction to be kept in mind in reviewing these chapters, therefore, is whether it is expression of overcontrolled anger or under-controlled anger that is the therapeutic target being discussed. Methods of anger control and stress management have been strongly recommended and studied, whereas methods of dealing with problems of overcontrol have been inadequately described and studied (Greenberg & Paivio, 1997). For example, it is surprising to see how little we know about sup-pressed anger and depression given the positive correlation between the two (Biaggio & Godwin, 1987; Gilbert, Gilbert, & Irons, 2004). Ultimately the problem lies in a uniformity myth that has dominated the anger treat-ment literature to date—that all anger is the same and should be treated in the same way. As the Harmon-Joneses point out, although there is a uniform cluster of phenomena we can call anger, how problems arise with anger is not uniform. As Eckhardt, Norlander, and Deffenbacher (2004) have noted, "what we know and we can measure concerning 'clinical anger' is woefully inadequate. . . . The research indicates that research on anger and hostility lags behind that of other emotional variables both in terms of quality and quantity" (p. 37). The myth that all anger needs to be controlled thus must be put to rest. Not all anger is the same and it should not all be treated in the same fashion. Paivio and Carriere offer a good start in the direction of differential treatment by suggesting an emotion-focused therapy process, a taxonomy of types of emotions that occur in therapy, and different ways of intervening with different classes of anger. In other research, Linden et al. (2003) have begun to differentiate different types of anger, suggesting that there is more to anger coping than anger-in or anger-out. In their Behavioral Anger Response Questionnaire they delineate six anger factors: direct anger-out, assertion, support seeking, diffusion, avoidance, and rumination. However, conceptualizations of anger often mix experience of anger, expression of anger, and anger-related problems, and these need to be distinguished from each other. The Clinical Anger Scale (Snell, Gum, Shuck, Mosley, & Hite, 1995), for instance, addresses the following symptoms: anger now, anger about the future, anger about failure, anger about things, angry-hostile feelings, annoying others, angry about self, angry misery, wanting to hurt others, shouting at people, irritated now, social interference, decision interference, alienating others, work interference, sleep interference, fatigue, appetite interference, health interference, thinking interference, and sexual interference. This scale mixes categories and emphasizes negative aspects of anger without balancing with positive aspects of anger.

Another useful distinction to make in relation to anger is whether inhibition occurs in the form of suppression of the internal experience or a mental representation of anger, or suppression of angry behaviors or actions. In therapeutic terms, this difference amounts to a distinction between experience and expression of anger. Therapeutically, the discussion of inhibition often does not clearly distinguish between the inhibition of emotional experience and emotional expression. Because the functions of emotional experience and expression serve different purposes, inhibition of each likely has different consequences. Within a functional view of emotion (e.g., Johnson-Laird & Oatley, 1992), the function of emotional experience is to indicate relevant actions or goals for people in their current situations. In this case, emotion provides people with important information. For example, anger is experienced in response to goal frustration or boundary violation, and it serves to mobilize the person to overcome the obstacle or protect against intrusion.

Anger also serves important social functions, ones that often are important to help people develop in therapy. Anger helps renegotiate boundaries and thereby repair relationships (Oatley, 1993, 1996). The Harmon-Joneses demonstrate clearly that anger is an approach emotion that has adaptive functions. According to a study by Averill (1982), most anger episodes occur between people who are close to each other. In 63% of the cases, anger was expressed to demonstrate authority and independence, thereby restoring the image of the self as strong. Most people in this study experienced their own anger as unpleasant. However, 62% of those who experienced anger, and even 70% of those at whom the anger was directed found the expression of anger helpful in regard to their relationships. In a similar study about marital conflict, 79% of the wives experienced conflict and the expression of anger as good and helpful with regard to their relationships (Jenkins, Smith, & Graham, 1989). Expression of anger thus serves communication functions, such as to indicate aggressive intent. Anger is the emotion that is best recognized in social interactions. Oatley and Larocque (1995) estimate that in 73% of all cases in which someone feels angry, the person who is interacted with can recognize anger; by contrast, five other emotions (happiness, fear, sadness, shame, and guilt) are recognized in less than half of the cases.

Clearly, Harmon-Jones and Harmon-Jones (chap. 4, this volume), writing from their neuro-affective science view, support an adaptive view of the basic function of anger, as do Paivio and Carriere (chap. 6, this volume) from a more therapeutic vantage point. If we view emotions as a functional means of information processing, such as a way to orient individuals to how they are doing with their current goals (Greenberg, 2002) and to motivate them to useful action (Frijda, 1986), then inhibition of an emotion such as anger would necessarily limit effectiveness.

In contrast to the functional point of view proposed by Harmon-Jones and Harmon-Jones, if emotions are seen as irrelevant or dysfunctional responses in most situations, related more to an individual's biochemical state than to purposes, then suppression would be helpful for effective problem solving or action. Further more, even if emotional experience is useful, inhibition of expression can be seen as beneficial in that it prevents others from anticipating our likely behavior, which can be beneficial in competitive social situations. Clearly, Olatunji, Lohr, and Bushman take the view that anger is disruptive and see venting as simply leading people to being more angry and aggressive.

In Olatunji et al.'s view (chap. 6, this volume), as in most of the anger literature, anger is predominantly understood in terms of quantity rather than quality: "Anger varies in terms of frequency, intensity, and duration" (p. 00). Most treatment programs then target these three components of the experience of anger, helping people to experience anger less often, less intensely, and for less time. What is lacking, however, is the meaning component of this experience. Even in the Kip Kinkle case that Olatunji et al. mention, Kip was said to have experienced anger without knowing why. The qualitative domain of the experience of anger—for instance, what the anger is about—has been neglected in studying anger. Driving anger and workplace anger are equated with clinical experiences of anger such as the promotion of the expression of suppressed childhood resentment by an adult to an imagined abusive parent in an empty chair in the safety of the therapy hour. The expression of driving anger and workplace anger, however, differs greatly from the expression of anger in therapy to alleviate depression or hopelessness and the role of suppressed anger in psychopathology.

Turning our attention to another issue, we have only just begun to understand how anger is related to psychopathology. How does psychopathology, for instance, narcissistic personality disorder or depression, influence when people feel angry and how they express that? Depression, for instance has been linked to hostility and anger suppression. How are psychopathological symptoms related to the experience of anger? In a study of bulimic behavior (Meyer et al., 2005), men appeared to engage in bulimic behaviors to reduce anger states, whereas woman appeared to use such behaviors to reduce the likelihood that anger states would arise. Patients with borderline personality disorder report states of aversive inner tension that they try to terminate by impulsive self-harming behavior. Three events—"failure," "being alone," and "rejection"—account for 39% of all events preceding a state of tension for patients with a diagnosis of borderline personality disorder (Stiglmayr et al., 2005). Also, patients' experience of tension is related to feelings of helplessness, whereas healthy controls experience tension in relation to stress and the pressure to perform well (Bischkopf et al., 2006). In order to further our understanding of the experience, expression, and function of anger in relation to psychopathology, we need categories that go beyond diagnostic labels. These could be events or experiences that lead to anger or processes that inhibit or enhance the expression of anger. Thus, a more individualized and process-oriented view is needed that frees the emotion of anger of its stigma of being bad and destructive either for the person experiencing it or for the person to whom the anger is directed. One problem with taking a process-oriented view of emotion is how to measure unstable, dynamic phenomena. For anger, a new measure, the Emogram Anger Scale, has been developed for a more longitudinal emergent perspective on the emotion of anger (Mudge, 2004). However, to understand how anger in psychotherapy emerges and is dealt with the best way is to look at actual therapy sessions and track the emotion of anger and its resolution in therapy (Greenberg, in press).

Olatunji et al.'s chapter (chap. 5, this volume) provides a range of experimental evidence related to a hydraulic model of anger and the adverse effects of venting. However, the generalizability of these findings to a clinical population may be limited, as no distinction between under- and overregulated anger was made. Most of the research did not study clinical populations. It is interesting to note, however, when and where these findings may be most applicable and useful, like in preventing workplace violence as opposed to emotional processing in therapy. The majority of the experiments, however, have poor ecological validity for understanding anger processes in psychotherapy. Experiments that involve evaluating a professor or show that aggression increases over a football season, and that they claim contradict catharsis theory, are not relevant to a theory of therapeutic change and are in no way a test of expression in therapy. Using these types of experiments to argue against something as complex as dealing with anger in psychotherapy does not illuminate how to deal with anger in therapy. Clearly these authors are concerned about the dangers of expressive methods as witnessed by their comment, "To date there is no documented harm caused by CBT for anger control" (p. 134). They see themselves as debunking the myth of the benefits of venting. With this we fully agree, but they should be careful not to throw out the baby with the bath water. In certain circumstances and for certain people, anger awareness, anger expression, or anger activation for transformation may be just what is needed. In general (and unfortunately), it is becoming more common that in claiming the superiority of CBT other views are discounted as invalid. The global promotion of the superiority of CBT seems motivated by considerations other than scientific ones. The goal of science is knowledge rather than power.

Thus, most of the writing on anger seems too static. It focuses on the problem of expressing too much anger or being too quick to anger as a problem in life rather than dealing with the rich meanings and functions anger may carry in and outside of therapy, not only for the person experiencing it, but also for his or her environment.

Some studies in the experimental tradition within social and personality psychology do support a more complex understanding of anger. Among these are (a) views of emotion regulation as a dynamic process (Chow, Ram, Boka, Fujita, & Clore, 2005); "Dynamics of emotional experience are much more complex than what snapshots at a particular time point could convey," p. 220), (b) subcategories of anger, and (c) the notion that "the word anger takes on a specific meaning in specific context" (Russell & Fehr, 1997, p. 203). Also it is clear that anger is not perceived only as dangerous; people confer more status and competence to targets who express anger than to targets who express sadness (Tiedens, 2001).

COMPLEXITY RATHER THAN UNIFORMITY

A simple prescription either to inhibit or to avoid inhibiting emotional experience and expression is not supported, clinically or empirically. Rather than looking only at quantity of anger, personal and contextual factors seem to determine whether inhibition will be beneficial or problematic (Consedine et al., 2002). Researchers are beginning to examine this more complex view of inhibition of anger, and several factors are hypothesized to influence the consequences of inhibition, including the developmental and social characteristics of the individual, cultural views on emotion expression, and characteristics of the experience being inhibited.

That is, negative health consequences as a result of inhibition may depend on our reasons for, and reactions to, inhibiting a particular experience or behavior (Gross, 1998; Kennedy-Moore & Watson, 1999). With respect to inhibition of anger, both personal and cultural factors have impact on the meaning of particular emotion expressions. This includes personally developed, familial, and culturally supported beliefs about expressiveness and containment.

For example, control exerted over emotions for social reasons is quite different from the chronic suppression of emotions. The former is an essential aspect of human social interactions and is not generally harmful to health as long as expression is possible in some contexts and with some people (Buck, 1984). If, however, emotional awareness is deficient, resulting in either a mislabeling of felt emotions or learning to withhold emotions under all conditions, emotional arousal will result in stress. Too much and too little expression is detrimental to effective emotional communication, and thus we need both inhibition and expression. In addition, individual characteristics, such as personal preferences and ethnicity, are proposed to play a role in the relation between inhibition and health.

Individuals who are chronically inhibited in their expression seem to benefit more from disclosure than less inhibited individuals (Derryberry & Rothbart, 1997). However, individuals' comfort with their level of expressivity, and the meaning their expression or inhibition has for them, seem to influence stress reactivity (Kennedy-Moore & Watson, 1999; Roloff & Ifert, 2000). Evidence suggests that the match between the level of expression and a person's preferred level of expression is important, in that physiological arousal is observed to be greatest for expression that does not match a person's preference (Engebretson, Matthews, & Scheier, 1989). Stress results more from ambivalence about suppressing or expressing a given experience than from the expression itself (King & Emmonds, 1990; Pennebaker, 1998). If we are ambivalent—perhaps because previous expression of a behavior was sometimes rewarded and sometimes punished—suppression requires much more effort than if we unequivocally desire to suppress the behavior.

Therapists often are aware of the ambivalence clients have toward expressing thoughts or feelings. For example, a client referred for therapy for depression began to tell stories about her mistreatment at the hands of her mother. She voiced her ambivalence by directly saying, "I want to talk about this, I think I need to . . . but every time I start I feel shame and fear, like I'm betraying my family and I remember my mother saying, 'Don't air your dirty washing in public.'" The strong ambivalence can also be demonstrated nonverbally, with clients struggling to say certain things and showing symptoms of stress as they talk about avoided material.

Individuals' early experience is also an important influence on whether inhibition or expression is valued. Such training is strongly influenced by cultural practices and parental responses to a child's emotions, which largely determine whether a child learns to habitually express or suppress emotional expression or experience (Buck, 1993; Krause, Mendelson, & Lynch, 2003). Therapists thus need to assist clients to understand these early influences and use this understanding to make changes in the way they deal with their emotions.

Another important moderator of the inhibition–health relationship is the characteristics of the inhibited experience itself. Emotion is a multi-dimensional phenomenon, including experience, physiology, and expression, so for any specific situation it is important to determine exactly which aspects of emotion should or should not be inhibited. Furthermore, different emotions signal different needs and serve different purposes and so the consequences of inhibition will likely differ for the different emotions. For example, emotions that extend over longer periods of time, such as grief, may require more resources to inhibit than emotions of shorter duration, such as anger. This is reflected in differential treatment for anger management and grief: Many anger management techniques are brief and oriented toward coping, whereas grief management techniques are slower, take longer to complete, and are oriented toward processing the emotion and creating new meaning (Greenberg & Watson, 2005). Similarly, intense anger may require more resources to inhibit than milder experiences of anger. Furthermore, if one is practiced in suppressing anger, inhibition may be less effortful than less frequently suppressed emotions. Also gender and gender stereotypes play a role in how people have access to their anger.

The experience of anger could be bad for our health (Hull et al., 2003), but cathartic expression could result in more illness than would be expected from the suppression of that emotion (Ecton & Feindler, 1990). Another question that is still unanswered, however, is what happens to suppressed anger over time. It is questionable whether "anger does eventually dissipate with time, regardless of what people do" as Olatunji et al. (chap. 5, this volume) suggest (p. 125). In studying emotional injuries and forgiveness, we came to believe that the distinction between old, past, lingering anger and fresh, present anger is clinically meaningful. However, we have only begun to understand what happens to an emotion over time and how one emotion changes into another. Moreover, there seem to be no easy answers, as all of this has to be understood in context.

In their chapter, Paivio and Carriere (chap. 6, this volume) use the notion of emotional processing and imaginal exposure to explain some of the process for dealing with anger. We support this view and suggest, however, that neither mere exposure nor exposure to new information is a complete way of understanding emotional processing. Rather, we have proposed that emotion is processed in a three-stage manner involving approach, utilization, and transformation (Greenberg, 2002; Greenberg & Watson, 2005; Pos, Greenberg, Korman, & Goldman, 2003). Stage 1 of this processing involves approach and mere exposure. This involves attending to emotional experience and activating, allowing, regulating, and tolerating being in live contact with emotions. Stage 2 involves integrating emotion and cognition by cognitively orienting to emotional experience as information. This involves active exploration, reflection on, and the making sense of emotion. Stage 3 involves transformation, which involves activating new emotions to change old emotions and the development of new narratives. This whole process includes exploring beliefs relating to experienced emotion, giving voice to emotional experience, and identifying needs that can motivate change in personal meanings and beliefs. If such exploration and reflection occurs, new emotional reactions and new meanings emerge, which then are integrated into and change existing affective-cognitive meaning structures. This involves more than habituation or mere exposure.

So, given the evidence on expression and inhibition, the question becomes when should we encourage our clients to express a behavior or actively think about an issue, and when should we encourage inhibition of such actions and thoughts? The evidence suggests that both too much and too little inhibition of anger can lead to psychological and physical health problems (Arbuthnott et al., 2006). Thus, therapists must be alert to both of these extremes, assisting clients to make informed decisions about when and where to inhibit, and developing plans to assist with inhibition of specific behaviors when clients are unable to self-regulate in this way.

Whether inhibition is problematic or beneficial to mental health thus depends on many factors: the type of inhibition (cognitive or behavior), what is being inhibited (a perceptual distractor or an emotion), individual characteristics (age and temperament), context (cultural mores, social situation), and individual choice (e.g., voluntary vs. habitual). Given this complexity, theories of the relation between inhibition and health must be specific and comprehensive, defining both the inhibitory target and the characteristics of the person and the situation before useful prescriptions about catharsis or containment can be given (Consedine et al., 2002).

In summary, containment (or distraction) and expression (or experience) are both useful under different circumstances (Arbuthnott et al., 2006). To change bad habits, to reduce our attention to unwanted thoughts and behaviors, or to deal with circumstances that are beyond our control, inhibition may be a valuable tool. Similarly, evidence seems to support the use of inhibition for the emotions of anger under some conditions. Expression of anger or grief can decrease well-being rather than increase it

(Bonanno & Kaltman, 1999; Bushman, 2002; Smith, 1992) unless very specific elements enable working through the emotion (Greenberg & Safran, 1987). However, for reasonable goals that are denied for social reasons (Krause et al., 2003), bringing such desires into awareness, expressing them in both emotional and decisional action, seems most useful. In this case, overcoming inhibition could enhance well-being.

An important part of many therapies is to enhance affect regulation (Greenberg, 2002), helping clients to both appropriately express and withhold emotion (a process often referred to as *self-regulation*). Psychotherapy is in large part the intricate dance and balance between inhibition and action in various aspects of human experience. Thus, we conclude that neither expression nor inhibition of anger, of its own accord, makes us better or worse. All therapies need to aid clients in developing and maintaining skills in the appropriate inhibition or expression of thoughts, emotions, and actions. Thus, clients who are relieved by disinhibiting their emotional expressiveness may not be a good match for a strictly cognitive behavioral approach, and clients who become ruminative and distressed after experiencing deep emotion may not be a good match for expressive therapies. This illustrates the need to get feedback concerning the effects of techniques with each client and for therapists to be able to shift approaches when the feedback dictates a need to do so.

CONCLUSION

Our major reaction to the preceding chapters, thus, is that if the field of anger treatment is to progress we now need to begin to form a far more differentiated classification system for studying and treating anger. What is needed, then, is (a) clearer understanding and definitions of the experience, expression, and consequences of anger, and (b) a process-oriented view of anger treatment that takes into account meaning, context, and sequences of emotional experiences in psychotherapy.

To understand anger as a complex phenomenon, we would suggest that the following factors be considered. First, at what is the anger directed? For example, is it anger within the self, essentially toward the self, anger toward others (in the past vs. in the present), or anger directed toward the therapist (e.g., in an alliance rupture). How is the experience of anger being dealt with in regard to emotion regulation? Is it assertive or rejecting anger, empowering or destructive? Is the anger overcontrolled and suppressed or is it expressed in an uncontrolled, destructive way such as in anger outbursts or anger attacks? Is the anger fused with other emotions and not clearly felt and expressed, as in complaints that fuse anger with sadness? Is the anger so fuzzy that it can be felt only as a more general feeling of inner tension? How can anger be understood in terms of the process of experiencing within psychotherapy? Is the anger primary, secondary, or instrumental? Is it productive expression (Greenberg & Watson, 2005)? That is, is it experienced in the present; is it a fresh new experienced anger rather than a repetitive experience of anger; is the person not stuck in it but rather is processing it further; is it related to the person's need in the situation and therefore functionally adaptive; is it not overwhelming and is the intensity appropriate to the situation; is it pure or clear, rather than mixed with other emotions; and is it meaningful, acknowledged, and owned? Or is anger unproductive, in which case it would not satisfy the aforementioned criteria and would be repetitive, not functional in meeting needs, overwhelming, fuzzy, not clearly acknowledged, or not meaningful? An additional factor to be considered would be how the anger is related to clients' personalities with regard to anger proneness and trait anger.

As with many things in life, wherever one goes poets or writers have been there before. Thus, Rohinton Mistry (2003) in *Family Matters* catches some of the nuances in anger when he writes, "He thought about his father's anger—not the flash that would blaze now and again, like thunder and lightening, then clear, and bring back a smile like sunshine. This dull rage, constant over days, was different. The last weeks puzzled him. It was quarrels and sarcastic comments all the time" (p. 184). In addition, Goleman (1995), who draws on Aristotle to note that it is easy to express anger, but that it takes intelligence to express it at the right time, in the right way, to the right person, has highlighted that emotional intelligence requires a differentiated view and use of anger. Authors and philosophers alike have long recognized the varieties of anger experience and their differential impact. We as psychologists and psychotherapists need to do the same.

REFERENCES

Afifi, W. A., & Guerrero, L. K. (2000). Motivations underlying topic avoidance in close relationships. In S. Petronio (Ed.), *Balancing the secrets of private disclosures* (pp. 165–179). Mahwah, NJ: Lawrence Erlbaum Associates.

Arbuthnott K., Arbuthnott D & Thompson, V(2006). *The mind in therapy: Cognitive science in practice.* Mahwah New Jersey, Lawrence Erlbaum Associates.

Averill, J.R. (1982). *Anger and aggression: An essay on emotion.* New York: Springer.

Bannon, S., Gonsalvez, C. J., Croft, R. J., & Boyce, P. M. (2002). Response inhibition deficits in obsessive-compulsive disorder. *Psychiatry Research, 110,* 165–174.

Barkley, R. A. (1997). Behavioral inhibition, sustained attention, and executive functions: Constructing a unifying theory of ADHD. *Psychological Bulletin, 121,* 65–94.

Biaggio, M. K., & Godwin, W. H. (1987). Relation of depression to anger and hostility constructs. *Psychological Reports, 61*, 87–90.

Bischkopf, J., Stiglmayr, C., Scheuer, S., Albrecht, V., Porzig, N. & Auckenthaler, A. (2006). Combining qualitative and quantitative research strategies for analysing the experience of aversive tension in different patient groups. In P. Mayring G. L. Huber, L. Gurtler, & M. Kiegelmann (Eds.), *Mixed methodology in psychological research*. Rotterdam:

Bonanno, G. A., & Kaltman, S. (1999). Toward an integrative perspective on bereavement. *Psychological Bulletin, 125*, 760–776.

Brody, C. L., Haag, D. A. F., Kirk, L., & Solomon, A. (1999). Experiences of anger in people who have recovered from depression and never-depressed people. *Journal of Nervous and Mental Disease, 187*, 400–405.

Brown, D., Scheflin, A. W., & Hammond, D. C. (1998). *Memory, trauma treatment, and the law*. New York: Norton.

Buck, R. (1984). *The communication of emotion*. New York: Guilford.

Buck, R. (1993). Emotional communication, emotional competence, and physical illness: A developmental-interactionist view. In H. C. Traue & J. W. Pennebaker (Eds.), *Emotion inhibition and health* (pp. 32–56). Seattle, WA: Hogrefe & Huber.

Bushman, B. J. (2002). Does venting anger feed or extinguish the flame? Catharsis, rumination, distraction, anger, and aggressive responding. *Personality and Social Psychology Bulletin, 28*, 724–731.

Chow, S., Ram, N., Boka, S. M., Fujita, F., & Clore, G. (2005). Emotion as a thermostat: Representing emotion regulation using a damped oscillator model. *Emotion, 2*, 208–225.

Consedine, N. S., Magai, C., & Bonanno, G. A. (2002). Moderators of the emotion inhibition–health relationship: A review and research agenda. *Review of General Psychology, 6*, 204–228.

Davey, A., Dey, L., & Howells, K. (2005). Anger, over-control and serious violent offending. *Aggression and Violent Behavior, 10*, 624–635.

Derryberry, D., & Rothbart, M. K. (1997). Reactive and effortful processes in the organization of temperament. *Development and Psychopathology, 9*, 633–652.

Eckhardt, C., Norlander, B., & Deffenbacher, J. (2004). The assessment of anger and hostility: a critical review. *Aggression and Violent Behavior, 9*, 17–43.

Ecton, R. B., & Feindler, E. L. (1990). Anger control training for temper control disorders. In E. L. Feindler & G. R. Kalfur (Eds.), *Adolescent behavior therapy handbook* (pp. 351–371). New York: Springer.

Engebretson, T. O., Matthews, K. A., & Scheier, M. F. (1989). Relations between anger expression and cardiovascular reactivity: Reconciling inconsistent findings through a matching hypothesis. *Journal of Personality and Social Psychology, 57*, 513–521.

Fava, M., Anderson, K., & Rosenbaum, J. F. (1990). "Anger attacks": Possible variants of panic and major depressive disorders. *American Journal of Psychiatry, 147*, 867–870.

Freud, S. (1957). The unconscious. In J. Strachey (Ed. & Trans.), *The standard edition of the complete psychological works of Sigmund Freud* (Vol. 14, pp. 159–215). London: Hogarth Press. (Original work published 1915)

Friedman, H. S., & Booth-Kewley, S. (1987). The "disease-prone personality": A meta-analytic view of the construct. *American Psychologist, 42*, 539–555.

Frijda, N. H. (1986). *The emotions*. Cambridge, England: Cambridge University Press.

Gilbert, P., Gilbert, J., & Irons, C. (2004). Life events, entrapments and arrested anger in depression. *Journal of affective disorders, 79*, 149–160.

Goleman, D. (1995). *Emotional intelligence*. New York: Bantam.

Greenberg, L. (2002). *Emotion-focused therapy: Coaching clients to work through feelings*. Washington, DC: American Psychological Association.

Greenberg, L. (in press). A guide to conducting a task analysis of psychotherapeutic change. *Psychotherapy Research*.

Greenberg, L. S., & Paivio, S. C. (1997). *Working with emotions in psychotherapy*. New York: Guilford.

Greenberg, L. S., Rice, L. N., & Elliott, R. (1993). *Facilitating emotional change: The moment-by-moment process*. New York: Guilford.

Greenberg, L. S., & Safran, J. D. (1987). *Emotion in psychotherapy: Affect, cognition, and the process of change*. New York: Guilford.

Greenberg, L., & Watson, J. (2005). *Emotion-focused therapy of depression*. Washington, DC: American Psychological Association.

Gross, J. J. (1998). The emerging field of emotion regulation: An integrative review. *Review of General Psychology, 2*, 271–299.

Harmon-Jones, E., Lueck, L., Fearn, M., & Harmon-Jones, C. (2005). *The effect of personal relevance and approach-related action expectation on relative left frontal cortical activity*. Manuscript under review.

Hull, L., Farrin, L., Unwin, C., Everitt, B., Wykes, T., & David, A. S. (2003). Anger, psychopathology, and cognitive inhibition: A study of UK servicemen. *Personality and Individual Differences, 35*, 1211–1226.

Jenkins, J. M., Smith, M. A., & Graham, P. (1989). Coping with parental quarrels. *Journal of the American Academy of Child and Adolescent Psychiatry, 28*, 182–189.

Johnson-Laird, P. N., & Oatley, K. (1992). Basic emotions, rationality and folk theory. *Cognition and Emotion, 6*, 201–223.

Kahn, S., & Greenberg, L. (1980). Beyond a cognitive-behavioral approach: Congruent assertion training. In C. S. Adamec (Ed.), *Sex-roles: Origins, influences and implications for women* (pp. 124–135). Montreal, Canada: Eden Press.

Kennedy-Moore, E., & Watson, J. C. (1999). *Expressing emotion: Myths, realties and therapeutic strategies*. New York: Guilford.

King, L. A., & Emmonds, R. A. (1990). Conflict over emotional expression: Psychological and physical correlates. *Journal of Personality and Social Psychology, 58*, 864–877.

Krause, E. D., Mendelson, T., & Lynch, T. R. (2003). Childhood emotional invalidation and adult psychological distress: The mediating role of emotional inhibition. *Child Abuse and Neglect, 27*, 199–213.

Larsen, R. J., & Prizmic, Z. (2004). Affect regulation. In R. F. Baumeister & K. D. Vohs (Eds.), *Handbook of self-regulation: Research, theory, and applications* (pp. 40–61). New York: Guilford.

Linden, W., Hogan, B. W., Rutledge, T., Chawla, A., Lenz, J. W., & Leung, D. (2003). There is more to anger coping than "in" or "out." *Emotion, 3*, 12–29.

Mayne, T. J. (1999). Negative affect and health: The importance of being earnest. *Cognition and Emotion, 13*, 601–635.

Meyer, C., Leung, N., Waller, G., Perkins, S., Paice, N., & Mitchell, J. (2005). Anger and bulimic psychopathology: Gender differences in a nonclinical group. *International Journal of Eating Disorders, 37,* 69–71.

Mistry, R. (2003). *Family matters* (Emblem editions). Toronto: McClelland & Stewart.

Mudge, S. D. (2004). Validation of the Emogram Anger Scale and the State-Trait Anger Expression Inventory–2 (STAXI–2): A correlational study. *Dissertation Abstracts International Section A: Humanities and Social Sciences, 65, 77.*

Oatley, K. (1993). Those to whom evil is done. In R. S. Wyer & T. K. Srull (Eds.), *Perspectives on anger and emotion* (pp. 159–165). Hillsdale, NJ: Lawrence Erlbaum Associates.

Oatley, K. (1996). Emotions: Communications to the self and others. In R. Harré & W. G. Parrot (Eds.), *The emotions: social, cultural and biological dimensions* (pp. 312–316.). London: Sage.

Oatley, K., & Larocque, L. (1995). Every-day concepts of emotions following every-other-day errors in joint plans. In J. A. Russel, J.-M. Fernandez-Dols, A. S. R. Manstead, & J. Wellenkamp (Eds.), *Everyday conceptions of emotions: An introduction to the psychology, anthropology, and linguistics of emotion (NATO ASI Series D 81).* (pp. 145–65). Dordrecht, Netherlands: Kluwer.

Pennebaker, J. W. (1997). Writing about emotional experiences as a therapeutic process. *Psychological Science, 8,* 162–166.

Pennebaker, J. W. (1998). Conflict and canned meat. *Psychological Inquiry, 9,* 219–220.

Perls, F., Hefferline, R. F. & Goodman, P. (1951). *Gestalt therapy.* New York: Dell.

Pos, A. E., Greenberg, L. S., Korman, L. M., & Goldman, R. N. (2003). Emotional processing during experiential treatment of depression. *Journal of Consulting and Clinical Psychology, 71*(6), 1007–1016.

Roffman, A. E. (2004). Is anger a thing-to-be-managed? *Psychotherapy: Theory, Research, Practice, Training, 41,* 161–171.

Rogers, C. R. (1942). *Counseling and psychotherapy.* Boston: Houghton Mifflin.

Roloff, M. E., & Ifert, D. E. (2000). Conflict management through avoidance: Withholding complaints, suppressing arguments, and declaring topics taboo. In S. Petronio (Ed.), *Balancing the secrets of private disclosures* (pp. 151–163). Mahwah, NJ: Lawrence Erlbaum Associates.

Russell, J. A., & Fehr, B. (1997). Fuzzy concepts in a fuzzy hierarchy: Varieties of anger. *Journal of Personality and Social Psychology, 67,* 186–205.

Smith, T. W. (1992). Hostility and health: Current status of a psychosomatic hypothesis. *Health Psychology, 11,* 139–150.

Smyth, J. M. (1998). Written emotional expression: Effect sizes, outcome types, and moderating variables. *Journal of Consulting and Clinical Psychology, 66,* 174–184.

Snell, W. E., Jr., Gum, S., Shuck, R. L., Mosley, J. A., & Hite, T. L. (1995). The Clinical Anger Scale: Preliminary reliability and validity. *Journal of Clinical Psychology, 51,* 215–226.

Stiglmayr, C. E., Grathwol, T., Linehan, M. M., Ihorst, G., Fahrenberg, J., & Bohus, M. (2005). Aversive tension in patients with borderline personality disorder:

A computer-based controlled field study. *Acta Psychiatrica Scandinavica, 111,* 372–379.

Tangney, J. P., Wagner, P. E., Barlow, D. H., Marschall, D. E., & Gramzow, R. (1996) Relation of shame and guilt to constructive versus destructive responses to anger across the lifespan. *Journal of Personality and Social Psychology, 70,* 797–809.

Tiedens, L. Z. (2001). Anger and advancement versus sadness and subjugation: The effect of negative emotion expressions on social status conferral. *Journal of Personality and Social Psychology, 80,* 86–94.

Williams, J. M. G. (1995). Depression and the specificity of autobiographical memories. In D. C. Rubin (Ed.), *Remembering our past: Studies in autobiographical memory* (pp. 244–270). Cambridge, England: Cambridge University Press.

III

THE ANGER–AGGRESSION RELATION IN VIOLENT CHILDREN AND ADOLESCENTS

The Roles of Anger, Conflict With Parents and Peers, and Social Reinforcement in the Early Development of Physical Aggression

James Snyder, Lynn Schrepferman, Monica Brooker,
and Mike Stoolmiller

Physical aggression and violence is a serious and prevalent health problem that engenders substantial personal and social costs (U.S. Department of Health and Human Services, 2001). Though considerable empirical effort has been made to understand the causes of aggression and to intervene to reduce its occurrence, it continues to be a major health issue. This chapter examines the origins of physical aggression and violence from a developmental perspective. It focuses on how anger regulation and social contingencies in parent–child and peer interaction contribute to early development of aggression, and how individual differences in children's attention deployment and impulsivity moderate these social processes. The implications of the findings are discussed in terms of early preventive interventions designed to reduce physical aggression.

Early Developmental Trajectories for Physical Aggression

Physical aggression normatively appears as part of early neuromotor maturation, and serves as one behavioral instrument by which young children can fulfill basic needs (Shaw, Owens, Giovannelli, & Winslow, 2001; Tremblay, 2003). Given the relative lack of more sophisticated self-regulatory and verbal abilities, the frequency of physical aggression normatively increases to ages 3 to 4 years. The frequency of aggression subsequently declines during childhood and adolescence as socialization efforts are effective and more constructive means of relating to other people are developed (Cairns & Cairns, 1994; Nagin & Tremblay, 1999). These normative trajectories suggest that individuals learn to inhibit physical aggression rather than learn how to aggress (Tremblay, 2003).

Three important variations are hidden in this normative picture. First, consistent group-average gender differences in the frequency of physical aggression become apparent around ages 3 to 4 years and persist throughout subsequent childhood, adolescence, and adulthood (Maccoby, 1998). Understanding the origins of these gender differences may usefully inform developmental models and interventions focusing on physical aggression.

Second, there are substantial individual differences in the developmental timing for the inhibition of aggression. For approximately 5% to 10% of all individuals, reductions in the frequency of physical aggression are substantially delayed until later childhood and adolescence (Broidy et al., 2003). In fact, chronically violent adolescents and young adults typically display high rates of aggression from an early age (Brame, Nagin, & Tremblay, 2001). Delays in the inhibition of aggression beyond ages 6 to 7 years powerfully increment risk for aggression and violence as well as other forms of antisocial behavior during adolescence—at least for boys (Broidy et al., 2003). Interventions to reduce physical aggression during early childhood provide an opportunity to reduce the incidence and prevalence of violence, but the efficacy of these interventions depends on a clear understanding of malleable risk factors operating at this point in development.

Third, although rates of physical aggression decline with age, the damage resulting from physical aggression increases as individuals become physically larger and stronger. Major social concerns about violence focus on adolescents and adults (U.S. Department of Health and Human Services, 2001) rather than on younger children, although it is clear that physical aggression and victimization are serious problems during childhood as well (Snyder, Schrepferman, Brooker, & Stoolmiller, 2003). The promise of a developmental approach is the creation of interventions to reduce physical aggression during early childhood before it becomes developmentally persistent and evolves to more assaultive and lethal dimensions in adolescence and adulthood.

A Social Learning Perspective on the Development of Physical Aggression

From a social learning perspective, socialization occurs in the cumulative, day-to-day interactions of children with their parents, siblings, peers, and teachers (Snyder, Reid, & Patterson, 2003). Two social processes operating in these interactions are particularly important to the inhibition of physical aggression and to the acquisition of more constructive social and instrumental skills: anger regulation and social reinforcement contingencies. Though both of these processes have received considerable theoretical and empirical attention, they have seldom been simultaneously explored as complementary social processes in relation to the early development of physical aggression.

Anger prepares individuals to attain goals or to respond to frustration and challenge by instigating sustained, energetic (and if needed, forceful) behavioral approach. During social interaction, anger may instigate coercive verbal and physical behavior (Snyder, Schrepferman, & St. Peter, 1997). This may particularly be the case when anger becomes dysregulated, floods effortful cognitive processing, and instigates the use of over learned coercive responses (Gottman, Fainsilber-Katz, & Hooven, 1997). Anger display by one person may also evoke reciprocal anger display by another, or anger contagion (Hatfield, Cacioppo, & Rapson, 1994). Given its instigative and contagion functions, the repeated experience and expression of anger by parties to social interaction may extend the duration of coercive exchange and escalate the amplitude of coercive behavior to physical aggression.

Disagreement, frustration, and conflict are part and parcel of residing in a social world (Shantz, 1994), and can be a source for the acquisition of constructive conflict resolution and social problem-solving tactics as well as for coercive behavior. Coercive behaviors are powerful social instruments and are displayed frequently insofar as they are maintained by short-term reinforcement contingencies that "pay off" better than socially skilled alternatives (Patterson, 1982; Patterson & Reid, 1970; Snyder & Patterson, 1995). Coercive behaviors are maintained by their functional value in attaining access to desired activities, materials, and social attention (positive reinforcement; Patterson, Littman, & Bricker, 1967), and in responding to social demands and disputes without capitulation (negative reinforcement; Snyder & Patterson, 1995).

Physical aggression typically occurs during extended social conflicts in which mild-intensity coercive acts (e.g., commands, noncompliance, and criticism) by one person are met with countercoercion by another (Patterson, 1982; Stoolmiller, 1992). As a coercive dyadic exchange extends over time, there is an escalation in the intensity of coercive tactics to include physical aggression (Reid, 1986; Snyder, Edwards, McGraw, Kilgore, & Holton, 1994). Escalation may be fueled by the experience and display of anger (Snyder, Stoolmiller, Wilson, & Yamamoto, 2003) by either or both parties involved in the conflict. Escalation may also be shaped by social contingencies. Increasingly harsh tactics used in an attempt to "win" a conflict may become increasingly preferred over time as they become routinely associated with the termination of conflict (Snyder et al., 1994).

This formulation suggests that failures to inhibit physical aggression during early childhood may result from children's repeated involvement in and exposure to extended and escalating coercive exchanges with parents and peers. If this formulation is supported by data, the prevention of serious physical aggression would entail fostering family and peer social environments that promote emotion regulation, provide contingencies supporting skillful social behavior, and reduce involvement in extended coercive social exchanges.

Child Characteristics and Trajectories for Physical Aggression

Social learning theory relies heavily on observable social interaction in family and peer settings to ascertain the proximal social processes that evoke, shape, maintain, and elaborate aggressive behavior. However, children bring a set of individual characteristics to these social exchanges that reflect prior learning history, genetic and maturational influences, and biological capacities. A variety of child characteristics have been offered as factors associated with risk for physical aggression (Coie & Dodge, 1998). One child characteristic that appears to be strongly linked to such risk is inattention-impulsivity (Moffitt, Caspi, Rutter, & Silva, 2001).

Children's ability to inhibit overlearned, prepotent responses supported by short-term reinforcement contingencies entails a set of executive functions mediated by the midline prefrontal cortex (Barkley, 1997; Nigg, 2000). Inhibition is critical to children's ability to deploy attention and to regulate emotional arousal in service of longer-term goals (Davidson, Jackson, & Kalin, 2000). Maturation of these executive functions precedes and may contribute substantially to the normative inhibition of physical aggression during the preschool years, although the sophistication of this functional system is itself sensitive to social-environmental experiences (Posner & Rothbart, 2000). Individual differences in inhibition may influence a child's capacity to respond in controlled and constructive ways to the recurring social disputes, challenges, and frustrations that are encountered during family and peer interaction in early childhood. Children with diminished capacity to inhibit responding and to deploy attention are likely to display more frequent and persistent aggressive behavior during early childhood.

Origins of Gender Differences in Physical Aggression

Gender differences in physical aggression have multiple determinants (Maccoby, 1998). The variables that may account for individual differences in physical aggression described in the previous two sections may also account for average gender differences in physical aggression (Moffitt et al., 2001). Developmental research indicates that boys relative to girls evidence slower average rates of maturation of executive functions mediating behavioral inhibition, emotion regulation, and the deployment of attention. Boys relative to girls are also slower to develop language skills during the toddler and preschool years. As a consequence, boys may be less equipped on average to inhibit physical aggression and to engage in more constructive modes of dealing with conflict (Keenan & Shaw, 1997).

Gender differences in physical aggression may also be shaped by social experiences in family and peer settings, including emotion arousal and regulation, involvement in coercive exchange, and the social consequences that accrue to coercive behavior. Previous research suggests the impact of family socialization on gender differences in physical aggression is modest. Boys relative to girls are more frequently involved in conflict with their parents, a difference that is especially pronounced for highly aggressive boys and girls (McFayden-Ketchum, Bates, Dodge, & Pettit, 1996). The contribution of coercive parent–child exchanges to the development of aggression may be amplified for boys as a result of delays in the maturation of their executive functions and verbal skills (Martin, 1981).

Research suggests that social experiences with peers during early childhood contribute more substantially to gender differences in physical aggression. During this period, children typically play in same-gender peer groups, and the social ecologies of boys' and girls' groups are quite different. Boys play in large groups and their interaction is characterized by rough play, verbal challenge, competition, and jockeying for dominance. Girls' interaction is more often dyadic, and is characterized by cooperation, verbal exchange, and mutual accommodation and perspective taking as a means of resolving conflict (Maccoby, 1998). Given these differences in peer ecologies, interaction among boys relative to girls is more likely to entail frequent displays of anger, involvement in more frequent and extended conflicts, and experience of peer contingencies that promote aggressive behavior. Boys and girls may evidence a different sensitivity to these risk-inducing peer processes given the same degree of exposure (Moffitt et al., 2001); boys' less sophisticated executive functions and verbal skills may exacerbate the impact of involvement in coercive peer interaction on physical aggression.

The Relative Role of Parents and Peers in the Development of Physical Aggression

Parents and peers play important but complementary roles in socialization. Parents provide early socialization experiences to promote children's emotion regulation, verbal control over behavior, and the ability to inhibit prepotent responses including physical aggression (Denham et al., 2000; Grusec, 2002). Skilled parents provide emotion coaching and social contingencies that help children learn how to constructively manage conflict (Snyder, Reid, & Patterson, 2003). In the relative absence of effective parenting, frequent and extended parent–child and sibling conflict is more likely to occur, to be infused with anger, and to shape and maintain a child's repertoire of coercive behavior. This coercive repertoire is carried over to the peer environment at the transition to child care or school.

Because young children's self-regulatory skills are still evolving, peer interaction in preschool and early elementary school is characterized by frequent disagreement, dispute, and conflict (Rudolph & Asher, 2000). In the relative absence of immediate adult supervision, the occurrence, duration, escalation, and resolution of conflict is powerfully determined by children's capacity for emotional and behavioral self-regulation and by natural peer contingencies. For children whose socialization in the family results in deficient verbal skills, reduced ability to inhibit prepotent responses, impaired capacity for emotion regulation, and deficits in social skills, the peer environment may powerfully facilitate the display of physical aggression (Snyder, Stoolmiller et al., 2003).

In summary, both parents and peers may contribute to delay and failure in the inhibition of aggression, but do so in different ways. Parents' contribution to children's persistent and frequent use of physical aggression during the preschool and early elementary school years may be indirect, mediated through children's difficulties in coping with the challenging peer environment. Given the nature of the early peer ecology, peer interaction may provide a more powerful, proximal, and direct training ground for the maintenance and shaping of physical aggression. However, prior socialization failures in the family may be a prerequisite to these peer effects. Finally, children with deficiencies in the executive functions needed to inhibit coercive behavior in family and peer environments may be at increased risk for frequent displays of physical aggression.

METHOD AND MEASURES

Data relevant to the proposed model of physical aggression were collected from 133 girls and 134 boys. Data collection was initiated when children were an average of 5.3 years of age (entry to kindergarten) and terminated at mean age of 9.2 years (third- to fourth-grade transition). A community sample was obtained by using a recruiting strategy targeting all kindergarten children ($N = 352$, participation rate = 76%) who enrolled in one elementary school during each of 3 consecutive years.

Twenty-nine percent of the children were minorities. At initial recruitment, 43% of children lived in intact households (two-biological parent), 28% in single- parent households(predominantly mother), 21% in blended households, and 7% in other family configurations. The median *per capita* family income per year was $8,300; 28% of the children lived in families with incomes below the poverty line. Forty-six percent of the parents had completed their high school education, 34% had education beyond high school, and 20% had less than a high school education.

Parent–child interaction was videotaped for 2 hours on each of two occasions during the children's kindergarten year. On each occasion, the parent and child engaged in a series of tasks, including learning to play a new game, problem solving, completing letter and number recognition drills, having a snack, and free play. All 4 hours of interaction were coded using the Family and Peer Process Code (FPPC; Crosby, Stubbs, Forgatch, & Capaldi, 1998) to ascertain the rates at which children and parents directed coercive behaviors toward one another. These behaviors range in severity from minor (e.g., commands, criticism, and noncompliance) to highly coercive (e.g., threats, demeaning name-calling, hitting) behaviors. The FPPC was also used to estimate the proportion of occasions on which parents negatively reinforced their children's coercive behavior during conflict episodes by capitulating to that behavior (see Snyder & Patterson, 1995, for more detail).

The first hour of the videotaped record from each of the two occasions was also coded by a second, independent set of coders using the Specific Affect Coding system (SPAFF; Gottman, McCoy, Coan, & Collier, 1996) to ascertain the rates at which parents and children displayed anger (summary of code categories for anger, contempt, and disgust) during their interaction. Cross-occasion mean rates per minute of parent and child coercive behavior from the FPPC and anger displays from the SPAFF were used as measured variables in the analyses.

One half hour of interaction of each child with two same-gender classmates (selected in semirandom fashion) was videotaped on three separate occasions during the kindergarten year. On each occasion, children spent 15 minutes playing a competitive game and 15 minutes in free play. Videotaped behavioral streams were coded using the FPPC and SPAFF and used to define measured variables of rates per minute of anger and of coercive behavior by the child and by peers in a manner similar to that described for parent–child interaction. Peers' reactions to children's talk about and modeling of aggression during play were coded either as approval/endorsement or as neutral/disapproving. The mean proportion of peer approval/endorsement across occasions provided a measured variable of peers' positive reinforcement of coercive behavior (Snyder, Stoolmiller et al., 2004).

Child impulsivity-inattention was assessed during the kindergarten year using multiple methods and informants: the mean of four scores (after each was transformed to a standard score) from two tests administered individually to children at school (Trail Making B, time and errors; Wechsler Intelligence Scale for Children–III [WISC–III], digits forward and backward); the mean of three separate classroom observations of children's academic engaged time (AET) as specified by percentage of time on task during periods of academic work; and ratings on two items (was inattentive, needed frequent redirection) made by assessors on each of three occasions of individual child assessment. The mean of these summary scores after their standardization was used to define a measured variable of impulsivity-inattention (Snyder, Prichard, Schrepferman, Patrick, & Stoolmiller, 2004).

Children's display of physical aggression was assessed at each of four developmental points, in the fall and spring of kindergarten and first grade, using rate per minute of observed physical aggression toward peers on the school playground (obtained on four to six occasions at each developmental point; Snyder, Schrepferman et al., 2003). Teacher ratings of child aggressive behavior (e.g., bullying, fights, physically attacks, threatens) were also obtained in the fall and spring of kindergarten and first grade. Finally, child self-report, parent-report, and teacher-report of children's overt and covert conduct problems were obtained in spring of third or fall of fourth grade.

RESULTS

The results are presented in several sections, each of which serves as a building block for a test of a final comprehensive model shown in Figure 8.3, which is discussed and displayed later in the chapter. Descriptive data relevant to the proposed social learning model are also provided.

Observed Family and Peer Processes, and Child Physical Aggression

Family and peer settings are two primary contexts for young children's socialization. However, children's experiences and behavior with their parents and with their peers are substantially different. The range of experiences encountered by children and the types of behaviors children display are also likely to be different for boys and girls. Rates per minute of anger displays, involvement in coercive social exchange, and social reinforcement contingencies encountered in family and peer interaction are shown separately by child gender in the top of Table 8.1. Anger during parent–child interaction was relatively infrequent; parents and children

TABLE 8.1
Setting and Gender Differences in Family and Peer Processes, and Child
Characteristics

Measure	Boys' Mean	Girls' Mean	Difference p <	
Parent–Child Interaction				
rpm anger by child	.11 (.15)	.10 (.15)	n.s.	
rpm anger by parent	.08 (.21)	.07 (.16)	n.s.	
rpm coercive by child	.63 (.23)	.58 (.28)	n.s.	
low-intensity	.61 (.22)	.58 (.25)	n.s.	
high-intensity	.02 (.02)	.01 (.01)	.10	B > G
rpm coercive by parent	1.52 (.56)	1.32 (.45)	.01	B > G
low-intensity	1.50 (.55)	1.31 (.45)	.01	B > G
high-intensity	.02 (.05)	.01 (.01)	.20	B > G
% parent negative reinforcement of child aversive behavior	47 (.21)	46 (23)	n.s.	
Peer–Child Interaction				
rpm anger by child	.59 (.22)	.42 (.24)	.01	B > G
rpm anger by peers	.48 (.27)	.32 (.22)	.01	B > G
rpm coercive by child	1.30 (.69)	1.01 (.48)	.001	B > G
low-intensity	1.11 (.56)	.94 (.44)	.01	B > G
high-intensity	.19 (.24)	.07 (.08)	.001	B > G
rpm coercive by peers	.87 (.26)	.68 (.24)	.001	B > G
low-intensity	.79 (.22)	.64 (.23)	.001	B > G
high-intensity	.09 (.10)	.04 (.04)	.001	B > G
% peer reinforcement of child aggressive behavior	38 (17)	36 (19)	n.s.	
Child Characteristics				
Impulsivity-Inattention[a]	5.14 (1.02)	4.85 (.98)	.05	B > G

Note: Standard deviations are shown in parentheses.
[a]Sum of multiple standardized measures.

displayed anger about once every 10 minutes. Rates of coercive behavior were more substantial, displayed about once every 2 minutes by children and between one and two times per minute by parents. Most coercive behavior during parent–child interaction was of low intensity (irritable "nattering") and only about 1% of children's and parents' coercive behavior escalated to more intense forms (i.e., threats, demands, and hitting). Rates of high-intensity coercive behavior by parents ($r = .28$, $p < .01$) and by children ($r = .38, p < .01$) were reliably correlated with rates of their own anger displays, but rates of low-intensity coercive behavior were unrelated to rates of anger display. This suggests that anger may contribute to escalation in parent–child conflict.

There were no significant differences in rates of parent and child anger displays or in child displays of low-intensity coercive behavior according to child gender. Parents directed more coercive behavior toward sons than daughters, especially low-intensity nattering ($t = 2.74, p < .01$). Boys tended to display high-intensity coercive behavior at higher frequencies than girls ($t = 1.85, p < .10$). On the average, parents' negatively reinforced (capitulated to) child coercive behavior about half of the time, with no reliable gender differences.

As shown in the bottom portion of Table 8.1, rates of children's display of anger during peer interaction were substantial, occurring once every 2 to 3 minutes. This represents an approximate fourfold increase over rates of anger observed in parent–child interaction. Child coercive behavior during peer interaction was displayed at approximately twice the rate of child coercive behavior in parent–child interaction, occurring about once every minute. Moreover, the proportion of high-intensity coercive behaviors (from 4% to 19%) during peer interaction was about five times that observed in parent–child interaction. Rates of children's anger displays were reliably correlated with rates at which they engaged in low-($r = .37, p < .01$) and high-($r = .39, p < .01$) intensity coercive behavior, and with rates at which their peers engaged in high-($r = .25, p < .05$) but not low-($r = .01$) intensity coercive behavior. Thirty-five to 40% of the occasions of children's talk and modeling of aggressive behavior during play resulted in peer approval.

Consistent gender differences in anger and coercive behavior were observed during peer interaction. Boys were more likely to display ($t = 2.37, p < .01$) and to be the targets of peer anger ($t = 2.05, p < .05$). Boys relative to girls were more likely to engage in and be the targets of coercive behavior, of both lower ($t = 2.74, p < .01; t = 4.78, p < .001$, respectively) and higher ($t = 5.20, p < .001; t = 5.94, p < .001$, respectively) intensity. Peer interaction, relative to parent–child interaction, appears to be powerfully imbued with anger and coercive exchange, and anger appears to fuel both lower and higher intensity coercive behaviors during peer interaction. Finally, as shown in the last line in Table 8.1, boys evidenced higher levels of impulsivity-inattention than girls.

Gender Differences and Growth of Physical Aggression During Early Childhood

Table 8.2 provides means and standard deviations for observed rates of physical aggression on the school playground and for teacher ratings of

TABLE 8.2
Gender Differences in Child Physical Aggression

Measure	Boys' Mean	Girls' Mean	Difference	p <
Observed Rate Per Minute on the Playground				
Fall kindergarten	.40 (.41)	.17 (.22)	.001	B > G
Spring kindergarten	.43 (.38)	.20 (.21)	.001	B > G
Fall first grade	.37 (.33)	.18 (.26)	.001	B > G
Spring first grade	.44 (.47)	.18 (.34)	.001	B > G
Teacher-Ratings[a]				
Fall kindergarten	.21 (.37)	.07 (.22)	.001	B > G
Spring kindergarten	.30 (.44)	.12 (.26)	.001	B > G
Fall first grade	.23 (.40)	.17 (.29)	.200	
Spring first grade	.27 (.44)	.20 (.42)	.150	

Note. Standard deviations are shown in parentheses.
[a]Represented as item means and standard deviations.

physical aggression in the fall and spring of kindergarten and first grade. Boys were observed to engage in higher rates of playground physical aggression than girls by a factor of two to three at each of the four measurement points. Boys relative to girls were rated by teachers as more physically aggressive in the fall and spring of kindergarten, but these gender differences were no longer apparent in first grade. At each developmental point for observed and teacher-rated physical aggression, boys evidenced larger variance in physical aggression than girls (F tests for equality of variances > 4.5, $p < .05$).

Aggregate scores were calculated at each developmental point from the observed rate per minute of aggressive behavior on the playground and from teacher ratings. This aggregation entailed the following steps. Scores for each of the measures in fall kindergarten were rescaled to have equivalent means and standard deviations and then summed so that each measure contributed equally to the aggregate score for initial levels of aggression (intercept in the growth model). The rescaling algorithm used in fall kindergarten was applied to each of the measures in the spring of kindergarten and in the fall and spring of first grade in order to weight the scores relative to the scaling used in fall kindergarten. These weighted, rescaled scores were summed to create a single score for each child in spring of kindergarten and in the fall and spring of first grade.

The fit of data to a growth model of physical aggression was good: $X^2_{(9,267)} = 21.90$, $p = .039$, TLI = .994, root mean square error of approximation

[RMSEA] = .056. The means (2.57 and 2.10, respectively) and the variances (.34 and .19, respectively) for fall kindergarten physical aggression were significantly different from 0 for both boys and girls (all Critical Ratio or CRs > 4.50). The mean slope for neither boys (–.002) nor girls (.005) was significant, indicating no group-average changes in physical aggression across the kindergarten and first-grade years. The variance of the slope for physical aggression was significant for boys (variance = .04, CR = 3.15) and for girls (.05, CR = 5.88), indicating reliable individual differences in the change in physical aggression during kindergarten and first grade. Boys relative to girls evidenced higher levels and more between-individual variability in physical aggression in fall kindergarten, but there were no significant gender differences in the slope parameters.

This growth model for physical aggression was also prospectively associated with a multiinformant (teacher, parent, and child) construct for overt and covert conduct problems at ages 9 to 10 years: $X^2_{(82, 267)} = 126.61$, $p = .001$, TLI = .981, RMSEA = .045. Specifically, fall kindergarten rates of physical aggression by girls (intercept) but not change over time (slope) reliably predicted the conduct problems construct ($b = .77$, CR = 3.79) at ages 9-10 years. Fall rates of aggression ($b = .65$, CR = 4.35) and change in aggression over time (slope; $b = .44$, CR = 2.12) by boys reliably predicted the conduct problems construct at ages 9 to 10 years.

Anger, Reinforcement, and Coercion Training in Parent–Child and Peer–Child Interaction

The relationship of anger and social reinforcement to coercive exchange in parent–child interaction is shown in Figure 8.1. The fit of the model to the data from observed parent–child interaction was good: $X^2_{(10, n = 266)} = 6.84$, $p = .740$, Comparative fit index [CFI] = .999, RMSEA = .001. The association of children's rate of expression of anger with their rates of coercive interaction toward parents (boys: $b = .17$, $p < .05$; girls: $b = .26$, $p < .05$), and of parents' rate of anger with their rates of coercive interaction toward their sons ($b = .50$, $p < .01$) are consistent with the notion that anger facilitates coercive behavior, especially for more intense or serious forms of coercive behavior. The reliable association between observed rates of parent and child anger (boys: $r = .36$, $p < .05$; girls, $r = .43$, $p < .01$) is consistent with the notion of anger contagion. Finally, the coercive behavior of parents is reliably associated with the coercive behavior of their children toward them (for boys: $b = .37$, $p < .01$; for girls: $b = .27$, $p < .01$). Although the association between parent and child coercion was tested as a directional path, this relationship is likely reciprocal. Finally, parents' capitulation to child coercive behavior (negative reinforcement) during social interaction was a reliable predictor of the rates at which boys ($b = .29$, $p < .05$)

and girls ($b = .21$, $p < .05$) engaged in coercive behavior during interaction with their parents. Children's coercive behavior toward parents appears to be facilitated by the consequences it engenders, by child anger displays, and by parent coercive behavior. These social processes appear to operate in an equivalent fashion for boys and girls despite some gender differences in the rates at which anger and coercive exchange were observed in parent–child interaction. The total variance in child coercive behavior explained by the model was 22% for boys and 19% for girls.

A test of a comparable model of the association of child anger, peer anger, and peer coercive behavior and social reinforcement with rates of child coercive behavior during peer interaction is shown in Figure 8.2. The fit of the model to the data was adequate: $X^2(10, n = 266) = 23.25$, $p = .010$, CFI $= .980$, RMSEA $= .070$. Rates of children's anger were reliably associated with the rates at which they directed coercive behavior toward peers (boys: $b = .45$, $p < .01$; girls: $b = .61$, $p < .01$). Peers' anger facilitated the rates at which they directed coercive behavior toward boys ($b = .17$, $p < .05$) and girls ($b = .31$, $p < .01$). As described earlier, anger was associated with low-and high-intensity coercive behaviors in peer interaction. There was evidence of reciprocity of anger expression or contagion (boys: $r = .19$, $p < .05$; girls: $b = .28$, $p < .01$). For boys ($b = .36$, $p < .01$) and girls ($b = .27$, $p < .01$), high rates of peer coercion evoked coercive behavior from children toward peers. Rates of child coercive behavior during peer interaction were tied to the positive social outcomes provided by peers for talking about and modeling of such behavior during play (boys: $b = .27$, $p < .01$; girls: $b = .25$, $p < .01$).

The peer model suggests that frequent anger, peer coercive behavior, and peer reinforcement contingencies are reliably associated with high rates of child coercive behavior during peer interaction. These social processes appear to operate in an equivalent fashion for boys and girls despite systematic gender differences in the rates at which anger and coercive exchange were observed in peer interaction. The total variance in child coercive behavior explained by the model was 33% for boys and 20% for girls.

The Contribution of Parent–Child and Peer Social Processes, and Child Inattention–Impulsivity to the Early Development of Physical Aggression

The full model for the joint contribution of coercive social exchange, anger, and child inattention-impulsivity to early trajectories for child physical aggression is shown in Figure 8.3. The top portion of the full model, labeled "Parent–Child Interaction," is the same model shown in Figure 8.1. The middle portion of the full model, labeled "Peer–Child

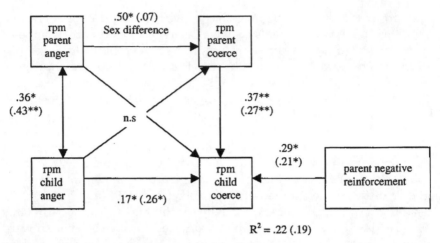

Parameters for girls are shown in parentheses
*p < .05, p < .01

$X^2_{(10, 267)}$ = 6.84, p = .740; TLI = .999, RMSEA = .001

FIGURE 8.1.   The roles of anger and social reinforcement in coercive
parent–child interaction.

Interaction," is the same model shown in Figure 8.2. The lower right portion of the full model in Figure 8.3 is the growth model for child physical aggression during kindergarten and first grade described earlier.

The new facet of the full model is shown in the lower left portion of Figure 8.3 and labeled "Child Inattention-Impulsivity." In addition to examining the main effects of inattention-impulsivity on physical aggression, interaction effects of inattention-impulsivity with four other measured variables were tested. The first two interaction terms ascertained whether child inattention-impulsivity exacerbated the contribution of coercive behavior (by parents or peers) to early trajectories of aggressive behavior. The second two interaction terms ascertained whether child inattention-impulsivity exacerbated the contribution of children's anger (toward parents or peers) to early trajectories of physical aggression. Each interaction term was tested separately. Only one of the four interaction terms, impulsivity-inattention × peer coercive behavior, was reliability associated with child aggression.

The full, multicomponent model shown in Figure 8.3 fit the data adequately: $X^2_{(184, n = 266)}$ = 203.28, p < .013, TLI = .975, RMSEA = .043. The rates at which children directed low-and high-intensity coercive behavior toward peers was reliably associated with physical aggression early in the kindergarten year (intercept) for boys (b = .28, p < .05) and for girls (b = .49,

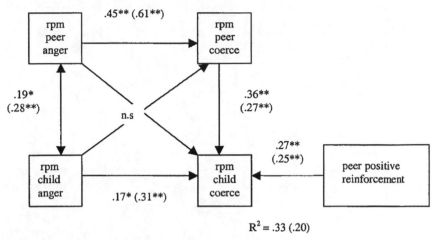

$R^2 = .33 (.20)$

Parameters for girls are shown in parentheses
*$p < .05$, $p < .01$

$X^2_{(10, 267)} = 23.25$, p = .010; TLI = .980, RMSEA = .070

FIGURE 8.2. The roles of anger and social reinforcement in coercive peer–child interaction.

$p < .01$). High rates of peer coercion were reliably associated with physical aggression in early kindergarten for boys ($b = .28$, $p < .05$) but not for girls. Inattention-impulsivity was associated with boys' ($b = .51$, $p < .01$) but not girls' physical aggression in the fall of the kindergarten year—a significant gender difference. Rates of children's coercion toward parents were indirectly rather than directly associated with physical aggression in early kindergarten. Both boys and girls who displayed high rates of coercive behavior toward parents were also more likely to display high rates of coercive behavior toward peers ($b = .31$, $p < .05$; and $b = .27$, $p < .05$, respectively). Involvement in coercive interaction with parents increments risk for physical aggression as a result of generalization of children's coercive tactics to the peer setting. The model accounted for 42% of the variance in boys' and 24% of the variance in girls' physical aggression in early kindergarten.

Change in physical aggression during kindergarten and first grade (slope) was predicted by a different set of gender-specific variables. High rates of child anger displays toward peers predicted growth in physical aggression for girls ($b = .51$, $p < .01$) and for boys ($b = .27$, $p < .05$), with a significant gender difference. For boys only, the interaction of peer coercive behavior X inattention-impulsivity ($b = .35$, $p < .05$) predicted growth

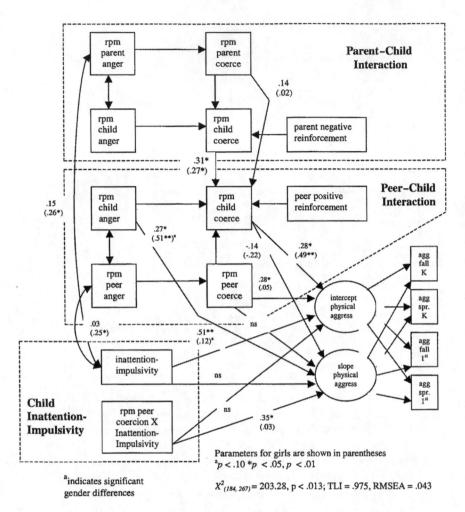

FIGURE 8.3.   The contribution of child impulsivity-inattention, and
child involvement in coercive interaction with parents and peers to the
development of physical aggression.

in physical aggression. The nature of this interaction effect is shown in
Figure 8.4. In the fall of kindergarten (top plot in Fig. 8.4), physical aggression increased as peer coercive behavior increased in a similar manner for
boys who were in the bottom and top third of the distribution on inattention-impulsivity. By spring of kindergarten (middle plot in Fig 8.4, physical aggression increased with exposure to higher rates of peer coercion
only for boys who evidenced high levels of inattention-impulsivity. By
spring of first grade (bottom plot in Fig. 8.4), increased physical aggression

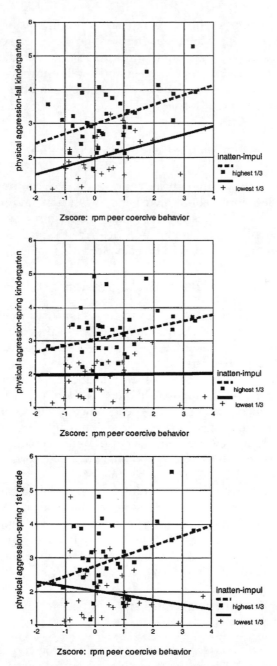

FIGURE 8.4.   The synergistic effects of boys' inattention-impulsivity and rates of exposure to peer coercive behavior on growth in physical aggression

was apparent for boys who were exposed to high rates of peer coercive behavior and who were high on inattention-impulsivity. In contrast, exposure to higher rates of peer coercion was associated with decreasing child physical aggression for boys low on inattention-impulsivity. The full model accounted for 23% of the variance in change in physical aggression over time for boys and 30% for girls.

DISCUSSION AND IMPLICATIONS

The findings derived from these analyses have clear implications for developmental theories about anger and aggression, and for early interventions to prevent aggressive behavior. The ensuing sections consider these implications in more detail, and describe the strengths and limitations of the findings reported in this chapter.

Early Development of Physical Aggression

The data presented in this chapter are consistent with previous research (Broidy et al., 2003; Nagin & Tremblay, 1999) and provide a clear picture of the early development of physical aggression. Physical aggression occurred at substantial rates during kindergarten and first grade, and clear individual differences in developmental trajectories for physical aggression were already apparent. Some children increasingly inhibited physical aggression from ages 5 to 7 years whereas other children showed persisting and increasing physical aggression. Failure to inhibit physical aggression early in development was also found to increase risk for the continuing use of physical aggression and other forms of antisocial behavior in late childhood. The persistence of physical aggression during early childhood may be one important developmental route to escalating violence and delinquency in adolescence (Patterson & Yoerger, 1993). These findings collectively suggest that successful universal or targeted interventions during early childhood may effectively reduce physical aggression before it becomes increasingly serious and dangerous during later development.

Coercive Interaction as a Training Ground
for Physical Aggression

Previous research has repeatedly shown that coercive interaction in family (Patterson, 1982) and peer settings (Coie & Dodge, 1998) predicts an array of child conduct problems. The data in this chapter extend these findings in two ways. First, these data demonstrate a specific linkage between the frequency of involvement in coercive exchange and the development of physical aggression at child ages 5 to 7 yeas of age. Second, the data allow us to estimate the relative contribution of coercive interaction with parents and peers to risk for aggression.

These as well as previous analyses (Patterson, Reid, & Dishion, 1992; Snyder, 2002; Snyder & Stoolmiller, 2002) indicate that children's daily interaction with family members and peers are replete with coercive behavior and conflict. Even though most coercive behavior is characterized by low-intensity irritability, the models suggest that the frequency of children's involvement in garden-variety, low-intensity conflicts reliably predicts individual differences in physical aggression. What processes account for this relationship? One interpretation might be labeled a "frequency" effect in that all low-intensity conflicts carry the seeds for physical aggression. Insofar as low-intensity coercive exchanges are encountered frequently, it is increasingly likely that an individual will be involved in exchanges that escalate to physical aggression. A second interpretation might be labeled "amplification" or "shaping." As low-intensity coercive exchanges are repeatedly experienced, the conditions engendering such exchanges may also facilitate their persistence and escalation.

Analyses presented in this chapter examined whether anger and social reinforcement may serve as the conditions that increment the frequency of involvement in coercive exchanges and also facilitate persistence and escalation of coercive exchanges toward high-intensity forms, including physical aggression. Anger was observed to be contagious, and its frequent display during children's interaction with parents and peers was related to high-rate involvement in coercive exchange in each setting. Rates of anger were also associated with the use of high-intensity coercive tactics or escalation in conflict. Frequent and dysregulated anger during peer and family interaction appears to fuel both the frequency and the intensity of coercive exchanges.

The frequency with which children engaged in coercive behavior was associated with the likelihood with which parents' and peers' reinforced that behavior, replicating previous research derived from smaller, convenience samples (Patterson et al., 1967; Snyder & Patterson, 1995). Naturally occurring social contingencies encourage children to "use what works" in relating to other people. Insofar as coercion "works" (i.e., is reinforced relative to constructive or skilled behavior) in the short run, coercive behavior is more likely to be used in subsequent interaction. Children's continuing display of coercive behavior is inherent in the definition of parent negative reinforcement of that behavior; negative reinforcement occurs when the child persists in coercive actions until the parent "backs down." The contribution of social contingencies to escalation of coercive behavior to higher intensity forms is less clearly supported by the data presented here.

However, sequential analyses of extended coercive exchanges using other data have shown that the escalation by children and parents is closely tied to the functional utility of high-versus low-intensity coercive tactics in terminating conflict (Snyder, et al., 1994).

Poor anger regulation and social contingencies appear to serve as interlocking, tandem social processes in evoking, maintaining, and escalating coercive exchanges. In addition, these processes appear to operate in both family and peer environments. Frequent and persisting physical aggression during early childhood is associated with residing in social environments in which lower and higher intensity coercive behaviors are used as common and functional tools to relate to other people. Although the same processes appear to contribute to persisting and escalating coercion in family and peer settings, the contribution of children's experiences with parents and with peers to trajectories for aggression are not equivalent—at least as they were assessed in this research.

The peer environment appears to be more challenging. Children's interaction with peers relative to that with parents was characterized by twice the rate of low-intensity coercive behavior, 5 to 10 times the rate of high-intensity coercive behavior, and 4 times the rate of anger. The intense "training ground" for persisting and escalating coercion in the peer ecology is the result of interaction between individuals who are still acquiring emotional and behavioral self-regulation. The intensity of peer training also reflects the relative lack of adult supervision and contingencies in relatively open settings such as the playground and backyard.

The strong and direct role of coercion training in peer interaction does not mean that the family environment is unimportant. Children's involvement in coercive processes with parents is also linked to the development of physical aggression, but this linkage appears to be more indirect and distal after children make the transition to elementary school. Anger regulation and reinforcement contingencies promoting the inhibition of coercive behavior and the acquisition of skilled behavior at home may be critical to children's success in navigating the challenging peer environment (Parke & Ladd, 1992).

Complementing ongoing social experiences, children's developing abilities to inhibit behavior and deploy attention predict decreasing rates of physical aggression during kindergarten and first grade—at least for boys. Deficits in inhibition, as reflected in impulsivity and inattention, have been clearly established as a risk factor for the development of early-onset conduct problems (Moffitt et al., 2001; Nigg, 2000) in both family (Kochanska, Murray, & Coy, 1997) and peer (Hughes, White, Sharpen, & Dunn, 2000) environments. The data described in this report replicate this finding and indicate that this risk operates in a specific fashion for physical aggression. The data also indicate that risk engendered by deficits or delays in inhibition may be gender-specific as well, as considered in the next section.

The Origins and Sources of Gender Differences in Physical Aggression

Clear gender differences in physical aggression were apparent at entry to kindergarten. Boys evidenced higher rates of aggression than girls according to teacher report but this difference was even more apparent on the playground. This replicates previous research (Broidy et al., 2003; Maccoby, 1998; Tremblay, 2003). However, significant between-individual differences in the persistence and change in physical aggression during kindergarten and first grade were also apparent for both boys and girls— a less well established finding.

A more critical question concerns the origins of boys' more frequent displays of physical aggression. In the models presented in this report, gender differences in aggression appeared to be the end result of similar social processes. Anger and reinforcement were related in similar ways to coercive behavior, and child coercive behavior was related in similar ways to physical aggression for boys and girls. However, large differences were observed in the mean rates of boys' and girls' expression of and exposure to anger and coercion in family and peer environments. Boys' greater involvement appears to provide more frequent and more intense training in coercion and its escalation, and to promote more frequent experience of social contingencies for coercive and aggressive behavior.

This increased involvement in coercion training may indicate that parents' socialization of boys and girls is different on average. Boys' increased involvement in coercion training more clearly reflects the very different social experiences of boys and girls in largely gender-segregated peer groups during early childhood. However, children actively contribute to the differences in the environments they experience. Inattention-impulsivity was powerfully associated with rates of physical aggression in early kindergarten for boys, but not for girls. This significant gender difference may operate in two ways. First, the risk for physical aggression imbued by inattention-impulsivity may be most apparent at the higher average levels of inattention-impulsivity displayed by boys. Second, the contribution of inattention-impulsivity to the development of physical aggression may be exacerbated under conditions of greater environmental challenge and may become increasingly apparent as children become older. This is supported by the age-incremental moderator effect of inattention-impulsivity for boys in the rough-and-tumble, dominance-oriented, same-gender peer environment during kindergarten and first grade. Physical aggression persisted and increased for boys whose self-regulatory capacities were insufficient to cope with coercive peer behavior, an insufficiency that became increasingly apparent with ongoing experience in the peer ecology. The absence of a comparable moderator effect for girls may reflect their better self-regulatory capacities, or the lower rates of coercive peer behavior may provide less challenge to their regulatory capacities.

In contrast, anger display processes may be a more important element in the development of physical aggression for girls than boys even though the rates of anger exchanged during interaction with parents and peers is lower for girls than boys. The importance of anger was most apparent in the strong prospective relationship of girls' rates of peer-directed anger to growth in physical aggression during kindergarten and first grade. Although statistically significant gender differences were not observed, girls' relative to boys' anger expression appears to be more closely linked to the anger displays of parents and peers, and to girls' own rates of coercive behavior. Anger seems to operate as a more powerful social signaling and coercion-facilitating process for girls than for boys. Boys get angry more often, but anger displays by girls may serve as a more potent social process. Parents' and peers' expressions of anger toward girls but not boys were correlated with girls' inattention-impulsivity even though on average it is lower than that of boys. Difficulties in girls' self-regulation, when they occur, may be relatively unexpected and socially dystonic, and consequently may evoke angry reactions from social partners. In a sense, "girls are supposed to be self-controlled." Girls with deficits in "expected" self-control may become engaged in a set of social processes that increase risk for physical aggression that are different than processes that mediate risk for boys.

Strengths, Limitations, and Extensions of the Current Analyses

The data and analyses presented in this chapter have several psychometric and methodological strengths. The observation of children's interaction with parents and peers provides real time estimates of rates of anger, low- and high-intensity coercive behavior exchange, and reinforcement contingencies as they occur in natural social ecologies. These observational data provide a relatively unbiased description of the social conditions associated with the development of physical aggression, and a balanced comparison of those conditions across family and peer settings. The data in this report displayed a full spectrum of variation so that range restriction was unlikely to bias the results. Finally, methods and informants used to define the social processes comprising the exogenous constructs in the final hypothesized model did not overlap with the methods and informants used to define growth models for child physical aggression.

However, the data and analyses also have several important limitations. The sample was derived from one school so that generalization of the findings needs to be demonstrated. The findings are derived from a passive longitudinal design so that inferences about causality are necessarily tentative and await stronger causal tests using experimental intervention designs. The role of anger displays and reinforcement contingencies on coercion training in family and peer interaction were ascertained as rates per minute. Finer grained, real-time, microsocial sequential or event history analyses are needed to more clearly delineate the dynamic and likely reciprocal relationships among anger, coercion, and reinforcement as they unfold during social interaction in family and peer settings.

Early Interventions to Reduce Violence: Potential Benefits and Malleable Social Risk

These as well as other data indicate that the serious physical violence during adolescence and young adulthood have identifiable origins in earlier development. Preventive interventions provide a means by which to reduce physical aggression prior to its more serious manifestations and increasing resistance to intervention in later development. The data in this chapter provide clues about how such interventions might be constructed and the developmental timing and ecologies in which interventions might be implemented. Both family and peer venues may usefully be targeted in early intervention efforts. Anger regulation and social contingencies are candidate processes that can be targeted in intervention.

Parenting skills training may be most usefully implemented during the preschool years, perhaps beginning as early as child age 2 or 3 (Shaw, Gilliom, Ingoldsby, & Nagin, 2003), especially for families with children who evidence difficulties in behavioral inhibition, irritability, and fearlessness, and with parents who evidence irritable and harsh discipline styles. Although contingency management is a central component of already-existing, efficacious parenting programs (Webster-Stratton, Reid, & Hammond, 2001), intervention modules that explicitly promote parental emotion coaching (Izard, 2002) may further enhance the efficacy of these programs. Given the difficulties in engaging parents in skills- training programs, especially those with the highest risk children (Miller & Prinz, 2003), sole reliance on parenting-skills training to alter trajectories for early physical aggression is likely not sufficient to address the public health problem of violence.

Interventions targeting aggression in peer interaction provide a second promising venue. The data in this chapter suggest that to have maximal impact peer interventions should: (a) target children during the early elementary school grades; (b) be implemented in the natural peer environment in which adult monitoring and contingencies supervision are typically minimal; (c) foster anger/emotion regulation skills; and (d) alter natural peer contingencies for coercive behavior.

Though many schools have implemented programs to reduce aggression (Espelage & Swearer, 2004), these programs tend to focus on small-group interventions that promote skills development and attitudes to minimize conflict and aggression. Many of these programs lack strong empirical validation (Leff, Power, Manz, Costigan, & Nabors, 2001). The recent emphasis on academic achievement increasingly precludes the often extensive programming and instructional time required by classroom-based interventions.

Early interventions that alter group contingencies for physical aggression and disruptive behavior (Embry, 2002) hold particular promise. These programs can be applied in hallways, lunchrooms, and playgrounds where adult monitoring and contingencies are often nonsystematic and minimal. These programs do not require extensive classroom or instructional time, and can be implemented by paraprofessionals. These programs most powerfully reduce peer-directed physical aggression for those children who demonstrate chronically high rates of such aggression (Stoolmiller, Eddy, & Reid, 2000). Contingency-based programs do not typically focus on emotion regulation, but may be augmented by the addition of "teaching moments" in which adults shape children's capacity for emotion recognition and regulation as "hot" disputes occur in the natural peer environment (Izard, 2002).

ACKNOWLEDGMENTS

This research was supported by National Institutes of Health Grant R01 MH57342, "Child Conduct Problems: Competing Theories of Socialization."

REFERENCES

Barkley, R. A. (1997). Behavioral inhibition, sustained attention, and executive functions: Constructing a unifying theory for ADHD. *Psychological Bulletin, 121,* 65–94.

Brame, B., Nagin, D. S., & Tremblay, R. E. (2001). Developmental trajectories of physical aggression from school entry to late adolescence. *Journal of Child Psychology and Psychiatry, 42,* 503–512.

Broidy, L. M., Nagin, D. S., Tremblay, R. E., Bates, J. E., Brame, B., Dodge, K. A., et al. (2003). Developmental trajectories of childhood disruptive behaviors and adolescent delinquency: A six-site, cross-national study. *Developmental Psychology, 39,* 222–245.

Cairns, R. B., & Cairns, B. D. (1994). *Lifelines and risks: Pathways of youth in our time.* New York: Cambridge University Press.

Coie, J., & Dodge, K. A. (1998). Aggression and antisocial behavior. In W. Damon (Series Ed.) & N. Eisenberg (Vol. Ed.), *Handbook of child psychology: Vol. 3. Social, emotional and personality development* (5th ed., pp. 779–862). New York: Wiley.

Crosby, L., Stubbs, J., Forgatch, M., & Capaldi, D. (1998). *Family and peer process code training manual.* Eugene: Oregon Social Learning Center.

Davidson, R. J., Jackson, D. C., & Kalin, N. H. (2000). Emotion, plasticity, context, and regulation: Perspectives from affective neuroscience. *Psychological Bulletin, 126,* 890–909.

Denham, S. A., Workman, E., Cole, P. M., Weissbrod, C., Kendziora, K. T., & Zahn-Waxler, C. (2000). Prediction of externalizing behavior problems from early to middle childhood: The role of parental socialization and emotion expression. *Development and Psychopathology, 12,* 23–46.

Embry, D. D. (2002). The Good Behavior Game: A best practice candidate as a universal behavioral vaccine. *Clinical Child and Family Psychology Review, 5,* 273–297.

Espelage, D. L., & Swearer, S. M. (2004). *Bullying in American schools: A social-ecological perspective on prevention and intervention.* Mahwah, NJ: Lawrence Erlbaum Associates.

Gottman, J. M., Fainsilber-Katz, L., & Hooven, C. (1997). *Meta-emotion: How families communicate emotionally.* Mahwah, NJ: Lawrence Erlbaum Associates.

Gottman, J. M., McCoy, K., Coan, J., & Collier, H. (1996). *The Specific Affect Coding System (SPAFF) for observing emotion communication in marital and family interaction.* Mahwah, NJ: Lawrence Erlbaum Associates.

Grusec, J. E. (2002). Parental socialization and children's acquisition of values. In M. Borstein (Ed.), *Handbook of parenting* (Vol. 3, pp. 143–168). Mahwah, NJ: Lawrence Erlbaum Associates.

Hatfield, E., Cacioppo, J. T., & Rapson, R. L. (1994). *Emotional contagion.* New York: Cambridge University Press.

Hughes, C., White, A., Sharpen, J., & Dunn, J. (2000). Antisocial, angry and unsympathetic: "Hard to manage" preschoolers' peer problems and possible cognitive influences. *Journal of Child Psychology and Psychiatry, 41,* 169–179.

Izard, C. E. (2002). Translating emotion theory and research into preventive interventions. *Psychological Bulletin, 128,* 796–824.

Keenan, K., & Shaw, D. S. (1997). Developmental and social influences on young girls' behavioral and emotional problems. *Psychological Bulletin, 121,* 97–113.

Kochanska, G., Murray, K., & Coy, K. C. (1997). Inhibitory control as a contributor to conscience in early childhood: From toddler to early school age. *Child Development, 68,* 263–277.

Leff, S. S., Power, T. J., Manz, P. H., Costigan, T. E., & Nabors, L. A. (2001). School-based aggression-prevention programs for young children: Current status and implications for violence prevention. *School Psychology Review, 30,* 343–360.

Maccoby, E. E. (1998). *The two sexes: Growing up apart, coming together.* Cambridge, MA: Harvard University Press.

Martin, J. A. (1981). A longitudinal study of the consequences of early mother–child interaction: A microanalytic approach. *Monographs of the Society for Research in Child Development, 46*(3, Serial No. 190).

McFayden-Ketchum, S. A., Bates, J. E., Dodge, K. A., & Pettit, G. S. (1996). Patterns of change in early childhood aggressive-disruptive behavior: Gender differences in predictions from early coercive and affectionate mother-child interactions. *Child Development, 67,* 2417–2433.

Miller, G. E., & Prinz, R. J. (2003). Engagement of families in treatment for childhood conduct problems. *Behavior Therapy, 34,* 517–534.

Moffitt, T. E., Caspi, A., Rutter, M, & Silva, P. A. (2001). *Sex differences in antisocial behavior, conduct disorder, delinquency and violence in the Dunedin Longitudinal Study.* New York: Cambridge University Press.

Nagin, D., & Tremblay, R. E. (1999). Trajectories of boys' physical aggression, opposition, and hyperactivity on the path to physically violent and nonviolent juvenile delinquency. *Child Development, 70,* 1181–1196.

Nigg, J. T. (2000). On inhibition/disinhibition in developmental psychopathology: Views from cognitive and personality psychology, and a working taxonomy. *Psychological Bulletin, 126,* 220–246.

Parke, R. D., & Ladd, G. W. (1992). *Family and peer relationships: Modes of linkage.* Hillsdale, NJ: Lawrence Erlbaum Associates.

Patterson, G. R. (1982). *Coercive family process.* Eugene, OR: Castalia.

Patterson, G. R., Littman, R. A., & Bricker, W. (1967). Assertive behavior in children: A step towards a theory of aggression. *Monographs of the Society for Research in Child Development, 32*(5), 1–43.

Patterson, G. R., & Reid, J. B. (1970). Reciprocity and coercion: Two facets of a social system. In C. Neuringer & J. L. Michael (Eds.), *Behavior modification in clinical psychology* (pp. 133–177). New York: Appleton–Century–Crofts.

Patterson, G. R., Reid, J. B., & Dishion, T. J. (1992). *Antisocial boys.* Eugene, OR: Castalia.

Patterson, G. R., & Yoerger, K. (1993). Developmental models for delinquent behavior. In S. Hodgins (Ed.), *Mental disorder and crime* (pp. 140–172). Newbury Park, CA: Sage.

Posner, M. I., & Rothbart, M. K. (2000). Developing mechanisms of self regulation. *Development and Psychopathology, 12,* 427–442.

Reid, J. B. (1986). Social interaction patterns in the families of abused and non-abused children. In C. Zahn-Waxler, E. M. Cummings, & R. Iannotti (Eds.), *Altruism and aggression: Biological and social origins* (pp. 238–255). New York: Cambridge University Press.

Rudolph, K. D., & Asher, S. R. (2000). Adaptation and maladaptation in the peer system: Developmental processes and outcomes. In A. J. Sameroff, M. Lewis, & Z. Miller (Eds.), *Handbook of developmental psychopathology* (pp. 157–175). New York: Kluwer.

Shantz, C. U. (1994). *Conflict in child and adolescent development.* New York: Cambridge University Press.

Shaw, D. S., Gilliom, M., Ingoldsby, E. M., & Nagin, D.S. (2003). Trajectories leading to school-age conduct problems. *Developmental Psychology, 39,* 189–200.

Shaw, D. S., Owens, E. B., Giovannelli, J., & Winslow, E. B. (2001). Infant and toddler pathways leading to early externalizing behavior: Ages 1 to 3. *Journal of the American Academy of Child and Adolescent Psychiatry, 40,* 36–43.

Snyder, J. (2002). Coercion and reinforcement mechanisms in the development of antisocial behavior: Peer relationships. In J. B. Reid, G. R. Patterson, & J. Snyder (Eds.), *Antisocial behavior in children and adolescents: A developmental analysis and model for intervention* (pp. 101–122). Washington, DC: American Psychological Association.

Snyder, J., Edwards, P., McGraw, K., Kilgore, K., & Holton, A. (1994). Escalation and reinforcement in mother-child conflict: Social processes associated with the development of physical aggression. *Development and Psychopathology, 6,* 305–321.

Snyder, J., & Patterson, G. R. (1995). Individual differences in social aggression: A test of a reinforcement model of socialization in the natural environment. *Behavior Therapy, 26,* 371–391.

Snyder, J., Prichard, J., Schrepferman, L., Patrick, M. R., & Stoolmiller, M. (2004). Impulsiveness-inattention, early peer experiences, and the development of early onset conduct problems. *Journal of Abnormal Child Psychology, 32,* 579–594.

Snyder, J., Reid, J. B., & Patterson, G. R. (2003). A social learning model of child and adolescent antisocial behavior. In B. B. Lahey, T. E. Moffitt, & A. Caspi (Eds.), *Causes of conduct disorder and juvenile delinquency* (pp. 27–48). New York: Guilford.

Snyder, J., Schrepferman, L., Brooker, M., & Stoolmiller, M. (2003). Observed peer victimization during early elementary school: Continuity, growth, and relation to risk for child antisocial and depressive behavior. *Child Development, 74,* 1881–1898.

Snyder, J., Schrepferman, L., & St. Peter, C. (1997). Origins of antisocial behavior: Negative reinforcement and affect dysregulation as socialization mechanisms in family interaction. *Behavior Modification, 21,* 187–215.

Snyder, J., & Stoolmiller, M. (2002). Coercion and reinforcement mechanisms in the development of antisocial behavior: The family. In J. B. Reid, G. R. Patterson, & J. Snyder (Eds.), *Antisocial behavior in children and adolescents: A developmental analysis and model for intervention* (pp. 65–100). Washington, DC: American Psychological Association.

Snyder, J., Stoolmiller, M., Patterson, G. R., Schrepferman, L., Oeser, J., Johnson, K., et al. (2004). The application of response allocation matching to understanding risk mechanisms in development: The case of young children's deviant talk and play, and risk for early onset antisocial behavior. *Behavior Analyst, 4,* 335–343.

Snyder, J., Stoolmiller, M., Wilson, M., & Yamamoto, M. (2003). Child anger regulation, parental responses to children's anger displays, and early child antisocial behavior. *Social Development, 12,* 335–359.

Stoolmiller, M. (1992, September). *Contagion models of social interaction.* Paper presented at the Oregon Social Learning Center Symposium on the Social Dynamics of Development and Psychopathology, Eugene.

Stoolmiller, M., Eddy, J. M., & Reid, J. B. (2000). Detecting and describing preventive intervention effects in a universal school-based randomized trial targeting delinquent and violent behavior. *Journal of Consulting and Clinical Psychology, 68,* 296–306.

Tremblay, R. E. (2003). Why socialization fails: The case of chronic physical aggression. In B. B. Lahey, T. E. Moffitt, & A. Caspi (Eds.), *Causes of conduct disorder and
juvenile delinquency* (pp. 182–226). New York: Guilford.

U.S. Department of Health and Human Services (2001). *Youth violence: A report of
the Surgeon General*. Rockville, MD: Author.

Webster-Stratton, C., Reid, M. J., & Hammond, M. (2001). Preventing conduct
problems, promoting social competence: A parent and teacher training partner-
ship in Head Start. *Journal of Clinical Child Psychology, 30,* 283–302.

Anger and Aggression: A Developmental Perspective

Karen L. Bierman

Developmental models of aggression highlight the central roles of parenting practices, social cognitions, and peer relations in the etiology and maintenance of aggressive behavior problems (Coie & Dodge, 1998). Research is accumulating to support the additional contribution of emotional functioning, in general, and anger regulation, in particular, to the development and maintenance of aggressive behavior problems (Eisenberg & Fabes, 1992), leading theorists to call for greater attention to emotional functioning in assessment and intervention planning (Izard, 2002). This chapter reviews developmental research linking emotional functioning and anger regulation with the development and maintenance of aggressive behavior problems in childhood and associated social-emotional maladjustment. Implications for prevention and early-intervention programs are discussed.

EMOTIONAL FUNCTIONING AND THE DEVELOPMENT OF "EARLY-STARTING" AGGRESSIVE BEHAVIOR PROBLEMS

Children who show high rates of chronic aggressive behavior problems typically experience multiple risks, which interact over time to impair adaptive development and maintain problem behaviors. Child characteristics (e.g., inattention, impulsivity, and negative affectivity) challenge parents, contributing to inconsistent and harsh parenting and coercive family interactions (Coie & Dodge, 1998; Patterson, 1986). Concurrent peer rejection and academic difficulties are common, and problems often occur in high-stress neighborhoods and school settings, where support resources are limited, and exposure to hostile environments fuels aggressive behavior (Dodge, Bates, & Pettit, 1990; Thornberry, Lizotte, Krohn, Farnworth, & Jang, 1994).

Emotional functioning in early childhood, including emotional understanding and emotion regulation, appears to interact with child characteristics and early parenting to predict "early-starting" aggressive behavior problems in grade school. Normatively, children display the highest levels of aggressive behaviors when they are first learning to get along with others (ages 2–4) (Hartup, 1983). Grabbing toys and pushing a peer away is the natural response of a 2-year-old who wants a toy; hitting or even biting is a common response to the frustration of someone blocking a goal. Under positive developmental conditions, rates of aggression decrease sharply during the preschool years, as children develop the verbal, emotional, and social skills that allow them to inhibit their first impulses, comply with social protocol, and "use their words" to voice dissatisfaction and resolve disagreements (Greenberg, Kusche, & Speltz, 1991). Parallel advances occur in cognitive and language development, fostering children's capacities to attend to and follow social rules, and supporting the anticipatory planning that allows them to consider the interpersonal consequences of their behaviors, and inhibit reactive aggression in favor of socially appropriate alternatives (Cole, Michel, & Teti, 1994). Critical aspects of emotional functioning that develop during the preschool years include the capacity to: (a) label one's feelings and recognize the feelings of others, promoting empathy and interpersonal understanding, (b) inhibit behavioral reactivity and cope with frustration and distress, and (c) communicate effectively to express feelings and resolve social problems.

Delays in the acquisition of these important social-emotional skills and corresponding deficits in social-emotional functioning (particularly poor emotional understanding, low levels of frustration tolerance, and low levels of prosocial behaviors) are linked concurrently with high levels of aggressive reactivity during the preschool years (Eisenberg & Fabes, 1992). These social-emotional skill deficits also predict elevated aggression as children move from preschool into elementary school (Dodge et al., 1990; Ladd, Kochendorfer, & Coleman, 1997; Vitaro, Tremblay, Gagnon, & Boivan, 1992), and across the first year of grade school, controlling for initial levels of aggression (Ladd & Profilet, 1996). Delays in the acquisition of emotional understanding and emotion regulation capabilities impede the social control of aggression by reducing the child's ability to identify their feelings and those of others, their capacity to inhibit reactive responding, and their ability to consider alternative socially appropriate approaches to dealing with frustration and solving interpersonal problems (Dodge, 1991).

Emotional Functioning and the Course of Grade School Aggression.

By school entry, aggressive children are at high risk for developing chronic behavior problems, along with corresponding difficulties in areas of academic achievement and peer rejection. Interestingly, however, not all aggressive children are at equal risk. Deficits in emotional functioning, and associated difficulties with attention control and interpersonal relationships, are important features characterizing those aggressive children most at-risk for chronic developmental problems.

For example, several studies have differentiated groups of aggressive children who are accepted by their peers from those who are rejected by peers (Cillessen, van Ijzendoorn, van Lieshout, & Hartup, 1992). Aggressive-rejected children are more likely to show stable behavior problems and negative outcomes than are aggressive-accepted children (Bierman & Wargo, 1995; Dubow, 1988; Miller-Johnson, Coie, Maumary-Gremaud, Bierman, & the Conduct Problems Prevention Research Group, [CPPRG], 2002). Aggressive-rejected children differ from their accepted-aggressive peers in the array of problem behaviors they show and, notably, in their emotional functioning. Aggressive children who are rejected by peers typically display a broad range of disruptive and oppositional behaviors that reflect difficulties in regulating emotions effectively and maintaining positive interpersonal relationships (Cillessen et al., 1992; Coie & Dodge, 1998; Pope & Bierman, 1999). Emotionally, these children are often irritable and unhappy, overly sensitive and easily annoyed by others, and angry and resentful, quick to blame others for their own mistakes. Aggressive-rejected children also show greater problems in the areas of attention deficits, emotional dysregulation, and internalizing problems than do aggressive children who are better accepted by peers (Bierman, Smoot, & Aumiller, 1993; Miller-Johnson et al., 2002; Pope & Bierman, 1999).

David Perry uses the terms *effectual* versus *ineffectual* aggressors to differentiate youth who appear to have more (or less) control over their aggressive behavior (Perry, Perry & Kennedy, 1992). In Perry's model, effectual aggressors are children who use force or verbal intimidation to achieve dominance, lead others, and get their own way. In contrast, ineffectual aggressors display an array of aggressive-disruptive behaviors that are highly reactive emotionally, and detrimental to their social relationships and skill acquisition. Ineffectual aggressors are likely to be rejected and/or victimized by peers. Emotional functioning appears to be a critical feature differentiating effectual and ineffectual aggressors. The reactive aggression exhibited by ineffectual aggressors is emotionally loaded, as when a child explodes in reaction to an assault or threat made

TABLE 9.1
Emotional Characteristics of Aggressive Children Who Are Rejected
and/or Victimized by Peers

- Irritable, unhappy, moody
- Easily upset, quick to blame others
- Angry outbursts, difficult to calm
- Low levels of emotional understanding
- Poor emotion recognition skills
- Insecure, socially anxious, distrustful

---

by someone else, or when a child has an angry outburst (a tantrum) following some frustrating or negative event (Coie & Dodge, 1998; Miller-Johnson et al., 2002).

Effectual aggressors, who are accepted by their peers, are significantly more likely to outgrow their aggressive behavior problems over time. In contrast, ineffectual aggressors, who are rejected by their peers, are at substantially higher risk for displaying chronic aggression and experiencing chronic peer problems (Bierman & Wargo, 1995). These findings suggest that emotional functioning and angry reactivity play a role in determining the social impact and longitudinal course of aggressive behavior problems.

Emotional functioning also contributes to child vulnerability to victimization by peers (see Table 9.1). For example, children who are victimized report low self-esteem and high levels of social insecurity and anxiety (Hodges & Perry, 1996), and show poor social skills and elevated levels of emotional reactivity (Schwartz, Dodge, & Coie, 1993). Ineffectual aggressors are often victimized by peers, and this victimization, in turn, may fuel escalations in their angry and reactive aggression toward peers (Schwartz et al., 1993).

Emotional functioning warrants attention in developmental models of early-starting aggressive behavior problems. Deficits in emotional understanding and emotion regulation show concurrent and predictive associations with aggressive behavior problems, and with social dysfunction (especially peer rejection and victimization). Poor social-emotional functioning, in turn, exacerbates the school adjustment difficulties associated with aggressive behavior problems and increases the likelihood that the aggressive behavior problems will become more severe, chronic, and debilitating.

EMOTIONAL FUNCTIONING AND AGGRESSION: MECHANISMS OF ACTION

Longitudinal studies provide strong empirical evidence to support social learning theory models that emphasize the role of parental discipline practices, along with child social cognitions, as key mechanisms promoting the development of early-starting aggressive behavior problems. These are important influences that warrant attention in intervention and prevention programs. In addition, recent research has highlighted the influence of emotion on child behavior in the context of parent–child relationships and the influence of emotional arousal on child social-cognitive functioning. The next sections provide a brief review of evidence supporting social learning theory models of aggressive behavior, and then consider the mechanisms of action whereby emotional functioning and angry arousal interact with cognitive processes and interpersonal contingencies to affect aggression.

Coercive Family Processes

Across a number of studies, longitudinal analyses have documented associations between punitive parental discipline and elevated levels of child aggressive behavior (Dodge et al., 1990; Patterson, 1986). In a near consensual model, researchers agree that certain child temperamental characteristics (e.g., inattention, impulsivity, and negative affectivity) can make parenting difficult during the toddler and early childhood years. When parents respond to these demands by using a high rate of negative commands, combined with inconsistent limit setting and inadequate follow-through, increases in child oppositional and defiant behaviors are likely (Campbell, 1990). Under these conditions, high-rate parental commands function like aversive events, and when children can successfully apply noncompliant or aggressive responding to terminate parental commands, their oppositional behavior is reinforced (Patterson, 1986). Over time, coercive interactions predominate in the parent–child relationship, as parents and children learn to use increasingly harsh and aggressive behaviors to gain control over each other, and positive interactions undergo a corresponding decline. When children find that they can use aggression to get what they want or to terminate negative behavior in their interactions with siblings or peers as well, their use of aggression generalizes across relationships and escalates (Asarnow, 1983).

"Biased" Social Cognitions

Social learning theory models posit that, in addition to the effects of immediate interpersonal contingencies, child behavior is also affected by the mental representations children form of their social world that lead to the generalization of aggressive responding across contexts. As articulated by Dodge in 1986, child social cognitions have the capacity to influence aggressive responding by affecting any one of five steps in social information processing: (a) *encoding*, the number and types of cues that are selectively attended to in the process of perceiving and appraising a social situation (processes influenced by the childs social goals, attention, cue utilization, and memory skills); (b) *representation*, the way in which those cues are interpreted and evaluated, including the attributions children make about others' motivations and intentions; (c) *response generation*, the number and type of possible responses that children consider prior to taking action, (d) *response selection*, the type of behaviors likely to be selected for action, based upon the child's perception of his/her ability to enact the strategy effectively and his or her beliefs about the efficacy of certain behaviors for achieving desired outcomes, and (e) *enactment*, the child's actual skill at converting response ideas into social performance. In Dodge's model, these steps of social information processing typically operate rapidly, at a level below consciousness, to affect social behavior.

A large number of studies suggest that significant differences do exist in the social information processing of aggressive and nonaggressive children in each of these areas. For example, in terms of *encoding processes*, investigators have found that aggressive children are more impulsive and less comprehensive in the way that they gather information about social situations, attending to fewer cues before moving on to make interpretations and attributions about the dynamics and motivations reflected in the situation (Dodge & Newman, 1981; Milich & Dodge, 1984). Aggressive children also appear more likely than nonaggressive children to focus selectively on aggressive and self-threatening cues in social situations, and to find it difficult to shift their attention away from those cues (Gouze, 1987). In addition, when asked to recall social scenarios presented via videotape, aggressive children show deficits in their memory for relevant social cues (Dodge, Pettit, McClaskey, & Brown, 1986). The way that aggressive children *represent and interpret* social events is also atypical, particularly when those social events involve negative outcomes and ambiguous interpersonal intentions. For example, in ambiguous situations, aggressive children are more likely than non aggressive children to attribute hostile intentions to peers (Dodge, Murphy, & Buchsbaum, 1984; Dodge et al., 1986; Graham & Hudley, 1994; Lochman, 1987). Characteristic *response search* and *response selection* biases are evident among aggressive children. Aggressive children tend to generate fewer prosocial and more aggressive responses than do nonaggressive children (Asarnow & Callan, 1985; Dodge, 1986). In evaluating possible responses, aggressive children tend to emphasize instrumental and personal gain over interpersonal goals (Dodge, Asher, & Parkhurst, 1989). In addition, they expect more positive outcomes and fewer negative sanctions for aggressive responding than do nonaggressive children (Hart, Ladd, & Burleson, 1990; Perry, Perry, & Rasmussen, 1986). Aggressive children are also more confident in terms of their perceived capacity to use aggressive responding effectively to attain their goals (Perry et al., 1986).

Each of these socia-information-processing tendencies increases the likelihood that aggressive children will select hostile or power-domination strategies to solve social problems, thus increasing the prevalence of their aggressive responding. Indeed, social-information-processing deficits show significant associations with measures of aggressive behavior problems and have demonstrated predictive validity when used to assess growth and change in aggressive behavior across time (Dodge, Pettit, Bates, & Valente, 1995).

Although often referred to as "biased" social-cognitive processing, theorists suggest that the tendency of aggressive children to emphasize aggressive and threatening cues in their social perceptions, as well as their positive beliefs about the utility of aggressive responding reflect their past interpersonal experiences, particularly the coercive family processes and negative sibling and peer relationships to which they have been exposed. Functionally, the value of developing social-cognitive schemas to organize information processing is to enhance one's capacity to predict and control one's environment, and to promote self-protection, supporting feelings of efficacy and motivation for active coping (Cairns, 1991; Epstein, 1991). Given that the histories of early-starting aggressors are characterized by interpersonal conflict and coercion, their heightened sensitivity toward personal threat and their readiness to take hostile action to protect themselves may have strategic value in terms of protecting their self-interests in the short-term (Patterson, 1986). Unfortunately, their hostile orientations are also likely to alienate new social partners (teachers and peers), thus undermining their social adjustment in the long run.

The Role of Emotion

In describing the development of aggressive behavior problems, social learning theory models focus on interpersonal contingencies (especially parenting) and information processing, but recognize that the emotional functioning of aggressive children affects and is affected by their interpersonal experiences. For example, in their reformulated model of social-cognitive processes, Crick and Dodge (1994) emphasize the role of an affect-laden informational database, influenced by past relationship experiences, that has an impact on social information processing at the levels of social perception and appraisal, causal interpretations, and decisionmaking. These affective biases operate at an unconscious level contributing to child sensitivity and reactivity to certain social cues (Crick & Dodge, 1994).

Some investigators, notably Izard (2002), Sroufe (1996), Greenberg and colleagues (Greenberg, Kusche, & Speltz, 1991), and Denham

(Denham & Burton, 2004) have argued that emotional functioning deserves even greater attention in models of aggressive behavioral development and a more explicit focus in corresponding interventions targeting reductions in aggression and improvements in social adjustment. This argument is based on evidence that aggressive behavior is influenced directly by emotional functioning, in three major areas: (a) by the way that past emotional experiences in parent–child relationships affect relational schemas and child interpersonal orientations and sensitivities, (b) through the influence of emotional understanding on social competence, and (c) by the impact of emotional arousal on information processing. They argue that the impact of emotional functioning on child aggression is not mediated fully by its impact on information processing, and relatedly, that emotional functioning requires more explicit attention in developmental and intervention models.

Emotionally Laden Relational Schemas

Sroufe (1990) points out that emotion plays a central role in motivating and regulating social interaction. Theorists have suggested that human infants are biologically oriented to pursue social interactions and that their early representations of their world are heavily influenced by the interactions they have with primary caregivers (Bowlby, 1969). Fueled by this innate motivation, infants develop internal working models that enable them to predict the behavior of primary caregivers in relation to themselves (Bowlby, 1969; Bretherton, 1995). These early experiences, along with later significant interactions with others, contribute to broader sets of relational schemas, which involve emotionally laden expectations regarding how others will behave toward them and their corresponding self-evaluations (Baldwin, 1992). Young children who develop insecure relational schemas, anticipating that others will not behave in ways that are supportive (or will behave in ways that are hostile), become vulnerable to social adjustment problems, as those beliefs affect their interpersonal reactions, perceptions, and behaviors (Baldwin, 1992; Sroufe, 1990).

Supporting the hypothesis that affect-laden relational schemas often accompany aggressive behavior problems, several investigators have documented associations between insecure parent–child attachments and aggressive acting-out behavior problems. For example, Speltz, Greenberg, and DeKlyen (1990) found that preschool-age children with aggressive and oppositional behavior problems were more likely to show evidence of insecure attachments in a maternal separation and reunion task than were their nonproblem peers (84% vs. 28%, respectively). They hypothesized that these children experienced inconsistent and insensitive caregiving situations that elicited feelings of insecurity, anxiety, and anger. By engaging in high-demand acting-out behaviors, these children were both reacting to and coping with their negative feelings, by compelling their mothers to attend and respond to them. Similarly, a longitudinal study conducted by Sroufe and Egeland (1989) documented predictive links between insecure attachment with caregivers in infancy and social adjustment problems (low levels of teacher-rated peer competence) in third grade.

In addition to the innate motivation to form relationships with others, the motivation to act with autonomy emerges during the second year of life and begins to energize and shape interpersonal behavior in characteristic ways. Autonomy reflects the individual's desire to direct his or her own behavior toward chosen goals and to control resources that allow him or her to do so (Deci & Ryan, 1985). Increases in autonomous child activity during the toddler years often set the stage for escalations in parent–child coercive interactions, if parents respond with punitive attempts at overcontrol of child behavior (Campbell, 1990). Emotionally, children may react to punitive control and autonomy restrictions with anger and frustration. Behaviorally, attempts to resist such control and preserve autonomy include oppositional-defiant and bossy behavior (e.g., wanting to do things their way), and high levels of reactivity in situations involving goal frustration (e.g., when they can't get what they want, when they lose a game).

The social-information biases documented for aggressive children are consistent with the hypothesis that they are hypervigilant and emotionally reactive to potential threats to their autonomy in their social interactions (see Table 9.2). For example, hypervigilance is evident in the selective attention aggressive children show to social cues involving interpersonal threat or power-domination (Gouze, 1987) and in their tendency to interpret the ambiguous behavior of peers as hostile (Dodge et al., 1984, 1986). The tendency to focus on instrumental gains rather than relationship goals in their social interactions (Dodge et al., 2002) likewise suggests the heightened value of autonomous functioning and resource control to aggressive (compared to nonaggressive) children. The emotional sensitivity to autonomy threats may both bias social information processing and motivate power-oriented behavior in social interactions. Notably, aggressive children tend to be competitive and argumentative in their play interactions, and they are highly reactive in the face of frustration or perceived threat, escalating quickly to a "fight" response if they feel that their control is threatened or their goals are thwarted.

Emotional Understanding and Social Competence.

In addition to evidence that aggressive children tend to be particularly sensitive and reactive to threats to perceived security (loss of interpersonal support) and/or threats to perceived autonomy and resource

TABLE 9.2
The Biased Social Cognitions of Aggressive Children

Biases associated with information processing:	• Impulsive and incomplete attending to social cues • Selectively vigilant for threats to self • Attribute hostile intent in ambiguous situations • Emphasize personal gain over concern for others • Believe aggressive behavior is often justified • Expect aggression can solve problems
Biases associated with emotional reactivity:	• Reactive to loss of support—threats to security • Reactive to external control—threats to autonomy

control, research also suggests that aggressive children, compared with nonaggressive children, are delayed in the development of emotional understanding and empathy (Dodge, Laird, Lochman, Zelli, & CPPRG, 2002). Emotional understanding involves the capacity to identify one's own emotional states and differentiate between related emotional states, such as anger, frustration, sadness, and anxiety. It also involves the capacity to recognize others' facial expressions and body cues, and includes knowledge regarding cultural guidelines for expressing and masking emotional displays in social interaction (e.g., display rules) (Cole, 1986; Parker et al., 2001).

Delays in the capacity to recognize and label emotions accurately are evident among aggressive children during the preschool and early elementary years. For example, Dodge and his colleagues (Dodge et al., 2002) assessed emotional understanding in a large sample of 387 second-grade children. Among these children, lack of emotion knowledge represented a distinct aspect of social cognition, and was correlated with aggressive behavior at home (as assessed by the Child Behavior Checklist and Parent Daily Reports of aggression) and also with teacher reports of aggression. Similarly, other researchers have documented associations between emotional understanding and children's behavioral control and social adjustment (Denham & Burton, 2004).

Several factors may account for this association. First, the capacity to use language to describe internal affective states provides a foundation for the inhibition of reactive behavior and the redirection of emotional arousal into alternative actions (Izard, 2002). Children then become able to share their feelings verbally with others, fostering new avenues for coping with frustrations and managing conflicts. In addition, the capacity to identify unpleasant arousal with specific labels empowers children to identify cause–effect sequences associated with those feelings, promoting anticipatory problem solving. Emotional understanding and corresponding language skills also allow the child to better understand the feelings of others, allowing them to be more sensitive and responsive in their peer interactions, thereby providing a foundation for mutually rewarding cooperation. Positive peer exchanges further motivate children to inhibit the impulsive and aggressive behaviors that might alienate their peers, fueling the identification of cause–effect links between their behavior and the interpersonal consequences. Conversely, low levels of emotional understanding increase the likelihood that children will fail to understand or will misinterpret the actions of others, thus fueling interpersonal conflicts and supporting negative attributional biases (Dodge et al., 2002).

In addition, Hubbard (2001) found that the capacity to show appropriate display and masking of anger was associated with social adjustment during early grade school. Studying second-grade children, Hubbard videotaped interactions during competitive games with a confederate. Children who were rejected by their peers expressed more anger in their facial expressions, as well as in their verbal interactions, whereas peer-accepted children were more able to regulate and mask their anger in this frustrating social interaction.

Emotional Arousal and Social Information Processing

Social information-processing models suggest that emotion affects behavior primarily by its impact on social appraisals, interpretation, and decision-making processes. However, Izard (2002) and others have argued that the relationship between emotional arousal and information processing is more transactional, such that arousal not only influences and biases, but sometimes derails or short-circuits cognitive processing in social interactions. Specifically, Izard agrees that emotions have a profound influence on perception, cognition, and action, but argues that the relationship between thinking and feeling is reciprocal, and that noncognitive processes associated with emotional experiences have not received sufficient attention in etiological or intervention models targeting child aggression.

For example, high levels of angry arousal often lead to preemptive "fight-or-flight" responding, in which children respond reactively with aggression to (or avoidance of) a perceived threat. It is believed that little active problem solving or reflection occurs under these conditions of affective arousal (sometimes termed "hot cognition"), but rather that children rely on overlearned and habitual self-protective responding. In this way, high levels of angry arousal magnify the deficits associated with social information processing among aggressive children, as they tend to react to upsetting events impulsively with aggression, without careful appraisal, or without thoughtful consideration of consequences or alternative behaviors.

Evidence suggests that aggressive children may be more easily aroused by negative emotional events than are nonaggressive children. In a valuable empirical examination of arousal processes, Hubbard and colleagues (2002) measured children's skin conductance and heart rate reactivity as they played a competitive game with a confederate who cheated. Skin conductance reactivity was linked with nonverbal displays of anger and with reactive aggression, and as arousal (skin conductance reactivity) increased during the course of the game, so did displays of nonverbal anger and aggressive reactions. Compared with nonaggressive children, reactively aggressive children showed evidence of greater angry arousal during the game, including larger increases in skin conductance from one turn to the next, and more sweating. These findings support the hypothesis that reactive emotional arousal fuels aggressive reactions, and that children who are habitually aggressive experience more physiological and emotional arousal under conditions of interpersonal threat.

Theoretically, child temperamental characteristics, combined with early experiences with insensitive, unresponsive, and punitive caregiving, increase child sensitivity and emotional reactivity to perceived rejection or lack of support by others, as well as their sensitivity to threats to autonomy. These emotional sensitivities contribute to a readiness for or vulnerability to increased physiological arousal and feelings of anxiety and anger in interpersonal contexts. Combined with low levels of emotional understanding and regulation and social information-processing deficits (including reduced cue utilization, biases that increase hostile attributions, and a reliance on aggressive responding), angry and anxious arousal increases the likelihood of aggressive and hostile social responding. In the next section, the issue of attending to emotional issues in the design of preventive and remedial interventions for aggressive children is discussed.

ATTENDING TO EMOTIONS IN INTERVENTIONS FOR AGGRESSIVE CHILDREN

Theoretical models and empirical studies suggest that emotion plays an important role in aggressive behavior problems and associated social adjustment difficulties. Intervention models targeting children's social-emotional skills focus primarily on social-cognitive coaching with concurrent behavioral management to exert growth in these skills and corresponding changes in child behavior. Emotional understanding and emotion regulation have been included as skills targeted for change in both prevention and intervention programs designed to reduce aggression. Examples and empirical findings are described in the following sections. In addition, future areas for program development and research are examined, including implications for considering emotional arousal in intervention processes and design.

Social-Cognitive Interventions.

Social-cognitive interventions designed to reduce aggressive behavior and improve social-emotional competencies have included both universal prevention programs and targeted intervention programs. Universal prevention programs are usually taught by classroom teachers and directed toward the entire classroom group to promote social-emotional learning and to reduce aggressive-disruptive behavior in school settings. Social-cognitive coaching programs have also been used as interventions for children already identified as having significant levels of aggressive behavior and related conduct problems. These intervention programs focus on remediating cognitive and emotional skill deficits to reduce the existing aggressive behavior problems. In recent years, universal prevention programs have been coordinated with indicated interventions, in order to provide an optimal "continuum" of services, in which social-emotional competencies are strengthened for all children (in the universal parts of the program) and additional practice and support are provided for aggressive children to remediate their deficits and support their families and teachers in fostering behavioral changes (Webster-Stratton & Taylor, 2001).

Universal social-emotional learning prevention programs and targeted social-cognitive coaching interventions share a common set of assumptions and strategies for teaching social-emotional skills. These programs begin with the assumption that children can learn social-emotional competencies in the same way that they learn cognitive skills, and that these competencies in turn, will provide them with the power to control and organize their behavior when they are emotionally distressed (Denham & Almeida, 1987). The learning process includes phases in which children learn the rudimentary behavioral and cognitive skill components, and then with ongoing support and practice, become better able to integrate and perform these components in increasingly complex and challenging situations, so that they eventually internalize a capacity for self-regulation and social regulation, using the skills in a flexible and socially appropriate way across a wide range of settings and affectively-charged interpersonal situations.

To teach these skills, prevention and intervention programs use four training components (Ladd & Mize, 1983). *First,* instructions, models, and rationales are provided to help children form a conceptual understanding of the target skill. Behavioral examples are illustrated and discussed, so that children can identify the target skill and explain the benefits of using that skill rather than behaving in a more impulsive or aggressive manner. Stories, videotapes, or role plays are typically used to build these skill concepts. *Second,* children are provided with multiple opportunities to practice the target skill under supportive condition. For example, roleplays, scripted sociodramatic play, or interaction tasks are structured to provide practice in specific skills. *Third,* adults provide performance feedback, giving specific praise to identify positive aspects of skill performance and helping the child to identify and redirect problematic aspects of poor skill performance. For the consolidation of social-emotional skills, the goal is to increase children's self-monitoring skills, and their sensitivity to social cues and feedback. *Fourth,* strategies are employed to enhance the generalization of new skills to naturalistic settings, including the classroom and playground context. This may include both the use of contingency management by teachers and parents, and also teacher and parent guidance in supporting flexible social problem solving and skill use when conflicts or problems arise in naturalistic settings.

The most effective programs are those that target skills that are "competence correlates" of positive social adjustment and aggression control, skill deficits that have been associated empirically with aggression and compensatory skills that are correlated with positive social behavior and peer relations (Bierman, 2004). For example, social-cognitive interventions for aggressive children have focused on reducing aggression by targeting the social information biases associated with aggressive responding—asocial goals, negatively biased social appraisals and attribution, and a reliance on domineering approaches to social problem solving. To address these distortions and deficits, coaching programs have focused on social problem-solving skills that teach children to inhibit their initial responses and to think more carefully about the causes and effects of their social behavior, fostering self-control and thoughtful interpersonal problem solving (Lochman & Lenhart, 1993). In addition, as research on the importance of emotional functioning for aggression control and positive social adjustment has accumulated, prevention and intervention programs have included emotional understanding and emotion regulation as key target skills. For example, to foster emotional understanding, interventions have focused on improving children's abilities to identify and label their feelings and to recognize and accurately identify the feelings of others. To enhance emotion regulation, interventions have included self-control skills, including inhibiting impulsive reactivity under conditions of emotional arousal, and coping effectively with feelings of anger. Approaches appear most effective when these skills are embedded within more comprehensive programs that also include prosocial friendship skills to foster positive social engagement and motivation. (Bierman, Greenberg, & CPPRG, 1996). As examples, one universal prevention program and one targeted intervention program with strong empirical evidence of effectiveness are described next; for more comprehensive reviews of prevention and intervention programs, see the Consortium on the School-Based Promotion of Social Competence (1994) and Bierman (2004).

Universal Prevention Program—PATHS

The Promoting Alternative Thinking Strategies (PATHS) program (Greenberg & Kusche, 1993) is a good example of a comprehensive social-emotional learning program designed to promote positive behavioral adjustment and reduce aggressive-disruptive behaviors in school settings. Designed to be taught two to three times per week by classroom teachers, the PATHS curriculum consists of developmentally sequenced lessons. The lessons, 20 to 30 minutes each, target specific social-emotional skills. They provide teachers with systematic materials to present skill concepts (e.g., posters, pictures, videotaped models, stories, and discussion topics) and provide opportunities for behavioral rehearsal (role plays, practice exercises, homework assignments). PATHS lessons target the skills of emotional understanding (identifying and labeling feelings, expressing feelings, assessing the intensity of feelings, understanding the difference between feelings and behaviors), emotion regulation (delaying gratification, controlling impulses, reducing stress, self-talk), and interpersonal problem solving (reading and interpreting social cues, understanding the perspectives of others, using steps for problem solving and decision making). In addition, self-esteem, communication, and friendship skills are covered in the curriculum. The program is designed to enhance student outcomes in areas of emotional literacy, self-control, social competence, positive peer relations, and interpersonal problem-solving skills, and thereby to prevent or reduce behavioral and emotional problems. Lessons also provide teachers with suggestions for formal and informal extension activities for use throughout the day and in integration with other academic units (e.g. language arts, social studies) in order to promote the generalization of key concepts of the curriculum. Teachers are the delivery agents of the PATHS curriculum, with consultation and support provided by PATHS consultants.

The PATHS curriculum has been evaluated in three randomized-controlled studies of early elementary school classrooms. Across studies, PATHS demonstrated positive effects for children in both regular-education and special-education classrooms (including behaviorally at-risk students), with documented improvements in teacher-rated behaviors (e.g., increased self-control, frustration tolerance, and emotional understanding, and reduced aggression), student self-reports (of sadness and depressive symptoms), and peer sociometric ratings (Conduct Problems Prevention Research Group, 1999; Greenberg & Kusche, 1998; Greenberg, Kusche, Cook, & Quamma, 1995). The program has been designated a model program for the prevention of violence (see Greenberg, Kusche, & Mihalic, 1998).

Targeted Intervention Program: Anger Coping and Coping Power

Skills for emotional understanding and regulation have also been incorporated into coaching programs designed for youth who have serious aggressive behavior problems. Some of these, such as Anger Coping (Lochman & Lenhart, 1993), and Coping Power (Lochman & Wells, 1996), specifically combine social-cognitive skill training with exposure to provocative situations, in order to enhance children's abilities to apply social-cognitive skills to inhibit aggressive reactivity when faced with frustrating and anger-inducing situations.

The Anger Coping program (Lochman & Lenhart, 1993) is a 12-session group program that utilizes social-cognitive coaching to promote self-control skills, anger management, and interpersonal problem-solving skills. The program is designed for use with collateral monitoring and behavioral management by classroom teachers, who provide children with contingent reinforcement for the inhibition of aggressive behaviors and the display of positive behaviors. The program is designed specifically for 8- to 12-year olds with anger and aggressive behavior problems. In addition to coaching in the social-cognitive skills associated with self regulation, anger management, and social information processing, the Anger Coping program includes role play exercises in which children practice maintaining their composure when exposed to provocative statements from others. The Coping Power Program (Lochman & Wells, 1996) incorporates the social-cognitive coaching program used in Anger Coping, but is longer in duration (15 months) and incorporates behavioral parent training along with child-focused skills training. Studies have demonstrated program effects on the reduction of aggressive behavior (reported by parents) and antisocial behavior (reported by participants) (see Lochman & Lenhart, 1993; Lochman & Wells, 1996).

Changing Emotional Reactivity

Although curriculum-based lessons on skills such as emotional under-standing and anger regulation may be helpful, these kinds of lessons still rely primarily on changes in children's cold cognitions (their capacity to think about and talk about feelings outside of a problem situation) as a mechanism for driving changes in the underlying feelings and motiva-tions that affect their functioning in the "hot cognition" conditions of real-life interactions. Although role play exercises are utilized to help children practice skills under conditions that simulate "real-world" aggravations, these exercises are still time-limited and contained, with cues that indicate to children that these are "pretend" rather than "actual" provocations. It may be that more naturalistic, experiential intervention strategies are also needed to "rewire" habitual reactive arousal and preemptive fight-or-flight reactivity in interpersonal situations perceived as threatening (par-ticularly those that threaten security or autonomy). As an addition to "cold cognition" lessons, scaffolded experiences that allow for commen-tary, inquiry, and support during "online" emotion-charged social inter-actions may provide critical learning opportunities (Bierman, 2004; Selman & Schultz, 1989).

At this point in time, the empirical literature provides a basis for spec-ulation concerning intervention components and processes that may help rewire or reconstruct children's affective reaction systems, particularly those that serve self-protective functions. However, intervention research is needed to validate these approaches. Here, three factors that warrant consideration are described: (a) the importance of attending to emotional comfort and interpersonal security in the context of intervention sessions to foster openness to emotional learning, (b) the value of inductive pro-cessing during intervention sessions to encourage affective self-regulation, and (c) the benefits of including in intervention programs graduated "exposure" to interpersonal situations that involve increasing levels of affective challenge, along with opportunities for self-reflection and verbal processing of emotional reactions.

Perceived Security in Intervention Sessions

Theoretically, an emotionally and socially supportive context may be important for enhancing the feelings of interpersonal security that allow a child to reduce their reactive reliance on self-protective strategies learned in the context of past relationships. Hence, characteristics of the group-coaching context and the quality of the therapist–child relationship may be important to producing change in emotional reactivity. Certain coach-ing processes and strategies may be particularly useful in strengthening children's feelings of security and connectedness in their peer relations, allowing for greater change in emotional reactivity during sessions. For example, high levels of coach warmth, displayed affection, sensitive responding, supportive social referencing, and frequent praise may all enhance the degree to which children feel supported by the coach and more comfortable trying new interaction strategies with peers. Physiologically, this feeling of security may promote greater social-cognitive learning (Izard, 2002) and reduce threat reactions in the context of peer interactions. The quality of therapist–child and teacher–child relationships as a mediator of change has been documented in other settings; it may be of similar importance as a predictor of emotional change for children in social-cognitive interventions focused on reducing self-protective reactivity and reactive aggressive responding.

Inductive Strategies to Encourage Affective Self-Regulation

The use of "inductive" behavior management strategies, in contrast to power-assertive strategies, may minimize perceived threats to autonomy and encourage children to self-regulate in appropriate ways, hopefully fostering internalized attributions to support generalized behavior change (Bierman, 2004). In contrast to power-assertive strategies (e.g. direct commands), which use adult instruction to redirect problematic child behavior, induction strategies involve verbal and nonverbal techniques designed to help children self-identify and redirect their own behavior. Theoretically, the use of more frequent inductive (rather than directive) strategies minimizes perceived threats to autonomy, thereby encouraging children to self-regulate in appropriate ways without eliciting negative arousal. Inductive strategies cue children to consider the impact of their problematic behavior and suggest alternative behaviors, but do not involve commands or power-oriented constraints that directly threaten a child's self determination.

One type of induction strategy involves providing children with information about desirable behaviors. For example, coaches may praise the positive behavior of others and label positive expectations, thereby identifying appropriate behavior for the target child while minimizing direct commands, which might trigger negative arousal associated with perceived threats to autonomy. Inductive strategies also provide information to enhance a child's awareness of the negative effects of his or her behavior, as with the use of "I-statements" or by eliciting feedback from peers to illustrate the negative (or positive) interpersonal effects of a behavior. Giving choices and pointing out consequences that matter for the child also provide guidance without coercion, which may elicit and encourage self-regulation.

Graduated Exposure With Reflection

A third area warranting consideration in intervention design involves the use of graduated exposure to interpersonal challenges, along with opportunities for emotional reflection. That is, the capacity to use social problem-solving skills in the context of "hot cognition" may require repeated practice opportunities that incorporate increasing levels of affective challenge. Although prior programs have included role play exercises that mimic exposure to insults or put-downs, the daily lives of children involve a much broader array of emotional challenges, ranging from small social slights (a peer did not save a seat at lunch; losing at a game) to direct hostile harassment. It may be important to include in sessions graduated exposure to the everyday hassles of childhood (competitive game play, dealing with unequal and scarce resources). Graduated opportunities to practice social problem-solving skills when aroused may be most effective when adults are available to enhance self-reflection and social-emotional reasoning, by providing commentary and eliciting feedback from others. With these techniques, coaches can cue self-regulation in the context of social challenge, and can also increase the predictability of the child's social experiences, making more explicit for the child the cause–effect relations between their behaviors and the interpersonal responses they receive.

Research has documented the important role that emotional understanding, reactive arousal, and emotion regulation play in the developmental course and expression of aggressive behavior. Hence, the field is challenged to attend to emotion in the design of universal prevention and targeted intervention programs focused on reducing aggression and improving social competence. Current intervention models emphasize social-cognitive skill training, using a combination of instruction, guided practice, feedback, and contingency management to improve social-information-processing skills and positive interaction skills. Emotional understanding and emotion regulation have been added as target skills in universal prevention and intervention programs (such as PATHS and Anger Coping) with a positive impact on behavioral outcomes. These lessons strive to improve emotional understanding and emotion regulation, but still rely on changes in children's "cold cognitions" (their capacity to think about and talk about feelings outside of a problem situation) as a mechanism for driving changes in the underlying feelings and motivations that affect their functioning in the "hot cognition" conditions of real-life interactions. The Anger Coping intervention and others like it have incorporated guided role-play practice in coping with peer provocations as a strategy to help children reduce reactive anger and apply positive coping strategies when aroused.

Additional strategies designed to help rewrite habitual reactive arousal and improve emotion regulation under conditions of duress deserve exploration and evaluation. For example, greater attention to emotional comfort and interpersonal security, the use of inductive strategies to encourage self-regulation, and the inclusion of graduated exposure to everyday hassles with increasing levels of affective challenge and opportunities to reflect on feelings during intervention sessions may enhance emotional learning. Future intervention research should include specific attention to emotion in both program design and evaluation, in order to determine whether such modifications improve the impact of coaching interventions, particularly for early-starting aggressive youth.

REFERENCES

Asarnow, J. (1983). Children with peer adjustment problems: Sequential and non-sequential analyses of school behaviors. *Journal of Consulting and Clinical Psychology, 51,* 709–717.

Asarnow, J. R., & Callan, J. W. (1985). Boys with peer adjustment problems: Social cognitive processes. *Journal of Consulting and Clinical Psychology, 53,* 80–87.

Baldwin, M. W. (1992). Relational schemas and the processing of social information. *Psychological Bulletin, 112,* 461–484.

Bierman, K. L. (2004). *Peer rejection: Developmental processes and intervention strategies.* New York: Guilford.

Bierman, K. L., Greenberg, M. T., & the Conduct Problems Prevention Research Group (1996). Social skills training in the Fast Track program. In R. D. Peters & R. J. McMahon (Eds.), *Preventing childhood disorders, substance abuse, and delinquency* (p. 65–89). Newbury Park, CA: Sage.

Bierman, K. L., Smoot, D. L., & Aumiller, K. (1993). Characteristics of aggressive-rejected, aggressive (nonrejected), and rejected (nonaggressive) boys. *Child Development, 64,* 139–151.

Bierman, K. L., & Wargo, J. (1995). Predicting the longitudinal course associated with aggressive-rejected, aggressive (non-rejected) and rejected (non-aggressive) status. *Development and Psychopathology, 7,* 669–682.

Bowlby, J. (1969). *Attachment and loss: Vol. 1. Attachment.* New York: Basic Books.

Bretherton, I. (1995). Attachment and psychopathology. In D. Cicchetti & S. L. Toth (Eds.), *Emotion, cognition, and representation* (Rochester Symposium on Developmental Psychopathology, Vol. 6, pp. 231–260). Rochester, NY: University of Rochester Press.

Cairns, R. B. (1991). Developmental epistemology and self-knowledge: Towards a reinterpretation of self esteem. In G. Greenberg & E. Tobach (Eds.), *Theories of the evolution of knowing* (pp. 69–86). Hillsdale, NJ: Lawrence Erlbaum Associates.

Campbell, S. B. (1990). *Behavior problems in preschool children: Clinical and developmental issues.* New York: Guilford.

Cillessen, A. H. N., van Ijzendoorn, H. W., van Lieshout, C. F. M., & Hartup, W. W. (1992). Heterogeneity of peer rejected boys. *Child Development, 63,* 893–905.

Coie, J. D., & Dodge, K. A. (1998). Aggression and antisocial behavior. In W. Damon (Ed.) (N. Eisenberg, Vol. Ed.), & *Handbook of child psychology, fifth edition. Vol. 3: Social, emotional, and personality development* (pp. 779–862). New York: Wiley.

Cole, P. M. (1986). Children's spontaneous control of facial expression. *Child Development, 57,* 1309–1321.

Cole, P. M., Michel, M. K., & Teti, L. O. (1994). The development of emotion regulation and dysregulation: A clinical perspective. *Monographs of the Society for Research in Child Development, 59,* 53–72.

Conduct Problems Prevention Research Group. (1999). Initial impact of the Fast Track prevention trial for conduct problems: II. Classroom effects. *Journal of Consulting and Clinical Psychology, 67,* 648–657.

Consortium on the School-Based Promotion of Social Competence. (1994). The school-based promotion of social competence: Theory, research, practice, and policy. In R. J. Haggerty, L. R. Sherrod, N. Garmezy, & M. Rutter (Eds.), *Stress, risk, and resilience in children and adolescents: Processes, mechanisms, and interventions* (pp. 268–316). New York: Cambridge University Press.

Crick, N. R., & Dodge, K. A. (1994). A review and reformulation of social information-processing mechanisms in children's social adjustment. *Psychological Bulletin, 115,* 74–101.

Deci, E. L., & Ryan, R. M. (1985). *Intrinsic motivation and self-determination in human behavior.* New York: Plenum.

Denham, S. A., & Almeida, M. C. (1987). Children's social problem-solving skills, behavioral adjustment, and interventions: A meta-analysis evaluating theory and practice. *Journal of Applied Developmental Psychology, 8,* 391–409.

Denham, S. A., & Burton, R. (2004). *Social and emotional prevention and intervention programming for preschoolers.* New York: Kluwer Academic/Plenum.

Dodge, K. A. (1986). A social information processing model of social competence in children. In M. Perlmutter (Eds.), *Cognitive perspectives on children's social and behavioral development* (pp. 77–125). Hillsdale, NJ: Lawrence Erlbaum Associates.

Dodge, K. A. (1991). Emotion and social information processing. In J. Garber & K.A. Dodge (Eds.), *The development of emotion regulation and dysregulation* (pp. 159–181). New York: Cambridge University Press.

Dodge, K. A., Asher, S. R., & Parkhurst, J. T. (1989). Social life as a goal coordination task. In C. Ames & R. Ames (Eds.), *Research on motivation in education* (Vol. 3, pp. 107–135). San Diego, CA: Academic Press.

Dodge, K. A., Bates, J. E., & Pettit, G. S. (1990). Mechanism in the cycle of violence. *Science, 250,* 1678–1683.

Dodge, K. A., Laird, R., Lochman, J. E., Zelli, A., and the Conduct Problems Prevention Research Group (2002). Multidimensional latent-construct analysis of children's social information processing patterns: Correlations with aggressive behavior problems. *Psychological Assessment, 14,* 60–73.

Dodge, K. A., Murphy, R. R., & Buchsbaum, K. (1984). The assessment of intention–cue detection skills in children: Implications for developmental psychopathology. *Child Development, 55,* 163–173.

Dodge, K. A., & Newman, J. P. (1981). Biased decision-making processes in aggressive boys. *Journal of Abnormal Psychology, 90,* 375–379.

Dodge, K. A., Pettit, G. S., McClaskey, C. L., & Brown, M. (1986). Social competence in children. *Monographs of the Society for Research in Child Development, 51*(3, Serial No. 213).

Dodge, K. A., Pettit, G. S., Bates, J. E., & Valente, E. (1995). Social information-processing patterns partially mediate the effect of early physical abuse on later conduct problems. *Journal of Abnormal Psychology, 104,* 632–643.

Dubow, E. F. (1988). Aggressive behavior and peer social status of elementary school children. *Aggressive Behavior, 14,* 315–324.

Eisenberg, N., & Fabes, R. A. (1992). Emotion, regulation, and the development of social competence. In M. S. Clark (Ed.), *Review of personality and social psychology: Vol. 14. Emotion and social behavior* (pp. 119–150). Newbury Park, CA: Sage.

Epstein, S. (1991). Cognitive-experiential self theory: Implications for developmental psychology. In M. R. Gunnar & L. A. Sroufe (Eds.), *Self processes and development: The Minnesota symposium on child psychology* (Vol. 23, pp. 79–123). Hillsdale, NJ: Lawrence Erlbaum Associates.

Gouze, K. R. (1987). Attention and social problem solving as correlates of aggression in preschool males. *Journal of Abnormal Child Psychology, 15,* 181–197.

Graham, S., & Hudley, C. (1994). Attributions of aggressive and nonaggressive African-American male early adolescents: A study of construct accessibility. *Developmental Psychology, 30,* 365–373.

Greenberg, M. T., & Kusche, C. A. (1993*). Promoting social and emotional development in deaf children: The PATHS project.* Seattle: University of Washington Press.

Greenberg, M. T., & Kusche, C. A. (1998). Preventive intervention for school-aged deaf children: The PATHS curriculum. *Journal of Deaf Studies and Deaf Education, 3,* 49–63.

Greenberg, M. T., Kusche, C. A., Cook, E. T., & Quamma, J. P. (1995). Promoting emotional competence in school-aged deaf children: The effects of the PATHS Curriculum. *Development and Psychopathology, 7,* 117–136.

Greenberg, M. T., Kusche, C. & Mihalic, S. F. (1998). *Blueprints for violence prevention: Promoting alternative thinking strategies (PATHS).* Boulder, CO: Center for the Study and Prevention of Violence.

Greenberg, M. T., Kusche, C. A., & Speltz, M. (1991). Emotional regulation, self control, and psychopathology: The role of relationships in early childhood. In D. Cicchetti & S. L. Toth (Eds.), *Internalizing and externalizing expressions of dysfunction: Rochester symposium on developmental psychopathology* (Vol. 2, pp. 21–66). Hillsdale, NJ: Lawrence Erlbaum Associates.

Hart, C. H., Ladd, G. W., & Burleson, B. (1990). Children's expectations of the outcomes of Social strategies: Relations with sociometric status and maternal disciplinary styles. *Child Development, 61,* 127–137.

Hartup, W. W. (1983). The peer system. In E. M. Hetherington (Ed.), *Handbook of child psychology: Vol. 4. Socialization, personality, and social development* (4th ed., pp. 102–196). New York: Wiley.

Hodges, E., & Perry, D. (1996). Victims of peer abuse: An overview. *Journal of Emotional and Behavioral Problems, 5,* 23–28.

Hubbard, J. A. (2001). Emotion expression processes in children's peer interaction: The role of peer rejection, aggression, and gender. *Child Development, 72,* 1426–1438.

Hubbard, J. A., Smithmyer, C. M., Ramsden, S. R., Parker, E. H., Flanagan, K. D., Dearing, K. F., et al. (2002). Observational, physiological, and self-report measures of children's anger: Relations to reactive versus proactive aggression. *Child Development, 73,* 1101–1118.

Izard, C. (2002). Translating emotion theory and research into preventive interventions. *Psychological Bulletin, 128,* 796–824.

Ladd, G. W., & Mize, J. (1983). A cognitive-social learning model of social skill training. *Psychological Review, 90,* 127–157.

Ladd, G. W., Kochenderfer, B. J., & Coleman, C. (1997). Classroom peer acceptance, friendship social adjustment. *Child Development, 68,* 1181–1197.

Ladd, G. W., & Profilet, S. M. (1996). The child behavior scale: A teacher measure of young children's aggressive, withdrawn, and prosocial behaviors. *Developmental Psychology, 32*(6), 1008–1024.

Lochman, J. E. (1987). Self and peer perceptions and attributional biases of aggressive and nonaggressive boys. *Journal of Consulting and Clinical Psychology, 55,* 404–410.

Lochman, J. E., & Lenhart, L. A. (1993). Anger coping intervention for aggressive children: Conceptual models and outcome effects. *Clinical Psychology Review, 13,* 785–805.

Lochman, J. E., & Wells, K. C. (1996). A social-cognitive intervention with aggressive children. In R. D. Peters & R. J. McMahon (Eds.), *Preventing childhood disorders, substance abuse, and delinquency* (pp. 111–143). Thousand Oaks, CA: Sage.

Milich, R., & Dodge, K. A. (1984). Social information processing patterns in child psychiatric populations. *Journal of Abnormal Child Psychology, 12,* 471–490.

Miller-Johnson, S., Coie, J. D., Bierman, K., Maumary-Gremaud, A., & Conduct Problems Prevention Research Group. (2002). Peer rejection and aggression and early-starter models of conduct disorder. *Journal of Abnormal Child Psychology, 30,* 217–230.

Parker, E. H., Hubbard, J. A., Ramsden, S. R., Relyea, N., Dearing, K. F., Smithmyer, C. M., et al. (2001). Children's use and knowledge of display rules for anger following hypothetical vignettes versus following live peer interaction. *Social Development, 10,* 528–557.

Patterson, G. R. (1986). Performance models for antisocial boys. *American Psychologist, 41*(4), 432–444.

Perry, D. G., Perry, L. C., & Kennedy, E. (1992). Conflict and the development of antisocial behavior. In C. Shantz & W. Hartup (Eds.), *Conflict in child and adolescent development* (pp. 301–329). Cambridge, England: Cambridge University Press.

Perry, D. G., Perry, L. C., & Rasmussen, P. (1986). Cognitive social learning mediators of aggression. *Child Development, 57,* 700–711.

Pope, A. W. & Bierman, K. L. (1999). Predicting adolescent peer problems and antisocial activities: The relative roles of aggression and dysregulation. *Developmental Psychology, 35,* 335–346.

Schwartz, D., Dodge, K. A., & Coie, J. D. (1993). The emergence of chronic peer victimization in boys' play groups. *Child Development, 64,* 1755–1772.

Selman, R. L., & Schultz, L. H. (1990). *Making a friend in youth: Developmental theory and pair therapy.* Chicago: University of Chicago Press.

Speltz, M. L., Greenberg, M. T., & DeKlyen, M. (1990). Attachment in preschoolers with disruptive behavior: A comparison of clinic-referred and nonproblem children. *Development and Psychopathology, 2,* 31–46.

Sroufe, L. A. (1990). An organizational perspective on the self. In D. Cicchetti & M. Beeghly (Eds.), *The self in transition: Infancy to childhood* (pp. 281–307). Chicago: University of Chicago Press.

Sroufe, L. A. (1996). *Emotional development: The organization of emotional life in the early years.* Cambridge, England: Cambridge University Press.

Sroufe, L. A., & Egeland, B. (1989, April). *Early predictors of psychopathology.* Symposium presented at the Biennial Meeting of the Society for Research on Child Development, Kansas City, MO.

Thornberry, T. P., Lizotte, A. J., Krohn, M. D., Farnworth, M., & Jang, J. J. (1994). Delinquency of peers, beliefs, and delinquent behavior: A longitudinal test of interactional theory. *Criminology, 32,* 47–83.

Vitaro, F., Tremblay, R. E., Gagnon, D., & Boivan, M. (1992). Peer rejection from kindergarten to Grade 2: Outcomes, correlates, and prediction. *Merrill–Palmer Quarterly, 38,* 382–400.

Webster-Stratton, C., & Taylor, T. (2001). Nipping early risk factors in the bud: Preventing substance abuse, delinquency, and violence in adolescence through interventions targeted at young children (0 to 8 Years). *Prevention Science, 2,* 165–192.

Multisystemic Treatment With Violent Youths and Their Families

Charles M. Borduin

Violent criminal acts and other serious crimes (i.e., index offenses) committed by youths present significant problems at several levels of analysis, and these problems argue for the development of effective treatment approaches. On a personal level, youths who commit serious crimes experience numerous psychosocial problems as well as reduced educational and occupational opportunities (Lyons, Baerger, Quigley, Erlich, & Griffin, 2001; Melton & Pagliocca, 1992). Moreover, serious criminal activity perpetrated by youths has extremely detrimental emotional, physical, and economic effects on victims, their families, and the larger community (Britt, 2000; Cohen & Miller, 1998; Gottfredson, 1989; Robinson & Keithley, 2000). Therefore, effective treatment may not only benefit the youth and his or her family, but may also save many persons from victimization.

On an epidemiological level, youths under the age of 18 years account for approximately 26% of all arrests for index offenses, including 23% of robberies and 17% of forcible rapes (Federal Bureau of Investigation, 2003), and such arrests greatly underestimate the prevalence of youth criminal activity (Elliott, Dunford, & Huizinga, 1987; Loeber, Farrington, & Waschbusch, 1998). In addition, although only about a fourth of youths arrested for delinquent acts could be characterized as serious offenders and even fewer (approximately 10%) as violent offenders, serious and violent juvenile offenders account for more than half of the total volume of youth crime in a community (Farrington, Ohlin, & Wilson, 1986; Loeber et al., 1998; Moffitt, 1993). Thus, if one purpose of treating juvenile offenders is to decrease crime, then serious and violent juvenile offenders are a logical target for intervention efforts.

On a social services level, juvenile offenders, especially those who are violent, consume much of the resources of the child mental health, juvenile justice, and special education systems and are overrepresented in the "deep end" of these systems (Cocozza, 1992; Melton, Lyons, & Spaulding, 1998), with considerable cost to the public treasury and intrusion on family integrity and youth autonomy. Moreover, youths who engage in violence and other serious forms of antisocial behavior often have continued contact with the mental health and criminal justice systems well into adulthood (Borduin & Schaeffer, 1998; Moffitt, 1993; Pajer, 1998). Therefore, the development of effective treatments for youth violence and criminality may help to free resources to address other important problems of children and their families.

Unfortunately, as numerous reviewers have concluded (e.g., Kazdin, 2000; Melton & Pagliocca, 1992; Tate, Reppucci, & Mulvey, 1995), the development of effective treatments for violence and criminality in youths has been an extremely difficult task. In part, this difficulty is due to the fact that serious antisocial behaviors, especially those involving aggression, tend to be highly stable in individuals (Loeber & Hay, 1996; Moffitt, 1993) and across generations (Hawkins et al., 1998; Huesmann, Lefkowitz, Eron, & Walder, 1984). However, an even more important reason for the general lack of effective treatments for youths who commit serious crimes is that most extant treatments do not address the multiple and changing mental health needs of these youth. Clearly, there is a pressing need to develop effective alternatives to the narrowly focused treatments that are commonly used with youths involved in violent and other serious antisocial behaviors.

Multisystemic therapy (MST; Borduin & Henggeler, 1990; Henggeler & Borduin, 1990) was developed to address major limitations of existing mental health services for juvenile offenders and has been viewed as a promising treatment for violence and criminality in youths (see, e.g., Kazdin, 2000; Larzelere, Kuhn, & Johnson, 2004; Levesque, 1996; Tate et al., 1995). Consistent with the theme of the present volume, this chapter considers how aggressive behavior and angry emotions are addressed within the context of MST interventions for violent youths. As background for discussing MST interventions, this chapter begins with a brief description of the empirical underpinnings and theoretical foundation of the MST approach. Next, an overview of clinical interventions in MST is provided, describing how MST is operationalized (i.e., specified), delivered to youths and families (using a home-based model of service delivery), and supported in the supervisory process. Findings from controlled evaluations that demonstrate the effectiveness of MST with violent and serious juvenile offenders are then summarized, and current and future studies of MST with violent juvenile offenders and other clinical populations are described. Finally, some implications of our work for the development of effective treatments for violent youths and their families are discussed.

EMPIRICAL FOUNDATIONS OF MST

Correlates of Serious and Violent Antisocial Behavior

A large number of studies have evaluated correlates of serious and violent antisocial behavior in youths. In general, these correlates pertain to the individual youth and to the key social systems (family, peers, school, neighborhood) in which the youth is embedded. Table 10.1 lists the correlates that have consistently emerged in the literature (for reviews, see Borduin & Schaeffer, 1998; Farrington & Loeber, 2000; Hawkins et al., 1998; Thornberry, Huizinga, & Loeber, 1995).

In light of the numerous correlates of violent and other serious antisocial behavior in youths, an ever-increasing number of research groups have developed empirically based multidimensional causal models of delinquent behavior. These research groups have used path analysis or structural equation modeling to examine the interrelations among variables from several of the psychosocial domains (i.e., individual, family, peers, school, neighborhood) that have been linked with serious antisocial behavior. Such causal modeling studies allow a determination of which variables have direct versus indirect effects on antisocial behavior, and which variables are no longer linked with antisocial behavior when the effects of other correlates are controlled. Findings across studies (e.g., Henry, Tolan, & Gorman-Smith, 2001; Herrenkohl et al., 2001; LeBlanc & Kaspy, 1998; Paschall & Hubbard, 1998) are relatively clear and consistent:

1. Involvement with deviant peers is virtually always a powerful direct predictor of violence and other serious antisocial behaviors.
2. Family relations predict serious antisocial behaviors either directly (contributing unique variance) or indirectly by predicting involvement with deviant peers.
3. School difficulties predict involvement with deviant peers.
4. Neighborhood and community support characteristics add small portions of unique variance or indirectly predict serious antisocial behaviors by, for example, affecting family, peer, or school behavior.

Thus, across studies and in spite of substantial variation in research methods and measurement, investigators have shown that youth violence is linked directly or indirectly with key characteristics of youths and of their social systems.

Clinical Implications of Findings

If the primary goal of treatment is to optimize the probability of decreasing rates of youth violent or other serious antisocial behavior, then treatment

TABLE 10.1
Correlates of Serious and Violent Antisocial Behavior

Individual youth characteristics

- Low verbal skills
- Favorable attitudes toward antisocial behavior
- Immature moral reasoning
- Cognitive bias to attribute hostile intentions to others

Family characteristics

- Lax and ineffective parental discipline
- Lack of parental monitoring
- Low affection and cohesion
- High conflict and hostility
- Parental difficulties, such as substance abuse, psychiatric conditions, and criminality

Peer relations

- High involvement with deviant peers
- Poor social skills
- Low involvement with prosocial peers

School factors

- Low commitment to education
- Poor academic performance
- Dropout
- Poor academic quality and weak structure of school

Neighborhood and community characteristics

- Low organizational participation among residents
- High mobility
- Low social support available from church, neighbors, and the like
- Criminal subculture (e.g., drug dealing, prostitution)

approaches must have the flexibility to address the multiple known determinants of such behavior. Indeed, there is a growing consensus among reviewers that the major limitation of most treatments for serious antisocial behavior is their failure to account for the multidetermined nature of such behavior and that effective treatments must have the capacity to intervene comprehensively, at individual, family, peer, school, and possibly even neighborhood levels (Borduin, 1994; Kashani, Jones, Bumby, & Thomas, 1999; Kazdin, 2000; Levesque, 1996; Melton & Pagliocca, 1992; Mulvey,

Arthur, & Reppucci, 1993). A critical feature of MST is its capacity to address the multiple determinants of violence or serious antisocial behavior in a comprehensive, intense, and individualized fashion.

THEORETICAL FOUNDATIONS OF MST

Family systems theory (Bateson, 1972; Hoffman, 1981; Minuchin, 1985) and the theory of social ecology (Bronfenbrenner, 1979) fit closely with research findings on the correlates and causes of serious antisocial behavior in youths and serve as a basis for case conceptualization and treatment planning in MST. Family systems theory views the family as a rule-governed system and an organized whole that transcends the sum of its separate parts. From this perspective, it is assumed that problematic individual behaviors and symptoms are intimately related to patterns of interaction between family members and must always be understood within the context of those interaction patterns. Although there are differences in how various schools of family therapy interpret systems theory, most attempt to understand how emotional and behavioral problems "fit" within the context of the individual's family relations and emphasize the reciprocal and circular nature of such relations. Thus, a therapist working from a family systems conceptual framework would consider not only how parental discipline strategies influence youth aggressive behaviors but also how the aggressive behaviors of the youth shape and guide the behaviors of the parents, and what function the misbehaviors might serve in the family.

The theory of social ecology (Bronfenbrenner, 1979) shares some of the basic tenets of family systems theory but encompasses broader and more numerous contextual influences within a youth's life. The youth is viewed as being nested within a complex of interconnected systems that include the individual youth, the youth's family, and various extrafamilial (peer, school, neighborhood, community) contexts (see Figure 10.1). The youth's behavior is seen as the product of the reciprocal interplay between the youth and these systems and of the relations of the systems with each other. Thus, although the interactions between the youth and family or peers are seen as important, the connections between the systems are viewed as equally important. It is assumed, then, that youth behavior problems such as aggression can be maintained by problematic transactions within any given system or between some combination of pertinent systems. Important to note, social-ecological theory emphasizes the significance of "ecological validity" in understanding behavior, that is, the basic assumption that behavior can be fully understood only when viewed within its naturally occurring context.

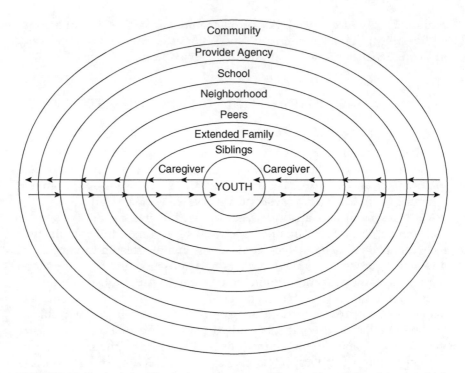

FIGURE 10.1. Social-ecological environment. The youth and family are embedded in multiple systems with dynamic and reciprocal influences (represented by arrows) on the behavior of family members. Violent behavior can be maintained by problematic transactions within and/or between any one or combination of these systems.

CLINICAL FOUNDATIONS OF MST

Model of Service Delivery

The provision of MST to violent youth is consistent with the family preservation model of service delivery (Nelson & Landsman, 1992). Family preservation is based on the philosophy that the most effective and ethical route to helping youth is through helping their families. Thus, families are seen as valuable resources, even when they are characterized by serious and multiple needs. A critical characteristic of the family preservation model is that interventions are delivered in the family's natural environment (home, school, neighborhood) to optimize ecological validity. Delivering interventions in the natural environment also greatly decreases barriers to service access in a population (i.e., families of adolescents presenting serious antisocial behavior) that has very high "no-show" and dropout rates from traditional institution-based services (for a discussion of this issue, see Snell-Johns, Mendez, & Smith, 2004). Indeed, working with families on their own "turf" sends a message of therapist commitment and respect that can greatly facilitate family engagement and the development of a therapeutic alliance—prerequisites for achieving desired outcomes.

MST is usually delivered by a master's-level therapist with a caseload of four to eight families. The MST therapist is a generalist who directly provides most mental health services and coordinates access to other important services (e.g., medical, educational, recreational), always monitoring quality control. Although the therapist is available to the family 24 hours a day, 7 days a week, therapeutic intensity is titrated to clinical need; thus, the range of direct contact hours per family can vary considerably. In general, therapists spend more time with families in the initial weeks of therapy (daily, if indicated) and gradually taper off (as infrequently as once a week) during a 3- to 5-month course of treatment.

MST Treatment Principles

MST does not follow a rigid protocol in which therapists conduct sets of predetermined tasks in an invariant sequence. Indeed, because MST is typically used with complex cases that present serious and diverse problems and that also evidence a wide variety of possible strengths, fully detailing treatment parameters for each possible combination of situations would be an impossible task. Nevertheless, in the absence of strong specification, the value of MST would be greatly diminished. Thus, rather than providing session-by-session breakdowns of recommended clinical procedures, we have developed treatment principles to guide therapists' case conceptualizations, prioritization of interventions, and implementation of intervention strategies in MST.

The nine treatment principles enumerated in the following serve as general guidelines for designing multisystemic interventions. Detailed descriptions of these principles, and examples that illustrate the translation of these principles into specific intervention strategies, are provided in a clinical volume (Henggeler & Borduin, 1990) and a treatment manual (Henggeler, Schoenwald, Borduin, Rowland, & Cunningham, 1998). MST therapists and supervisors often refer to the principles while planning interventions, and treatment fidelity can be evaluated by measuring therapist adherence to the principles.

> **Principle 1. The primary purpose of assessment is to understand the "fit" between the identified problems and their broader**

systemic context. The goal of MST assessment is to "make sense" of aggression and other antisocial behaviors in light of their systemic context. Consistent with both the empirically established correlates/causes of youth violence and with systemic/social-ecological theories, MST assessment focuses on understanding the factors that contribute directly or indirectly to behavioral problems such as aggression. In general, these features pertain to characteristics of the individual youth (e.g., distortions and deficiencies in social cognition) and to transactions between the youth and the multiple systems in which he or she is embedded (e.g., family, peer, school, and neighborhood). Thus, the MST therapist attempts to determine how each factor, singularly or in combination, increases or decreases the probability of youth aggression and other behavior problems.

The assessment of fit proceeds in an inductive manner, systematically examining the strengths and needs of each system and their relationship to identified problems. The MST therapist examines perceived strengths and needs from the perspectives of key informants in the youth's social ecology, including family members, school personnel, possibly neighbors and family friends, probation officers, peers, and so forth. The integration of information from multiple sources, each containing unique forms of bias, is not a simple task. MST therapists must be able to resolve inconsistencies between the views of different respondents and know when the information obtained does not "make sense" of the problems.

After obtaining the information needed to understand fit, the therapist in collaboration with the treatment team and clinical supervisor develops testable hypotheses (i.e., the underlying constructs or relevant factors are concrete and measurable). MST therapists initially give priority to hypotheses that are based on proximal causes of behavior prior to hypothesizing more distal causes. Nevertheless, proximal effects may mask more distal and indirect effects, and these distal effects often become initial targets of intervention. For example, a youth's aggression toward his or her siblings may be linked proximally with ineffective parental discipline strategies. Factors contributing to the ineffective discipline strategies (i.e., proximal determinants) may include high family stress, low parent–youth bonding, parental drug abuse or psychiatric condition, lack of knowledge regarding effective parenting, a weak social support network, and marital distress; these proximal determinants of ineffective discipline are the more distal determinants of the youth's aggression.

Targets of intervention in MST are derived from the hypotheses formulated from the assessment data. These hypotheses are then tested through the implementation of interventions, and hypotheses are either confirmed or refuted based on outcomes of interventions. As information supporting or refuting hypotheses is gathered over the course of treatment, understanding of the fit of aggression or other problems should remain or change accordingly. That is, the therapist and treatment team develop a process of ruling in or ruling out the various hypotheses thought to explain the youth's and family's behavior. Thus, the concept of fit is used in the development of hypotheses and the design of interventions in an ongoing fashion.

Principle 2. Therapeutic contacts emphasize the positive and use systemic strengths as levers for change. Identifying strengths begins during the MST assessment and focuses on the broad ecology of the youth and family. Staying strength-focused means that MST therapists realistically appraise family members' ability to use their strengths to accomplish tasks while working to develop additional strengths to accomplish goals. Moreover, a consistent and ongoing emphasis on fostering strength-focused attitudes and communications among MST therapists, supervisors, administrators, and professionals from other agencies is critical to the reinforcement of strength-focused therapist–family interactions.

Principle 3. Interventions are designed to promote responsible behavior and decrease irresponsible behavior among family members. Conceptualizing the purpose of MST as enhancing responsible behavior is a point of view that can be readily communicated and understood by diverse groups of individuals, including family members, school personnel, agency colleagues, judges, and legislators. For all parties involved, increasing the responsible behavior of youths and parents is a less daunting and more achievable task than treating "psychopathology," which, as reflected in diagnostic labels such as conduct disorder, borderline personality disorder, and so forth, implies a fixed, diseaselike, and potentially intractable entity ("the disorder") as the target of treatment.

Responsible youths engage in behaviors and activities that help them to become competent members of their families, communities, and society. Responsible parents engage in behaviors that prepare their youths to become competent members of these systems. Improvement in parental responsibility is almost always linked with improved youth behavior; thus, MST therapists devote a great deal of time to developing and maintaining parental responsibility.

Principle 4. Interventions are present focused and action oriented, targeting specific and well-defined problems. MST interventions emphasize changing the family's present circumstances as a step toward changing future functioning. In light of the serious nature of the problems presented by youths and families referred for MST, interventions aim to activate the family and their social ecology to make multiple, positive, observable changes. Making and sustaining such changes within the brevity of MST requires a high-energy and action-oriented focus. Targeting well-defined problems (i.e., objective, measurable, and jargon free) and setting well-defined treatment goals keeps family members, therapists, and other participants fully aware of the direction of treatment, the criteria used to measure success, and the effectiveness of various interventions.

Principle 5. Interventions target sequences of behavior within and between multiple systems that maintain the identified problems. This principle orients the MST practitioner toward modifying those aspects of family relations and of the social ecology that are linked with identified problems. Thus, whether addressing problematic family interactions or helping to build the family's relations with extrafamilial systems (e.g., family–school interface, family–peer interface), MST focuses on interpersonal transactions as the mechanism for achieving treatment goals.

Principle 6. Interventions are developmentally appropriate and fit the developmental needs of the youth. Youths and their caregivers have different needs at different periods of their lives, and MST interventions are designed in consideration of such. For example, the nature of family-based interventions will vary with the developmental level of the youth. For children and younger adolescents, considerable efforts may be extended to increasing parental control. For older adolescents (e.g., 17-year-olds), interventions might be more viable if they focus on preparing the youth for entry into the adult world. The developmental stage of the caregiver is also an important factor when designing interventions. For example, a grandparent who is thrust into the the role of primary caretaker may have different developmental needs than a traditional parent.

Principle 7. Interventions are designed to require daily or weekly effort by family members. A basic assumption of MST is that therapists can help families resolve their problems more quickly if everyone involved (e.g., caregivers, extended family, siblings, friends, neighbors, and social service personnel) works together diligently. This assumption is predicated on the family and therapist agreeing on and collaborating with the goals of treatment and, by default, agreeing to address any barriers that interfere with achieving these goals. Because intervention tasks occur daily, family members have frequent opportunities to receive positive feedback and praise in moving toward goals. Such reinforcers promote family motivation and maintenance of change. In addition, family empowerment is supported as families learn that they are primarily responsible for and capable of progressing toward treatment goals.

Principle 8. Intervention effectiveness is evaluated continuously from multiple perspectives with providers assuming accountability for overcoming barriers to successful outcomes. This principle ensures that the MST therapist will have a continuous and relatively accurate view of treatment progress and, therefore, receive ongoing and prompt feedback regarding the viability of interventions. If an intervention is not working, prompt feedback allows the therapist and family to consider alternative interventions or alternative conceptualizations of the targeted problem. Problems can usually be resolved in multiple ways, and MST therapists are encouraged to consider alternative solutions when the present ones are not effective.

Principle 9. Interventions are designed to promote treatment generalization and long-term maintenance of therapeutic change by empowering caregivers to address family members' needs across multiple systemic contexts. Ensuring that treatment gains will generalize and be maintained when treatment ends is a critical and continuous thrust of MST interventions. To promote treatment generalization and maintenance, MST therapists (a) teach relevant behaviors or skills in the environments and under the conditions in which clients will eventually behave, (b) encourage and reinforce the development of family members' problem-solving skills, (c) find individuals in the ecology who can and will reinforce family members' new behaviors and skills across settings (e.g., home, school, and community), (d) alert significant others (e.g., teachers, probation officers, and case managers) to the new behaviors of the family members, (e) provide reinforcement when generalization occurs, and (f) allow clients to do as much of the development and implementation of interventions as they can. Thus, through emphasizing family empowerment and the mobilization of indigenous youth, family, and community resources, the MST therapist aims to set the stage for lasting therapeutic change.

Findings from several studies indicate that therapists' adherence to the MST treatment principles is directly related to clinical outcomes with violent youths. For example, in an MST clinical trial with youth who were violent and chronic offenders, Henggeler, Melton, Brondino, Scherer, and Hanley (1997) found that parent, youth, and therapist reports of high treatment fidelity (assessed with a 26-item measure of MST adherence; Henggeler & Borduin, 1992) were associated with low rates of rearrest and incarceration for adolescents at a 1.7-year follow-up. Other, related studies (Huey, Henggeler, Brondino, & Pickrel, 2000; Schoenwald, Henggeler, Brondino, & Rowland, 2000) have supported the view that therapist adherence to the MST principles influences those processes (e.g., family relations, association with deviant peers) that sustain youth violent and serious antisocial behavior. Thus, significant empirical support is emerging for the association between treatment adherence and clinical outcomes in MST.

MST Interventions Targeting Aggression (and Anger in Some Cases)

MST interventions target identified youth and family problems within and between the multiple systems in which family members are embedded. The overriding goals of MST are to empower parents with the skills and resources needed to independently address the inevitable difficulties that arise in raising youths and to empower youths to cope with familial and extrafamilial problems. Using well-validated treatment strategies derived from strategic family therapy, structural family therapy, behavioral parent training, and cognitive-behavioral therapy, MST directly addresses intrapersonal (e.g., cognitive), familial, and extrafamilial (i.e., peer, school, neighborhood) factors that are known to contribute to youth serious and violent antisocial behavior. Biological contributors to identified problems (e.g., major depression, attention deficit hyperactivity disorder) in family members are also identified, and, when appropriate, psychopharmacological treatment is integrated with psychosocial treatment. Because different contributing factors are relevant for different youths and families, MST interventions are individualized and highly flexible.

Although the exact nature and sequence of interventions in MST can vary widely from family to family, several types of ecologically and systemically oriented interventions are commonly used with violent youths and their parents. At the family level, MST interventions generally aim to remove barriers to effective parenting (e.g., low social support, high stress, marital conflict), to enhance parenting knowledge, and to promote affection and communication among family members. At the peer level, interventions frequently are designed to decrease affiliation with delinquent and drug-using peers and to increase affiliation with prosocial peers (e.g., through church youth groups, organized athletics, after-school activities). Such interventions are optimally conducted by the youth's parents, with the guidance of the therapist, and often consist of active support and encouragement of associations with nonproblem peers (e.g., providing transportation, increased privileges) and substantive discouragement of associations with deviant peers (e.g., applying significant sanctions). Likewise, under the guidance of the therapist, the parents often develop strategies to monitor and promote the youth's school performance or vocational functioning; interventions in this domain typically focus on establishing positive communication lines between parents and teachers and on restructuring after-school hours to promote academic efforts.

Usually, aggressive behaviors diminish in frequency and intensity when systemic interventions are implemented in MST. In some cases, however, a violent youth may continue to display aggressive behavior in one or more contexts (e.g., in the classroom, with certain peers, and with siblings) after systemic interventions have been consistently implemented by parents, teachers, and other relevant persons in the youth's natural ecology. In such instances, youth cognitive distortions (e.g., attributing the behavior of others to hostile intentions even when that behavior is neutral) and cognitive deficiencies (e.g., coming up with fewer verbally assertive and more physically aggressive solutions to social problems) are assessed as possible contributing factors to the aggressive behavior. Jim, for example, had often angrily threatened to "pound" his brother Sam whenever he used an item belonging to Jim and had recently punched Sam after threatening him. As it turned out, Jim perceived Sam's behavior as intentional stealing and thought that his anger and aggression toward Sam were reasonable retaliation. The usual MST approach to a problem such as one family member using the belongings of another family member without permission would be to develop family consensus regarding rules for such behavior with consequences for violations. If such family interventions were not effective in curbing Jim's aggression with his brother, however, individual interventions helping Jim identify and correct his attributions about Sam's behavior would be considered.

From an MST perspective, interventions targeting youth cognitive distortions or deficiencies provide opportunities to prevent angry outbursts and, as such, are preferable to interventions that rely solely on helping the youth to manage the anger after it occurs. The MST therapist uses cognitive-behavioral interventions to help the youth think through and behaviorally practice solutions to the specific interpersonal problems targeted for change. The main objectives of the individual sessions are to identify and address those distortions and deficiencies that compromise the youth's ability to develop, choose, and implement solutions to interpersonal problems—distortions and deficiencies that result in negative outcomes for the youth or others even when ecological interventions are in place. Cognitive-behavioral interventions to acomplish these aims generally draw on strategies such as modeling, role-play and perspective-taking exercises, behavioral contingencies, self-monitoring, and self-instruction.

There are also some circumstances in which MST therapists engage in individual treatment with a parent on a continuous, albeit time-limited basis. Decisions to pursue individual treatment with parent figures most often pertain to problems that interfere with parental functioning, such as depression, anxiety disorders, substance abuse, and recent or past victimization. When investigating the role of individual factors in the fit of presenting problems, the practitioner's task is always to determine whether and how the factors constitute critical barriers to a parent's capacity to engage in MST. The therapist should have evidence that the individual problem, as opposed to other factors (e.g., marital problems, practical needs, skill or knowledge deficits, a history of adversarial relations with school officials), is a powerful predictor of the youth's aggressive behavior. In such cases, cognitive-behavioral interventions are often a first choice for individual treatment of a parent in the context of MST. Other interventions are also used in some cases (e.g., psychopharmacological treatment for a serious psychiatric disturbance, multicomponent behavior therapy for substance abuse).

Clinical Supervision in MST

Treatment fidelity in MST is maintained by weekly group supervision meetings involving three to four therapists and a doctoral-level clinical supervisor (usually a child psychologist or child psychiatrist). During these meetings, the treatment team (i.e., therapists, supervisor, and, as needed, a consulting psychiatrist) reviews the goals and progress of each case to ensure the multisystemic focus of therapists' intervention strategies and to identify obstacles to success. Important to note, the treatment team accepts responsibility for engaging families in treatment and for effecting therapeutic change. Thus, when obstacles to successful engagement or to therapeutic change are identified, the team develops strategies to address those obstacles and to promote success.

The clinical supervisor plays a critical role in the MST treatment process. The primary focus of the MST clinical supervisor is on the therapist's thinking, behavior, and interactions with the family and with the systems in which the family is embedded. Clinical supervisors ensure that therapists adhere to the nine principles of MST in all aspects of treatment (i.e., engagement and alignment, conceptualization of the causes of referral problems, design and implementation of interventions, overcoming barriers to intervention effectiveness, and assessment of outcomes). In addition, supervisors must be able to assess and promote the development

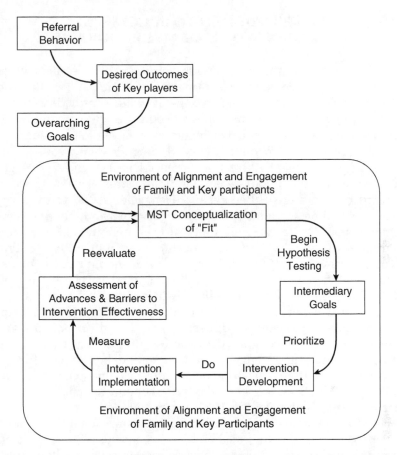

FIGURE 10.2.   The MST analytical process. MST supervisors ensure that therapists are able to (a) develop and refine a multisystemic conceptualization of the causes of identified problems, (b) identify barriers to the successful engagement of key participants (family members, school personnel, sources of parental social support) and implement strategies to overcome these barriers, (c) logically and clearly connect intermediary goals to overarching goals, (d) design and effectively implement intervention strategies to meet intermediary and overarching goals, and (e) identify barriers to the successful implementation of interventions and implement strategies to overcome them.

of therapists' MST-like conceptualization and intervention skills across cases (generalization). To facilitate therapists' implementation of MST and the attainment of favorable family outcomes, supervisors reinforce critical thinking about all aspects of treatment. Figure 10.2 depicts the various aspects of treatment, the relationships among them, and the analytical process used to identify and execute them.

ISSUES RELATED TO SUCCESSFUL
IMPLEMENTATION OF MST PROGRAMS

MST programs for youths who commit violent and other serious offenses are typically implemented by public (mental health, juvenile justice, social welfare) or private service organizations in order to provide a community-based alternative to incarceration and other out-of-home placements. Although the preceding clinical elements are believed to be fundamental to the successful implementation of MST programs with youth violent offenders (see the following section on effectiveness), an MST program cannot be successful without several key administrative elements as well. As discussed elsewhere (Schoenwald & Henggeler, 2002), a service organization (including key administrators, supervisors, and therapists) must be fully committed to the philosophical (e.g., definition of the mental health professional's role) and empirical (e.g., accountability for clinical outcomes) framework of the MST approach and should receive intensive training and ongoing consultation in the MST model. The MST program should have distinct, dedicated staff (i.e., 100% time MST therapists) and include a clinical supervisor who has credible authority regarding clinical decisions. Substantial changes in agency policies and in staff members' work routines are often required to successfully implement the clinical approach of MST, and concrete support should be evident from the administration of the service organization (e.g., implementing flex-time and comp-time policies for staff, scheduling supervision and consultation times, providing highly competitive salaries and incentives).

Successful implementation of an MST program also requires initiative in developing and maintaining collaborative relationships with other agencies in the community (i.e., schools, juvenile justice, social welfare, mental health, and substance abuse) that are involved in the lives of adolescent violent offenders (Schoenwald & Henggeler, 2002). Indeed, a strength of the MST approach is that it assumes accountability as the single point of responsibility for ensuring that the broad needs of violent youths and their families are met. Thus, the main purpose of coordinating MST activities with those of other agencies is to produce favorable long-term clinical outcomes. Moreover, given that the funding mechanisms in many communities include disincentives for public agencies to use community-based services in lieu of out-of-home placements, an MST program is unlikely to attain a sufficient referral base and concomitant funding without first seeking the support and cooperation of key agencies and stakeholders in the community. One mechanism for funding used in MST programs at different sites across the United States has involved shifting local or state children's services monies allocated for residential treatment or other out-of-home placements (e.g., foster care) to the MST program.

CLINICAL AND COST-EFFECTIVENESS OF MST WITH VIOLENT YOUTHS AND THEIR FAMILIES

Clearly, for both ethical and pragmatic reasons, it is important that mental health services for youths who engage in violent and serious crimes be evaluated rigorously. Evaluation of outcomes produced by MST has been a high priority since the initial development of this treatment model in the late 1970s.

Two early clinical trials established the the promise of MST with challenging clinical problems. First, Henggeler et al. (1986) evaluated the effectiveness of MST with inner-city juvenile offenders ($N = 80$), whose arrest histories included relatively serious violent and nonviolent crimes (M [Mean] = 2.1 arrests). At posttreatment, MST was more effective than usual community treatment in decreasing youth behavior problems, decreasing youth association with deviant peers, and improving family communication and warmth. Second, in a study (Brunk, Henggeler, & Whelan, 1987) contrasting MST versus behavioral parent training with abusive and neglectful families ($N = 43$), MST was more effective at restructuring problematic parent–child relations. Although these studies are modest in scope by today's standards (e.g., no follow-up or cost analysis), the favorable effects of MST supported the viability of conducting further studies of the effects of MST in treating serious clinical problems.

Violent and Chronic Offenders

Two different randomized clinical trials have demonstrated the effectiveness of MST with youth violent and chronic offenders. In the first study, Henggeler, Melton, and Smith (1992) compared MST and usual services (provided by a state agency) in the treatment of 84 youth serious offenders (54% violent offenders), who averaged 3.5 previous arrests and 9.5 weeks of prior incarceration. Findings at posttreatment showed that MST improved family relations (i.e., increased cohesion) and peer relations (i.e., decreased aggression) of the youths and their families. In addition, at a 59-week postreferral follow-up, adolescents who received MST had significantly fewer rearrests ($Ms = .87$ vs. 1.52) and weeks incarcerated ($Ms = 5.8$ vs. 16.2) than did adolescents who received usual services; the cost per adolescent for treatment in the MST group was also substantially lower than the average cost in the usual services group ($2,800 vs. $16,300). Important to note, results from a 2.4-year follow-up (Henggeler, Melton, Smith, Schoenwald, & Hanley, 1993) showed that MST doubled the survival rate (i.e., percentage of adolescents not rearrested) of these violent and chronic offenders when compared with usual services.

In the most comprehensive and extensive evaluation of MST to date, Borduin et al. (1995) examined the long-term effects of MST versus individual therapy (IT) on violent offending and other criminal offending in 200 adolescent serious offenders, who averaged 4.2 previous arrests. Results from multiagent, multimethod assessment batteries conducted before and after treatment showed that MST was more effective than IT in improving key family correlates of antisocial behavior and in ameliorating adjustment problems (including problems with anger) in individual family members. An ancillary analysis completed for the present chapter also showed that youths who received MST evidenced significant decreases in temper and impulsivity in their peer relations, whereas their counterparts who received IT evidenced no change. Moreover, results from a 4-year follow-up of rearrest data showed that youths treated with MST were significantly less likely to be rearrested (26.1 % vs. 71.4%) than youths treated with IT. In addition, an examination of recidivists from each group revealed that MST youths arrested during follow-up were less likely to be arrested for violent (i.e., rape, attempted rape, sexual assault, aggravated assault, assault/battery) and other serious crimes (i.e., burglary, larceny, auto theft, arson) than were comparison counterparts.

More recently, in a 13.7-year follow-up of the youths (now in their late 20s and early 30s) who participated in the Borduin et al. (1995) clinical trial, Schaeffer and Borduin (2005) found that participants treated with MST evidenced 59% fewer rearrests for violent crimes and 56% fewer arrests for other serious crimes than did participants treated with IT. In addition, MST participants were sentenced to 57% fewer days (Ms = 582.25 vs. 1,356.53 days) of confinement in adult detention facilities than were comparison counterparts. Applying a cost–benefit model for criminal justice programs (Washington State Institute for Public Policy, 2001) to the results of this long-term follow-up, Klietz and Borduin (2004) estimated that the net present value of MST ranged from $40,329 (taxpayer benefits only) to $201,858 (taxpayer and crime victim benefits combined) per participant.

Substance Use and Abuse in Violent Offenders

Prior to the completion of the two MST trials with youth violent and chronic offenders (Borduin et al., 1995; Henggeler et al., 1992), Henggeler et al. (1991) examined the effects of MST on reductions in substance use and abuse in the offenders participating in these studies. Analyses of self-report data from the Henggeler et al. (1992) sample showed that youth offenders in the MST condition reported significantly less soft-drug use (i.e., alcohol, marijuana) at posttreatment than did offenders who received usual services. Similarly, analyses of arrest data from the Borduin et al.

(1995) sample indicated that youths who participated in MST had a significantly lower rate of substance-related arrests 4 years following treatment than did youths who participated in IT (i.e., 4% vs. 16%); this lower rate of substance-related arrests for MST participants relative to IT participants was also observed 13.7 years following treatment (Schaeffer & Borduin, 2005), although the rates of arrest had increased for both groups (i.e., 13% for MST vs. 33.3% for IT).

Aggressive Sexual Offenders

Though modest in scope and size (N = 16), Borduin, Henggeler, Blaske, and Stein (1990) was the first published randomized trial with juvenile sexual offenders. Youths and their familes were randomly assigned to treatment conditions: home-based MST delivered by doctoral students in clinical psychology versus outpatient individual therapy delivered by community-based mental health professionals. Recidivism results at a 3-year follow-up revealed that MST was more effective than IT in reducing rates of rearrest for aggressive sexual crimes (12.5% vs. 75.0%) and in reducing the mean frequency of rearrests for both sexual crimes (0.12 vs. 1.62) and nonsexual crimes (0.62 vs. 2.25). The favorable effects of MST supported the viability of conducting a second evaluation of MST with juvenile sexual offenders.

In a recently completed clinical trial, Borduin, Schaeffer, and Heiblum (2004) used a multiagent, multimethod assessment battery to evaluate instrumental (i.e., theory driven) and ultimate (i.e., common to all treatments of juvenile sexual offenders) outcomes in aggressive (i.e., sexual assault, rape) and nonaggressive (i.e., molestation of younger children) juvenile sexual offenders (N = 48) who were randomly assigned to MST or usual services (i.e., group and individual therapy). Compared to youths who received usual services, youths who received MST showed improvements on a range of instrumental outcomes, including fewer behavior problems, less criminal offending (self-reported), improved peer relations (i.e., more emotional bonding with peers, less involvement with deviant peers), improved family relations (i.e., more warmth, less conflict), and better grades in school, and their parents showed decreased adjustment problems (including problems with anger). Although the improvements on instrumental outcomes were largely consistent across aggressive and nonaggressive sexual offenders in MST, it is noteworthy that MST was especially effective in reducing angry feelings (i.e., hostility) and peer-directed aggression in aggressive sexual offenders. Most important, a 9-year follow-up of ultimate outcomes revealed that aggressive sexual offenders who participated in MST were less likely than their usual services counterparts to be arrested for sexual (16.7% vs. 58.3%) and nonsexual (33.3% vs. 75.0%) crimes and spent one fifth as many days incarcerated as adults; a similar pattern of findings emerged for the nonaggressive sexual offenders in the two groups. In a cost–benefit analysis of these follow-up results, Borduin and Klietz (2003) estimated that the net present value of MST ranged from $171,882 (taxpayer benefits only) to $262,271 (taxpayer and crime victim benefits combined) per aggressive sexual offender, and from $67,615 to $103,307 per nonaggressive sexual offender.

Current and Future Evaluations

The refinement of MST with youth violent and serious offenders is a continuous, ongoing, and dynamic process (see Henggeler et al., 1998). Current projects are examining treatment processes and potential moderators of MST effectiveness in families of violent juvenile offenders (Schaeffer & Borduin, 2004), the integration of MST into juvenile drug courts (Randall, Halliday-Boykins, Cunningham, & Henggeler, 2002), and the integration of MST with empirically based drug and violence prevention programs in urban middle school settings (Cunningham & Henggeler, 2001). We also recently began another randomized trial with juvenile sexual offenders (Borduin, Letourneau, Henggeler, & Swenson, 2003) using a larger sample ($N = 160$) than in our prior trials. Another current project is evaluating the transportability and dissemination of MST to various community settings serving adolescent violent and chronic offenders (see Schoenwald & Hoagwood, 2001); a major task in our dissemination research is to evaluate those factors (e.g., therapist characteristics, supervisory behaviors, agency policies) that are linked with treatment adherence and with clinical outcomes. Finally, we are planning to conduct an 18-year follow-up of the violent and chronic juvenile offenders who participated in the Borduin et al. (1995) randomized trial; a major component of the follow-up is an assessment of each participant's service utilization (mental health, juvenile justice, social welfare, education) during the follow-up period and a delineation of the costs of such services in order to more fully evaluate the cost-effectiveness of MST.

Additional evaluations of MST are currently under way in an effort to adapt and extend the treatment model to other populations with serious clinical problems. Recent work has been evaluating the clinical and cost effectiveness of MST as an alternative to inpatient psychiatric hospitalization for adolescents presenting mental health emergencies (e.g., suicidal behavior, psychosis). To date, the findings from this work (see, e.g., Henggeler et al., 1999; Schoenwald, Ward, Henggeler, & Rowland, 2000) have been very promising and suggest that an intensive, well-specified, and evidenced-based treatment model such as MST can effectively serve as a family- and community-based alternative to the emergency psychiatric hospitalization of adolescents. Another project, in collaboration with the Annie E. Casey Foundation, is currently under way in Philadelphia, Pennsylvania to evaluate the clinical and cost-effectiveness of an MST-based continuum of care for adolescents with serious emotional disturbances. This project will allow us to better understand which components of treatment are most essential for maintaining such youths safely in the community.

IMPLICATIONS FOR DEVELOPING EFFECTIVE TREATMENTS FOR VIOLENT YOUTHS AND THEIR FAMILIES

The results of our clinical trials suggest that MST is relatively effective in reducing both aggressive behavior and angry emotions in violent youths. Aggressive behavior is virtually always a direct target of interventions in MST with violent youths because such behavior is usually the reason for referral to treatment. It is possible that systemic (e.g., family, peer) interventions that directly target aggressive behavior also play an important role in reducing (i.e., preventing) angry outbursts by addressing the sequence of interactions (and associated cognitive distortions) that led to the anger (and aggression). Of course, as described earlier, angry feelings are directly targeted in MST in those instances when systemically oriented interventions for aggression have not proven successful. Nevertheless, given that interventions targeting angry feelings are not routinely used in MST and that MST is not always effective in altering the criminal trajectories of violent youths (as described in the prior section on effectiveness), it seems reasonable to ask whether increased attention should be devoted in MST to interventions that directly target anger in family members. To begin to answer this question, research is needed to evaluate the influence of treatment-related changes in key domains of functioning (e.g., family relations, peer relations, cognitions, emotions) on youth outcomes in MST. After central change mechanisms (i.e., both direct and indirect effects on youth outcomes) in MST have been identified, these "active ingredients" could be distilled and refined to further enhance therapy outcomes for violent youths (see Weisz, Huey, & Weersing, 1998).

The relative effectiveness of MST in reducing violence and criminality in youths has important implications that can help guide the development of potentially more effective interventions for such youths. If, as suggested earlier, a major shortcoming of most interventions for treating violence and other serious antisocial behavior has been their neglect of the multiple determinants of such behavior, then the success of MST may be linked with its comprehensive and flexible nature; that is, the results of MST may be due to its explicit focus on ameliorating key social-ecological factors associated with serious antisocial behavior, including behavior problems, parental disturbance, problematic family relations, association with deviant peers, and poor school performance. In light of the multidetermined nature of youth violence and serious antisocial behavior, it is unrealistic to expect even the best conceived office-based treatments to be effective due to their relatively narrow focus.

Another important aspect of MST pertains to the accessibility and ecological validity of services. Traditionally, mental health services for juvenile offenders either have been inaccessible (i.e., office based) or have provided interventions (e.g., residential treatment centers, wilderness programs, boot camps, incarceration) that have little bearing on the real-world environmental conditions that led to the youth's criminal behavior and to which the youth will eventually return (see Melton & Pagliocca, 1992). In contrast, by using the family preservation model of service delivery, MST is provided in natural community contexts (e.g., home, school, recreation center). The delivery of services in youths' natural environments enhances family cooperation, permits more accurate assessment of identified problems and of intervention results, and promotes long-term maintenance of therapeutic changes (Henggeler & Borduin, 1990). Indeed, there is a growing consensus that providers of children's mental health services should recognize the natural ecology of the child and diminish barriers to service access (e.g., Burns & Hoagwood, 2002; Cauce et al., 2002; Roberts, 1994; Snell-Johns et al., 2004; Stroul, 1996). Likewise, other aspects of MST (e.g., intensive training and supervision of therapists, development of collaborative interagency relationships) may also contribute to the positive clinical outcomes that have been obtained with many violent youths and their families.

In conclusion, our work indicates that a comprehensive intervention, intensively addressing the multiple determinants of serious antisocial behavior in youths' naturally occurring systems, can successfully reduce violent offending and other criminal activity in youths and can result in considerable cost savings for taxpayers and crime victims. Of course, extensive validation and replication are needed for even the most promising treatment approaches. Nevertheless, given the many problems that youth violent offenders present for our society, as well as the significant costs of providing these youths with treatments that do not produce durable changes, it is time that priority be placed on the evaluation of promising treatment models such as MST.

REFERENCES

Bateson, G. (1972). *Steps to an ecology of the mind*. New York: Ballantine.

Borduin, C. M. (1994). Innovative models of treatment and service delivery in the juvenile justice system. *Journal of Clinical Child Psychology, 23*(Suppl.), 19–25.

Borduin, C. M., & Henggeler, S. W. (1990). A multisystemic approach to the treatment of serious delinquent behavior. In R. J. McMahon & R. Dev. Peters (Eds.), *Behavior disorders of adolescence: Research, intervention, and policy in clinical and school settings* (pp. 62–80). New York: Plenum.

Borduin, C. M., Henggeler, S. W., Blaske, D. M., & Stein, R. (1990). Multisystemic treatment of adolescent sexual offenders. *International Journal of Offender Therapy and Comparative Criminology, 34*, 105–113.

Borduin, C. M., & Klietz, S. J. (2003, August). *Multisystemic therapy with juvenile sexual offenders: Clinical and cost effectiveness*. Paper presented at the meeting of the American Psychological Association, Toronto.

Borduin, C. M., Letourneau, E. J., Henggeler, S. W., & Swenson, C. C. (2003). *Treatment manual for multisystemic therapy with juvenile sexual offenders and their families*. Unpublished manuscript.

Borduin, C. M., Mann, B. J., Cone, L. T., Henggeler, S. W., Fucci, B. R., Blaske, D. M., et al. (1995). Multisystemic treatment of serious juvenile offenders: Long-term prevention of criminality and violence. *Journal of Consulting and Clinical Psychology, 63*, 569–578.

Borduin, C. M., & Schaeffer, C. M. (1998). Violent offending in adolescence: Epidemiology, correlates, outcomes, and treatment. In T. Gullotta, G. Adams, & R. Montemayor (Eds.), *Delinquent violent youth: Theory and interventions* (pp. 144–174). Newbury Park, CA: Sage.

Borduin, C. M., Schaeffer, C. M., & Heiblum, N. (2004). *Multisystemic treatment of juvenile sexual offenders: Effects on adolescent social ecology and criminal activity*. Manuscript submitted for publication.

Britt, C. L. (2000). Health consequences of criminal victimization. *International Review of Victimology, 8*, 63–73.

Bronfenbrenner, U. (1979). *The ecology of human development: Experiments by nature and design*. Cambridge, MA: Harvard University Press.

Brunk, M., Henggeler, S. W., & Whelan, J. P. (1987). Comparison of multisystemic therapy and parent training in the brief treatment of child abuse and neglect. *Journal of Consulting and Clinical Psychology, 55*, 171–178.

Burns, B. J., & Hoagwood, K. (Eds.). (2002). *Community treatment for youth: Evidenced-based interventions for severe emotional and behavioral disorders*. New York: Oxford University Press.

Cauce, A. M., Domenech-Rodriguez, M., Paradise, M., Cochran, B. N., Shea, J. M., Srebnik, D., et al. (2002). Cultural and contextual influences in mental help health seeking: A focus on ethnic minority youth. *Journal of Consulting and Clinical Psychology 70*, 44–55.

Cocozza, J. J. (Ed.). (1992). *Responding to the mental health needs of youth in the juvenile justice system*. Seattle, WA: National Coalition for the Mentally Ill in the Criminal Justice System.

Cohen, M. A., & Miller, T. R. (1998). The cost of mental health care for victims of crime. *Journal of Interpersonal Violence, 13,* 93–110.

Cunningham, P. B., & Henggeler, S. W. (2001). Implementation of an empirically based drug and violence prevention and intervention program in public school settings. *Journal of Clinical Child Psychology, 30,* 221–232.

Elliott, D. S., Dunford, F. W., & Huizinga, D. (1987). The identification and prediction of career offenders utilizing self-reported and official data. In J. D. Burchard & S. N. Burchard (Eds.), *Prevention of delinquent behavior* (pp. 90–121). Newbury Park, CA: Sage.

Farrington, D. P., & Loeber, R. (2000). Epidemiology of juvenile violence. *Child and Adolescent Psychiatric Clinics of North America, 9,* 733–748.

Farrington, D. P., Ohlin, L., & Wilson, J. Q. (1986). *Understanding and controlling crime.* New York: Springer-Verlag.

Federal Bureau of Investigation, U. S. Department of Justice. (2003). *Uniform crime reports.* Washington, DC: Author.

Gottfredson, G. D. (1989). The experiences of violent and serious victimization. In N. A. Weiner & M. E. Wolfgang (Eds.), *Pathways to criminal violence* (pp. 202–234). Newbury Park, CA: Sage.

Hawkins, J. D., Herrenkohl, T., Farrington, D. P., Brewer, D., Catalano, R. F., & Harachi, T. W. (1998). A review of predictors of youth violence. In R. Loeber & D. P. Farrington (Eds.), *Serious and violent juvenile offenders: Risk factors and successful interventions* (pp. 106–146). Thousand Oaks, CA: Sage.

Henggeler, S. W., & Borduin, C. M. (1990). *Family therapy and beyond: A multisystemic approach to treating the behavior problems of children and adolescents.* Pacific Grove, CA: Brooks/Cole.

Henggeler, S. W., & Borduin, C. M. (1992). *Multisystemic therapy adherence scales.* Unpublished instrument, Department of Psychiatry and Behavioral Sciences, Medical University of South Carolina.

Henggeler, S. W., Borduin, C. M., Melton, G., Mann, B., Smith, L., Hall, J., et al. (1991). Effects of multisystemic therapy on drug use and abuse in serious juvenile offenders: A progress report from two outcome studies. *Family Dynamics of Addiction Quarterly, 1,* 40–51.

Henggeler, S. W., Melton, G. B., Brondino, M. J., Scherer, D. G., & Hanley, J. H. (1997). Multisystemic therapy with violent and chronic juvenile offenders and their families: The role of treatment fidelity in successful dissemination. *Journal of Consulting and Clinical Psychology, 65,* 821–833.

Henggeler, S. W., Melton, G. B., & Smith, L. A. (1992). Family preservation using multisystemic therapy: An effective alternative to incarcerating serious juvenile offenders. *Journal of Consulting and Clinical Psychology, 60,* 953–961.

Henggeler, S. W., Melton, G. B., Smith, L. A., Schoenwald, S. K., & Hanley, J. H. (1993). Family preservation using multisystemic treatment: Long-term follow-up to a clinical trial with serious juvenile offenders. *Journal of Child and Family Studies, 2,* 283–293.

Henggeler, S. W., Rodick, J. D., Borduin, C. M., Hanson, C. L., Watson, S. M., & Urey, J. R. (1986). Multisystemic treatment of juvenile offenders: Effects on adolescent behavior and family interaction. *Developmental Psychology, 22,* 132–141.

Henggeler, S. W., Rowland, M. D., Randall, J., Ward, D., Pickrel, S. G., Cunningham, P. B., et al. (1999). Home-based multisystemic therapy as an alternative to the hospitalization of youths in psychiatric crisis: Clinical outcomes. *Journal of the American Academy of Child and Adolescent Psychiatry, 38*, 1331–1339.

Henggeler, S. W., Schoenwald, S. K., Borduin, C. M., Rowland, M. D., & Cunningham, P. B. (1998). *Multisystemic treatment of antisocial behavior in children and adolescents.* New York: Guilford.

Henry, D. B., Tolan, P. H., & Gorman-Smith, D. (2001). Longitudinal family and peer group effects on violence and nonviolent delinquency. *Journal of Clinical Child Psychology, 30,* 172–186.

Herrenkohl, T. I., Huang, B., Kosterman, R., Hawkins, J. D., Catalano, R. F., & Smith, B. H. (2001). A comparison of social development processes leading to violent behavior in late adolescence for childhood initiators and adolescent initiators of violence. *Journal of Research in Crime and Delinquency, 38,* 45–63.

Hoffman, L. (1981). *Foundations of family therapy.* New York: Basic Books.

Huesmann, L. R., Lefkowitz, M. M., Eron, L. D., & Walder, L. O. (1984). Stability of aggression over time and generations. *Developmental Psychology, 20,* 1120–1134.

Huey, S. J., Henggeler, S. W., Brondino, M. J., & Pickrel, S. (2000). Mechanisms of change in multisystemic therapy: Reducing delinquent behavior through therapist adherence and improved family and peer functioning. *Journal of Consulting and Clinical Psychology, 68,* 451–467.

Kashani, J. H., Jones, M. R., Bumby, K. M., & Thomas, L. A. (1999). Youth violence: Psychosocial risk factors, treatment, prevention, and recommendations. *Journal of Emotional* and Behavioral Disorders, 7, 200–210.

Kazdin, A. E. (2000). Treatments for aggressive and antisocial children. *Child and Adolescent Psychiatric Clinics of North America, 9,* 841–858.

Klietz, S. J., & Borduin, C. M. (2004). *Cost–benefit analysis of multisystemic therapy with life-course-persistent offenders.* Manuscript submitted for publication.

Larzelere, R. E., Kuhn, B. R., & Johnson, B. (2004). The intervention selection bias: An unrecognized confound in intervention research. *Psychological Bulletin, 130,* 289–303.

LeBlanc, M., & Kaspy, N. (1998). Trajectories of delinquent and problem behavior: Comparison of social and personal control characteristics of adjudicated boys on synchronous and nonsynchronous paths. *Journal of Quantitative Criminology, 14,* 181–214.

Levesque, R. J. R. (1996). Is there still a place for violent youth in juvenile justice? *Aggression and Violent Behavior, 1,* 69–79.

Loeber, R., Farrington, D. P., & Waschbusch, D. A. (1998). Serious and violent juvenile offenders. In R. Loeber & D. P. Farrington (Eds.), *Serious and violent juvenile offenders: Risk factors and successful interventions* (pp. 13–29). Thousand Oaks, CA: Sage.

Loeber, R., & Hay, D. F. (1996). Key issues in the development of aggression and violence from childhood to early adulthood. *Annual Review of Psychology, 48,* 371–410.

Lyons, J. S., Baerger, D. R., Quigley, P., Erlich, J., & Griffin, E. (2001). Mental health service needs of juvenile offenders: A comparison of detention, incarceration, and treatment settings. *Children's Services: Social Policy, Research, and Practice, 4,* 69–85.

Melton, G. B., Lyons, P. M., & Spaulding, W. J. (1998). *No place to go: The civil commitment of minors.* Lincoln, University of Nebraska Press.

Melton, G. B., & Pagliocca, P. M. (1992). Treatment in the juvenile justice system: Directions for policy and practice. In J. J. Cocozza (Ed.), *Responding to the mental health needs of youth in the juvenile justice system* (pp. 107–139). Seattle, WA: National Coalition for the Mentally Ill in the Criminal Justice System.

Minuchin, P. P. (1985). Families and individual development: Provocations from the field of family therapy. *Child Development, 56,* 289–302.

Moffitt, T. E. (1993). Adolescence-limited and life-course-persistent antisocial behavior: A developmental taxonomy. *Psychological Review, 100,* 674–701.

Mulvey, E. P., Arthur, M. A., & Reppucci, N. D. (1993). The prevention and treatment of juvenile delinquency: A review of the research. *Clinical Psychology Review, 13,* 133–167.

Nelson, K. E., & Landsman, M. J. (1992). *Alternative models of family preservation: Family-based services in context.* Springfield, IL: Thomas.

Pajer, K. A. (1998). What happens to "bad" girls? A review of the adult outcomes of antisocial adolescent girls. *American Journal of Psychiatry, 155,* 862–870.

Paschall, M. J., & Hubbard, M. L. (1998). Effects of neighborhood and family stressors on African American male adolescents' self-worth and propensity for violent behavior. *Journal of Consulting and Clinical Psychology, 66,* 825–831.

Randall, J., Halliday-Boykins, C. A., Cunningham, P. B., & Henggeler, S. W. (2002). *Integrating evidence-based substance abuse treatment into juvenile drug courts: Implications for outcomes.* Manuscript submitted for publication.

Roberts, M. C. (1994). Models for service delivery in children's mental health: Common characteristics. *Journal of Clinical Child Psychology, 23,* 212–219.

Robinson, F., & Keithley, J. (2000). The impacts of crime on health and health services: A literature review. *Health, Risk, and Society, 2,* 253–266.

Schaeffer, C. M., & Borduin, C. M. (2004). *Moderators and mediators of therapeutic change in multisystemic treatment of violent juvenile offenders.* Manuscript submitted for publication.

Schaeffer, C. M., & Borduin, C. M. (2005). Long-term follow-up to a randomized clinical of multisystemic therapy with serious and violent juvenile offenders. *Journal of Consulting and Clinical Psychology, 73,* 445–453.

Schoenwald, S. K., & Henggeler, S. W. (2002). Mental health services research and family-based treatment: Bridging the gap. In H. Liddle, G. Diamond, R. Levant, J. Bray, & D. Santisteban (Eds.), *Family psychology intervention science* (pp. 259–282). Washington, DC: American Psychological Association.

Schoenwald, S. K., Henggeler, S. W., Brondino, M. J., & Rowland, M. (2000). Multisystemic Therapy: Monitoring treatment fidelity. *Family Process, 39,* 83–103.

Schoenwald, S. K., & Hoagwood, K. (2001). Effectiveness, transportability, and dissemination of interventions: What matters when? *Psychiatric Services, 52,* 1190–1197.

Schoenwald, S. K., Ward, D. M., Henggeler, S. W., & Rowland, M. D. (2000). MST vs. hospitalization for crisis stabilization of youth: Placement outcomes 4 months post-referral. *Mental Health Services Research, 2*, 3–12.

Snell-Johns, J., Mendez, J. L., & Smith, B. L. (2004). Evidence-based solutions for overcoming access barriers, decreasing attrition, and promoting change with underserved families. *Journal of Family Psychology, 18,* 19–35.

Stroul, B. A. (Ed.). (1996). *Children's mental health: Creating systems of care in a changing society.* Baltimore: Brookes.

Tate, D. C., Reppucci, N. D., & Mulvey, E. P. (1995). Violent juvenile delinquents: Treatment effectiveness and implications for future action. *American Psychologist, 50,* 777–781.

Thornberry, T. P., Huizinga, D., & Loeber, R. (1995). The prevention of serious delinquency and violence: Implications from the program of research on the causes and correlates of delinquency. In J. C. Howell, B. Krisberg, J. D. Hawkins, & J. J. Wilson (Eds.), *A sourcebook: Serious, violent, and chronic juvenile offenders* (pp. 213–237). Newbury Park, CA: Sage.

Washington State Institute for Public Policy. (2001). *The comparative costs and benefits of programs to reduce crime.* Olympia: Evergreen State College.

Weisz, J. R., Huey, S. J., & Weersing, V. R. (1998). Psychotherapy with children and adolescents: The state of the art. In T. H. Ollendick & R. J. Prinz (Eds.), *Advances in clinical child psychology* (Vol. 20, pp. 49–91). New York: Plenum.

The Anger–Aggression Relation in Violent Children and Adolescents

Julie A. Hubbard, Meghan D. McAuliffe,
Ronnie M. Rubin, and Michael T. Morrow

The three preceding chapters provide distinct yet overlapping perspectives on the relation between anger and aggression in children and adolescents. To integrate these perspectives, we divide this commentary into three broad sections designed to follow the overarching themes of this edited volume. In the first section, we focus on the relation between aggression and emotion in children and adolescents. In the second section, we narrow this focus to examine the link between aggression and the specific emotion of anger. Finally, the third section emphasizes applications of our knowledge of the anger–aggression relation to intervention programs for aggressive children and adolescents.

THE RELATION BETWEEN AGGRESSION AND EMOTION IN CHILDREN AND ADOLESCENTS

Until the past 10 to 15 years, researchers did not pay much attention to emotion when striving to understand and treat children's and adolescents' aggressive behavior disorders.[1] Instead, our field was driven by the social information-processing (SIP) model originally posited by Dodge, Pettit, McClaskey, and Brown (1986). This model provided an incredibly useful and strongly evidenced-based conceptualization of the importance of social cognitive mechanisms in children's aggressive behavior.

---

[1] For the sake of simplicity, hereafter, both children and adolescents are referred to as "children."

More recently, we have seen a dramatic shift toward examining the emotional mechanisms, in addition to the social cognitive mechanisms, that underlie children's aggressive behavior. However, this shift has been characterized by a continuing reliance on the SIP model, with researchers fitting emotion constructs into the SIP framework. For example, Crick and Dodge (1994) incorporated emotion constructs into their reformulation of the SIP model, particularly in the affect-laden database, which they hypothesized develops through an accumulated history of social experiences and influences each step of social information processing. A few years later, Lemerise and Arsenio (2000) expanded on this idea by describing explicitly how emotion constructs could function as part of each step of the SIP model. Interestingly, in each of the three preceding chapters, the authors continue to integrate emotion into the SIP model. Bierman as well as Snyder and colleagues emphasize that emotional arousal, and perhaps anger arousal in particular, makes adaptive social information processing more difficult. Conversely, Borduin stresses that maladaptive social information processing (particularly hostile attributional biases) is, at least in part, responsible for children's angry feelings.

Integration of emotion constructs into the SIP model is clearly an important goal for our field. Such an integrated model may more adequately describe the multiple mechanisms driving children's aggression. However, it is our belief that we also need to "think outside the SIP box" in considering how emotion and aggression may relate. Emotion may influence children's aggression in ways that are unrelated to social information processing. Consideration of the relation between emotion and aggression, independent of social information processing, has been called for by several researchers and interventionists (e.g., Denham & Burton, 2004; Greenberg, Kusche, & Speltz, 1991), as Bierman (chap. 9, this volume) noted. Additionally, the work of prominent emotions theorists supports the idea that emotion is not necessarily inherently intertwined with cognition. For example, in a highly influential paper, Izard (1993) posited that emotion is not always activated by cognition, and he specified three systems (neural, sensorimotor, and motivational) that he believes activate emotion independent of cognition.

In considering the relations between emotion and aggression independent of social cognition, it is useful to begin with a model that lays out the essential components of children's emotional functioning. One such theory is the model of affective social competence (ASC) proposed by Halberstadt, Denham, and Dunsmore (2001). In a recent chapter, we reviewed components of the ASC model that have been solidly empirically linked to children's aggressive behavior (Hubbard & Dearing, 2004). In brief, we found strong empirical support for the hypothesis that aggressive children have difficulties with emotion regulation, in that they are more likely than their peers to be physiologically reactive to emotion-evoking social situations, to express negative emotions, and to display high levels of negative emotionality. We also found that there are several areas in which more research on the links between aggression and emotional functioning are needed. In particular, relatively little empirical work has related aggression to children's understanding of emotion. Existing research on the connection between aggression and emotion understanding is highlighted in Bierman's chapter. Overall, though, this work is scarce and our empirical knowledge base on the relation between emotion and aggression could clearly benefit from more attention to this important area.

THE RELATION BETWEEN AGGRESSION AND ANGER IN CHILDREN AND ADOLESCENTS

Although we began by focusing on the relation between aggression and emotion in general, the topic of the current book is more narrowly focused on the relation between aggression and anger specifically. The findings presented in the Snyder chapter (chap. 8, this volume) are an important contribution to furthering our understanding of this relation. In particular, Snyder and his colleagues demonstrated that when a child displays anger, this display increases the likelihood that he or she will receive coercive feedback from others, which in turn increases the likelihood that the child will respond by behaving aggressively. These data suggest that anger and aggression occur in the context of dynamic and transactional relationships between two or more individuals, a theme that is repeated throughout all three preceding chapters. Moreover, the data suggest that anger and aggression are actually linked through sequential dyadic relationship processes, involving feedback that is elicited from others in response to the display of anger. Thus, if children's displays of anger are met with negative or antagonistic responses, then children are likely to escalate from anger to aggression. Conversely, if anger displays are not matched with coercive responses, then it is less likely that this escalation will occur. These relational sequences make intuitive sense; however, these findings are actually quite novel for our field and thus hold significant importance in advancing our understanding of the link between anger and aggression in children.

Snyder's data remind us of an important point that Averill (1982) made years ago about the relation between anger and aggression, a point that has guided much of the work in our own laboratory. In his essay, Averill stressed that not all anger results in aggression, and that not all aggression is the result of anger. Snyder's data clearly fit with the first half of this idea, in stressing the importance of coercive feedback in children's spiral from anger to aggression.

The second concept, that not all aggression is the result of anger, brings to mind the distinction between reactive and proactive aggression (Dodge, 1991; Vitaro & Brendgen, 2005). Reactive aggression is anger-driven, defensive, retaliatory, and in response to real or perceived provocation. Proactive aggression, on the other hand, is displayed to reach a goal, whether the goal involves material or territorial gain (proactive instrumental aggression) or social dominance (proactive bullying aggression). Throughout the years, researchers and theorists have used different labels to describe this distinction. Their terms have included hostile/instrumental, retaliatory/predatory, and the effectual/ineffectual distinction mentioned by Bierman (chap. 9, this volume). However, each of these pairs of labels refers to the same basic idea. Essentially, across all of these labels, researchers are recognizing that, when children (or adults or even animals) display aggression, their behavior sometimes seems driven by anger and impulsivity, whereas at other times, they seem cool, deliberate, and purposeful.

In our opinion, the distinction between reactive and proactive aggression is critical to understanding the relation between anger and aggression. This distinction suggests that some episodes of children's aggressive behavior are strongly driven by anger, whereas other instances of aggressive behavior are markedly lacking in anger, being driven instead by a desire to achieve an instrumental or social goal. Thus, learning more about the distinction between reactive and proactive aggression is essential to developing a greater understanding of the complex relation between anger and aggression.

Researchers originally hypothesized that distinct groups of aggressive children existed, with one group displaying primarily reactive aggression and the other group displaying primarily proactive aggression (Dodge, 1991). However, in most studies to date, the correlation between reactive and proactive aggression ranges from .65 to .80. These strong correlations imply that the two subtypes of aggression tend to co-occur, with most aggressive children displaying some degree of both reactive and proactive aggression. In other words, the subtypes of aggression are most accurately conceptualized as continuous dimensions that exist to varying degrees in each child, rather than as categories into which children are exclusively placed.

Important to note, a number of unique correlates have been identified for both reactive and proactive aggression. These findings suggest that children's level of reactive aggression is related to variations in their level of particular behavioral, social cognitive, social, emotional, and physiological variables (e.g., hostile attributional biases, peer rejection, depression). At the same time, their level of proactive aggression is related to variations in the level of other, quite distinct, variables (e.g., positive outcome expectations for aggression, instrumental goal orientation, deviant friendships). Cronbach (1951) argued that two measures that do not relate to other variables in the same way must represent distinct constructs, even when they are highly correlated. Thus, this growing literature on the differential correlates of the subtypes of aggression provides one indication that the distinction between reactive and proactive aggression is valid, despite their high correlation.

The correlate most relevant to the current volume is anger. A number of researchers have found that anger is related to reactive aggression, but not to proactive aggression (Dodge & Coie, 1987; Hubbard et al., 2002; Little, Brauner, Jones, Nock, & Hawley, 2003; Little, Jones, Henrich, & Hawley, 2003; Price & Dodge, 1989). In these studies, anger has been assessed through adult ratings, peer ratings, observations, and even psychophysiological methods.

Unfortunately, this work linking anger uniquely to the reactive subtype of aggression is lacking in several important areas. Our first concern is that new measures of reactive and proactive aggression are sorely needed. Existing measures, including adult rating scales and laboratory-based measures, are psychometrically weak, lack face validity, do not adequately reflect theory, and confound the two subtypes of aggression with each other or with correlates. For example, by far the most commonly used measure of reactive and proactive aggression is a six-item teacher-rating scale developed by Dodge and Coie (1987). One primary concern that we have with this scale is that the reactive aggression items describe anger as much as they describe aggression. This approach may inflate the relation between anger and reactive aggression that is found across many studies that use the scale.

Our second concern is that longitudinal studies of reactive and proactive aggression are scarce. Only five published studies of reactive and proactive aggression have used a longitudinal design, and they were drawn from only three data sets (Brendgen, Vitaro, Tremblay, & Lavoie, 2001; Dodge, et al., 2003; Dodge, Lochman, Harnish, Bates, & Pettit, 1997; Vitaro, Brendgen, & Tremblay, 2002; Vitaro, Gendreau, Tremblay, & Oligny, 1998). Unfortunately, none of these studies assessed the subtypes of aggression at more than one time point. Assessments of reactive and proactive aggression across time are needed, because the temporal stability of the subtypes of aggression has never been examined in a published study. Moreover, multiple measures over time of both the subtypes of aggression and their correlates would allow us to (a) examine developmental changes or consistency in the correlates of the subtypes of aggression, (b) partial out the effects of earlier aggression or correlates when examining longitudinal relations between the two, and (c) investigate whether correlates function more strongly as precursors or outcomes of the subtypes of aggression.

Our third concern is that very little empirical work has examined the psychophysiological profiles associated with reactive and proactive aggression. When theorists describe the subtypes of aggression, they use terms such as "hot-headed" to refer to reactive aggression and "cold-blooded" to refer to proactive aggression. Thus, differing physiological underpinnings are central to theory, with reactive aggression characterized by sympathetic arousal and proactive aggression characterized by low-baseline physiological activity (Dodge, 1991; Dodge & Pettit, 2003; Vitaro & Brendgen, 2005). Empirical evidence of this characterization would greatly bolster support for the validity of the distinction between reactive and proactive aggression. Unfortunately, though, only one study of the psychophysiology of the subtypes of aggression has been conducted (Hubbard et al., 2002, 2004).

Clearly, researchers face many challenges and considerable work before we will fully understand and effectively use the distinction between reactive and proactive aggression. However, in our view, this distinction may be the critical link in untangling the complex web of relations between anger and aggression.

THE ANGER–AGGRESSION RELATION AND INTERVENTIONS FOR CHILDREN AND ADOLESCENTS

In the final section of this commentary, we would like to provide some thoughts on integrating our knowledge of the anger–aggression relation more fully into intervention and prevention programs for aggressive children and adolescents. The original idea behind this book was that incorporation of current empirical work on the anger–aggression relation may improve the efficacy of intervention and prevention programs for violence and aggression. This idea makes great intuitive sense to us, and in this section, we describe some of the issues and challenges we foresee with this integration.

A good place to start is by recognizing that empirical support for the multisystemic therapy (MST) intervention described in Borduin's chapter (chap. 10, this volume) is undeniably impressive. The results of numerous efficacy and effectiveness trials are particularly striking because Borduin and his colleagues work with the most entrenched violent adolescent offenders and because they achieve results on objective outcomes such as recidivism rates.

Unfortunately, and paradoxically, we have not been as successful in preventing and treating developing aggressive behavior problems in younger children. In the 1970s and 1980s, efforts to intervene with aggressive children produced disappointing results (see Kazdin, 1987, for a review), at least partially because the interventions were usually short-term and involved only a single component (e.g., social-skills training, parent management training). However, in the past decade, long-term, multicomponent interventions have been developed, and these treatments have shown more promise (see, for reviews, Catalano, Arthur, Hawkins, Berglund, & Olson, 1998; Elliott, Hamburg, & Williams, 1998; Greenberg, Domitrovich, & Bumbarger, 2001).

These successes have brought some measure of hope to researchers invested in developing effective preventive treatments for aggressive children. However, there is general agreement that room for improvement exists in several respects. First, although these interventions have demonstrated effects on some constructs, these effects are by no means pervasive across all constructs assessed or even across different sources of data for the same construct. Furthermore, even those effects that are obtained are sometimes not maintained at future assessments. Finally, the amount of time, money, and labor required to obtain these effects is quite significant.

A long-term goal for our field is to develop intervention and prevention programs for aggressive children that demonstrate greater efficacy, and at the same time that are cheaper, shorter, and easier to administer. Another way to think about this goal is that we should strive to keep as many children as possible from developing into adolescents in need of interventions such as MST. Admittedly, this is a huge task. However, one possible pathway toward enhancing current intervention and prevention efforts for aggressive children may be to incorporate our knowledge of the anger–aggression relation into these programs. What follows are our preliminary ideas for how to do so.

In keeping with the importance of the SIP model as a driving force in basic research on the mechanisms underlying childhood aggression, many current intervention and prevention programs for aggressive children have a strong social cognitive focus. This emphasis is clearly appropriate and important, given the wealth of empirical support for the role of social cognitive processes in children's display of aggressive behavior. In addition, as research on emotional mechanisms underlying childhood aggression has emerged, interventionists have worked to incorporate emotion into intervention and prevention programs for aggressive children, with both emotion understanding and emotion regulation processes playing central roles. Lochman's Coping Power Program (e.g., Larson & Lochman, 2002) and Greenberg's PATHS program (Greenberg & Kusche, 1993, 1998) are important examples of this shift.

In part, the inclusion of emotion in these programs is in the service of enhanced social information processing. If children have well-developed emotion understanding skills, they will likely interpret social situations more accurately, particularly social situations that are ambiguously provocative. Similarly, if children have strong emotion regulation capabilities, they may be able to "cool down their angry feelings," allowing for more effortful and adaptive social information processing. However, if emotion indeed influences childhood aggression, independent of its connection to social information processing, then the inclusion of emotional-skills training in intervention and prevention programs may play a role in reducing children's aggression that extends beyond the impact of emotion on social information processing.

One possible way to incorporate the anger–aggression relation more fully into treatments for childhood aggression may be to develop differential interventions for reactive aggression and proactive aggression. Separate interventions for reactive and proactive aggression have been suggested by numerous researchers (e.g., Brown & Parsons, 1998; Crick & Dodge, 1996; Dodge, 1991; Dodge & Coie, 1987; Dodge & Schwartz, 1997; Larson, 1994; Little et al., 2003; McAdams, 2002; Phillips & Lochman, 2003; Poulin & Boivin, 1999; Salmivalli & Niemenen, 2002; Vitaro & Brendgen, 2005; Vitaro et al., 2002; Waschbusch, Willoughby, & Pelham, 1998; Weinshenker & Siegel, 2002). These treatment packages could target the specific correlates of each subtype of aggression. For example, a reactive aggression intervention could emphasize anger regulation training, hostile attributional bias reduction, social problem solving, improved peer relations and social skills, and reductions in internalizing symptoms. In contrast, treatment for proactive aggression could stress the negative consequences of aggressive behavior, the importance of social goals, and the development of empathy for others. Aggressive behavior may be decreased more effectively if the specific behavioral, social, social-cognitive, emotional, and physiological underpinnings of each subtype of aggression are targeted separately.

Given the high correlation between the subtypes of aggression, many aggressive children might benefit from both treatment packages. However, a differentiated approach to the treatment of the subtypes of childhood aggression may make sense not only for those aggressive children who display primarily one subtype of aggressive behavior, but for those children who display both subtypes as well. The idea is that careful targeting of the mechanisms driving each subtype of aggression may enhance the efficacy of our intervention efforts with all aggressive children.

Within an intervention for reactive aggression, we would be wise to include a strong element of exposure to anger, as Bierman (chap. 9, this volume) so soundly suggests. Thus, after children have been taught basic skills for regulating their angry feelings, situations should be structured within the context of the intervention group that will purposefully elicit angry feelings in the children. Adult leaders can then encourage children to practice their developing anger regulation skills, while coaching and supporting as much as is necessary. The "taunting circles" that Lochman uses in his Coping Power Program (Larson & Lochman, 2002) probably come closest to Bierman's concept of exposure to anger. Other examples would be to ask children to negotiate the allocation of scarce resources or to play competitive games. If a group of aggressive children must divide up too few snacks, decide who gets to play with a Gameboy first, or handle losing a game, the opportunity to practice anger regulation skills will arise almost without fail.

Exposing children to actual anger-inducing experiences provides them with an opportunity to practice their anger regulation skills online. Roleplays and other forms of simulated practice are important in the initial stages of teaching children skills and techniques for regulating anger. However, Bierman believes, and we agree, that we should also challenge children to use their emerging anger regulation skills online in situations where they experience high levels of angry arousal.

Creating interventions that incorporate these types of anger-inducing situations will require substantial innovation, planning, foresight, and courage. And, clearly, opportunities for children to practice anger regulation skills online would need to be accompanied by considerable support, coaching, and scaffolding. We believe, though, that this sort of real-world practice is at the heart of what is missing from current approaches to teaching children how to regulate their anger. And, it may be the key to obtaining faster and longer-lasting generalization of anger regulation skills from the treatment setting to home and school environments.

Why, then, have we shied away from exposing children to their strong angry feelings in the context of our intervention programs? One possibility is that the taboo against anger that exists in our society is being perpetuated by the very researchers who study and treat children's aggression. In spite of encouraging children to believe that "all feelings are okay," many of us do not feel comfortable with children's anger, especially if we feel responsible for it. We may even believe that the goal of our intervention programs is to prevent children from ever becoming angry, rather than teaching children adaptive ways of coping with the anger that they all experience. Snyder's data (chap. 8, this volume) speaks eloquently to this point, by providing clear evidence of just how normative anger is in interactions between children and both their parents and their peers. If children indeed experience anger many times a day, then our goal should be to help children learn effective and constructive ways to manage angry feelings, rather than pursuing the unrealistic goal of banishing angry feelings altogether.

It is also likely that we have avoided giving children full-fledged opportunities to practice their anger regulation skills in our interventions because we worry about the ethics and pragmatics involved in doing so. When children become angry, they are sometimes going to resort to aggression, no matter how much coaching and scaffolding we provide. How do we keep all of the children in our intervention groups safe under these circumstances? Many of us are already doing so. Anyone who has worked with groups of aggressive children has experience in planning for the disagreements and scuffles that inevitably result. Most of us use as much scaffolding, praise, and support as possible, but we also use as many time-outs and as much "safe holding" as necessary. We also make sure that our groups are adequately staffed to allow for individual attention when children require it. Planning for exposure to anger is not really any different from planning for these naturally occurring altercations; in fact, it is in some ways easier, because we can more readily predict when aggressive episodes may occur.

The risks involved in exposing children to anger are obvious. However, in our opinion, the benefits may well justify these risks. Only when children are placed in actual anger-provoking situations are they allowed the opportunity to practice their anger regulation skills, to learn that they can actually control their angry feelings, and to experience the power of feeling angry but not resorting to aggression. In the cognitive-behavioral tradition, these experiences may fundamentally change the meaning of anger for aggressive children. Through success experiences such as these, aggressive children may learn that anger is something that they can control, not something that controls them. For all of these reasons, we fully agree with Bierman's suggestion that interventions for aggressive children would do well to include greater exposure to angry feelings.

Finally, as described previously, increasing attention is being paid to the importance of including anger in the child component of intervention and prevention programs for aggressive children. However, Snyder makes the important point that little attention has been paid to incorporating a focus on anger into work with the parents of aggressive children. Parent-focused interventions are still largely behavioral, with emphasis on training parents to spend positive time with children, praise positive behaviors, ignore minor misbehaviors, give clear and consistent commands, and use time-out effectively. As Snyder (chap. 8, this volume) suggests, two means of incorporating anger constructs into work with parents come readily to mind. The first approach would be to train parents to coach children in emotion understanding skills and anger regulation techniques. The second approach would be to train parents in effective ways to manage their own angry feelings when interacting with their children. Both of these ideas seem like logical extensions of the work that is being done with children. Furthermore, it is likely that these approaches would serve to increase the generalizability of children's own anger regulation skills from the intervention setting to homes and neighborhoods.

CONCLUSION

In conclusion, the authors of the three preceding chapters have given us much to think about when considering the importance of the relation between anger and aggression in understanding and treating children's aggressive behavior problems. The distinction and connection between anger and aggression has long been misunderstood. We believe, though, that consideration of the complex interplay between these two constructs is essential to moving forward in our work with violent children and adolescents. We hope that our comments have provided some additional insight into this work, and we look forward to a continuing focus on the anger–aggression relation in our own research and in that of our colleagues.

REFERENCES

Averill, J. R. (1982). *Anger and aggression: An essay on emotion.* New York: Springer-Verlag.

Brendgen, M., Vitaro, F., Tremblay, R. E., & Lavoie, F. (2001). Reactive and proactive aggression: Predictions to physical violence in different contexts and moderating effects of parental monitoring and caregiving behavior. *Journal of Abnormal Child Psychology, 29,* 293–304.

Brown, K. S., & Parsons, R. D. (1998). Accurate identification of childhood aggression: A key to successful intervention. *Professional School Counseling, 2,* 135–140.

Catalano, R. F., Arthur, M. W., Hawkins, D. J., Berglund, L., & Olson, J. J. (1998). Comprehensive community- and school-based interventions to prevent antisocial behavior. In R. Loeber & D. P. Farrington (Eds.), *Serious & violent juvenile offenders: Risk factors and successful interventions* (pp. 248–283). Thousand Oaks, CA: Sage.

Crick, N. R., & Dodge, K. A. (1994). A review and reformulation of social-information-processing mechanisms in children's social adjustment. *Psychological Bulletin, 115,* 74–101.

Crick, N. R., & Dodge, K. A. (1996). Social information-processing mechanisms on reactive and proactive aggression. *Child Development, 67,* 993–1002.

Cronbach, L. J. (1951). Coefficient alpha and the internal structure of tests. *Psychometrika, 16,* 297–334.

Day, D. M., Bream, L. A., & Pal, A. (1992). Proactive and reactive aggression: An analysis of subtypes based on teacher perceptions. *Journal of Clinical Child Psychology, 21,* 210–217.

Denham, S. A., & Burton, R. (2004). *Social and emotional prevention and intervention programming for preschoolers.* New York: Kluwer Academic/Plenum.

Dodge, K. A. (1991). The structure and function of reactive and proactive aggression. In D. J. Pepler & K. H. Rubin (Eds.), *The development and treatment of childhood aggression* (pp. 201–218). Hillsdale, NJ: Lawrence Erlbaum Associates.

Dodge, K. A., & Coie, J. D. (1987). Social-information-processing factors in reactive and proactive aggression in children's peer groups. *Journal of Personality and Social Psychology, 53,* 1146–1158.

Dodge, K.A., Lansford, J. E., Burks, V. S., Bates, J. E., Pettit, G. S., Fontaine, R., et al. (2003). Peer rejection and social information-processing factors in the development of aggressive behavior problems in children. *Child Development, 74,* 374–393.

Dodge, K. A., Lochman, J. E., Harnish, J. D., Bates, J. E., & Pettit, G. (1997). Reactive and proactive aggression in school children and psychiatrically impaired chronically assaultive youth. *Journal of Abnormal Psychology, 106,* 37–51.

Dodge, K. A., & Pettit, G. S. (2003). A biopsychosocial model of the development of chronic conduct problems in adolescence. *Developmental Psychology, 39,* 349–371.

Dodge, K. A., Pettit, G. S., McClaskey, C. L., & Brown, M. (1986). Social competence in children. *Monographs of the Society for Research in Child Development* (Serial 213, Vol. 51, No. 2).

Dodge, K. A., & Schwartz, D. (1997). Social information processing mechanisms in aggressive behavior. In D. M. Stoff & J. Breiling (Eds.), *Handbook of antisocial behavior* (pp. 171–180). New York: Wiley.

Elliott, D. S., Hamburg, B. A., & Williams, K. R. (Eds.) (1998). *Violence in American schools: A new perspective.* New York: Cambridge University Press.

Greenberg, M. T., Domitrovich, C., & Bumbarger, B. (2001). The prevention of mental disorders in school-aged children: Current state of the field. *Prevention and Treatment, 4.*

Greenberg, M. T., & Kusche, C.A. (1993). *Promoting social and emotional development in deaf children: The PATHS project.* Seattle: University of Washington Press.

Greenberg, M. T., & Kusche, C. A. (1998). Preventive interventions for school-age deaf children: The PATHS curriculum. *Journal of Deaf Studies and Deaf Education, 3,* 49–63.

Greenberg, M. T., Kusche, C. A., & Speltz, M. (1991). Emotional regulation, self control, and psychopathology: The role of relationships in early childhood. In D. Cicchetti & S. L. Toth (Eds.), *Internalizing and externalizing expressions of dysfunction: Rochester Symposium on Developmental Psychopathology* (Vol. 2, pp. 21–66). Hillsdale, NJ: Lawrence Erlbaum Associates.

Halberstadt, A. G., Denham, S. A., & Dunsmore, J. C. (2001). Affective social competence. *Social Development, 10,* 79–119.

Hubbard, J. A., & Dearing, K. F. (2004). Children's understanding and regulation of emotion in the context of their peer relations. In J. B. Kupersmidt & K. A. Dodge (Eds.), *Children's peer relations: From development to intervention* (pp. 81–99). Washington, DC: American Psychological Association Press.

Hubbard, J. A., Parker, E. H., Ramsden, S. R., Flanagan, K. D., Relyea, N., Dearing, K. F., et al. (2004). The relations between observational, physiological, and self-report measures of children's anger. *Social Development, 13,* 14–39.

Hubbard, J. A., Smithmyer, C. M., Ramsden, S. R., Parker, E. H., Flanagan, K. D., Dearing, K. F., et al. (2002). Observational, physiological, and self-report measures of children's anger: Relations to reactive versus proactive aggression. *Child Development, 73*, 1101–1118.

Izard, C. E. (1993). Four systems of emotion activation: Cognitive and noncognitive processes. *Psychological Review, 100*, 68–90.

Kazdin, A. E. (1987). Treatment of antisocial behavior in children: Current status and future directions. *Psychological Bulletin, 102*, 187–203.

Larson, J. (1994). Cognitive-behavioral treatment of anger-induced aggression in the school setting. In M. J. Furlong & D. C. Smith (Eds.), *Anger, hostility, and aggression: Assessment, prevention, and intervention strategies for youth* (pp. 393–440). Brandon, VT: Clinical Psychology.

Larson, J., & Lochman, J. E. (2002). *Helping schoolchildren cope with anger: A cognitive-behavioral intervention. The Guilford school practitioner series.* New York: Guilford.

Lemerise, E. A., & Arsenio, W. F. (2000). An integrated model of emotion processes and cognition in social information processing. *Child Development, 71*, 107–118.

Little, T. D., Brauner, J., Jones, S. M., Nock, M. K., & Hawley, P. H. (2003). Rethinking aggression: A typological examination of the functions of aggression. *Merrill–Palmer Quarterly, 49*, 343–369.

Little, T. D., Jones, S. M., Henrich, C. C., & Hawley, P. H. (2003). Disentangling the "whys" from the "whats" of aggressive behavior. *International Journal of Behavioral Development, 27*, 122–133.

McAdams, C. (2002). Trends in the occurrence of reactive and proactive aggression among children and adolescents: Implications for preparation and practice in child and youth care. *Child & Youth Care Forum, 31*, 89–109.

Phillips, N. C., & Lochman, J. E. (2003). Experimentally manipulated change in children's proactive and reactive aggressive behavior. *Aggressive Behavior, 29*, 215–227.

Poulin, F., & Boivin, M. (1999). Proactive and reactive aggression and boys' friendship quality in mainstream classrooms. *Journal of Emotional and Behavioral Disorders, 7*, 168–177.

Price, J. M., & Dodge, K. A. (1989). Reactive and proactive aggression in childhood: Relations to peer status and social context dimensions. *Journal of Abnormal Child Psychology, 17*, 455–471.

Salmivalli, C., & Nieminen, E. (2002). Proactive and reactive aggression among school bullies, victims, and bully-victims. *Aggressive Behavior, 28*, 30–44.

Vitaro, F., & Brendgen, M. (2005). Proactive and reactive aggression: A developmental perspective. In R. E. Tremblay, W. M. Hartup, & J. Archer (Eds.), *Developmental origins of aggression* (pp. 178–201). New York: Guilford.

Vitaro, F., Brendgen, M., & Tremblay, R. E. (2002). Reactively and proactively aggressive children: Antecedent and subsequent characteristics. *Journal of Child Psychology & Psychiatry & Allied Disciplines, 43*, 495–506.

Vitaro, F., Gendreau, P. L., Tremblay, R. E., & Oligny, P. (1998). Reactive and proactive aggression differentially predict later conduct problems. *Journal of Child Psychology and Psychiatry and Allied Disciplines, 39*, 377–385.

Waschbusch, D. A., Willoughby, M. T., & Pelham, W. E. (1998). Criterion validity and the utility of reactive and proactive aggression: Comparisons to attention deficit hyperactivity disorder, oppositional defiant disorder, conduct disorder, and other measures of functioning. *Journal of Clinical Child Psychology, 27,* 396–405.

Weinshenker, N. J., & Siegel, A. (2002). Bimodal classification of aggression: Affective defense and predatory attack. *Aggression and Violent Behavior, 7,* 237–250.

IV

THE ANGER–AGGRESSION RELATION IN VIOLENT FAMILIES

Anger and Anger Attacks as Precipitants of Aggression: What We Can Learn from Child Physical Abuse

Oommen K. Mammen, Paul A. Pilkonis, David J. Kolko, and Alexandra Groff

More than two decades ago, in a paper titled "Child Abuse as an Area of Aggression Research," Knutson (1978) suggested that because child physical abuse (CPA) involves an aggressive act directed at the child, the wealth of research on aggression in other groups may help to better understand and treat CPA. Such an endeavor has the potential for dramatically increasing the fund of knowledge applicable to CPA, or as pointed out by Frude (1979): "An alignment of aggression theory and explanations of child abuse might be highly productive" (p. 703). Reversing this logic, the literature on CPA can be used to illustrate various aspects of aggression in general. Here we use this latter approach to illustrate the role of anger as a precipitant of aggression. We address the treatment implications of anger in aggression, with a specific focus on pharmacological interventions. Other chapters in this volume address psychosocial interventions to reduce anger. Given their different mechanisms of action, pharmacological treatment has the potential for augmenting recognized psychosocial treatments. Indeed such integrated treatment has been described and used before in family violence (e.g., Maiuro & Avery, 1996). Finally, the limitations of focusing on anger and aggression are described.

DEFINITIONS OF ANGER AND AGGRESSION

Inconsistencies in the use of the terms *anger, aggression, irritability,* and *hostility* have made it difficult to interpret the research literature, so it is important to define and consistently use these terms (Eckhardt, Barbour, & Stwart, 1997). The following definitions offered by Spielberger and Sydeman (1994) are useful: *Anger* is an emotion that may or may not be associated with aggressive impulses and behaviors, whereas *aggression* refers to behaviors that are destructive or punitive. Thus anger is an internal experience whereas aggression is a behavior. *Hostility* refers to a cognitive set including the perception of having been treated unfairly, bitterness about this treatment, feelings ranging from low trust to cynicism about people, and also feelings that range from suspiciousness to ideas of references and paranoia. *Irritability* refers to a low threshold for an angry response or a readiness to become angry at minor provocations.

Human aggression is broadly classified as instrumental (incentive motivated) or reactive (annoyance motivated; Baron & Richardson, 1994). *Instrumental aggression* is purposeful, not accompanied by strong emotion, and the aggressive act itself serves another goal (e.g., a planned assassination, assault solely for the purpose of theft). *Reactive aggression* occurs in response to a perceived provocation and the goal of the aggressive act is to harm the recipient. Because reactive aggression is accompanied by strong emotion (typically anger) and is not premeditated it is also called *impulsive or emotional aggression* (Berkowitz, 1997). In interpersonal contexts, aggression is typically "reactive" (Averill, 1983). Because parent-to-child aggression in CPA tends to occur in response to aversive child behavior (Herrenkohl, Herrenkohl, & Egolf, 1983; Kadushin & Martin, 1981), it is likely often reactive.

In practice, however, aggressive incidents are not easily classified as reactive or instrumental. Thus when Dietrich, Berkiowitz, Kadushin, and McGloin (1990) classified descriptions of the abusive incident that brought parents to the attention of Child Protective Services, they found that a third of the abusive incidents were rated as instrumental, a third impulsive, and the remainder had qualities of both instrumental and impulsive aggression. Similar proportions were found in a study of prison inmates (Barratt & Slaughter, 1998), consistent with the view that instrumental and impulsive aggression are opposite ends of a continuum, with emotion contributing to varying degrees at different points in the continuum (Huesmann, 1998).

Because many aggressive acts cannot be clearly classified as instrumental or reactive, Bushman and Anderson (2001) suggest that it is more accurate and useful to view aggressive acts as having attributes that lie on a continuum from "automatic" to "controlled" information processing. According to this classification scheme, aggressive acts are characterized by controlled processing when they have following four attributes: consciousness of what the control will achieve, feeling of control, effort used to control the action, and monitoring of the outcomes of the control. In aggression characterized by automatic processing, one or more of the preceding attributes of controlled processing are absent. This latter approach to describing aggressive acts applies very well to disciplinary acts by parents, which can range from a controlled act of verbal or physical aggression to modify child behavior in a parent motivated by anger caused by child misbehavior to explosive out-of-control physical aggression in CPA that may have started out as an act of discipline to modify child behavior (Dix, 1991). As the automatic/controlled aggression classification has not been applied to CPA research, in this paper we use the terms *reactive* and *instrumental aggression*.

Anger attacks are a set of symptoms that have received little attention in the research and clinical literature. These attacks are characterized by a rapid onset of intense anger and a crescendo of autonomic arousal that occurs following a provocation that is described as trivial by the individual. Anger attacks are important because of their association with feeling out-of-control, overt aggressive behaviors and interpersonal problems (Fava et al., 1993; Gould et al., 1996). Anger attacks are typically "ego-dystonic": They are described as uncharacteristic of oneself, cause much subjective distress, and are followed by guilt and regret (Fava et al., 1993). Anger attacks are a particular problem for parents, because anger and aggression tend to be directed primarily at immediate family members rather than others (Mammen et al., 1999). For example, in a sample of pregnant and postpartum women with mood and anxiety disorders, 60% reported anger attacks in the prior month (Mammen et al., 1999). Among these participants, anger attacks were associated with verbally attacking others in 93%, feeling like physically attacking others in 81%, physically attacking others in 33%, and throwing or destroying objects in 47%. Anger attacks in the month prior to assessment were significantly more likely to be provoked by immediate family members than by someone from outside the immediate family. The anger attacks were typically described as uncharacteristic of the self, were followed by guilt and regret, and were associated with worry over having anger attacks and attempts to prevent them. From a clinical standpoint, anger attacks are of interest because they may respond well to treatment with serotonergic antidepressants (e.g., Fava et al., 1993, 1996).

ANGER, AGGRESSION, AND THEORY OF EMOTIONS

Specific types of emotions tend to be aroused by specific categories of events that are personally meaningful to the individual (Campos, Mumme, Kermoran, & Campos, 1994). Emotions have neural substrates and distinctive motor expressive patterns and subjective experiences (or feelings) that enable the person to respond adaptively to the events or stimuli that provoked the emotion (Damasio, 1998; Izard, 1993). The motor expressive pattern of emotions include "action tendencies" that create an impulse and preparedness to act in ways congruent with the signal function of the emotion (Frijda, Kuipers, & ter Schure, 1989). For example, threatening stimuli cause the experience of fear and the action tendency to flee (LeDoux, 1995). Therefore the emotion of fear is a signal to the individual of impending threat and the fear creates a preparedness to take protective measures. Similarly, other emotions have characteristic signal functions and action tendencies that foster adaptive responses (Roseman, Wiest, & Swartz, 1994). Though emotions are clearly influenced by experience, they also appear to be "preadapted" and not entirely contingent on experience. This is suggested by their conservation across phylogeny (i.e., across species), appearance early in ontogeny (i.e., in early infancy), and relative consistency across cultures (Cicchetti, Ackerman, & Izard, 1995). These characteristics cause emotions to be motivators to respond in adaptive ways (Campos et al., 1994) and they impart to emotion "survival value" from an evolutionary perspective (Izard, 1978). However, emotions can also contribute to dysfunction, as in the anxiety disorders where the qualitative and quantitative aspects of fear make it maladaptive (Ohman, 1993). Similarly, as described later, anger can be both adaptive and maladaptive.

Anger is aroused when a person feels thwarted or treated unfairly and is therefore a signal that something is amiss (Lazarus, 1991). Because the action tendency associated with anger is the impulse to rectify the situation that provoked the anger, the outcome of expressed anger is often positive (Averill, 1983). Parental anger is often adaptive because anger provoked by child behavior helps parents respond rapidly with disciplinary responses vital to child safety and social development (Dix, 1991). In fact, the experience of anger in adults is far more common than actual acts of aggression (Averill, 1983). Similarly, anger is highly prevalent in mothers of young children, but most do not abuse their children (Frude & Goss, 1979).

Anger can be maladaptive when there is an imbalance between the strength of the aggressive impulse and the capacity for restraint, when it is disproportionate to the provocation, and when its expression is poorly regulated (Berkowitz, 1997; de Koning & Mak, 1991; Feindler & Ecton, 1986). High levels of anger can contribute to reactive aggression by contributing to the strength of aggressive impulses (Sonnemans & Frijda, 1994), and also by decreasing cognitive controls (Zillmann, 1994; Zillmann, Bryant, Cantor, & Day, 1975). Indeed, research shows that angered and distressed individuals can direct aggression at persons who have not caused the distress (Berkowitz, 1993).

The "frustration–aggression" hypothesis is frequently invoked to explain reactive aggression. As originally described, this hypothesis

(Dollard, Dools, Miller, Mowrer, & Sears 1939) was a simple stimulus–response model in which individuals respond with aggression when frustrated by being blocked from achieving an expected goal. Current conceptualizations of the frustration–aggression relationship include internal experiences and a definition of frustration that has been broadened to include various types of aversive experiences, including ones that are interpersonal or physical (Berkowitz, 1989). Applying the frustration–aggression hypothesis to reactive aggression reveals the following sequence of events: a trigger precipitating emotion (typically anger) with its attendant aggressive action tendencies and aggressive behavior as an outcome when the aggressive impulse is not controlled (de Koning & Mak, 1991). The angry feelings precipitated by the trigger often result from the manner in which the triggering event is interpreted (Coie & Dodge, 1998; Feindler & Ecton, 1986), and the aggressive impulse can be controlled by cognitions such as awareness of consequences for aggression, recognition of mitigating factors that caused the trigger, and personal values that proscribe aggression (Berkowitz, 1993). Further details on the role of cognitions in reactive aggression are described later in this chapter.

In summary, according to emotion theory, the action tendency associated with anger will result in anger contributing to aggression. Consistent with this, in the cross-sectional study of 50 pregnant and postpartum women with mood and anxiety disorders described earlier, state anger contributed significantly to parent-to-child aggression after controlling individually for the effects of depressive symptoms, partner verbal aggression, satisfaction with social support, and number of children (Mammen, Pilkonis, & Kolko, 2000).

ANGER AND AGGRESSION
IN CHILD PHYSICAL ABUSE

Although CPA and parenting behavior in general are multiply determined (Azar, 1991; Belsky, 1984), here we emphasize the role of anger and aggression. The text that follows is organized as follows: First, we describe how anger may contribute to etiologic models that seek to explain CPA. Useful overviews of etiologic models of CPA have already been provided by Azar (1991) and Ammerman (1990). Thus, rather than review these models, we describe how anger may contribute to the models. Next, we briefly describe the limited data on anger in CPA. Then we describe the potential role for integrated psychotherapeutic and pharmacological treatment in CPA. After discussing the limitations of a primary focus on anger and aggression, we end with suggestions and questions that may be useful to examine in research.

Anger and Etiologic Models of Child Physical Abuse

The following observation by Gelles and Straus (1979) regarding their attempt to integrate theories purporting to explain CPA is still valid more than two decades later: "At many points in the integration of the theories is the frustration–aggression hypothesis, i.e., the tendency to respond to frustration and/or stress by aggression" (p. 570). Because of the association between anger and aggression, next we describe how anger may contribute to etiologic models that seek to explain CPA.

Dual-Component Model. The first "component" of this model (Vasta, 1982) refers to parental disciplinary actions that are reinforced because they stop aversive child behaviors. The second "component" refers to the "explosive rage, loss of control, and lashing out" that results in CPA (Vasta, 1982, p. 131). The second component of the model results from abusive parents' tendency to increased physiologic arousability: The deleterious effects of heightened arousal on cognitive controls reduce the capacity for restraint, which in turn increases the intensity of emotion and disciplinary actions. Consistent with this model, laboratory studies suggest increased physiologic arousability in abusive parents and non-parents at risk for abuse (see review by McCanne & Milner, 1991).

There was no role described for anger in Vasta's (1982) model. However, anger could contribute to the model's second component because of its association with aggressive action tendencies and because heightened anger itself can reduce cognitive controls over behavior (Dix, Reinhold, & Zamburano, 1990; Zillmann, 1994). Also, the events described in the dual-component model parallel those seen in the phenomenon of "escalation of aggression," in which aggressive episodes go through escalating sequences leading to a crescendo followed by resolution (Potegal & Knutson, 1994). Berkowitz (1994) has also described the role of anger in escalated aggression, again suggesting a role for anger in the dual-component model of CPA. Lastly, the subjective experience of uncontrollable anger and reactive aggression described by abusive parents (Knutson, 1978; Vasta, 1982) bears a striking resemblance to anger attacks. We are not aware of any published data on anger attacks in parents who have physically abused their child. In one study, 42.3% of parents who had physically abused or neglected their child reported anger attacks (Mammen et al., unpublished data).

Social-Information-Processing Model. This model posits that the cognitive biases of abusive parents predispose them to view ambiguous or neutral child behavior as provocative, annoying, and warranting discipline (Azar, 1997). The resulting disciplinary encounter has the potential to escalate into an abusive episode because of the parent's limited disciplinary skills (Milner, 1993). Research has shown that abusive parents have such cognitive biases in multiple realms and that these biases are related to the use of more physical discipline (Azar, 1997; Milner, 1993).

The possible effects of depression and anxiety on information processing in CPA have been described (Milner, 1993), but similar attention has not been paid to anger. Emotions can influence social cognition in two ways (Forgas, 1994). In "affect-as-information," the signal function of the emotion influences cognition (e.g., concluding something is unfair because one feels angry). In "affect priming," information is processed with a bias toward congruence with experienced affect, such that the affects' valence influences attentional focus, memory retrieval, and the making of interpretations and associations. Most work on the effect of negative affect on social cognition has been with anxiety and depression, but studies suggest that anger also influences social cognition. For example, studies show that anger is associated with diminished reliance on objective appraisal (Bodenhausen, Sheppard, and Kramer, 1994) and with parents attributing hostile intentions to child behavior (Dix et al., 1990). Thus, anger could make it more likely that the abusive parent would see the child as needing to be disciplined, and the disciplinary encounter could escalate into an abusive episode.

Stress-Coping Model.   This model posits that individual differences in the appraisal of situations determine whether an event will be experienced as stressful and that these differences explain why only some individuals respond to stressors with CPA (Hillson & Kupier, 1994). According to this model, abusive parents are more likely to experience stress because they tend to perceive events as personally meaningful ("primary appraisal problem") and are less likely to use adaptive coping strategies to handle problems ("secondary appraisal problem"). Also, this model describes enduring, traitlike "dispositional coping strategies" that influence parental behavior in response to stress. According to Hillson and Kuiper, abusive parents have coping styles characterized by anger and emotional venting that "may culminate more often in explosive outbursts of physical abuse" (p. 274). The model does not address the possibility that anger may increase the likelihood that stress may result in aggression through the effects of anger on primary and secondary appraisal (e.g., Deffenbacher, 1992; Dix et al., 1990). Also this model does not specify a relationship between anger and aggression. The absence of a salient role for emotion in this model may be because it was derived from the work of Lazarus (1991, 1993) in which emotions are seen as resulting from cognitive appraisals. Because this chapter is concerned with the role of emotion in CPA, we describe next non-cognitive mechanisms by which emotions can be aroused.

The precise boundaries between emotion and cognition are the focus of extensive debate (Fridja, 1993; Izard, 1989; LeDoux, 1989). Zajonc (1998) has provided a useful summary of differences between emotion and cognition. Experimental work has shown that there are noncognitive origins for emotions and that "noncognitively" aroused emotions influence behavior (Berkowitz, 1993; Izard, 1993; LeDoux, 1995). Izard (1993) has suggested a useful approach to this issue: viewing cognition as a form of information processing, while recognizing that not all forms of brain information processing are cognitive. According to this approach (Izard, 1993), emotion-relevant information processing in the brain occurs at the following levels: (a) cellular (such as drug-induced mood changes and genetically based personality traits of emotionality); (b) organismic (preprogrammed and independent of experience, such as infants' anger responses to pain and disgust responses to bitter tastes); (c) biopyschological (presumed to occur on the basis of preprogrammed phylogenetically preserved traits, such as disgust reactions to excreta and the development of fear responses in spite of lack of prior exposure to the stimulus); and (d) cognitive (emotion generated by appraisal that a stimulus is personally relevant). In summary, according to this approach information processing occurs along a continuum from cellular to cognitive and an event is seen as cognitive if it is based on factors such as experience, knowledge, and memory (Izard, 1993). Considering noncognitive origins for emotion does not imply that emotions are more salient than cognitions. Rather, it is a means of calling attention to the importance of emotion in influencing behavior. Recent data on the effects of stress on brain neurotransmitters (e.g., serotonin) associated with negative affects including anger also suggest "noncognitive" means by which stress may contribute to aggression through increasing the general level of negative affect. Thus, research has shown a direct relationship between socioeconomic status (which is related to stress) and brain serotonin responsivity in physically and psychiatrically healthy adults, paralleling findings from research on stress in animals (Matthews, Flory, Muldoon, & Manuck, 2000). If replicated, findings such as this may partly explain the relationship between stressful ecological factors and parental irritability, given the association between decreased brain serotonin and anger and aggression (Coccaro & Kavoussi, 1997; Manuck et al., 1998; Matthews et al., 2000).

Disciplinary Model.   This model posits that CPA is a manifestation of parental disciplinary tactics gone awry. It is based on observations that physical abuse tends to occur within the context of disciplinary encounters and that abusive parents are less effective in stopping problematic child behaviors (Reid, 1986). It uses the social-interactional perspective on disciplinary breakdown, according to which parent and child use increasingly coercive behaviors to gain control over the other. During escalating coercive cycles, parents vulnerable to CPA lose control and abuse the child. Patterson (1983) described two paths into these coercive disciplinary encounters, which he also called "irritability cycles": One path is driven by parental frustration that results from difficulty controlling child misbehavior, whereas in the other path high levels of parental anger drive the disciplinary encounter. We are not aware of studies specifically testing this two-path hypothesis. Reid (1983, cited in Reid & Kavanagh, 1985) observed that abusive parents reported more anger during disciplinary confrontations than nonabusive parents, and that behaviorally based treatment-induced improvement in disciplinary techniques was associated with a decline in anger to the level of a nonabusive control group (Reid & Kavanagh, 1985). However, the dropout rate from this study was 45% and improvement in disciplinary techniques took much longer than with nonabusive families (Reid & Kavanagh, 1985). Thus, it is not clear if this finding on reduction in anger with discipline-focused treatment is generalizable.

Anger may contribute to the disciplinary model by increasing the likelihood of aversive parental aggressive responses at every stage of the extended coercive cycles, by the mechanisms described earlier. Additionally, it is possible that parents with problems of anger may limit interactions with their children so as to avoid becoming angry with them, as found in sample of mothers with mood and anxiety disorders (Mammen et al., 1999). This avoidance could increase aversive child behaviors that compel the parent to respond, in accordance with Wahler's (1994) social-continuity hypothesis. This hypothesis views disruptive behavior as a means of engaging inattentive and erratic parents and the child's success in engaging the parent reinforces the child's aversive behavior, thereby setting the stage for even more disciplinary encounters that have the potential to become abusive (Cerezo, 1997). To the best of our knowledge, such a proposed path from anger related avoidance to parental aggression has not been studied.

Psychopathological Model and Substance Abuse. The psychopathological model posits that there must be a serious problem such as a psychiatric disorder that would cause a parent to abuse a child (see Azar, 1991). It fell into disfavor because early studies did not find specific psychiatric disorders associated with CPA (Wolfe, 1985) and because of increasing recognition of the role of stressful ecological factors in the etiology of CPA (Azar, 1991; Belsky, 1993). However, more recent research has found an association between CPA and parental psychiatric disorders (Belsky, 1993). The Epidemiologic Catchment Area survey found that 58.5% of abusive parents had a history of lifetime psychiatric disorder and that psychiatric diagnosis was a more powerful predictor of CPA than sociodemographic variables (Egami, Ford, Greenfield & Crum, 1996). Therefore we describe next the relationship between anger, aggression, CPA, and two of the most prevalent groups of psychiatric disorders (unipolar depressive disorders and anxiety disorders; Kessler et al., 1994). Focusing on these disorders in abusive parents is important because they are common and treatable (Chaffin, Kelleher, & Hollenberg, 1996). Also, depression and anxiety along with anger constitute "negative affect," which has been implicated in both CPA (Belsky, 1993) and aggression (Berkowitz, 1993).

Improved research methodology may explain the association between depressive disorders and CPA found in more recent studies (e.g., Bland & Orn, 1986; Chaffin et al., 1996; Famularo, Barnum, & Stone, 1986; Famularo, Kinscherff, & Fenton, 1992; Kelleher, Chaffin, Hollenberg & Fischer, 1994) but not in older studies reviewed by Wolfe (1985; Belsky, 1993). The association between depression and CPA may be partly explained by the observation that anger and aggression are frequent in depressive disorders (Fava et al., 1993, 1996) and that the aggressive acts are more frequently directed at family rather than those outside the family (Mammen et al., 1999).

There has been less research on anxiety in CPA, though correlational data suggest it is worthy of research attention (Milner, 1993) because abusive parents (compared to nonabusive controls) have been found to have higher levels of self-reported anxiety (Brunnquell, Crichton & Egeland, 1981; Perry, Wells, & Doran, 1983; Whipple & Webster-Stratton, 1991). Given the association between CPA and depression noted previously, high rates of anxiety disorders are likely in abusive parents because depression and anxiety are highly comorbid (Wetzler & Katz, 1989). In the Epidemiologic Catchment Area Survey, when anxiety disorders were comorbid with depressive disorders, the rates of depression-associated aggression almost tripled from 3.45% to 11.09% (Swanson, Holzer, Ganju, & Jono, 1990). This survey may have underestimated the association between anxiety disorders and aggression because it did not assess for posttraumatic stress disorder (PTSD), in which anger and aggression can be major problems (Chemtob, Hamada, Roitblat, & Muraoka, 1994). Famularo, Fenton, Kinscherff, Ayoub, and Barnum (1994) found that in 109 abusive mothers, 15.6% met criteria for current PTSD and 36.7% for past PTSD, and that the children of mothers with PTSD experienced an earlier age of onset of abuse.

There is also a clear relationship between substance abuse and both aggressive behavior (Steadman et al., 1998; Swanson et al., 1990) and CPA (Chaffin et al., 1996; Famularo et al., 1986), but research has yet to establish the causal links explaining these relationships (Miller, Maguin, & Downs, 1997; White, 1997). Varying amounts of data support the following proposed causal mechanisms: (a) Substance use causes aggression by affecting brain chemistry and by fostering aggression to support the drug habit, (b) aggressive individuals are drawn to substance use and the proneness to aggression is exacerbated by ecological factors related to drug use, (c) there is a reciprocal relationship between Factors 1 and 2, and (d) the relationship is an epiphenomenon of other factors that contribute to substance abuse and aggression (see review by White, 1997). Anger may contribute to the substance abuse–CPA relationship by predisposing the individual to substance abuse and by increasing the likelihood that the individual will respond aggressively while intoxicated. Longitudinal and cross-sectional studies show that for some individuals aggressive behavior and irritability antedate substance use (e.g., Brook, Whiteman, & Finch, 1990; Moeller et al., 1997; Tarter, Blackson, Brigham, Moss, & Caprara, 1995). As anger contributes to aggression and irritability, it is possible that anger may be a problem for these individuals. In this regard, high levels of anger have been reported among persons with substance abuse (e.g., Walfish, Massey, & Krone, 1990) and persons with high trait anger consume more alcohol than those with low trait anger (Deffenbacher, 1992).

DATA ON ANGER IN CHILD PHYSICAL ABUSE

There are surprisingly few data on parental anger in CPA, given that the literature is replete with references to a role for anger in CPA (e.g., Ammerman, 1990; Belsky, 1993; Kadushin & Martin, 1981; Peterson, Gable, Doyle, & Ewigman, 1997; Reid, 1986; Wolfe, 1987a). The following data suggest a role for anger in CPA, though it must be noted that the data are limited, some sample sizes are small, and many of the studies were not conducted with parents who were recruited based on their being abusive.

Nomellini and Katz (1983) studied four parents in anger control treatment for having abused their child or for fearing they would do so and found that mean pretreatment anger scores on the Novaco Anger Scale (Novaco, 1976) were higher than the mean scores for a normative group and for a group of hospitalized psychiatric inpatients. Acton and During (1992) found that both pre- and posttreatment scores of trait anger on the State-Trait Anger Scale (Spielberger & Sydeman, 1994) were higher than normative scores in 29 abusive parents enrolled in aggression management behavioral treatment. In a treatment study with 38 abusive families, Kolko (1996b) found that parental self-reports of anger were positively correlated with the use of force in physical discipline. Kolko also found that mean ratings of anger throughout treatment were significantly correlated with scores on the Child Abuse Potential Inventory, an index of risk for CPA (Milner, 1994).

Rodriguez and Green (1997) examined the associations among parental anger (on the State-Trait Anger Expression Inventory; Spielberger & Sydeman, 1994), parental stress (on the Parenting Stress Index; Abidin, 1990), and scores on the Child Abuse Potential Inventory (Milner, 1994) in two nonabusive samples. In both samples, the amount of variance explained increased significantly when anger was added to the regression equation following the entry of parental stress. Also, DiLillo, Tremblay, and Peterson (2000) reported that maternal anger mediated the effects of childhood sexual abuse on Child Abuse Potential Inventory scores in a community sample of 290 mothers of young children. These mothers were considered at risk on the basis of low socioeconomic status and education, self-reported high anger during discipline, and use of corporal punishment on at least one occasion. The authors controlled for the effects of childhood physical abuse in all their analyses.

Peterson and colleagues (1994) examined the role of anger in low-income mothers' choice of disciplinary strategy (physical vs. nonphysical) in response to vignettes of child misbehavior. Self-reports of anger in response to the vignettes did not correlate with whether verbal or physical disciplinary techniques were used. However, mothers' rating of anger in response to the vignettes was significantly correlated with describing their own child as having behavior problems, and rating their child as having behavior problems was related to the frequency with which mothers reported spanking their child. The authors noted that because discipline intensity was not measured, the results did not preclude the possibility of anger affecting the intensity of discipline, an important contributor to CPA.

Whiteman, Fanshel, and Grundy (1987) reported a treatment study on anger control for parents who were abusive or "at risk for abuse." Active treatment was provided to 42 parents and 13 parents were controls. Posttreatment parental anger for the entire sample (controls and those receiving active treatment) showed significant, positive one-tailed correlations with self-reports of harsh discipline and irritation over child behavior.

With regard to the disciplinary model of CPA, Reid (1983, cited in Reid, 1986) found that abusive parents compared to nonabusive parents experienced more anger during disciplinary confrontations, and Patterson (1985) found angry affect to be associated with an increased likelihood of mothers reacting with and persisting in aversive behavior in response to child behaviors. Similarly, in a sample of physically abusive parents enrolled in a treatment study, hostility on the BSI (Brief System Inventory, Derogatis, 1993) was significantly correlated with Minor Physical Violence on the Conflict Tactics Scale, but not Severe Physical Violence (Mammen, Kolko, & Pilkonis, 2002).

Greenwald, Bank, Reid, and Knutson (1997) examined the determinants of punitive punishment in a community sample of lower socioeconomic status families recruited to study the determinants of antisocial behavior (not child abuse specifically). Using structural equation modeling, the relative contributions of the following variables to punitive parenting were examined: parental irritability (a composite measure of anger), discipline style, family stress and coercive child behavior. In testing the measurement model, it was revealed that (a) parent irritability correlated with discipline style, (b) discipline style was correlated with punitive parenting, but that (c) parent irritability was not related to punitive parenting. When the discipline mediated model was tested, parent irritability did not contribute to discipline style. However when the composite parent discipline measure was divided into its constituents (parenting effectiveness and nattering) it was found that (a) parent irritability was significantly correlated with parenting effectiveness, and (b) parenting effectiveness was in turn correlated with punitive parenting. Thus a role for anger was partially supported. However, the authors questioned whether method variance may have contributed to this last finding. Also, punitive punishment was measured as a dichotomous variable, and therefore the question of whether anger contributed to the frequency and intensity of punitive parenting could not be examined.

In summary, there are sound theoretical reasons to hypothesize a relationship between anger and CPA, anger is widely cited as contributing to CPA, and anger is often a focus of treatment in CPA (as described later). Nevertheless, the available research described earlier does not permit us to conclude whether or not anger contributes to CPA.

Anger as a Mediator Between Aggression and Its Predictors

As noted previously, anger is aroused when a person feels thwarted or treated unfairly and is a signal that something is amiss. Because the action tendency associated with anger is aggression, anger may serve as a mediator between attributions for aversive experiences and aggression (Geen, 1996). There has been little research on the potential role of anger as a mediator. To truly examine the role of anger as mediator would require a study in which anger is manipulated. We are not aware of such studies, but there are limited data that, although not confirming mediation, suggest mediation. In the study of pregnant and postpartum women described earlier, results were consistent with anger in the prior 2 weeks mediating the effects of depressive symptoms, partner aggression directed at the mother, satisfaction with social support, and number of children on parent-to-child aggression (Mammen et al., 2000). Developmental psychopathology studies have shown that parental stress disrupts disciplinary actions through their effects on parental negative emotions (e.g., Conger, Ge, Elder, Lorenz, & Simons, 1994; Conger, Patterson, & Ge, 1995). These studies suggest a mediational role for anger because disrupted parental discipline typically involves verbal aggression and because assessed negative emotions such as depressive symptoms frequently coexist with anger. In summary, theory would suggest that anger is an ideal candidate to be a mediator between aversive experiences and aggression, but there are inadequate data to confirm this.

Potential Clinical Implications

There is heterogeneity in the factors that lead to abuse in individual families and this heterogeneity calls for individualized assessments and treatment plans (Kolko, 1996). Interventions need to focus on child safety, the factors (parental and environmental) contributing to the abuse, and optimization of child outcomes through child-focused interventions (Kolko, 1996a). A review of assessment and treatment in cases of CPA has been the focus of various papers (e.g., Kolko, 1996a; R. K. Oates & Bross, 1995; Wolfe & Wekerle, 1993) and is beyond the scope of this report.

Treatment for abusive families is typically psychosocial. Broadly, interventions consist of behavioral and cognitive-behavioral programs and comprehensive/multiservice programs (Wolfe & Wekerle, 1993). Multiservice programs use a comprehensive intervention package to address the various ecological and parental problems afflicting the family (Wolfe & Wekerle, 1993). As behavioral and cognitive-behavioral therapies are widely used and well recognized in the treatment of CPA, they are not described further here.

Though standard treatment for CPA generally includes anger control interventions, not all parents are helped by current approaches (Wolfe & Wekerle, 1993). For example, in a study with abusive parents, Kolko (1996a) found that 31% of parents reported high anger late in the course of the 12-week treatment. Also, in a study targeting aggressive behavior in abusive parents Acton and During (1992) found that parents' anger decreased but that anger scores were higher than normative scores even at the end of the treatment. Lack of universal response to cognitive-behavioral therapy for anger is also seen in other groups. For example, the success rate was 67% in the meta-analysis by Beck and Fernandez (1998). This suggests the need for alternate approaches to treatment.

Alternative psychotherapeutic approaches to anger have been well described (e.g., Brondolo, DiGiuseppe, & Tafrate, 1997; Ornstein, 1999; Paivio, 1999; Robins & Novaco, 1999) and are not a focus of this chapter. Rather, we focus on pharmacological approaches because they have not been described adequately in the literature on CPA. Pharmacological treatment targeting anger and aggression in abusive parents may have a role for several reasons. First, a number of parents are not helped by current psychotherapeutic and psychosocial interventions (Wolfe & Wekerle, 1993). Second, medication responsive mood and anxiety disorders are prevalent in abusive parents (e.g., Egami et al., 1996; Famularo et al., 1994; Kelleher et al., 1994) and these disorders can be associated with anger and aggression. Third, data suggest that antidepressants reduce anger and aggression independent of their effects on depression and anxiety (Coccaro & Kavoussi, 1997; Salzman et al., 1995). Fourth, pharmacological treatment may reduce impulsivity as suggested by studies on the treatment of impulse control disorders (Stein, Hollander, & Liebowitz, 1993) and may also reduce physiologic arousability as suggested by studies on the treatment of PTSD (Katz, Fleisher, Kiernisted, & Milanese, 1996). This is relevant as parental impulsivity and heightened physiological arousability have been implicated in CPA (Milner & Chilamkurti, 1991). Fifth, because cognitive-behavioral therapy and medications have different mechanisms of action, medications may prove to be a useful adjunct to psychotherapeutic interventions. Lastly, abusive parents often suffer from various social adversities that are impediments to psychotherapy and much time is required to address relationship difficulties and cognitive disturbances acquired over a lifetime (Wolfe, Edwards, Manion, & Koverola, 1988; Wolfe & Wekerle, 1993). For such individuals, medication to reduce anger and aggressive action tendencies "may facilitate psychotherapy and resocialization measures" (de Koning & Mak, 1991). Medication-induced reductions in anger and aggression may be especially important in abusive families if homes are made safe sooner for children at risk. Reductions in parental anger and aggression, and thus greater safety, will in turn enable parents to practice behavioral and cognitive-behavioral skills with the child still in the home. As noted by R. K. Oates and Bross (1995), many interventions for CPA are ideally implemented with the child in the home, a limitation for parents whose children have been removed.

The only study of pharmacological treatment for physically abusive parents was conducted more than two decades ago (Rosenblatt, Schaeffer, & Rosenthal, 1976). At the time, abusive parents were considered suitable for a trial of medication with antiaggressive potential because of contemporaneous reports in which abusive parents described CPA as occurring during "rage attacks." The clinical trial of phenytoin did not show positive effects (Rosenblatt et al., 1976) and subsequent studies with this agent in other groups provided mixed results (Fava, 1997).

Though research on the pharmacological treatment of anger and aggression has lagged behind pharmacologic research in other areas, available data suggest a role for such treatment (Fava, 1997). In considering the treatment of aggression, it helps to distinguish between instrumental and reactive aggression, because pharmacological agents help the latter and not the former (Barratt & Slaughter, 1998). Much of this work has been with antidepressants, the anger and aggression reducing effects of which have been reported in case reports and small open-label studies (Fava, Anderson, & Rosenbaum, 1993; Kavoussi, Liu, & Coccaro, 1994; Rubey, Johnson, Emmanuel, & Lydiard, 1996). These effects have been found in persons with major depressive disorder (Fava, 1997; Fava et al., 1993), bipolar depression (Mammen, Pilkonis, Chenguppa, & Kupfer, 2004), borderline personality disorder (Salzman et al., 1995), personality disorder without current major depression (Coccaro & Kavoussi, 1997), and in the absence of psychiatric disorder (Fava et al., 1993, Mammen, Shear, Jennings, & Popper, 1997). Of these studies, the two randomized double-blind placebo-controlled trials found the antidepressant fluoxetine to be effective in reducing anger (Salzman et al., 1995) and aggression (Coccaro & Kavoussi, 1997). In these controlled trials, antidepressants reduced anger and aggression independent of their effects on depression and anxiety. Subjects who failed to improve on the antidepressant fluoxetine in the Coccaro and Kavoussi study were subsequently found to respond to open-label treatment with the mood-stabilizing agent valproic acid (Kavoussi & Coccaro, 1998).

Another approach to treating impulsive aggression involves medications from the class of "mood-stabilizing agents" used to treat bipolar disorder or manic depressive illness (McElroy, 1999). These agents include lithium and the anticonvulsants used in the treatment of bipolar disorder (e.g., valproic acid, carbamezapine). The rationale underlying the use of mood stabilizers is that (a) they have been shown empirically to reduce impulsive aggression (Donovan et al., 2000; Malone, Delaney, Luebbert, Carter, & Campbell, 2000), and (b) high levels of impulsive aggression in the form of intermittent explosive disorder and bipolar disorder frequently coexist in psychiatric settings (McElroy, 1999). McElroy has suggested a clinically useful algorithm for the pharmacological treatment of impulsive aggression. Briefly, this algorithm suggests initially using serotonin reuptake inhibitor antidepressants (e.g., fluoxetine) because of their relative ease of administration, but using mood stabilizers as an initial treatment if there is coexisting bipolar disorder. Fava (1997) has reviewed the effects of other medications (e.g., beta-blockers) in reducing aggression.

Given the association between substance abuse and CPA described previously, it is noteworthy that medication trials are being increasingly conducted with people actively abusing drugs and alcohol (e.g., Cornelius et al., 1997). For people with coexisting depressive disorders and substance abuse, antidepressant treatment is associated with reductions in consumption of alcohol (Cornelius et al., 1997) and possibly even marijuana, cocaine, and opiates (Cornelius et al., 1999; Nunes et al., 1995, 1998). It is possible therefore that for abusive parents with substance abuse problems, pharmacological treatment may help treat underlying mood and anxiety disorders, while also reducing anger, aggression, and substance use.

The following caveats are warranted when considering pharmacological treatment for impulsive aggression. First, because there has been limited research in this area, it is advisable to inform patients that these medications have not been approved for treating aggression. Second, though the available data suggest that serotonergic antidepressants reduce aggression, there are case reports of violent offenders claiming these agents caused them to aggress (Myers & Vondruska, 1998). Although such reports are extremely uncommon compared to the rates of effective serotonergic antidepressant use, and though no cause-and-effect relationship has been established (Fuller, 1996; Heiligenstein, Beasley, & Potvin, 1993), it is useful to check for increased aggression when using medication to treat aggression.

In summary, the literature discussed previously suggests there may be a role for medication treatment targeting anger and aggression in abusive parents. It must be noted, however, that none of this pharmacological research has been conducted with abusive parents. Also, the number of rigorous trials of pharmacological treatment targeting anger and aggression in is very limited.

Summary

Because CPA involves an aggressive act by the caregiver or parent to the child, we used the research literature on CPA to illustrate the anger–aggression relationship. Though the literature is replete with references to a role for anger in CPA, and though there is a long history of focusing on anger and aggression in behavioral and cognitive-behavioral treatment for CPA, there are limited data on anger in CPA. Nevertheless, we found sound theoretical grounds to hypothesize a role for anger in CPA. This and the finding that emotions can be aroused by "noncognitive" factors suggest that it may be important to focus on anger in aggression. Lastly, our survey of treatment of aggression in other groups suggests that there may be a role for pharmacological treatment specifically aimed at reducing anger and aggression in abusive parents.

It is useful however to consider the limitations of focusing on anger and aggression in CPA. First, it is important to attend to causes of heightened anger in individual parents. Ignoring potential causes of justifiable anger such as partner violence and major psychosocial stress could result in a failure to identify treatable causes of anger. Also, an exclusive focus on anger under such circumstances could result in "blaming of the victims," and could augur a return to older etiologic models of CPA that are "parent blaming." The challenge for researchers and clinicians is to look for social problems contributing to anger while ensuring that such a search does not result in a failure to offer and study effective psychotherapeutic and pharmacological treatments for anger and aggression.

Second, etiologic models to explain CPA have increased in complexity from early, single-factor models to contemporary process models (Azar, 1991). It is important that the focus on anger and aggression not result in a return to the single-factor approach to understanding CPA. As noted by Azar, the initial move away from viewing CPA as a problem of aggression was that it failed to take into account the multiple factors that contribute to CPA. The task then is to take advantage of focusing on anger and aggression, while recognizing and working with complex interplay of factors contributing to CPA.

Third, physical aggression is only part of the problem facing the victimized child: The aggression typically occurs in the context of serious parenting problems and social adversity. Consequently, CPA has been conceptualized as an "extreme deviation on a continuum of parenting adequacy" (Ammerman, 1990, p. 248; see also Wolfe, 1985) or an extreme form of parenting dysfunction (Belsky &Vondra, 1989). Because of this, adverse child outcomes associated with CPA are not simply a consequence of parental aggression but are also related to parenting dysfunction and social adversity (Azar, 1997). Therefore, optimizing child outcomes entails much more than stopping parental aggression or reducing anger (Azar, 1997; Kolko, 1996a).

Fourth, pharmacologic treatment in family violence is not without controversy, even though it has previously been suggested for abusive parents (Christmas, Wodarski, Smokowski, 1996) and though there has been a call for research into the pharmacologic treatment of "anger arousal" in abusive parents (Kolko, 1996). Mauiro and Avery (1996) have discussed these controversies with regard to male spousal batterers. At its heart, the concern is that using medication is a form of reductionism and subscription to a biomedical view of family violence, and that medication treatment will result in "oversimplifying and underestimating the scope of interpersonal violence, promoting the disavowal of personal responsibility due to 'diminished capacity,' as well as ignoring important sociocultural and psychological bases for such behavior" (Maiuro & Avery, 1996, p. 240). The authors point out that rather than avoid potentially helpful medications, these legitimate concerns should cause practitioners to provide pharmacological treatment integrated with psychosocial and psychotherapeutic measures in such a way as to minimize concerns about using medication (Maiuro & Avery, 1996).

CONCLUSIONS AND POTENTIAL RESEARCH IMPLICATIONS

The following comments by Eckhardt et al. (1997) on research in the area of marital violence is applicable to CPA and aggression in general: "The anger-leads-to-aggression equation simply makes intuitive sense (cf. Tavris, 1989) . . . it is unfortunately difficult to offer sound conclusions about the actual role of anger" (p. 353).

From a research standpoint it would be useful to document the role of anger in aggression, given that it is frequently cited as an etiologic factor, in spite of limited evidence. Evidence to date typically documents correlations between anger and aggression. In future research, it would be ideal to examine the causal role of anger within the context of studies in which anger is manipulated. Intervention studies targeting anger and studies on the intergenerational transmission of aggression (e.g., Conger, Neppl, Kim, & Scarmellan, 2003) would be ideal for such purposes. In conducting such research, it will be crucial to be rigorous and consistent in defining and measuring anger and aggression. It would also be useful to anchor such research in theoretical models such as the ones described earlier, so that the role of anger relative to other variables may be examined. Also, as described previously, anger frequently coexists with anxiety disorders and depressive disorders. It would be useful to learn whether anger is simply an associated feature of these disorders as suggested by the current psychiatric nosology (American Psychiatric Association, 1994) or whether anger is an independent clinical problem (Kassinove, 1995). Relatedly, it may be worthwhile to examine the status of anger attacks relative to other psychiatric disorders, and also to develop data-based criteria for anger attacks (Morand, Thomas et al., 1998).

Investigators have frequently commented on the need to identify subgroups among aggressive persons as that may help guide treatment choices (Eichelman & Hartwig, 1991; Keefe, 1995). Unlike domestic-violence research (Holtzworth-Munroe, Meehan, Herron, Rehman, & Stuart, 2000), such work is limited in CPA (e.g., Francis, Hughes, & Hitz, 1992; M. R. Oates, 1979; Oldershaw, Walters, & Hall, 1989; Sloan & Meier, 1983). Thus, Wolfe's (1987b) observation from over a decade ago is still valid: "Unfortunately, over the past 25 years these rationally derived subtypes of child-abusive parents have received little empirical validation" (p. 95). To some extent this observation may also be applied to other areas of aggression research. In this regard, it may also be useful to systematically examine aggressive acts and aggressive groups based on the controlled versus automatic processing dichotomy described by Bushman and Anderson (2001) and presented previously.

Another area of research importance is examining whether medications with antiaggressive potential in other groups (reviewed by Fava, 1997) will help abusive parents. Establishing a role for medications targeting aggression in abusive parents would pave the way to examining the effectiveness of integrated psychotherapy and pharmacology treatments. In such research with abusive parents and also other groups with problems of aggression, it would be ideal to establish aggression as an outcome and anger as mediator of treatment effects. This would be in contrast to research on anger attacks, where there has been no study in which the anger attacks themselves are the focus of treatment trial. Rather, the only data on the treatment of anger attacks come from the response of anger attacks during the course of the pharmacological treatment of mood disorders (e.g., Fava et al., 1993).

Though much work remains to be done, this is an opportune time to conduct research on anger and aggression because of increased research attention to anger and emotions in general, improvements in measures of anger (DiGiuseppe, Eckhardt Tafrate, & Robin, 1994; Eckhardt et al., 1997), and the availability of pharmacological and psychotherapeutic treatments for anger (e.g., Deffenbacher, Oetting, Huff, Cornell, & Fava et al., 1993; Dallager, 1996; Rubey et al., 1996).

ACKNOWLEDGMENTS

This work was supported in part by National Institute of Mental health Grant MH01678.

REFERENCES

Abidin, R. R. (1990). *Parenting Stress Index*. Charlottesville, VA: Pediatric Psychology Press.

Acton, R. G., & During, S. M. (1992). Preliminary results of aggression management training for aggressive parents. *Journal of Interpersonal Violence, 7*(3), 410–417.

American Psychiatric Association. (1994). *Diagnostic and Statistical manual for mental disorders*. Washington, DC: Author.

Ammerman, R. T. (1990). Etiological models of child maltreatment: A behavioral perspective. *Behavior Modification, 14*(3), 230–254.

Averill, J. R. (1983). Studies on anger and aggression: Implications for theories of emotion. *American Psychologist, 38*(11), 1145–1160.

Azar, S. T. (1991). Models of child abuse: A metatheoretical analysis. *Criminal Justice & Behavior, 18*(1), 30–46.

Azar, S. T. (1997). A cognitive behavioral approach to understanding and treating parents who physically abuse their children. In D. A. Wolfe & R. J. McMahan (Eds.), *Child abuse: New directions in prevention and treatment across the lifespan. Banff international behavioral science series, Vol. 4.* (pp. 79–101). Thousand Oaks, CA: Sage.

Baron, R. A., & Richardson, D. R. (1994). Aggression: Definitions and perspectives. In *Human aggression* (pp. 1–38). New York, Plenum.

Barratt, E. S., & Slaughter, L. (1998). Defining, measuring, and predicting impulsive aggression: A heuristic model. *Behavioral Sciences & the Law, 16*(3), 285-302.

Beck, R., & Fernandez, E. (1998). Cognitive-behavioral therapy in the treatment of anger: A meta-analysis. *Cognitive Therapy & Research, 22*(1)a, 63–74.

Belsky, J. (1984). The determinants of parenting: A process model. *Child Development, 55*(1), 83–96.

Belsky, J. (1993). Etiology of child maltreatment: A developmental-ecological analysis. *Psychological Bulletin, 114*(3), 413–434.

Belsky, J., & Vondra, J. (1989). Lessons from child abuse: The determinants of parenting. In D. Cicchetti & V. Carlson (Eds.), *Child maltreatment: Theory and research on the causes and consequences of child abuse and neglect* (pp. 153–202). New York: Cambridge University Press.

Berkowitz, L. (1989). Frustration–aggression hypothesis: Examination and reformulation. *Psychological Bulletin, 106*(1), 1–15.

Berkowitz, L. (1993). Towards a general theory of anger and emotional aggression: Implications of the cognitive-neoassociationistic perspective for the analysis of anger and other emotions. In R. S. Wyer, Jr. & T. K. Srull (Eds.), *Perspectives on anger and emotion. Advances in social cognition (Vol. 6, pp. 1–46).* Hillsdale, NJ: Lawrence Erlbaum Associates.

Berkowitz, L. (1994). On the escalation of aggression. In M. Potegal, J. F. Knutson (Eds.), *The dynamics of aggression: Biological and social processes in dyads and groups* (pp. 33–41) Hillsdale, NJ: Lawrence Erlbaum Associates.

Berkowitz, L. (1997). On the determinants and regulation of impulsive aggression. In S. Feschbach & J. Zagrodzka (Eds.), *Aggression: Biological, development, and biological perspectives.* (pp. 187–211). New York: Plenum.

Bland, R. C., & Orn, H. (1986). Psychiatric disorders, spouse abuse and child abuse. *Acta Psychiatrica Belgica, 86*(4), 444–449.

Bodenhausen, G. V., Sheppard, L. A., & Kramer, G. P. (1994). Negative affect and social judgment: The differential impact of anger and sadness. *European Journal of Social Psychology, 24*(1), 45–62.

Brondolo, E., DiGiuseppe, R., & R. Tafrate (1997). Exposure-based treatment for anger problems: Focus on the feeling. *Cognitive & Behavioral Practice, 4*(1), 75–98.

Brook, J. S., Whiteman, M. M., S. Finch (1990). Childhood aggression, adolescent delinquency, and drug use: A longitudinal Study. *Journal of Genetic Psychology, 153*(4), 369–383.

Brunnquell, D., Crichton, L., B. Egeland (1981). Maternal personality and attitude in disturbances of child rearing. *American Journal of Orthopsychiatry, 51*(4), 680–691.

Bushman, B. J., & Anderson, C. A. (2001). Is it time to pull the plug on hostile versus instrumental aggression dichotomy? *Psychological Review 108*(1): 273–279.

Campos, J. J., Mumme, D. L., Kermoran, R., & Campos, R. G. (1994). A functionalist perspective on the nature of emotion. *Monographs of the Society for Research in Child Development, 59*(2–3), 284–303.

Cerezo, M. A. (1997). Abusive family interaction: A review. *Aggression & Violent Behavior, 2*(3), 215–240.

Chaffin, M., Kelleher, K., Hollenberg, J. (1996). Onset of physical abuse and neglect: Psychiatric, substance abuse, and social risk factors from prospective community data. *Child Abuse & Neglect, 20*(3), 191–203.

Chemtob, C. M., Hamada, R. S., Roitblat, H. L., & Muraoka, M. Y. (1994). Anger, impulsivity, and anger control in combat-related posttraumatic stress disorder. *Journal of Consulting & Clinical Psychology, 62*(4), 827–832.

Christmas, A. L., Wodarski, J. S., & Smokowski, P. R. (1996). Risk factors for physical child abuse: A practice theoretical paradigm. *Family Therapy, 23*(3), 233–248.

Cicchetti, D., Ackerman, B. P., Izard, C. E. (1995). Emotions and emotion regulation in developmental psychopathology. *Development & Psychopathology, 7*(1), 1–10.

Coccaro, E. F., & Kavoussi, R. J. (1997). Fluoxetine and impulsive aggressive behavior in personality-disordered subjects. *Archives of General Psychiatry, 54*(12), 1081–1088.

Coie, J. D., & Dodge, K. A. (1998). Aggression and antisocial behavior. In W. Darwin & N. Eisenberg (Eds.), *Handbook of child psychology: Vol. 3. Social emotional, and personality development* (pp. 787–786). New York: Wiley.

Conger, R. D., Ge, X., Elder, G. H., Jr., Lorenz, F. D. & Simons, R. L. (1994). Economic stress, coercive family process, and developmental problems of adolescents. *Child Development, 65*(2), 541–565.

Conger, R. D., Neppl, T., Kim, K. J., & Scaramella, L. (2003). Angry and aggressive behavior across three generations: a prospective, longitudinal study of parents and children [see comment]. *Journal of Abnormal Child Psychology, 31*(2), 143–160.

Conger, R. D., Patterson, G. R., Ge, X. (1995). It takes two to replicate: a mediational model for the impact of parents' stress on adolescent adjustment. *Child Development, 66*(1), 80–97.

Cornelius, J. R., Perkins, K. A., Salloum, I. M., Thase, M. E., & Moss, H. B. (1999). Fluoxetine versus placebo to decrease the smoking of depressed alcoholic patients. *Journal of Clinical Psychopharmacology, 19*(2), 183–184.

Cornelius, J. R., Salloum, I. M., Ehber, J. G. Jarrett, P. J., Cornedius, M. D., Perel, J. M., et al. (1997). Fluoxetine in depressed alcoholics. A double-blind, placebo-controlled trial.[see comment]. *Archives of General Psychiatry, 54*(8), 700–705.

Damasio, A. R. (1998). Emotion in the perspective of an integrated nervous system. *Brain Research Reviews, 26*(2–3), 83–86.

de Koning, P., & Mak, M. (1991). Problems in human aggression research. *Journal of Neuropsychiatry & Clinical Neurosciences, 3*(2), 561–565.

Deffenbacher, J. L. (1992). Trait anger: Theory, findings, and implications. *In* C. D. Spielberger & J. N. Butcher (Eds.)., *Advances in personality assessment (pp. 177–201)*. Hillsdale, NJ: Lawrence Erlbaum Associates.

Deffenbacher, J. L., Oetting, E. R., Huff, M. E., Cornell, G. R. & Dallager, C. J. (1996). Evaluation of two cognitive-behavioral approaches to general anger reduction. *Cognitive Therapy & Research, 20*(6), 551–573.

Derogatis, L. R. (1993). *BSI (Brief Symptom Inventory): Administration, Scoring, and procedures manual*. Minneapolis, National Computer Systems, Inc.

Dietrich, D., Berkowitz, L., Kadushin, A., & McGloin, J. (1990). Some factors influencing abusers' justification of their child abuse. *Child Abuse & Neglect, 14*(3), 337–345.

DiGiuseppe, R., Eckhardt, C. I., Tafrate, R., & Robin, M. (1994). The diagnosis and treatment of anger in a cross-cultural context. *Journal of Social Distress and the Homeless, 3*, 229–261.

DiLillo, D., Tremblay, G. C., Peterson, L. (2000). Linking childhood sexual abuse and abusive parenting: The mediating role of maternal anger. *Child Abuse & Neglect, 24*(6), 767–779.

Dix, T. (1991). The affective organization of parenting: Adaptive and maladaptive processes. *Psychological Bulletin, 110*(1), 3–25.

Dix, T., Reinhold, D. P,. & Zambarano, R. J. (1990). Mothers' judgment in moments of anger. *Merrill–Palmer Quarterly, 36*(4), 465-486.

Dollard, J., Doob, L. W., Miller, N. E., Mowrer, O. H., & Sears, R. R. (1939). *Frustration and aggression*. New Haven, CT: Yale University Press.

Donovan, S. J., Stewart, J. W., Nunes, E. V., Quitkin, F. M., Parides, M., Daniel, W., et al. (2000). Divalproex treatment for youth with explosive temper and mood lability: a double-blind, placebo-controlled crossover design [erratum appears in 2000 Jul; *157*(7), 1192]. *American Journal of Psychiatry, 157*(5), 818–820.

Eckhardt, C. I., Barbour, K. A., & Stuart, G. L. (1997). Anger and hostility in maritally violent men: Conceptual distinctions, measurement issues, and literature review. *Clinical Psychology Review, 17*(4), 333–358.

Egami, Y., Ford, D. E., Greenfield, S. F. & Crum, R. M. (1996). Psychiatric profile and sociodemographic characteristics of adults who report physically abusing or neglecting children. *American Journal of Psychiatry, 153*(7), 921–928.

Eichelman, B., & Hartwig, A. (1991). Application of the Carolina Nosology of Destructive Behavior. *Journal of Neuropsychiatry & Clinical Neurosciences, 3*(2), S15-S21.

Famularo, R., Barnum, R., & Stone, K. (1986). Court-ordered removal in severe child maltreatment: An association to parental major affective disorder. *Child Abuse & Neglect, 10*(4), 487–492.

Famularo, R., Fenton, T., Kinscherff, R., Ayoub, C., & Burnam, R. (1994). Maternal and child posttraumatic stress disorder in cases of child maltreatment. *Child Abuse & Neglect, 18*(1), 27–36.

Famularo, R., Kinscherff, R., & Fenton, T. (1992). Psychiatric diagnoses of abusive mothers: A preliminary report. *Journal of Nervous & Mental Disease, 180*(10), 658–661.

Fava, M. (1997). Psychopharmacologic treatment of pathologic aggression. *Psychiatric Clinics of North America, 20*(2), 427–451.

Fava, M., Alpert, J., Nierenberg, A. A., Ghaemi, N., O'Sullivan, R., Tedlow, J. et al. (1996). Fluoxetine treatment of anger attacks: A replication study. *Annals of Clinical Psychiatry, 8*(1), 7–10.

Fava, M., Anderson, K., & Rosenbaum, J. F. (1993). Are thymoleptic-responsive anger attacks a discrete clinical syndrome? *Psychosomatics, 34*(4), 350–355.

Fava, M., Rosenbaum, J. F., Pava, J. A., McCarthy, M. K., Steingard, R. J., & Bouffides, E. (1993). Anger attacks in unipolar depression: I. Clinical correlates and response to fluoxetine treatment. *American Journal of Psychiatry, 150*(8), 1158–1163.

Feindler, E. L., & Ecton, R. B. (1986). *Adolescent anger control: Cognitive-behavioral techniques.* New York: Pergamon.

Forgas, J. P. (1994). The role of emotion in social judgments: An introductory review and an Affect Infusion Model (AIM). *European Journal of Social Psychology, 24*(1), 1–24.

Francis, C. R., Hughes, H. M., & Hitz, L. (1992). Physically abusive parents and the 16–PF: A preliminary psychological typology. *Child Abuse & Neglect, 16*(5), 673–691.

Fridja, N. H. (1993). Appraisal and beyond. *Cognition and Emotion, 7*(¾), 225–231.

Frijda, N. H., Kuipers, P., & ter Schure, E. (1989). Relations among emotion, appraisal, and emotional action readiness. *Journal of Personality & Social Psychology, 57*(2), 212–228.

Frude, N. (1979). The aggression incident: A perspective for understanding abuse. *Child Abuse & Neglect, 3*, 903–906.

Frude, N. & Goss, A. (1979). Parental anger: a general population survey. *Child Abuse & Neglect, 3*, 331–333.

Fuller, R. W. (1996). The influence of fluoxetine on aggressive behavior. *Neuropsychopharmacology, 14*(2), 77–81.

Geen, R. G. (1996). Affective and nonaffective mediation of motivation: A broader context: Comment. *Psychological Inquiry, 7*(3), 230–232.

Gelles, R. J., & Straus, M. A. (1979). Determinants of violence in the family: Toward a theoretical integration. In W. R. Burr, R. Hill, F. I. Nye, & I. L. Reiss (Eds.), *Contemporary theories about the family: Research-based theories* (pp. 549–581). New York: The Free Press.

Gould, R. A., Ball, S., Kaspi, S. P., Otto, M. W., Pollack, M. H., Shekhar, A. et al. (1996). Prevalence and correlates of anger attacks: A two site study. *Journal of Affective Disorders, 39*(1), 31–38.

Greenwald, R. L., Bank, L., Reid, J. B., & Knutson, J. F. (1997). A discipline-mediated model of excessively punitive parenting. *Aggressive Behavior, 23*(4), 259–280.

Heiligenstein, J. H., Beasley, C. M., Jr., & Potvin, J. H. (1993). Fluoxetine not associated with increased aggression in controlled clinical trials. *International Clinical Psychopharmacology, 8*(4), 277–280.

Herrenkohl, R. C., Herrenkohl, E. C., & Eglof, B. P. (1983). Circumstances surrounding the occurrence of child maltreatment. *Journal of Consulting & Clinical Psychology, 51*(3), 424–431.

Hillson, J. M. C., & Kupier, N. A. (1994). A stress and coping model of child maltreatment. *Clinical Psychology Review, 14*(4), 261–285.

Holtzworth-Munroe, A., Meehan, J. C., Herron, K., Rehman, U., & Stuart, G. L. (2000). Testing the Holtzworth-Munroe and Stuart (1994) batterer typology. *Journal of Consulting & Clinical Psychology, 68*(6), 1000–1019.

Huesmann, L. R. (1998). The role of social information processing and cognitive schema in the acquisition and maintenance of habitual aggressive behavior. In R. G. Geen & E. Donnerstein (Eds.), *Human aggression: Theories, research, and implications for social policy* (pp. 73–109). San Diego, CA: Academic Press.

Izard, C. E. (1978). Emotions as motivations: An evolutionary-developmental perspective. *Nebraska Symposium on Motivation, 26*, 163–200.

Izard C. E. (1989). Editorial: Studies of development of emotion cognition relations. *Cognition and Emotion, 3*(4), 257–266.

Izard, C. E. (1993). Four systems for emotion activation: Cognitive and noncognitive processes. *Psychological Review, 100*(1), 68–90.

Kadushin, A., & Martin, J. A. (1981). *Child abuse: An interactional event.* New York: Columbia University Press.

Kassinove, H. (Ed.). (1995). *Anger disorders: Definition, diagnosis, and treatment.* (The series in clinical and community psychology). Washington, DC: Taylor & Francis.

Katz, L., Fleisher, W., Kjernisted, K., & Milanese, P. (1996). A review of the psychobiology and pharmacotherapy of posttraumatic stress disorder. *Canadian Journal of Psychiatry—Revue Canadienne de Psychiatrie, 41*(4), 233–238.

Kavoussi, R. J., & Coccaro, E. F. (1998). Divalproex sodium for impulsive aggressive behavior in patients with personality disorder. *Journal of Clinical Psychiatry, 59*(12), 676–680.

Kavoussi, R. J., Liu, J., & Coccaro, E. F. (1994). An open trial of sertraline in personality disordered patients with impulsive aggression. *Journal of Clinical Psychiatry, 55*, 137–141.

Keefe, R. S. E. (1995). The contribution of neuropsychology to psychiatry. *American Journal of Psychiatry, 152*(1), 6–15.

Kelleher, K., Chaffin, M., Hollenberg, J., & Fischer, E. (1994). Alcohol and drug disorders among physically abusive and neglectful parents in a community-based sample. *American Journal of Public Health, 84*(10), 1586–1590.

Kessler, R. C., McGonagle, K. A., Zhao, S., Nelson, C. B., Hughes, M. Eshelman, S. el al. (1994). Lifetime and 12–month prevalence of DSM–III–R psychiatric disorders in the United States: Results from the National Comorbidity Study. *Archives of General Psychiatry, 51*(1), 8–19.

Knutson, J. F. (1978). Child abuse as an area of aggression research. *Journal of Pediatric Psychology, 3*(1), 20–27.

Kolko, D. J. (1996a). Child physical abuse. In J. Briere, L. Berliner, J. A. Bulkley, C. Jenny, & T. Reid (Eds.). *The APSAC handbook on child maltreatment* (pp. 21–50). Thousand Oaks, CA: Sage.

Kolko, D. J. (1996b). Clinical monitoring of treatment course in child physical abuse: Psychometric characteristics and treatment comparisons. *Child Abuse & Neglect, 20*(1), 23–43.

Lazarus, R. S. (1991). Progress on a cognitive-motivational-relational theory of emotion. *American Psychologist, 46*(8), 819–834.

Lazarus, R. S. (1993). From psychological stress to the emotions: A history of changing outlooks. *Annual Review of Psychology, 44*, 1–21.

LeDoux J. E. (1989). Cognitive-emotional interactions in the brain. *Cognition and Emotion, 3*(4), 267–289.

LeDoux, J. E. (1995). Emotion: Clues from the brain. *Annual Review of Psychology, 46*, 209–235.

Maiuro, R. D., & Avery, D. H. (1996). Psychopharmacological treatment of aggressive behavior: Implications for domestically violent men. *Violence & Victims, 11*(3), 239–261.

Malone, R. P., Delaney, M. A., Luebbert, J. F., Carter, J., & Campbell, M. (2000). A double-blind placebo-controlled study of lithium in hospitalized aggressive children and adolescents with conduct disorder. *Archives of General Psychiatry, 57*(7), 649–654.

Mammen, O. K., Kolko, D. J., & Pilkonis. P. A. (2002). Negative affect and parental aggression in child physical abuse. *Child Abuse & Neglect, 26*(4), 407–424.

Mammen, O. K., Pilkonis, P. A., Chengappa, K. N., & Kupfer, D. J. (2004). Anger attacks in bipolar depression: predictors and response to citalopram added to mood stabilizers. *Journal of Clinical Psychiatry, 65*(5), 627–633.

Mammen, O. K., Pilkonis, P. A., & Kolko, D. J. (2000). Anger and parent-to-child aggression in mood and anxiety disorders. *Comprehensive Psychiatry, 41*(6), 461–468.

Mammen, O., Shear, K., Jennings, K., & Popper, S. (1997). Case study: ego-dystonic anger attacks in mothers of young children. *Journal of the American Academy of Child & Adolescent Psychiatry, 36*(10), 1374–1377.

Mammen, O. K., Shear, M. K., Pilkonis, P. A., Kolko, D. J., Thase, M. E. & Greeno, C. G. (1999). Anger attacks: Correlates and significance of an underrecognized symptom. *Journal of Clinical Psychiatry, 60*(9), 633–642.

Manuck, S. B., Flory, J. D., McCaffery, J. M., Mathews, K. A., Mann, J. J. Maldaon M. P. (1998). Aggression, impulsivity, and central nervous system serotonergic responsivity in a nonpatient sample. *Neuropsychopharmacology, 19*(4), 287–299.

Matthews, K. A., Flory, J. D., Muldaon, M. F., & Manuck, S. B. (2000). Does socio-economic status relate to central serotonergic responsivity in healthy adults? *Psychosomatic Medicine, 62*(2), 231–237.

McCanne, T. R., & Milner, J. S. (1991). Physiological reactivitiy of physically abusive and at-risk subjects to child-related stimuli. In J. S. Milner (Ed.), *Neuropsychology of aggression* (pp. 147–166). Boston: Kluwer Academic.

McElroy, S. L. (1999). Recognition and treatment of DSM–IV intermittent explosive disorder. *Journal of Clinical Psychiatry, 60*(Suppl 15), 12–16.

Miller, B. A., Maguin, E., & Downs, W. R. (1997). Alcohol, drugs, and violence in children's lives. In M. Galanter (Ed.), *Recent developments in alcoholism: Vol. 13. Alcohol and violence: Epidemiology, neurobiology, psychology, family issues* (pp. 357–385). New York: Plenum.

Milner, J. S. (1993). Social information processing and physical child abuse. *Clinical Psychology Review, 13*(3), 275–294.

Milner, J. S. (1994). Assessing physical child abuse risk: The Child Abuse Potential Inventory. *Clinical Psychology Review, 14*(6), 547–583.

Milner, J. S., & Chilamkurti, C. (1991). Physical child abuse perpetrator character-istics: A review of the literature. *Journal of Interpersonal Violence, 6*(3), 345–366.

Moeller, F. G., Dougherty, D. M., Rustin, T. Swann, A. C., Allen, T. J., Shah, N., et al. (1997). Antisocial personality disorder and aggression in recently abstinent cocaine dependent subjects. *Drug & Alcohol Dependence, 44*, 175–182.

Morand, P., Thomas, G., Bungener, C., Ferreri, M., & Jouvent, R. (1998). Fava's anger attacks questionnaire: Evaluation of the French version in depressed patients. *European Psychiatry, 13*(1), 41–45.

Myers, W. C., & Vondruska, M. A. (1998). Murder, minors, selective serotonin reuptake inhibitors, and the involuntary intoxication defense. *Journal of the American Academy of Psychiatry & the Law, 26*(3), 487–496.

Nomellini, S., & Katz, R. C. (1983). Effects of anger control training on abusive parents. *Cognitive Therapy & Research, 7*(1), 57–67.

Novaco, R. W. (1976). The functions and regulation of the arousal of anger. *American Journal of Psychiatry, 133*(10), 1124–1128.

Nunes, E. V., McGrath, P. J., Quitkin, F. M., Ocepek-Welikson, K., Steward, J.W., Koenig T., et al. (1995). Imipramine treatment of cocaine abuse: possible boundaries of efficacy. *Drug & Alcohol Dependence. 39*(3), 185–195.

Nunes, E. V., Quitkin, F. M., Donovan, S. J., Deliyannides, D. Ocepek-Welikson, K., Kuenig, T., et al. (1998). Imipramine treatment of opiate-dependent patients with depressive disorders. A placebo-controlled trial. *Archives of General Psychiatry, 55*(2), 153–160.

Oates, M. R. (1979). A classification of child abuse and its relation to treatment and prognosis. *Child Abuse & Neglect, 3*, 907–915.

Oates, R. K., & Bross, D. C. (1995). What have we learned about treating child physical abuse? A literature review of the last decade. *Child Abuse & Neglect, 19*(4), 463–473.

Ohman, A. (1993). Fear and anxiety as emotional phenomena: Clinical phenomenology, evolutionary perspectives, and information-processing mechanisms. In M. Lewis, & J. Haviland (Ed.), *Handbook of emotions* (pp. 511–536). New York: Guilford.

Oldershaw, L., Walters, G. C., & Hall, D. K. (1989). A behavioral approach to the classification of different types of physically abusive mothers. *Merrill–Palmer Quarterly, 35*(3), 255–279.

Ornstein, P. H. (1999). Conceptualization and treatment of rage in self psychology. *Journal of Clinical Psychology, 55*(3), 283–293.

Paivio, S. C. (1999). Experiential conceptualization and treatment of anger. *Journal of Clinical Psychology, 55*(3), 311–324.

Patterson, G. R. (1983). Stress: A change agent for family process. In N. Garmezy & M. Rutter, (Eds.), *Stress, coping, and development in children* (pp. 235–264). Baltimore: Johns Hopkins University Press.

Patterson, G. R. (1985). A microsocial analysis of anger and irritable behavior. In M. A. Chesney & R. H. Rosennan (Eds.) *Anger and hostility in cardiovascular and behavioral disorders* (pp. 83–100). Washington, DC: Hemisphere.

Perry, M. A., Wells, E. A., & Doran, L. D. (1983). Parent characteristics in abusing and nonabusing families. *Journal of Clinical Child Psychology, 12*(3), 329–336.

Peterson, L., Ewigman, B., Doyle, C., & Ewigman, B. (1994). Role of parental anger in low-income women: Discipline strategy, perceptions of behavior problems, and the need for control. *Journal of Clinical Child Psychology, 23*(4), 435–443.

Peterson, L., Gable, S. (1997). Beyond parenting skills: Battling barriers and building bonds to prevent child abuse and neglect. *Cognitive & Behavioral Practice, 4*(1), 53–74.

Potegal, M., & Knutson, J. F. (Eds.). (1994). *The dynamics of aggression: Biological and social processes in dyads and groups.* Hillsdale, NJ: Lawrence Erlbaum Associates.

Reid, J. B. (1986). Social-interactional patterns in families of abused and nonabused children. In C. Zahn-Waxler, E. M. Cummings, & R. J. Iannotti (Eds.), *Altruism and aggression: Biological and social origins* (pp. 238–255). Cambridge, England: Cambridge University Press.

Reid, J. B., & K. Kavanagh, (1985). A social interactional approach to child abuse: Risk, prevention, and treatment. In M. A. Chesney & H. Rosenman (Eds.), *Anger and hostility in cardovascular and behavioral disorders* (pp. 241–257). Washington, DC: Hemisphere.

Robins, S., & Novaco, R. W. (1999). Systems conceptualization and treatment of anger. *Journal of Clinical Psychology, 55*(3), 325–337.

Rodriguez, C. M., & Green, A. J. (1997). Parenting stress and anger expression as predictors of child abuse potential. *Child Abuse & Neglect, 21*(4), 367–377.

Roseman, I. J., Wiest, C., & Swartz, T. S. (1994). Phenomenology, behaviors, and goals differentiate discrete emotions. *Journal of Personality & Social Psychology, 67*(2), 206–221.

Rosenblatt, S., Schaeffer, D., & Rosenthal, J. S. (1976). Effects of diphenylhydantoin on child-abusing parents: A preliminary report. *Current Therapeutic Research, 19*(3), 332–336.

Rubey, R. N., Johnson, M. R., Emmanuel, N., & Lydiard, R. B. (1996). Fluoxetine in the treatment of anger: An open clinical trial. *Journal of Clinical Psychiatry, 57*(9), 398–401.

Salzman, C., Wolfson, A. N., Schatzberg, A. Looper, J., Henle, R. Albanese, M. et al. (1995). Effect of fluoxetine on anger in symptomatic volunteers with borderline personality disorder. *Journal of Clinical Psychopharmacology, 15*(1), 23–29.

Sloan, M. P., & Meier, J. H. (1983). Typology for parents of abused children. *Child Abuse & Neglect, 7*(4), 443–450.

Sonnemans, J., & Frijda, N. H. (1994). The structure of subjective emotional intensity. *Cognition & Emotion, 8*(4), 329–350.

Spielberger, C. D., & Sydeman, S. J. (1994). State-Trait Anxiety Inventory and State-Trait Anger Expression Inventory. In M. E. Maruish (Ed.), *The use of psychological tests for treatment planning and outcome assessment* (pp. 292–321). Hillsdale, NJ: Lawrence Erlbaum Associates.

Steadman, H. J., Mulvey, E. P., Monahan, J., Robbins, P. C., Appelbaum, P. S., Grisso, T., et al. (1998). Violence by people discharged from acute psychiatric inpatient facilities and by others in the same neighborhoods. *Archives of General Psychiatry, 55*(5), 393–401.

Stein, D. J., Hollander, E., & Liebowitz, M. R. (1993). Neurobiology of impulsivity and the impulse control disorders. *Journal of Neuropsychiatry & Clinical Neurosciences, 5*(1), 9–17.

Swanson, J. W., Holzer, C. E., III, Ganju, V. K., & Jono, R. T. (1990). Violence and psychiatric disorder in the community: Evidence from the Epidemiologic Catchment Area surveys. *Hospital & Community Psychiatry, 41*(7), 761–770.

Tarter, R. E., Blackson, T., Brigham, J. Moss, H., & Caprara, G. (1995). The association between childhood irritability and liability to substance abuse in early adolescence: A 2–year follow-up study of boys at risk for substance abuse. *Drug & Alcohol Dependence, 39*, 253–261.

Vasta, R. (1982). Physical child abuse: A dual-component analysis. *Developmental Review, 2*(2), 125–149.

Wahler, R. G. (1994). Child conduct problems: Disorders in conduct or social continuity? *Journal of Child & Family Studies, 3*(2), 143–156.

Walfish, S., Massey, R., & Krone, A. (1990). Anxiety and anger among abusers of different substances. *Drug & Alcohol Dependence, 25*(3), 253–256.

Wetzler, S., & Katz, M. M. (1989). Problems with the differentiation of anxiety and depression. *Journal of Psychiatric Research, 23*(1), 1–12.

Whipple, E. E., & Webster-Stratton, C. (1991). The role of parental stress in physically abusive families. *Child Abuse & Neglect, 15*(3), 279–291.

White, H. R. (1997). Alcohol, illicit drugs, and violence. In D. M. Stoff, J. Breiling, & J. D. Maser (Eds.), *Handbook of antisocial behavior* (pp. 511–523). New York: Wiley.

Whiteman, M., Fanshel, D., & Grundy, J. F. (1987). Cognitive-behavioral interventions aimed at anger of parents at risk of child abuse. *Social Work, 32*(6), 469–474.

Wolfe, D. A. (1985). Child-abusive parents: An empirical review and analysis. *Psychological Bulletin, 97*(3), 462–482.

Wolfe, D. A. (1987a). The development of severe parent–child conflict and abuse. In D. A. Wolfe (Ed.), *Child abuse: Implications for child development and psychopathology* (pp. 41–68). Newbury Park, CA: Sage.

Wolfe, D. A. (1987b). Psychological characteristics of abusive parents. In D. A. Wolfe (Ed.), *Child abuse: Implications for child development and psychopathology* (pp. 69–96). Newbury Park, CA: Sage.

Wolfe, D. A., Edwards, B., Manion, I., & Koverola, C. (1988). Early intervention for parents at risk of child abuse and neglect: A preliminary investigation. *Journal of Consulting & Clinical Psychology, 56*(1), 40–47.

Wolfe, D. A., & Wekerle, C. (1993). Treatment strategies for child physical abuse and neglect: A critical progress report. *Clinical Psychology Review, 13*(6), 473–500.

Zajonc, R. B. (1998). Emotions. In D. T. Gilbert & S. T. Fiske (Eds.), *The handbook of social psychology* (4th ed., Vol. 1, pp. 591–632*).* Boston: McGraw-Hill.

Zillmann, D. (1994). Cognition-excitation interdependence in escalation of anger and angry aggression. In M. Potegal & J. F. Knutson (Eds.), *The dynamics of aggression: Biological and social processes in dyads and groups* (pp. 45–71). Hillsdale, NJ: Lawrence Erlbaum Associates.

Zillmann, D., Bryant, J., Cantor, J. R., & Day, K. D. (1975). Irrelevance of mitigating circumstances in retaliatory behavior at high levels of excitation. *Journal of Research in Personality, 9*(4), 282–293.

The Association Between Anger and Male Perpetration of Intimate-Partner Violence

Amy Holtzworth-Munroe and Kahni Clements

Husband-to-wife violence is a serious problem in this country. Data from nationally representative surveys suggest that, each year, one out of every eight married men will be physically aggressive toward his wife and nearly 2 million women will be severely assaulted by their male partners (Straus & Gelles, 1990). Though both men and women engage in physical aggression in their intimate relationships, the majority of available studies demonstrate that male aggression has more negative consequences than female aggression, including higher rates of physical injury, fear, and other psychological consequences, such as depression and marital dissatisfaction (see reviews in Archer, 2000; Holtzworth-Munroe, Smutzler, & Bates, 1997). Thus, the focus of both our research and this chapter is male physical violence perpetrated against an intimate female partner. For ease of presentation, we refer to this problem as "husband violence," although some of the studies we review included either married or cohabiting couples.

In understanding husband violence, it is important to study correlates of male aggression. Such research may identify factors that could be risk markers for violence, factors that cause or precipitate violence, or variables that need to be clinically addressed to help reduce violent behavior. One correlate that has received empirical attention is male anger and hostility, as several theoretical models suggest a link between anger, hostility, and aggression.

For example, in frustration–aggression theory, Dollard et al. (1939) posited that the nonfulfillment of an expected gratification leads to frustration, which can, in turn, instigate aggression. Their theory was criticized on the grounds that only some frustrations (i.e., illegitimate and arbitrary barriers to attaining one's goal) produce aggressive inclinations (Berkowitz, 1988). Thus, in a modification of the original theory, Averill (1982) and Weiner (1985) proposed that response to a frustrating event depends on the appraisal of that event and on the interpretation of its cause. Relevant to this focus on interpretation of events, research has demonstrated that violent husbands are more likely than nonviolent husbands to attribute hostile intent to their wives' negative behaviors (Holtzworth-Munroe & Hutchinson, 1993); theoretically, this could lead to increases in their frustration and an elevated risk of violence perpetration during marital conflicts.

Indeed, social learning models of husband violence assume that high levels of anger and hostility increase the risk of violence. For example, in a social information processing model of husband violence, Holtzworth-Munroe (1992) suggested that anger can inhibit "rational" cognitive processing and result in skills deficits (e.g., hostile attributional biases, inability to generate competent responses) that escalate a marital conflict toward violence.

The role of anger in the occurrence of husband violence can also be understood using Bowlby's (1977) attachment theory (Dutton, 1995a). Unmet attachment needs may produce frustration that, in turn, leads to proneness to react with high levels of anger and aggression when attachment is threatened. According to this theory, an assaultive man's violence is a form of protest behavior aimed at his adult attachment figure (i.e., his intimate female partner) when he perceives possible separation and abandonment.

Consistent with models positing a role of anger in marital violence, many available clinical interventions for batterers, particularly behavioral-cognitive treatments, include anger management training. These interventions usually involve teaching men to recognize their anger and to take steps (e.g., time-out procedures, cognitive restructuring, relaxation) to avoid the escalation of negative behavior when angry (e.g., Hamberger, 1996; Tolman & Saunders, 1988).

Interestingly, however, other theorists suggest that anger may not play a central role in husband violence and that the emphasis on anger management in batterer intervention programs is misplaced. Feminist theorists have proposed that violence is an expression of control and domination that is not necessarily associated with high levels of anger (e.g., Dobash & Dobash, 1977). Such theorists contend that although husbands act violently toward their although to control and intimidate them, they may later report high levels of anger only to justify their violent behavior (Gondolf & Russell, 1986).

To address such issues, in the current chapter, we review some of the available data on the relationship between men's anger and hostility and their perpetration of physical violence against a female intimate partner.

Eckhardt, Barbour, and Stuart (1997) conducted an earlier review of this issue; the present review includes studies they reviewed, along with more recent research. In addition, as part of a more extensive review of a wide variety of risk factors for male-to-female partner physical abuse, Schumacher, Feldbau-Kohn, Slep, and Heyman (2001) briefly reviewed studies of violent husbands' anger and hostile behavior; the present review focuses exclusively on anger and hostility.

In conducting a research review of this topic, it is important to note that there are theoretical differences between anger and hostility. Anger usually refers to a subjective, phenomenological, emotional state, whereas hostility refers to an attitude involving dislike and negative evaluation of others, cynicism, and mistrust (e.g., see discussion of this distinction by Eckhardt et al., 1997; Eckhardt, Norlander, & Deffenbacher, 2004). However, most available measures assess both constructs, without clear differentiation between them, and there are not many data to suggest that these constructs are independent (Eckhardt et al., 2004). Similarly, many marital violence researchers have included measures of both anger and hostility, without differentiating between these constructs, in their studies. Thus, despite theoretical differences between anger and hostility, at the current time, available data do not allow a determination of whether one of these constructs is more useful in understanding husband violence than the other.

Similarly, anger is often viewed as a multidimensional construct, including physiological, cognitive, phenomenological, and behavioral aspects (see Eckhardt et al., 2004). Again, however, most of the available research findings do not differentiate between these theoretical dimensions. Thus, at this time, it is difficult to draw definitive conclusions regarding whether certain dimensions of anger, but not others, are related to husband violence. Instead, our review focuses on studies of hostility and multiple dimensions of anger.

QUESTIONNAIRE MEASURES OF GENERAL ANGER AND HOSTILITY

The earliest, and the most common, research on the relationship between husband violence and anger/hostility involves studies using questionnaires assessing men's self-reported levels of general anger and hostility. Such measures have the advantage of being standardized, thus allowing comparisons of findings across studies using the same measures. Such measures, however, also have some disadvantages. They do not directly assess men's anger at their intimate female partners, which, intuitively, would be the assessment target with the most theoretical relevance to the study of marital violence. Indeed, measures that assess anger or hostility in general often do not specify the situation or person toward whom one gets angry; thus, it is unclear if study participants are considering their wives or not when they complete such measures. As a result, when violent versus nonviolent group differences are found on these measures, one cannot be sure whether violent and nonviolent men differ in general levels of anger, levels of anger directed at their wives, or some combination of both types of anger and hostility. Such limitations should be kept in mind when reviewing these studies (see Table 13.1).

Overall, the available evidence clearly suggests a link between men's levels of general anger/hostility and their engagement in violence toward an intimate female partner. The data also suggest a positive correlation between the level of men's general anger/hostility and the level of the intimate partner violence they perpetrate. These findings are consistent across differing questionnaire measures (e.g., STAXI, MAI, BDHI) and samples of violent men (e.g., clinical or community samples). Significant group differences are almost always found in studies comparing violent to nonviolent men, without further differentiation among the nonviolent comparison samples, and in studies comparing violent to nonviolent/ happily married men. In addition, the majority of studies, but not all, comparing violent men to nonviolent but maritally distressed men yield at least some significant group differences. In contrast, group differences are not consistently demonstrated in research comparing maritally violent men to men who are generally violent; this should not be surprising, given that these studies examine general anger and hostility levels.

NEWER RESEARCH DIRECTIONS USING QUESTIONNAIRE MEASURES OF GENERAL ANGER AND HOSTILITY

Going beyond cross-sectional studies comparing violent men to various nonviolent comparison samples, researchers have begun to conduct new lines of research on the role of general anger and hostility in husband violence. First, as researchers have increasingly recognized variability among samples of maritally violent men, some have begun to consider the possibility that maritally violent men may be heterogeneous with respect to anger problems. Indeed, in some of the research already reviewed, findings demonstrated that within samples of maritally violent men individual difference variables were related to anger level. For example, batterers with fearful attachment have been found to have the highest anger levels (Dutton, Saunders, Starzomski, & Bartholomew, 1994), and batterers with posttraumatic stress disorder (PTSD) personality profiles scored higher on measures of anger than other batterers (Dutton, 1995b). Differing subsamples of batterers also tend to vary in their anger scores: Batterers

TABLE 13.1

Questionnaire Measures of General Anger and Hostility, General Findings, and Limitations

Measure	Findings	Study Considerations
Psychiatric Symptom Checklist 90 Hostility Subscale (Derogatis, Lipman, Covi, and Rickles, 1971)	McKenry, Julian, & Gavazzi, 1995: Hostility related to level of husband physical aggression	Did not compare violent to nonviolent men
Multidimensional Anger Inventory (MAI; Siegel, 1986)	Anger of martially violent men related to wife report of psychological abuse and severe violence	Did not compare violent to nonviolent men
	Dutton et al., 1994; Dutton, 1995b, Dutton, Starzomski, & Ryan, 1996: Men in treatment for marital violence higher than demographically matched nonviolent comparisons	Did not control for marital distress; overlapping samples across studies
	Boyle & Vivian, 1996: All three clinic groups moderately higher than happily married community group on Hostility scale	Compared a nonviolent and happily married sample of men to three groups of couples seeking marital therapy
Buss–Durkee Hostility Inventory (BDHI; Buss & Durkee, 1957)	Leonard & Blane, 1992: Hostility related to self-reports of hitting female partner even after sociodemographics controlled	• Did not control for marital distress
	Leonard & Senchak, 1993: Hostility related to premarital husband aggression	
	Maiuro, Cahn, & Vitaliano, 1986: Maritally violent men higher on Overt (motoric aggression) and Covert	• Did not compare marital distress

TABLE 13.1 (Continued)

Measure	Findings	Study Considerations
	aggression (internal affective experience) and six of seven other subscales	
	Maiuro, Cahn, & Vitaliano, 1988: Violent men higher on Overt and Covert Aggression, Assault, Irritability, Resentment, and Suspicion subscales	Compared three violent groups (martially violent, assaultive, and both violent and assaultive) to nonviolent controls
Buss–Durkee Hostility Guilt Inventory (BDHGI; Buss & Durkee, 1957)	Barnett, Fagan, & Booker, 1991: Violent men not in treatment higher on the Resentment scale and higher than all but violent offenders on Assault and Indirect Hostility scales	Compared violent groups to nonviolent controls
Hostility and Direction of Hostility Questionnaire (HDHQ: Caine, Foulds, & Hope, 1967)	Else, Wonderlich, Beatty, Christie, & Staton, 1993: Maritally violent men higher on Acting-out Hostility and Self-Criticism	Did not control for marital distress
	Maiuro, Cahn, Vitaliano, & Wagner, 1988: Violent men higher on Extrapunitive, Acting Out Hostility, and Critize Others subscale	Compared three violent groups (martially violent, assaultive, and both violent and assaultive) to nonviolent controls
Brief Anger-Aggression Questionnaire (BAAQ)	Maiuro, Vitaliano, & Cahn, 1987: Violent men higher than non violent men but not significantly from each other	Compared three violent groups (martially violent, assaultive, and both violent and assaultive) to nonviolent controls

TABLE 13.1 (*Continued*)

Measure	Findings	Study Considerations
Modified Novaco Anger Scale (Novaco, 1975)	Telch & Lindquist, 1984: No differences were found between violent, nonviolent/distressed, and nonviolent satisfied couples	• Small sample size (fewer than 20 couples per group) • Compared between couples rather than men
Spielberger State-Trait-Anger Expression Inventory (STAXI; Spielberger, 1988)	Beasley & Stoltenberg, 1992: Violent men significantly higher than the nonviolent men on measures of both state and trait anger	Compared martially violent to nonviolent/distress men
	Boyle & Vivian, 1996: Three clinic groups higher than happily married group on Trait Anger scale; moderately violent men higher than nonviolent clinic men on Trait Anger scale	• Nonviolent and happily married comparison sample • Used three groups of couples seeking marital therapy (presumed marital distress)
	Barbour, Eckhardt, Davison, & Kassinove, 1998: Maritally violent men higher on Trait Anger and Anger Out measures and lower on Anger Control than both nonviolent comparison groups	• Compared maritally violent, nonviolent/maritally distressed, and nonviolent/nondistressed men. • Community sample

self-referred to treatment had higher anger scores than court-referred batterers (Dutton & Starzomski, 1994), batterers not in treatment had the highest hostility scores (Barnatt, Fagan, & Booker, 1991), and severely violent men had higher anger/hostility scores than other maritally violent men (Boyle & Vivian, 1996).

Examining this issue more closely, it is useful to consider typologies of batterers, which often identify several subtypes of maritally violent men (see review in Holtzworth-Munroe & Stuart, 1994). One subtype, which we have labeled *Family Only* (FO), usually engages in lower levels of marital violence, is not usually violent outside the home, and evidences little, if any, psychopathology. In sharp contrast, another subtype, which we labeled *Generally Violent/Antisocial* (GVA), engages in high levels of marital violence and high levels of violence outside the home and has characteristics of antisociality and associated psychological problems (e.g., criminal behavior, substance abuse problems). A third subtype, labeled *Borderline/Dysphoric* (BD), has high levels of marital violence, but moderate levels of violence outside the home; these men are the most likely to report psychological distress (e.g., depression) and to evidence characteristics of borderline personality disorder, including difficulties with jealousy, overdependence on their wives, and insecure attachment.

Some early batterer typology researchers considered possible subtype differences in anger. Interestingly, in these early studies, evidence on the level of anger experienced by FO and GVA men was mixed. In contrast, BD men were more consistently found to experience high levels of general anger, to be volatile in their anger expression, and to overreact to situations with often explosive anger. (See early batterer typologies by Cadsky & Crawford, 1988; Elbow, 1977; Faulk, 1974; Hamberger & Hastings, 1986; Hershorn & Rosenbaum, 1991; Saunders, 1992, as reviewed in Holtzworth-Munroe & Stuart, 1994).

In a study involving a community sample of 102 violent men, Holtzworth-Munroe, Rehman, and Herron (2000) compared batterer subtypes to each other and to 61 nonviolent comparison men on standardized measures of general anger (Speilberger's 1998, STAXI Trait and Expression scales; the Hostility Subscale of the Buss–Perry Aggression Questionnaire, Buss & Perry, 1992). In general, BD and GVA men (i.e., the two subgroups with the highest levels of marital violence) self-reported the highest levels of general anger and hostility, whereas FO men had the lowest levels. Indeed, on most measures, FO men did not differ significantly from nonviolent but maritally distressed men. Holtzworth-Munroe, Rehman, and Herron (2000) had hypothesized that GVA men, who engage in more general violence outside the home than the other subtypes, would have the highest levels of general anger and hostility; the data did not support this prediction.

Given such data, it is increasingly clear that not all maritally violent men are alike with respect to anger and hostility levels. Some subgroups (e.g., FO, who have lower levels of violence and psychopathology) may not have elevated levels of anger, particularly relative to nonviolent but maritally distressed men. Other subgroups, including more severely violent men with more psychopathology (GVA and BD men), clearly have higher levels of general anger and hostility then nonviolent men. Future researchers should more systematically examine whether men who engage in high levels of general violence against others besides their partners (e.g., GVA men) have higher levels of general anger/hostility than men whose violence is primarily confined to the home (e.g., BD men), although this did not prove to be the case in the one study examining this issue (Holtzworth-Munroe, Rehman et al., 2000), perhaps due to the problem of ambiguity regarding the target of one's anger on general anger and hostility questionnaires.

A second new development in this research area has been to move to longitudinal research. O'Leary, Malone, and Tyree (1994) studied approximately 270 couples from premarriage to 30 months postmarriage. They found that husbands' premarriage scores on the aggression scale (i.e., tendency to act angrily, argumentatively, and vengefully) of the Jackson Personality Research Form (Jackson, 1974) predicted husbands' psychological aggression toward wives at 18 months postmarriage, which in turn predicted husbands' use of physical aggression at 30 months. Using the same sample, Heyman, O'Leary, and Jouriles (1995) found that husbands' premarital aggressive personality scores were related to husband violence at 18 months (but not at 30 months) postmarriage, both directly and in interaction with husbands' drinking (i.e., drinks consumed). Men with aggressive personality traits who drank more were the most likely to engage in physical aggression.

In a longitudinal study of 541 newlywed couples, Leonard and Senchak (1996) examined husband and wife hostility (as measured with the STAXI Trait Anger Scale and the Assault subscale of the BDHI) as predictors of husband violence 1 year later. At the univariate level, husband hostility predicted husband violence longitudinally, but it did not continue to do so once level of premarital aggression was entered first into the prediction equations. The longitudinal relationship between husband violence and most of the predictor variables, including husband hostility, tended to be mediated through marital conflict styles and the husband's alcohol consumption.

Thus, both the Leonard and Senchak (1996) and Heyman et al. (1995) studies suggest the potential pathway of husband anger/hostility leading to husbands' drinking and escalating marital conflict, which then results in physical violence perpetration. Future researchers studying men's anger and hostility might do well to also include measures of alcohol use and abuse and escalating marital conflict.

QUESTIONNAIRE (AND INTERVIEW) MEASURES OF SPOUSE-SPECIFIC ANGER

To understand husband violence, rather than men's general anger and hostility, it is potentially more useful to examine directly men's anger and hostility at their own wives (i.e., spouse-specific anger and hostility). This strategy can help disentangle potential confusion resulting from the use of general anger/hostility measures, as spouse-specific measures direct study participants to consider their intimate partner when answering questions about anger. Few such studies have been conducted to date. Given the strength of their findings (as reported next), we urge future researchers to compare systematically violent and nonviolent men's general versus spouse-specific anger/hostility.

Boyle and Vivian (1996) created a measure of spouse-specific anger from two interview questions (they gathered reports of the husband's spouse-specific anger from both the husband and the wife) and a measure of spouse-specific hostility from the men's self-reports on the Spouse-Specific Assertiveness Scale (O'Leary & Curley, 1986). Boyle and Vivian then compared scores on these measures across a nonviolent comparison sample of 49 men and three groups of couples seeking marital therapy—100 severely violent men, 69 moderately violent men, and 94 nonviolent men. All three of the clinic groups (violent or not) scored higher than the community group on all of the spouse-specific measures. Comparing the three marital therapy clinic samples to each other, both severely and moderately violent men had higher self-reported spouse-specific hostility than the nonviolent men. Severely violent men also had higher levels of self-reported spouse-specific anger than did nonviolent men, and their wife-reported levels of spouse-specific anger were higher than those of both the moderately violent and nonviolent clinic men.

In another study of this issue, Holtzworth-Munroe, Rehman et al. (2000) compared four subtypes of batterers and two samples of nonviolent men (one maritally distressed and one not), all recruited from the community, on questionnaires assessing anger and hostility directed at one's partner. The researchers rewrote questions on the Buss–Perry Hostility Subscale and the STAXI Trait Anger and Anger Expression Scales to refer to one's partner. Holtzworth-Munroe, Rehman, et al not only asked men to self-report on their spouse-specific anger, but also asked the men's wives to report on how angry/hostile they believed their husbands were toward them. Interestingly, in analyses comparing men's general versus spouse-specific anger, the "target" of anger main effect never reached statistical significance, suggesting that group differences are similar for men's general and spouse-specific anger. As was found with men's general anger (reviewed previously), more severely violent men (i.e., GVA and BD men) usually reported the highest levels of anger, whereas men who engaged in less violence (FO men) reported less anger/hostility and often did not differ significantly from the nonviolent comparison groups. Wives' reports of their husbands' spouse-specific anger also differentiated the subtypes of maritally violent men. Again, the more violent subtypes (BD and GVA) reported the highest levels of spouse-specific anger, which were always significantly higher than the nonviolent and maritally satisfied group, but not always significantly higher than men in the nonviolent but maritally distressed comparison group. Thus, the data suggest that future researchers should consider that maritally violent men may be heterogeneous with respect to levels of spouse-specific anger and hostility.

It may be surprising how little research has been conducted using questionnaire measures of spouse-specific anger and hostility. The two studies that have done so indicate that maritally violent men, particularly severely violent men, may experience high levels of spouse-specific anger and hostility. A strength of these research findings is the use of both men's self-reports and reports from the men's wives (i.e., multiple informants). Future research on spouse-specific anger/hostility is needed to better understand the relationship between men's general and spouse-specific anger. In doing so, it may be necessary for researchers to first develop standardized, reliable, and valid measures of spouse-specific anger and hostility.

RESPONSES TO SIMULATED CONFLICT VIGNETTES

In addition to studies using questionnaire measures of anger and hostility, a few researchers have demonstrated that violent husbands experience more anger than nonviolent husbands in response to simulated conflict vignettes. Such work may be viewed as gathering "online" measures of anger during potentially anger-arousing situations.

To our knowledge, only one research group (i.e., Holtzworth-Munroe, Rehman et al., 2000) has compared violent and nonviolent men's anger in response to vignettes depicting conflicts with individuals besides the wife, as a measure of general anger. In that study, men were presented with hypothetical situations (e.g., involving a boss or friends) and asked how they would respond. Their audiotaped responses were later coded for level of anger. GVA men were found to express the most anger, significantly more than that expressed by the FO men and both nonviolent comparison groups (i.e., maritally distressed and nondistressed). Among violent subtypes, FO men expressed the least anger and did not differ significantly from either nonviolent comparison sample of men.

Other researchers using simulated vignettes have presented men with marital conflict situations. Thus, the data reviewed here can be considered evidence regarding the relationship between husband violence and spouse-specific anger and hostility. In an early study of this type, Dutton and Browning (1988) presented men with videotaped depictions of marital conflicts. They found that relative to nonviolent men violent husbands were more likely to report feeling angry, particularly in response to vignettes depicting possible abandonment by the wife.

Eckhardt, Barbour, and Davison (1998) have argued that because emotion-relevant cognitions are more accessible during activation of a relevant mood state, cognitive distortions related to anger are best assessed during anger arousal. Thus, Eckhardt et al. used the Articulated Thoughts in Simulated Situations paradigm (ATSS; Davison, Feldman, & Osborn, 1984; Davison, Robins, & Johnson, 1983) to examine possible cognitive distortions exhibited by men in response to hypothetical marital conflict situations designed to increase angry arousal. During ATSS procedures, participants listen to audiotapes of emotion-eliciting scenarios. The tapes are paused after short segments (e.g., 10–20 seconds), at which time the participants are prompted to articulate their thoughts and feelings during a 30-second interval. Trained raters later code transcripts of the participants' articulated thoughts along a variety of dimensions.

Barbour, Eckhardt, Davison, and Kassinove (1998) and Eckhardt et al. (1998) used the ATSS procedure with a sample of 31 maritally violent men, 23 nonviolent but maritally distressed men, and 34 nonviolent and nondistressed men. Participants completed the ATSS procedures while listening to a nonarousing control scenario and two anger-arousing scenarios. In the control scenario, each man was asked to imagine that he and his partner were playing a game with a competitive and annoying couple, but that the source of the annoyance had nothing to do with the wife. One of the anger-arousing scenarios was designed to depict potential wife abandonment; in this scenario, the participant imagined that he overheard his wife criticizing him and expressing uncertainty about remaining in the relationship. The other anger-arousing scenario was designed to elicit jealousy; the participant was asked to imagine that he returns home and overhears his wife talking flirtatiously with a male acquaintance. Interestingly, no group differences were found on the total number of angry verbalizations (Barbour et al., 1998). However, Barbour et al. found that compared to the two nonviolent groups, maritally violent men articulated a greater number of insulting, demeaning, and belligerent aggressive verbalizations. In addition, Eckhardt et al. found that maritally violent men articulated significantly more irrational thoughts and cognitive biases during anger arousal than did the two nonviolent comparison groups. Compared to the other two groups, maritally violent men were also found to articulate more hostile attribution biases across all of the scenarios. Given these findings, Eckhardt et al. (1998) have argued that maritally violent men may lack the skills to assertively express their anger and thus, instead may engage in verbally aggressive and belligerent forms of communication.

Eckhardt and colleagues found there were some differences between violent and nonviolent groups even in response to what was supposed to be the control or non-anger-arousing scenario. In an explicit examination of the question of whether violent men are more angry than nonviolent husbands in a wide variety of marital situations, not just negative marital conflicts, Holtzworth-Munroe and Smutzler (1996) recruited a clinical sample of 25 maritally violent men, a group of 21 maritally violent men from the community, and two nonviolent community comparison samples (i.e., 23 nonviolent but maritally distressed men and 28 nonviolent and nondistressed men). All men were presented with a series of video-taped and written depictions of various wife behaviors. Some of the wife behaviors were clearly aggressive (i.e., hostility or anger directed at the husband), but others were not. Instead, some scenarios depicted wife irritation at someone besides the husband, some wife statements were depressive in nature (e.g., wife is sad about her weight), and some were even facilitative (e.g., complimenting the husband). Men were asked to rate, in response to each depicted wife behavior, how they would feel and respond in these situations. In general, across a wide range of wife behaviors (not just wife aggression directed at the husband), violent men were more likely than nonviolent men to report that they would experience anger and irritation and would be more likely to respond by saying something hostile to their wives or by arguing with her. In contrast, there were no violent versus nonviolent group differences in levels of nonangry, negative emotions (i.e., sadness or anxiety), suggesting that violent men may have specific problems with anger.

These findings, along with those of Eckhardt's research team, suggest that violent husbands may experience more hostility and anger, not only during marital conflict but also in response to marital interactions that most men do not find anger arousing. As suggested by Holtzworth-Munroe and Smutzler (1996), this lack of predictability (i.e., never knowing when one's husband will become angry or aggressive) may be a key component in making male violence frightening and controlling for women.

Holtzworth-Munroe, Rehman et al. (2000), in a study described earlier, used marital situation vignettes to compare subtypes of maritally violent men to each other and to two nonviolent comparison groups (one maritally distressed and one maritally satisfied). They also asked men's wives to report how their husbands would respond to the marital conflict vignettes. The responses were later coded for level of anger. Consistent with questionnaire data from this study, the more severely violent subgroups (GVA and BD) were found to express the most anger in response to marital conflict vignettes, expressing significantly more anger than men who engaged in lower levels of violence (FO) and men in nonviolent comparison samples; FO men did not always differ significantly from the nonviolent comparison samples.

Although there has been a lack of questionnaire data regarding spouse-specific anger, there are studies of spouse-specific anger as assessed by men's reactions to simulated marital conflict vignettes. These data suggest that violent men may be more likely than nonviolent men to experience feelings of anger. The data also demonstrate that violent men are more likely than nonviolent men to indicate that they would express their anger using hostile behavior in response to such situations. Of course, cognitions and behavioral intentions, as measured in these studies, do not necessarily match actual behavioral responses to real-life situations. Thus, it is useful to turn our attention to studies that have coded men's anger during nonsimulated marital interactions with their partners.

OBSERVATIONAL STUDIES OF
MARITAL COMMUNICATION

The studies reviewed earlier involved questionnaires or responses to simulated vignettes. Other researchers, however, have directly examined men's angry and hostile behavior during actual marital interactions, usually occurring in the lab. In such studies, researchers videotape couples having a discussion (usually, but not always, regarding relationship problems) and later code the behaviors displayed during the interactions. The findings can be used to compare the extent to which violent and nonviolent husbands express anger or engage in hostile behaviors during such interactions. Given the focus of this chapter, our brief review of this research area focuses on angry and hostile behavior and does not systematically review data on other husband behaviors (e.g., sadness, withdrawal, affection, problem solving). In addition, we focus our review on findings regarding husbands', not wives', behavior.

Observational Research by Margolin, Burman, and Colleagues

From the community, Margolin and colleagues recruited three types of conflictual couples (i.e., physically aggressive, verbally aggressive, and withdrawing) and a comparison group of nonviolent and nondistressed couples. Across multiple assessment sessions, the researchers gathered several types of marital interaction data (e.g., problem discussions in the lab, reenactments of past conflictual discussions in the couples' homes) and used different analyses (e.g., frequency counts, sequential analyses). Results of this study have been presented in several publications (Burman, John, & Margolin, 1992; Burman, Margolin, & John, 1993; Margolin, Burman, & John, 1989; Margolin, John, & Gleberman, 1988; Margolin, John, & O'Brien, 1989). Examining problem-solving discussions in the laboratory, Margolin et al. (1988) noted that group differences were found mainly among husbands. Physically aggressive men expressed more offensive negative behaviors (e.g., signs of dismissal, threatening or mimicking gestures, and negative physical contact) and more negative voice tone (e.g., irate, angry, and accusatory) than verbally aggressive or withdrawing husbands. Burman et al. (1992) further studied the laboratory problem discussions using sequential analyses and found that physically aggressive couples, compared to other groups, displayed interaction patterns that increased the probability of further aggression.

Margolin et al. (1989) asked their sample to reenact in their home two problem discussions. In this setting, aggressive husbands were found to display more overt hostility (e.g., blaming, disapproval, anger, raised voice) than men in the comparison groups. During the last third of the discussions, physically aggressive couples were more likely to maintain their hostile behavior and to increase their patronizing behavior, whereas spouses in the other groups decreased these behaviors. Burman et al (1993) used sequential analyses to further investigate couples' home reenactments of marital conflicts. Physically aggressive couples displayed more hostile affect than verbally aggressive or withdrawing couples and also engaged in "a number of contingent behavior patterns involving anger" (p. 36). The findings suggest that physically aggressive couples engage in reciprocal patterns of hostile affect in which angry/contemptuous behavior by one partner increases the likelihood of the same behavior in the other partner. For the physically aggressive couples, this exchange of hostile affect continued for more lags than for the other conflictual, but nonviolent, couples.

Finally, in addition to directly observing men's angry and hostile behavior, Margolin et al. (1988) examined men's subjective experiences of anger in response to laboratory-based marital problem discussions. Consistent with observations of men's behavior during the interactions, the researchers found that relative to nonviolent men, physically aggressive husbands' self-reported more anger and more physiological symptoms of anger or arousal.

Observational Research by Jacobson, Gottman, and Colleagues

Jacobson and his colleagues also collected observational data in a study comparing the communication patterns of violent/distressed, nonviolent/distressed, and happily married couples recruited from the community. Researchers coded couples' behaviors during laboratory-based discussions of problems in their relationship. This project led to several published papers regarding couples' communication patterns.

Cordova, Jacobson, Gottman, Rushe, and Cox (1993) studied a subsample of couples in this study and found that violent/distressed couples showed a greater tendency to engage in negative reciprocity patterns than distressed/nonviolent or happily married couples. The violent husbands displayed more aversive negative behavior than men in the comparison groups. Jacobson et al. (1994) analyzed data from the full sample and found that violent husbands displayed more anger than the distressed/nonviolent group. In addition, the violent husbands expressed more contempt and belligerence than the distressed/nonviolent men. Examining the same sample, Berns, Jacobson, and Gottman (1999) again found that violent husbands were significantly more negative (i.e., a composite score including anger, distrust, contempt, domineering, belligerence, fear, whining, sadness, tension, defensiveness, and stonewalling) than nonviolent but maritally distressed husbands during their marital problem discussions; both the violent and nonviolent/distressed men were significantly more negative than happily married and nonviolent husbands.

Observational Research by Holtzworth-Munroe and Colleagues

Using one sample, Holtzworth-Munroe and colleagues published two studies comparing the marital interaction behaviors of four groups of couples (each group had 25 couples) recruited from the community—husband violence with marital distress, husband violence without marital distress, nonviolent husbands with marital distress, and nonviolent husbands without marital distress. Holtzworth-Munroe, Smutzler, and Stuart (1998) compared the groups' behavior using the standard laboratory-based marital problem discussion paradigm. Significant group differences were found on two codes related to hostility—blaming and contempt during discussions of wife-initiated topics. Violent/distressed spouses were significantly more blaming than nonviolent/nondistressed spouses and engaged in significantly more contempt than both nonviolent comparison samples; also, violent/nondistressed spouses engaged in more contempt than nonviolent/nondistressed couples.

Considering that Eckhardt et al. (1998) and Holtzworth-Munroe and Smutzler (1996) found that violent men express more anger than nonviolent men in response to a wide variety of wife behaviors, at least as portrayed in simulated situation vignettes, Holtzworth-Munroe, Stuart, Sandin, Smutzler, and McLaughlin (1997) examined the idea that high levels of husband hostility may characterize other types of marital discussions. Specifically, they asked the couples in their study to engage in a social support discussion in which they were to discuss the wife's personal (not relationship) problems (e.g., weight, career, friends). Relative to nonviolent men, violent husbands displayed more contempt/disgust, anger/frustration, and belligerent/domineering behavior. Again, these findings suggest that the angry and hostile behavior of maritally violent men may be expressed in a broad range of situations rather than being limited to marital conflicts or problem discussions.

Observational Studies That Consider Alcohol

Given the overlap between alcohol use problems and husband violence (e.g., O'Farrell & Murphy, 1995), some researchers have begun to examine the interplay among marital interaction behavior, alcohol use, and aggression. For example, among a sample of newly abstinent, treatment-seeking male alcoholics, Murphy and O'Farrell (1997) compared the marital interaction behavior of nonviolent couples to that of couples with a physically aggressive husband. They found that the aggressive husbands displayed more negative reciprocity, being more likely to respond negatively to their wives' prior negative behavior. Leonard and Roberts (1998) compared the marital interactions of maritally aggressive and nonaggressive men under a baseline condition and then after the husband received no alcohol, a placebo (i.e., the couple thought the husband was receiving alcohol but he was not), or alcohol. Similar to other studies, at baseline, the aggressive couples had more negative behavior and higher levels of negative reciprocity than nonaggressive couples. Alcohol, but not the placebo, led to increased negativity.

Observational Studies of Batterer Typologies

Recently, researchers also have begun to code marital interactions in an effort to compare the behavior of various subtypes of maritally violent men. Examining the Jacobson and Gottman sample (introduced earlier), Gottman et al. (1995) derived a typology of two male batterer subtypes (based on heart rate responses during marital interactions) and compared the marital interaction behavior of these subtypes. They found that Type I batterers (i.e., those whose heart rate lowered during marital interaction and appeared to be more antisocial and generally violent) engaged in more verbal aggression toward their wives than did the other subtype (i.e., Type II). In another study of this sample, Coan, Gottman, Babcock, and Jacobson (1997) found that Type I batterers were more likely than Type II batterers to respond to low-level, negative wife affect with escalated negativity; Type II men, in turn, were more likely than nonviolent but maritally distressed men to do so. Both subgroups of violent men were more likely than nonviolent men to reciprocate high levels of wife negativity.

In a replication study, Meehan Holtzworth-Munroe, and Herron (2001) were able to derive the same two subtypes as identified by Gottman et al. (1995) using the same methods (i.e., heart rate reactivity to the marital interaction) among a different sample of men (from Holtzworth-Munroe, Meehan, Herron, Rehman, & Stuart, 2000). Meehan et al. compared these two subtypes on laboratory based marital interaction behavior. Unlike Gottman et al. they found no differences between Type I and Type II men's emotionally aggressive behavior during marital interactions. Thus, until further replications are done, Meehan et al. suggested that it may be premature to use the Gottman et al. typology.

In contrast, using the same sample, Holtzworth-Munroe, Meehan et al. (2000) did find some group differences in marital interaction behaviors across the Holtzworth-Munroe and Stuart (1994) subtypes and two nonviolent comparison samples. The more violent subgroups (e.g., GVA and BD) scored highest on a negative behavior summary code that included contemptuous, belligerent, and domineering behavior. On this summary code, FO men did not differ significantly from either of the nonviolent comparison groups. In a more detailed examination of the data, Holtzworth-Munroe, Rehman et al. (2000) found that GVA men had the highest levels of contemptuous/belligerent behavior. When examining men's anger, significant group differences did not emerge during discussion of a wife-selected topic; however, during discussion of a husband-selected topic, the more severely violent men and the nonviolent but maritally distressed men had the highest levels of anger, whereas the FO men and happily married, nonviolent men displayed the least anger.

In a more recent batterer typology study, Chase, O'Leary, and Heyman (2001) categorized 60 maritally violent men as either reactive or proactive relationship aggressors. Chase et al. compared the behavior of these two subtypes during a videotaped interaction with the spouse. Reactive men were found to display more anger than proactive men (proactive men were more dominant).

In summary, though some controversy still surrounds the issue of which subtypes of maritally violent men demonstrate the most anger and hostility during marital interactions, all of the typology studies suggest there are definite differences in such behaviors across various subtypes of violent husbands. Thus, future researchers must keep in mind that samples of maritally violent men may be quite heterogeneous in their level of angry and hostile behavior during marital interactions and that some subtypes (particularly those engaging in low levels of marital violence) may not differ systematically from nonviolent men, particularly nonviolent but maritally distressed.

Other Possible Issues That Might Be Explored in Future Observational Research

Observational research methods could be used to examine other interesting controversies regarding the role of anger in husband violence. Two such issues are briefly introduced to illustrate the potential usefulness of observational research.

First, it has been suggested that anger may represent a motivated approach state that is likely to alternate with withdrawal as the threat of punishment for one's anger (e.g., anger and aggression or rejection and abandonment by one's interactional partner) increases (Cavell, 2004). Observational methods could be employed to study this notion. Indeed, there have been a limited number of observational studies comparing the demand and withdraw behaviors of violent and nonviolent couples during videotaped marital problems discussions. In at least one of these studies, couples experiencing husband violence and marital distress engaged in the highest levels of both demanding and withdrawing behavior, relative to nonviolent comparison samples (Holtzworth-Munroe et al., 1998). Sequential analyses were not used so the issue was not directly examined, but these findings suggest that violent husbands may be demanding when angry and hostile, but may then withdraw when the fear of reprisal or wife abandonment or anger becomes too high. Certainly, observational research methods could be used to examine more systematically such hypotheses.

Second, observational methods might be used to examine the relationship between anger and power within marital relationships. As noted in the introduction, there is controversy regarding whether batterers actually are angrier than other men or whether they use violence in a systematic attempt to influence their wives but claim anger as a post hoc excuse for their aggressive and domineering actions. A few systems for coding power and control behavior during observed marital interactions have been developed (see Herron & Holtzworth-Munroe, 2006, for a discussion of such methods). Thus, observational research holds the potential to examine systematically men's displays of anger and hostility in relation to their use of power and control tactics during marital interactions.

Longitudinal Observational Research

Data from longitudinal studies have shown that premarital communication negativity may predict marital dissatisfaction (Rogge & Bradbury, 1999) but not husband violence (Smith, Vivian, & O'Leary, 1991). Yet, in a longitudinal study of husbands who were already moderately to severely violent, men who displayed more negativity (i.e., belligerence, contempt, defensiveness, domineering) during a marital problem discussion were less likely than others in the sample to decrease their level of violence over time (Jacobson, Gottman, Gortner, Berns, & Shortt, 1996).

Taken together, the body of research examining the marital interaction behavior of violent husbands suggests (a) that maritally violent men display more angry and hostile behavior than nonviolent men, (b) that spouses in violent relationships are more likely to get trapped in patterns of negative reciprocity, and (c) that among samples of violent men, there are differing levels of anger and hostility observed during marital interactions. In addition, understanding the complex interaction among men's anger/hostility, their perpetration of marital violence, and other potentially related variables (e.g., demand–withdraw behavior, power and control, alcohol use) may be facilitated by the use of observational methods.

WIVES' ANGER AND HOSTILITY: AN UNDERSTUDIED ISSUE

One issue that is politically sensitive, but that ultimately must be considered in any marital research, is the role of not only the husband's, but also the wife's, anger and hostility. There are at least two sensitive issues regarding wives' anger/hostility to be considered.

The first such issue is whether women who perpetrate physical aggression against their male intimate partners are more angry and hostile than women who are nonviolent in their intimate relationships. This issue is complicated by the political furor surrounding the question of whether or not female aggression is a serious problem, deserving of scientific attention, or whether studies of female aggression will only distract attention and resources from the more important public health problem of male aggression (for a brief discussion of this controversy, see Holtzworth-Munroe, 2005). As mentioned in the introduction to this chapter, we believe that the current data consistently demonstrate that male aggression has more negative consequences than female aggression. Thus, we have focused this chapter on maritally violent men, not maritally violent women. If, however, we had been interested in reviewing data on the anger/hostility of maritally violent women, we probably would have been unable to do so, as studies comparing maritally violent and nonviolent women's levels of anger and hostility do not exist.

Even if one agrees that male violence is a more important problem than female aggression, a second politically charged issue still remains. That is the question of whether one should study the anger/hostility levels of women who are married to violent men, regardless of whether or not the wife is violent. In other words, when attempting to understand what could be a dyadic process (i.e., male violence in the context of marital conflicts), should researchers compare the anger/hostility levels of women in violent relationships to those of women in nonviolent relationships? This question is controversial given concerns about the potential misuse of any data demonstrating negative characteristics of wives in violent relationships. For example, if researchers were to find that wives of violent husbands are more angry than wives of nonviolent husbands, such data might be used to blame the victim, leading some to conclude that wives provoke, and thus possibly deserve, the abuse they receive from their husbands. Perhaps given such concerns, to our knowledge, there are few if any studies of wife anger using either questionnaires or simulated situation vignettes.

In contrast, in the marital observation studies reviewed previously, researchers have examined wife behavior during videotaped marital interactions. Although space does not allow a review of these data, it is interesting to note that many of these observational studies revealed that both spouses in husband-violent relationships engage in more negative behavior, including more hostile behavior, than spouses in nonviolent relationships. Of course, one does not know if such anger preceded the onset of husband violence or is a consequence of it (e.g., a battered woman's anger may be one of many attempts she makes to counter or prevent her husband's violence; note, however, that such a question could also be asked regarding male anger/hostility). Future researchers must grapple with the question of how to examine further the role of women's anger in dyadic interactions in a research area that is primarily concerned with male violence and in a manner that does not unfairly blame victims of violence.

Anger/Hostility: An Individual Characteristic or a Dyadic Interaction Variable?

Putting political concerns aside, such a question is potentially scientifically exciting, as marital and family interactions may afford an unique opportunity to examine the complex interplay of anger, hostility, and aggression between individuals. In contrast, most questionnaire measures of general anger and hostility assume that only the respondent's anger is problematic or of interest. In much research using such measures, anger and hostility are viewed as individual difference variables or personality characteristics. In contrast, more careful examination of marital interactions, particularly as they unfold over time, could allow us to consider how anger and hostility, as both an individual characteristic and a reaction to another individual's characteristics or to particular situational stimuli, are more likely to emerge in certain contexts than in others.

As one example of research that could be conducted at this level of analysis, consider the study of batterer typologies. Holtzworth-Munroe, Meehan, Herron, Rehman, and Stuart (2003) hypothesized that the relationship violence of severely violent men (BD and GVA men) is related to the stable individual characteristics of those men. In other words, the characteristics of some men put them at high risk for perpetrating severe relationship violence and, in their relationships, these men are the "cause" of the relationship violence; presumably such men are likely to carry their violence forward, over time and across relationships. In contrast, Holtzworth-Munroe et al. also hypothesized that low levels of violence perpetrated by FO men, although reflecting some individual characteristics (e.g., lack of communication skills), may be more strongly related to dyadic factors (e.g., marital conflict), life stressors, or other external factors (e.g., the cultural acceptability of low levels of relationship aggression). If correct, then FO men should use violence inconsistently, both across situations within a marriage and across differing relationships. Studies that examine, over time, the interactions of maritally violent men with differing individuals (e.g., a spouse vs. a stranger), across differing situations within a relationship (e.g., marital problem discussions vs. social support discussions or pleasant conversations), or across differing intimate partners, will be necessary to test such hypotheses. Such work would help to disentangle the role of the man's anger/hostility, his partner's anger/hostility, and both spouses' perpetration of violence. We would urge future researchers to undertake such studies, despite the political controversy such work might engender.

FUTURE RESEARCH DIRECTIONS: USING METHODS DEVELOPED FOR GENERAL ANGER RESEARCH

When people report experiencing a particular emotion, they also tend to engage in distinctive patterns of interpretation and evaluation of context consistent with their emotional state. For example, individuals may identify particular instigators of anger (e.g., feeling blamed or unfairly treated), engage in distinct cognitive processing (e.g., obsessive thinking about the angering event), experience corresponding physiological reactivity (e.g., increased heart rate or blood pressure), and engage in particular types of behaviors (e.g., aggression or attempts to control their anger) (e.g., Averill, 1982; Fletcher & Fitness, 1993; Russel & Fehr, 1994; Shaver, Schwartz, Kirson, & O'Connor, 2001). Thus, there is a large range of variables that can be examined to better understand anger, and researchers who study general anger have been developing new methods to examine these variables. Unfortunately, researchers studying husband violence have generally underutilized strategies developed in the general field of anger research. Thus, to encourage more innovative research on the role of anger in husband violence, we provide examples of research methods and paradigms that might be considered by those who research husband violence.

Attention Allocation and Anger Induction

Individuals are known to allocate attentional and cognitive resources to stimuli that are self-relevant and of high importance. Thus, it is assumed that individuals with anger problems allocate attention to anger-relevant stimuli. To our knowledge, however, this issue has not been directly examined in marital violence research. Therefore, we offer an example from the general anger research literature.

Cohen, Eckhardt, and Schagat (1998) found differences in task performance between high- and low-trait-anger individuals during a visual search task for positive, neutral, or angry distracter words. Participants who were high in trait anger had longer response times when distracter words were anger related and when target words were surrounded by anger-related distracters, relative to positive-emotion distracters. These findings suggest that high trait anger individuals allocate more attentional resources to anger cues than do low trait anger participants.

Such a study demonstrates group differences under relatively neutral conditions. Yet, it is also assumed that individuals allocate attention to emotion-congruent stimuli, so that it might be best to study the impact of anger on subjects when subjects are in fact angry. However, with few exceptions (e.g., see work of Barbour et al., 1998, and Eckhardt et al., 1998, reviewed earlier), the majority of research comparing the information processing of maritally violent and nonviolent men either has not used anger induction techniques or has only done so indirectly. For example, in the observational studies reviewed previously, a man may or may not become angered when discussing a marital problem with his wife (see Holtzworth-Munroe, 2000, for a review of social information processing studies comparing maritally violent and nonviolent men in response to hypothetical marital conflicts that might indirectly induce anger). Using anger induction might provide a more accurate picture of violent versus nonviolent men's information processing, as researchers could observe men's attention allocation under conditions presumed to be similar to real-life situations involving violence perpetration (e.g., an angry marital conflict).

An illustrative study from the general anger literature was conducted by Eckhardt and Cohen (1997). The researchers used the emotional Stroop paradigm to examine subjects' task performance (i.e., response latency to name the color of words) when reading anger words, positive-emotion words, or neutral words. Undergraduate study participants were divided into high trait anger and low trait anger individuals. In addition, participants were assigned randomly to receive (or not receive) an insult (i.e., the anger induction condition) before completing the color-naming task. Among all participants who were not insulted, there was no effect of word type. In contrast, among those who were insulted, anger words interfered with the task performance of high trait anger individuals but not the performance of low trait anger individuals. The results suggest that anger led to difficulties in attention allocation among high trait anger subjects, leading to group differences in performance not observed in a non-anger inducing context.

Such studies suggest a more accurate understanding of the effects of anger on information processing is possible when anger induction techniques are used. It should be noted, however, that the lack of any other negative emotion words in the studies by Eckhardt and Cohen leaves unanswered the question of whether high trait anger individuals become distracted only in response to anger-relevant stimuli or in response to any negative stimuli, such as depression or anxiety-relevant stimuli.

Given the findings just reviewed, we recommend that future marital violence researchers incorporate anger induction techniques into their studies to better understand the effects of anger on information processing and attention allocation among violent husbands. We also recommend that marital violence researchers use a variety of methods for studying information processing and attention allocation, such as those used by Eckhardt, Cohen, and colleagues.

Researchers can use these methods to examine differences between general and spouse-specific anger. For example, it would be interesting to examine whether anger induced by someone other than one's spouse would affect attention allocation in marital relevant tasks. We would hypothesize that violent spouses may be particularly likely to react with aggression and anger during marital interactions, even when the source of the anger is not relevant to their marriage. Of course, we also believe that it will be beneficial to incorporate methods that examine anger induced by the spouse or by violent husbands' interpretations of their spouses' behavior. For example, spouses' experience of anger during marital conflicts may influence their attention and interpretation of contextual cues during such conflicts, facilitating spouses' hostile or aggressive responses toward their partner.

A final example of an issue to consider is the question of possible differences across subtypes of maritally violent men, both in terms of what induces anger and in terms of possible variations in emotionally relevant tasks that demand attention allocation. For example, the BD subtype of batterer has been hypothesized to be particularly sensitive to criticism or rejection from his wife and to possible wife abandonment. Thus, we might hypothesize that BD men, following anger induction prior to an emotional Stroop task, would evidence longer response latencies to words relevant to interpersonal rejection or criticism by an intimate partner.

Another potentially promising avenue to better understanding social information processing differences of maritally violent versus nonviolent men is to investigate basic social cues, such as voice cues or facial-affect recognition, that lead to anger or to the misinterpretation of anger. For example, various aspects of voice cues have been shown to be related to individuals' perception of others' emotions (e.g., Frick 1985; see Johnstone, Van Reekum, & Scherer, 2000; Frick, 1985; Murray & Arnott, 1993). Moreover, Juslin and Laukka (2001) found that the intensity of expressed emotion influences perceivers' accuracy in identifying the emotion being portrayed. Interestingly, there are large individual differences in both encoding and decoding accuracy (Pakosz, 1983). Given that previous studies of social information processing deficits have found that maritally violent men attribute hostile intent to their wives' behavior (e.g., Holtzworth-Munroe & Hutchinson, 1993), it seems plausible that violent husbands would also overattribute anger to their wives during emotion recognition tasks. Moreover, it is possible that the degree to which violent husbands perceive hostility or anger from contextual cues is likely to increase following anger induction. It would be interesting to examine whether such differences, if found, would be related only to wives' emotional cues, to those of all women, or even to those of both men and women.

Biological Measures

It also may be valuable to examine individual differences in anger response styles in combination with differences in psychophysiological responses and coping potential. For example, studies using samples of maritally violent men have shown that violent men have more intense psychophysiological responses during marital conflict than nonviolent men (e.g., Jacobson et al., 1994), but few such studies have been conducted.

Other researchers have investigated the relationship between prefrontal cortical activity and negative emotions (e.g., see Davidson, 1995;

Davidson, Jackson, & Kalin, 1999), and anger in particular (e.g., Harmon-Jones, Sigelman, Bohlig, & Harmon-Jones, 2003; Harmon-Jones & Harmon-Jones, chap. 4, this volume). There has been some debate about the conceptual relationship between asymmetrical frontal cortical activity and motivation for emotional processes. One view suggests that positive affect is associated with increased left frontal activity whereas negative affect is associated with increased right activity (e.g., Ahern & Schwartz, 1985; Heller, 1990; Heller & Nitschke, 1998). It has also been argued that increased left frontal cortical activity is related to approach motivation, whereas increased right frontal cortical activity is related to withdrawal motivation (e.g., Harmon-Jones, 2003; Harmon-Jones et al., 2003; Harmon-Jones & Allen, 1998). Davidson (1998) has argued that relative to right frontal cortical activity, increased left activity is related to both positive affect and approach motivation, whereas increased right activity is related to withdrawal motivation and negative affect. Anger, which is both a negative emotion and is associated with approach motivation, has been shown to be associated with increased relative left frontal cortical activation among college students following an insult (Harmon-Jones & Sigelman, 2001). Participants who reported feeling the most anger also exhibited increased relative left frontal activity and behaved the most aggressively. According to the authors, these results suggest that relative left frontal activity is related to approach motivation, regardless of emotion. Harmon-Jones et al. (2003) examined affective and midcortical activity among students in response to the anger-inducing situation. Among students given the opportunity to take action to alleviate the angering situation (i.e., sign a petition), they found that relatively greater left midcortical activity was related to students' signing the petition. These findings raise the question of whether maritally violent men, who experience high levels of anger, exhibit increased relative left prefrontal cortical or midcortical activity during negative interactions, which in turn might be related to their motivation to aggress against their wives or to their failure to control their aggressive behavior.

Such work is still in its infancy and, to our knowledge, has never been applied to the study of husband violence. But further developments in our understanding of the relationships among anger, psychophysiological responding, and cortical functioning may lead to interesting future research possibilities in the marital violence area.

CLINICAL IMPLICATIONS AND FUTURE RESEARCH

As noted in the introduction, there has been some controversy regarding the role that anger plays in husband violence (i.e., whether it is a precipitating event or a post hoc excuse for violence) and, correspondingly, whether anger needs to be a primary focus of batterer intervention programs. The reviewed studies clearly indicate a link between husband violence and husband anger/hostility, but such data do not definitively resolve this conflict. We suggest that to make further progress a variety of clinically relevant issues must be considered.

Diagnosis and Assessment Issues

Perhaps one reason for a lack of systematic research on the problem of anger and hostility among maritally violent men is the lack of DSM–IV–TR (American Psychiatric Association, 2000) diagnoses for anger-related problems (e.g., Eckhardt et al., 2004). In contrast to anger, there are multiple diagnoses involving other negative emotions, such as depression and anxiety. Interestingly, anger is listed among the diagnostic criteria for some Axis II personality disorders, including two (antisocial personality disorder and borderline personality disorder) that are represented in the batterer typology of Holtzworth-Munroe and colleagues (Holtzworth-Munroe, Holtzworth-Munroe & Stuart, 1994; Meehan et al., 2000; 2003). Researchers have begun to call for more careful consideration of anger in future diagnostic systems (e.g., Eckhardt & Deffenbacher, 1995; Eckhardt et al., 2004; Widiger & Mullins-Sweatt (2004). Such considerations might lead to more research and clinical attention being directed toward the problem of anger, both to better understand this emotion and to develop more effective treatments for it.

Another problem is that some of the currently available assessment methods are methodologically weak. Eckhardt et al. (2004) reviewed problems with many of the self-report questionnaire measures of general anger and hostility, concluding that, "The scales discussed varied widely in their theoretical underpinnings, psychometric quality, and construct validity" (p. 35). Eckhardt et al. argue that greater understanding of the relationship between anger experience and anger expression may emerge from studies conducted in the context of anger-arousal. Thus, Eckhardt et al. present possible assessment alternatives to self-report questionnaires, including self-monitoring, interviews, and the ATSS paradigm. We would add to this list the behavioral observation of marital interactions along with gathering data on spouses' subjective experiences during these interactions. Eckhardt et al. also suggest that in clinical settings, it may be informative for clinicians to engage clients in role plays or anger memory induction tasks to provide a more complete understanding of their anger during actual anger-arousal states. Observations of marital problem discussions could also provide an indirect method of anger induction. The utility of such methods deserve further research attention.

Treatment Issues

Many of the available batterer intervention programs include an anger management component. Unfortunately, overall, batterer intervention programs have not proven very effective (see Babcock, Green, & Robie, 2004, for a recent meta-analysis of batterer intervention outcome studies). Thus, we must consider why such programs may be ineffective.

It is possible that such programs do not give enough attention to anger or may be addressing anger in a formal, relatively sterile clinical environment, rather than allowing men to grapple with their behavior during anger-arousing situations. In other words, a violent man may be able to calmly discuss nonviolent ways of responding to situations when sitting in a therapy group, but whether or not he can actually implement such responses in a real-life, anger-arousing situation is unclear. Thus, as suggested by Eckhardt et al. (2004), we urge therapists to consider anger induction methods for role plays.

Though controversial, and perhaps inappropriate for severely violent couples, the need to help violent men learn to control their anger "online" would be one possible argument for the use of conjoint couples therapy to treat husbands who are violent. Indeed, we have found couples therapy very useful in the treatment of mild to moderately violent couples (e.g., see Holtzworth-Munroe, Clements, & Farris, 2005). The conflicts experienced by such couples inevitably arise during treatment sessions, allowing the clinician a chance to encourage the use of time-outs and other anger management methods under therapist supervision, in addition to helping couples immediately consider different cognitive interpretations of the situation and to practice different behavioral responses.

It is also important to consider the data, reviewed earlier, demonstrating differing levels of anger and hostility across subtypes of maritally violent men. These data suggest that men who engage in low levels of violence (e.g., FO men) may not have any more difficulty than nonviolent men, particularly nonviolent but maritally distressed men, in handling their anger. Indeed, even nonviolent couples, particularly maritally distressed couples, sometimes experience difficulty controlling their anger and hostility. Thus, anger management might be an appropriate intervention for FO men and for their nonviolent, maritally distressed counterparts.

For subtypes of severely violent men, who appear to have elevated levels of anger and hostility, it is still theoretically possible that their anger is in reaction to differing issues. For example, we have theorized that GVA men would be most likely to engage in marital violence when their partners challenge their authority or frustrate their immediate goals and plans (Holtzworth-Munroe & Meehan, 2005). Such violence might be related to anger or might be a more "cold-blooded," calculated method to get their own way during marital conflicts. In contrast, we have hypothesized along with others (Dutton, 1995a) that the violence of BD men likely derives from their fear of abandonment and from anxiety over threats to their attachment to their partners, although it is again unclear whether such violence represents emotional dysregulation and loss of control (in the face of overwhelming insecurity) or a calculated attempt to prevent the wife from leaving (Holtzworth-Munroe & Meehan, in press). As these hypothesized subgroup differences illustrate, researchers and clinicians need to outline more carefully the attitudinal, cognitive, physiological, and subjective experiences of anger across batterer subtypes, in addition to the situations that elicit anger. Only through a careful functional analysis will clinicians eventually be able to tailor general anger management treatments to meet the clinical needs of varying subtypes of violent husbands.

Further Future Directions

In considering directions for future research, it is important to end with some caveats—concerns that should give us pause in our rush to consider the relevance of anger and hostility to husband violence. First, it must be noted that, at this time, we do not understand how men's anger and hostility relate to husband aggression. In other words, we simply do not understand the role of anger/hostility in male violence toward intimate female partners or the mechanisms involved in translating such anger and hostility into physical aggression.

A second, related concern requires one to think even more broadly. Specifically, one should note an important point made in an earlier review of this research literature (Eckhardt et al., 1997): Men's violence against female partners may have a variety of causes, with anger being just one of the many possible causes. Indeed, to further our understanding of male-to-female marital violence, we must consider the full range of reasons why men may abuse their wives, including such factors as individual psychopathology (including alcohol abuse), a desire for power and control, societal sanctioning of such actions, and a lack of social skills, as just a few possibilities that have been discussed in the literature. It is likely that such factors will interact with each other, and with anger/hostility, requiring multidimensional, multiconstruct models to fully understand why an individual man perpetrates marital violence and how to best help him change his destructive behavior.

REFERENCES

Ahern, G. L., & Schwartz, G. E. (1985). Differential lateralization for positive and negative emotion in the human brain: EEG spectral analysis. *Neuropsychologia*, 23, 745–755.

American Psychiatric Association. (2000). *Diagnostic and statistical manual of mental disorders* (4th ed., text revision). Washington, DC: Author.

Archer, J. (2000). Sex differences in aggression between heterosexual partners: A meta-analytic review. *Psychological Bulletin, 126*(5), 651–680.

Averill, J. R. (1982). *Anger and aggression: An essay on emotion.* New York: Springer-Verlag.

Babcock, J. C., Green, C. E., & Robie, C. (2004). Does batterers' treatment work? A meta-analytic review of domestic violence treatment. *Clinical Psychology Review, 23*(8), 1023–1053.

Barbour, K. A., Eckhardt, C. I., Davison, G. C., & Kassinove, H. (1998). The experience and expression of anger in maritally violent and maritally discordant-nonviolent men. *Behavior Therapy, 29*(2), 173–191.

Barnett, O. W., Fagan, R. W., & Booker, J. M. (1991). Hostility and stress as mediators of aggression in violent men. *Journal of Family Violence, 6*(3), 217–241.

Beasley, R., & Stoltenberg, C. D. (1992). Personality characteristics of male spouse abusers. *Professional Psychology: Research & Practice, 23*(4), 310–317.

Berkowitz, L. (1988). Frustrations, appraisals, and aversively stimulated aggression. *Aggressive Behavior. Special Issue: Current Theoretical Perspectives on Aggressive and Antisocial Behavior, 14*(1), 3–11.

Berns, S. B., Jacobson, N. S., & Gottman, J. M. (1999). Demand–withdraw interaction in couples with a violent husband. *Journal of Consulting & Clinical Psychology, 67*(5), 666–674.

Bowlby, J. (1977). The making and breaking of affectional bonds: I. Aetiology and psychopathology in the light of attachment theory. *British Journal of Psychiatry, 130*, 201–210.

Boyle, D. J., & Vivian, D. (1996). Generalized versus spouse–specific anger/hostility and men's violence against intimates. *Violence & Victims, 11*(4), 293–317.

Burman, B., John, R. S., & Margolin, G. (1992). Observed patterns of conflict in violent, nonviolent, and nondistressed couples. *Behavioral Assessment, 14*(1), 15–37.

Burman, B., Margolin, G., & John, R. S. (1993). America's angriest home videos: Behavioral contingencies observed in home reenactments of marital conflict. *Journal of Consulting & Clinical Psychology, 61*(1), 28–39.

Buss, A. H., & Durkee, A (1957). An inventory for assessing different kinds of hostility. *Journal of Criminal Psychology, 21*, 343–349.

Buss, A. H., & Perry, M. (1992). The Aggression Questionnaire. *Journal of Personality & Social Psychology, 63*(3), 452–459.

Cadsky, O., & Crawford, M. (1988). Establishing batterer typologies in a clinical sample of men who assault their female partners. *Canadian Journal of Community Mental Health. Special Issue: Wife Battering: A Canadian Perspective, 7*(2), 119–127.

Caine, T. M., Foulds, G. A., & Hope, K. (1967). *The Hostility-Direction of Hostility Questionnaire.* London: London University Press.

Cavell, T. (2004). *Opening comments.* Anger and Aggression Conference, University of Arkansas, Fayetteville.

Chase, K. A., O'Leary, K. D., & Heyman, R. E. (2001). Categorizing partner-violent men within the reactive-proactive typology model. *Journal of Consulting & Clinical Psychology, 69*(3), 567–572.

Coan, J., Gottman, J. M., Babcock, J., & Jacobson, N. (1997). Battering and the male rejection of influence from women. *Aggressive Behavior. Special Issue: Appeasement and reconciliation, 23*(5), 375–388.

Cohen, D. J., Eckhardt, C., & Schagat, K. D. (1998). Attention allocation and habituation to anger-related stimuli during a visual search task. *Aggressive Behavior, 24*(6), 399–409

Cordova, J. V., Jacobson, N. S., Gottman, J. M., Rushe, R., & Cox, G. (1993). Negative reciprocity and communication in couples with a violent husband. *Journal of Abnormal Psychology, 102*(4), 559–564.

Davidson, R. J. (1995). Cerebral asymmetry, emotion, and affective style. In R. J. Davidson & K. Hugdahl (Eds.), *Brain asymmetry* (pp. 361–387). Cambridge, MA: MIT Press.

Davidson, R. J. (1998). Anterior electrophysiological asymmetry, emotion, and depression: Conceptual and methodological conundrums. *Psychophysiology, 35,* 607–614.

Davidson, R. J., Jackson, D. C., & Kalin, N. H. (2000). Emotion, plasticity, context, and regulation: Perspectives from affective neuroscience. *Psychological Bulletin, 126,* 890–909.

Davison, G. C., Feldman, P. M., & Osborn, C. E. (1984). Articulated thoughts, irrational beliefs, and fear of negative evaluation. *Cognitive Therapy & Research, 8*(4), 349–362.

Davison, G. C., Robins, C., & Johnson, M. K. (1983). Articulated thoughts during simulated situations: A paradigm for studying cognition in emotion and behavior. *Cognitive Therapy & Research, 7*(1), 17–39.

Derogatis, L. R., Lipman, R. S., Covi, L., & Rickels, K. (1971). Neurotic symptom dimensions: As perceived by psychiatrists and patients of various social classes. *Archives of General Psychiatry, 24*(5), 454–464.

Dobash, R. E., & Dobash, R. P. (1977). Wives: The appropriate victims of marital violence. *Victimology, 2*(3/4), 426–442.

Dollard, J., Doob, L. W., Miller, N. E., Mowrer, O. H., Sears, R. R., Ford, C. S., et al. (1939). *Frustration and aggression.* New Haven, CT: Yale University Press.

Dutton, D. G. (1995a). Intimate abusiveness. *Clinical Psychology: Science & Practice, 2*(3), 207–224.

Dutton, D. G. (1995b). Trauma symptoms and PTSD-like profiles in perpetrators of intimate abuse. *Journal of Traumatic Stress, 8,* 299–316.

Dutton, D. G., & Browning, J. J. (1988). Concern for power, fear of intimacy, and aversive stimuli for wife assault. In G. T. Hotaling, D. Finkelhor, J. T. Kirkpatrick, & M. A. Straus (Eds), *Family abuse and its consequences: New directions in research.* (pp. 163–175). Thousand Oaks, CA: Sage.

Dutton, D. G., Saunders, K., Starzomski, A., & Bartholomew, K. (1994). Intimacy-anger and insecure attachment as precursors of abuse in intimate relationships. *Journal of Applied Social Psychology, 24*(15), 1367–1386.

Dutton, D. G., & Starzomski, A. J. (1994). Psychological differences between court-referred and self-referred wife assaulters. *Criminal Justice & Behavior, 21*(2), 203–222.

Dutton, D. G., Starzomski, A., & Ryan, L. (1996). Antecedents of abusive personality and abusive behavior in wife assaulters. *Journal of Family Violence, 11*(2), 113–132.

Eckhardt, C. I., Barbour, K. A., & Davison, G. C. (1998). Articulated thoughts of maritally violent and nonviolent men during anger arousal. *Journal of Consulting & Clinical Psychology, 66*(2), 259–269.

Eckhardt, C. I., Barbour, K. A., & Stuart, G. L. (1997). Anger and hostility in maritally violent men: Conceptual distinctions, measurement issues, and literature review. *Clinical Psychology Review, 17*(4), 333–358.

Eckhardt, C. I., & Cohen, D. J. (1997). Attention to anger-relevant and irrelevant stimuli following naturalistic insult. *Personality & Individual Differences, 23*(4), 619–629.

Eckhardt, C. I., & Deffenbacher, J. L. (1995). Diagnosis of anger disorders. In H. Kassinove, Anger desorders: Definition diagnosis, and treatment (pp. 27–47). Washington, DC: Taylor & Francis.

Eckhardt, C. I., Norlander, B., & Deffenbacher, J. (2004). The assessment of anger and hostility: A critical review. *Aggression & Violent Behavior, 9*(1), 17–43.

Elbow, M. (1977). Theoretical considerations of violent marriages. *Social Casework, 58*(9), 515–526.

Else, L., Wonderlich, S. A., Beatty, W. W., Christie, D. W., & Staton, R. D. (1993). Personality characteristics of men who physically abuse women. *Hospital & Community Psychiatry, 44*(1), 54–58.

Faulk, M. (1974, July). Men who assault their wives. *Medicine, Science, and the Law, 14*(3), 180–183.

Fletcher, J., & Fitness, J. O. G. (1993). Love, hate, anger, and jealousy in close relationships: A prototype and cognitive appraisal analysis. Journal *of Personality & Social Psychology, 65*(5), 942–958.

Frick, R. W. (1985). Communicating emotion: The role of prosodic features. *Psychological Bulletin. 97*(3), 412–429.

Gondolf, E. W., & Russell, D. (1986). The case against anger control treatment programs for batterers. *Response to the Victimization of Women & Children, 9*(3), 2–5.

Gottman, J. M., Jacobson, N. S., Rushe, R. H., & Shortt, J. W., Babcock, J., LaTaillade, J. J., et al. (1995). The relationship between heart rate reactivity, emotionally aggressive behavior, and general violence in batterers. *Journal of Family Psychology, 9*(3), 227–248.

Hamberger, L. K. (1996). Group treatment of men who batter their female partners. *In Session: Psychotherapy in Practice, 2*, 49–62.

Hamberger, L. K., & Hastings, J. E. (1986). Personality correlates of men who abuse their partners: A cross-validation study. *Journal of Family Violence, 1*, 323–341.

Harmon-Jones, E. (2003). Clarifying the emotive functions of asymmetrical frontal cortical activity. *Psychophysiology, 40*(6), 838–848.

Harmon-Jones, E., & Allen, J. J. B. (1998). Anger and prefrontal brain activity: EEG asymmetry consistent with approach motivation despite negative affective valence. *Journal of Personality and Social Psychology, 74*, 1310–1316.

Harmon-Jones, E., & Sigelman, J. (2001). State anger and prefrontal brain activity: Evidence that insult-related relative prefrontal activation is associated with experienced anger and aggression. *Journal of Personality and Social Psychology, 80*, 797–803.

Harmon-Jones, E., Sigelman, J. D., Bohlig, A., & Harmon-Jones, C. (2003). Anger, coping, and frontal cortical activity: The effect of coping potential on anger induced left frontal activity. *Cognition and Emotion, 17(1)*, 1–24.

Heller, W. (1990). The neuropsychology of emotion: Developmental patterns and implications for psychopathology. In N. L. Stein, B. Leventhal, & T. Trabassa (Eds.), *Psychological and biological approaches to emotion* (pp. 167–211). Hillsdale, NJ: Erlbaum Associates.

Heller, W., & Nitschke, J. B. (1998). The puzzle of regional brain activity in depression and anxiety: The importance of subtype and comorbidity. *Cognition and Emotion, 12*, 421–447.

Herron, K., & Holtzworth-Munroe, A. (Manuscript in preparation). *A multi-faceted examination of power in couples experiencing husband violence.*

Hershorn, M., & Rosenbaum, A. (1991). Over vs. undercontrolled hostility: Application of the construct to the classification of maritally violent men. *Violence & Victims, 6(2)*, 151–158.

Heyman, R. E., O'Leary, K. D., & Jouriles, E. N. (1995). Alcohol and aggressive personality styles: Potentiators of serious physical aggression against wives? *Journal of Family Psychology, 9(1)*, 44–57.

Holtzworth-Munroe, A. (1992). Social skill deficits in maritally violent men: Interpreting the data using a social information processing model. *Clinical Psychology Review, 12(6)*, 605–617.

Holtzworth–Munroe, A. (2000). Social information processing skills deficits in maritally violent men: Summary of a research program. In J. P Vincent, & E. N. Jouriles, (Eds.), *Domestic violence: Guidelines for research-informed practice* (pp. 13–36). Jessica Kingsley.

Holtzworth-Munroe, A. Female perpetration of physical aggression against an intimate partner: A controversial new topic of study. An invited commentary on the articles in a special issue on female-to-male intimate partner violence, edited by L.K. Hamberger. *Violence and Victims*, 20, 253–261.

Holtzworth-Munroe, A., Clements, K., & Farris, C. (2005). Working with couples who have experienced physical aggression. In M. Harway (Ed.) *Handbook of couples therapy* (pp. 289–312). Hoboken, NJ: Wiley.

Holtzworth-Munroe, A., & Hutchinson, G. (1993). Attributing negative intent to wife behavior: The attributions of maritally violent versus nonviolent men. *Journal of Abnormal Psychology, 102(2)*, 206–211.

Holtzworth-Munroe, A., & Meehan, J. C. (2005). Partner violence and men: A focus on the male perpetrator. In W. M. Pinsof & J. Lebow (Eds.), *Family psychology: The art of science* (pp. 169–190). *Oxford, England:* Oxford University Press.

Holtzworth-Munroe, A., Meehan, J. C., Herron, K., Rehman, U., & Stuart, G. L. (2000). Testing the Holtzworth-Munroe and Stuart (1994) batterer typology. *Journal of Consulting and Clinical Psychology, 6(68)*, 1000–1019.

Holtzworth-Munroe, A., Meehan, J. C., Herron, K., Rehman, U., & Stuart, G. L. (2003). Do subtypes of maritally violent men continue to differ over time? *Journal of Consulting and Clinical Psychology, 71(4)*, 728–740.

Holtzworth-Munroe, A., Rehman, U., & Herron, K. (2000). General and spouse-specific anger and hostility in subtypes of martially violent men and nonviolent men. *Behavior Therapy, 31(4)*, 603–630.

Holtzworth-Munroe, A., & Smutzler, N. (1996). Comparing the emotional reactions and behavioral intentions of violent and nonviolent husbands to aggressive, distressed, and other wife behaviors. *Violence & Victims, 11*(4), 319–339.

Holtzworth-Munroe, A., Smutzler, N., & Bates, L. (1997). A brief review of the research on husband violence. Part III: Sociodemographic factors, relationship factors, and differing consequences of husband and wife violence. *Aggression & Violent Behavior, 2*(3), 285–307.

Holtzworth-Munroe, A., Smutzler, N., & Stuart, G. L. (1998). Demand and withdraw communication among couples experiencing husband violence. *Journal of Consulting & Clinical Psychology, 66*(5), 731–743.

Holtzworth-Munroe, A., & Stuart, G. L. (1994). Typologies of male batterers: Three subtypes and the differences among them. *Psychological Bulletin, 116*(3), 476–497.

Holtzworth-Munroe, A., Stuart, G. L., Sandin, E., Smutzler, N., & McLaughlin, W. (1997). Comparing the social support behaviors of violent and nonviolent husbands during discussions of wife personal problems. *Personal Relationships, 4*(4), 395–412.

Jackson, D. (1974). *Personality research form manual.* Goshen, NY: Research Psychologists Press.

Jacobson, N. S., Gottman, J. M., Gortner, E., Berns, S., & Shortt, J. W. (1996). Psychological factors in the longitudinal course of battering: When do the couples split up? When does the abuse decrease? *Violence & Victims, 11*(4), 371–392.

Jacobson, N. S., Gottman, J. M., Waltz, J., Rushe, R., Babcook, J., & Holtzworth-Munroe, A. (1994). Affect, verbal content, and psychophysiology in the arguments of couples with a violent husband. *Journal of Consulting & Clinical Psychology, 62*(5), 982–988.

Johnstone, T., Van Reekum, C. M. & Scherer, K. R. (2001). Vocal expression correlates of appraisal processes. In K. R. Scherer, A. Schorr, (Eds.), *Appraisal processes in emotion: Theory, methods, research. Series in affective science* (pp. 271–284). London: Oxford University Press.

Juslin, P. N., & Laukka, P. (2001). Impact of intended emotion intensity on cue utilization and decoding accuracy in vocal expression of emotion. *Emotion, 1*(4), 381–412.

Leonard, K. E., & Blane, H. T. (1992). Alcohol and marital aggression in a national sample of young men. *Journal of Interpersonal Violence, 7*(1), 19–30.

Leonard, K. E., & Roberts, L. J. (1998). The effects of alcohol on the marital interactions of aggressive and nonaggressive husbands and their wives. *Journal of Abnormal Psychology, 107*(4), 602–615.

Leonard, K. E., & Senchak, M. (1993). Alcohol and premarital aggression among newlywed couples. *Journal of Studies on Alcohol, (11),* 96–108.

Leonard, K. E., & Senchak, M. (1996). Prospective prediction of husband marital aggression within newlywed couples. *Journal of Abnormal Psychology, 105*(3), 369–380.

Maiuro, R. D., Cahn, T. S., & Vitaliano, P. P. (1986). Assertiveness deficits and hostility in domestically violent men. *Violence & Victims, 1*(4), 279–289.

Maiuro, R. D., Cahn, T. S., Vitaliano, P. P., Wagner, B. C., & Zegree, J. B. (1988). Anger, hostility, and depression in domestically violent versus generally assaultive men and nonviolent control subjects. *Journal of Consulting & Clinical Psychology, 56(1),* 17–23.

Maiuro, R. D., Vitaliano, P. P., & Cahn, T. S (1987). A brief measure for the assessment of anger and aggression. *Journal of Interpersonal Violence, 2*(2), 166–178.

Margolin, G., Burman, B., & John, R. S. (1989). Home observations of married couples reenacting naturalistic conflicts. *Behavioral Assessment. Special Issue: Coding marital Interaction, 11*(1), 101–118.

Margolin, G., John, R. S., & Gleberman, L. (1988). Affective responses to conflictual discussions in violent and nonviolent couples. *Journal of Consulting & Clinical Psychology, 56*(1), 24–33.

Margolin, G., John, R. S., & O'Brien, M. (1989). Sequential affective patterns as a function of marital conflict style. *Journal of Social & Clinical Psychology, 8*(1), 45–61.

McKenry, P. C., Julian, T. W., & Gavazzi, S. M. (1995). Toward a biopsychosocial model of domestic violence. *Journal of Marriage & the Family, 57*(2), 307–320.

Meehan, J. C., Holtzworth-Munroe, A., & Herron, K. (2001). Maritally violent men's heart rate reactivity to marital interactions: A failure to replicate the Gottman et al. (1995) typology. *Journal of Family Psychology, 15*(3), 394–408.

Murphy, C. M., & O'Farrell, T. J. (1997). Couple communication patterns of maritally aggressive and nonaggressive male alcoholics. *Journal of Studies on Alcohol, 58*(1), 83–90.

Murray, I. R., & Arnott, J. L. (1993). Toward the simulation of emotion in synthetic speech: A review of the literature on human vocal emotion. *Journal of the Acoustical Society of America. 93(2),* 1097–1108.

Novaco, R. W. (1975). *Anger control: The development and evaluation of an experimental treatment.* Lexington, MA: Heath.

O'Farrell, T., & Murphy, C. M. (1995). Marital violence before and after alcoholism treatment. *Journal of Consulting & Clinical Psychology, 63*(2), 256–262.

O'Leary, K. D., & Curley, A. (1986). Assertion and family violence: correlates of spouse abuse. *Journal of Marital and Family Therapy, 12,* 284–289.

O'Leary, K. D., Malone, J., & Tyree, A. (1994). Physical aggression in early marriage: Prerelationship and relationship effects. *Journal of Consulting & Clinical Psychology, 62*(3), 594–602.

Pakosz, M. (1983). Attitudinal judgments in intonation: Some evidence for a theory. *Journal of Psycholinguistic Research, 12*(3), 311–326.

Rogge, R. D., & Bradbury, T. N. (1999). Till violence does us part: The differing roles of communication and aggression in predicting adverse marital outcomes. *Journal of Consulting & Clinical Psychology, 67*(3), 340–351.

Russel, J. A., & Fehr, B. (1994). Fuzzy concepts in a fuzzy hierarchy: Varieties of anger. *Journal of Personality & Social Psychology, 67(2),* 186–205.

Saunders, D. G. (1992). A typology of men who batter: Three types derived from cluster analysis. *American Journal of Orthopsychiatry, 62*(2), 264–275.

Schumacher, J. A., Feldbau–Kohn, S., Slep, A. M. S., & Heyman, R. E. (2001). Risk factors for male–to–female partner physical abuse. *Aggression & Violent Behavior. Special Issue: Risk Factors for Family Violence, 6*(2–3), 281–352.

Shaver, P., Schwartz, J., Kirson, D., & O'Connor, C. (2001). Emotion knowledge: Further exploration of a prototype approach. In W. G. Perrott (Ed.), *Emotions in social psychology: Essential readings* (pp. 26–56). Philadelphia: Psychology Press.

Siegel, J. M. (1986). The Multidimensional Anger Inventory. *Journal of Personality & Social Psychology, 51*(1), 191–200.

Smith, D. A., Vivian, D., & O'Leary, K. D. (1991). The misnomer proposition: A critical reappraisal of the longitudinal status of "negativity" in marital communication. *Behavioral Assessment. Special Issue: Negative Communication in Marital Interaction: A Misnomer?, 13*(1), 7–24.

Spielberger, C. D. (1988). *State–Trait Anger Expression Inventory Manual.* Odessa, FL: Psychological Assessment Resources.

Straus, M. A., & Gelles, R. J. (1990). *Physical violence in American families.* New Brunswick, NJ: Transaction.

Telch, C. F., & Lindquist, C. U. (1984). Violent versus nonviolent couples: A comparison of patterns. *Psychotherapy: Theory, Research, Practice, Training, 21*(2), 242–248.

Tolman, R. M., & Saunders, D. G. (1988). The case for the cautions use of anger control with men who batter. *Response, 11,* 15–20.

Weiner, B. (1985). An attributional theory of achievement motivation and emotion. *Psychological Review, 92*(4), 548–573.

Widiger, T., Mullins-Sweat, S. N. (2004). A typology of maritally violent men: A discussion of Holtzworth–Munroe and Meehan. *Journal of Interpersonal Violence, 10,* 1396–1400.

When Family Values Clash With Therapist's Goals and Treatment Delivery

Sandra T. Azar and Kerry N. Makin-Byrd

When we work in the realm of family relationships, we are inherently working in the murky realm of values. Indeed, this chapter could have just as easily been titled "When Therapist Values Clash With Family's Goals and Wishes for Treatment Delivery." It is only the vantage point of being the professional with some documented "expertise" (clearly a form of "egocentrism") that keeps us from seeing it as being the other way around. This stance as the "expert" may be particularly problematic in work with families touched by aggression and violence. Although therapists label some actions within families as evidence of "violent" and "unacceptable behavior," parents, spouses, and youth who have been referred for treatment often label many of the same actions as being within what they believe are "normative" bounds, based on their individual life experiences and circumstances. Therapists argue that families habituate to the violence and need to be shown the errors of their ways; whereas, from their vantage point, families look in disbelief at therapists' suggestions of using reasoning, problem solving, or empathic and reflective statements to get through difficult times. This contrast in world views is most clearly seen in cognitive-behavioral theories of aggression, which see aggression as having its origin in the irrational beliefs held by clients. Not a word, however, is said regarding clients' experiencing therapists' views as similarly "irrational." After all, families' "training" and "expertise" tells them the therapists are wrong.

This chapter starts from the idea that such disparities in views are associated with much emotion on both the client's *and* the therapist's part and impede constructive therapeutic work. It argues that it is crucial that therapy begin with the therapist acknowledging and accepting these differences with no attempt to honor one view over the other. Although most traditional views of therapeutic ruptures blame the client's pathology as the main source of difficulties,[1] we present two alternative formulations of therapeutic ruptures that place greater weight on the therapist role (Azar, 1996). The first formulation focuses on "cultural" disparities that produce dissonance in therapy work (e.g., therapists' cognitive problems such as unrealistic expectations, schemas about family life that are disparate from that of clients' families, overvaluing of the rituals of therapy). The second formulation focuses on the idea that disparities may actually be experienced by clients as prejudices being expressed by therapists. Ruptures in this latter formulation may represent experiences of stigmatization occurring on client's parts. In these two views, therapeutic ruptures can be seen as places where alliance breeches may occur that are not repairable. In work with aggressive clients, therapists need to be better at identifying when such clashes in values occur, understanding their own cognitive and affective responses to them, and then managing both better. In the last part of this chapter, we attempt to discuss potential strategies for lessening the impact of and negotiating these values-based clashes. Although there is evidence available from other areas of family violence research (e.g., marital abuse), our discussion draws heavily on work with child-abusing parents where discussions of disparities in relational schemas in therapy have already taken place (Azar, 1996; Azar, Nix, & Makin-Byrd, 2005; Peterson, Gable, Doyle, & Ewigman, 1997).

---

[1]This view is captured well in discussion of Strupp's (1973) social-influence model of psychotherapy. He argues that:

> The fundamental difference between the client and therapist is that the client subscribes to maladaptive beliefs while the therapist subscribes to more adaptive beliefs. The client enters treatment with a well-worn path of neurotic behaviors. Interventions present an alternative route, a detour from the frequently traveled road. A rupture in therapy highlights this fork in the road; faced with irreconcilable options, the client cannot, at once, continue to engage in the neurotic behavior and remain connected to the therapist ... for the client,] the lure of the novel path is only as strong as the positive valence of the relationship with the therapist. (as cited in Maramba & Castanguay 2004, p. 1)

Strupp goes on to say: "In the final analysis the patient changes out of love for the therapist. ... The patient trades a symptom or a maladaptive from of behavior for ... the love or approval of an authority" (pp. 140–141).

A Need to Consider Therapist Emotion in Work With Aggressive Clients

In thinking about connecting therapeutically with individuals and families, two terms have been used—working alliance and ruptures. The *working alliance* is the positive outcome of the client–therapist relationship; whereas *ruptures* indicate that the positive course of client–therapist relationship has been disrupted. Early ruptures may be particularly problematic. Even though ruptures are described as "co-constructed," significantly less attention has been paid to therapists' role in producing them other than ineptness (Safran, 1993). Maramba and Castonguay (2004) note that ruptures that occur later in the therapeutic work may be easier to negotiate in that therapists can draw on the positive relationship already developed and the fact that past ruptures have been successfully negotiated (and have already enhanced the alliance because of their successful outcomes). Evidence exists, for example, that early dropouts have more frequent and more severe ruptures prior to leaving therapy (Hynan, 1990). Moreover, poor treatment outcomes are associated with therapists caught in a negative interactional cycle with their clients (Safran, 1993) and client negativity that is met with counterhostility—coldness, distancing, and other forms of rejection (Strupp, 1980).

In the general psychotherapy literature, attrition is said to peak after a few sessions (Maramba & Castonguay, 2004). This is particularly true of families that have problems with aggressive patterns of behavior. It is telling that attrition rates appear highest during the assessment phase when clients are engaging with treatment agents for the first time. It may be here that there is a serious "disconnect." While therapists are conducting an assessment of the case, clients are also engaged in an assessment. In early stages of therapeutic work, therapists are generally "an object of scrutiny rather than a partner in pursuit of relief" (Maramba & Castinguay, 2004). For involuntary referrals, a common characteristic of cases involving aggression (i.e., child protection services, courts, and the juvenile system refer them to us), the scrutiny might be heightened. The bar for failure is lower than when the relationship is more developed and clients feel the full brunt of our missteps (Maramba & Castanguay, 2004).

As in all new relationships, demand characteristics require us to mask negative experiences occurring early in therapy. Safran and his colleagues (Safran, Crocker, McMain, & Murray, 1990), who have written about the different forms that ruptures may take, argue that for clients who are not comfortable with expressing negative emotions, ruptures are most likely to take the form of avoidance. Although aggressive family members could be seen as potentially more "comfortable" with expressing such negative emotions, they also "know" firsthand that such emotions might lead to more "dangerous" consequences that could be especially problematic with outsiders to the family. Consequently, members of such families may be especially prone to engage in avoidance or nonresponsiveness. If they do not avoid, and actually confront, their methods for doing so may be jarring for a therapist. Given aggressive clients' non-normative ways of expressing negative affect, clinicians could find it difficult to remain neutral, perhaps recoiling at these distressing moments in treatment and leaving therapy derailed.

"Resistance," the potential for therapeutic ruptures, and the emotion generated by those ruptures, thus, may be seen as key issues in working with families where violence is the presenting problem. Patterson and others have shown that three out of four parents of children with conduct problems exhibit significant resistance to intervention, more than typically found in other populations (Chamberlain, Patterson, Reid, Kavanagh, & Forgatch, 1984; O'Dell, 1982; Patterson & Chamberlain, 1988). Although ruptures are seen as evidence of "trouble' in the therapeutic relationship, they are also seen as a natural part of the change process. Indeed, in some intervention work, ruptures are more likely during the most critical phase of intervention (i.e., when the therapist is training the very skills needed to affect change), where parents show what Patterson and Chamberlain call "I can't" and "I won't" symptoms, clear examples of *direct* evidence of a treatment rupture in a typology offered by Saffran and colleagues (Saffran, et al., 1990). In Patterson and Chamberlain's discussion, we see hints that therapists must be wary of how they respond at this point. Parents' responses are seen as potentially undermining therapist motivation and efforts to remain engaged in the process of change. Disengagement has been shown to result in decreased liking for and support to parents, in withdrawal of efforts to teach new skills, in failures to confront parents about their resistance, and in loss of interest in parents' progress and whether they even keep appointments. Therapists essentially may let their client fail (Patterson & Chamberlain, 1988, p. 194).

Working with clients with histories of violence has also been said to impact strongly the affective state of the therapist. Therapists often hear verbal descriptions of violence or may even witness firsthand the consequences of their clients' violence. For example, in work with child-abusing families, the clinician may arrive at the home for a parent-training session and find a bruised and crying child just after an abusive incident has occurred. Vicarious trauma responses have been documented in professionals who work with those who perpetrate and are victims of violence (Figley, 1995; McCann & Pearlman, 1990; Miller, 1998). The first author has further suggested that escalating affective dysregulation may be a common reaction among such therapists and, over time, if not addressed, may lead to overly negative or disengaged interactions with clients. In the extreme, vicarious trauma responses might even disrupt the course of clinical supervision designed to rectify such situations (Azar, 2000). Ultimately, therapist "burnout" may result, but not before much damage is done to the therapy process. Thus, in line with the other discussions in this volume, this is yet another area where emotion and perhaps anger specifically must be considered in treatment work with violent clients. Emotion could negatively impact the work with any given family, but it also may affect the longevity of professionals in the field.

Negative Affect in Therapists

Although most discussions of clashes with clients have focused on emotion in the client (transferential reactions), less has been said about emotion within the therapist (the exception being discussions of counter-transference). Early in the field of cognitive-behavioral work, for example, this topic was ignored. Indeed, cognitive therapeutic work has been faulted for its lack of attention to emotion in general. As Leahy (2001) put it: "Our underlying assumption was, 'if the transference doesn't touch you, don't touch the transference.' Certainly if we ignored the transference, we would ignore our own counter-transference. Perhaps we were overly optimistic about the power of the techniques, treatment plans, and "professionalism" that our approach offered" (p. 240). Yet, even when emotion-laden clashes in treatment are discussed, the focus is still almost exclusively on the client. In Leahy's volume on resistance in CBT work, seven chapters are devoted to client resistance and only two to counter-transference. Even these two chapters return to clients' difficulties as triggers and the need for therapists to "protect" themselves from clients' pathology-based reactions.

In a rare, direct look at therapist negative emotion, object relations theorists have gone so far as to discuss therapist "hate" of the client who behaves in ways that are experienced by therapists as primitive and regressed. Again, blaming the client's "pathology," Winnicott (1949) argued that such clients place an emotional burden on the therapist. However, he also argued that such "hate" is crucial and must be sorted out and "stored" for later interpretation, potentially to be fed back to clients as part of the therapeutic work. Thus, Winnicott saw acceptance and acknowledgment of such negative emotions as important, but he did not go so far as to consider what in the therapist may account for the rupture. Safran (1993) does mention the idea that therapists' poorly timed interventions can trigger a rupture, but then continues to focus on client-based process issues to understand those ruptures.

Negative Affect in Clients

Clients' emotions are also high at points of rupture. It has been argued in the therapy engagement literature that ruptures require clients to confront therapists with their disappointment or distress and then to negotiate the discordance they feel—with a heightened alliance resulting if all goes well (Maramba & Castonguay, 2004). The very same capacities needed to identify and address a rupture successfully—the ability to recognize one's own negative affect and the reasons for this affect, and to address it in a ways that improve the situation—are all capacities with which aggressive clients have difficulty. Thus, ruptures may be much harder for them to identify, to confront, and to negotiate. Addressing ruptures in relationships, it could be argued, is central to therapy with clients who engage in violent behavior. As Safran (1993) argues, the therapeutic relationship is a "meeting between adults" and it is these "adult" moments in treatment where therapists and clients assume responsibility for breaches in the alliance that change can occur. Therefore, it is crucial to have frameworks for understanding therapeutic ruptures when working with families where violence has occurred.

Unfortunately, there is ample evidence that we, as therapists, are not negotiating ruptures well. For example, attrition rates in therapy are generally high. In child psychotherapy, specifically, there is a 15% to 35% no-show rate for the first appointment following the initial telephone request for service (Kourany, Garber, & Tournusciolo, 1990). Across various parent-training studies, between 28% and 59% of families drop out of treatment (Forehand, Middlebrook, Rogers, & Steffe, 1983; Gould, Shaffer, & Kaplan, 1985; Kazdin, 1996). However, families whose members are prone to violence account for the highest rates. For example, in parent-training studies, the worst attrition rates are found for families with children who have externalizing problems (e.g., conduct disorder). Kazdin and Mazurick (1994) found that children's history of antisocial behavior and the variety of their conduct disorder symptoms were both significant predictors of dropout rates. In treating children with persistent conduct disorder problems, Luk, Staiger, Mathai, Wong, Birleson, and Adler (2001) reported dropout rates of 36% and 48%. These findings suggest there are factors specific to families with aggressive children that increase the likelihood of early therapy termination. High parental stress, a common characteristic found across families where violence is an issue, also appears to be associated with high dropout rates. This pattern is also evident in work with adults in violent families, including families with abusive parents (e.g., dropout rates from 32% to 87%; Reid, 1985; Wolfe, Aragona, Kaufman, & Sandler, 1980) and violent husbands (e.g., noncompletion rates in the 90% range; DeHart, Kennerly, Burke, & Follingstad, 1999; Gondolf & Foster, 1991).

Even if clients stay in treatment, therapists might also complain of noncompliance with their efforts. That is, attendance does not equate with quality of participation. The first author has actually witnessed clients attending parenting groups to address child maltreatment issues doing crossword puzzles during therapy sessions or staring out the window. Problems with homework compliance and lack of involvement in sessions are common (Azar & Wolfe, 1998). One batterer study found that only about one fifth of the women reported that partners involved in the intervention program had actually attempted to implement strategies learned at home (Gregory & Erez, 2002).

It also appears that when the "bottom-line" measure of treatment change is considered, we are not very successful in changing the behavior of violent families. Between 20% and 70% of parents who engage in child maltreatment reabuse or reneglect their children (Williams, 1983). In the domestic violence literature, only 20% to 40% of batterers cease their abusive behavior over a 2-year follow-up period (Aldarondo & Sugarman, 1996; Quigley & Leonard, 1996). In one study, 20% of female partners of men participating in batterer intervention programs reported that treatment actually increased conflict in the relationship and overall (Gregory & Erez, 2002). Rearrest rates for serious youth offenders in traditional individual therapy can run as high as 71%[2] and even in comprehensive multisystem interventions (i.e., multi systemic therapy [MST]), rearrests can still be 22% (Henggeler, Melton, & Smith, 1992). We are clearly not being very effective with violent clients.

Why Is Treatment Adherence and Effectiveness So Poor?

Given evidence that the therapeutic alliance is a prerequisite for change (Safran, 1993), one possible explanation for the attrition and recidivism data presented earlier is that we are not connecting with clients. That is, we in some way "turn them off" or fail to engage them in the change process (see Fig. 14.1). Examination of the little data on treatment process provides some support for this conclusion. Although client characteristics have been associated with attrition (e.g., severity of problems, demographic characteristics, contextual issues such as stress level), clients' reactions to therapy have been found to play an important role in treatment adherence. For example, high dropout rates found in conduct disorder are associated with self-reports of parental dissatisfaction and with

---

[2]As can be seen later, interventions that attend to the systemic needs of aggressive clients may be seen as therapists being sensitive to the negative influence of their life circumstances and thus, indicate common ground on which to build alliances (e.g., MST does this; Henggeler, Melton, & Smith, 1992).

| **Therapist's original culture** (e.g. racial and ethnic heritage, class) | **Culture of** psychology (e.g. assumed expertise, rules) | 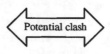 Potential clash | **Client culture** (e.g. ethnicity, race, class, traditional ways of addressing conflict, negative experiences with government agencies) |

Potential assumption clashes:
a) The nature of roles of family members
b) How family members should relate to one another
c) Who one should be asked for help and how one should relate to therapists
d) Most important, what strategies are acceptable and effective for conflict resolution

Failure to identify values-based rupture
1. Both therapist and client experience negative affect
2. Therapist empathic failure, bias toward labeling as evidence of client "pathology," or further stigmatizing response
3. Client:
   a. Withdrawal
   b. Resistance
   c. Noncompliance
   d. Disengagement
   e. And risk of attrition & recidivism

Successfully identify values-based rupture
1. Identify values clash and acknowledgment of therapist contribution to rupture
2. Explore the rupture with the client
3. Negotiate resolution with client
4. Alliance repair

FIGURE 14.1.   Values-based therapeutic ruptures

lower clinician ratings about the projected success of treatment (Luk et al., 2001). Is it possible that parents were dissatisfied with treatment specifically because of their own sense that therapists doubted therapy would be successful? This suggests that dropout rates in violent families may be associated with therapist factors. The field has long blamed clients for ruptures in clinical work when in fact it may be therapists' behavior that needs to be given more scrutiny. If we can identify and address therapist factors, we can develop interventions for violent families with a greater chance of success (Azar, 1996; Maramba & Castonguay, 2004).

The most frequently cited explanation for alliance problems with violent clients is that these clients are mandated consumers of our services. They are not voluntary clients, but are sent to us by the child protection system and by adult, family, and juvenile court systems. These clients do not define themselves as having a problem; rather, someone else has defined this for them. Yet, data suggest that with external pressure our violence-prone clients tend to stay in treatment at higher rates. Indeed, data both with child-abusing parents and with batterers show that having attendance monitored by others predicts better attendance (DeHart et al., 1999; Wolfe et al., 1980). So, we cannot be comforted by the notion that their involuntary status is the problem. We would suggest a more discomforting possibility.

We suggest that there is a clash of values or belief systems that leads to "empathic failures" on therapists' part, which then leads to negative affect and ultimately to breaches in therapeutic alliance. First, we discuss at length the idea that ruptures are evidence of assumption differences between therapist and client (disparities in deeply held beliefs/values). The points at which assumptions clash include (a) the nature of roles of family members, (b) how family members should relate to one another, (c) who one should go to for help and how one should relate to therapists, and most important, (d) what are acceptable and effective conflict-resolution strategies. Potential differences in assumptions come from a mix of demographically based factors on which aggressive clients differ from therapists (socioeconomic status, ethnic and racial background differences, and what follows from these—life experiences, deeply held patterns of operating) and prejudices therapists hold because of our sanctioned role as healers and the collective beliefs set forth by our profession. This model argues that therapists can negotiate ruptures more effectively and maintain better alliances with clients if we viewed dispassionately the fact that we are operating from different assumptive foundations.

Second, we present a contrasting model drawn from social-psychological theories that places greater weight on therapists' emotional reactions and behavior. This model would require conceiving of therapists rupture-triggering behaviors as evidence of "prejudice" from the family's perspective.

This second model outlines the nature of this perceived threat and the conditions under which persons experiencing prejudice are likely to confront those who are being prejudicial. From this model, we can understand why clients do or do not leave treatment or engage in avoidant and nonresponsive behavior, and thus provide a place where their perceived prejudice can be worked through and alliances strengthened.

Evidence for Values Clash: Racial/Ethnic and Social-Class Differences and Unique "Culture" of Violent Families

It has been said that mental health professionals observe families through "cultural filters" that operate outside their awareness (Watzlawick, 1976) and that these filters can persist in spite of clear evidence to the contrary. Cultures delineate the nature of roles in families (e.g., how children and parents, as well as husbands and wives, should relate to each other and what their respective "job" descriptions are), how help seeking should take place, and what the relationships should be with helpers outside the family (e.g., who is an allowable helper, how much control one should have in the help-seeking transaction, the directness, and indeed the moment-by-moment process of contact) (Azar & Benjet, 1994). Similar discussions have taken place regarding social class as well, although our cultural belief in a "classless" society seems to preclude mention of social class as an issue in therapeutic work.[3] In previous decades where the issue of class was briefly a more acceptable part of clinical dialogue (1970s), therapy research went so far as to discuss therapy preparation work, to socialize the client to the therapeutic process (Heitler, 1976). As can be seen below, we suggest that perhaps therapy preparation work around social class is needed for therapists as well, as is often discussed around training in cultural sensitivity.

First, most therapists are not members of the same social class or ethnic/racial group as clients. Indeed, the paucity of minority clinicians is striking: Only 9.6% of mental health professionals in the workforce were minorities in 2002 (American Psychological Association, 2002), compared to 20% to 30% in the general population. The "right" minorities are also lacking. For example, in California, which had 300,000 refugees in the 1990s, a survey identified only 18 licensed mental health care providers in public settings familiar with Southeast Asian language and culture (10 psychiatrists, 8 social workers; all Vietnamese; none were Cambodian,

---

[3]The Supplement to the Surgeon General's Report on Mental Health (U.S. Department of Health and Human Services, 2001) cites social-class differences as underlying what may appear to be cultural, racial, and ethnic biases in clinicians' treatment of clients and that it is these biases that may act as barriers to service utilization (p. 33).

Laotian, Hmong, or Mieng) (cited in Gong-Guy, Cravens, & Patterson, 1991). The wide gap of cultural experiences between professionals and the clients they serve cannot help but lead to misunderstandings, and these sociocultural disparities are likely to be overrepresented among clients referred because of their violent behavior.

The "culture" of families touched by violence also represents a worldview of relationships that is disparate from that held by most therapists. Such differences may be the source of the strongest fissures in the family–therapist relationship. A father who says his child is "his" (meaning his property) and he "can do what he wants with him" (including breaking his legs), or a mother who leaves her infant in a crib while she goes out drinking with her friends, can seem like aliens to mental health professionals who, if anything, are overly empathic with their children and hold higher standards of parental conduct than is typical of society as a whole. For example, Peterson, Ewigman, and Kivlahan (1993), in studying standards for supervision of children, found that although there was some overlap in views between professionals and parents, professionals clearly ascribed to a greater need for supervision than parents. Examples of gross disparities in worldviews are easily identified, but a continuum of disparities may exist and more subtle ones could result in unconscious and negative "moral" judgments on the part of professionals. Although recognizing cultural, racial, or social-class differences is difficult and may improve with sensitivity training, being sensitive and understanding about these differences when they concern family violence may be nearly impossible at times.

Therapeutic ruptures catch therapists off guard and thus, they are not prepared to deal with them when they happen. Human information processing is automatized and ruptures may be too quickly labeled as "resistance" and as the client's fault (e.g., a lack of investment or lack of desire for change, sabotaging treatment). Azar and Benjet (1994) provide many examples where potential for bias may surface in working with parents who are living in poverty or with parents who are from ethnic and racial minority groups. Some of these examples are listed later to provide a starting point for predicting when therapeutic ruptures might happen and for preventing them in the first place. In these examples, one can easily see what might be labeled as evidence of "resistance." Those involving ethnicity, race, and social class are listed first followed by ones that are often labeled "irrational" beliefs within families touched by violence. Readers should notice that the first set of examples includes both client and therapist elements. Although not as apparent in the area of irrational beliefs, evidence exists for a range of such beliefs in our society, suggesting some validation of what might be considered our clients "more irrational" beliefs in their everyday lives.

The Changing Face of America's Families: Differing Beliefs, Family Practices, and Ways of Relating to Therapists

A discussion of values requires a delineation of the nature of the populations with whom we deal. In the United States, our society is in the process of undergoing a massive transformation in its demographic characteristics. In 1990, approximately 30% of all American children were members of minority groups and this will increase to about 50% by the year 2030 (National Research Council, 1998). One fifth of the children in America are either immigrants or the sons and daughters of immigrant parents, with the majority of Hispanic or Asian origin (National Research Council, 1998).[4] One in five children in this country also live in poverty and more of these children come from minority families.

Parenting, Child Maltreatment, and, Conduct Disorder. Ethnic and racial minorities and families from lower socioeconomic status (SES) backgrounds are disproportionately represented among child abuse cases. In 2001, one fourth of all child maltreatment cases were African American; 15% were Hispanic. American Indian/Alaska Natives accounted for 2% of victims, and Asian/Pacific Islanders accounted for 1% of victims (Administration on Children, Youth and Families, 2001; http://nccanch.acf.hhs.gov/pubs/factsheets/canstats.cfm). This group is overwhelmingly from lower SES backgrounds (Pelton, 1994).

There also is an overrepresentation of minorities and low-SES teens in those diagnosed with conduct disorder. African American youth are also overrepresented among those arrested for violent crimes (Reiss & Roth, 1993). African American youth account for 52% of youth arrested for violent crimes, even though they make up only 15% of the juvenile population (Dryfoos, 1990).[5] Poverty is also one of the strongest predictors of youth violence (Centerwall, 1984), although its impact appears to occur through disrupted parenting and changes it produces in family life (Guerra, Huesmann, Tolan, Van Acker, & Eron, 1995).

The parenting styles and practices of lower SES parents are different from those of middle-class ones, and these differences must be considered as potential sources of value clashes when working with child-maltreating

---

[4]It should be noted that within each of the labels, Hispanic and Asian, are embedded multiple subcultures, all of which may have slightly different ideas about family life and relationships with professionals, even though we treat them as somewhat homogeneous in our discussion.

[5]It must be noted, however, that the data on self-reported offenses demonstrate a much narrower difference between the prevalence of violence between Blacks and Whites (Elliot, 1994). This fact may not be lost on minority families and may contribute to potential for ruptures (e.g., perceiving that their children are being discriminated against).

parents and with families of conduct-disordered youth. That is, some of the patterns of interaction exhibited by families touched by violence are ones shared with other members of their social-class group. Some of these patterns could reflect commonly held religious or cultural values (e.g., "spare the rod and spoil the child"). As therapists, we may, because of our cultural perspective, view these patterns as reflective of parenting attitudes and behaviors that are nonmainstream or maladaptive. Our attempts to induce "healthier" functioning could contradict parents' own experience of being "normal" relative to families surrounding them and could require, in some cases, giving up deeply held religious convictions. Thus, from the perspective of some families, it is the therapist who is "wrong" (note that the idea of abusive parents falling on a continuum with other parents is not held by all researchers in the field; see Azar & Wolfe, 1998).

The parenting styles of poor parents are often qualitatively different from those of middle-and upper-class parents, although it must be pointed out that there is as much variability among poor families as there is between poor and other families (Hess, 1970). Differences might reflect differing priorities in lower-class work environments that value and reward obedience and respectfulness more than independence (Kohn, 1963). Parents with these priorities might tailor their socialization practices to what they "know" will ensure their children's "competence" in the world in which they will live (i.e., they are acting as "competent" socialization agents). Lower SES parents also report feeling less control over the later outcomes of their children. Working-class parenting is oriented more toward obedience and order, less democratic, more authoritarian and parent centered, and more permissive (Azar, 1996). These are not the climates touted by developmental psychologists as "good" for children's adjustment and well-being. Note, however, there are some data that some of these characteristics may in fact predict better adjustment in inner-city, urban, and high-risk neighborhoods (A. Baldwin, Baldwin, & Cole, 1990). Thus, the very parenting behaviors we as therapists do not value may be useful for children under some conditions. Like verbal style, parenting practices differ and therapists may not see the leap they are asking some parents to make, believing erroneously that what is recommended is "natural" and, therefore, should be adaptive and easy to master.

Our own research has found evidence that mothers' perceptions of and responses to their children's behavior vary depending on ethnicity and SES. For example, we have found that in a general sample of families, lower SES parents from Asian and Latino cultures tend to make more external attributions for their children's aggressive and antisocial behavior (Diriwachter & Azar, 2002). Therapists may view this tendency as failing to instill in children "taking responsibility for one's actions."

Ethnically diverse parents are also likely to respond to certain types of aggressive behavior more strongly (i.e., in ways that appear more extreme and less coherent from clinicians' perspective) and will use techniques that are atypical in our clinically traditional lexicon of parenting (e.g., Asian parents use of "the silent" treatment). Even efforts to get parents to "manage" children's behavior may fly in the face of worldviews that consider this not within parental control but due to factors external to the family (Lieh-Mak, Lee, & Luk, 1984).

Couple Relationships and Domestic Violence. Although space constraints limit the discussion of SES, racial, and ethnic differences in worldviews regarding marital and cohabiting relationships, similar disparities may occur in work with clients referred for domestic violence. Families living in poverty and racial and ethnic minorities are similarly overrepresented in incidence rates of domestic violence (Greenfield et al., 1998; Raphael, 1997; West, 2004;). Studies suggest that domestic violence is viewed differently across racial and ethnic groups (Locke & Richman, 1999; Nayak et al., 2003). Ideas about marriage and gender roles also tend to vary. For example, the balance of power in marital relationships is often viewed as tipped strongly in favor of men in many minority cultures (e.g., Latino and Middle Eastern cultures). In other subgroups, because of the typical composition of households, women are more often the decision maker (e.g., a high percentage of female-headed households in low-SES African American families). Another example is the use of "love" as a motivator for change in marital therapy. Some cultures place greater emphasis in marriage on the legal contract, guaranteeing a family's economic and social welfare (e.g., in arranged marriages) or on the joining of families or of the continuation of the family. At best, these differing assumptions could lead to interactions that are confusing to therapists and at worst, to ones that are seen as resistant.

Relationships With Helpers. Along with influencing relationships within the family, social class and culture can also lead to potential differences in relationship formation with therapists and other professional helpers. These differences could lead to failures to buffer therapeutic relationships from the inevitable "disappointments" that occur and from efforts to repair these ruptures. In many cultures, one does not go outside the family with problems, but rather to relatives. Talking to strangers about family relationships and one's feelings could be seen as inappropriate, making clients' interactions with therapists appear disengaged or difficult. For some subgroups, going to see a therapist is associated with having medical or physical problems and the expectation of receiving medicine as opposed to talk therapy (Gong-Guy et al., 1991). This perception alone could produce a rupture (e.g., disappointment in clients). Attendance at therapy could also carry with it risks for members of some cultural groups. For example, having a mental illness could affect the marriageability of other members of the family (Gong-Guy et al., 1991) and thus should be avoided at all costs. Therapists who are not sensitive to such issues might misinterpret families' response to interventions as well as their level of participation.

Cultures also see psychotherapy differently. Psychotherapy reflects not only a society's conceptualizations of illness and health, but also its values. Ethnic groups, therefore, are likely to approach therapy differently. Frank (1985) argues, for example, that in American psychotherapy, patient and therapist are generally required to work at some form of mutual activity to justify spending time together and increased autonomy is regarded as an important feature of mental health. Other cultures might find these attitudes astonishing. For them, simply being together is a worthwhile end in itself and dependency on others is a valued feature of life (Neki, 1973; Pande, 1968). Therapists might regard such families as "killing time" and not "really engaged." They may also be seen as not making progress in that they may be "obligated" culturally to portray a dependence on the therapist out of "respect." Such tendencies could also affect the handling of ruptures in treatment. Clients from cultures in which authority is greatly revered might be unwilling to admit when they don't understand or agree with therapists, further complicating the therapeutic process. Cultural scripts dictating respectful politeness could result in apparent acquiescence despite clients not understanding or intending to go along with recommendations (Casas, 1992). Immigrant families from countries with repressive governments that prohibited openly disputing authorities could be reticent to dispute therapists' assertions, thereby reducing the potential for ruptures to lead eventually to alliance building.

Testifying to the importance of a common worldview between clients and therapists is the fact that ethnic match and "cultural-sensitivity" services have been shown to be linked to success in therapy. For example, data from a health prevention program with Hispanic clients suggest that the provision of materials in Spanish and messages aimed at culturally relevant motivation (e.g., reminding participants of their role as behavioral referents to their children) are more successful with individuals who are less acculturated and more dependent on Spanish to communicate (Marin, Perez-Stable, Sabogal, & Otero-Sabogal, 1990). Data from a study of family coordinators doing prevention work with children at risk for conduct disorder showed that both the quantity and quality of parent participation was predicted by SES match and commonality of life experiences (Orrell-Valente, Pinderhughes, Valente, & Laird, 1999). These investigators found that racial and SES similarity and commonality of life experiences for parents and family coordinators were highly associated with therapeutic engagement. Engagement was in turn associated with rate of parental attendance at group training sessions. So engagement may in part be determined by experiencing a sense that intervention agents know what families' life is like and how they might view issues.

The "Values," Beliefs, and Social-Interaction Patterns of Families Touched by Violence

So far we have addressed ways in which SES, ethnicity, and race affect the ways families organize themselves and interact with professional helpers. These culturally specific differences could also account for why the inter- action patterns of violence-prone families are seen by therapists as con- fusing or somewhat "alien." However, violent families could also have their own unique set of beliefs and relational practices that are disparate from those of therapists, including how families should be organized, whether "violence" has indeed been perpetrated (i.e., whether the behav- ior in fact needs changing), and whether its cause is intrinsic to family members or is caused by others external to the family. It is rare to find a family member who sees his or her recurring pattern of aggressive behav- ior as the core problem.

Where therapists see "violence," parents, spouses, and youth from violence-prone families are likely to see "acceptable" conflict resolution strategies and expressions of emotion that fall within normative bounds (e.g. "normative" for their immediate/extended family, their racial/ ethnic group, their social class). It is noteworthy that child-maltreating fam- ilies are often socially isolated, like families living on an island where the larger cultures' norms touch them little. Indeed, social isolation is charac- teristic of many families touched by violence. No contact means fewer chal- lenges to family norms. Such "island" life is not just physical but also cognitive such that families are less open to new input. Indeed, some clients describe in a neutral tone incident after incident that clinicians would see as very abusive and violent. The first author has family members keep diaries of conflict situations and it is only through recording over and over again such incidents and reading them aloud in therapy sessions that families begin to see the pattern of violence that is occurring.

Intergenerational data on relationship violence clearly support clinical observations of ingrained differences in how families define the problem. The likelihood that maltreated children will maltreat their own children has been estimated to be as high as 25% (Kaufman & Zigler, 1987). In ret- rospective report studies, women and men who grow up with domestic violence report heightened rates of violence in their dating or marital relationships (Ehrensaft et al., 2003; Kalmuss, 1984). Exposure to violent role models seems to lead to violence as an acceptable part of couple and family life. Indeed, O'Leary, Malone, and Tyree (1994) found that women in stable violent relationships tended to discount the significance of aggression directed toward them. That is, couples in highly stable aggressive relationships did not identify themselves as less relationally dissatisfied. Thus, individuals' exposure to violence can influence beliefs about what is acceptable (or tolerated) relationship behavior.

Further evidence that what therapists label as aberrant might be part of the family "culture" is the high degree of overlap between battering and child abuse in families. Physical child abuse is committed at high rates by both batterers (between 47% and 54%) and victims of battering (between 28% and 35%; Saunders, 1994). Even though women have directly experienced the effects of violence concurrently and historically in their childhood, they are still prone to engaging in it with their own children. Violence is also a highly stable part of relationship interactions, as indicated by the high recidivism rates noted earlier in both domestic violence and child maltreatment. Such families may in fact be "comfortable" with the occurrence of high levels of aggression: One study found that 37% of men and 43% of women reported aggressing against their married and cohabiting partner in the last year (O'Leary et al., 1989).

Another piece of evidence that suggests the "dangerous" meaning of violence is not the same as might be perceived by therapists is the fact that men who batter their partners do not appear to protect their children from observing it. It has been estimated that between 3.3 million and 10 million children in the United States witness at least one violent incident directed at their mother (Fantuzzo & Mohr, 1999). Moreover, some of these children report becoming involved in the incidents. Thus in violence-prone families, aggressive conflict resolution strategies appear to be a stable and continuous part of family life and all members are participating.

There are other beliefs about family relationships that differ for violent and nonviolent families (Azar & Twentyman, 1986). Clinically, maltreating parents have shown to possess a set of schemas regarding children, parental roles, and how parents and children interact that are different from those found in nonmaltreating parents (Azar, 1986, 1989, 1997a; Azar et al., 2005). The schemas of maltreating parents appear to have more unrealistic, less flexible, and more negatively toned elements. Even young children are viewed as functionally equivalent in their capacities to those of adults, as able to take care of their own needs and those of the parent. These schemas also include beliefs in their children's having higher levels of social-cognitive and physical-care abilities: beliefs that a 3-year-old can comfort parents when they are upset, that a 4-year-old can pick out the right clothing for the weather, or that a teenager can help patch up parents' marital problems (Azar, Robinson, Hekimian, & Twentyman, 1984; Azar & Rohrbeck, 1986; Haskett, Scott, Grant, Ward, & Robinson, 2003). Parent groups at risk for other forms of aggression (e.g., substance-abusing mothers) show similar difficulties (Spieker, Gilmore, Lewis, Morrison, & Lohr, 2001).

Also disparate is maltreating parents' schema about their roles as parents. They believe more strongly that punishment is what a parent "should do" and that power-assertive strategies will be effective and that inductive ones will be less effective (Caselles & Milner, 2000). They are likely to hold a role definition of parenting that requires them to have absolute control over their children (Peterson et al., 1997). This belief may stem from a tendency to perceive themselves as having less control as a parent (i.e., children having more power over outcomes than they do) and an overly generalized concern regarding dominance (Bugental, Blue, & Cruzcosa, 1989). It has been argued that parents with low perceived control have stored schemas regarding power that can be activated by merely anticipating child difficulties. This hypersensitivity to potential dominance concerns could contribute to negative responses to therapists' suggestions for more benign disciplinary interventions.

Maltreating parents are also more likely to experience their children as engaging in aversive behavior with negative intent (Haskett et al., 2003; Larrance & Twentyman, 1983). Abusive mothers are also likely to have an expectation of being negatively evaluated by others, including therapists (Shorkey, 1980). Such expectations have been shown to increase self-criticism, which can disrupt cognitive processing and produce negative affect, contributing to less effective interaction and task performance (M. W. Baldwin, 1997). Again, this suggests a greater potential for interpreting therapist feedback as criticism. Indeed, when such parents are faced with their child's tantrums in a grocery store, their attention is focused on others' likely judging them negatively instead of on efforts to manage their child's distress and behavior.

Evidence for "biased" information processing has also been found for other groups contributing to the level of violence within a family. Qualitative work with couples in battering relationships has revealed the use of mutually acceptable stories about the battering that function as a "neutralizing" technique that allows the couple to stay together (Dutton, 1986; Hyden, 1994). Eisikovits, Goldblatt, and Winstok (1999) argue that these narratives might balance the negative impact of the violent act by altering its meaning or focusing instead on hope for a good life. In studying the narratives of a small group of violent couples, Elsikovitz et al. found that couples typically began their stories asserting that their expectations were those of the normative culture. Couples then reframed their use of violence in acceptable terms that defused the intent ("I pushed her unintentionally. She got hit by the wall, fell, and lost consciousness."); the severity ("I hit her gently."); and the frequency ("It's seldom ever that I hit her. I wouldn't call that violence.") of the violence. The mutuality of these defusing narratives is well illustrated by the following two accounts that one couple provided for the cause of a violent incident. The man explained: "I slapped her only because the situation became risky. You know, it's my responsibility to protect us from dangerous things." His partner agreed: "He slapped me to get me back on track ... Who knows what would have happened without this?" (Eisikovitz et al., 1999, p. 612). A traditional gender role of "protector" is used here to normalize a behavior that therapists are not likely to view as normal.

This example illustrates the tendency for battering men to have unusual beliefs regarding women and male–female relationships, in addition to exhibiting a negative attributional bias when processing couple interactions (Hastings, 2000; Holzworth-Munroe & Hutchinson, 1993). Aggressive youth also hold normative beliefs about the social appropriateness of aggression (Huesmann & Guerra, 1997) as well as information-processing biases such as attributing hostile motives to others and foreseeing meaningful benefits to aggressive solutions (Arnaldo, Dodge, Lochman, & Laird, 1999).

Families who experience intense conflict and violence are likely to view disagreements as potentially dangerous and to doubt the worth of "talking out" differences of opinion. Men who batter women are also more likely to see disagreement in relationships as more destructive than their nonviolent counterparts. These tendencies could make disagreeing with therapists problematic and make therapists' request to discuss relationship problems during a session especially difficult. If batterers also believe that women enjoy humiliating men, they could also be more sensitive to the slights when working with female therapists.

Therapists might label divergent beliefs as evidence of social-cognitive "problems," but to the families involved, these "problems" are just what they believe. If therapists are to have a foothold for challenging maladaptive beliefs, they will need to titrate how they respond emotionally and "accept" clients' beliefs as coming from a "different" belief system than that of the therapist. As therapists, we will also need to accept the possibility that families may see our beliefs as "problematic."

The "Culture" of Therapists: Challenges to Expert Role, Offensive Behavior, and Power Differential

We forget, at times, that therapists have "cultures" as well. As noted earlier, mental health professionals' ethnic and racial mix, and in most cases their social class, are likely to differ from that of most clients. As a result, many life experiences are not shared by clients and therapists. There is also the tendency for therapists to hold idealized notions about how families should operate, given training in what are optimal ways for families to function. As therapists, we see ourselves as the "experts" when it comes to family life. But families, despite coming to us for help, will not always acknowledge this "expertise." In areas where we have less knowledge, we might even question our expertise and, thus, experience some threat. When coupled with values disparities, threatened expertise can mean the potential for missteps and for failures in neutrality are great. There is also the potential for our "helping" behavior to be experienced by clients as "offensive." Real threat behavior on clients' parts (e.g., yelling or being mildly belligerent) could produce emotional reactions that further compromise neutrality. We also hold "power" over families or we are perceived as having power (e.g., we may be required to report to authorities clients' progress). Without some added effort at humility on our part, this perceived power could make it difficult for families to believe that therapists are on their side or even neutral. These issues are explored briefly later.

The psychological knowledge base specific to working with minorities and family violence remains somewhat limited. For example, only 3% to 8% of articles in major child development journals from 1979 to 1993 were devoted to families who were racially or ethnically diverse (Cauce, Ryan, & Grove, 1998; Graham, 1992). Data on the effectiveness of interventions with racial and ethnic minorities generally, and in the context of parent training or marital work in particular, is sparse (Armistead et al., 2004; Azar, 1989; Forehand & Kotchik, 1996; Leslie & Morton, 2001; Malgady, Rogler, & Constantino, 1987; Saks-Berman, 1989). In addition to limited knowledge about treating family violence, many therapists do not have the training needed to do this work (Azar & Wolfe, 1998; National Research Council, 1993). This lack of "expertise" could lead to discomfort and lessen therapists' sense of efficacy as they work.

If therapists are "in the dark" about what works, then their sense of being an "expert" is more tenuous and even typical challenges to this expertise will be difficult to negotiate. When roadblocks occur in treatment, a self-protective bias could lead therapists to blame families rather than attributing ruptures to a failure to understand families' diverse cultural beliefs and values, limitations in training, community-level factors that interfere with service utilization, or even justifiable mistrust of so-called "experts" from the majority culture (Azar, 1996; Forehand & Kotchik, 1996; Snell-Johns, Mendez, & Smith, 2004). Although perhaps a natural reaction for therapists, it becomes problematic when therapists do not recognize it as their responsibility and instead continue to blame the client.

Clients who violate the rituals of treatment represent additional challenges to therapists' "expertise." For example, in assessing whether clients have complied with treatment, therapists typically consider—in addition to evidence of changes in behavior—attendance at sessions, responsiveness to feedback, ability to form relationships with professional caregivers, integration of information provided (e.g., demonstration of new skills), and ongoing help-seeking behavior. Here again, because of ethnic and racial differences in the meaning of these behaviors, these data would not necessarily reflect families' investment or progress in treatment. Cultural groups vary in their tolerance for strangers doing parent training in the home, in the emphasis placed on formal appointments, or in the ease by which they seek help from nonfamily members (Kim, McLeod, & Shantzis, 1992). Attending treatment regularly also requires resources that are not available on a consistent basis for all social classes (e.g., a car that works, being able to leave work early). These differences might inappropriately color the impression formed by professional caregivers.

Some immigrant groups came to the United States after facing repressive governmental intrusions, which can influence how they react to bureaucratic system representatives. For example, the Children's Defense Fund in New York City has begun a campaign to get immigrant families to sign up for medical care to which their children are entitled. In assessing barriers to signing up for such benefits, fear of deportation was cited as a major obstacle—even for legal immigrants (Children's Defense Fund, 2003). Therapists who engage in authoritarian behavior could invoke such fears and produce unexpected ruptures in therapeutic alliance or slow the progress of therapy. Therapists should be aware that that seemingly "subtle" transgressions of cultural scripts can add up and lead to mild frustration or irritation, to hampering the formation of the client–therapist relationship, and to erroneous attributions about the cause of therapeutic ruptures.

Language barriers can also influence therapists' judgments about families' responsiveness to treatment. Using relatives or community members as interpreters can add complexity to the therapeutic relationship and slow process. This practice could also be seen by family members as a violation of privacy, which can produce emotional distance and lead to unrecognized resentment on the professional's part.

Therapists' scripts for interpersonal interactions could be viewed by families as dissonant and at times offensive. For example, getting right down to business without polite small talk, using first names, having children be translators, and directly demanding personal disclosures could all be seen as offensive to Hispanic parents (Barbosa, Carr, & Johnson, 1992; Falicov, 1982; Garcia-Preto, 1982). At the same time, applying stereotyped cultural views to all families blindly (e.g., the view that all Mexican fathers will be resistant to therapy) could lead to self-fulfilling prophecies (Falicov, 1982). Therapists have been shown to be quite adept at predicting which families will drop out of interventions (Bischoff & Sprenkle, 1993; Russell, Lang, & Brett, 1987), but it may be therapists' expectations that produce this outcome (Snell-Johns et al., 2004). Therapy techniques could also fly in the face of family religious beliefs (Peterson et al., 1997). Religion, prayer, and spirituality can be of varying importance to families' coping style and if treatment does not encourage or respect families' views, members may not feel accepted and may "resist" treatment (Snell-Johns et al., 2004).

Fear on the part of therapists could also influence their judgment and lead to missteps in treatment. Working with minority families may involve going into violent neighborhoods or interviewing individuals who are angry and suspicious. The feelings engendered by these situations could lead to psychological distancing and difficulty forming a working relationship. A qualitative study of British child protection caseworkers suggested that when fathers were the perpetrator, caseworkers quickly shifted their attention over the course of work to mothers and their parenting (Farmer & Owen, 1998). It was suggested that caseworkers are fearful of violent men and in response change the target of their intervention. Unfortunately, this strategy reinforces the "norms" of the family (e.g., mom is to blame, dad can't be changed; dad's power is absolute and even the therapist knows it) and may reduce potential for change.

Social-psychological studies suggest that even low-prejudice individuals may behave in manners connoting prejudice when faced with conversations with minorities around "hot topics" (e.g., discussions of discrimination). Because of the topic, fear of behaving in a prejudicial manner changes their behavior. For example, in a laboratory study involving yet unmet minority partners, Goff (2004) found that when Caucasians anticipated having conversations on race relationships, they placed chairs farther apart than when they anticipated discussing a topic that was not so charged. If physical distancing when discussing heated topics extends to therapist–client interactions, this response could be viewed by clients as prejudicial behavior and responded to in accord with that labeling.

Overall, therapist behavior during family treatment has received little research attention. In an excellent review of evidence-based solutions for overcoming access barriers, decreasing attrition, and promoting change with underserved families, Snell-Johns et al. (2004) devoted only one paragraph to monitoring therapist behaviors and expectations, and empirical evidence was not presented. What has been studied is the effectiveness of changes in the structure of service delivery (e.g., home-based services) and in techniques (e.g., motivational interviewing) that prepare families—but not therapists—for the "culture" of treatment.

Conclusions

There may be a cumulative effect from family–therapist disparities in values and beliefs due to culture/class/race, disparities in normative beliefs and strategies for resolving conflict, and disparities in values inherent to therapeutic training (seeing oneself as the "expert"). We argue that these disparities help explain heightened levels of therapeutic ruptures in therapy with families touched by violence, and that these ruptures, in turn, lead to attrition and to noncompliance with or nonacceptance of therapeutic strategies. We also believe these disparities lead to heightened affect in both therapist and family members, and we see a need for greater attention to therapist-based ruptures if practitioners are to be effective in dealing with violence-prone clients. In the following section, we focus on therapist affect when "cultural" clashes occur. Anger and frustration are key emotional issues, but also fear and, at times, disgust at clients' behavior. Each can potentially influence whether therapy ruptures are negotiated or not.

THERAPIST-BASED FORMULATIONS OF RUPTURES

Before a discussion of therapist-caused ruptures can occur, it is important to make two points. First, therapists are not perfect; they are human. We humbly offer the ideas in this chapter as a way for clinicians to improve their practice, to better serve families who are struggling, and to help families function in ways that facilitate the development of all members. We would deeply regret misinterpretations of our thoughts as saying therapists are wrong to struggle with sadness, fear, anger, shock, and bewilderment when dealing with family members who have engaged in violent behavior. These are all natural reactions that speak to therapists' human caring about the safety of family members and about their own safety. Our purpose is to help clinicians identify how these emotional reactions can hinder further progress if their sources are not labeled correctly. If negative emotional reactions are embedded in the experiences of the therapist and not simply the difficulties of the family, and then incorrectly labeled, then these reactions could be deflected inappropriately onto the family and onto the therapy relationship. Second, because of the emotions generated in working with such families, the potential for therapy ruptures is great; these ruptures represent opportunities for strengthening the alliance or places where alienation and misinterpretation can occur. We argue that viewing and labeling ruptures as client resistance, rather than something emanating from the therapist, cuts off avenues for therapists to grow in their capacity to temper strong emotional reactions and decrease the likelihood of triggering ruptures in the first place.

To date, the ways in which therapeutic ruptures and alliance failures have been described and understood have been top-heavy with discussions of clients' pathology (e.g., Strupp, 1973). It is the therapeutic relationship that powers change, yet a relationship cannot exist unless family members feel their viewpoints are respected as being potentially "viable" (at least for the moment) and not dismissed too quickly. Feeling respected (and not "disrespected") is especially important for many minority-group members and for families who have encountered systems where they feel they have little power.

We would like to propose two other formulations that focus more squarely on therapists as the source of alliance ruptures. The first focuses on identifying and perhaps restructuring therapists' cognitions, in particular erroneous assumptions about client families and unrealistic expectations about what members *should* be doing (Azar, 1996). The second formulation takes this idea a little further and it is based on a frame that therapist–family disparities and subsequent negative emotional reactions are so great that therapy creates "stigmatizing" moments in which clients perceive therapists as being "prejudiced" toward them. With this latter formulation, we can draw on social psychological research on stigma and the determinants of outcomes once prejudice is experienced by individuals from a marginalized group.

These alternative formulations might be experienced negatively by clinicians reading this chapter. Indeed, these views resulted in noticeable angst when first presented at a recent conference. As one participant put it, "Are you saying we should *blame* the therapist?" Clearly, we do not intend that therapists engage in self-hostility as a reaction to our formulations. Indeed, hostility directed to the self by therapists will lead inevitably to hostility toward the client (Henry, Strupp, Butler, Schact, & Binder, 1993) and thus, exacerbate the problem. However, we argue that a process of disengaged self-questioning has merit. Based on critical race theory, members of majority cultures are often oblivious to when they are being prejudiced and their position of social power gives them privilege to label those who do not have power as "pathological" (Harris, 1995). Therefore, the potential for engaging in stigmatizing behavior is not so obvious to therapists.

Ruptures as the Result of Therapists' "Irrational Beliefs" or "Negatively Toned Schemas"

As noted earlier, when compared to families whose lives are touched by violence, therapists are likely to have very different assumptions about how families *should* work and how clients *should* relate to professionals. We believe that therapists are more likely to experience incongruence with deeply held schemas when working with diverse and lower SES families (Azar, 1996; Azar & Benjet, 1994) and with families who are also violent (Azar, 2000; Azar et al., 2005). Information-processing models of human judgment suggest this incongruence can introduce biases into clinicians' thinking. When others' behavior fails to fit our own schemas, we are likely to experience moments of dysynchrony in our interactions with them, we might experience negative affect, and we are more likely to attribute fault to something internal in the other (i.e., the fundamental attributional error). If the schemas one holds are inappropriate, overly narrow, or inflexible, error can be introduced into judgments made about others, resulting in faulty decision making and maladaptive responses. For example, studies conducted by the first author suggest that parents who have rigid expectations regarding children tend to label developmentally "normal" behavior as misbehavior and as intended to annoy them, which can lead to feeling distress and anger and to inappropriate discipline (Azar, 1986, 1989). Therapists are not immune from such cognitive errors (Dumont & Lecomte, 1987) nor from the negative affect and behavior that results from those errors.

It has been argued that therapists underestimate the influence of their own beliefs/values and affect on alliance development (Azar, 1996, 2000; Maramba & Castonguay, 2004). Schemas regarding poor and minority clients, in particular, can influence professionals' expectations and play a major role in failures to work effectively with them (Azar, 1996; Azar & Benjet, 1994). A history of trauma (not uncommon for clients who are affected by or involved in family violence) can result in responses that could also violate substantially therapists' expectations. These violated expectancies can produce affective dysregulation within the therapist that can affect their judgment and slow their work. For example, individuals exposed to high levels of aggression and violence, rather than finding closeness to others as positive, might experience it as threatening and thus react in ways that do not fit therapists' "scripts" for client behavior. Moments of ambiguity occur at such times and schema-based reactions can be activated. Therapists are human and are apt to respond in line with schemas based on their own unique "cultural beliefs" about threats to self and to their professional role (e.g., an "expertise" violation). These biased schemas come from a number of sources: media, therapists' professional training, as well as a frame for research knowledge that focuses on the risk status of poor and minority clients rather than strengths (Azar & Cote, 2002; Lorion, 1978; Polakow, 1993).[6] When therapy cases are not going well, these negative schemas are more likely to be activated (i.e., act as availability heuristics that, because of their vividness, act as prototypes), potentially distracting therapists from their work with families.

Furthermore, we know that experts will search their environment for those cues that elicit the greatest amount of information, shortening the decision tree used to reach a judgment (Fiske & Taylor, 1991). Labels such as "violent" or "aggressive" are associated with large amounts of vivid data, which could lead to premature and erroneous judgments about the meaning of interactions. These misjudgments include making disposi-tional attributions (e.g., moral failings, a disturbed personality) and using physical cues to form impressions (e.g., threatening looks, belligerent stances, loud voices). Individuals who have little experience with an out-group are also likely to make extreme inferences (Fiske & Taylor, 1991). Thus, clinicians inexperienced in work with marginalized populations could be even more susceptible to these processes.

There are other sources of biases in therapists' views that can emerge, particularly when working with violence-prone families. Therapists typi-cally are working in concert with agencies charged with enforcing laws, determining guilt, and engaging in punitive responses to exact restitution (i.e., child protection, court systems). Unfortunately, with constant com-merce with professionals from these other agencies, boundary problems can emerge and the thinking of therapists can come to parallel that of the legal community, resulting in a more punitive and moralizing stance toward our clients (Azar & Soysa, 1999). For example, an investigatory style as opposed to an information-gathering one can emerge when assessing families. This style can lead families to situate the therapist in the camp of those who are "against" the family. From the mandate to report abusive incidents to realistic fears for family members' safety, the pressure for therapists to drift in this direction is enhanced.

As therapists, it appears that our internal models of families who are touched by violence and our role in helping them may be overly simple, negatively toned, and inaccurate in many respects. Furthermore, clients

---

[6]Our clients are not unaware of such views. For example, a young teenage mother on public assistance with whom the first author worked, angrily noted how people looked neg-atively at her in the grocery store: "You could see it in their eyes . . . like I'd made a big mis-take. Like I screwed up my life and there was no way I could be a good mother." Such experiences of perceived overt disdain could lead families to be reluctant to seek treatment where such views are likely to be reinforced.

are often aware of these biases and limitations and if these are triggered in therapy, it could set up barriers to forming and sustaining collaborative relationships. These working models tend to operate outside of therapists' awareness and begin very early when processing cues presented by clients (Dumont & Lecomte, 1987). Seen in this light, alliance ruptures may have as much to do with therapists' "pathological" thinking as clients'.

Ruptures as Stigmatizing Moments in Treatment

Psychotherapy process research has suggested that the alliance is strengthened when clients confront their therapist with their discomfort during therapy ruptures and when these moments are successfully negotiated (Maramba & Castonguay, 2004; Safran, 1993). However, if one adopts the idea that therapeutic ruptures represent a clash in values (in the extreme), which is then perceived as stigmatizing by client, then it can be seen that confronting one's therapist can have both costs and benefits for some clients and families. For client groups marginalized because of minority status or SES or because their behavior is deemed to be non-normative by legal authorities, the costs may outweigh the benefits (Crosby, 1993; Shelton & Stewart, 2004). For example, out-groups often differ in their level of preparedness and sense of entitlement regarding their views and opinions. Lareau (2002) notes that from an early age, middle-class individuals are socialized to gain an emerging sense of entitlement in family life, whereas, lower-class and impoverished families and, in particular, minority families do not provide this same sense of entitlement when socializing their offspring. Lareau argues that this sense of entitlement gives middle-class individuals more resources for negotiating with professionals, leading to a cumulative advantage over the life course. Out-group members lack this advantage and the power required to confront a therapeutic rupture. Instead of a sense of entitlement, they carry a greater fear of negative repercussions.

Confronting one's therapist is further complicated when clients have poor impulse control. The consequences of clients' feeling frustrated or distressed are typically a negative affective discharge that can lead to detrimental behavior (e.g., violence). Thus, "leaving the scene" might be seen as "safer" for all concerned. Even in laboratory studies, if an out-group member does confront, it is likely to involve indirect actions such as nonverbal signs of disgust or sarcasm (Shelton & Stewart, 2004; Swim & Hyers, 1999).

At best, confrontation coping by out-group members will potentially lead to derogation by the target (i.e., the therapist, in this case), or worse, aggression and thus compounds the problem (Dodd, Giuliano, Boutell, &

Moran, 2001; Kaiser & Miller, 2001, 2003; Shelton & Stewart, 2004). On the other hand, social-psychological research also indicates that if individuals believe strongly that they should confront prejudice, failing to do so could make them feel worse about themselves and lead to intrusive thoughts about the situation (Shelton & Stewart, 2004 as cited by Swim & Thomas, 2005). Applied to the context of therapy, we would hypothesize that intrusive thoughts could lead to client disengagement and to avoidance of the relationship, thereby slowing the process of therapy or, if families feel deeply wronged, their dropping out of treatment entirely.

The therapeutic stance can also contribute to this sense of stigma. In fact, some approaches add to the reality of experiencing the therapist as stigmatizing (Leahy, 2001). Cognitive-behavioral work, often employed in anger management, "conceives of client problems as errors, distortions, and biases that when corrected cease to be problems. To describe someone's thinking as 'distorted' is not far from implying that he or she is less intelligent than the person doing the describing" (Leahy, 2001, p. 59). The family touched by violence has had more than its share of authority figures intruding on and judging their family life (e.g., courts, child protection, probation officers). These authority figures label them as troubled, dysfunctional, and maladaptive, and threaten actions that might break up their family. At times, therapists' actions have them joining this crowd in indicting the families they are to help.

Violence in families can produce strong emotional reactions in therapists, which can give rise to responses that add further to clients' sense of being stigmatized. For child abuse in particular, it is difficult for clinicians to maintain a neutral stance. Therapists often experience strong feelings about what parents have done, including disgust, anger, the urge to scold parents (Steele, 1975). Domestic violence and youth aggression can lead to similar negative reactions. Therapists might also experience fear when clients become belligerent or fail to express regret at causing harm to another, especially when it is a person whom they purport to love. Feelings of fear could lead to therapists to issue threats (e.g., plans to call child protective services or the courts, "If you continue, you will put me in the position of . . . ") or to disengage in order to control their emotional reaction. At the very least, therapists' expressions of real disappointment could be felt by family members as shame producing. Less experienced therapists' reactions are the most apparent (e.g., "How could they do that . . . I really thought they were trying," or when a man's wife showed up for a marital therapy session with a black eye, "He really had me fooled . . . I liked him"). Strong aversive reactions could lead therapists to dehumanize the perpetrator in order to further distance themselves from the idea that someone "so like" them could do such a thing. Ruptures may be inevitable at these moments, but they are accounted for by both client and therapist

Low-Prejudice Individual	**High-Prejudice Individual**
Prejudiced Response	Prejudiced Response
↓	↓
Identify error & experience aversive affective state (e.g., discomfort, guilt, & self-criticism)	Do not identify error
↓	↓
Behavioral inhibition & learning that is crucial to avoiding future prejudicial errors takes place	No learning
↓	↓
Better identification of risk of prejudicial responses and better avoidance of errors	Continued prejudicial responses (if confronted by target of prejudice, experience feeling of threat and discomfort; blame placed on target)

FIGURE 14.2   Social-psychological stigma model (based on Monteith, 1993).

emotional reactions. Further deepening these ruptures are verbal and nonverbal responses that imply stigma.

Social-psychological research has also shown that negative affective and cognitive reactions are commonly experienced by low-prejudice individuals (a label that might be applied to therapists) when they find themselves engaging in responses that are prejudicial. For example, when dominant-group members experience a prejudiced-related discrepancy (i.e., when their actual behavior toward a stigmatized group is at odds with their personal standards), they often report strong feelings of discomfort, guilt, and self-criticism (Devine, Monteith, Zuwerink, & Elliot, 1991; Zuwerink, Devine, Monteith, & Cook, 1996) and an increase in self-discrepant thoughts (Monteith, 1993; see Fig. 14.2). Slowed responses are also likely to occur with such feelings of compunction and a heightened self-focus (M. J. Montieth, 1993). Although aversive, this state can produce greater attention to relevant information in low-prejudice individuals and over time function to decrease prejudiced responding (M. J. Monteith, 1993). Thus, negative affect has adaptive value if its source is labeled as prejudice and self-discrepant thoughts occur (i.e., a violation of standards set for the self). Indeed, it has been suggested that change might be a function of this self-directed affect.

If, however, this aversive state is attributed to a personal attack or to client pathology, then the reaction may be to denigrate the client. And when confronted by clients for having engaged in prejudicial behavior, therapists who make such attributions are likely to respond by labeling the confronter negatively. If therapists have strongly held beliefs about family violence (e.g., "People who would hit their children are . . .") and are thus behaving like high-prejudice individuals (i.e., having stereotyped meanings regarding categories of people), then feelings of discomfort and threat are more likely than feelings of guilt. A sense of threat might explain why rupture experiences would not instigate self-regulatory processes nor reduce the likelihood of prejudiced responses following a discrepancy experience (M. J. Monteith, 1993). Even low-prejudice individuals, who typically avoid prejudiced responses, are likely to detect subtle biases but blame their biased behavior on external factors related to the target of their bias (M. J. Monteith, Voils, & Ashburn-Nardo, 2001). This pattern helps explain why researchers develop theories that foster blaming client pathology for asynchrony in therapeutic interactions.

IMPLICATIONS FOR NEGOTIATING THERAPEUTIC RUPTURES

Both of the proposed formulations imply that therapists working with violence-prone families are subject to emotional reactions that can interfere with therapeutic engagement and that might require personal work. Earlier in this chapter, however, we noted that psychotherapy process research finds evidence that successfully negotiated ruptures can strengthen the therapeutic alliance. If true, then the existence of the therapy relationship and the formation of a healthy working alliance can challenge families' operating assumptions about the use of violence to resolve conflicts, thus creating opportunities for change to occur. Negotiation of the rupture also allows for *in vivo* modeling and rehearsal of nonaggressive conflict resolution strategies. In contrast to the traditional view of ruptures as resistance, the formulations we have presented suggest that some ruptures are not founded entirely in client pathology, but rather in therapists' difficulties. If clients are merely reacting and not resisting, then some ruptures are preventable.

Given the two formulations presented, what are the implications for approaching therapy ruptures? Patterson and Chamberlain (1994) and others have suggested that encountering resistance in family work means therapists are going in the right direction. The proposed formulations suggest a slightly different perspective. Drawing on solution-focused approaches, we argue that therapists need to see prolonged and frequent therapeutic ruptures as places of potential "failure" on their part. Rather than indicating a move in the right direction and a cue to press forward, these moments are signals to make a dead stop and to take time to assess where one is in therapy. Indeed, there might be times when more "personal" work needs to be done before therapists press forward in the work.

Containment of therapists' negative affect (e.g., hostility, disgust, disappointment) is the first crucial goal. Because of potential value differences, cognitive restructuring—similar to that done in anger and stress management training with aggressive clients—might be needed to ensure greater neutrality in therapists' reactions to clients' values (Azar, 1996). Our second formulation requires a more sensitive response and even greater humility on therapists' part—a concession that they behaved in a way that could be construed as prejudicial and that triggered the rupture. Here the underlying affective response would be related to having violated their own standards of behavior. This approach could be harder to carry out in practice. It requires clinicians to question whether they are experiencing guilt and negative reactions to the self.

Patterson and Chamberlain (1994) recognize therapist disengagement and dislike of clients as potentially detrimental reactions, but they supply little in the way of resolutions for therapists except to press forward in the work with the idea that success will eventually result and the situation will be negotiated successfully. How one contains the hostility that may be engendered at those moments and how this event can be prevented in future work are not given much attention. Indeed, their formulation almost necessitates the occurrence of ruptures in the process of change. The formulations we propose do not cast all ruptures as necessary for change to occur or as evidence of families' resisting change. Also, pressing forward might not work if emotion is still hanging in the air. Indeed, if therapists cannot reengage their client, they might become disappointed in themselves and engage in the kind of self-hostility that can lead to hostility directed at clients. Winnicott's (1949) notion that "hate" of clients is inevitable when they violate what therapists see as basic "human" principles could help therapists endure such moments and accept the depth of negative affect experienced. In some cases, the "hate" may be beyond what is acceptable for even the most well-trained professional, perhaps requiring that the case be referred elsewhere. However, in most cases, we would expect that therapists have the capacity to contain their affect when it interferes with the therapeutic alliance.

A second goal when responding to therapy ruptures is for therapists to identify what values-based clashes underlie the rupture and to deal with them directly. Perhaps most harmful to the therapy process are those involving therapists' expectations for "success," "expertise," and "control." Azar (2000) argues that such expectations, if held too rigidly, can lead to therapist burnout. Such beliefs include the following:

1. Family problems are always manageable and we professionals have the tools to be helpful.
2. I know *exactly* what my role is in relation to the families and children I serve.
3. Parents and children will always want my help and will view my efforts positively.
4. Because of my role as helper, I will always be safe.
5. I will do no harm.

Leahy (2001) argues that clients who are perceived as resistant could actually be activating in therapists a number of maladaptive schemas. These include overgeneralization (e.g., "I didn't help this family. I can't help any of these families."), all-or-nothing thinking (e.g., "Nothing works with this family."), labeling the patient (e.g., "This father is a pain to deal with. He really doesn't care about his family."), or labeling the self (e.g., "I must be a lousy therapist; she won't leave this abusive guy."). Clients who present with issues and themes involving abuse, devaluation, betrayal, demandingness, or exploitation can activate therapists' own vulnerabilities. Leahy provides a useful typology of therapist schemas that can influence emotional reactions toward clients. He labels these *demanding standards, judgmental, helplessness,* and *control.* An example of a judgmental schema would be: "Some people are basically bad people. People should be punished if they do wrong things" (p. 256). Following from such schemas, Leahy argues, are behaviors that are apt to be "punishing" toward clients (e.g., shaming) and to lead to retaliation or withdrawal.

Both Leahy (2001) and Azar (1996) offer rational responses to counter these distortions. For example, Leahy offers self-statements such as the following

> This person is a human being who is suffering. He doesn't want to suffer and the difficulty and resistance that the patient expresses is probably causing him more discomfort than it is causing me. Try to see life through his eyes and develop a shared curiosity with the patient about the current problem; There are some people you work well with and others that you don't. Even the "famous" therapists make mistakes. No therapist is perfect. (p. 265)

Azar also offers self-statements to counteract therapists' own dysfunctional thinking and labeling of families. Examples include: "Families do the best they can"; "Change is dangerous"; and "Change is slow."

Social-psychological studies of stigma suggest other solutions. In an article titled "Putting the Brakes on Prejudice," J. J. Monteith, Ashburn-Nardo, Voils, and Czopp (2002) suggest that people expressing prejudicial behavior develop "cues for control" to self-regulate and to reduce the potential for automatic stereotyped responses. Monteith et al. invoke a neuropsychological concept, *behavioral inhibition* (i.e., shift from automatic to controlled processing), to explain how this might happen. Behavioral inhibition requires identifying cues that activate the stereotyped schema (self-regulatory responses). For example, low-prejudice individuals who label their behavior as prejudicial can enhance learning through the process of behavioral inhibition. Because responding in a way that is negative or discrepant from one's beliefs can lead to a negative experience of the self, activation of behavioral inhibition is enhanced by an increase in one's arousal and a momentary pausing or interruption of ongoing behavior (Gray, Buhusi, & Schmajuk, 1997). This interruption allows one to pay increased attention to stimuli that are relevant to the discrepant response (i.e., retrospective reflection). The likely result is identification of environmental stimuli that predict future occurrences of the discrepant response. Associations form around these stimuli and cues for control can be established. When these cues are encountered again, behavioral inhibition occurs along with prospective reflection (e.g., more careful consideration of how to respond; careful execution of responses, and ultimately the generation of responses that do not constitute discrepancies). Thus a transition from automatic to controlled processing is triggered. Of course, use of this strategy requires that therapists label family members' emotion responses as reactions to therapists' own prejudicial behavior. However, therapists who are high in prejudice (i.e., hold negatively toned and biased standards) are more likely to experience discomfort that is not rooted in violation of a self-standard. If any labeling of behavior as prejudicial occurs, it is seen as originating in the judgments of others, not rooted in reality. This stance does not trigger the process of behavioral inhibition and learning is not facilitated. Instead, therapists are more likely to engage in denigrating behavior toward the clients.

We suspect there are times when therapists working with clients who engage in violent behavior are more like the high-prejudice individual whose motivation to engage in reflective thinking is often short-circuited. After all, a parent who hits their child or a man who hits his wife must be an awful person, right? All that such individuals do is subject to being part of that "awfulness" and we have done nothing to get them upset. But if for a brief moment we try on the label of "prejudiced," we might be able to engage in a search for alternative interpretations of therapy ruptures, or at least struggle with families in trying to understand what has occurred between we and they.

Finally, therapists should strive to create therapeutic moments when clients feel more comfortable with confrontation and are better able to suppress behaviors that produce disengagement and avoidance. A recent chapter by Swim and Thomas (2005) provides hints at how this might be done. The authors focus on motivational goals that need to be activated in order for confrontation to occur and cite Fiske's (2004) core social goals (i.e., the need *to belong, to be trusted, to be understood, to feel in control, and for self-enhancement*) as key factors in facilitating or impeding whether stigmatized members of a group confront the perpetrator of prejudice. These goals, it might be suggested, also need to be considered when therapists think about how to negotiate the confrontation. For therapists, the need for trust, self-enhancement, and control might be primary for negotiating the rupture; for the client, the need to belong and to be understood could be crucial. From this framework, one can see that examples provided earlier of a violent husband's invoking a traditional role of "protector" to explain his abusive behavior could be seen as an effort to maintain "belonging" with the interviewer.

This perspective would also suggest that clients' initial resistance is perhaps a reaction to experiencing stigmas (evaluative judgments) that block one of these core social goals. Increased "resistance" could also be repeated attempts to achieve those social goals, which, if not satisfied, might lead to dropout. Such moments require that therapists identify which of their clients' motivational goals have been threatened while also containing their own affective responses by identifying which of their social goals have been threatened. Therapists will use cognitive restructuring strategies with themselves, evaluating whether the threat to their social goals is real or not, or as great as they perceive it to be. Useful self-statements include, "I don't have to be the expert here" and "We have to struggle with this situation together." Therapists also need to consider how they may have threatened a client's social goals and how they can defuse that threat: "It feels like I may have done something that made you feel not understood"; "Perhaps what I just said came out too harsh. I have to admit I think differently about such matters"; or "I am not sure what just happened here. Perhaps, you can help me understand it." At a subsequent session, therapists can offer, "I went home after our last session and realized I may have offended you when I said. ..." Such statements should facilitate clients' being more candid or at least convey a sense of "I am struggling with you" as opposed to "I am against you." Other strategies that might be useful are positive reframing as well as ways to focus on efficacy building to restore a sense of self during such moments (Berg & Jaya, 1993; DuCharme, Atkinson, & Poulton, 2000).

One final caution is needed before our discussion ends. Leahy (2001) suggests there are times when therapists who work with abusive clients have to act to protect the self. Such work can erupt into family members yelling, being physically belligerent, or using abusive language toward the therapist. Such behavioral displays of value differences can be too damaging to the therapeutic relationship, and clients should not be allowed to engage in fear-inducing or abusive behavior toward therapists.

Thus, we are not suggesting that therapists "think" their way out of all aversive situations or tolerate all violations of their values. "Tolerating" abusive behavior could inadvertently reinforce it. Indeed, in family work, it is crucial to model for the nonviolent members of the family the setting of firm limits. To continue this work in the face of intimidation, Leahy argues, could make it difficult to remain in the professional role with the family and possibly indicate a maladaptive therapist schema (e.g., self-sacrificing or approval-seeking schema). He argues that establishing clear guidelines and client "time-outs" might be necessary during sessions (this is similar to instructions to violent domestic partners to leave the home when they cannot contain violent behavior by other means). In line with our earlier discussions, Leahy suggests that the first item on the agenda for the next meeting should be a discussion of "respect." In this way, the collaborative relationship is highlighted and hopefully preserved and the alliance deepened.

CONCLUSIONS

Given the lack of psychotherapy process research on families that are prone to violence, the formulations we have suggested in this chapter are tentative ones. However, we know from the general psychotherapy process literature that alliance predicts outcome best when measured by the client's report (Barber et al., 1999; Horvath & Symonds, 1991; Tichenor & Hill, 1989) and when assessed early in treatment(Barber et al., 1999; Horvath & Symonds, 1991; Tichenor & Hill, 1989). Furthermore, it has been observed that therapists and clients are often not aware of the interpersonal rifts that occur between them (Castonguay & Constantino, in press). Clients are likely to drop out of treatment if there are too many early ruptures (Maramba & Castonguay, 2004). These kinds of ruptures might also be harder for therapists to identify, especially if tied to basic assumptions about how families should operate or how therapy should occur, or if linked to evidence about the self that therapists would rather not know.

It has been said that therapists underestimate the influence of their beliefs on alliance development (Maramba & Castonguay, 2004). Yet, therapy is a co-constructed relationship. In discussing another professional relationship, that between parents and teachers, Azar (1997b) has suggested that members of this dyad have different internal models about their roles in children's lives and about how each of them "work." These differing role schemas lead to transactions marked by an adversarial tone rather than a collaborative one. As parents offer their view of the problem and how they respond, as well as how they think teachers should respond, there will likely be a "disconnect" with how teachers view these same factors. We have argued that similar difficulties are in play when working with families who are violence prone and we have offered formulations for countering those difficulties.

Future research with violence-prone families should include process studies that test these formulations and the implications these formulations have for the conduct of therapy. Therapy process work should also assess the level of negative emotions (e.g., hostility) experienced by therapists in such cases and the manner in which these emotions are expressed and contained. Advising clinicians to focus solely on alliance building and to press forward in the face of their dislike for clients is not enough. And comforting clinicians with the idea that client pathology is the cause of resistance could actually induce a rupture if families sense a lack of respect or experience efforts to press forward as therapists ignoring their experiences of prejudice. Social-psychological research on strategies for interrupting automatized and stereotyped processing of interpersonal interactions offers great promise to those who train clinicians working in this area.

REFERENCES

Administration on Children, Youth and Families (2001). *10 years of reporting on child maltreatment.* Washington, DC: U.S. Department of Health & Human Services.

Aldarondo, E., & Sugarman, D. B. (1996). Risk marker analysis of the cessation and persistence of wife assault. *Journal of Consulting and Clinical Psychology, 64,* 1010–1019.

American Psychological Association. (2002). Characteristics of recent doctorates in psychology: 2001. Retrieved December, 13, 2004, from http://www.apa.org/monitor/feb04/number.html

Armistead, L. P., Clark, H., Barber, C. N., Dorsey, S., Hughley, J., Favors, M., et al. (2004). Participant retention in the Parents Matter! Program: Strategies and outcomes. *Journal of Child and Family Studies, 13,* 67–80.

Arnaldo, Z., Dodge, K. A., Lochman, J. E., & Laird, R. D. (1999). The distinction between beliefs legitimizing aggression and deviant processing of social cues. *Journal of Personality and Social Psychology, 77,* 150–166.

Azar, S. T. (1986). A framework for understanding child maltreatment: An integration of cognitive behavioral and developmental perspectives. *Canadian Journal of Behavioral Science, 18,* 340–355.

Azar, S. T. (1989). Training parents of abused children. In C. E. Shaefer & J. M. Briesmeister (Eds.), *Handbook of parent training* (pp. 414–441). New York: Wiley.

Azar, S. T. (1996). Cognitive restructuring of professionals' schema regarding women parenting in poverty. *Women and Therapy, 18,* 149–163.

Azar, S. T. (1997a). A cognitive behavioral approach to understanding and treating parents who physically abuse their children. In D. Wolfe & R. McMahon (Ed.),

Child abuse: New directions in prevention and treatment across the life span (pp. 78–100). New York: Sage.

Azar S. T. (1997b). Parents and children: Representations of family: Understanding parents' and teachers' internal working models of their roles in children's lives. *Journal of Education Policy, 20,* 1–10.

Azar, S. T. (2000). Preventing burnout in professionals and paraprofessionals who work with child abuse and neglect cases: A cognitive behavioral approach to supervision. *JCLP/In-Session: Psychotherapy in Practice, 56,* 1–21.

Azar, S. T., & Benjet, C. L. (1994). A cognitive perspective on ethnicity, race and termination of parental rights. *Law and Human Behavior, 18,* 249–268.

Azar, S. T., & Cote, L. R. (2002). Sociocultural issues in the evaluation of the needs of children in custody decision-making. What do our current frameworks for evaluating parenting practices have to offer? *International Journal of Law and Psychiatry, 25,* 193–217.

Azar, S. T., Nix, R. L., & Makin-Byrd, K. N. (2005). Parenting schemas and the process of change. *Journal of Marriage and Family Therapy, 31,* 45–58.

Azar, S. T., Robinson, D. R., Hekimian, E., & Twentyman, C. T. (1984). Unrealistic expectations and problem solving ability in maltreating and comparison mothers. *Journal of Consulting and Clinical Psychology, 52,* 687–691.

Azar, S. T., & Rohrbeck, C. A. (1986). Child abuse and unrealistic expectations: Further validaton of the Parent Opinion Questionnaire. *Journal of Consulting and Clinical Psychology, 54,* 867–868.

Azar, S. T., & Soysa, K. (1999). Legal and system issues in the assessment of family violence involving children. In R. T. Ammerman & M. Hersen (Eds.), *Assessment of family violence: A clinical and legal sourcebook* (2nd ed. (pp. 48–72). New York: Wiley.

Azar, S. T., & Twentyman, C. T. (1986). Cognitive-behavioral perspectives on the assessment and treatment of child abuse. In P. C. Kendall (Ed.), *Advances in cognitive-behavioral research and therapy* (Vol. 5, pp. 237–267). New York: Academic Press.

Azar, S. T., & Wolfe, D. A. (1998). Child abuse and neglect. In E. G. Mash & R. A. Barkley (Eds.), *Behavioral treatment of childhood disorders* (2nd ed., pp. 501–544), New York: Guilford.

Baldwin, A., Baldwin, C., & Cole, R. E. (1990). Stress-resistant families and stress-resistant children. In J. E. Roff, A. S. Masten, D. Cicchetti, K E. Wechterlein, & S. Weintraub (Eds.), *Risk and protective factors in the Development of psychopathology* (pp. 257–280). New York: Cambridge University Press.

Baldwin, M. W. (1997). Relational schema as a source of if-then self inference procedures. *Review of General Psychology, 1,* 326–335.

Barber, J. P., Luborsky, L., Chris-Chistoph, P. Thase, M.E., Weiss, R., Frank, A., et al. (1999). Therapeutic alliance as a predictor of outcome in treatment of cocaine dependence. *Psychotherapy Research, 9,* 54–73.

Barbosa, J., Carr, T. F., & Johnson, E. (1992). Cultural factors and considerations in the investigation of care and protection petitions. In C. Ayoub et al. (Eds.), *Court investigations in care & protections.* Boston: American Professional Society on the Abuse of Children.

Berg, I. S., & Jaya, A. (1993). Different and same: Family therapy with Asian-American families. *Journal of Marital and Family Therapy, 19,* 31–38.

Bischoff, R. J., & Sprenkle, D. H. (1993). Dropping out of marriage and family therapy. *A critical review of Research. Family Processes, 32,* 353–375.

Bugental, D., Blue, J., & Cruzcosa, M. (1989). Perceived control over caregiving outcomes. Implications for child abuse. *Developmental Psychology, 25,* 532–539.

Casas, M. S. (1992). A culturally sensitive model for evaluating alcohol and other drug abuse prevention programs. A Hispanic perspective. In M. Orlandi (Ed.), *Cultural competence for evaluators* (pp. 75–116). Washington, DC: U.S. Department of Health and Human Services.

Caselles, C. E., & Milner, J. S. (2000). Evaluation of child transgressions, disciplinary choices, and expected child compliance and a crying infant condition in physically abused and comparison mothers. *Child Abuse & Neglect, 24,* 477–491.

Castonguay, L. G., & Constantino, M. J. (in press). Engagement in psychotherapy: Factors contributing to the Facilitation, demise, and restoration of the working alliance. In D. Castro-Blanco (Ed.), *Treatment engagement with adolescents.* Washington, DC: American Psychological Associaton.

Cauce, A. M., Ryan, K. D., & Grove, K. (1998). Children and adolescents of color, where are you? Participation, selection, recruitment, and retention in developmental research. In V. C. McLoyd L. Steinberg (Eds.), *Study minority adolescents: Conceptual methodological, and theoretical issues* (pp. 147–166). Mahwah, NJ: Lawrence Erlbaum Associates.

Centerwall, B.S. (1984). Race, socioeconomic status, and domestic homicides, Atlanta, 1971–2. *American Journal of Public Health, 74,* 813–815.

Chamberlain, P., Patterson, J. R., Reid, J. B., Kavanagh, K., & Forgatch, M. S. (1984). Observation of client resistance. *Behavior Therapy, 15,* 144–155.

Children' Defense Fund. (2003). *Health insurance in New York City: Is it working for immigrant families?* Retrieved December 25, 2004 from. http://www.cdfny.org/RR/reports/ImmigrantReport_ New.pdf.

Crosby, F. J. (1993). Why complain. *Journal of Social Issues, 49,* 169–184.

DeHart, D., Kennerly, R., Burke, L., & Follingstad, D. (1999) Predictors of attrition in a treatment program for battering men. *Journal of Family Violence, 14,* 19–34.

Devine, P., Monteith, M., Zuwerink, J., & Elliot, A. (1991). Prejudice with and without compunction. *Journal of Personality and Social Psychology, 60,* 817–830.

Diriwachter, R., & Azar, S. T. (2002, March). T*he role of poverty in parents' disciplinary responses.* Paper presented at the annual meeting of the Eastern Psychological Association, Boston.

Dodd, E. H., Giuliano, T. A., Boutell, J. M., & Moran, B. E. (2001). Respected or rejected: Perceptions of women who confront sexist remarks. *Sex Roles, 45,* 567–577.

Dryfoos, J. G. (1990). *Adolescents at risk: Prevalence and prevention.* New York: Oxford University Press.

DuCharme, J., Atkinson, L., & Poulton, L. (2000). Success based, noncoercive treatment of oppositional behavior in children from violent homes. *Journal of the American Academy of Child and Adolescent Psychiatry, 39,* 995–1004.

Dumont, F., & Lecomte, C. (1987). Inferential processes in clinical work. *Professional Psychology, Research, and Pracice, 18,* 433–438.

Dutton, D. G. (1986). Wife assaulter's explanations for the assault: The neutralization of self-punishment. *Canadian Journal of Behavioral Science, 18,* 381–390.

Ehrensaft, M. K., Cohen, P., Brown, J., Smailes, E., Chen, H., & Johnson, J. G. (2003). Intergenerational transmission of partner violence: A 20-year prospective study. *Journal of Consulting and Clinical Psychology, 71*, 741–753.

Eisikovits, Z., Goldblatt, H., & Winstok, Z. (1999). Partner accounts of intimate violence: Toward a theoretical model. *Families in Society,* 606–619.

Elliott, D. S. (1994). Serious violent offenders: Onset, developmental course, and termination. The American Society of Criminology 1993 Presidential Address. *Criminology, 3,* 1–21.

Falicov, C. (1982). Mexican American families. In M. McGoldrick, J. Pearce, & J. Giordano (Eds.), Ethnicity and family therapy (pp. 134–163). New York: Guilford.

Fantuzzo, J. W., & Mohr, W. K. (1999). Prevalence and effects of child exposure to domestic violence. *The Future of Children, 9,* 21–32.

Farmer, E., & Owen, M. (1998). Gender and the child protection process. *The British Journal of Social Work, 28,* 545–564.

Figley, C. R. (1995). *Compassion fatigue: Coping with secondary traumatic stress disorder in those who treat the traumatized.* New York: Bruner/Mazel.

Fiske, S. T. (2004). Social beings: A core social motives approach to social psychology. Hoboken, NJ: Wiley.

Fiske, S. T., & Taylor, S. E. (1991). *Social cognition.* New York: McGraw-Hill.

Forehand, R., & Kotchick, B. (1996) Cultural diversity: A wake-up call for parent training. *Behavior-Therapy, 27,* 187–206.

Forehand, R. Middlebrook, J., Rogers, T., & Steffe, M. (1983). Dropping out of parent training. *Behaviour Research and Therapy, 21,* 663–668.

Frank, J. D. (1985). Therapeutic components shared by all psychotherapies. In M. J. Mahoney & A. Freeman (Eds.), *Cognition and psychotherapy* (pp. 49–80). New York: Plenum.

Garcia-Preto, N. (1982). Puerto Rican families. In M. McGoldrick, J., Pearce, & J. Giordano (Eds.), *Ethnicity and family therapy* (pp. 134–164). New York: Guilford.

Goff, P. A. (2004, April). *When what's inside is not what counts: Stereotype threat and White identity. Invited presentation,* Department of Psychology, Pennsylvania State University, University Park.

Gondolf, E., & Foster, R. (1991). Pre-program attrition in batterer programs. *Journal of Family Violence, 6,* 337–349.

Gong-Guy, E., Cravens, R. B., & Patterson, T. E. (1991). Clinical issues in mental health service delivery to refugees. *American Psychologist, 46,* 642–648.

Gould, M., Shaffer, D., & Kaplan, D. (1985). The characteristics of dropouts from a child psychiatry clinic. *Journal of American Academy of Child Psychiatry, 24,* 316–328.

Graham, S. (1992). Most of the subjects were white and middle class. *American Psychologist, 47,* 629–639.

Gray, J. A., Buhusi, C. V., & Schmajuk, N. (1997). The transition from automatic to controlled processing. *Neural Networks, 10,* 1257–1268.

Greenfeld, L., Rand, M., Craven, D., Klaus, P., Perkins, C., Ringel, C., et al. (1998). *Violence by intimates.* U.S. Department of Justice. Retrieved December 13, 2004. from http://www.ojp.usdoj.gov/bjs/pub/pdf/vi.pdf.

Gregory, C., & Erez, E. (2002). The effects of batterer intervention programs. *Violence Against Women, 8,* 206–232.

Guerra, N. G., Huesmann, L. R., Tolan, P. H., Van Acker, R., & Eron, L. D. (1995). Stressful events and individual beliefs as correlates of economic disadvantage and aggression among urban children. *Journal of Consulting and Clinical Psychology, 63*, 518–528.

Harris, C. L. (1995). Whiteness as property. In K. Crenshaw, N. Gotanda, G. Peller, & K. Thomas (Eds.), Critical race theory. *The key writings that formed the movement* (pp. 276–291). New York: The New Press.

Haskett, M. E., Scott, S. S., Grant, R., Ward, C. S., & Robinson, C. (2003). Child related cognitions and affective functioning of physically abusive and comparison parents. *Child Abuse & Neglect, 27*, 663–686.

Hastings, B. (2000). Social information processing and the verbal and physical abuse of women. *Journal of Interpersonal Violence, 15*, 651–664.

Heitler, J. B. (1976). Preparatory techniques in initiating expressive psychotherapy with lower-class unsophisticated patients. *Psychological Bulletin, 83*, 339–352.

Henggeler, S. W., Melton, G. B., & Smith, L. A. (1992). Family preservation using multisystemic therapy. An effective alternative to incarcerating, serious juvenile offenders. *Journal of Consulting and Clinical Psychology, 60*, 953–961.

Henry, W. P., Strupp, H. H., , Butler, S. F., Schact, T. E., & Binder, J. L. (1993). The effects of training in time limited dynamic psychotherapy: Changes in therapist behavior. *Journal of Consulting and ClinicalPsychology, 61*, 434–440.

Hess, R. D. (1970). Social class and ethnic influences upon socialization. In P. H. Mussen (Ed.), *Carmichael's manual of child psychology* (Vol. II, pp. 457–557). New York: Wiley.

Holtzworth-Munroe, A., & Hutchinson, G. (1993). Attributing negative intent to wife behavior: The attributions of maritally violent versus nonviolent men. *Journal of Abnormal Psychology, 102*, 206–211.

Horvath, A. O., & Symonds, D. B. (1991). Relationship between working alliance and outcome in psychotherapy. A meta-analysis. *Journal of Counseling Psychology, 38*, 139–149.

Huesmann, L. R., & Guerra, N. G. (1997). Children's normative beliefs about aggression and aggressive behavior. *Journal of Personality and Social Psychology, 72*, 408–219.

Hyden, M. (1994). Woman battering as a marital act: Interviewing and analysis in context. In C. K. Riessman (Ed.), *Qualitative studies in social work* (pp. 95–111). Newbury Park, CA: Sage.

Hynan, D. J. (1990). Client reasons and experiences in treatment that influence termination of psychotherapy. *Journal of Clinical Psychology, 46*, 891–895.

Kaiser, C. R., & Miller, C. T. (2001). Stop complaining! The social costs of making attributions to discrimination. *Personality and Social Psychology Bulletin, 27*, 254–263.

Kaiser, C. R., & Miller, C. T. (2003). Derogating the victim: The interpersonal consequences of blaming events on discrimination. *Group Processes and Intergroup Relations, 6*, 227–237.

Kalmuss, D. (1984). The intergenerational transmission of marital aggression. *Journal of Marriage and the Family, 46*, 11–19.

Kaufman, J., & Zigler, E. (1987). Do abused children become abusive parents? *American Journal of Orthopsychiatry, 57*, 186–192.

Kazdin, A. (1996). Dropping out of child psychotherapy: Issues for research and implications for practice. *Journal of Clinical Child Psychology and Psychiatry, 1*, 133–156.

Kazdin, A., & Mazurick, J. (1994). Dropping out of child psychotherapy: Distinguishing early and late dropouts over the course of treatment. *Journal of Consulting and Clinical Psychology, 62*, 1069–1074.

Kim, S., McLeod, J. H., & Shantzis, C. (1992). Cultural competence for evaluators working with Asian-Americans. In M. Orlandi, (Ed.), *Cultural competence for evaluators: A guide for alcohol and other drug abuse prevention practitioners working with ethnic and racial communities* (pp. 203–260). Washington, DC: U.S. Department of Health and Human Services.

Kohn, M. L. (1963). Social class and parent–child relationship. *American Journal of Sociology, 68*, 471–480.

Kourany, R. F., Garber, J., & Tournusciolo, G. (1990). Improving first appointment attendance rates in child psychiatric outpatient clinics. *Journal of the American Academy of Child and Adolescent Psychiatry, 29*, 657–660.

Lareau, A. (2002). Invisible inequality: Social class and childrearing in Black families and White families. *American Sociological Review, 67*, 747–776.

Larrance, D. T., & Twentyman, C. T. (1983). Maternal attributions in child abuse. *Journal of Abnormal Psychology, 92*, 449–457.

Leahy, R. L. (2001). *Overcoming resistance in cognitive therapy*. New York: Guilford.

Leslie, L. A., & Morton, G. (2001). Family therapy's response to family diversity. *Journal of Family Issues, 22*, 904–921.

Lieh-Mak, F., Lee, P. W., & Luk, S. L. (1984). Problems encountered in teaching Chinese parents to be behavior therapists. *International Journal of Psychology in the Orient, 27*, 56–54.

Locke, L., & Richman, C. L. (1999). Attitudes toward domestic violence: Race and gender issues. *Sex Roles, 40*, 227–247.

Lorion, R. (1978). Research on psychotherapy and behavior change with the disadvantaged. In S. L. Garfield & A. E. Bergin (Eds.), *Handbook of psychotherapy and behavior change* (pp. 903–938). New York: Wiley.

Luk, E., Staiger, P., Mathai, J., Wong, L., Birleson, P., & Adler, R. (2001). Children with persistent conduct problems who dropout of treatment. *European Child and Adolescent Psychiatry, 10*, 28–36.

Malgady, R. G., Rogler, L. H., & Constantino, G. (1987). Ethnocultural and linguistic bias in mental health evaluation of Hispanics. *American Psychologist, 42*, 222–234.

Maramba, G. G., & Castonguay, L. G. (2004, November). *Beliefs and early alliance ruptures*. Paper presented at the meeting of the North American Society for Psychotherapy Research, Springdale, AZ.

Marin, G., Marin, B.V., Perez Stable, S., Sabogal, F., & Otero Sabogal, R. (1990). Change in information as a function of a culturally appropriate smoking cessation community intervention for Hispanics. *American Journal of Community Psychology, 18*, 847–864.

McCann, I. L., & Pearlman, L. A. (1990). *Psychological trauma and the adult survivor: Theory therapy, and transformation*. New York: Brunner/Mazel.

Miller, L. (1998). Our own medicine: Traumatized psychotherapists and the stresses of doing therapy. *Psychotherapy, 35*, 137–146.

Monteith, J. J., Ashburn-Nardo, L., Voils, C. L., & Czopp, A. M. (2002). Putting the brakes on prejudice: On the development and operation of cues for control. *Journal of Personality and Social Psychology, 83,* 1029–1050.

Monteith, M. J. (1993). Self-regulation of prejudiced responses: Implications for progress in prejudice reduction efforts. *Journal of Personality and Social Psychology, 65,* 469–485.

Monteith, M. J., Voils, C. I., & Ashburn-Nardo, L. (2001). Taking a look underground: Detecting, interpreting, and reacting to implicit racial biases. *Social Cognition, 19,* 395–417.

National Research Council. (1993). *Understanding child abuse and neglect.* Washington, DC: National Academy Press.

National Research Council. (1998). *From generation to generation: The health and well-being of children in immigrant families.* Washington, DC: National Academy Press.

Nayak, M. B., Byrne, C. A., Martin, M. K., & Abraham, A. G. (2003). Attitudes toward violence against women: A cross national study. *Sex Roles, 49,* 333–342.

Neki, J. S. (1973). Guru–chela relationship: The possibility of a therapeutic paradigm. *American Journal of Orthopsychiatry, 32,* 755–766.

O'Dell, D. (1982). Enhancing parent involvement training: A discussion. *The Behavior Therapist, 5,* 9–13.

O'Leary, D. K., Barling, J., Arias, J., Arias, I., Rosenbaum, A., Malone, J., et al. (1989). Prevalence and stability of physical aggression between spouses. A longitudinal analysis. *Journal of Consulting and Clinical Psychology, 57,* 263–268.

O'Leary, D. K., Malone, J., & Tyree, A. (1994). Physical aggression in early marriage: Pre-relationship and relationship effects. *Journal of Consulting and Clinical Psychology, 62,* 594–602.

Orrell-Valente, J. K., Pinderhughes, E. E., Valente, E., & Laird, R. D. (1999). If it is offered, will they come? Influences on parents' participation in a community-based conduct problems prevention program. *American Journal of Community Psychology, 27,* 753–783.

Pande, S. K. (1968). The mystique of "Western" psychotherapy: An Eastern view. *Journal of Nervous and Mental Disease, 146,* 425–432.

Patterson, G. R., & Chamberlain, P. (1988). Treatment process: A problem at three levels. In L. C. Wynne (Ed.), *The state of the art in family therapy research: Controversies and recommendations* (pp. 189–226). New York: Family Process Press.

Patterson, G., & Chamberlain, P. (1994). A functional analysis of resistance during parent training therapy. *Clinical Psychology: Science and Practice, 1*(1), 53–70.

Pelton, L. H. (1994). The role of material factors in child abuse and neglect. In G. B. Melton & F. D. Barry (Eds.), *Protecting children from abuse and neglect: Foundations for a new national strategy* (pp. 131–181). New York: Guilford.

Peterson, L., Ewigman B., & Kivlahan, C. (1993). Judgments regarding appropriate child supervision to prevent injury: The role of environmental risk and child age. *Child Development, 64,* 934–950.

Peterson, L., Gable, S., Doyle, C., & Ewigman, B. (1997). Beyond parenting skills. *Cognitive and Behavioral Practice, 4,* 53–74.

Polakow, V. (1993). *Lives on the edge: Single mothers and their children in the other America.* Chicago: University of Chicago Press.

Quigley, R. M., & Leonard, K. E. (1996). Desistance of husband aggression in the early years of marriage. *Violence and Victims, 11*, 355–370.

Raphael, J. (1997). Understanding women's poverty. Law and Policy, *19*, 117–123.

Reid, J. B. (1985). Behavioral approaches to intervention and assessment with child abusive families. In P. H. Bornstein & A. Kazdin (Eds.), *Handbook of clinical behavior therapy with children* (pp. 772–802). Homewood, IL: Dorsey.

Russell, M. N., Lang, M., & Brett, B. (1987). Reducing dropout rates through improved intake procedures. Social Casework: *The Journal of Contemporary Social Work, 68*, 421–425.

Safran, J. D. (1993). Breaches in the therapeutic alliance: An arena for negotiating authentic relatedness. *Psychotherapy, 30*, 11–24.

Safran, J. D., Crocker, P., McMain, S., & Murray, P. (1990). The therapeutic alliance rupture as a therapy event for empirical investigation. *Psychotherapy, 27*, 154–165.

Saks-Berman, J. R. (1989). A view from rainbow bridge: Feminist therapist meets changing women. *Women & Therapy, 8*, 65–78.

Saunders, D. G. (1994). Child custody decisions in families experiencing woman abuse. *Social Work, 39*, 51–59.

Shelton, J. N. & Stewart, R. E. (2004). Confronting perpetrators of prejudice: The inhibitory effects of social cost. *Psychology of Women Quarterly. 28*(3), 215–223.

Shorkey, C. T. (1980). Sense of personal worth, self esteem, and anomie of child abusing mothers and controls. *Journal of Clinical Psychology, 36*, 817–820.

Snell-Johns, J., Mendez, J. L., & Smith, B. H. (2004). Evidence-based solutions for overcoming access barriers, decreasing attrition, and promoting change with underserved families. *Journal of Family Psychology, 18*, 19–35.

Spieker, S. J., Gilmore, M. R., Lewis, S., Morrison, D. M., & Lohr, M. J. (2001). Psychological distress and substance use by adolescent mothers. *Journal of Psychoactive Drugs, 33*, 83–93.

Steele, B. F. (1975). Working with abusive parents: A psychiatric view. *Children Today, 4*, 3–5.

Strupp, H. H. (1973). Psychotherapy: *Clinical, research, and theoretical issues.* New York: Aronson.

Strupp, H. H. (1980). Success and failure in time-limited psychotherapy. A systematic comparison of two cases. *Archives of General Psychiatry, 37*, 595–603.

Swim, J. K., & Hyers, L. L. (1999). Excuse me—What did you just say?! Women's public and private responses to sexist remarks. *Journal of Experimental Social Psychology, 35*, 68–88.

Swim, J. K., & Thomas, M. A. (2005). Responding to everyday discrimination: A synthesis of research on goal directed, self-regulatory coping behaviors. In S. Levin & C. Van Laar, (Eds.), *Stigma and group inequality: Social psychological Approaches, Claremont Symposium on Applied Social Psychology* (pp. 105–126). Mahwah, NJ: Lawrence Erlbaum Associates.

Tichenor, V., & Hill, C. E. (1989). A comparison of six measures of working alliance. *Psychotherapy: Theory, Research, and Practice, 26*, 195–199.

U.S. Department of Health and Human Services. (2001). *Mental health: Culture, race, and ethnicity. A supplement to mental health: A report of the Surgeon General.* Washington, DC: Author, U.S. Department of Public Health.

Watzlawick, P. (1976). *How real is real?* New York: Random House.

West, C. (2004). Black women and intimate partner violence. New directions in research. *Journal of Interpersonal Violence, 19,* 1487–1493.

Williams, G. (1983). The urgency of authentic prevention. *Journal of Clinical Child Psychology, 12,* 312–319.

Winnicott, D. W. (1949). Hate in the counter-transference. *The International Journal of Psychoanalysis, 30,* 69–74.

Wolfe, D. A., Aragona, J., Kaufman, K., & Sandler, J. (1980). The importance of adjudication in the treatment of child abuse: Some preliminary findings. *Child Abuse & Neglect, 4,* 127–135.

Zuwerink, J. R., Devine, P. G., Monteith, M. J., & Cook, D. A. (1996). Prejudice toward Blacks: With and without compunction? *Basic and Applied Social Psychology, 18,* 131–150.

15

Understanding Anger: Key Concepts From the Field of Domestic Violence and Child Abuse

David A. Wolfe

The previous chapters (Mammen, Pilkonis, Kolko, & Groff; Holtzworth-Munroe & Clements; and Azar & Makin-Byrd, chaps. 12, 13, and 14, respectively) offer an up-to-date look at how the study of anger requires an integration of wide-ranging areas of research, from the study of emotional development and expression to the understanding of anger and arousal in the context of close relationships. Most significantly, the authors have explored the most difficult aspects of anger, from normal to extreme expressions that lead to aggressive behavior. The chapters highlight the various ways that clinicians can measure or observe the expression of anger, ranging from self-report questionnaires (simple but very limited in assessing extreme emotion) to in vivo observations and anger induction tasks (very revealing but ethically challenging and risky). As emphasized by Holtzworth-Munroe and Clements (chap. 13, this volume), the expression of anger within an intimate relationship (such as husband to wife) is qualitatively different from persons with a more general anger problem, reminding us that anger is not a uniform concept. These chapters provide a comprehensive look at the theories of anger and aggression, as well as the significance of different subtypes that underlie this complex emotion.

The chapters by Azar and Makin-Byrd (chap 14, this volume) and Mammen et al. (chap. 12, this volume) provide experienced, down-to-earth discussion of the promise and pitfalls of working with violent families. These chapters offer seasoned advice for those working with troubled or aggressive families, such as meeting them at their own level (i.e., recognizing their patterns of interaction and coping, good and bad), timing the intervention for maximum effect, and choosing realistic treatment goals. Working with issues of anger and aggression, whether they involve parent–child or husband–wife interactions, requires clinicians to be sensitive to far-reaching dynamics and power differentials in the family that preclude simple or straightforward forms of counseling or training. Many clients do not understand the "system" of intervention and may lack the effective skills to ask for and receive proper help.

For example, Azar and Makin-Byrd (chap. 14, this volume) describe the culture of families touched by violence as involving a worldview of relationships that differ immensely from the view of most therapists. That is, family members may see the world in more black-and-white terms, such as victims and victimizers, or male privilege and rights, which serve to excuse or justify anger and aggression. Similarly, many clients with anger and aggression problems are not prepared for the therapeutic process, which they see as foreign, disruptive, and sometimes culturally irrelevant. When our lab began work with child-abusive families in the late 1970s, for example, we quickly discovered that we often had to accept the abusive parent's perception of the child and his or her behavior at the beginning of treatment, right or wrong, simply to initiate the therapeutic process. Their veil of anger made them vigilant for signs of blame or chastisement, and would quickly interfere with the establishment of a therapeutic relationship. A delicate balance was struck between blaming the child for the abuse (something we never allowed) and permitting the parent to vent his or her frustration with the child, their limited resources, and the perceived harshness of the child welfare system's response to their distress. Although we found that avoiding a confrontation at the beginning was an essential step in the treatment process involving parents and children, a different dynamic with woman-abusing husbands often dictates a more unilateral strategy of his responsibility and accountability.

A central thesis of these chapters is the connection between early child-rearing experiences, such as poor attachment, being exposed to angry adult models, and the ensuing inability on the part of the child to develop appropriate forms of emotion regulation. To reflect on this point, I review some research on how we have come to understand anger, especially in relation to developmental psychopathology across the life span.

UNDERSTANDING ANGER

Three psychological factors have been consistently linked to adult responses to stressful events: (a) control, or the ability to make coping responses during stress, (b) the amount of feedback or information one receives following an aversive event or the response to that event, and (c) the degree of predictability one has of the stressor (Levine, 1983).

Control is often considered to be the most important psychological factor mediating the impact of stress and emotional arousal, for it allows the individual to avoid or escape the undesired event. As Levine sums up this relationship, "Having control is helpful, losing control is aversive, and previous experience with control can significantly alter the ability to cope with subsequent aversive stimuli" (p. 115). Feedback also serves a facilitative function in managing stress and arousal, as it conveys to the individual whether he or she has done the right thing and whether or not it has been effective. Predictability, on the other hand, is less clear-cut but seems to be related to the individual's *sense* of control; that is, an event may be perceived as less stressful if one believes that he or she can exercise personal choice, which is predicted on the basis of prior experience.

Two psychological processes are particularly important for an understanding of the escalation from anger to aggression: the effects of mood states and emotional arousal on aggression, and the individual's perceptions of stressful events or provocation, such as perceived loss of control or placement of blame for feelings of discomfort. Both of these processes serve to disinhibit one's control of aggression, as discussed next.

The Effects on Aggression of Mood States and Arousal

Social-psychological studies regarding the primacy of mood or affect on behavioral responses and studies on the development and expression of aggressive behavior offer some insight into the connection between anger and aggression. Laboratory studies of mood and behavior have shown that when a positive mood is artificially induced, people are better able to postpone gratification and are more willing to comply with the requests of others. Moreover, many emotionally arousing experiences have affective "tags" when stored in memory, such that when these experiences are recalled at some later point in time the recollection of the actual event is biased by the person's mood that was present at the time. Similarly, if a person's current mood is one of sadness or depression, he or she is more likely to recall other previously sad or depressing events (Bower, 1981).

This relationship between mood, affect, and memory sheds considerable light on our understanding of the behavior of abusive or violent adults. Anger and aggression not only can be elicited not only by the immediate stressor (e.g., a child's behavior) but may be greatly exacerbated by one's memory of similar circumstances from previous stressful encounters. For example, a parent's previous mood of distress and anger toward the child is recalled by the child's current behavior or expression, leading to an overgeneralized (i.e., more angry, more aggressive) response by the parent. In effect, the parent's affective state at the time of an aversive encounter with the child is *classically conditioned* to particular aspects of the child's behavior and/or appearance, such as voice tone, facial expression, or loud crying. When these child behaviors return, the conditioned emotional response of anger, irritation, or rage quickly reappears and contributes to the parent's inability to maintain self-control and rational thought. Presumably, the adult is responding to cues that have been previously associated with frustration or anger, and the adult's behavior toward the child may be powerfully influenced by these conditioning experiences (Wolfe, 1999).

Appropriate inhibition typically evolves throughout childhood and early adulthood as the individual learns to discriminate between aggressive and assertive behavior, to develop self-control abilities, and to use prosocial means of attaining his or her goals. Because these counteraggressive abilities are learned in large part through family interactions, it stands to reason that the family of origin is a prime suspect in the initial failure to establish inhibitory controls for anger and aggressive behavior. This assumption is supported by studies showing the abuser's family of origin as a training ground for interpersonal violence and lowered social competence (Wekerle & Wolfe, 2003). Modeling of aggressive problem-solving tactics via marital violence and corporal punishment, rehearsal and reinforcement (or lack of effective punishment) of aggressive behavior with siblings and peers, the absence of opportunities to learn appropriate problem resolution approaches, and the establishment of a cognitive viewpoint that adheres to strict family roles and low self-efficacy all contribute to impaired self-regulation and disinhibition of aggressive behavior.

Part of the answer to why a child or spouse may become the victim of unmitigated anger and aggression also comes from experiments with normal subjects. Anger, which is a precursor of aggression, is a highly interpersonal emotion that typically involves a close affectional relationship between the angry person and the target (Averill, 1983). The person's level of arousal and his or her beliefs about the *source* of arousal play a critical role in determining the actual expression of aggression. A person may become aroused, such as hyperalert, tense, anxious, or in a state of high emotion, from a number of sources, including frustration, extraneous physical arousal from exercise or exertion, or threat. Once a family member feels provoked by someone or something following arousal from one of the aforementioned sources, aggressive behavior becomes more likely if the adult misattributes his or her anger and arousal to the current provocation, such as the child's behavior. This process, termed *transfer of arousal*, may account for episodes of abuse that occur in response to mild provocation from the child or spouse. An abusive adult may become angered and aroused by a previous encounter with someone else (an employer, neighbor, motorist, etc.), which lowers his or her threshold for anger and aggression with family members.

In brief, a person must believe he or she has a reason to be angry, or to have some form of justification for anger. A vicious cycle is formed between anger and aggression: Feelings of anger, often derived from various sources, create a need for justification. Once the anger has been justified, such as blaming the child for causing the parent to feel angry, upset, and hassled, this justification in return encourages further anger and aggression. As arousal turns into physical punishment or aggression, such behavior may be prolonged and the act itself can become invigorating or cathartic. Thus, negative arousal interferes with rational problem solving and reduces one's ability to control aggressive or excessive reactions. Because arousal itself is normal, cognitive-behavioral processes such as attribution for arousal and awareness of alternative, nonabusive responses are essential components in understanding why some parents and marital partners become abusive and others do not, under similar circumstances. Furthermore, factors that influence their level of anger and arousal may have a cumulative and multiplicative effect over time, underscoring the importance of early recognition and prevention.

Developmental Considerations

In addition to the psychological factors of mood, affect, and memory in determining the escalation of anger and aggression, the field of developmental psychopathology has added greatly to our knowledge of emotion regulation across the life span. Emotion regulation, a key concept in understanding an individual's pattern of poor management of anger and arousal, refers to the manner in which a child learns to identify and regulate emotional reactions from an early age, relying on caregivers and the environment to provide the necessary guidance and control. During childhood, self-regulation of affect involves the ability to modulate, modify, redirect, and otherwise control one's emotions, especially intense ones, in a way that facilitates adaptive functioning. Emotion regulation problems tend to involve modulation difficulties, such as an inability to alter emotion intensity with self-soothing strategies, as well as experiential avoidance. In the latter type, an individual may have limited ability to accept or tolerate affect and therefore tries to avoid, control, or suppress emotional experiences (Cicchetti, Ackerman, & Izard, 1995).

Among abused children, affective issues seem in particular to involve difficulties with modulation, resulting in experiencing affective extremes and diminished awareness of body states or physiological responses. Modulation difficulties can be seen in extreme depressive reactions and intense angry outbursts, not only in children but in adults as well. Adults who suffered trauma or heightened emotional reactions in childhood, and who lacked appropriate adult guidance in regulating their reaction to such events, often have considerable difficulties regulating their mood and affect throughout their life course. This latter notion is well documented in follow-up studies of physically and sexually abused children, who tend to suffer from high rates of depression, substance abuse, posttraumatic-stress-related symptoms, and similar problems related to poor affect regulation well into adulthood (Widom, 1999; Wolfe, Francis, & Straatman, 2006).

The ability to regulate strong emotions such as fear and anger in turn affects children's ability to relate to others. A main relational theme in these children's lives is a power imbalance in which there is a helpless (victim) versus hostile/controlling (victimizer) dichotomy associated with relationships. Such experiences pair anger and fear as being a major part of close relationships, and may establish one's views of others in terms of being threatening, abandoning, and not trustworthy. Consequently, adolescents who grow up in a family atmosphere of abuse and violence are more likely to alternate between victim and victimizer roles during the course of an argument or conflict with peers or dating partners, and to have difficulty regulating their emotions. (Dodge, Pettit, & Bates, 1994).

As a result of their early childhood experiences, adolescents with histories of maltreatment are especially at risk for relationship-based difficulties (Bank & Burraston, 2001), and have more than three times the risk of being involved in adult domestic violence (Coid et al., 2001). Studies of the development of maltreated children draw connections between maltreatment and difficulties inferring emotions and intent of others, which in turn results in coercive interactions with peers and dating partners (Rogosch, Cicchetti, & Aber. 1995; Wolfe, Wekerle, Reitzel-Jaff & Lefebvre, 1998). As well, some teens with maltreatment histories acquire a generalized tendency toward domineering and controlling behavior, which reemerges in the context of intimate relationships. Due to these challenges, peer and social-dating relationships among maltreated youth are more likely to be accompanied by poor interpersonal adjustment, typified by fear, mistrust, and hostility toward others, and limited personal resources such as poor problem solving, lower self-efficacy, and distorted beliefs about relationships. These factors further tax their ability to form healthy, nonviolent relationships (Wolfe, Scott, Wekerly, & Pittman, 2001).

Our research team has been investigating the connection between child maltreatment and the emergence of dating violence in adolescence, with a particular emphasis on anger and trauma-related symptoms. We divided 1,400 high school students into those with maltreatment or nonmaltreatment backgrounds, and examined their current adjustment difficulties. Compared to their nonmaltreated counterparts, youths who grew up in maltreating families reported more hostility and interpersonal sensitivity, such as self-deprecation and feelings of uneasiness, and lower self-efficacy in solving interpersonal problems. They also had higher self- and teacher ratings of peer aggression. Past maltreatment was significantly related to boys becoming perpetrators (as well as victims) of physical violence and threats, and to girls being recipients of such violence in adolescence. Specifically, girls with a history of maltreatment were about nine times as likely to report symptoms of emotional distress relative to girls without such histories, including symptoms of anger, depression, anxiety, and post-traumatic stress-related problems. Boys with histories of maltreatment also reported symptoms of emotional distress, but not to the same extent as the girls. Boys with maltreatment history were about three times as likely to report clinical levels of depression and posttraumatic stress as boys without. Notably, only the boys from maltreating families had a significantly greater risk of using threatening behaviors or physical abuse against their dating partners. As expected, past maltreatment experiences influenced adolescent relationships and well-being, with a differential pattern for girls and boys (Wolfe et al., 2001). We followed these adolescents a year later, and found that boys and girls who experienced maltreatment in their families continued to have higher levels of dating aggression and trauma-related emotional problems, such as anxiety and anger. These symptoms, in turn, significantly predicted their abusive behavior toward dating partners over time (Wolfe, Wekerle, Scott, Straatman, & Grasley, 2004).

Anger and aggression are also mediated by cognitive variables such as attitudes, beliefs, attributions, motives, and faulty information processing. These factors can include hostile attribution bias (i.e., one sees hostility where none exists), quick judgment, omission of important cues, and incorrect prediction of outcomes (Dodge & Pettit, 2003). Two types of attributions have been studied with abusive men, in particular: men's attributions about their own violence and men's attributions of wife intent. In general it has been found that violent husbands attribute negative intentions to their wives and blame their wives for their own violence, as noted by Holtzworth-Munroe and Clements (chap. 13, this volume).

Finally, in considering developmental influences and pathways leading to anger and aggression, it is important to draw attention to the emerging findings related to psychophysiological processes associated with emotion regulation. Maltreated children, as compared to socio-demographically matched, nonmaltreated children, show more clinical-level internalizing behavior problems, such as elevated self-report of depression or teacher-rated internalizing problems (Cicchetti & Rogosch, 2001). Further more, higher cortisol levels were noted in the morning, afternoon, and on daily average among the maltreated children, as opposed to the normal pattern of higher levels at the time of awakening with decline to low levels by sleep onset. Because cortisol levels would be elevated in response to acute trauma, maltreated, internalizing childrens' patterns suggest chronic hyperactivity of the limbic-hypothalamic-pituitary-adrenal (LHPA) axis and may indicate the presence of brain impairment (e.g., neuronal damage, neuronal loss in the hippocampus, retarded myelination, atypical synaptic pruning). DeBellis, Baum et al. (1999) similarly found that maltreated prepubertal children with post-traumatic stress disorder and comorbid depressive disorder had dysregulation of the LHPA axis.

CONCLUSIONS

In conclusion, the study of anger and aggression has considerable significance for the overlapping fields of domestic violence and child abuse. Knowledge of the dynamics underlying emotional regulation and aggression are leading to greater inroads in treatment and prevention, such as child management skills training (among abusive parents), stress and anger management training, and cognitive restructuring approaches. Advanced knowledge of developmental psychopathology, including early brain development and impairments related to trauma, are also bringing us closer to understanding the precursors to anger problems, and offer additional choices for intervention and prevention. Nonetheless, evidence to date suggests that "correcting" one's anger expression and regulation of emotion is a very difficult task, due to the individual's long history of negative exposure. Consequently, treatment methods, such as anger management, must involve more than recognizing and controlling anger impulses; treatment must attempt to replace impulsive patterns of anger and emotional arousal with more appropriate methods of self-regulation, which have often been missing from an early age. The person's cognitive distortions and lack of skills in handling arousal form the most promising basis for treating this developmentally related problem.

REFERENCES

Averill, J. R. (1983). Studies on anger and aggression: Implications for theories of emotion. *American Psychologist, 38,* 1145–1160.

Bank, L., & Burraston, B. (2001). Abusive home environments as predictors of poor adjustment during adolescence and early adulthood. *Journal of Community Psychology, 29,* 195–217.

Bower, G. H. (1981). Mood and memory. *American Psychologist, 36,* 129–148.

Cicchetti, D., Ackerman, B. P., & Izard, C. E. (1995). Emotions and emotion regulation in developmental psychopathology. *Development and Psychopathology, 7,* 1–10.

Cicchetti, D., & Rogosch, F. A. (2001). The impact of child maltreatment and psychopathology on neuroendocrine functioning. *Development and Psychopathology, 13,* 783–804.

Coid, J., Petruckevitch, A., Feder, G., Chung, W., Richardson, J., & Moorey, S. (2001). Relation between childhood sexual and physical abuse and risk of revictimisation in women: A cross-sectional survey. *The Lancet, 358,* 450–454.

DeBellis, M. D., Baum, A., Birmaher, B., Keshavan, M., Eccard, C. H., Boring, A. M., et al. (1999). Developmental traumatology. Part I: Biological stress systems. *Biological Psychiatry, 45,* 1259–1270.

Dodge, K. A., & Pettit, G. S. (2003). A biopsychosocial model of the development of chronic conduct problems in adolescence. *Developmental Psychology, 39*(2), 349–371.

Dodge, K. A., Pettit, G. S., & Bates, J. E. (1994). Effects of physical maltreatment on the development of peer relations. *Development and Psychopathology, 6,* 43–55.

Levine, S. (1983). A psychobiological approach to the ontogeny of coping. In N. Garmezy & M. Rutter (Eds.), *Stress, coping, and development in children* (pp. 107–131). New York: McGraw-Hill.

Rogosch, F. A., Cicchetti, D., & Aber, J. L. (1995). The role of child maltreatment in early deviations in cognitive and affective processing abilities and later peer relationship problems, *Development & Psychopathology, 7,* 591–609.

Wekerle, C., & Wolfe, D. A. (2003). Child maltreatment. In E. J. Mash & R. A. Barkley (Eds). *Child psychopathology 2nd ed.,* (pp. 632–684). New York: Guilford.

Widom, C. S. (1999). Posttraumatic stress disorder in abused and neglected children grown up. *American Journal of Psychiatry, 156,* 1223–1229.

Wolfe, D. A. (1999). *Child abuse: Implications for child development and psychopathology (2nd Ed.).* Thousand Oaks, CA: Sage.

Wolfe, D. A., Francis, K. J., & Straatman, A. (2006). Child abuse in religiously-affiliated institutions: Long-term impact on men's mental health. *Child Abuse & Neglect, 30,* 205–212.

Wolfe, D. A., Scott, K., Wekerle, C., & Pittman, A. (2001). Child maltreatment: Risk of adjustment problems and dating violence in adolescence. *Journal of the American Academy of Child and Adolescent Psychiatry, 40,* 282–298.

Wolfe, D. A., Wekerle, C., Reitzel-Jaffe, D., & Lefebvre, L. (1998). Factors associated with abusive relationships among maltreated and non-maltreated youth. *Development and Psychopathology, 10,* 61–85.

Wolfe, D. A., Wekerle, C., Scott, K., Straatman, A., & Grasley, C. (2004). Predicting abuse in adolescent dating relationships over one year: The role of child maltreatment and trauma. *Journal of Abnormal Psychology, 113,* 406–415.

AUTHOR INDEX

A

Abeles, R. P., 9, 53
Aber, J. L., 398, 401
Abidin, R. R., 294, 302
Abraham, A. G., 362, 390
Abramowitz, J. S., 129, 130, 138
Abramson, L., 103, 115
Ackerman, B. P., 286, 304, 397, 400
Acton, R. G., 293, 296, 302
Adler, R., 354, 357, 389
Administration on Children, Youth and Families, 360, 384
Afifi, W. A., 167, 179
Aggleton, J. P., 20, 43
Ahern, G. L., 338, 341
Albanese, M., 297, 298, 310
Albrecht, V., 173, 180
Aldarondo, E., 355, 384
Alessandri, S. M., 103, 106, 108, 115
Allan, S., 152, 162
Allcorn, S., 137
Allen, J. J. B., 22, 48, 103, 109, 115, 338, 344
Allen, T. J., 293, 308
Almeida, M. C., 227, 235
Alpert, J., 285, 292, 305
Alpert, N. M., 112, 114
American Psychiatric Association, 120, 137, 301, 302, 339, 342
American Psychological Association, 158, 358, 384
Ammerman, R. T., 287, 293, 300, 302
Amrhein, P. C., 92, 95
Anastasi, A., 79, 95

Anderson, C. A., xix, xxii, 11, 44, 69, 70, 73, 91, 95, 284, 302, 304
Anderson, K., 22, 28, 43, 47, 170, 180, 298, 305
Anderson, S., 152
Appelbaum, P. S., 23, 29, 34, 48, 51, 292, 310
Aragona, J., 354, 357, 392
Arbuthnott, D., 168, 177, 179
Arbuthnott, K., 168, 177, 179
Archer, J., 313, 342
Arias, I., 365, 390
Arias, J., 365, 390
Aristotle, 68, 73
Armistead, L. P., 368, 384
Arnaldo, Z., 367, 384
Arnott, J. L., 337, 347
Arsenio, W. F., 268, 279
Arthur, M. A., 243, 264
Arthur, M. W., 273, 277
Asarnow, J., 219, 220, 234
Ashburn-Nardo, L., 378, 380, 390
Asher, S. R., 192, 212, 220, 235
Atkinson, L., 382, 386
Auckenthaler, A., 173, 180
Aumiller, K., 217, 234
Averill, J. R., ix, xxii, 11–14, 17, 24, 43, 47, 171, 179, 269, 277, 284, 286, 302, 314, 335, 342, 396, 400
Avery, D. H., 283, 300, 301, 307
Ayoub, C., 292, 297, 305
Azar, S. T., xvi, 287–289, 291, 300, 303, 350, 353, 355, 357–359, 361, 365, 366, 368, 372–374, 379, 380, 383–386, 393, 394
Azrin, N. H., 57, 75, 76

SUBJECT INDEX